P9-AGR-158

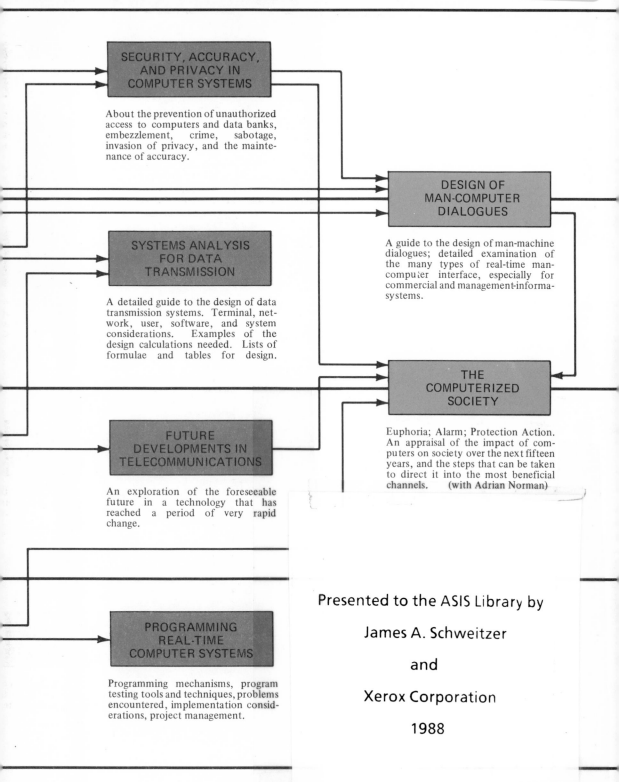

SECURITY, ACCURACY, AND PRIVACY IN COMPUTER SYSTEMS

About the prevention of unauthorized access to computers and data banks, embezzlement, crime, sabotage, invasion of privacy, and the maintenance of accuracy.

DESIGN OF MAN-COMPUTER DIALOGUES

A guide to the design of man-machine dialogues; detailed examination of the many types of real-time man-computer interface, especially for commercial and management-informa-systems.

SYSTEMS ANALYSIS FOR DATA TRANSMISSION

A detailed guide to the design of data transmission systems. Terminal, network, user, software, and system considerations. Examples of the design calculations needed. Lists of formulae and tables for design.

THE COMPUTERIZED SOCIETY

Euphoria; Alarm; Protection Action. An appraisal of the impact of computers on society over the next fifteen years, and the steps that can be taken to direct it into the most beneficial channels. (with Adrian Norman)

FUTURE DEVELOPMENTS IN TELECOMMUNICATIONS

An exploration of the foreseeable future in a technology that has reached a period of very rapid change.

PROGRAMMING REAL-TIME COMPUTER SYSTEMS

Programming mechanisms, program testing tools and techniques, problems encountered, implementation considerations, project management.

SECURITY, ACCURACY, AND PRIVACY IN COMPUTER SYSTEMS

Prentice-Hall
Series in Automatic Computation
George E. Forsythe, Editor

Aho, editor, *Currents in the Theory of Computing*
Aho and Ullman, *Theory of Parsing, Translation, and Compiling*
Andree, *Computer Programming: Techniques, Analysis, and Mathematics*
Anselone, *Collectively Compact Operator Approximation Theory and Applications to Integral Equations*
Arbib, *Theories of Abstract Automata*

Bates and Douglas, *Programming Language/One,* 2nd ed.
Blumenthal, *Management Information Systems*
Bobrow and Schwartz, editors, *Computers and the Policy-Making Community*
Bowles, editor, *Computers in Humanistic Research*
Brent, *Algorithms for Minimization without Derivatives*

Ceschino and Kuntzman, *Numerical Solution of Initial Value Problems*
Cress et al., *FORTRAN IV with WATFOR and WATFIV*

Daniel, *The Approximate Minimization of Functionals*
Desmonde, *A Conversational Graphic Data Processing System*
Desmonde, *Computers and Their Uses,* 2nd ed.
Desmonde, *Real-Time Data Processing Systems*
Drummond, *Evaluation and Measurement Techniques for Digital Computer Systems*

Evans et al., *Simulation Using Digital Computers*

Fike, *Computer Evaluation of Mathematical Functions*
Fike, *PL/1 for Scientific Programmers*
Forsythe and Moler, *Computer Solution of Linear Algebraic Systems*

Gauthier and Pronto, *Designing Systems Programs*
Gear, *Numerical Initial Value Problems in Ordinary Differential Equations*
Golden, *FORTRAN IV Programming and Computing*
Golden and Leichus, *IBM/360 Programming and Computing*
Gordon, *System Simulation*
Greenspan, *Lectures on the Numerical Solution of Linear, Singular, and Nonlinear Differential Equations*
Gruenberger, editor, *Computers and Communications*
Gruenberger, editor, *Expanding Use of Computers in the 70's*
Gruenberger, editor, *Fourth Generation Computers*

Hartmanis and Stearns, *Algebraic Structure Theory of Sequential Machines*
Hull, *Introduction to Computing*

Jacoby et al., *Iterative Methods for Nonlinear Optimization Problems*
Johnson, *System Structure in Data, and Programs, and Computers*

Kanter, *The Computer and the Executive*
Kiviat et al., *The Simscript II Programming Language*

Lorin, *Parallelism in Hardware and Software: Real and Apparent Concurrency*
Louden and Ledin, *Programming the IBM 1130,* 2nd ed.

Martin, *Design of Man–Computer Dialogues*
Martin, *Design of Real-Time Computer Systems*
Martin, *Future Developments in Telecommunications*
Martin, *Introduction to Data Transmission*
Martin, *Programming Real-Time Computer Systems*
Martin, *Security, Accuracy, and Privacy in Computer Systems*
Martin, *Systems Analysis for Data Transmission*
Martin, *Telecommunications and the Computer*
Martin, *Teleprocessing Network Organization*
Martin and Norman, *The Computerized Society*
Mathison and Walker, *Computer and Telecommunications: Issues in Public Policy*
McKeeman et al., *A Compiler Generator*
Meyers, *Time-Sharing Computation in the Social Sciences*
Minsky, *Computation: Finite and Infinite Machines*
Moore, *Interval Analysis*

Plane and McMillan, *Discrete Optimization: Integer Programming and Network Analysis for Management Decisions*
Pritsker and Kiviat, *Simulation with GASP II: A FORTRAN-Based Simulation Language*
Pylyshyn, editor, *Perspectives on the Computer Evaluation*

Rich, *Internal Sorting Methods: Illustrated with PL/1 Program*
Rustin, editor, *Algorithm Specification*
Rustin, editor, *Computer Networks*
Rustin, editor, *Debugging Techniques in Large Systems*
Rustin, editor, *Design and Optimization of Compilers*
Rustin, editor, *Formal Semantics of Programming Languages*

Sackman and Citrenbaum, editors, *On-Line Planning: Toward Creative Problem-Solving*
Salton, *The SMART Retrieval System: Experiments in Automatic Document Processing*
Sammet, *Programming Languages: History and Fundamentals*
Schaefer, *A Mathematical Theory of Global Optimization*
Schultz, *Digital Processing: A System Orientation*
Schultz, *Spine Analysis*
Schwarz et al., *Numerical Analysis of Symmetrical Matrices*
Sherman, *Techniques in Computer Programming*
Simon and Siklossy, editors, *Representation and Meaning: Experiments with Information Processing Systems*
Snyder, *Chebyshev Methods in Numerical Approximation*
Sterling and Pollack, *Introduction to Statistical Data Processing*
Stoutemyer, *PL/1 Programming for Engineering and Science*
Strang and Fix, *An Analysis of the Finite Element Method*
Stroud, *Approximate Calculation of Multiple Integrals*
Stroud and Secrest, *Gaussian Quadrature Formulas*

Taviss, editor, *The Computer Impact*
Traub, *Iterative Methods for the Solution of Polynomial Equations*

Uhr, *Pattern Recognition, Learning, and Thought*

Van Tassel, *Computer Security Management*
Varga, *Matrix Iterative Analysis*
Vazsonyi, *Problem Solving by Digital Computers with PL/I Programming*

Waite, *Implementing Software for Non-Numeric Application*
Wilkinson, *Rounding Errors in Algebraic Processes*
Wirth, *Systematic Programming: An Introduction*

Ziegler, *Time-Sharing Data Processing Systems*

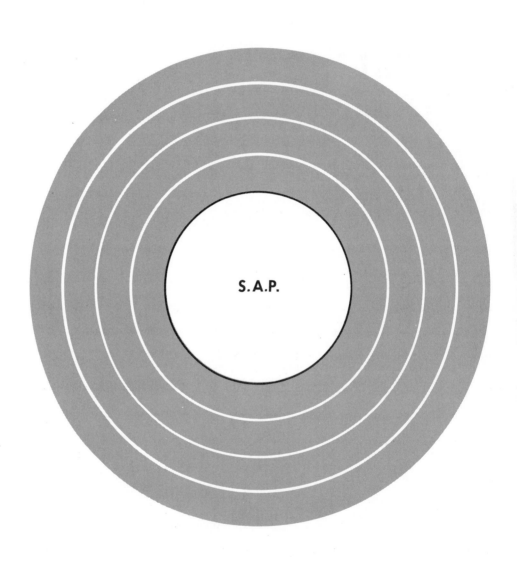

SECURITY, ACCURACY, AND PRIVACY IN COMPUTER SYSTEMS

JAMES MARTIN

IBM Systems Research Institute

PRENTICE-HALL, INC., ENGLEWOOD CLIFFS, NEW JERSEY

Library of Congress Cataloging in Publication Data

Martin, James
   Security, accuracy, and privacy in computer systems.

   (Prentice-Hall series in automatic computation)
   Includes bibliographical references.
   1. Electronic data processing department—Security
measures. 2. Electronic data processing. 3. Privacy,
Right of. I. Title.
HF5548.2.M342   658.4'7   73–14961
ISBN 0–13–798991–1

10 9 8 7 6 5

Printed in the United States of America

Prentice-Hall International, Inc., *London*
Prentice-Hall of Australia, Pty., Ltd., *Sydney*
Prentice-Hall of Canada, Ltd., *Toronto*
Prentice-Hall of India Private Limited, *New Delhi*
Prentice-Hall of Japan, Inc., *Tokyo*

ACKNOWLEDGMENTS

Any book about the state of the art in a complex technology draws material from a vast number of sources. While many sources are referenced in the text, it is impossible to cite all of the pioneering projects that have contributed to the development of new techniques. To the many systems engineers and others who have contributed to this body of knowledge, the author is indebted.

I am very grateful for the time spent reviewing this book and for the helpful suggestions of Dr. P.H. Sterbenz, Mr. I. Gavrilovic, Mr. C.T. Fike, Mr. R. Courtney, Mr. A.R.D. Norman, Mr. L. Fuller, an anonymous critic at the Bell Telephone Laboratories, innumerable people who have demonstrated system failings to me, and my wife. I am particularly grateful for detailed assistance from two partners of Arthur Andersen & Co., Mr. G. E. Hemmings in London and Mr. P. Tom in New York.

It is intended to improve the class questions and problems in this and my other books in later printings and editions. If any professors or students would like to suggest class questions or problems that have proved effective in practice, for inclusion in this or my other books, I should be very grateful. They may be sent to C. Howland Anders, 198 Shore Road, Old Greenwich, Connecticut 06870.

I am immensely grateful to my wife for compiling the index, and to Miss Cora Tangney for organizing the typing.

James Martin

THE STRUCTURE OF THE BOOK

I. The Nature of the Problem

II. Design of the Computer System

III. Design of Physical Security

IV. Design of Administrative Controls

V. Design of the Legal and Social Environment

CONTENTS

TO CHARITY

FOREWORD

Electronic computers have been with us for about twenty years now. The industry, and we who serve in it, are coming of age. Society on the whole seems to welcome the newcomer, but not without some misgivings. Increasingly we hear warning noises that we will be judged as much for the responsibility and respect we show in our use of computers as for our technical brilliance and imaginative innovations. The million dollar payroll check or the threatening letter for an already settled bill can be laughed off for a while as the growing pains of adolescence. It will be less funny if the computer is allowed to become an intrusion on our privacy or a pollutant of our lives.

For this reason I believe this book is particularly welcome and appropriate. Accuracy, Security, and Privacy may not be the most glamorous aspects of computing but they are the essence of responsibility and respect for humanity. James Martin has performed a valuable and difficult service in codifying the best information we have at present in these fields.

And this brings me to my second main observation. After only twenty years or so, we do not have the final answer to all these problems. Our knowledge concerning Accuracy is very highly developed, concerning Security (other than in national defence) it is young but growing fast, and concerning Privacy it is still rudimentary. I think these different stages of development are well reflected in this book.

I have a personal and particular interest in the Privacy issue. I have been a member of the Privacy and Public Welfare Committee of the British Computer Society for two years. What I have learned is that there is a real fear that computers will adversely affect our privacy but that this fear is ill defined and that practical evidence to substantiate this fear is slight. At the present moment it is impossible to lay down hard and fast rules or guidelines. All we can do is make people in the industry alert to the danger and trust them to act in a responsible fashion. This book makes a valuable contribution in pointing out the problems. If our industry does not achieve effective self-regulation, governments will legislate.

On the issues of Accuracy and Security, I do think we have knowledge based on enough practical experience to be reliable. Unfortunately, the frequency which one comes across systems that show a total disregard for good practice in these areas makes it only too apparent that a codification of this knowledge was urgently needed. James Martin has filled this need and I am sure that the effect of this book will be significant.

Giles E. Hemmings,
Partner,
Arthur Andersen & Co.
London

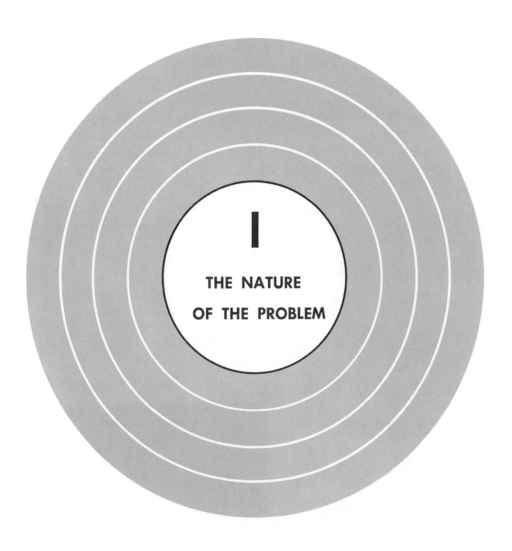

I

**THE NATURE
OF THE PROBLEM**

1 INTRODUCTION

As computers emerge from their years of infancy, they are taking on increasingly responsible work. We do not know how far this process will go or how responsible the computer will eventually become in society. We can only observe its prodigious growth in capability and potential. The more vital the work of the computer becomes, the more important it is to protect it from failure and catastrophe, and from criminals, vandals, incompetents, and people who would misuse its power.

The following cases are typical:

1. A large city uses a computer for controlling its police operations. All police vehicles and ambulances are dispatched by men using terminals that inform them of the current emergencies and vehicle locations. If the computer system was put out of action, many of the operations could not be controlled.
2. A corporation uses a real-time system for controlling many of its activities. So vital to the operations are the computer programs that the corporation could no longer function if they ceased to exist. Data-processing executives refer to the system's reliability using the phrase "you bet your business!" Nevertheless, there are an increasing number of recorded cases of sabotage directed at corporate computers.
3. 747s approaching a congested airport are prevented from colliding by a computerized air traffic control system. The air traffic density has been allowed to increase to such a level that it could not be handled without the computer system.
4. The clearing banks in London have computers that process checks totaling almost 100 million pounds a day in value. A set of small, related changes in the programs could produce history's most profitable robbery.

5. Commercial data banks contain trade secrets and other information that could be worth many millions of dollars to competitors, for example, the results of oil or mineral prospecting. There are several recorded cases of such data being stolen.

6. A variety of nuclear weapon systems are under computer control. The decision to launch a defensive nuclear attack is made by men reacting quickly to information from computer systems. The computer system controlling the ABM is among the most complex ever constructed.

7. There are nearly 2000 types of U.S. government files holding personal information about individuals. More than a third of these have no guarantee of confidentiality. The number in the commercial world is far greater. Unless new privacy safeguards are employed, the concepts of personal privacy will change completely in a fully computerized society.

8. To slow the growth in check processing, the means of making payments in advanced countries must soon incorporate electronic fund-transfer systems in which cash transfers are initiated directly from terminals and take place entirely within the computer systems. A "checkless" payments mechanism will be fully dependent on the security and accuracy of data processing and transmission.

If computers are to assume such vital functions in our society and industry, one assurance must be demanded. It can be stated simply:

The data-processing function shall not lose vital data, introduce errors into them, or permit data to be read or modified without authorization.

To accomplish this involves a variety of different techniques, because the data must be protected in some fashion from unintentional occurrences, such as negligence, machine failures, fire, flood, program errors, transmission errors, and operator errors, and also from willful human acts involving vandalism, sabotage, curiosity, or crime. The problem is made more interesting by the fact that the human malefactors may be diabolically clever. The crime of the century will probably not be the Great Train Robbery but could be a silent extended operation in which graduates change bits in a data bank.*

The illustrations given above are spectacular ones, but the problem of security and accuracy is one that must concern management in any corporation or organization which uses data processing. The question of privacy will be of increasing public concern as data banks grow.

Security, accuracy, and privacy *can* be achieved in computer systems. A series of technical and administrative measures is needed. *The three subjects are related in their technical solutions and hence should be considered together in the planning of computer installations.* They affect all aspects of the system design, including files, terminals, software, operating procedures, and physical installation planning, and hence should be understood by all systems analysts and data-processing managers. The techniques need to be clearly

*Written before the $100,000,000 Equity Funding fraud came to light.

understood by auditors (but frequently are not), and general management needs to be aware of the potential problems and types of solution available.

When we discuss accuracy controls, the discussion will frequently invoke considerations of security, and no system can be considered secure without tight controls on accuracy. Privacy cannot be ensured without security, and most of the technical methods for achieving privacy are also essential for security.

BEYOND THE
DATA-PROCESSING
DEPARTMENT

Two definitions make clear the important distinction between privacy and security:

Data security refers to *protection of data against accidental or intentional disclosure to unauthorized persons, or unauthorized modifications or destruction.*

Privacy refers to *the rights of individuals and organizations to determine for themselves when, how, and to what extent information about them is to be transmitted to others.*

Although the technology of privacy is closely related to that of security, privacy is an issue that goes far beyond the computer center. To a large extent it is a problem of society. To preserve the privacy of data about individuals, solutions are needed beyond the technical solutions. Future society, dependent upon a massive use of data banks, will need new legal and social controls if the degree of privacy of personal information that is cherished today is to be maintained.

Accuracy also becomes a social problem when it affects the lives of citizens. Information in the data banks is employed when an individual uses his credit card, asks for a mortgage to buy a house, or applies for a job. It may be used by the policeman in the radio car following you, or by your doctor administering a potentially dangerous drug. The newspapers have been flooded with horror stories about leases being terminated incorrectly, pornography being mailed to children, old ladies having their electricity cut off in midwinter, and even a surgeon removing the wrong part of a patient, all because of computer errors.

It has become fashionable to blame the anonymous computer for all such occurrences, as though they were not the fault of *people* at all. In fact, in most such cases there was nothing wrong with the machine or its programming. The fault was that the data fed to the machine were incorrect. The *system* was to blame to some extent, because it accepted and preserved the incorrect data and then used them in a damaging way without any form of double check. There has been a tendency in recent years to build systems that use their power carelessly. Many systems have not employed the important controls described in Sections II and III. One management consultant is proclaiming that America is becoming a nation of "sick systems." It is important for the computer industry as a whole that irresponsibility in system design should cease.

The question of security also extends beyond the data-processing center. Access to classified or sensitive data needs to be controlled wherever the data are in the organization. In a corporation, corporate-wide control is needed of information that is confidential or secret, and this control extends into the computer center, to its terminals, and far beyond.

A major failure in the computer center would make its effects felt far beyond the data-processing section. In the worst cases it could bring the downfall of the corporation (and has in a few cases). It is therefore important that a level of management above the data-processing management should concern itself with security.

LAYERS OF PROTECTION   The nucleus of the methodology for control of security and accuracy lies in the design of the computer system and its programs. Without tight control in the system itself, no other precautions can make the system secure. The controls that should be built into the computer system are the subject of Section II, the major section of this book. They are summarized in Appendix D.

Design of a tightly controlled computer system, however, is not enough by itself. As indicated in Fig. 1.1., it must be surrounded by layers of control external to the system design. The layer of technical controls is surrounded by that of *physical security*. This refers to locks on the doors, guards, alarms, and other means of preventing unauthorized access, fire precautions, protection of stored data files, and so on. This layer is the subject of Section III.

The next layer is that of *administrative controls* to ensure that the system is used correctly. The programmers and data-processing staff must be controlled so that they do not misuse the system. Controlled computer-room and program-testing procedures must be enforced. The administrative controls extend beyond the data-processing section to the user departments, the auditors, and general management. In Section IV we discuss administrative controls. Appendix D gives a checklist for auditors and also provides questions that management should ask.

The layers in Fig. 1.1 are not entirely separate. Physical security is not irrelevant when designing system techniques. The question of what data volumes should be stored off the premises affects both system design and physical security. Prevention of wiretapping is partially a matter of preventing

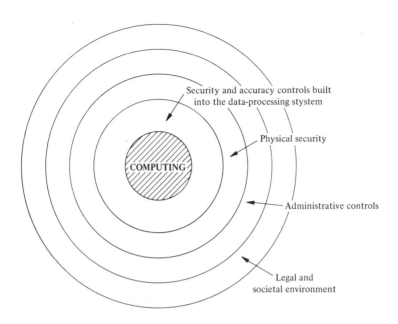

Figure 1.1. Four layers of control.

physical access to junction boxes and private branch exchanges on the user's premises, and partially a question of system techniques, including cryptography. The administrative procedures are very much related to the system design, especially with a real-time or terminal-based system. The auditors need to be involved in the system design, and the views of general management concerning security very much affect the system design.

The outermost layer in Fig. 1.1 is by far the most problematical. When the computer and telecommunications revolution has run its full course (and today it is only just beginning), society will be very different. Many controls will no doubt have evolved, seeking to maximize the benefits and minimize the dangers of a technology of which George Orwell never dreamed. In Section V we discuss some of the laws that have been proposed which relate to the issues of privacy and accuracy in data banks. This subject is more fully explored in the author's book *The Computerized Society* (coauthor, Adrian R. D. Norman).

COST   *Absolute* security is unattainable. No matter how
EFFECTIVENESS   good the protective measures, there will always be
                    some means of damaging the computer or its data.
We shall never be talking about absolute security, but about minimizing the

exposure that an installation faces. The highest levels of security are pro-hibitively expensive. However, a substantial measure of protection can cost very little. Many of the most effective measures discussed in this book are not expensive.

It is desirable to have a security budget of reasonable proportions—say, not more than 5 per cent of the total data-processing budget—and to spend that budget as effectively as possible. Some systems need much more security than others. A large number of techniques for enhanced security, privacy, and accuracy are given in this book, and most of them are summarized in the tables at the end. Not all will be used in any one installation. It is necessary to select those which give the best value for the money in each particular installation.

Some firms have reacted to the question of computer security on the spur of the moment, and have selected measures that are far from giving the best value. One manufacturing company, for example, appointed a computer security officer and told him to do whatever was necessary to make the system secure. He installed a guard post, closed-circuit television surveillance, and a costly electronic door system. All of these measures were expensive, but at the same time the machine room had no security-oriented operating procedures and was open to clerical personnel. Neither the tape control pro-cedures nor the file backup was adequate. The high expenditure had not bought a reasonable measure of security.

The level of expenditure needs to be related to the degree of vulner-ability of the computer and the value of the data in question. If the effects of loss or damage could be extremely expensive to a corporation, it is worth a substantial expenditure to prevent them from occurring. In a corporate data bank there are usually some data that are vital to corporate operations; if they were lost or incorrect, replacement could be very expensive. At the same time, the majority of information in the data bank is less important; if it were lost or incorrect, it would be inconvenient but not disastrous. In such a case the vital items in the file might be copied onto tape every night, and the copy stored securely away from the computer site. Programs would exist for reconstructing the vital items in the file. The less vital items would be copied less frequently or not at all.

The degree of vulnerability of the organization needs to be assessed for the effect of various calamities that could occur. How vulnerable is it if cer-tain data items are incorrect? How vulnerable if certain files or records are destroyed? How vulnerable if the computer center is burned down?

Vulnerability to a certain event may be defined as *the cost that an organization would incur if that event took place.* It is the duty of the data-processing department to minimize the vulnerability of the organization to all foreseeable disasters, failures, errors, and breaches of privacy or security.

The *likelihood* of these occurrences needs to be considered. There may be a very low probability of a sabotage attack on a certain installation, for example. The probability of fire or embezzlement can be reduced by various precautions. The degree of exposure that an organization faces for each event is a combination of the vulnerability and probability of that event occurring.

For the sake of specific discussion in the chapters ahead, *exposure* to a stated event may be defined as *the vulnerability to that event multiplied by the probability of its occurrence within a given time.* The overall exposure of an organization to its data-processing facility is the sum of the exposures for the various events that could occur. The limited budget that an installation may have for security (or for accuracy control) should be spent to minimize the overall exposure.

This theme of spending money where *exposure* is greatest should be kept in mind throughout all the technical discussions that form the body of this book.

2 SECURITY EXPOSURE

In August 1971, the French satellite Eole was launched by NASA as part of a cooperative French-American space program. The satellite was designed to gather data from 115 balloons, each carrying an instrument package around the earth at an altitude of 38,000 feet. On command from Eole, the balloons could transmit their information to the satellite, which in turn would relay the data to a computer center for analysis. The balloons all carried explosive charges which could detonate on a command from the satellite. On the 346th orbit of the satellite, a French programmer error caused the "destruct" command to be sent to the satellite instead of the "interrogate" command.

The error was discovered quickly, but before the instruction could be rescinded, the satellite had hurtled over the horizon, beyond control. A NASA spokesman said "I couldn't tell you what happened after that; sort of chaos broke loose in the station" [1]. Eole destroyed 72 of the 115 balloons, all of those in its path on that orbit. NASA officials said the mistake resulted in some "procedural changes" at mission control and the possible demise of "one dumb computer programmer."

The press headlines have contained many alarming stories about damage to computer systems. They range from bomb explosions to Boy Scouts with magnets. Shareholders have been robbed. Bank computers have paid money into phony accounts. Antiwar protestors erased 1000 tapes at Dow Chemical. A Mariner space shot plunged into the Atlantic because of a programming error. Fires have gutted installations. A New York brokerage programmer transferred $250,000 to his own account and was not caught until 8 years later when he was a vice-president of the firm.

In spite of the dramatic headlines, by far the most common and most probable causes of computer calamities are human carelessness and accidents. Carelessness has sometimes had spectacular results. One company reported a "$2.8 million deficiency" caused by a error in cutover. Usually, however, failures are less spectacular and more frequent.

A security program must therefore be designed to protect an installation both from calamitous events that rarely occur, such as fires and major embezzlements, and from relatively minor events, such as damage to individual records, which occur on some systems several times a week.

THREE-LEVEL ATTACK   Each security exposure must be attacked in three ways:

1. *Minimize the probability of it happening at all.* A major part of fire precautions should be preventive, and this is just as important with all other security breaches. Would-be embezzlers should be discouraged from ever beginning.
2. *Minimize the damage if it does happen.* A fire, once started, should be prevented from spreading. A disk that has been dropped and bent should be prevented from damaging a read head, which in turn could damage other disks. An intruder who succeeds in bypassing the physical or programmed controls that were intended to keep him out should still be very restricted in what he can accomplish. If the security procedures are compromised, it must be possible to limit the harm that could result. Some security designers have made the grave error of supposing that their preventive measures will always work.
3. *Design a method of recovering from the damage.* It *must* be possible to recover from a disastrous fire sufficiently quickly to keep the business running. It must be possible to reconstruct vital records or whole files if they become accidentally or willfully damaged or lost. If an unauthorized person obtains a security code or a file of security codes, it must be possible to change these quickly so that they are of no use to him. It is important to attack the security problem *in depth*, and recovery procedures are vital to the overall plan. The designers of the preventive mechanisms must not be allowed to become so infatuated with their schemes that they neglect recovery techniques.

TYPES OF EXPOSURE   Table 2.1 lists the main types of incident for which protection is needed. They fall under five headings: acts of God, hardware and program failure, human carelessness, malicious damage, and crime. Invasion of privacy, which may not necessarily represent a security breach, has also been included.

The result of the incident may fall into one or more of five categories: loss of single records, modifications of records, loss of an entire file, loss of ability to process a file, and unauthorized reading or copying of records.

Table 2.1. Types of Security Exposure*

	Inability to Process	Loss of Entire File	Loss of Single Records	Modification of Records	Unauthorized Reading or Copying
Acts of God					
Fire	2	2			
Flood	2	2			
Act of war	2	2			
Other catastrophe	2	2			
Hardware and program failures					
Computer outage	5				
File unit damages disk track			3		
Tape unit damages part of tape			3		
Disk, or other volume, unreadable		3			
Hardware/software error damages file		2	4	5	
Data transmission error not detected			4	6	
Card (or other input) chewed up by machine			6	5	
Error in application program damages record			4	5	
Human carelessness					
Keypunch error			4	7	
Terminal operator input error			5	7	
Computer operator error		3	4	5	
Wrong volume mounted and updated		3		3	
Wrong version of program used		3		3	
Accident during program testing		3	4	4	
Mislaid tape or disk		3			2
Physical damage to tape or disk		3	3		
Malicious damage					
Looting	2	2			
Violent sabotage	2	2			
Nonviolent sabotage (e.g., tape erasure)	2	2	3	3	
Malicious computer operator		2	3	3	
Malicious programmer			3	3	3

*The numbers in the table are merely examples and would have to be evaluated anew for any specific application. One data-processing manager rated several of the probabilities an order of magnitude higher.

Table 2.1. Types of Security Exposure (*cont'd*)

	Inability to Process	Loss of Entire File	Loss of Single Records	Modification of Records	Unauthorized Reading or Copying
Malicious tape librarian		2			
Malicious terminal operator		2	3	3	
Malicious user (e.g., punches holes in returnable card)			3	3	
Playful malignancy (e.g., misusing terminal for fun)		2	3	3	3
Crime					
Embezzlement			3	4	4
Industrial espionage					3
Employees selling commercial secrets					3
Employees selling data for mailing lists					3
Data-bank information used for bribery or extortion					3
Invasion of privacy					
Casual curiosity (e.g., finding out employee salaries)					4
Looking up data of a competing corporation					4
Obtaining personal information for political or legal reasons					3
Nondeliberate revealing of private information					4
Malicious invasion of privacy					4

Key to the numbers in Table 2.1

P : *Rating for the probability of an event occurring*:

0 : Virtually impossible
1 : Might happen once in 400 years
2 : Might happen once in 40 years
3 : Might happen in 4 years (1000 working days)
4 : Might happen once in 100 working days
5 : Might happen once in 10 working days
6 : Might happen once a day
7 : Might happen 10 times a day

It is worthwhile to check this list when planning the security procedures for an installation, and to estimate, approximately, the probability of the listed occurrences. The estimate will differ from one installation to another. The probability of one type of event will differ very widely from that of another. The probability can be estimated only very approximately, and it may be unreasonable to ask that it should be estimated more accurately than by picking one of eight grades from the following list.

P : *Rating for the probability of an event occurring*:

0 : Virtually impossible
1 : Might happen once in 400 years
2 : Might happen once in 40 years
3 : Might happen once in 4 years (1000 working days)
4 : Might happen once in 100 working days
5 : Might happen once in 10 working days
6 : Might happen once a day
7 : Might happen 10 times a day

EXPOSURE   Management, preferably management beyond the
ESTIMATE   data-processing department, should make some esti-
                      mate of the potential cost of the damage that might
be done by the problems listed in Table 2.1. Like the probability, the cost can be estimated only vaguely in many cases, and the best that can be done might again be to select one grade from a set of eight, where the eight have the following meanings:

D : *Rating for the amount of damage the event causes in lost business, cost of correcting the data, and other costs*:

0 : Negligible (about $1)
1 : On the order of $10
2 : On the order of $100
3 : On the order of $1,000
4 : On the order of $10,000
5 : On the order of $100,000
6 : On the order of $1,000,000
7 : On the order of $10,000,000

If these rating scales are used, a quantitative rating for *exposure* may be calculated (multiplying vulnerability by probability) that corresponds to the probable average damage per year.

If E is the exposure rating, P the rating for probability of an event occurring, and D the rating for the damage the event causes, then (when P and $D \neq 0$): $E = \dfrac{10^{(P+D-3)}}{4}$ dollars per year.

If a certain type of problem is estimated to cause \$1000 worth of harm and to have a probability such that it might happen once every 100 working days, then $P = 4$ on the scale, $D = 3$, and the exposure, E, may be assessed at \$2500 per year. If a fire in the computer center can cause \$1 million worth of harm but is thought to be such an improbable event that it might happen once in 400 years, the exposure for this might be assessed at $\dfrac{10^{(1+6-3)}}{4} = \$2500$ per year, also. On the other hand, a \$10 problem occurring 10 times per working day costs \$25,000 per year. It may be worthwhile to spend 10 times as much of the budget on the latter as on the former two problems.

In some cases it may be felt desirable to calculate the exposure more precisely than with these rating scales. Some persons prefer the formula: $E = \dfrac{\text{Damage an event causes (\$)}}{\text{Mean time between events occurring (years)}}$. Whatever the method, some such exercise should be done to set the security requirements into perspective.

MULTIPLICATION OF IMPROBABLES   As we commented earlier, *absolute* security is unattainable. The objective is to minimize the exposure at a reasonable cost. Most successful security measures are based on the compounding of low probabilities. If two eventualities are each improbable, and both of them must occur to cause a security failure, the probability of this happening will be the product of the two probabilities, which will be extremely low. For example, a system may store a backup copy of a vital file in a secure location away from the computer site. For a catastrophic data loss to occur, the records in the computer center have to be destroyed at the same time as the destruction of the backup copy. Either of these is unlikely by itself. The probability of both losses occurring simultaneously is very low. If the probability of either happening on a given day is 0.001 (might happen once in 4 years on average), the probability of both events happening *independently* is 0.000001 (might happen once in 4000 years on average). If a third copy was stored in another separate location, the probability of all three happening together *independently* would be 0.001 × 0.001 × 0.001. The search for security will be a search for inexpensive methods of multiplying probabilities of unlikely occurrences in this way.

A key word in the above paragraph was *independently*. If the data in the computer room and that in the backup store were both attacked together in a deliberate planned fashion, the events would not be independent and the probabilities could not be multiplied. To lessen the chances of this happening, the location of the backup store should be kept secret from all but those persons who need to know. Similar reasoning will apply to many aspects of security. The security designer must make it valid to multiply the low probabilities.

When the concern is about a deliberate attack for reasons of malice, embezzlement, procurement of trade secrets, invasion of privacy, and so on, the likelihood of its succeeding is reduced by restricting knowledge of various aspects of the system to persons with a *need to know*. The security procedures themselves should be classified. The technical manuals and documents describing the system and its programs should be locked away. The contents of the data files should be revealed only to those with a *need to know*.

EMBEZZLEMENT   A security problem which needs to be singled out for special attention is that of fraud and embezzlement. *White-collar crime* in the United States (which includes many crimes other than embezzlement) has been estimated to amount to nearly 1 per cent of the Gross National Product. The amount stolen by embezzlers is much greater than that by burglars, pickpockets, armed robbers, auto thieves, and the like. Less than 1/30 of the known losses due to employee dishonesty are actually recovered. More than 100 firms go into bankruptcy every year because of internal embezzlement.

Some computer crimes have been so simple that it is amazing that the perpetrator was not caught; certainly he would have been if the system had had adequate controls. In other cases, the crimes are masterpieces of ingenuity. The majority (of those *detected*) do not fall into the latter category.

In one crime the address of an approved, but no longer used, supplier was changed to that of the embezzler, and the computer was programmed to print fake invoices for that supplier. In another, the computer posted all the positive rounding errors to the programmer's account. In one case a transport manager with the aid of the computer arranged that the delivery vehicles worked 2 days a week for the firm that employed him, and the rest of the time for his own private trucking company. A programmer in a bank raised his own overdraft limit by three digits to $200,000, and lived in splendor until they caught him. Another bank programmer opened a bogus account and made the computer pay the over-the-counter sundry deposits into it. Yet another closed those accounts with very low activity, gambling that the account owners would not attempt to use them, and kept the proceeds.

When a major British chemical company centralized the accounts for its three main divisions, the chief programmer spotted that one division was selling chemicals to another without the 40 per cent intracompany discount that it should have used. In collusion with the chief buyer, he started a bogus subsidiary. By doing this, they could offer their customers not only a 40 per cent discount but also extended credit. After operating their "subsidiary" for some months they were selling chemicals to 60 outside companies, undercutting their own company. They made $360,000 profit in $2\frac{1}{2}$ years (and paid corporation tax on this sum). Eventually, they even sold chemicals to the division of their own company that was not receiving the 40 per cent intracompany discount it should have. They were finally caught and dismissed, but their business was so profitable that the parent company decided to legitimize it, and at the time of writing it is a booming success!

Each month a substantial number of people are convicted for computer-oriented crimes, and the number is rising rapidly. Those who are being caught, however, do not in general look like the smart ones. Their crimes are mostly simpleminded. This suggests that the brighter computer criminals are not being caught. As Brandt Allen, a business school specialist on the subject, puts it, "One can't help wondering what the really clever ones are doing." Furthermore, much computer fraud is never heard about as corporations usually prefer to keep it quiet.

The computer, if appropriate controls are used, can do much to prevent the traditional forms of embezzlement. The clerks and accountants who could falsify ledgers do not know how to falsify computer records. If they make a naive attempt, the machine controls will probably catch them.

While computers close many doors, they open others. The potential gain in embezzling a computer system is often greater because so many records are concentrated together. The likelihood of detection is lower if the computer controls are bypassed, because the records are hidden away. The modifications made to records can be more frequent or more audacious, because they will not pass under the eyes of innumerable clerks. Auditors are often less likely to find the falsification. There will be no fingerprints, erasure marks, or missing ledger pages. The falsifying program routine can disappear as quickly as it appeared. The evidence of what happened can be erased simply from the tapes and disks. There is no need to burn the books. The skills required are greater and the detection mechanisms are more subtle, but the stakes are higher. As one errant technician expressed it: "The quality of the game has been raised."

TWELVE ELEMENTS   In the area of embezzlement the controls needed
OF FRAUD CONTROL   for security merge with those needed for accuracy.
                       The accuracy controls, discussed mainly in Chapters 6, 7, and 23, protect the system both from accidental and intentional

errors. On most systems only certain of the data items are vulnerable to the attacks of embezzlers. Often these are a low proportion of the total. They should be singled out for special checks. The expense of these special controls is not necessary on the nonfraudworthy records.

The exposure to possible fraud can be reduced drastically without major expense by anticipating the possible ways in which it can be committed and devising system controls to catch any such attempt. Twelve elements necessary in the design and operation of a system well protected from fraud are:

1. *Balances of cash and accountable items* will be taken frequently and in such a way that they form interlocking controls. Balances of items entered from terminals, for example, teller terminals in a bank, will be checked against overall file balances. To change the file fraudulently, an embezzler would have to alter the balancing program as well as the file updating programs, and these are kept separately.

2. *Validity checks* will be applied to all input items, as described in Chapters 6 and 7. An input/output control section will ensure that the controls on input are used correctly and that no items are lost.

3. *The tape and disk library will be carefully controlled* to ensure that files are not borrowed by unauthorized persons and possibly modified.

4. *The on-line data files will be controlled*, possibly by off-line scanning runs or batch operations, as described in Chapter 23, to ensure that no records have been tampered with.

5. *Control over the promotion of programs* to operational status will be rigorous, and this includes any program changes. (See Fig. 34.6.) Programs not on the official program file will never be used. Unauthorized routines or modifications must be kept out of the system.

6. *The actions of the computer operator will be logged* in such a manner that he cannot take any action with the system (such as loading a program) without its being recorded.

7. *Access to the computer room will be restricted* to the official operators.

8. *Access to the computer via terminals will be controlled* by positive identification of the person making the access (Chapter 11) and also in some cases positive identification of the terminal (Chapter 12).

9. *Physical access to the data-processing area will be restricted* by means of locked doors, burglar alarms, and possibly guards. Overtime working will be restricted.

10. *The responsibilities of users and staff will be divided* in such a way that *collusion is necessary* between entirely separate groups in order to embezzle the system. The controls should be such that no one man or group can do it on his own.

11. *Knowledge of the system will be divided and restricted* so that only the smallest number of people will have enough knowledge to carry out a successful embezzlement. Technical manuals and program descriptions and listings will be carefully locked away. The high level of system complexity is a great asset in protecting the system.

12. *An internal audit group will check all aspects of the system*, including the design of
   its accuracy and security procedures (Fig. 37.1).

DANGER   There are a variety of different aspects to making a
SIGNS   system secure. If any one of them has been neglect-
                  ed, then that represents a security loophole. There
are a number of characteristics of certain installations that make them particularly vulnerable. Data-processing management and general management
should be on the lookout for the following warning signs:

1. *Lack of an overall security program.* One person should have overall responsibility for
   security. It is necessary for an individual or a team to establish the overall security and
   accuracy controls in an integrated manner, as discussed in this book. If there is no program for this, the system may be vulnerable.
2. *Lack of balance in the security efforts.* Sometimes attention has been focused on one
   aspect of security, but not on others. Management sometimes stresses aspects of security in a sporadic manner because of internal politics, press reports, or because of a
   catastrophe in another organization. Overreacting to the current security fashion often
   results in the security budget being spent unevenly, leaving gaping holes in certain
   areas. A high expenditure on guards and gadgets is sometimes found with no controls
   on the data-processing staff. The attitude toward security of the typical policeman or
   ex-military man often neglects the programmed controls, because he does not fully
   understand them. Some consulting firms approach security with a one-sided attitude,
   especially those with certain devices to sell, or those in which a man with a background
   in a highly specialized security area is peddling his capability.
3. *An open-shop computer center.* A security computer room should be closed to all persons except the official operators. An open-shop computer center in which programmers can run their own programs cannot be as secure as one where only operators have
   access.
4. *Untidy operations.* An ill-controlled computer room with tape reels and card decks
   lying about, operators having lunch at the console (few things do more harm to a
   printer than spilt Coca-Cola), untidy keypunch rooms, and generally bad housekeeping
   can result in lost documents, lost control, and inability to recover from disasters. The
   most dangerous form of untidy operation is inadequate control of tapes, disks, and
   vital documents.
5. *Poor documentation and untidy programming.* The programs on some systems have
   become a labyrinth of undebuggable patches, like a garden reverting to jungle if left unattended. On many systems the program documentation is quite inadequate for an auditor or new programmer to understand what is going on. Apart from being inefficient
   and leading to excessive maintenance costs, such a situation is insecure. Vital programs
   may cease to operate correctly. Fraudulent modifications may be virtually undetectable. When a programmer leaves, it may be almost impossible to make necessary modifications to his programs. On-line updating of the *systems* programs without thorough
   control should be avoided.

6. *Inadequate backup planning.* Effective means must be available to reconstruct any important file if it is damaged. Spare copies of programs must be fully up to date with the latest modifications. Contingency plans must be worked out in detail for what happens if a disaster puts the computer out of action. Can a computer in a nearby installation be used? And does it have the requisite devices and special features? To neglect such questions is to court disaster.

7. *Low employee morale.* Low employee morale is almost certain to lead to carelessness, and in some cases has resulted in programmers or other staff deliberately damaging the system. It is unquestionably a danger sign.

8. *Inadequate division of responsibilities.* Division of responsibilities is necessary so that no man has control of all the steps required for an embezzlement. It is standard procedure in accounting, but has often been neglected in data processing. Segregation of programming responsibilities is necessary to prevent embezzlement by programming. (See Table D.19.)

9. *Shopwindow installation.* A computer that is vital to the operations of a corporation should have low visibility. It should not be labeled with an attention-attracting sign and should not be a shopwindow installation, as many have been in the past. It should not be a center for visitors to be taken to, such as stockholders or Boy Scout troops. Demonstrations should be carefully controlled. Nobody can be sure when a rash of student protests about computers or corporations will break out. Many computer centers have been attacked. Perhaps future generations of machines will be designed so that the computers and data banks can be in a concrete vault and operated remotely.

10. *Lack of internal auditing of all security aspects.* An internal audit group should audit *all* security aspects of an installation, including its physical security. If this is not done, management should instigate it. An auditing checklist, something like that in Table D.30, should be used.

REFERENCE

1. "L'Affaire Eole," *Science,* 29, Oct. 1971.

3 COMPUTER ERRORS

As with security violations, there have been innumerable stories in the press about computers making monumental and often comic errors.

A leader writer in the London *Daily Mail* [1] described how he received "in the natural course of computerized living" a gas bill 1800 per cent too high. He complained to the Gas Board and an official eventually came around to check, admitting that their computer was at fault. The official was carrying "some hundreds" of cards, each one referring to a similar error.

The gas bills of an acquaintance in Canada arrived in the form of credits rather than debits for some months. The authorities, perhaps reluctant to admit the error, permitted him to keep the money in his account. He joyously claimed that it was rather like winning a national lottery—the only trouble was that he could only spend the money on more gas!

London's *Daily Telegraph* [2] described how children in Birmingham who had failed their "11-plus examination" were nevertheless offered places in the schools they desired to enter by an errant computer. The Birmingham authorities agreed to honor the offer. Korvette's in New York City advertised a carpet sale with the headline, "Computer Runs Wild! Huge Overstock of Luxury Carpets." Perhaps less beneficial, a computer producing labels for magazine mailing printed the same address on each, with the result that several truckloads of that issue of the magazine were delivered to the house of one startled subscriber.

It is to be hoped the glut of such stories will come to an end and be regarded as part of the early growth pains of the computer industry. They are mainly the fault of programming errors, operating errors, and of wrong data fed to the machine. Preventive methods exist but on some systems the controls have not been adequately employed. To omit them can only be regarded as unprofessional systems design or implementation.

SEVEN SOURCES   There are seven types of reasons for computer
OF ERROR   errors, as illustrated in Fig. 3.1.

1. Hardware Errors

The first type of reason, hardware errors, is rare today. Error-detecting circuits and error-detecting codes catch virtually all the hardware errors in the computer. Computers are likely to become increasingly error-proof as the cost of logic circuitry drops and hardware technology increases in reliability.

The most error-prone hardware components of systems are the telecommunication lines. There are techniques for eliminating transmission errors that can be made highly effective even on the noisiest line when used correctly. These are discussed in Chapter 8, and with inexpensive mass production of logic for terminals, using large-scale-integration circuits, we can look forward to telecommunication channels as error free as tape and disk channels.

2. Software Errors

Software, especially in its initial versions, sometimes contains subtle undetected errors. It is more likely to cause machine failures or cause a job to be rejected than cause errors in output.

Techniques are now becoming better understood for controlling the reliability of software.

3. Application-Program Errors

When a computer does something *spectacularly* stupid, the cause is usually an application programming error.

The prime answer to this problem is *very* thorough program testing. On real-time systems with multithread operation, the errors remaining in a system often involve the relative timing of two transactions. This type of error

HARDWARE ERRORS
Very infrequent. Hardware can be designed to
detect virtually all its own errors.

SOFTWARE ERRORS
Especially in new software
that has had little "field" testing. A nuisance but not
a major cause of errors in output.

ERRORS IN APPLICATION PROGRAMS
The usual cause of wild behavior in a
computer system. The cure: thorough
program testing.

OPERATOR ERRORS
For example, an operator incorrectly recovering
from a card jam or other failure.
Solution: foolproof operating procedures.

DATA-INPUT ERRORS
"Garbage in: Garbage out. Cause:
errors in keypunching, terminal entry or
other manual input; use of wrong data.
Necessary: keypunch verification, input
controls, accuracy tests. Faulty input is the
biggest cause of "computer errors"

INAPPROPRIATE PROGRAM DESIGN
Invalid decision-making process. Neglect of important
parameters. For example: inappropriate method of
setting overbooking limits in an airline may result in
passengers being stranded at the airport.

QUESTIONABLE SYSTEM PHILOSOPHY
For example, the system is insufficiently flexible to handle unanticipated
events; the system methodology imposes undesirable constraints
on the operating environment; the effects of invalid data
are acted upon without a double check (e.g., consumer's
electricity is incorrectly cut off).

Figure 3.1. Sources of computer errors.

can be very difficult to repeat exactly, and so tracking down is very difficult. The type of program that might be subject to nonrepeatable errors requires a lengthy period of *saturation testing* designed to produce the maximum number of potential error conditions. The system should be hammered with all varieties of test data to ensure that programs behave properly before they are let loose on the system users. Unfortunately, in the pressure to make the computer economical or to gain on a slipping schedule, program testing has sometimes not been done with the time-consuming thoroughness that it needs. In some systems, a few residual bugs do not matter too much; in others they can be catastrophic. It is necessary to differentiate between these cases.

4. Operator Errors

One typical newspaper story described telephone bills on which the charge for the same call had been entered more than once. This was possibly caused by a computer operator mishandling a card jam. It would have been prevented if adequate controls had been used.

The operator of a large computer system has a highly responsible job. It is frightening to reflect how much damage an operator *could* do—files of vital data accidently erased, financial records mistakenly updated twice with the same data, wrong tapes or programs used, and so on. Computer operators are generally difficult to recruit and quick to leave a position, a situation that enhances the possibility of errors. It is desirable for systems analysts to devise controls which guard against the sorts of mistakes that operators can make. Several systems have come close to disaster because the operators processed an out-of-date file (kept for backup purposes). On one system this resulted in a day's transactions being omitted. The computer had printed a console message to the operator warning him of his mistake, but he had ignored it. The computer program can be written so that it will not read or update data until it has checked that it has the correct file. The program can total certain fields on the transactions it processes, and compare the result with an expected total to ensure that no card has been lost. The program can be designed so that it will not run until the operator has carried out certain checking actions.

Installations with well-planned controls generally do not suffer from damage caused by operator errors. Where such controls have not been applied, however, results have sometimes been chaotic. Once data are lost or wrongly updated on a system without controls, recovering from the trouble can be difficult and expensive.

5. Data-Input Errors

The largest cause of "computer errors" is not failure in programs or hardware, but incorrect input. Garbage in, garbage out.

There is a variety of controls that can be placed on input. They include card verification, batch total controls, self-checking numbers, consistency checks, and others.

A well-planned computer system is normally more accurate than its clerical predecessor. When terminals were installed in one factory for data collection from the shop floor, the error rate dropped from 2.5 per cent with the previous manual system to 0.5 per cent. These terminals were off line, and the move from off-line to on-line data collection has similarly reduced the number of errors by a factor of 5 or so. When a real-time system is in use, the computer can check data as they are entered—against known facts. When a worker keys in information about the status of the job he is working on, the machine checks that the worker *should* have been on that job at this stage and that the status report is as expected; if not, the machine may notify a supervisor, who checks what is happening and sees whether an error has been made. In this way much tighter control of shop information has been achieved than was possible before the computer was used.

The trouble with computers is that, whereas the errors may be fewer than on a clerical system, they can be spectacular. The various manual stages in a clerical system give plenty of opportunities for spotting absurd errors or misplaced decimal points. The clerks would be unlikely to send a householder a telephone bill for $10,000. The computer needs to be given a sense of the absurd by programming reasonableness checks into various stages.

Some systems have been designed to take aggressive action against the public without adequate checking. A system that causes an old lady's electricity to be cut off, because her account number is incorrectly recorded on the files and it appears that she never pays, deserves the adverse press reporting it receives. So do the credit-card organizations and book clubs whose computers print abusive letters to their subscribers when the computer system is in error. Such system design is grossly irresponsible.

6. Inappropriate Program Design

A system with happily working bug-free programs and good hardware and operator controls is still not necessarily devoid of problems. The method it is using may be inappropriate to the situation in question. A program for stock control, for example, commonly decides when to reorder stock and what quantities to order. It uses equations for determining these, employing such parameters for the item in question as stock turnover, delivery time, orders in hand, and sales forecast. However, the equations may have been poorly chosen. They may neglect certain parameters, or produce results that do not minimize costs or that run too high a risk of a stock shortage.

An inappropriate choice of equations may simply fail to maximize profitability; in some cases, however, a poor choice of equations could be more serious. On an international airline, for example, many cancellations of reserved seats occur in the few days before the flight. The same seats are often sold two or three times because of such cancellations. The airline may therefore allow a limited amount of overbooking in an attempt to fill as many seats as possible. The amount of overbooking permitted decreases as the takeoff date nears. If, in this situation, a reservations computer uses inappropriate equations for setting limits on overbooking, the airline runs the risk of stranding passengers at the airport. In one such case there was a fistfight at the airport!

This type of problem is somewhat more difficult to solve than the earlier ones, and requires an elaborate study of the situation in question.

7. Questionable System Philosophy

The airline reservations situation could be put right by modifying a small element of the decision-making process. The system may have been fundamentally sound, but needed "tuning" or adjusting to the environment it worked with. This is often the case when a system makes elaborate decisions or takes control actions—based, for example, on probability calculations of some form.

A potentially worse situation is one in which the overall philosophy of the system is questionable. The system may, for example, be insufficiently flexible to handle unanticipated events properly. This has been the case in some systems for production control; the computer laid down a schedule that became difficult to maintain when unforeseen circumstances arose, such as a batch of material being abandoned, a foreman deciding to give an apprentice certain types of work not on the schedule, or a panic occurring to complete a particular customer's order. Shop-floor personnel may consequently begin ignoring the computer's work schedule and start making their own decisions. When one part of the schedule is ignored, other parts are usually invalidated. The shop personnel thus lose confidence in the computer, and before long the machine's orders are being disobeyed completely.

Here, the entire scheme is at fault, and no amount of tuning would make it sufficiently adaptable. Instead, a scheme is needed that either permits shop foremen a measure of decision-making responsibility, or else deals in turn with each new circumstance on the shop floor as it occurs, rescheduling if necessary. The latter procedure requires real-time collection of data from the shop floor and a computer that reschedules the work every time its current schedule is overridden by unforeseeable events.

Again, in a system which gathers statistics, produces summaries, or uses statistics to influence events, one would like guarantees that the final figures do indeed represent the facts. This, however, can be more difficult than it may appear at first sight. The method used for collecting or condensing the information will often hide or distort facts. There is a variety of such *methodological distortions*. Data easily collected may be incomplete, or may reflect a bias inherent in the method of collection. Decision making based upon data so collected reflects this bias.

DESIGN FOR ACCURACY

Several steps are necessary to design accuracy into computer systems. First, the overall philosophy of the system needs to be appropriate. It should avoid using algorithms that are inherently dubious. When errors occur, the system should be self-healing as far as possible, rather than making the error worse or taking extreme actions based on dubious data. When extreme actions are taken (like cutting off a person's gas, telephone, or credit, or canceling a customer's order or booking) and there is a remote possibility of error, a human double check is required to find out whether the action is really warranted.

Given a sound system philosophy, good hardware and software, powerful error-detecting techniques on data transmission (Chapter 8), and very thorough program testing are all needed. These are basic essentials for an error-free system.

There then remains the question of controlling the accuracy of the input. A variety of techniques for controlling input accuracy are discussed in Chapters 6 and 7. These techniques will be backed up by procedures for checking the accuracy of the data files, discussed in Chapter 23. The data files may be checked on an off-line scan of critical records, which takes cash totals and other control totals and performs specific accuracy checks. The file scan is a check on both accuracy and security, as it is designed to check that there has been no unauthorized file modification. On real-time systems the off-line file scan can combine with the validation and totaling of input to form a tight interlinking set of controls.

On batch-processing systems various batch totals are taken and must agree in the different batch runs. The totals taken by the computer must agree with totals of the input taken by the user department. In addition to control totals, a variety of validation checks can be applied to input transactions, and reasonableness checks can be applied to output.

COSTS OF
ERROR CORRECTION

It is possible to spend much money on accuracy controls. As with security, the question arises, how much is it worth spending. The basic controls, such as batch totaling, are inexpensive and indispensible. A substantial measure of control is bought at low cost. Again, as with security, diminishing returns set in when *all* the possible controls are considered. One large commerical user states that 50 per cent of the company's total programming effort is spent on validating and identifying data. A U.S. Air Force installation estimates that 40 per cent of its programming time is spent incorporating checks and controls. Another user claims that 25 per cent of his machine time is spent on validity and control operations. At the other extreme, some installations spend almost no machine time or programming effort on accuracy controls. It has been the experience of many installations that they have had to steadily increase the thoroughness of their validation and checking routines as experience indicated that this was necessary. The overall cost would have been lower *if they had been built in to begin with.*

The cost of correcting errors should be compared with the cost of letting them slip through. To catch 95 per cent of input errors may be inexpensive. To catch 100 per cent of them may be extremely costly. It is generally true that the cost of catching an error should not exceed the cost that would be incurred if it slipped through. This is not always the case. For example, it would usually be inacceptable to print slightly wrong payroll checks to avoid the cost of correcting them. On the other hand, in certain types of statistical files a low proportion of erroneous items does not matter much.

The costs of error detection and correction include the following:

1. Programming
2. Debugging time
3. Computer memory
4. Throughput time
5. Manual error correction
6. Reentry time for corrected records

The savings, which offset these costs, include the elimination of reruns by facilitating continuous processing, the reduction of maintenance programming, and the avoidance of problems that would have been caused by undetected errors.

An intangible cost incurred by letting errors slip through is the loss of confidence in the system by company management and customers.

REFERENCES

1. *The Daily Mail* (London), March 18, 1968.

2. "Computer Mixes Up 11-Plus Results," *The Daily Telegraph* (London), Aug. 1, 1967.

4 COMMERCIAL SECRETS AND INDIVIDUAL PRIVACY

As we commented in Chapter 1, privacy is an issue of society that goes far beyond the controls of any data-processing installation. It refers to how data about individuals is used, and by whom. The spread of massive data banks and teleprocessing makes the subject of privacy of particular concern to the computer industry.

PRIVACY OF COMMERCIAL DATA
In industry there is often more concern with the privacy of commercial data than with the privacy of individuals. Industrial espionage and the unauthorized selling of competitive data are increasing substantially at the time of writing.

Encyclopaedia Britannica sued three of the computer operators on their night shift for $4 million for copying nearly 3 million names from tapes of the company's "most-valued" customer list and selling them to a direct-mail advertiser. A major manufacturer sued a person for copying a tape with details of all its customers and prospects on the East Coast and selling this to other manufacturers. British Overseas Airways Corporation had the programs and technical details of its $100 million system stolen and offered for sale to rival airlines. Information Systems Design, a California computer service firm, filed a $6 million suit against University Computing Co., charging an employee with stealing computer programs by long-distance telephone.

There are many other such cases. Often they are unsuccessful in court. The laws in many countries relating to the theft of commercial secrets give little protection. When data are copied onto the thief's own tape, nothing *physical* is stolen. Often it is difficult to prove the theft. In some cases the grounds for dismissing a case were that the data were *insufficiently safe-guarded* by the firm from whom they were stolen.

The computer makes theft of industrial information more profitable because it concentrates the information. In some cases immensely valuable information, such as machine specifications or geological prospecting data, can reside in a single tape or disk.

INTERNATIONAL　　　　International espionage used to concentrate mainly
ESPIONAGE　　　　　　on government and military secrets. Today large
　　　　　　　　　　　　sums of money are being spent to obtain industrial secrets. To quote *Newsweek* [1],

> Increasingly, the KGB is turning its attention to a new kind of spying: technological, commercial and industrial espionage. The field is less glamorous than traditional undercover pursuits, but it is probably more vital to the Soviet Union.... One of the KGB's new assignments is to help close the technology gap between the Soviet Union and more advanced nations—and to prevent even less developed enemies from catching up. Sometimes, this calls for extreme measures.

Newsweek went on to say that the KGB is by far the biggest of the world's secret services and that its head, Yuri Andropov, had higher rank in the Politburo than Foreign Minister Andrei Gromyko or Defense Minister Andrei Grechko.

In September 1971, 105 Soviet spies were expelled from England in one coup, and most were engaged in ferreting out industrial secrets. One of their main methods was to bribe or blackmail British citizens into obtaining industrial information, particularly on electronics and computers. *The London Observer* commented [2]:

> The factory and the laboratory have become major priority areas for modern spies. Nor is it difficult to see why a country like Russia, still technologically so far behind Britain, should invest so much money in this kind of spying, and court the kind of risks that exploded with such impact in their face. The cost of initiating and developing new technological processes is immensely expensive, and it is obviously quicker and cheaper to steal what knowledge one can from those who have made the initial investment in capital and knowledge.
>
> Russia would obviously be far better off if, instead of having to import expensive computers and scientific instruments, it could gain access to information that would enable it to produce these goods for itself.

In this case specific details were revealed of how Russians stole the plans for the Concorde, so the obvious similarities between the Russian and Anglo-French supersonic transports caused persons in the aircraft industry to dub the Russian plane the "Concordeski."

International espionage probably takes place between entirely friendly nations. Peter Hamilton in his book *Espionage and Subversion in an Industrial Society* [3] states that schools for industrial spies exist in Switzerland and Japan, the Japanese being the more important of the two.

EXPENDITURE ON PROTECTING DATA   There are a variety of techniques for keeping unauthorized persons out of computer files. They are listed in the tables in Appendix D, and are discussed in detail in Sections II to IV. Often, many of the techniques in the table will be used in combination, and a high level of protection against unauthorized eyes can be built up.

It is much less expensive to build protection against an amateur data thief than against a well-equipped professional attack, and, again, an organization needs to decide what is a reasonable level of expenditure. The approach discussed in Chapter 2 is of value with most commercial files. The potential cost in losing the data is estimated and the cost/effectiveness of the safeguards is evaluated.

When we discuss the privacy of individuals, however, the cost/effectiveness approach is usually irrelevant. It is difficult to assess how much an individual's privacy is worth. A cynical businessman may decide that it is not worth much. If it costs money to safeguard information about individuals in, say, a hotel-booking system, an airline-reservation system, or credit-information system, the managers with tight budgets may decide not to use the safeguards. It does not affect their profitability if private information is obtained by detectives or other persons.

Unless there are laws that enforce the protection of the individual, privacy depends upon the morality or social conscience of the organization in question. Pressures may be brought to bear on government agencies to safeguard records about individuals (often they have not). In private industry there may be little or no such pressure.

FOUR LEVELS OF SAFEGUARD   There are four levels of safeguards needed to protect the privacy of individuals. The first is the locking up of data in the system so that unauthorized persons cannot read or copy them. This safeguard is technological in nature and is discussed at length in this book.

The second is an appropriate system philosophy. There are certain ways in which a system should not be used if privacy is of concern, and there are certain types of data that should not be collected. The purpose of a system containing sensitive data should be defined and data not relevant to that purpose should not be in the files. Controls over which persons are authorized to access sensitive data should be carefully established. It is important to distinguish between statistical data banks and data banks containing information about specific individuals. The former should be designed in such a way that information about *individuals* cannot be extracted from the data bank by asking the right questions (Chapter 12). Controls on the misuse of statistical data banks are necessary. The subject of system philosophy is treated in Chapter 38.

The third level is administrative controls within a corporation. Within government, for example, there are tight controls on who has access to census data. Controls are needed on what data one agency can obtain from another agency's files, and how the data can be used. Within a corporation, general access to some of the personnel data will usually be restricted. Only certain persons will be able to obtain salary information. Details of a person's past police convictions may be withheld from his manager or from other managers interviewing him for a possible transfer. This subject is discussed in Chapter 38.

The last level is legal controls. Without appropriate laws there are no means of enforcing the other controls that are necessary. Systems will be built without technical safeguards on privacy because they can be cheaper. Mailing lists containing private data will be fully distributed. (Certain computer dating firms sell the answers to their questionnaires, for example.) Governments will be free to use data for purposes other than those for which they are collected. Chapter 39 discusses legal controls.

PUBLIC CONCERN
A great public concern is growing over the possible invasion of privacy that computers and data banks may bring. The former U.S. Attorney General, Ramsey Clark, in an article called "The Death of Privacy" [4] says

> In times past, privacy has seemed both plentiful and indestructible, and its value has been largely ignored. Now we are losing it, and once lost, it may never be regained. Crush privacy for a generation and it may be gone forever.... If we lose the right to be let alone, we will lose everything—our individuality, our dignity, our liberty, and our capacity for loving.

The individual already leaves a trail of computer records in many of his daily activities. Table 4.1 lists some of the types of data banks that hold

Table 4.1. Some Types of Data Bank Holding Personal Information

Category	Types of Data Bank
Police	FBI Security clearances Police-information systems Defense Department surveillance of citizens
Regulatory	Tax Licensing Vehicles
Planning	Property owners Vehicles Economic data Business information
Welfare	Medical Educational Veterans Job openings and unemployment
Financial	Credit bureaus Savings-and-loan associations Banks
Market	Mailing lists
Organizational	Personnel files Membership lists Professional bodies Armed forces Corporation employee dossiers recording intelligence, aptitude, and personality tests, and appraisals and attitudes
Social	Computer dating Marriage bureaus Hobby data
Research	Medical case histories Drug usage Psychiatric and mental-health records
Travel	Airline reservations with full passenger details Hotel reservations Car rentals
Service	Libraries Information-retrieval profiles Insurance records
Qualifications	Educational records Professional expertise Membership of professional groups Results of I.Q. and aptitude tests

personal information. There are innumerable others. In the next decade the cost of on-line storage will drop by a factor of 100, and access to data banks by teleprocessing will become commonplace. In a society filled with such technology there is reason for concern about individual privacy.

There are excellent reasons for needing to collect and store data about individuals. It would be a retrograde step to limit the use of data banks. What is needed are controls on the data banks so that respect for the privacy of individuals can be enforced.

The situation is effectively summed up in a speech made in April 1968 by Thomas J. Watson, Jr., then Chairman of the Board of International Business Machines [5]. The remainder of this chapter quotes his speech.

Do we in our time face "an end to all privacy"—the right, in the words of Samuel D. Warren and Louis Brandeis, "to enjoy life, the right to be let alone?"

Today I should like to discuss that question and some of the things I believe we can do about it. And I should like to concentrate specifically on its relation to the twentieth century technological marvel I know best—the electronic computer, which enables us to mass in centralized systems Gargantuan quantities of information about everything, and most particularly about people.

All of us, I feel certain, have heard about such repositories—present and planned—of:

university social scientists;

retail credit agencies and employment services;

state and local crime and education and welfare agencies.

We all remember the computerized data center in Martinsburg, West Virginia, which holds a file on every one of us, belonging to the Internal Revenue Service.

And we have all read about the proposal for a National Data Center in Washington, which would pull together in one place economic and social statistics now scattered about in more than twenty separate federal agencies.

Now, centralizing information is nothing new. Every book, every file cabinet, every library is a repository to some extent centralized. The bigger the library, the greater the centralization, and the greater the repository's usefulness to us all.

The thrust toward centralizing is the thrust toward knowledge itself.

And the thrust toward knowledge is the thrust toward a better life for everyone.

With big enough and detailed enough repositories of information on people, for example:

> doctors could spot the first appearance in a community of a new disease and cure it before it raged into an epidemic;

> community welfare professionals could identify first tendencies within a particular neighborhood toward juvenile delinquency and move in to help before delinquency turned to crime;

> educators could identify throughout our society brilliant children barred for some reason from a chance at a college education, and try to help that child's family remove the obstacle—an obstacle which deprives us all.

Given such uses of information, the arguments for centralizing it by electronic means are forthright and compelling.

To a social worker it means fewer hours filling out paper forms and more hours working with people.

To consumer credit agencies, it means faster and more accurate reporting—reporting which spurs economic advance.

To the person looking for work or the organization looking for talent, the centralizing of personnel data can help match the right man with the right job, on an assembly line or in the President's cabinet.

To people here in California—with the State Highway Patrol's Autostatis System, and with the police information network in the Bay area—centralizing data means new strength in the fight against crime.

Specifically, to the state trooper who has flagged down a speeder, it means knowing—as he approaches the stopped car—whether he's about to confront a happy-go-lucky teenager or a trigger-happy escaped convict.

And that knowledge can save his life.

In a time when cities expand and people move about as never before, the electronic centralization of data helps local governments know what is going on—helps them see problems coming, before they boil over in traffic snarls, glutted school buildings, and even bloodshed.

And finally, the centralizing of data permits the study in unprecedented new ways of detailed quantitative information—mountains of information, all meaningful and useful, of the sort federal agencies just couldn't use in the past after they complied their aggregates.

For example, government statisticians today cannot put together in one pool for study the dollar volume of construction underway in the U.S., collected by one survey, plus the number of people employed in the industry, collected by another, plus the number of construction workers out of work, collected by a third.

Centralization would end .such blocks to knowledge. It would give sociologists and economists new funds of fact to combine and recombine electronically, at speeds impossible and in quantities unthinkable with pencil and paper.

And thus it would offer us all a more incisive insight into the workings of our society and our economy than we have ever had.

These are the promises of the information repositories—clear, compelling, unassailable.

Given these promises, you might expect they would produce only enthusiasm. But they haven't. Instead they have evoked deep anxiety and often rage.

You have seen the headlines on the National Data Center. From coast to coast editorial writers, politicians and academicians—left, right, and center—have commented not on what it was designed to be—a carefully limited repository of statistics for study.

Instead they have concentrated on what, under evil management, they fear it might become: a monster machine containing everything ever known about every one of us, deliverable at the push of a button to an all-powerful government.

And that is the point:

Today the Internal Revenue Service has our tax returns.

The Social Security Administration keeps a running record on our jobs and our families.

The Veterans Administration has medical records on many of us; and the Pentagon our records of military service.

So in this scatteration lies our protection.

But put everything in one place, computerize it, and add to it without limit, and a thieving electronic blackmailer would have just one electronic safe to crack to get a victim's complete dossier, tough as that job would be.

And a malevolent Big Brother would not even have to do that: he could sit in his office, punch a few keys, and arm himself with all he needed to know to crush any citizen who threatened his power.

Therefore, along with the bugged olive in the martini, the psychological test, and the spike microphone, the critics have seen "data surveillance" as an ultimate destroyer of the individual American citizen's right to privacy—his right to call his soul his own.

Now, on this controversy, let me say just two things:

First, I applaud the statistical purposes of a National Data Center, and I respect the intelligence and sensitivity of the men who devised it. They never dreamed of advocating it as a jack boot to stamp our privacy.

Second, I believe the critics have a point. And I share their concern, particularly when it focuses not on the National Data Center alone, but on the prospect of a decades-long trend ahead toward more and more and more centralizing, in many forms—Federal, state and local, public and private.

That trend, I believe, does give us a conflict: a promise and a threat.

The first is to become intellectual Luddites: to ban technology, to admit we cannot control the machines, to assert that if we proceed on our present course they will enslave us.

That course, I believe, is foolhardy—a road to obscurantism and defeat.

We cannot stand pat.

No. For as far ahead as we can see, we are going to need all the information we can get, need it fast and need it right.

In the racial agonies of previous summers—we may well read, in part, the penalties of knowing too little too late about the lives and living of our people.

Such penalties of ignorance—and many others—we cannot continue to accept.

We have no choice—absolutely no choice.

So we turn to another possible answer: to get the information we need at all cost, relax our concern, and go flat out with computerized centralizing—centralizing without restriction, without care for the individual, without any purpose but efficiency.

This course, I believe, is if anything even worse than the first.

For it is a call to glorify the machine and to fold, spindle, and mutilate the human being.

It could indeed threaten to put us into chains.

And it could, in the end, drive a watched people to revolt.

We must face up to the threat to privacy.

And to that end the first requisite is understanding—massive and incisive public understanding.

Fortunately, academicians and lawyers and government officials—as well as industry groups—have already launched a number of driving inquiries into the problem—at Columbia and Harvard Universities, for example; and in committee hearings on Capitol Hill, under Congressman Cornelius Gallagher, Senator Edward Long, and Senator Sam Ervin.

I applaud such studies, and I hope we shall see many more like them.

But they are only the beginning.

For to translate understanding into action, responsibilities fall upon us all.

And let me begin close to home.

I believe we in industry must continue to improve existing technological safeguards which limit access to information stored in electronic systems; and we must devise new ones as the needs arise.

Safeguards, present and planned, like these:

devices which will shut out anyone who does not identify himself by a password or by a badge which can be inserted into a terminal;

crypotographic techniques which will protect information transmitted from a computer to a distant terminal over telephone lines;

techniques for recording every request for information.

Moreover, I believe we in industry must offer to share every bit of specialized knowledge we have with the users of our machines—the men who set their purposes—in a determination to help secure progress and privacy, both together.

I have every confidence that our industry will discharge these responsibilities to the full.

But we cannot do the job alone.

No manufacturer can make a system proof against human corruption.

Some human being can somehow get at everything stored in any system, however ingenious.

Therefore a heavy responsibility falls foursquare upon us—every one of us as citizens—to do this: help devise new public policies—laws, ethical codes, standards of business practice—to meet this new public problem.

Already suggestions for such policies as these have entered the record:

new professional ethical standards for computer programmers and machine room operators;

rigid penalties for unauthorized access to information;

prohibition of the indiscriminate transfer of information on individuals from one agency to another.

opportunity for the individual to read and rebut any information in any file on him that exists.

These make an exemplary beginning.

We shall need many more.

And we shall need, above all, a keen public determination to choose the best ones and write them into effect.

This responsibility you and I cannot abdicate.

For the problem of privacy in the end is nothing more and nothing less than the root problem of the relation of each one of us to our fellow men.

What belongs to the citizen alone?

What belongs to society?

Those, at bottom, are the questions we face—timeless questions on the nature and place and destiny of man.

All of us together must seek the answers: answers which will make the force of technology—the wealth of great repositories of information—the servant of the individual, to run his cities, to cure his diseases, to lighten his darkness with education, and above all to confirm and strengthen him in freedom.

In our twentieth-century world—so rich in promise and reward, so bright in things to better the lives of its people; and yet so dark in its capacity to hedge in the single citizen, to fence his room to live and breathe and move —even in this twentieth-century world of technological miracles I believe we can retain—triumphantly retain—those ancient liberties which have been ours for nearly 200 years.

With thought and concern and action, I believe we can assure ourselves and our children both progress without precedent and, coupled with it, in the ringing words of Louis Brandeis, "that right most valued by civilized men"— the right to privacy.

We can. We must. And I am convinced we will.

REFERENCES

1. *Newsweek*, Oct. 5, 1971.

2. *The London Observer*, Oct. 3, 1971.

3. Peter Hamilton, *Espionage and Subversion in an Industrial Society*, Hutchinson Publishing Group Ltd., London, 1967.

4. Ramsey Clark, "The Death of Privacy," *McCall's*, Feb. 1970.

5. "Technology and Privacy," an address by Thomas J. Watson to the Commonwealth Club of America, San Francisco, California, April 5, 1968.

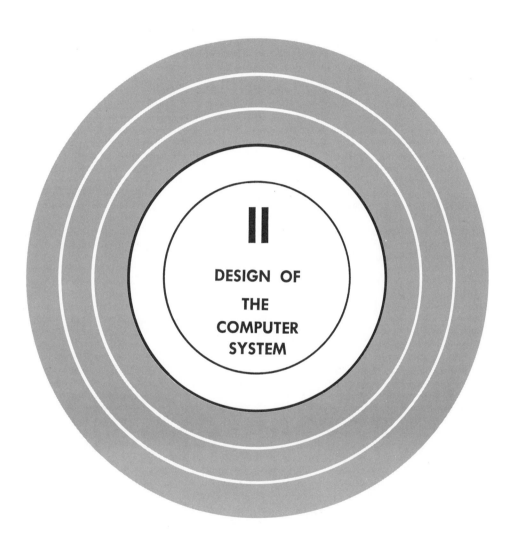

II

**DESIGN OF
THE
COMPUTER
SYSTEM**

5 DESIGN PROCEDURE

Table 5.1 gives an overall design procedure. Most of the detail lines in the table are themselves expanded in the Appendix tables, and these are referenced. Table 5.1 also gives the chapters in which the details are discussed, and the reader may use the table as a guide to his reading of the book.

The first step in the procedure suggested is to establish an overall control philosophy. Higher-level management must establish how tight they want the security to be. On some military and intelligence systems an extremely high level of security is needed, and expensive measures can be employed to keep out intruders. At the other extreme, some commercial systems can afford to take a minimal posture on security, especially if they are systems not vulnerable to embezzlement. In a library information retrieval system, for example, it is not worth taking expensive measures to ensure security. Disciplined operation, good fire precautions, and backup files so that the data cannot be destroyed are about all that is needed. In some systems there may be special reasons for maintaining a high level of security for certain files. The question of privacy of personal information is largely an ethical one, and a decree from higher management may be needed to make a data-processing manager spend his precious budget on it.

Security and accuracy controls increase the cost of a computer system and in some cases degrade its performance somewhat. Furthermore, they do not give absolute safety, but a measure of it. The higher the measure of security gained, the higher may be the cost, in terms of both expenditure and

Table 5.1. Procedure for the Design of the Necessary Controls

	Chapter
1. Establish the overall control philosophy.	Section I
2. Determine who will have the overall responsibility for security.	30
3. Establish the value of protection and the potential exposures. (Develop tables such as Tables 2.1 and 5.1).	2, 5
4. Establish a budget for security and accuracy controls.	5
5. Establish the responsibility for technical design.	
(a) Accuracy controls:	
Determine the accuracy controls on batch operations (Table D.8).	7
Determine the accuracy controls on real-time operations (Table D.9).	7
Determine the error controls for teleprocessing (Table D.12).	8
Determine the controls built into off-line file operations (Table D.10).	23
Determine the controls to bridge periods of failure (Table D.11).	9
(b) Security controls:	
Determine the techniques for identifying the terminal users (Table D.16).	11, 12
Determine the structures of authorization schemes.	13, 14
Determine whether cryptography should be used. (Table D.18)	19, 20, 21
Determine what locks and alarms will be used to detect invalid entry (Table D.17).	10, 16
Determine the means of establishing security in systems programs.	17
Determine what controls are built into the use of statistical files.	15
Determine what controls are built into off-line file-scanning operations (Table D.10).	23
Determine surveillance methods.	16
Determine what methods will be used to recover from file damage (Table D.22).	22
6. Establish the responsibility for procedural controls:	
Determine the nature and functions of the input/output control section.	6, 7
Determine how quality control is achieved.	
Determine computer-room procedures.	
Determine tape/disk library procedures.	
Determine how conversion to the new system will be controlled.	
7. Establish the responsibility for the control of programs:	
Determine the techniques to prevent unauthorized programs being used (Table D.19).	34
Determine how program maintenance and promotion are controlled (controls to prevent unauthorize, undocumented program changes) (Table D.20).	34
Determine program-testing procedures.	
8. Establish the responsibility for physical security (Table D.25).	
Establish fire precautions (Table D.27).	26
Establish physical locks, alarms, guards, and sabotage protection.	24, 27
Establish an off-site data storage and means of conveyal (Tables D.25 and D.26).	
Consider precautions against wiretapping and system eavesdropping (Table D.7).	28, 29
9. Establish the responsibility for administrative controls:	
Establish a vital records program (Table D.24).	32
Incorporate controls for classified documents (Table D.23).	31
Take out insurance (Table D.28).	
Establish backup procedures in case of catastrophe.	22, 32
10. Involve the auditors:	
The auditors should check the controls planned at the design stage.	37
Audit trails must be designed, along with other technical aids to auditing.	37
All aspects of the system should be audited (Fig. 38.1) (Table D.29).	
A checklist should be prepared for future audit (Table D.30).	

performance degradation. However, like putting a lock on an office door, *a substantial measure of protection may be bought at little cost.*

As we commented in Chapter 1, the first step in designing features for security, accuracy, and privacy is to determine what degree of protection is needed. This level of protection should then be built into all facets of the system. As with other aspects of computer design, the security system needs to be well balanced. It would be poor design to build a high measure of security into part of the system while leaving wide loopholes elsewhere. This, however, has often happened. The design team may pay great attention to making the computer invulnerable to terminal users or to guarding the physical installation, and yet leave the system open to attack from an application programmer.

One man should have the overall responsibility for security. He should be outside the DP department and should report at a high level in the organization. Different persons will have responsibility for different aspects of the security design but will operate under his overall supervision.

Developing the technical design will be the work of systems analysts. It is necessary to develop procedural controls, which may be the job of the data-processing manager. The design of physical security may be passed on to a specialist in that area. The programming manager may be responsible for the controls on programs and programmers. The auditors should check the system plans to ensure that they are satisfied with the controls, ensure that the system is auditable, and develop procedures for auditing all aspects of it.

When an overall control philosophy has been agreed upon, a budget needs to be established for security and accuracy controls.

A first step in establishing a reasonable budget is to assess the nature of the exposure. What are the different categories of data? Who or what are we protecting the data from? What is the value of the data and how much will it cost if the data are lost, damaged, or inappropriately disclosed?

Figure 5.1 suggests a procedure for approaching these questions. As we have commented, there is some commonality between the controls needed for security, privacy and accuracy. An integrated set of measures need to be selected.

**CATEGORY OF
INTRUDER**
The costs of measures that could protect a system from people who might harm it or misuse it range from very small to astronomical. To select appropriate measures it is necessary to determine from whom we are protecting it. Protection against casual snoopers is easy. Protection against James Bond or the Central Intelligence Agency will need much more ingenious and expensive measures.

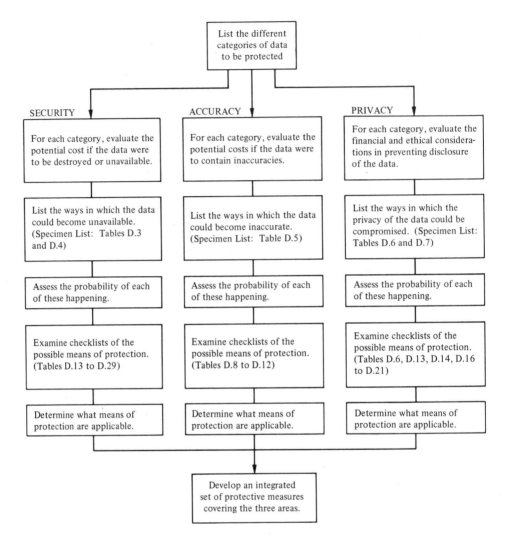

Figure 5.1

To set the security measures discussed in this book into perspective, we shall refer to six categories of unauthorized penetration:

1. *Accidental disclosure of secure information.* A computer user may be accidentally delivered a printout intended for someone else, and may accidentally obtain another person's data at a terminal.

2. *Casual entry by unskilled persons.* It is necessary to prevent clerks, policemen, managers, and government employees from casual browsing in files of sensitive data. The clerk with a terminal should not be able to look up his manager's salary. The government official should not be able to look up information about people, other than that intended for him. A secretary in the personnel department should not be able to read confidential reports on employees. There is no difficulty in "locking" the files against such prying eyes.

3. *Casual entry by skilled technicians.* As we increase the level of technical knowledge of the supposed marauder, so we need more elaborate safeguards to keep him out. A man at a terminal with a detailed knowledge of the system might find ingenious ways of making it respond to his questions. Programmers frequently entertain themselves by making a system do something it was not intended to do.

4. *Entry by persons who stand to gain financially, but are not professional criminals.* If we assume that the intruder stands to gain financially, we can assume that he might spend substantial money attempting to invade the system, which the casual intruder would not. He might infiltrate the programming staff, buy a compatible terminal, use wiretapping methods, plant bugs, have duplicate keys to the computer room made, and so on. We might be talking about a private detective agency or a hired intruder. We can assume that he will have both technical knowledge and technical equipment. This further raises the cost of defense.

5. *Attack by well-equipped criminals.* We may have assumed in the last category that the intruder was not prepared to break the law blatantly. (In this case the laws we shall discuss in Section V would offer some measure of protection.) Here we assume that a major criminal operation may be underway. It can be an employee embezzling his firm. It may be a highly paid industrial spy. It may be the big bank robbery of the computerized society. No masked bandits pull guns on the tellers; instead, a technically expert team changes the data on the computer files.

6 *Attack by organizations with massive funds.* Extremely elaborate methods are reported to have been devised for obtaining information from computer systems by the military and intelligence agencies. These include, for example, the detection of electromagnetic radiation from computer centers by using powerful antennas in a specially equipped truck. Such methods can involve almost unlimited expense, and the defense against them requires an equivalent level of expenditure and capability.

EFFECTIVENESS　　　　　Protection against category 1 is largely a question
OF THE　　　　　　　　　of good hardware design, good computer-room pro-
SAFEGUARDS　　　　　　cedures, and thorough program testing. Although
　　　　　　　　　　　　　accidental disclosures of private or secure information may occasionally occur, it will be rare on a well-controlled system for them to be catastrophic.

Protection against category 2 is easy and its cost is barely significant. Protection against categories 3 and 4 needs to be more elaborate, but can be made highly effective. Cost now becomes significant.

In protection against category 5 the battle becomes interesting. The security system must encompass hardware, software, programmers, operators, computer-room safeguards, physical security, and tight administrative controls. It is always a mistake to underestimate the ingenuity of our cleverest criminals. Given time, patience, and money, they will probably penetrate very well-defended systems occasionally, just as they do into bank vaults and jewel safes today. However, with a professional approach to computer security and the right hardware and software, we can make systems exceedingly difficult to penetrate.

If the enemy is in category 6, the cost of security will become extremely high and can only be achieved with personnel who are elaborately security cleared and known to be loyal. The techniques described in this book generally relate to commercial and government systems where the enemy does not have the resources of the CIA!

The staff and consultants of the quality found in an ordinary data-processing installation today should, if they tackle it seriously, be able to protect the data from anyone other than the National Security Agency or an organization with similar funds and skills. On rare occasions an ingenious and persistent criminal may slip through the defenses.

VALUE OF
THE DATA

In practice, the degree of protection taken, and hence its cost, will depend upon the assessment of the potential intruders, and this, in turn, will depend upon the sensitivity of the data and its possible value to an outsider. If an outsider is likely to spend money to steal the data, then money must be spent to protect it.

Much of the data stored in computer files are of no value to the potential embezzler. The first categorization of data, then, may relate to whether there can be any direct financial gain from unauthorized modification of certain records. If there can be, steps must be taken, first to prevent such modification, and second to detect it if it occurs. Cash amounts and other accountable quantities should be balanced at appropriate intervals to ensure that nothing is missing. The balancing controls should be designed so that it is difficult for the would-be embezzler to add cash to an account, or remove it, without this being detected. We shall discuss these controls in more detail later. The system designer and the auditors must pay special attention to records containing cash fields or other records that could be used in theft.

In designing a system, the following costs and values may be established:

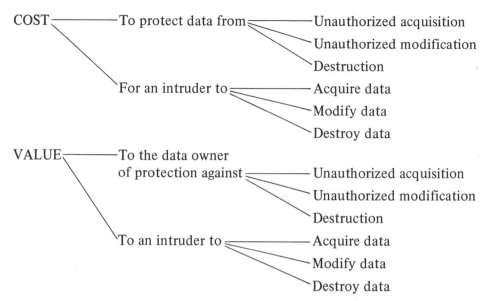

It will usually be possible to make a rough estimate of the *costs* in the above chart, but will sometimes be impractical to estimate the *values* of protection and intrusion. Sometimes the value of the data can be clearly assessed For example, seismic survey data could be extremely valuable to the acquirer. Some people may be willing to spend large sums to get it, if there is a reasonable probability of success. The cost of protection should not be large in comparison. On the other hand, obtaining information about workload in a factory from the production control system would be of little value to competition and not worth the expense of elaborate security procedures.

In some cases the factors involved are too subjective to have a price tag attached. Sometimes nonquantifiable factors determine the level of security that is used. This is often the case when privacy is involved, rather than business data of identifiable value. A cynical owner of a data base might assess as zero the value to him of keeping personal data private. An organization storing data about individuals might spend no money to prevent unauthorized reading of its records.

No one should be expected to spend more to break into a data-processing system than he would have to spend to acquire the data in any other way. Implicit here is the assumption that the intruder is aware of these other ways and that the risks and time factors are included in his calculations as elements of cost. For example, if active wiretapping in a particular situation would involve an expenditure of $1000 and it is believed possible to acquire the services of a disloyal employee with access to the desired data for less than that, say, $300, the wiretapper should be expected to use the services of this person, unless there are complicating factors such as greatly increased risk in attempting to locate the disloyal employee. If the data owner is unaware that anyone is interested in acquiring his data, and if attempts to locate disloyal employees result in loyal ones putting the employer on his guard, the intruder will be well advised to use the more expensive wiretapping approach with the higher probability of success than to jeopardize the entire effort by alerting the employer. Similarly, if the potential wiretapper can get the required data immediately by connections to communication lines but will require several days to obtain the services of a dishonest employee, he may still elect the higher cost of wiretapping to deliver the data in a more timely fashion.

COST OF LOSING DATA   Sometimes the cost to an organization of losing the capability to process data can be high, independent of whether the data were lost or whether the harm was caused deliberately or not. The cost of fire, machine failure, or damage caused by malfunctioning programs should be estimated.

The categories of harm used in Table 2.1 might be evaluated for the various different files:

1. Inability to process the data
2. Loss of the entire file
3. Loss of single records
4. Modification of records
5. Unauthorized reading or copying

If the harm is caused intentionally the estimates may be different from harm caused by accident. Deliberate modification of a record, for example, may have diabolical results, whereas an accidental modification may be merely a nuisance that is easily corrected.

As we commented earlier, it is sometimes difficult to establish a dollar value for data files, and the suggestion that it should be done is sometimes greeted with skepticism. Nevertheless, it provides an effective way to place security and other data-base problems into perspective. A file owner who is unprepared to place a precise dollar value on his data will usually agree that its value falls within one of a group of broad ranges. He may therefore fill in a chart such as Table 5.2 with the eight value categories discussed in Chapter 2.

Table 5.2

Type of file	Modification would permit embezzlement or theft?	Category of intruder that protection is designed for	Intentional Effect					Accidental Effect				
			Inability to process	Loss of entire file	Loss of single records	Modification of records	Unauthorized reading or copying	Inability to process	Loss of entire file	Loss of single records	Modification of records	Unauthorized reading or copying
_____												
_____												
_____												
_____												
_____												
_____												

A = Accidental
B = Casual entry by unskilled persons
C = Casual entry by skilled technicians
D = Persons who stand to gain financially
E = Well-equipped criminals
F = Organizations with massive funds

0 = Negligible
1 = On the order of $10
3 = On the order of $100
4 = On the order of $1000
5 = On the order of $10,000
6 = On the order of $100,000
7 = On the order of $1 million
8 = On the order of $10 million

BUDGET
DETAILS
When the values of the files have been examined, budget details may be established for the expenditures thought to be reasonable for security and accuracy controls.

It might be reasonable to say that not more than 5 per cent of the total computer budget will be spent on security. Guidelines may also be set for technical expenditure: for example, not more than 5 per cent of the programming effort shall relate to security controls and not more than 10 per cent to accuracy controls; not more than 10 per cent of the processing time or main memory shall be used for security and accuracy controls; the controls shall not increase the response time by more than 10 per cent. These figures will vary from one type of system to another. (Some systems spend *much* more than 10 per cent of the programming budget on accuracy controls.)

Guidelines may also relate to the users of the system, limiting the level of inconvenience that the controls can inflict. They may say, for example, that the actions necessary for a terminal operator shall not be increased by more than two entries per transaction. *It is particularly important that the controls do not cause inconvenience to the user.* In cases where they have, the user has tended to bypass them.

With such guidelines in mind the detailed controls may then be selected as indicated in Table 5.1. The detailed responsibility may fragment into separate areas such as the six shown in lines 5 to 10 of Table 5.1. The techniques in different areas should be under the coordination of one man to ensure that the security system is balanced and no loopholes remain.

6 ACCURACY CONTROLS ON BATCH PROCESSING

This chapter and the following three discuss methods of detecting and correcting errors in computer systems. Readers primarily interested in security controls might skip these four chapters on the first reading.

In this chapter we discuss the controls that are used on batch-processing systems. Their prime purpose is to control the accuracy of the operation, ensuring that no transaction is lost or accidentally processed twice, thereby erroneously updating files twice. A second purpose is to prevent embezzlement. The controls should make it impossible for a clerk to enter felonious items of his own, and difficult for a programmer to steal by modifying a program. We shall discuss various aspects of the control of embezzlement in later chapters, and many of them link into the basic batch-processing controls described here.

As far as possible the controls should be a by-product of the computer runs so that they pose little extra burden on the data-processing procedures. The auditors will need to be left information so that they can make appropriate checks that the system is being used correctly. These will also be discussed later, but again they must relate to the batch controls.

The prime type of control for preventing embezzlement and accidental loss is the taking of batch totals and balances to ensure that no amount is inserted or missing. In addition to the totals and balances, there are many types of validation checks that can be applied to the input and output.

**VERIFICATION
OF KEYING**

Important data are *verified* after punching by operators at verifier machines. The verifier operator keys in the same data as the card punch operator, and the machine compares what is keyed with the punching on the cards. If any character fails to agree, the machine stops and a correction must be made. On every card that has been correctly verified, the machine cuts a notch at the end. By glancing at a deck of cards an operator or control clerk can see immediately whether all the notches have been cut. The deck will not be processed until they have all been cut.

In many installations, card punching is being replaced by on-line data entry. Operators keying in data typically sit at a keyboard with a screen. The data they key in are checked by a program and written directly on tape or disk. In this type of input operation a separate verification operation is usually dispensed with, thereby saving up to half the manpower. Instead of a verification operation the data are inspected using the programmed checks discussed in this and the following chapter. Any errors found will be brought to the keying operator's attention immediately and will be corrected. The machine may record the accuracy of each operator. This process tends to make operators more accurate, and catches some errors on the source documents that a verification operation would not catch. On the other hand, some keying errors that would be caught by a verifier operator slip through the on-line checks.

**INPUT
VALIDATION**

The checks built into the programming should be designed so that they can be applied at all stages in the operation. A particularly important set of checks, however, is that used at the start of the operation when new input is first received. Every effort should be made to detect any erroneous or invalid input before it is processed.

The validation checks on new input may be carried out either in the first run which processes the data, or, before that, in a separate data validation run, or in an on-line keying operation. The disadvantage of a separate validation run is that it takes extra time. Its advantage, or that of on-line keying, is that invalid data can be repunched before the main processing begins, as shown in Fig. 6.1. In the majority of systems the advantages of having separate input validation outweigh the disadvantages. This editing may perform other functions, such as splitting up the data to go to different programs, blocking records for greater efficiency, and writing tables for the

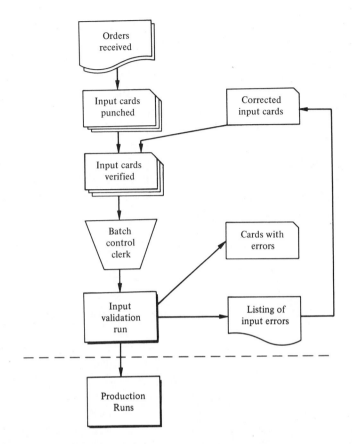

Figure 6.1. Many installations use a separate input validation run before the production runs. As many errors as possible are removed before the production runs begin.

control of magnetic tapes. When card punching is used, the input validation run will produce an error listing for the repunching and control of erroneous items.

TYPES OF DATA VALIDATION CHECKS   There are four categories of data validation checks:

1. Those applied to individual *characters.*
2. Those applied to individual *fields.*
3. Those applied to complete *records* or *transactions.*
4. Those applied to a *batch* of records.

A second important categorization is whether the check in question can be performed by itself in the input validation run or whether it requires the examination of another record on a different file. An example of the latter is a check that a part number in the input is in fact a current part number on the components file. If the components file is on-line and directly accessible, this check could be made during the input validation run. If, on the other hand, it is on tape, it will not be possible to make the check until later, when the input file is run against the components-file tape.

We shall call the first type of check an *immediate* check, and the second type a *deferred* check. An immediate check is one that can be made when the input is initially read, and a deferred check is one that must wait until a later state in the processing of the input.

CHARACTER   Typical of the checks applied to *characters* in input
CHECKS   data are

1. *Test for numeric.* Some characters should always be numeric, or possibly numeric or blank.
2. *Test for alphabetic.* Some characters should always be alphabetic. Some may be alphabetic or numeric. Some may be alphabetic or text punctuation characters. If alphabetic characters not vital to the processing are incorrect in the batch operation, the processing of the item may be permitted to continue and a correction made later.
3. *Test for special characters.* A character may have to be one of a limited set. For example, the letters A through F may be used to indicate course grades or initial letters to indicate seat classes. If a character is found not to be a member of such a set, an error indication may be given.
4. *Test for blanks.* Some characters in punched cards or other records are required to be blank. Sometimes they may be blank or zero, or are required to be blank because of the presence of another character.
5. *Test for sign.* A check may be made on the position in a numeric field requiring a sign.

FIELD   Typical of the checks applied to *fields* in input
CHECKS   data are

1. *Limit test.* A check may be made that a field is not above or below a certain limit. A bill, for example, may not be expected to exceed $100. Sometimes the limit varies depending upon previous items. A salary check, for example, may be examined to see that the sum paid is not more than 15 per cent of what was previously paid. In this case, however, the limit check is a deferred validation check rather than an immediate one.

2. *Range test.* A range check is often applied to a numeric field to ensure that it lies within both upper and lower limits. It is occasionally used in non-numeric fields where the collating sequence can be employed. Tables are sometimes employed in range checks.

3. *Reasonableness test.* A test may be made that the value of a field represents a normal situation. Sometimes this may be a simple range check. Sometimes it may depend upon the value of another field. For example, a charge of $500 might be reasonable on a corporation's electricity bill but not on an individual's bill. The reasonableness of the item may depend upon the value of previous items, as with positioning data for a space vehicle. Some exceptional items may be entered that are known to violate a given reasonableness check. These items may contain an indicator saying that the reasonableness check must be bypassed.

4. *Test for valid item.* A test may be made that a field represents a valid item, for example, a valid part number, a valid code, or a number of an actual account or employee, In some cases the validity may be established without going to the files, by means of a table look-up or a checking algorithm. In some cases invalidity is only established when the relevant record is read. Details of a job number are punched, for example, and it is found when an attempt is made to update the record for the job that no such job exists.

5. *Test for consistency.* Two or more fields may be checked in a related fashion to ensure that they follow certain consistency rules. In an airline booking to Chicago the transaction may be checked to ensure that the flight number in it does in fact go to Chicago. An order from a customer may be checked to ensure it is consistent with specified credit terms. Many consistency checks are deferred rather than immediate checks. In some cases the transactions are specifically designed so that consistency checks can be built in.

6. *Sequence check.* Sometimes the fields in sequential items must be in a given sequence for further processing. The sequence can be checked.

7. *Special tests.* Some fields can have tests unique to them because of the field structure. For example, dates may be checked to ensure that the month is between 1 and 12, that the day is between 1 and 28, 29, 30, or 31, depending upon the month, that it is not a Saturday or Sunday, and that it lies within a certain period. Many other types of fields are amenable to special tests.

SELF-CHECKING   An important form of checking is the use of self-
NUMBERS   checking numbers. A field that is to be made self-
          checking has an additional character or characters added to it, which are derived from the other characters by some algorithm. The process is usually applied to numeric fields such as part numbers or account numbers, and usually one extra digit is added. A six-digit account number may be made into a seven-digit number. The extra digit is derived arithmetically from the other digits. When an error occurs, the additional check digit is usually not the same as that derived from the other digits, and

hence reveals that the number is in error. The process of deriving the check digit is chosen so as to give the maximum probability of its catching any error. The probability would be higher if more than one check digit were employed. As with all error-detecting codes, there is a trade off between the degree of redundancy and the probability of letting an error escape undetected.

In some cases account numbers or other numbers are checked *as they are punched* or entered into a computer system. This may be done by a device on a keypunch that *automatically* checks the check digit as it is punched. It may be done by a computer with a terminal for on-line data entry. In either case, the operator punching a wrong number will be alerted immediately and will have a chance to correct his mistake.

A typical method of calculating a check digit is shown in Fig. 6.2. This is the method that has most commonly been used on IBM keypunches. The calculation proceeds as follows: The digits of the original number, from right to left, are individually multiplied by the following factors: 2, 3, 4, 5, 6, 7, 2, 3, 4, ... The results (in step 3 of Fig. 6.2) are added. The resulting sum is divided by 11, and the remainder of the division is subtracted from 11. The resulting digit is the check digit, which is attached to the original number to form the self-checking number.

1. The digits of the original number:		6	5	0	4	2	1	3	9
2. The digits employed to generate the check:	3	2	7	6	5	4	3	2	
3. The products of these:		18	10	0	24	10	4	9	18
4. The sum of the products: 93									
5. This sum divided by 11: 8 plus a remainder of 5									
6. The remainder subtracted from 11: 6									
7. 6 becomes the check digit and so the number becomes 650421396									

Figure 6.2. The steps used to generate a self-checking number (modulus 11 method).

Two more examples are

Original number: 456267; self-checking number: 4562674.
Original number: 107248695; self-checking number: 1072486958.

Once a self-checking number is assigned to an account, a part, an employee, or other entity, it may be checked whenever it is used. It is claimed that the method detects more than 97 per cent of all errors made in keypunching the number. Certain errors slip through the check when the operator accidentally interchanges two or more digits in a compensating fashion.

TRANSACTION
CHECKS
The transaction checks that may be applied are much more variable than the character, field, and batch checks, because they are dependent on the nature of the application and its transactions. Typical types of checks are

1. *Test for completeness.* A test may be made to check that no mandatory fields are missing. Some fields may be mandatory items and others not. Sometimes, when the fields are of variable length, a simple field count is used.

2. *Test for internal consistency.* Many different types of checks are made on the internal consistency of records or transactions. The transaction may be designed to facilitate such checks. The presence of a category indicator may, for example, make it necessary to check the presence of certain fields. The transaction may contain fields that deliberately double check each other, such as customer number *and* name. It may contain the cost of items in an order *and* the total of these costs.

3. *Test for external consistency.* The items in the transaction may be compared in a deferred check with other items on the files to ensure some type of consistency between transactions.

4. *Sequence checks.* Sometimes certain fields within one transaction must conform to an established sequence, for example, times of a scheduled set of machine operations, or geographical continuity when a journey is planned. Again transactions may be specifically designed so that continuity checks can be made.

5. *Serial number checks.* When it is important that every record be accounted for, they may be given serial numbers. This is usually done with bank checks and often with other items containing financial information. The input validation run should check the serial numbers.

6. *Test for valid item.* A test may be made to check that the item is valid. In some cases this may be a security check rather than an accuracy check. Is such a transaction permitted from the source in question? Is such a transaction permitted to read, or to modify, the particular record it requires? Is a correct security code included?

7. *Check for false punching.* When punched cards are returned by the public, as for example with telephone bills, the computer may check that punch holes have not been maliciously added.

BATCH
CHECKS
The most common, and perhaps the most important, controls in batch processing are those which test the completeness and accuracy of the batch as a whole. They include the following:

1. Transaction Count

A count is made of the number of records or transactions in a batch. This might, for example, be the number of punched cards in the batch. The cards are counted when they are keypunched, and the count may be entered into a final batch control card. An error in the record count indicates that a card has been lost or accidentally double processed—possibly when a jam occurred in the card reader.

The count will remain with the batch for the various runs that are made with it. After a sort, for example, a count of the records in the new sequence will be compared with the original count.

2. Batch Control Totals

The batch control card or record will contain several other items that may be checked at the end of each run, in addition to the record count.

All quantitative fields are accumulated to produce a set of batch totals. This will be done after each run to ensure that nothing has been lost. An error in a batch total without an error in the record count would indicate a fault in the processing. Simultaneous errors in count and totals would usually indicate that a card had been lost.

The total fields may be originally summed when keypunched or entered. The manually established totals must then agree with the computed totals. Sometimes the totals are originally obtained in the first input validation run.

3. Hash Totals

Totals may be made not only in quantitative fields where the total has some meaning, but in fields where the total is meaningless. For example, the account numbers may be summed. Alphabetic fields may be summed by stripping of the "zone" bits or otherwise converting the letters into numbers. Such sums are called *hash totals*. They are used solely for checking purposes.

If the record count is out by 1, a hash total of the record identification, such as account number, provides a valuable indication of which record in a batch has been lost or double processed. If the hash total of account numbers is short by 527168, the missing record is that for account 527168.

4. Batch Number Checks

The number of the batch may be in all the records in the batch. The records will then all be checked to ensure that they are part of the batch in question.

**ON-LINE
DATA ENTRY**

For the first 20 years of commercial computing, data were punched into cards (or paper tape) and fed to the computer. Now a variety of alternatives is available. Source data may be keyed directly to magnetic tape or disk. It may be entered into the computers on line. The possible advantages of employing on-line data entry are

1. Miskeying can be detected on line in many cases and corrected immediately. The verification operation used with card punching can be avoided or shortened with on-line data entry because of the on-line checking.
2. The data-entry process is usually speeded up. Often less data need to be entered because the computer can produce some of the requisite data from its on-line files.
3. Because of the faster operation and on-line error detection, fewer operators may be needed. In one typical case, throughput per operator was increased by 40 per cent over that with card punching. The terminals in some cases are cheaper than keypunches and verifiers. On-line data entry for many applications is cheaper than punched-card data entry. This is usually the key advantage. Cost is the determining factor.
4. The data-entry locations may be remote and scattered, connected to the computer by teleprocessing links.
5. Data reach the computer more quickly, because the cycles of operations concerned with handling, balancing, verifying, and correcting punched cards are avoided.

In one case a magazine publisher had a problem with excessive costs for correcting punched-card input errors. Fifteen per cent of all his transactions were in error for reasons that included keying errors, misspelled names, wrong addresses, and a variety of mismatches with the master file. Eighty per cent of his input costs resulted from retrieving the source documents, repunching and rebatching the cards, and then reprocessing the error transactions. On-line data entry enabled him to catch input errors as they were made and correct them at that time.

Some disadvantages of on-line data entry are

1. Programming and maintenance of the data-entry routines are needed.
2. The teleprocessing costs or central-processing-unit costs may be high.
3. Equipment backup may be needed or the data-entry operators will be idle when the computer is down.

In increasing numbers of installations the advantages are outweighing the disadvantages.

CHECKS ON   The programs may make certain checks on the
PROCESSING   correctness of the processing. Checks on the
                         performance of the hardware are less important
with well-designed modern computers than they were in the early days of
computing, because the machines are designed to detect their own faults.
The checks on processing are there mostly to ensure that the *programs* are
doing what was intended. The types of checks include

1. Arithmetic Checks

Early computer programs used to contain checks on the arithmetic of
single items, such as cross-footing checks, checking a multiplication by dividing, and so on. Such tests are infrequently used today, because computer
arithmetic can be assumed to be consistent. If the programs are thoroughly
tested, this should be enough. Arithmetic checks are used today to ensure
that such items as total quantities and costs are in agreement, and debits
balance with credits. The total quantity of an item sold may be added, for
example, and the equation "total quantity of items sold × price per item =
total charge" would be checked. Such checks are used to prevent items being
lost and to make it likely that attempts at embezzlement by removing an
item will be caught.

2. Rounding Errors

In some cases rounding errors have been used to steal money from a
computer system. Table 6.1 gives an example of the way rounding errors can
accumulate. An item has a price of 1.75 per unit quantity. Eight orders are
shown in which the amount charged for this item is the **quantity ordered** ×
1.75. Fractions of cents are eliminated by using normal rounding rules for
adjusting the price to the nearest cent. One might expect the small rounding
errors, each a fraction of a cent, to balance out over many orders, but in fact
they do not. The price of the item is such that the charges before rounding
end in a multiple of 0.0025. The charges ending in 0.0025 may balance out
those ending in 0.0075, but the ones ending in 0.0050 are rounded up by
half a cent, and no charges are rounded down by half a cent. The discrepancy in Table 6.1 is 2.25 cents. With many thousands of orders, the discrepancy would become substantial. Unless controls are planned to take care of
such rounding errors, a programmer might arrange to keep them and nobody
would be any the wiser.

Table 6.1. Rounding Errors

Sales of Item A:

Quantity	Price	Amount (after rounding)	Amount (before rounding)	Rounding error
1.33	1.75	2.33	2.3275	+0.0025
0.74	1.75	1.30	1.2950	+0.0050
0.91	1.75	1.59	1.5925	−0.0025
1.82	1.75	3.19	3.1850	+0.0050
1.22	1.75	2.14	2.1350	+0.0050
0.87	1.75	1.52	1.5225	−0.0025
1.10	1.75	1.93	1.9250	+0.0050
0.86	1.75	1.51	1.5050	+0.0050

Total Quantity __8.85__ Total Amount __15.51__ Total Rounding Error __+0.0225__

Total quantity X price = 15.4875

Total error = 15.51
              −15.4875
            =   0.0225

In some cases the fractions are always rounded *in the same direction*, in which case the discrepancy is larger.

The totals that might be used as a check on the calculation do not balance. The **total quantity** X **price** in Table 6.1 is 15.4875 and the **total amount charged** is 15.51. Such is generally the case when rounding is used. A common solution to this problem has been to permit a certain error in the totals of rounding fields when the batch totals are evaluated. Such a practice, however, is asking for trouble. A better solution is to keep a separate total of the rounding errors, as in Table 6.1, and then use the balancing equation: **total quantity** X **price** = **total amount charged** + **total rounding error**.

3. Reasonableness Checks

An overall reasonableness check is often applied to the output as with the input. When electricity bills are being sent, for example, a check may be made that the sum lies within a certain range expected for that customer.

4. Artificial Transactions

In some systems artificial transactions are included in the batch, for which known results are expected. When all the operations are completed, the results of processing the artificial transaction are checked. The artificial transaction may be inserted by the initial input validation run, and automatically checked by the run that produces the final output. A confirmation that the check is correct, along with a set of results, will be printed out. For example, in an invoicing run an artificial invoice may be printed. If this is incorrect, it indicates that the operations have not gone according to plan.

CONTINUOUS OPERATION

It is desirable that the checks employed should not significantly slow down the operations. In particular, if transactions are rejected or fail one of the validation tests, the run should continue and the problem should be dealt with later. The run should not stop unless it is useless to continue.

To achieve nonstop operation, a transaction may be set aside for processing at a later time. It may be saved for the next cycle of the operation, perhaps on the following day. The batch controls and totals in such a case must still be made to balance, and procedures must be devised to ensure that the rejected items cannot be lost or forgotten.

Sometimes an artificial value is assumed for a field in order to complete a run or a cycle of operations. When an electricity meter reading is not available, a value is sometimes assumed that is the average of previous values. An appropriate correction is made the following month, and usually the customer does not notice.

Again, if a nonvital alphabetic field is found invalid, it may be used regardless, and instructions left that it should be corrected the next time the program is run. This procedure could be used with any field that does not affect the current processing.

EXTERNAL CONTROLS

The input to the computer and the output from it will normally go via a control group (Fig. 6.3). This may be one control clerk on a small system or a group of people on a large system. The input/output control group is the interface between the user departments and the computer operations. It will ensure that the user departments submit work as intended, on schedule, with appropriate controls, and will receive all the output from the computer. It will verify the counts, control totals, and other checks on computer output, and will send it to the user departments, appropriately burst or bound, and with unwanted items removed.

The input/output control group will often submit work for keypunching and control this operation. Often, also, it will obtain tapes and disks from the library and control the operations that are performed on these. The

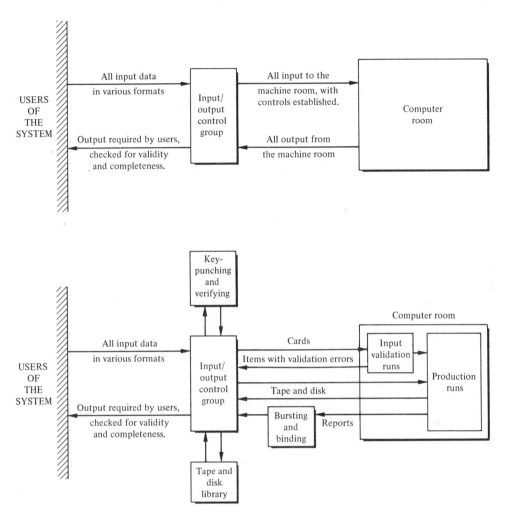

Figure 6.3. Input/Output control group: the key to external controls.

control group will receive the results of the input validation run and will ensure that the erroneous items are repunched with appropriate controls.

Typical of the responsibilities of the control group are

1. Receive work for processing from the user departments.
2. Record the receipt of the work along with the document counts and control totals.
3. Notify the user department that the work has been received and inform them whether the count and totals are correct. If they are not, hold the work until the matter has been investigated.

4. Note any work not received from the user departments on schedule and inform the department.

5. Note and initiate action on any improper preparation by the user departments, such as failure to provide counts or totals.

6. Submit documents to be keypunched or entered into tape or disk. This may include optical scanning or magnetic ink character recognition. Ensure that no documents are lost in this operation.

7. Check the results of the input validation run and arrange for any erroneous items to be repunched or reentered.

8. Balance the totals of the input validation run with those sent by the user departments, and record them.

9. Obtain necessary tapes or disks from the tape library and return them when they are used.

10. Submit jobs for processing to the operations department and record their submission. Several batches from the users may be combined into one batch. The batch numbers and new totals and counts must be recorded.

11. Receive the output of the computer runs and check that the counts and control totals are correct. If they are not, initiate investigation of the cause, and rerun the job.

12. Record details of the run, possibly filing the last page of the application-program printout, which prints the count and totals, and the last page of the listing on which the operating system prints details of the run.

13. Forward the output to the users after removing any items that are unwanted by them. The output should be appropriately burst and bound.

**CONTROLS
ON OUTPUT**
Certain controls should also be established on the output of the computer.

1. *Reasonableness checks* and other checks on the calculations, already mentioned, are one type of control on output.

2. *Serial numbers*, already mentioned, on bank checks or financial documents to assist in auditing and accountability external to the system. Other documents that might be used in computer-related robberies, such as stores requisitions, should also be serial numbered. When serial numbering is used, the last page or document should be marked as such.

3. *A control record* should be written at the end of a run. This may be a printed document or it may be a *trailer label* for a serial file on tape or disk. If a trailer label is written, it may also be printed so that it can be checked by the input/output control section. A trailer label should contain information such as
    (a) Label identifier
    (b) File number
    (c) Batch number

(d)　Creation date
(e)　Retention cycle (son, father, grandfather, etc.)
(f)　Real number
(g)　A count of the records on the reel
(h)　Batch controls
(i)　Hash totals of all important fields

TYPICAL
EXAMPLE

Figure 6.4 shows a typical example of a simple batch operation and the accuracy controls that are used.

QUALITY
CONTROL

Well-controlled installations establish a *quality-control* function to sample the accuracy of data both before and after processing. Errors should be analyzed by source, type, quantity, magnitude, age, and any other factors that might help to control them and pinpoint problems. Some installations maintain a computerized file of detected errors. When errors are detected by programmed checks, statistics can be maintained automatically. Machine halts, computer operator interventions, or other trouble indications should be analyzed. The objective of the quality-control operation should be to find where to exert pressure to minimize the number of errors.

Sometimes trends will be detected in the error rates. When the numbers of a certain category of errors are increasing, action may be taken to reverse the trend. Sometimes, in this way, a minor problem will be detected before it becomes major. At other times the statistics gathered point to a simple solution, such as additional training, better supervision, or new programmed checks.

Quality control on on-line files is especially important. As we shall discuss in Chapter 7, systems in which files are updated from terminals can be particularly vulnerable to errors if appropriate controls are not used. The tape and disk library needs to be carefully controlled, and special attention is needed to the quality of the programs. Control of the promotion of programs to the operational program library is discussed in Chapter 34. The computer operations need to be surrounded by the controls shown in Fig. 6.5 on page 69.

THE TYPES OF CONTROLS THAT ARE USED

EXTERNAL CONTROLS:

  * Number of documents are counted.
  * Total cash value is established.
  * Other totals may be used also.

  * Input cards are verified.
  * Self-checking numbers may be checked by
    the keypunch.

  * Input/output control section agrees with the
    record count and external totals.
  * Account number (or other) hash totals
    may be established.

  * The computer performs character, field, and record checks.
  * The records are counted.
  * The external control totals agree.
  * A complete set of hash totals is established.
  * A tape trailer label is written containing these totals.
  * A tape header label is written that will identify the tape.
  * Details of the count, control totals, hash totals and other
    checks are printed for the control desk.

  * Check the identification of the tape on its header label.
  * Check the record count.
  * Check all control totals.
  * Write tape trailer label.

  * Check the identification of both tapes.
  * Deferred validation checks to ensure that the
    input product data is correct.
  * Checks on processing.
  * Check record count and all control totals on
    New Order Tape.
  * Ditto on Product Master Tape.
  * Write tape trailer label giving record count and all
    control totals.

  * Check tape identification.
  * Check record count and all control totals.
  * Write tape trailer label.

  * Identification checks on both tapes.
  * Deferred validation checks to ensure that the
    input customer data is correct.
  * Checks on processing.
  * Check record count and all control totals on
    New Order Tape.
  * Ditto on Customer Master Tape.
  * Write tape trailer label giving record count and
    all totals.
  * Reasonableness checks on output.
  * Print the record count and all hash totals.
  * Serial number the invoices.
  * Mark the last invoice.

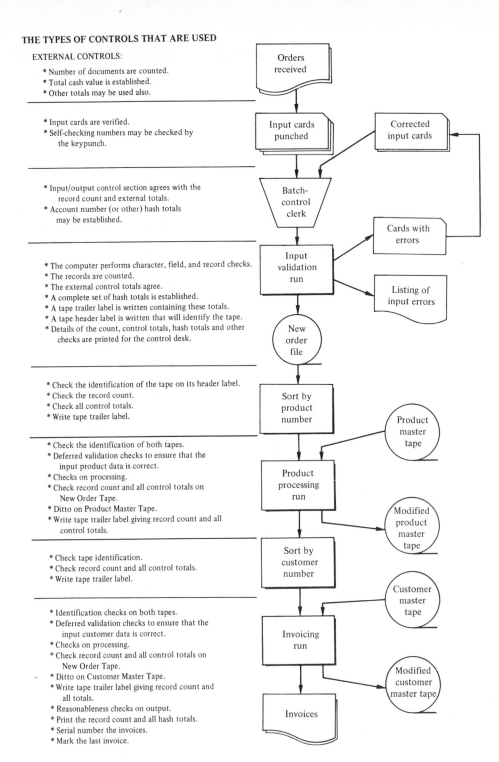

Figure 6.4. Typical set of controls used on a sequence of batch-processing operations.

68

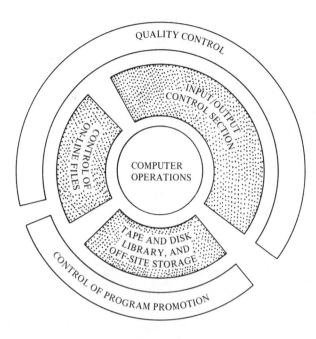

Figure 6.5

7 ACCURACY CONTROL ON REAL-TIME SYSTEMS

On real-time systems the transactions are often entered one at a time, independently, from terminals. In this case the batch controls that involve counting the items in a batch and developing a variety of batch totals cannot be used. The input/output control section cannot be similar to that in Fig. 6.3. However, terminal operators are always going to make errors and it is essential to protect the computer system from these errors. It is also necessary to leave audit trails so that the system can be audited and to take balances of certain files to ensure their accuracy. The transaction posting must be designed so that the files are capable of being balanced. The file balances will often be checked on off-line file-scanning runs, and these will be discussed in Chapter 23.

On systems in which the operator does not modify the data stored, it is not difficult to protect the system from operator errors. The files will be "locked," as described in later chapters, so that they cannot be overwritten, and if the terminal operator writes programs, these will be confined to one protected partition of an operating system so that they cannot interfere with any other programs. The main problem is that of helping the operator to find the information he wants when he uses the terminal incorrectly.

The control of errors is of much greater concern when the operators modify the data base, or are responsible for building up the information in the data base. In some systems *all information stored* originates from the terminal operators. Sometimes the terminal operators work in a fairly casual manner, compared with the card-punch operators and verifiers of batch data processing. Clearly, the viability of the concept of building up a data base in this way depends upon whether we can control the accuracy of the terminal input, catching the errors that occur.

On certain systems the errors are cumulative. The files contain information about a set of items that is kept for several months and is updated periodically be terminal operator actions. If occasional operator actions cause errors in the files, as the months pass by the files will steadily collect more and more inaccuracies. This situation could clearly bring the system into disrepute, and controls must be devised to prevent it.

A number of factors make real-time systems worse than batch systems for the control of accuracy. First, there are likely to be more terminal operators creating the input and they are scattered over many areas. They tend to be more diverse and less controllable than the operators in a keypunch room. Second, the verification operation found in a keypunch room is usually not employed. Third, batch totals and other batch controls often cannot be used, as the transactions originate singly, not in batches. Fourth, equipment failures will be experienced. It is often when a terminal, line, or computer fails, or during the recovery period, that errors originate.

We do, however, have one factor that is strongly in our favor on real-time systems. This is that in an appropriately designed dialogue most of the errors made can be caught *in real time*—as the operator makes them. The mistake or discrepancy is then rectified on the spot. If the accuracy of an item is questioned, as when a customer telephones to query his bill, the item in question can be investigated immediately. The distinction made in Chapter 6 between immediate and deferred checks often ceases to be significant, because the checks that were deferred in batch processing can now be handled in real time; the necessary files are on line. The effectiveness of such real-time error detection is highly dependent on the design of the man-machine dialogue.

There are eight vital aspects to the battle for accuracy on real-time systems:

1. The psychological considerations in dialogue design must be planned so as to minimize the probability of terminal operator errors.
2. The dialogue must be structured in such a way as to catch as many errors as possible, immediately.
3. The system must be planned so as to facilitate immediate correction of errors caught.
4. The real-time error-detection process must be backed up with off-line file inspection and, if applicable, balancing routines.
5. Self-checking operations must be built into both the real-time dialogue and the linkage of this dialogue to the file-inspection routines.

6. Transactions and posting procedures must be devised so that transaction balances and file balances can be taken where they are useful.

7. Procedures must be worked out to bridge all periods of system failure and recovery in such a way that errors are not introduced here.

8. Careful controls must be devised to prevent unauthorized persons from modifying the files or making entries at terminals.

ERROR PSYCHOLOGY   Psychological considerations and the structure of the man-machine interface are discussed in the author's book *Design of Man-Computer Dialogues.* It is desirable in the dialogue design to steer a course between boredom and bewilderment. Operator overload on the one hand, and lack of motivation on the other, will lead to errors.

When errors occur, the operator should be notified immediately, rather than later. Studies of the human learning process have shown that positive response to correct actions and admonition of incorrect actions *within seconds* gives by far the best reinforcement. The conscientious operator will learn from the response to his incorrect actions. The response, however, should not be overly abrupt. A split-second error response in midthought is jarring and "rude." The operator should be permitted to finish his thought before the error response is sent. A "dedicated" operator who spends much of his working day at the terminal may tolerate and learn from abrupt, abbreviated error messages, although some psychologists [1] recommend a response time of not less than 2 seconds. A "casual" operator, who uses the terminal only as an occasional adjunct to his job, is likely to require more dignified treatment. Figure 7.1 shows an error message worded with appropriate politeness on a system used by legislators.

There is one danger in giving real-time error responses. This is that the operator may develop the attitude that he does not need to be careful because the system picks up all his mistakes anyway. This must clearly be discouraged, and in many systems an appropriate way to do it is to log the error messages sent and analyze them. The operator, told that the system is keeping check on the mistakes he makes, will try to improve his performance.

TYPES OF ACCURACY CHECKS   The mainstay of batch processing—an input/output control group checking batch totals—does not exist. Instead, the types of accuracy checks that can be used are:

1. *Simple transaction checks.* An isolated transaction can usually be checked more completely than in batch processing, and this becomes the primary form of checking. The

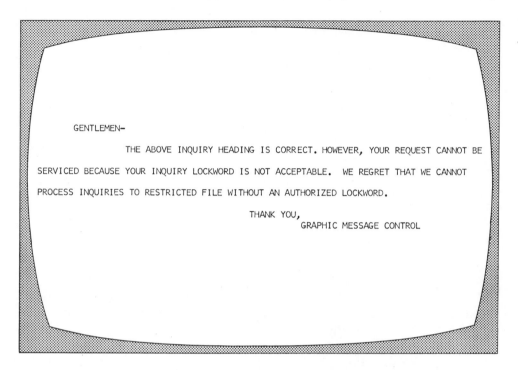

Figure 7.1. Error messages to "casual" operators should be worded with clarity and politeness; otherwise operator antagonism will result.

transaction and the dialogue must be structured so that there is some form of built-in redundancy, or some means of comparing the transaction with what was anticipated. There are a wide variety of ways of doing this, and they vary, necessarily, with the nature of the application.

2. *Group transaction checks.* The single-transaction checks will be backed up by a periodic check on a *group of transactions* when possible. In a bank, for example, the cash handled and entered by a teller will be balanced periodically to ensure that it is still correct. In a lengthy data entry dialogue relating to a single complex item, the status will be summarized at intervals to ensure that all appears correct.

3. *Checks made at a later time.* In many systems a transaction being entered can be used to check the accuracy of an earlier entry or of a record on file. The transactions should be designed so that there are cross-checks of this type.

4. *Off-line controls and file scanning.* These transaction checks will themselves be backed up by off-line accuracy controls, and the structure of the system and its processing must be designed to make these as effective as possible. Again taking the example of a bank, an end-of-day file scan will balance the cash from each teller and each branch, ensuring that it is correct. This will take place on other systems in which cash is involved. On some other systems the file scan will ensure that no record has been

accidentally deleted, and will check for certain types of undesirable circumstances. The same file scan that is used as an accuracy check can be employed to enhance the security procedures, and so we shall leave a detailed discussion of file scanning until Chapter 23, after the description of security procedures.

5. *Location validation reports.* On some systems a summary of the records relating to a branch location is prepared periodically, perhaps daily, and must be compared with records at that location. Thus a cash summary or inventory summary may be sent. A salesman may be sent a summary of his orders. The progress of a job through a factory may be checked.

6. *Checks on the operators.* Check will be made that only authorized terminal operators are using the system. This subject also relates to security, and will be left for later chapters.

Let us examine some of these checks in more detail.

SINGLE-TRANSACTION   We shall list a number of types of single-transaction
CHECKS   checks. The list is illustrative, not exhaustive, as
                           there is a wide difference in what is possible on different applications. The transaction designer should survey all the possibilities he can, and select a set of them to check the input as tightly as possible.

1. Descriptive Read Back

When the operator keys in a number or a mnemonic, an alphabetic read back should be given saying what it relates to, if possible. If he keys in 734912 instead of 743912, the response will inform him that he was ordering a snowplow (when in fact he intended to order a pair of sunglasses).

When a *menu-selection* technique is used with a visual display, the operator often responds to a menu screen by typing one digit. He may type the wrong digit, and so the subsequent screen should have a heading stating the item he has selected.

2. Character and Field Checks

The character and field validation checks discussed in Chapter 6 are applicable to real time and are possibly more important there than in batch processing.

3. Link to Earlier Transaction

Sometimes a transaction can be linked to an earlier transaction for error-control purposes. When a customer takes his passbook into a savings bank, for example, it should contain the balance at the end of the previous transaction. This redundant information may be keyed in by the teller. The computer checks the previous balance on the record for this customer. If it is not in agreement, this may indicate that the teller has made a mistake; it may indicate that something earlier has gone astray. If the latter, it should be sorted out there and then. There are many other examples in which the dialogue is designed to give continuity between separate transactions relating to the same entity.

4. Check for a Valid Sequence of Transactions

Sometimes events should happen only in a certain fixed sequence. A deviation from this sequence will indicate an error, and so sequence checks will be made when each transaction is entered. Such is the case in a production-control system. Workers on a factory shop floor enter into terminals details of jobs they start, complete, or, for some reason, leave. They may enter their man number, the job number, and the number of the machine tool that they are using. If they leave a job, they may indicate that it is 20 per cent complete, or whatever the figure is. The computer may maintain three sets of records, each of which is updated at this point—a record for the man, a record for the job, and a record for the machine tool. When an entry is made, the computer will check that *that* man should have been working on *that* job, using *that* machine tool. If he reports that the job is 20 per cent complete, the computer will check that this is a viable figure. If the job had not been reported as started, or had already been reported 50 per cent complete, an error message would result. In practice, these continuity checks result in almost all the data-entry errors being detected at one time or another. As soon as the computer's picture of what is occurring on the shop floor deviates from what is reported, action is taken.

5. Use of Machine-Readable Documents

On production-control and data-entry systems, badges are commonly used with information punched into them. A badge is used to give the employee number. Sometimes a badge travels around the factory with the job, giving the job number. Sometimes a badge is used for giving the machine-tool number. The use of such badges ensures that no mistake is made in the entry of these numbers, as it might be if the worker keyed them in.

A number of other forms of machine-readable documents are in use for similar reasons. It is likely that we may see a massive use of machine-readable credit cards in the future. A credit card with data about its owner encoded on a magnetic stripe is now in use.

6. Check for Internal Contradictions

A false entry may be detected by the fact that it contradicts other known data, or a set of entries may contain some inconsistency. In a system controlling railroad cars a terminal entry stating the movement of a car would first be checked to ensure that *that* car was in *that* location and possible that it *was* loaded with the goods stated. If any entry on an airline system is made to change a booking, the computer will first check that the passenger *was* booked on the stated flight.

In many cases the dialogue can be designed to enhance the checks that can be made. In an airline-reservation dialogue, for example, in which a multistop journey is being booked, it is desirable to do a location continuity check and also a date-time continuity check. Unfortunately, however, many passengers do not book continuous journeys. A man might, for example, make a booking from New York to Los Angeles, drive to San Francisco, and fly back from there to New York. The airline knows nothing about how he travels from Los Angeles to San Francisco, and so the continuity checks at first sight may seem valueless. The airline overcomes this problem by booking a false segment to bridge the gap. It is known as an ARUNK segment, meaning ARRIVAL UNKNOWN. The ARUNK segment is booked from Los Angeles to San Francisco, and then the computer can check the whole booking for location continuity and date-time continuity. There are other types of applications in which an invention like an ARUNK segment would be worthwhile.

There are many ways of building double checks into a dialogue structure. It is up to the designer to find them.

7. Check That All Facts Have Been Entered

The facts about a situation will often be entered in a variable rather than a fixed sequence. This will often be the case when the facts are being obtained from a potential customer over the telephone. The computer must then check that all the facts have been entered. Usually the entry of a subset of facts is mandatory. If the operator attempts to close the dialogue before these have been entered, he must be asked by the computer for the missing data. If one item of the set is not applicable, for example, the customer does not have a telephone number, a NIL entry should be made.

GROUP-TRANSACTION   The error checks may be applicable to a group of
CHECKS   transactions rather than to single transactions:

8. Periodic Item Balances

On systems in which cash is handled, an interim balance may be taken at fairly small intervals. On some systems several different accumulators are used to give a multiple balance. A similar approach is used with some systems handling items other than cash.

9. Running Totals

On some systems, running totals are kept. The terminal maintains a printout giving the totals of certain items entered. The totals may be broken down by category. At intervals, or at the end of the day, the totals will be compared with totals obtained by the computer.

Running totals are especially valuable during periods of equipment failure. The terminal goes dead, but customers still have to be dealt with. At some later time, one hopes not too much later, the terminal returns to life, and the transactions made in some makeshift manner while it was out are entered into the system. The running totals are maintained during the period of outage. When the transactions are then entered into the system, these totals will be compared with those obtained by the computer. In this way the running totals bridge the gap of terminal outage.

10. Checkpoints

When an operator is entering separate related items, each perhaps requiring some decision-making dialogue, he may be made to inspect a summary of his progress at intervals. At this checkpoint he must inspect the status summary and verify that he thinks it is correct. The checkpoint procedure may be designed to be optional so that the operator can use it when he thinks fit. It is probably better, however, to make it mandatory, forcing him to check at intervals that no misunderstanding or omission has occurred.

ERRORS CAUGHT AT A LATER TIME   On occasions an error may not be caught at the time it is made, but becomes apparent at some later time. It should, in fact, be given every opportunity to make itself manifest later. When an operator is given a display of a set of previously stored facts, he should be asked to verify that they are correct.

If the operator at this stage makes a correction entry, it is often advisable to keep a copy of the original. This is certainly so if the operator making the correction is different from the operator who made the original entry. On airline-reservation systems the passenger records are kept in two parts. One part gives details of the current status for that passenger, and the other is a "history record" showing what changes in the record have been made. The original may be stored in the lowest-cost level of storage.

There are some types of real-time systems in which a discrepancy is unlikely to survive undetected for long, provided that the data on the files are checked against each succeeding entry. As each change in status of an entry is recorded, it is compared with the previous information that the computer had about that entity.

ERRORS CORRECTED BY A SPECIALIZED OPERATOR   Sometimes when an entry triggers off an error indication, the best person to deal with it would not be the operator who originated the entry, but a different person who has an overall knowledge of the situation. In other words, it pays on some systems to have a specialist, or group of specialists, for dealing with certain types of errors.

The error-handling staff would sit at terminals through which they would receive notification of discrepancies. They will in some cases be close to the computer room and may use listings prepared each night on file-scanning runs. They will use their terminals for making corrections to the files when necessary.

Each major file may have a man assigned to it who would be responsible for its accuracy. As we shall discuss later, he may also be responsible for its security—insuring that unauthorized persons do not read items they should not or make changes to the records. We shall call this person the *file owner*. One person may have responsibility for more than one file. He will understand its structure, addressing, and the on-line and off-line checks that are made upon it. He will receive real-time notification of suspected discrepancies and will investigate them, making such changes as are appropriate.

The file owners may be gathered together in a room, which we shall call the *information control room.* A variety of other operations are likely to take place in such a room, and it is an essential adjunct to certain real-time systems.

INDIRECT
FEEDBACK

Most errors are best dealt with by the operator making the transaction. The feedback to this operator is of great importance. In some systems, however, direct and immediate feedback is not possible. The two main cases in which this is so are, first, when the operator is off line, and, second, when the operator has an inexpensive terminal not capable of giving verbal feedback. The first case occurs when messages are sent by teletype to the computer in a machine-readable code, but from an off-line operator, perhaps in a different organization. This occurs, for example, when one airline sends a teletype message to another about reservations. If the message turns out to be machine unreadable or contains a detectable error, it will be referred to an operator. Sometimes the operator will be able to see an obvious miscoding that can be put right on the spot. Sometimes he must compose a message to the originator requesting clarification.

The most common use of terminals that cannot give a detailed error message is in data-collection stations in a factory, warehouse, or other work location. Such applications often use a large number of terminals, and it is desirable to make the terminal as inexpensive as possible. For this reason no printing or other character response mechanism is used. Figure 7.2 illustrates a typical terminal of this nature.

Figure 7.2. Data-entry terminals with no printing or other response mechanism.

The user of such a terminal will make errors, and the systems designer must construct a mechanism for dealing with these. One solution is to place in the vicinity of the work stations a terminal that *is* capable of dialogue. This might be situated in a foreman's office, for example, and the foreman would sort out the problems. Another possibility is to have a shop-floor expediter, or roving problem solver, who is directed from the information control room.

Figure 7.3 shows a configuration that worked particularly well in practice in a factory data-collection system. Erroneous transactions from the work station terminals are detected by the computer and details of them are printed at the terminals in the information control room. The specialists there investigate the errors and can sometimes take care of them themselves. When they need the help of the roving shop-floor representative, they send a radio signal to him. He has a radio beeper in his belt, and when it sounds he goes to the nearest terminal. This has a telephone jack wired to the information control room. The control-room specialist tells the shop-floor man what is wrong, and the shop-floor man goes to the worker in question, finds out the correct situation, and makes appropriate corrections at the terminal.

This three-way linkage works well because it is highly flexible, and because the workers know that if they make mistakes at the terminal they will be visited by the shop-floor representative. They normally try to avoid such visitations. They can, however, ask for help at the terminal and, in effect, call for the representative.

Figure 7.4 shows some typical printouts received in the management control room in this example. In the first one a worker is claiming a job to be 20 per cent complete when the computer record says it has already been claimed 100 per cent complete. It is unclear how this has arisen, so the control-room specialist will ask the shop-floor representative to investigate and report the correct situation.

In the second example the same transaction is entered twice by the worker. The second one is ignored and no action is taken.

In the third example, the worker is claiming the start of a job, but the computer cannot find the record for that manufacturing order when it attempts to read the files. There could be several possible reasons for this. The manufacturing order number might be in error; a record for that manufacturing order number may have never been set up; or the record may have been accidentally destroyed, perhaps by a programming error. The control-room specialist examines the files, diagnoses the trouble, and may modify or create a record.

In the fourth example, the entry is made in an invalid sequence. The worker is claiming that his job is 100 per cent complete, but he is already in

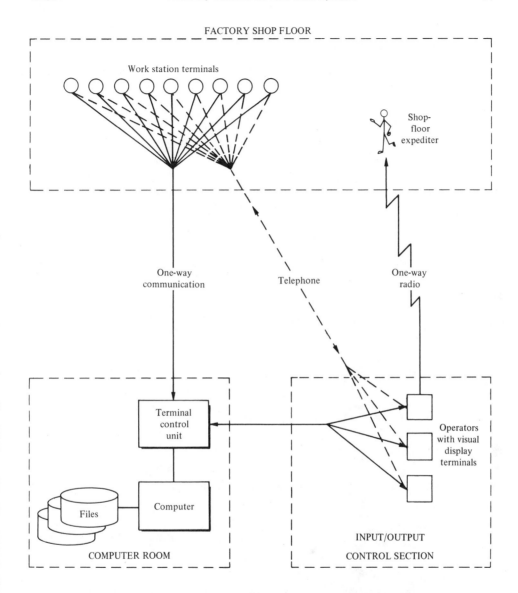

Figure 7.3. The input/output control section on a real-time system may be remote from the computer room; and more than one such section might be used. These sections are located close to the site of user activity.

"claim" status for a different job. The computer prints out information that will enable the control-room specialist to examine the appropriate files.

The last illustration in Figure 7.4 shows a worker asking for help because he has run out of parts. The message reaches the control-room specialist and he radios the shop-floor representative to take corrective action.

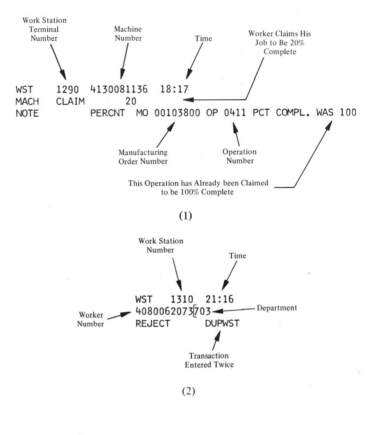

(1)

(2)

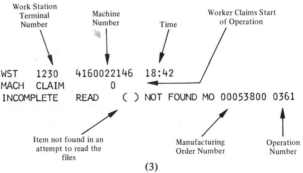

(3)

Figure 7.4

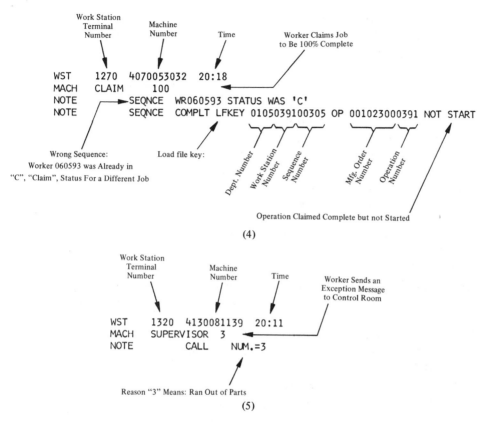

Figure 7.4 (cont'd)

INPUT/OUTPUT CONTROL SECTION   The input/output control section discussed in Chapter 6 does not exist in the same form when the input is received from terminals and the output is sent back to terminals. Nevertheless, a control section, which is sometimes given the same name, is employed on certain systems for the control of accuracy.

One difference with real-time systems is that there may be more than one input/output control section. The control sections may be sited in the locations where transactions originate, such as a factory area, and would be connected to the system by telecommunication links. In this way they may be better able to deal with local problems.

This section may have the following functions:

1. It will be notified in real time of any suspected errors not resolved in the man-terminal dialogue. It will investigate and correct them either by instructing that the transaction be reentered, or by reentering a correction from the input/output control room. This

operation is particularly important when the terminals do not have adequate dialogue capability, as with the data-entry terminals in the previous example.

2. When group-transaction checks are used, such as periodic terminal balances, the control section will be notified automatically of any imbalances or any failures on the part of the terminal operators to conform to the standards laid down.

3. The control section may monitor the terminal activity and may be informed automatically of any action by operators that breaks the rules.

4. The control section may be responsible for the overall accuracy of the data files. Suspected errors in the files may be detected by the computer during the processing of transactions or by a terminal operator. The control section will be notified and will investigate. It will sometimes be desirable for the control section to modify an erroneous item or create a record on the file that appears to be missing. This will be done in order that processing can continue as smoothly as possible, but a log of all such modifications will be kept for later reconciliation. (Record reconstruction is discussed in Chapter 22.)

5. Off-line operations will often be used to enhance or control file accuracy (and are discussed in Chapter 23). The input/output control section will ensure that these balancing or file-scanning operations are performed, and will deal with any discrepancies that might arise.

6. The control section may also be responsible for monitoring the security controls that the system uses. It would then be notified in real time of any suspected security violations, and would check the security logs, as will be discussed in Chapter 16.

7. The control section on some systems is concerned about whether certain operations happen on schedule. This is true, for example, in a production-control system in which jobs are being routed through a machine shop according to a specified schedule. If no report is received on a given operation by a preestablished time, the control section will automatically be notified and must investigate.

8. Often the control section takes on other functions that are entirely application oriented. It may be responsible for the control of flight loading in an airline or for progress monitoring in a factory. In some cases the control of accuracy is regarded as a secondary function, which would have been needed anyway.

EXCEPTION JOURNAL

The staff in the input/output control section may interact directly with a variety of different types of system users or other personnel. Many of these interactions will be triggered by messages from the computer detailing errors or suspected errors. The procedures should be specified in detail, saying who contacts whom and what action is taken.

The computer should keep an *exception journal* logging the exception messages, such as those in Fig. 7.4, that are sent to the input/output control room, and recording what action was taken concerning each of these.

The procedures by which the input/output control section interfaces with other personnel may be diagrammed on charts, such as those in Fig. 7.5. The charts in this illustration relate to a production-control system, such as that shown in Fig. 7.3. The shaded blocks are those in which the computer develops a transaction journal and a log of the exception conditions that arise. Both may be kept on disk so that the control section can read them and make inquiries, but not update them.

The first chart shows the handling of an invalid transaction. The second shows a condition in which a negative balance is produced in a part inventory record. There could be several reasons for this:

1. The transaction being processed when the condition occurred was in error.

INVALID TRANSACTION

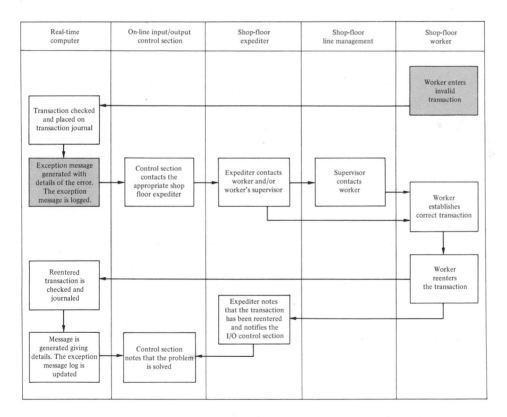

Figure 7.5. Part I. Incorrect choice of job at work station.

INCORRECT INVENTORY BALANCE IS FOUND

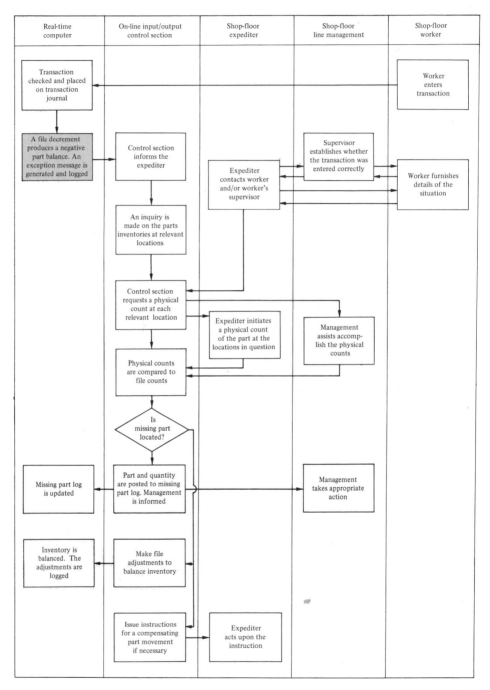

Figure 7.5. Part II. Transaction generates an exception condition.

TRANSACTION GENERATES AN EXCEPTION CONDITION

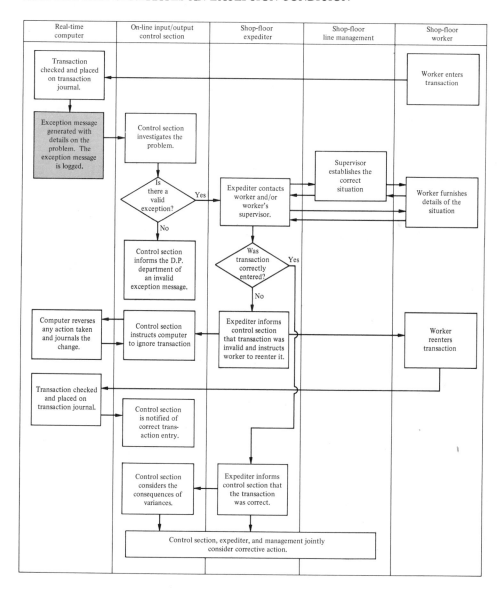

Figure 7.5 (cont'd)

INCORRECT CHOICE OF JOB AT WORK STATION

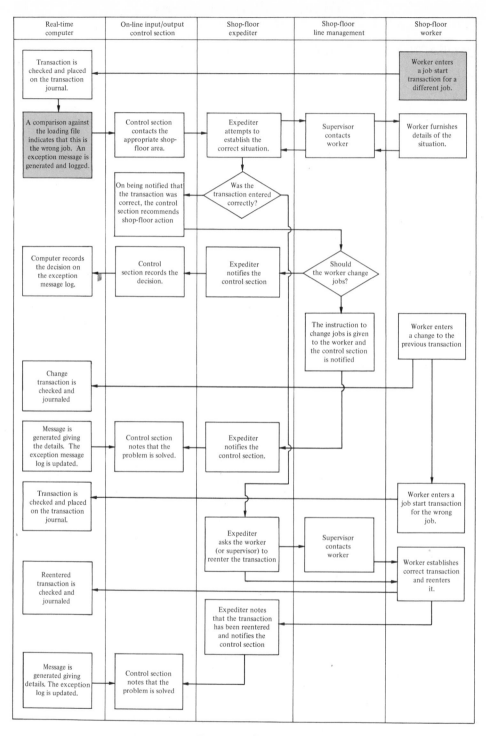

Figure 7.5 (cont'd)

2. The quantity recorded in the file record is in error.
3. There was an error in an earlier transaction relating to a move of parts out of the area in question.
4. There was an error in an earlier transaction relating to a move of parts into the area in question.
5. An improper movement of parts has taken place—possibly a theft.

The input/output control section will attempt to establish the reason for the discrepancy message, and will initiate immediate inventory counts for the part, if this is thought necessary, checking the file records against the physical stock. If a genuine parts shortage is found, management will be informed, and the computer files will be adjusted. The missing quantity will be posted to a *missing parts file* so that the files still balance, and balancing checks can be made on them periodically.

The third chart shows a general exception condition generated by an incoming transaction. The fourth chart shows what happens when a worker starts an incorrect job. There are many other error conditions, which must be charted in a similar fashion.

MORAL   Effective error control requires three system elements that interlink together:

1. A dialogue designed to catch the maximum possible number of errors with effective feedback to the operators.
2. Off-line file balancing, scanning, and policing operations.
3. Intelligent and flexible human action to detect and correct errors that do slip through.

Designing the man-machine interface to avoid errors will require perhaps 10 per cent more programming and 10 per cent more operator actions; sometimes a greater percentage than this. It has been discovered (the hard way!) on many systems in operation today is that this extra effort is very well worthwhile.

REFERENCE

1. Robert B. Miller, "Response Time in Man-Computer Conversational Transaction," Book Company, Washington, D.C.

8 ACCURACY CONTROLS IN TELEPROCESSING

On most data paths in a computer system the user justifiably expects the data transfers to be error-free. The one exception to this is the telecommunication channels. Transmission errors occur sufficiently frequently to be of concern, and it is necessary to detect them and take corrective action.

Error detection and correction are of vital concern when certain types of data are being transmitted, such as:

1. financial data
2. critical figures
3. programs

With other types of data they are less important, for example, telementry data from a space vehicle when one reading of a parameter is soon followed by the next reading, and successive readings differ little. When the transmitted data come from operators using real-time terminals, it is likely that far more errors will occur in the operator's keying than in the transmission process. The checks used on the accuracy of the operators will catch most transmission errors also.

The foundation stone for any means of controlling errors in teleprocessing is an *error-detecting code*. Some error-detecting codes are very powerful and will detect virtually any error that may occur. But not all codes are this effective.

Given a means to detect errors, there are several procedures that may be taken. These are summarized in Table 8.1 on pages 92 and 93, and are discussed in more detail in the two books referred to in the table: *Systems Analysis for Data Transmission* and *Teleprocessing Network Organization* (both written by James Martin; published in 1972 and 1970, respectively, by Prentice-Hall, Inc., Englewood Cliffs, N. J.).

The most common approach is to transmit a block of data, which may contain one or more records or messages. Often it is from one terminal, but sometimes it is from a group of terminals that share a control unit or concentrator. The block contains a number of characters, or a pattern of bits, derived from the data that are being transmitted so as to give a means of detecting errors in that data. If an error is found by the receiving device, the device ignores the block and sends a request to the transmitting machine requesting retransmission. If the same block is received in error several times in succession, a different type of action is taken. Examples of such types of action are:

1. Attempting to transmit at lower speed
2. Waiting for a given time and then attempting retransmission
3. Calling an operator

It is important for designers of data-transmission systems to realize that a very high measure of protection from transmission errors can be achieved. Codes can be constructed which are so effective that it would be unlikely that *any* error would slip through undetected. However, this is certainly not true with many of the error-detecting methods that are in common use. The powerful error-detecting codes do not necessarily introduce a higher proportion of checking bits than do the poorer codes that are in common use. The more successful codes, however, do require more logic in the encoding and decoding circuits.

As well as error-detecting codes, error-*correcting* codes are sometimes used. An error-correcting code contains more redundancy than an error-detecting code so that it can attempt to correct the errors that occur. This process does not require a reverse channel, as is needed with the request for retransmission when error-detecting codes are used. The process is therefore sometimes referred to as *forward error correction.*

The remainder of this chapter discusses the codes that may be used for error control.

Table 8.1. Techniques for Controlling Line Errors

Technique	Usage	Book	Chapter
1. Ignore line errors.	Used where proportion of operator errors is far greater than line errors. Used in verbal message transmission.	SYSTRAN	9
2. Common error-detection codes. — Character coding (e.g., 4-out-of-8 code)	Less commonly used today. Less effective than block codes.	NETWORK	2
Parity checks	Commonly used but of little value (especially with higher-speed transmission).	SYSTRAN	15
Vertical and longitudinal checks	Commonly used. Simple circuitry. Less efficient than polynomial codes.	SYSTRAN	15
Polynomial checks on blocks / Checks on groups of records	Exceedingly efficient block error detection is possible with polynomial codes.	NETWORK	5
3. Error detection without automatic retransmission.	Manually initiated retransmission is used when the proportion of operator errors is high (e.g., on airline reservation systems).	SYSTRAN	15
4. Error detection with automatic retransmission. Retransmit one character / Retransmit one word / Retransmit one message or record / Retransmit several messages or records / Retransmit a batch	The safest method, given a good error-detecting code. Some form of message storage is needed at the terminal. Echo check. Word check. Probably the most common. Block check on the message or record. Possibly checked with a high-order polynomial code. Possibly checked with a batch hash total.	SYSTRAN	15
Note:	It pays to select optimum block size or batch size.	SYSTRAN	35

Technique	Usage	Book	Chapter
5. Retransmit at a later time.	For example, after a periodic or daily balancing or policing run.	SYSTRAN	15
6. Retransmit several times if first attempt fails.	Normally done.	SYSTRAN	15
7. Retransmit several times with variable time delays.	To circumvent lengthy periods of line noise.	SYSTRAN	15
8. Retransmit with modem switched to lower speed.	Can be done automatically on certain terminals with built-in modems. Otherwise the modem speed may be switched manually.	SYSTRAN	14
9. Loop check. ⎯⎯ Characters returned to terminal ⎯⎯ Characters sent twice by terminal	Simple where loop transmission is employed. Used on in-plant loops with capacity to spare.	SYSTRAN	15
10. Forward-error correction.	Less efficient and less safe than error detection. Used on one-way links and on links with abnormally high error rates such as long-wave and short-wave radio, and telephone-line modems operating at 9600 bits per second.	SYSTRAN	15
11. Combination of forward-error correction and error detection with retransmission.	Forward-error correction is added to error-detection schemes when the proportion of retransmission becomes high enough to degrade throughput significantly.	SYSTRAN	35

*"NETWORK" refers to the author's *Teleprocessing Network Organization*. "SYSTRAN" refers to the author's *Systems Analysis for Data Transmission*.

93

CRITERIA FOR   The merit of any scheme for correcting transmis-
CHOICE OF CODE   sion errors is a function of three properties that
                          are listed below:

1. What is the efficiency of the code in detecting errors? How many incorrect messages does the code let through? Ideally, we would like a scheme that will be able to catch all errors.
2. How much does it reduce the line throughput? Both redundant bits and retransmission lessen the total data throughput on the line.
3. How much does it cost?

We can swing the design between these parameters by the choice of different coding methods. In some systems high accuracy is all important, and a high price will be paid for it if necessary. It is very rare, however, to find those codes that give the highest measures of protection in use today. Systems usually settle for a reasonably high measure of protection and a cost that is not too high. Line throughput is usually not too much of a worry in selecting a code. Higher-speed modems can be used if necessary, or more lines can be added. For this reason simple codes have been used that have a high degree of redundancy but that do not inflate terminal costs too much. In some systems, in the author's view, the systems analysts have paid too little attention to transmission accuracy.

The balance is swinging in favor of the more complex codes. In the early days of computing, the circuitry for composing the error check and for examining it after transmission was expensive. Circuit cost dominated the choice of code. Today, however, and especially in view of *large-scale-integration* technology, the cost associated with the more complex codes is much lower. Furthermore, more systems need a high degree of protection because they are transmitting data that should not be allowed to acquire errors—programs or financial data, for example. It would seem worthwhile to mass produce circuits that handle the high-order polynomial codes discussed at the end of this chapter, especially as these do not introduce a high level of redundancy and hence throughput degradation.

Terminal cost assumes great importance on some of today's systems with very large numbers of terminals. Therefore, one sometimes finds a cheap-to-implement code used at the terminal, but a more complex code giving better transmission throughput on the concentrators, or on control units handling many terminals.

With error-detecting codes it is not necessary, as we shall see, to have a very high proportion of redundancy in order to achieve a very high measure of protection. If we transmit a long block of data, we can protect it very well with relatively few bits. The error-detecting power depends primarily on the number of checking bits in a group rather than on the percentage of redundancy. Therefore, it gives more efficient coding if long blocks are sent and protected by one group of bits so that there is a high ratio of data bits to check bits. The error-detecting power, however, is *highly* dependent on the nature of the code.

As we shall see, we can transmit 100-character messages with only about 10 per cent redundancy, and can detect virtually all errors if we use a sufficiently powerful code.

ERROR-CORRECTING
CODES

The ability of a code to *correct errors* is related to its ability to *detect* them. A code that can detect double errors can correct *single* ones. If a single error occurs, the receiving machine could attempt to correct it, for example, by changing the bits one at a time. If the receiving machine could detect *all* double errors, then it could detect when the single erroneous bit had been modified correctly. Similarly, a device that can detect quadruple errors can *correct* double ones; a device that can detect $2x$ errors can correct.

Similarly, some codes can detect two error bursts of length b bits, in which bits within the burst may or may not be correct; such codes could *correct* one such burst.

In theory, an error-correcting code could be formed from a set of tables. If a set of bits representing a character, word, or block is received, the receiving machine could look up this set in a table which gives the correct character, word, or block that is the most likely to be the original. To construct such a table would require a knowledge of the most probable types of errors. In practice, we need something very much easier to implement than this.

Whatever way we implement an error-correcting code, there is always a probability that it will miscorrect. Sometimes it will turn a correct bit into an incorrect bit because the particular error pattern that occurred was not one that the code was designed to correct. If the bits in error were randomly distributed, this would not be much of a problem. It would happen very rarely. However, they are not. The noise is likely to come in bursts in which almost any error pattern could occur.

During a period of excessive noise, a good detection and retransmission scheme would increase the number of messages that were rejected, lowering the throughput until the noisy period ended. A forward error-correction system, on the other hand, would not degrade throughput but *would* increase the number of erroneous messages that it let slip through. For most computer systems the latter would be undesirable. Detection and retransmission are to be preferred.

Furthermore, because the bit errors tend to come in clusters, the number of messages that need retransmission is less. Suppose that we transmit blocks of 1000 bits on a line with an error rate of 1 bit in 10^5. If the errors were randomly distributed, one block in 100 would need to be retransmitted. However, if the errors are clustered, we might receive one block with 10 errors, and then 10^6 bits without error. The retransmission rate may thus have dropped to one block in 1000.

The cost of schemes for forward error correction is generally greater than that for effective detection. The number of redundant bits required for the same measure of protection as a good error-detection code is *much* higher. Error detection and retransmission therefore give better value for the money, and better value for bandwidth. It could be argued that retransmission necessitates the return path; however, this is almost invariably needed anyway for control of the machines and for responses.

Error-*checking* codes are of great value in protecting records on magnetic tape, disk, or other media when an error is detected and the original is unobtainable. With data transmission, however, the original still exists in the transmitting machine, and can easily be re-sent.

With computer data transmission over full-duplex, voice-grade, or sub-voice-grade lines, and with today's state of the art, forward error-correction systems have less merit for all of our three criteria—throughput, cost, and (especially) reliability.

Forward error correction has one important role to play, however. It is desirable on some systems to use modems that give as high a data rate as possible over a given line. For example, it is desirable to transmit at speeds ranging from 4800 to 9600 bits per second over a voice line. The modulation techniques which can achieve these speeds unfortunately produce a much higher proportion of transmission errors than the techniques used in lower-speed modems. The error rate becomes so high that a substantial amount of the available transmission time must be spent in retransmission. (See the author's book, *Systems Analysis for Data Transmission,* Chapter 35.) To overcome this problem, forward error correction is employed in the modem.

Forward error correction, as we have commented, does not correct all the errors. To achieve error-free transmission, it must therefore be backed up with error-*detecting* codes and retransmission of blocks in error. The role of forward error correction is to lessen the amount of retransmission needed, and hence improve the overall throughput. With transmission over a voice line at 9600 bits per second, this improvement is substantial.

On half-duplex lines, used at high speed, the line turnaround time becomes long compared to the character transmission time, and so here forward error correction is more attractive. The remainder of this chapter describes error-*detecting* codes.

PARITY
CHECKS

It is common to find two kinds of check on transmitted data, one on each character, and one on each message, message segment, or block. Many systems have both. Some systems have only character checks; this is generally not very secure. Some systems have only the message or block check, and this, as we shall see, can be made extremely secure, given a good code.

The simplest check, and one of the most commonly used because it is inexpensive to implement, is the parity check. However, one single parity check will fail to detect an error if that error damages an even number of bits. In data transmission a single noise pulse or dropout (loss of signal) is frequently of greater duration than the length of one bit. This is more likely to be so when a high bit rate is used. Even at low bit rates, double errors are common. A CCITT study* of 50-baud telegraph lines gave the following figures:

Isolated single-bit errors	50–60 per cent
Error bursts with two erroneous bits	10–20 per cent
Error bursts with three erroneous bits	3–10 per cent
Error bursts with four erroneous bits	2– 6 per cent

A burst was defined here as bits in error separated by less than 10 nonerroneous bits.

Curves published by American Telephone & Telegraph showing errors on their switched public network† indicate that when 1200-bit-per-second

*CCITT Special Study Group A (Data Transmission), Contribution 92, Annex XIII, p. 131, October 18, 1963.

†"Error Distribution and Error Control Evaluation," Extracts from Contribution GT. 43, No. 13, February 1960, *CCITT Red Book*, Vol. VII, The International Telecommunication Union, Geneva, 1961.

transmission is used, about 49 per cent of the error bits have another error following within 7 bits. If the error bit in question is the first one of an 8 bit character, there is a 49 per cent chance that the parity check will fail to detect the error (if the possibility of having 3 or more bits in error is ignored). For the character as a whole, the curves can be used to calculate that there is about a 30 per cent chance that the single parity check will fail. Such figures are very approximate estimates of code performance. Tests made on transmission lines with parity-checked characters have confirmed that this can hardly be regarded as a satisfactory way to protect data (although, surprisingly, it is used as such on some machines).

A parity check on a character is sometimes referred to as a *vertical* parity check. A parity bit checking all the equivalent bits in a message is referred to as a *horizontal* or *longitudinal* check. They are also referred to as *row* and *column* parity checks. Used in conjunction with each other, they provide a measure of protection much greater than either vertical or horizontal parity checks alone.

THE U.S. ASCII　　　　The American Standards Institute recommendation
RECOMMENDATION　　for checking on the ASCII code is to use horizontal
　　　　　　　　　　　　　and vertical parity bits. The level of redundancy
needed is fairly high. If x characters are sent, the ratio of check bits to data bits is

$$\frac{x + 8}{7x}$$

Thus, for a 20-character message, one fifth as many check bits as data bits is needed. A very long message needs about one seventh. This is a higher ratio than with the polynomial codes, which will be discussed shortly.

For an undetected error to occur, the bits changed must be self-compensating, as shown in Fig. 8.1. This type of check can detect all messages with 1-, 2-, 3-bit errors, all with an odd number of errors and some with an even number of errors. The probability of self-compensating errors occurring is low.

When the transmission system is prone to double errors, there will be a higher probability of self-compensating errors occurring. Some transmission schemes are designed in such a way that double-bit errors can occur. In some modulation schemes the bits are represented by a *change* in state of the carrier, rather than by the state of the carrier itself. This is referred to as *transition coding*, rather than *state coding*. For example, a change of phase in one direction represents a 1 bit, and a change of phase in the opposite

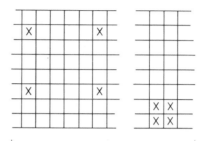

	Data character 1	Data character 2	Data character 3	Longitudinal check character
Bit position 1	1	0	1	0
Bit position 2	0	0	0	0
Bit position 3	0	0	1	1
Bit position 4	0	0	0	0
Bit position 5	0	1	0	1
Bit position 6	0	0	0	0
Bit position 7	1	1	1	1
Parity bit	1	1	0	0

A message of three data characters in ASCII code, with ASCII checking

For an undetectable error to occur an even number of bits, greater than three, must be changed, in compensating positions

Figure 8.1

direction represents a 0 bit. Here an erroneous phase change on the line may cause two errors rather than one. A second similar occurrence shortly afterward may give the compensating error that is undetectable by the vertical and horizontal parity checks.

Again, on some modems, data are coded into pairs of bits (di-bits) rather than single bits. The carrier may be in one of four possible states at one instant, conveying one of four possible bit pairs. A noise impulse is then likely to change a pair of bits. Two such impulses could give a compensating error.

We see, then, that the error-detecting power of this checking is dependent on the method of modulation being used. (It will be lower with transition coding than with state coding, and lower if di-bits rather than single bits are encoded.)

Measurements of the effectiveness of coding with a vertical and horizontal parity check indicate that it lessens the number of undetected errors by a factor ranging from 100 to 1000. A telephone line with an error rate of 1 to 10^5 might have an undetected error rate of from 1 to 10^7 to 1 in 10^8. During periods of abnormal noise on the lines, the undetected error rates will be much higher.

_M_-OUT-OF-_N_
CODES

Many transmission schemes have coded characters so that a fixed number of bits per character must be used. If a number of bits other than this is received, an error is recognized.

In one such code, 8-bit characters are transmitted, each of which must have four 1 bits and four 0 bits. This gives 70 possible combinations, much fewer than the 256 combinations when all bits are used or the 128 combinations when 1 bit is used to check parity.

A similar system used extensively in radio telegraph circuits (the van Duuren ARQ system) uses a 3-out-of-7 code.

In general, an _M_-out-of-_N_ code permits

$$\frac{N!}{M!(N-M)!}$$

combinations out of 2^N possible ones.

If all errors in a noise burst were the same type of change—for example, if they were all 0's changed to 1's—then the _M_-out-of-_N_ code would be very secure. It might be easy to imagine that this is the case, if we visualize noise impulses as always an increase in voltage on the line, for example, which would always change 0's to 1's when amplitude modulation or baseband signaling was in use.

Unfortunately, however, noise is often of an oscillating nature, a peak in voltage being followed by a dip in voltage. It is not uncommon that when a 0 is changed to a 1, a nearby 1 is changed to a 0. If this happens, the _M_-out-of-_N_ code loses its effectiveness. Similarly, where transition coding is used, or di-bits rather than bits are encoded, an undetectable compensating error can occur.

Experiments were performed by IBM using a 4-out-of-8 code transmitted over a voice line at 1200 bits per second. By comparing what was received with the original, the number of errors undetected by this code were counted. The results were compared with those for characters protected by a parity check, transmitted over the same line. It was found that the percentage of undetected errors for the parity-checked characters was about 1.9 times greater than with the 4-out-of-8 code. This ratio was approximately the same with both state coding and transition coding. The 4-out-of-8 code was, then, an improvement over the parity check, but, in view of the extra redundancy needed, was not a spectacular improvement.

Clearly, it would not be secure to transmit characters coded in 4-out-of-8 code without some form of longitudinal redundancy check. In practice, a longitudinal parity check is commonly employed on such messages, as with those using character parity.

POLYNOMIAL CODES

After M-out-of-N codes and codes with parity checks, vertical and longitudinal, the next most common class of codes are specific examples of polynomial codes, including the Hamming codes, the Bose-Chaudhuri codes, the Fire codes, the codes of Melas, various interleaved codes, and, for that matter, the simple parity check. (See bibliography for detailed references to all these.)

All these codes can be described in terms of the properties of divisions of polynomials.* Polynomial codes can be made to perform with very high efficiency.

Let us suppose that the data block that has to be transmitted is composed of k bits. We can represent this by a polynomial in a variable x, having k terms—a polynomial of order $(k - 1)$. If we represent the bits in the data block by the terms $a_{k-1} + a_{k-2} + \cdots + a_2 + a_1 + a_0$, the polynomial is then

$$M(x) = a_{k-1}x^{k-1} + a_{k-2}x^{k-2} + \cdots + a_2 x^2 + a_1 x + a_0$$

As an example, if the data message being sent is 1010001101, the polynomial representing it is

$$x^9 + 0 \cdot x^8 + 1 \cdot x^7 + 0 \cdot x^6 + 0 \cdot x^5 + 0 \cdot x^4 + 1 \cdot x^3 + 1 \cdot x^2 + 0 \cdot x + 1$$
$$= x^9 + x^7 + x^3 + x^2 + 1$$

The high-order term of the polynomial is the bit that is transmitted first.

This is simply a convenient mathematical way of expressing the message to be sent. We shall manipulate this using the laws of ordinary algebra, except that modulo 2 addition must be employed. This uses binary addition with no carries, as follows:

Example

Addition in Modulo 2 Arithmetic:

$x^7 + x^6 + x^5 + \qquad\qquad x^2 + 1$	$1\,1\,1\,0\,0\,1\,0\,1 +$
$x^7 + \qquad x^5 + x^4 + x^3 + x^2$	$1\,0\,1\,1\,1\,1\,0\,0 =$
$x^6 \qquad\quad + x^4 + x^3 \qquad\qquad 1$	$0\,1\,0\,1\,1\,0\,0\,1$

---

*W. W. Peterson and D. T. Brown, "Cyclic Codes for Error Detection," *Proceedings of the IRE*, January 1961.

Multiplication in Modulo 2 Arithmetic:

$$
\begin{array}{llll}
(x^7 + x^6 + x^5 + x^2 + 1)\,(x + 1) & & = & \begin{array}{l} 1\,1\,1\,0\,0\,1\,0\,1 \quad \times 1\,1 = \\ 1\,1\,1\,0\,0\,1\,0\,1\,0 + \end{array} \\
x^8 + x^7 + x^6 \qquad\quad + x^3 \qquad + x & & & \\
+ \quad\;\; x^7 + x^6 + x^5 \qquad\quad + x^2 \qquad + 1 & = & & 0\,1\,1\,1\,0\,0\,1\,0\,1 \qquad = \\
\;\; x^8 \qquad\qquad\quad + x^5 + x^3 + x^2 + x + 1 & & & 1\,0\,0\,1\,0\,1\,1\,1\,1
\end{array}
$$

To transmit the data block, we need a second polynomial, referred to as the *generating polynomial*, $P(x)$. $P(x)$ is of degree r, where this is less than the degree of the message polynomial $M(x)$, but is greater than zero. $P(x)$ has a unity coefficient on the x^0 term (i.e., the lowest-order term is 1).

Thus to transmit the above message,

$$M(x) = x^9 + x^7 + x^3 + x^2 + 1$$

we might use a generating polynomial:

$$P(x) = x^5 + x^4 + x^2 + 1$$

The steps involved in the transmission are, in effect,

Step 1: The data message $M(x)$ is multiplied by x^r, giving r 0's in the low-order positions.

Step 2: The result is divided by $P(x)$. This gives a unique quotient $Q(x)$ and remainder $R(x)$:

$$\frac{x^r \cdot M(x)}{P(x)} = Q(x) \oplus \frac{R(x)}{P(x)}$$

($\oplus$ is the sign for addition in modulo 2 arithmetic.)

Step 3: The remainder is added to the message, thus placing up to r terms in the r lower-order positions.

This is the message that is transmitted. Let us call it $T(x)$.

$$T(x) = x^r M(x) \oplus R(x)$$

As an example, suppose that the generating polynomial $P(x) = x^5 + x^4 + x^2 + 1$ is used, for which $r = 5$. The data block to be sent is the above 1010001101. We have

Step 1: $x^r M(x) = x^5 (x^9 + x^7 + x^3 + x^2 + 1)$

$$= x^{14} + x^{12} + x^8 + x^7 + x^5$$

which is equivalent to 101000110100000.

Step 2: This is divided by $P(x) = x^5 + x^4 + x^2 + 1$, which gives $x^9 + x^8 + x^6 + x^5 + x^2$ and a remainder of $x^3 + x^2 + x$, which is equivalent to 01110. Figure 8.2 shows the division.

Step 3: The remainder is added to $x^r M(x)$. This gives the bit pattern 101000110101110, which is the message transmitted.

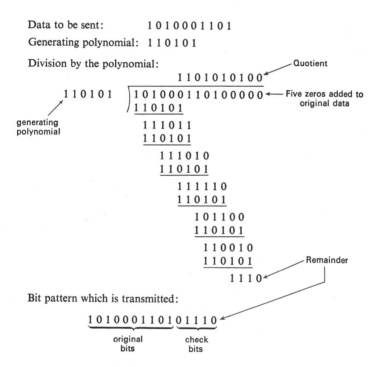

Figure 8.2. Check bits for a polynomial code.

We are thus sending the original bit pattern with 5 bits accompanying it for error detection. The bits are transmitted from left to right, the 5 check bits last.

The division is represented by the equation

$$\frac{x^r \cdot M(x)}{P(x)} = Q(x) \oplus \frac{R(x)}{P(x)}$$

Therefore,

$$x^r \cdot M(x) = Q(x) \cdot P(x) \oplus R(x)$$

Subtraction is the same as addition in modulo 2 arithmetic (no carries); therefore,

$$x^r \cdot M(x) \oplus R(x) = Q(x) \cdot P(x)$$

Hence the message transmitted is given by

$$T(x) = x^r \cdot M(x) \oplus R(x) = Q(x) \cdot P(x)$$

The message transmitted is therefore exactly divisible by the generating polynomial P(x). It is this property that we shall check in attempting to see whether an error has occurred. The receiving machine, in effect, divides the message polynomial it receives by $P(x)$. If the remainder is nonzero, an error has occurred. If it *is* zero, either there is no error or an undetectable error has occurred.

When the message is transmitted, a number of bits may be changed by noise. We may refer to this pattern of error bits by another polynomial $E(x)$. Thus for a message in error $T(x) + E(x)$ will be received. If $T(x) + E(x)$ is exactly divisible by $P(x)$, the error will not be detected.

It follows that if $E(x)$ is divisible by $P(x)$, the error will not be detected. On the other hand, if $E(x)$ is not divisible by $P(x)$, we will detect it. Knowing the characteristics of the communication lines, we must, therefore, pick our generating polynomial $P(x)$ such that it is very improbable that the pattern of error bits will be divisible by it.

ERROR-DETECTION PROBABILITIES The choice of generating polynomial should be dependent on a knowledge of the error patterns that are likely to occur on the channel in question. There are certain error characteristics that we can be sure to protect the data from:

1. Single-Bit Errors

If the data message or block protected by our polynomial code has one single bit in error, this can be represented by $E(x) = x^i$, where i is less than the total number of bits in the message, n.

If we give our generating polynomial more than one term, then x^i cannot be divided by it exactly. All single-bit errors will be detected.

2. Double-Bit Errors

Double-bit errors can be represented by the polynomial $E(x) = x^i + x^j$, where i and j are both less than n. If $i < j$, we can write $E(x) = x^i(1 + x^{j-i})$.

For the error to be detected, neither x^i nor $(1 + x^{j-i})$ may be divisible by the generating polynomial. If this polynomial has a factor with three terms, this will be so and all double errors will be detected.

3. Odd Numbers of Errors

If the error message contains an *odd* number of bits in error, the polynomial that represents it is not divisible by $(x + 1)$.

This can be proved as follows: Suppose that a message is represented by a polynomial $E(x)$, which is divisible by $(x + 1)$.

We can write $E(x) = (x + 1)Q(x)$. Substituting $x = 1$ into this, we have

$$E(1) = (1 + 1)Q(x)$$

Therefore, $E(1) = 0$. $(1 + 1 = 0$ in binary arithmetic with no carries.) Therefore, $E(x)$ must contain an even number of terms.

Hence, if we employ a generating polynomial $P(x)$ with a factor $(x + 1)$, then *any* message with an odd number of errors will be caught.

Any polynomial of the form $(x^c + 1)$ contains a factor $(x + 1)$, since $(x^c + 1) = (x + 1)(x^{c-1} + x^{c-2} + \cdots + 1)$. Therefore, any generating polynomial of the form $(x^c + 1)$ will detect all errors with an odd number of bits incorrect.

4. Bursts of Errors

A burst of errors refers to a group of incorrect bits within one data message or block. We shall define the length of a burst b as being the number of bits in a group having at least its first and last bits in error. Thus if $E(x)$ represents the error pattern 00000101001110000, this contains an error burst of length $b = 7$.

We can factorize $E(x)$ as

$$E(x) = x^i E_1(x)$$

where i is less than the number of bits in the message.

Thus the above error pattern is represented by

$$E(x) = x^{10} + x^8 + x^5 + x^4$$

and would be written $x^4(x^6 + x^4 + x^1 + 1)$. Since x^i is not divisible by $P(x)$ because it is a single term, the error will go undetected only if $E(x)$ is exactly divisible by $P(x)$.

When the length of the burst b is less than the length of $(r + 1)$ of $P(x)$, the generating polynomial $E_1(x)$ cannot be detected. Thus if we use a generating polynomial of 13 bits, all bursts of length 12 bits or less will be detected. To achieve this we shall have to use 12 redundant bits in the message [maximum size of the remainder $R(x)$].

When the number of bits in the burst b is equal to the number of bits in the generating polynomial $(r + 1)$ (13 in the above example), the error will go undetected if and only if the burst is identical to the generating polynomial. The first and last bits in the burst are error bits, by definition. Therefore, the remaining $(r - 1)$ bits must be identical. If we regarded all combinations of bits as equally possible, the probability of an error being undetected would be the probability that $(r - 1)$ independent bits are identical with the generating polynomial. This is $(1/2)^{(r-1)}$. In the above case $r = 12$, and so the probability of an undetected error is $1/2^{11} = 0.00049$, given that the block contains a burst of length 13 bits (a very rare event).

When the number of bits in the burst b is greater than $(r + 1)$, there is a variety of possible error patterns that are divisible by $P(x)$. If $E_1(x)$ is divisible by $P(x)$, we can write

$$E_1(x) = Q_1(x)P(x)$$

where Q_1 is the quotient obtained by dividing $E_1(x)$ by $P(x)$.

$E_1(x)$ is a polynomial of degree $(b - 1)$; $P(x)$ is a polynomial of degree r; therefore, the degree of the polynomial $Q_1(x)$ must be $(b - 1) - r$.

The number of bits represented by $Q_1(x)$ is, therefore, $(b - 1 - r) + 1 = b - r$. The first and last terms of $E_1(x)$ are always 1, and this causes the first and last terms of $Q_1(x)$ to be always 1. There are, therefore, $b - r - 2$ terms in $Q_1(x)$ that can alternate in value. This means that there are $b - r - 2$ ways in which $E_1(x)$ is divisible by $P(x)$.

As above, there are $2^{(b-2)}$ possible combinations of $E_1(x)$. If all combinations are equally probable, the probability of an error being undetected in this case is

$$\frac{2^{(b-2-r)}}{2^{(b-2)}} = 2^{-r}$$

In the above case in which $r = 12$ the probability of an undetected error is $2^{-12} = 0.00024$, given that the block contains a burst of length greater than 13 bits (again, a rare occurrence).

To Summarize: If we choose a polynomial having $(x + 1)$ as a factor, and one factor with three or more terms, then the following protection will be given:

Single bit errors:	100 per cent protection.
Two bits in error (separate or not):	100 per cent protection.
Odd number of bits in error:	100 per cent protection.
Error burst of length less than $(r + 1)$ bits:	100 per cent protection.
Error burst of exactly $(r + 1)$ bits in length:	$[1 - (\frac{1}{2})^{(r-1)}]$ probability of detection.
Error burst of length greater than $(r + 1)$ bits:	$[1 - (\frac{1}{2})^{r}]$ probability of detection.

The latter two terms assume an equal probability of any error pattern. In practice, some error patterns are more prevalent than others, so some generating polynomials of a given r are better than others.

It will be seen that polynomial codes can provide a high measure of protection. As r becomes larger, so the measure of protection against bursts becomes greater. This is especially so as long bursts are rarer than short bursts on telephone and telegraph lines.

Unfortunately, on typical voice lines there is a fairly high proportion of long bursts—greater than 30 bits, for example. This means that *some* errors are not going to be caught by the polynomial checks, or for that matter by any other checking schemes that are reasonable to implement.

We could, however, if it were necessary, make r very large, in other words, we could use a high-order generating polynomial. In this way we could produce a very *high* measure of protection indeed.

**RESULTS OBTAINED
IN PRACTICE**   Results obtained in practice with polynomial codes on telephone lines have been reasonably close to the theoretical prediction. Often the number of undetected errors has been slightly lower than predicted. To gather statistics on undetected errors, a large quantity of random data are transmitted, and the data received are compared with the original. In this way the effectiveness of different polynomials has been tested.

Table 8.2 shows a typical set of results. These measurements were made on a leased voice line from London to Rome transmitting random-bit messages in blocks of 729 bits. The transmission speed was 2000 bits per second:*

*Data taken with permission from "Data Transmission Test on a Multipoint Telephone Network in Europe," *CCITT Blue Book*, Vol. VIII, Data Transmission, Third Plenary Assembly, Supplement No. 37, The International Telecommunication Union, Geneva, 1964.

Table 8.2

Generating Polynomial Used	Fraction of Undetected Error Messages	
	Expected	*Actual*
$x^6 + 1$	0.0156	0.0107
$x^6 + x^5 + 1$	0.0156	0.0075
$x^6 + x + 1$	0.0156	0.0066
$x^7 + x^3 + 1$	0.0078	0.0035
$x^{12} + 1$	0.0003	0.0021
$x^{12} + x^{11} + 1$	0.0003	0.0003
$x^{12} + x + 1$	0.0003	0.0004

ENCODING AND DECODING CIRCUITS
Polynomial coding and decoding requires circuitry more complex than the use of vertical and horizontal parity bits. It is still not very complex, and, indeed, one of the advantages claimed for these codes is that of ease of coding and decoding.

The necessary division, such as that in Fig. 8.2, can be performed with a series of 1-bit shift registers and modulo 2 adders (exclusive OR circuits). The number of shift register positions is the same as the degree of the divisor, $P(x)$–five for the division in Fig. 8.2. The number of exclusive OR circuits is equal to (the number of 1 bits in the divisor $-$ 1)–three for the divisor in Fig. 8.2.

POLYNOMIAL CHECKING ON VARIABLE-LENGTH MESSAGES
When polynomial checking is used, the messages checked can be of fully variable length. On IBM's "binary synchronous" mode of data transmission, found on a wide range of different machines, the checking characters are placed at the end of records within a block. This range of equipment can either use the ASCII code with its recommended vertical and horizontal parity checks, or it can use polynomial checking. In another scheme 6-bit data characters are sent and two 6-bit checking characters are used, giving 12 check bits. A generating polynomial of order 12 will, therefore, be used ($T = 12$). When 8-bit data are sent, two 8-bit checking characters enable a generating polynomial of order 16 to be used.

The polynomials used are

$$x^{16} + x^{15} + x^2 + 1 = (x + 1)(x^{15} + x + 1)$$

and

$$x^{12} + x^{11} + x^3 + x^2 + x + 1 = (x + 1)(x^{11} + x^2 + 1)$$

It will be seen from the above theory that these will catch all messages with one or two errors, all with an odd number of errors, all with single bursts of less than 16 and 12 bits, respectively, and most of the few messages with larger bursts. In practice they have been found to perform slightly better than the above theory.

TO ACHIEVE A VERY HIGH MEASURE OF PROTECTION
We commented that is is possible to achieve a *very* high measure of protection with polynomial codes if a generating polynomial of sufficiently high order is used. Let us look at this a little more closely.

For the sake of discussion, suppose that when one is transmitting fixed-length blocks of 100 data characters (800 bits) over a certain telephone line there is a probability of 10^{-3} that a block will be perturbed by an error burst of length greater than 17 bits (pessimistic). If we make $r = 16$ and use 16 redundant bits for protection, the probability that the burst greater than 17 bits is detected is $[1 - (\frac{1}{2})^{16}] = (1 - 1.5 \times 10^{-5})$. The probability of having an undetected error is, then, theoretically of the order of $10^{-3} \times 10^{-5} = 10^{-8}$.

If we make $r = 80$, the probability that burst of length greater than 81 bits will be detected is $[1 - (\frac{1}{2})^{80}] = (1 - 0.83 \times 10^{-24})$. Bursts of less than 80 bits will always be detected. So now our probability of undetected error is at least $10^{-3} \times 10^{-24} = 10^{-27}$.

This is a much higher degree of protection than is needed for most practical purposes. If we had transmitted data protected in this way from all the locations in the world where there is now a telephone, transmitting at the maximum speed of a voice line, and if we had been transmitting nonstop since the time of Christ (with no equipment failures), it is unlikely that there would yet have been an undetected error anywhere in the world!

Furthermore, we had to add only 10 redundant characters to a message of 100 data characters. So the transmission efficiency is quite high—higher, indeed, than using the ASCII horizontal and vertical parity checking. The cost of the encoding and decoding equipment would have been higher. However, if it were mass produced in great quantities in *large-scale-integration* circuitry, it might not be significantly higher.

BIBLIOGRAPHY

1. W. W. Peterson, *Error Correcting Codes,* The M.I.T. Press, Cambridge, Mass.; John Wiley & Sons, Inc., New York, 1961.

2. F. F. Sellers, Jr., M-Y. Hsiao, and L. W. Bearnson, *Error Detecting Logic for Digital Computers*, McGraw-Hill Book Company, New York, 1968.

3. D. T. Tang and R. T. Chien, "Coding for Error Control," *IBM Systems Journal,* Vol. 8, No. 1 (1969).

4. R. W. Hamming, "Error Detecting and Error Correcting Codes," *Bell System Technical Journal* (April 1950).

5. P. Fire, "A Class of Multiple-Error-Correcting Binary Codes for Non-Independent Errors," Stanford Electronics Laboratories, Technical Report No. 55, April 24, 1959.

6. N. Abramson, "A Class of Systematic Codes for Non-Independent Errors," *IRE Transactions on Information Theory*, IT-5, 150 (1959).

7. L. H. Zetterberg, "Cyclic Codes from Irreducible Polynomials for Correction of Multiple Errors," *IRE Transactions on Information Theory*, IT-8, 13 (1962).

8. S. H. Rieger, "Codes for the Correction of 'Clustered' Errors," *IRE Transactions on Information Theory*, IT-6, 16 (1960).

9. M. Melas, "A New Group of Codes for Correction of Dependent Errors in Data Transmission," *IBM Journal*, Vol. 4, 58 (1960).

10. R. Bose and D. Ray-Chaudhuri, "A Class of Error-Correcting Binary Group Codes," *Information and Control*, Vol. 3 (March 1960).

11. D. Hagelbarger, "Error Detection Using Recurrent Codes." Presented at the AIEE Winter General Meeting, Feb. 1960.

12. W. Peterson and D. Brown, "Cyclic Codes for Error Detection," *Proceedings of the IRE* (Jan. 1961).

9 WHEN FAILURES OCCUR

The computer and its attachments are occasionally going to fail. How often will depend upon the degree of reliability that has been engineered into the system. The designer of the accuracy and security procedures must consider *all the possible* categories of failure and decide what should happen when each occurs. He must devise steps to ensure that no important data are lost or accidentally entered twice in such a way that they are added to a file record twice. He must devise procedures for reconstructing files in case the file records become permanently damaged (as has often occurred in practice). He must consider what could happen when a failure occurs in the equipment that is to be used for security purposes or file reconstruction. Chapter 22 discusses file reconstruction.

CHECKPOINTS On batch-processing systems, in which records are *rewritten* on a different volume (e.g., tape) when they are updated, failures present little difficulty. The run on which a computer failure occurs may be rerun. If it is a long run, it is desirable not to have to start again at the beginning, and so it is divided into short segments. At the end of each segment a *checkpoint* is taken, meaning that enough data are recorded to restart the run at that point. At the checkpoint all the totals that are being accumulated for batch control are recorded, so that the overall batch totals will be correct despite the interruption in the processing of the batch.

111

Checkpoints are also used in teleprocessing when a long string of items is being entered at a terminal, but on real-time systems the situation is more complex.

GRACEFUL   The failure of a computer system may be total.
DEGRADATION   Often it is only partial. A terminal or its line may
                          go dead, in which case the failure can appear total
to the terminal operator. An on-line data file may become unavailable. The main computer may go out, but peripheral line-control computers are still capable of giving a limited response to the terminal. In other situations, functions for which a fast response to terminals is not mandatory may be temporarily shelved.

The term *fallback* is used to mean that the system modifies its mode of operation to circumvent the error. In doing so it may give a degraded form of service, but still carry out the urgent part of its job. A real-time system may have a hierarchy of fallback procedures to deal with different eventualities, each circumventing an interruption of the more important functions of the system.

The term *fail softly* is used to mean that, when a component goes out, the system uses an alternative means of processing rather than collapsing completely. The euphemism "graceful degradation" is also employed for this, and implies that the system should be planned so that fallback procedures cause as little disturbance as possible to the more vital work, and especially the more vital real-time functions.

It is desirable that the fallback techniques used cause no change in the structure of the man-machine dialogue. Certain types of messages will no longer be permissible when the failure occurs, but the formats of those that are permissible should be unchanged. A full-time operator will be trained to deal with the fallback condition, and should be given detailed written instruction in the terminal operator's manual. A "nondedicated" operator will have to be guided by the terminal itself.

BYPASS   When a system does fail and terminals become in-
PROCEDURES   operative, the terminal users must still have some
                          means of dealing with the situations that confront
them. The bank teller must still be able to deal with customers who come in and ask to withdraw money. The insurance clerk, the shop foreman, and the telephone salesgirl must have some standby procedure that enables them to carry on their work without real-time assistance from the computer.

The computer may make periodic printouts of the key information in its files in anticipation of failure. These may be transmitted to the terminal operators at night or when the terminal is not in use. In a bank, for example, the balances of all branch accounts containing more than $500 may be printed at that branch, so that no amount greater than this will be paid out when the terminal is inoperative without checking the listing.

Alternatively, the terminal operator may make a telephone call to a central location to obtain key information. The terminal may be used off-line to obtain replies from staff at a central location. In most cases the terminal operator carries on as best as possible, and the computer sorts out what has happened when it comes back on the air. When the computer is used to control in an optimum fashion the events that are happening, the events will still go on when the machine has failed, but will no longer be optimized. The nonoptimum bypass procedure in such cases represents a loss in revenue, which may be roughly calculable.

CONTROLS DURING FAILURE PERIODS It is important that the system controls do not allow errors to be entered into the files, or information to be lost, during the brief periods of difficulty when failures are being encountered.

Some of the checks discussed in Chapter 7 can be designed so that they are continuous throughout the failure period. This is especially important with systems handling cash or accountable items.

When a bank teller's terminal ceases to obtain on-line responses, he can, on most systems, use the same terminal *off-line* to print transactions that are dealt with while the system is out. He saves these until the system is back on the air and then enters them. The check totals or running totals that are kept should be used to control this off-line procedure, ensuring that nothing is lost or double entered. The terminal in a system well designed for control has its own accumulators. When the computer failure occurs, the teller makes the terminal print out control totals, kept in its own accumulators, showing net cash. These will also have been recorded in the computer up to the time when the failure occurred. The off-line operation continues, and, when the computer becomes usable again, the operator prints the totals. He then enters all the transactions into the computer, which updates its files accordingly. The computer totals are then printed and must agree with the terminal's off-line ones.

Continuity of the use of control totals or other checks throughout the period of bypass operation is important to ensure that nothing is misprocessed during this difficult period.

MESSAGE   Every message sent by a terminal operator should
ACKNOWLEDGMENT   receive an acknowledgment, even if only a very
rudimentary one like printing an asterisk to show
correct receipt of the message. This is important for psychological reasons.
It is particularly important when failures occur. Appropriately designed message acknowledgments are necessary for the tight control that prevents
accidental loss of transactions.

On a well-designed system, the acknowledgment of correct message
receipt will be a programmed, rather than an automatic, hardware function,
because the computer withholds message acknowledgment until the message
is in the core of the main processor or, better, until it is written on a logging
tape or file. It may withhold acknowledgment until file records have been
updated. Doing this ensures that, if a fault occurs, either the operator will
have had no acknowledgment and so will repeat the message, or the computer
will have reached such a point that, when a restart or switchover occurs, it
can finish processing the message.

There is a danger when a transaction updates a file that an outage may
occur at such an instant that the record is not updated. The above answer-
back removes this danger but leaves the equally undesirable possibility that
the operator may reenter the transaction and cause the record to be updated
twice, for example, a bank withdrawal subtracted twice from the customer's
account record.

When an abrupt computer failure occurs, it will probably not be possible
to tell how far the application programs had gone in handling their message
or messages. They may or may not have updated the relevant files. It is therefore necessary to place some form of indication on the files at the time they
are updated so that either the programs or the operator can tell whether the
record in question has been updated. This may be a sequential number allo-
cated either by the computer or by the operator. Sometimes the operator
can tell from the data themselves. In a savings-bank system, for example, he
will record the old balance that was on the record before the transaction in
question was made. After the hardware failure is repaired he will again key
in this transaction along with the old balance and, if there is disagreement,
he will know that the record was in fact updated before. He must then check
whether the teller total on a separate record is correct. Similarly, an airline
agent can tell whether his booking for Mr. So-and-So was in fact recorded by
attempting to display the Passenger Name Record for this passenger.

SWITCHOVER   Sometimes, when a piece of equipment fails, a
switchover to a substitute occurs. This may be
automatic or manual. The switchover process must be planned so that no

item is lost or double entered, and to do this may involve the terminal operator, depending upon the system. Generally, in a multiprocessing system where each transaction is held in more than one computer, possibly first in a line-control computer and then in the main processing computer, a switchover procedure can be devised that automatically prevents loss or double updating. When this is not so, the terminal operator will be involved and must have a rigorously laid down set of instructions to follow. In general, if good error detection procedures are used, the entry of transactions on line should give rise to fewer errors than similar keying off line into cards or paper tape, or the writing of documents. The entry of transactions at their source with immediate checking enables errors to be controlled and minimized.

OPERATOR-ADDED SERIAL NUMBERS   On some systems, control against loss is achieved by giving serial numbers to the transactions. This is commonly the case, for example, on message-switching systems. Each operator gives a sequential number, of not more than three digits, to each message sent. On receiving messages, the computer checks that the number from that operator is in fact one higher than the last and stores the message along with the address of the sender. If a breakdown occurs and the system restarts after a period of downtime, each operator will resend his last message. The computer will check that there is no gap in the number sequences and no messages stored twice. Conversely, on output the machine will maintain a sequential number for each operator it sends messages to. The operator must check that the messages received are sequentially numbered. If an outage occurs, he must be particularly careful to ensure that there is no break in the number sequence.

COMPUTER-ADDED SERIAL NUMBERS   In other systems it is not the operator who gives the item a serial number but the computer itself. The sequential number is written temporarily on the file records which this transaction causes to be updated. If the question then arises in the restart procedures, Has such and such a record been updated by transaction no. XXX?, this can be answered. If a duplexed system is used, a scheme such as this will be used to protect the transactions when a switchover occurs, assuming that none are lost or entered twice.

Another variation on the theme is for the computer to compose transaction numbers and send these to the operator. Consider a system in which transactions are first received by a programmed transmission control computer and then, when checked out, are passed to a main processing computer as it asks for them. The sequence of events might be as follows (Fig. 9.1):

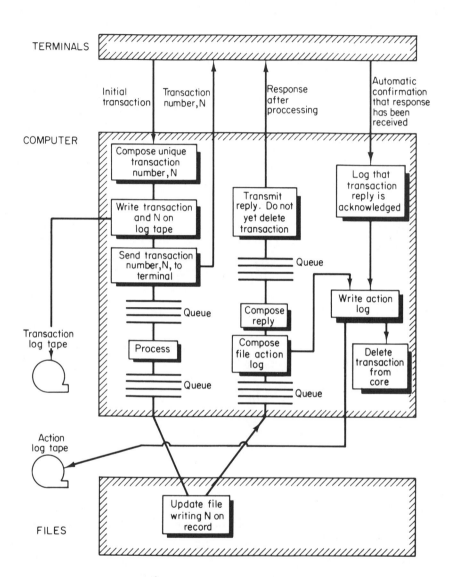

Figure 9.1. Use of a transaction number for maintaining security.

1. The terminal operator sends the message.
2. It is received in the transmission control computer. This adds a unique number to it and stores the transaction and its number in a table.
3. The items are checked, edited, and then queued in the transmission control computer. The main computer reads them from the transmission control computer one at a time.
4. The main computer stores the transaction with its number in a table or message-reference block.
5. As soon as the transmission control computer receives confirmation that the main computer has received the transaction correctly, it sends the transaction number to the terminal operator.
6. The main computer processes the transaction and prepares to update the files.
7. The unique transaction number is written on each file record updated, and remains there until it is again updated by a different transaction.
8. The main computer composes the reply.
9. The transmission control computer transmits the reply, noting this in its transaction table.
10. When the hardware signals that the terminal has correctly received the answer-back, the transaction number is deleted in the transmission control computer's table and the message is deleted from the core of the main computer.

The terminal operator is given the following instructions on what to do if a breakdown occurs: If she has received (or partially received) a reply giving the number of the transaction, she should not enter it again. If she has not received this, she should enter it when the system returns to operation. With this rule the system can be programmed to recover from the failure of a single unit without risk of not updating or double updating the file. This is so whenever the failure occurs in the above sequence of events.

If, however, both the main computer and the transmission control computer fail at once—if, for example, there is a power failure at the computer room—then the recovery procedure is different. If the terminal operator has received the message number but not the answer-back, she must key in both the message number and the message. All the terminal operators involved do this, and again the system can be programmed to resume in safety.

Schemes such as this, but differing in detail, must be thought out for each system that updates vital files in an on-line manner.

JOURNALING   The accuracy control on many on-line systems is built around a *journal* that is constantly kept to record the transactions being processed. (It is also called a *log*, and, somewhat misleadingly, an *audit trail*.) In its simplest form, the journal simply records input transactions received by the computer. Each item is written on tape or disk before it is processed, or at least before any critical file is updated. This action by itself, however, is insufficient to ensure that no item is lost because the terminal operator, recovering from a failure, does not know whether the file was updated before the failure occurred. It is therefore necessary to enter details of a record being updated in a journal. Some systems, in fact, use two journals: a *transaction journal* for recording the incoming transactions, and a *file-action journal* for recording the updating of the records. After a failure has occurred, the restart procedures center around the use of these journals.

It is usually not necessary to record all messages in the journal, but only those parts of a transaction that are used in updating the record. Similarly, it is often not necessary to journal the entire record. In an inventory system, for example, a note of all records updated would be journaled; these entries would include the item number, old balance, and new balance. The terminal number or operator number would be recorded as would, in some cases, the time of day. In order to correlate the *transaction* and *file-action* journal items, the transaction will be given a serial number by the computer and this will be recorded on both.

It is desirable that the writing of the transaction journal should be the first action taken after the transaction is received. This action may be taken by a priority routine that deals with the transaction as soon as its reception by the computer is complete. The transaction journal might be kept by the transmission control computer if this is separate from the main computer. Because it is necessary to write the journal item immediately, no blocking of this record should take place.

Similarly, the intention to update a record should be journaled immediately—that is, before the record is written. Notification that the updating has been completed should be journaled immediately after this has occurred. The modified contents of the record will be journaled before and after modification. It is then not necessary to write a serial number on the file, as was shown in Fig. 9.1.

The synchronization of events is important in this use of journaling. When a terminal operator updates a record the sequence may be as shown in Fig. 9.2. The terminal operator may be told, in this case, that *if he does not receive a transaction number, he must reenter the transaction. If he has received a transaction number, then the transaction should not be reentered.* The recovery programs will take the item from the transaction journal, inspect the file action journal, and if no transaction of that number is recorded *after* updating, the recovery program will proceed to use the application

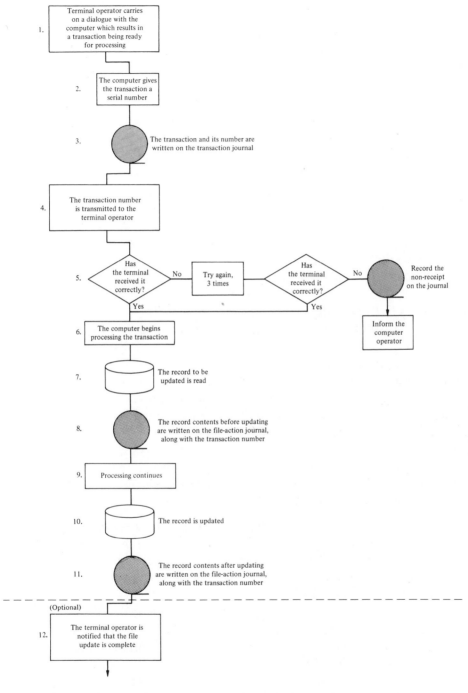

1. Terminal operator carries on a dialogue with the computer which results in a transaction being ready for processing

2. The computer gives the transaction a serial number

3. The transaction and its number are written on the transaction journal

4. The transaction number is transmitted to the terminal operator

5. Has the terminal received it correctly?
   No — Try again, 3 times — Has the terminal received it correctly?
   No — Record the non-receipt on the journal
   Yes
   Yes → Inform the computer operator

6. The computer begins processing the transaction

7. The record to be updated is read

8. The record contents before updating are written on the file-action journal, along with the transaction number

9. Processing continues

10. The record is updated

11. The record contents after updating are written on the file-action journal, along with the transaction number

(Optional)

12. The terminal operator is notified that the file update is complete

Figure 9.2. Journals written to provide a safe means of recovering from system failure. The computer can fail at any point in this sequence.

program in question to update the file. It is possible that the file *has already* been updated but that a failure has occurred between points 10 and 11 in Fig. 9.2; the update, in other words, has not been recorded in the file-action journal. The updating, therefore, does not begin with the contents of the record on the file, but with the contents of the record in the journal before updating (step 8 in Fig. 9.2). For this reason, three separate items must be written on the journal tape or tapes—the transaction, the record before updating, and the record after updating. The three items will be separated on the journal tape by other items being processed. They must therefore be associated by writing the transaction serial number with each of the three items.

Step 12 in Fig. 9.2 is not strictly necessary. The system can be designed to recover automatically if it has passed Step 4, without further attention from the terminal operator. Notification of the operator that the record updating is complete is done on some systems to provide a more complete terminal log. In this case, if the system fails before the update is complete, the operator should be notified, during the recovery process, of the successful completion of the update.

It is also not essential to send the terminal operator the transaction number in Step 4. He need not even know that the transaction was given a number. The transaction number can, however, be used to recover from an operator error. If he entered a wrong transaction or changed his mind he can key in the transaction number and the system can be programmed to "unprocess" the transaction, using the journals. Other updates of the same record may have taken place since his error. These can be corrected with the aid of the journals.

Journals have a variety of uses other than recovering from system failures. We will return to the subject of journaling in Chapter 23, after we have discussed other security requirements.

CHECKPOINTS   The taking of checkpoints is common practice on batch-processing systems. At intervals the status of the run in question is recorded on tape or file. If then a failure occurs, or the run is stopped for some reason, the operation returns to the previous checkpoint and can be restarted from there.

Checkpoints for restarting are still useful for some on-line and real-time systems, although on others they are a clumsy and unsatisfactory way of maintaining control. Certainly, when batches of work are sent over communication links, it is a good idea to have the checkpoints at fairly frequent intervals in the processing so that not too much has to be reprocessed, or possibly retransmitted, when a failure occurs. When single transactions are sent, it is more difficult. However, some single-transaction systems do maintain checkpoints.

As transactions flow through a typical system, the programs maintain tables giving the status of various lines and terminals, and recording the stage of processing that the various transactions have reached. One way of maintaining checkpoints is to dump these tables onto tape, drum, or disk at regular intervals, perhaps every 30 seconds or so. The tables may be dumped onto two alternating areas of a drum or disk, for example, at time intervals determined by a real-time clock. This will be fast and will not use much storage space. If a computer failure or stoppage occurs, the restart procedures will return to the previous checkpoint and examine what was on the tables at that time. The latest checkpoint tables will be reloaded into core, and the programs will determine which messages had been processed or are in such a state that the processing can be completed. The computer will complete the processing on these and will send messages to the terminal operators telling them to retransmit all messages sent after the message with such and such a serial number. Using the serial numbers, it will check carefully that it is not causing a file to be updated twice.

For on-line systems, transaction journaling is generally preferable to the use of checkpoints because it permits recovery from a variety of failures and human errors long after the harmful incident has occurred. Checkpoint recording, on the other hand, uses rather less machine and channel time, and slows down processing less. It tends to be used where speed and efficiency are of more concern, and long term recovery less so.

TERMINAL DIALOGUE INTERRUPTIONS   When the terminal user's dialogue is interrupted, it is sometimes advantageous that he should be able to start it again where he left off. If it is a lengthy dialogue, for example the reordering of complex machinery, it is certainly desirable that he should not have to go back to the beginning. For this reason, checkpoints may be built into the dialogue structure. At intervals the decisions made up to that point in the dialogue will be reviewed (and can be changed if necessary). When the operator agrees that they are correct, they will be recorded. If anything goes wrong from that point onward, the operator will be able to restart the dialogue at the previous checkpoint.

In most terminal "conversations" there are certain stages at which the set of decisions recorded up to that point can be agreed upon as correct. Sometimes this can be regarded as a mental *closure* in the decision-making process. Sometimes it is merely an arbitrary stage in data entry. Periodically, either at a natural closure or not, the operator should be given a recap of what has been established up to that point and asked to check it. If the operator is carrying out a complex data-entry sequence, the record being built up might be checked once every 10 screens, or every few minutes. When the operator has agreed that this is correct, the computer will store it.

This checkpoint is often of more value for operator failures than for machine failures. The operator will sometimes make mistakes or become confused in a lengthy dialogue, and the checkpoint will give him a point from which to recover. We do, in fact have *two entirely different types of checkpoint: one intended for accuracy control and recovery from hardware failure, the other primarily intended for bewilderment control and recovery from human dialogue failure*. With some dialogue structures the two checkpoints can be the same.

DIALOGUE BACKTRACK In many man-terminal dialogues the operator wants
CAPABILITY   something better than the ability to return to a
                        checkpoint of 10 screens ago. He would like to be
able to backtrack over the recent course of the dialogue. This is true if there has been a brief mechanical interruption in the dialogue. However, it is true much more frequently when the operator's mind wanders and he forgets where he was or forgets facts from the previous screens. If he is interrupted by conversation or by a telephone ringing, his thread of thought will be lost, and he will need to backtrack if the dialogue was other than the simplest. When the dialogue takes place at a printing terminal, he can backtrack by looking at the printout. When it took place at a screen, he will need help from the system.

Dialogue backtrack capability can be provided from the input message journal, or the system may be programmed so that each operator has dialogue assembly records, and these are used when backtracking is requested. The operator should have some simple means at the terminal of making backtracking possible, for example, by pointing to a word or mark with a light pen, or by employing a special-function key.

CONTROLS ON   Tight discipline on the operators of an on-line sys-
OPERATORS   tem is one of the important factors in maintaining
                  security and accuracy. This should be maintained
by programmed checks and strong supervision. The ability of the computer to detect many types of errors as soon as they are made and to check for the completeness of transactions will aid in this.

During periods when part of the equipment fails, detailed and well-rehearsed instructions to operators are vital. Fallback and bypass tactics to meet all circumstances should be mapped out in advance and documented clearly.

During periods of switchover or computer outages, it may be especially important to have tight controls on the terminal operators. When the terminals are being used merely for inquiries, there is normally no problem about transactions being lost. If the user wants an answer to his inquiry, he will reenter it when the computer is back "on the air." However, if he is entering data that must not be lost, it is worthwhile to derive checks on each individual operator. In a banking system, for example, the daily totals entered by the teller are added up first by the teller or his terminal and also by the computer. The totals are compared to ensure that nothing has been lost, and the methods for totaling bridge any period of switchover or outage. On other systems, totals of this type are kept, but are compared at much more frequent intervals, say, every hour. In this case, if any discrepancy is discovered, it will not take so long to put it right. The system may be designed so that the operator can check every time he has an idle period to ensure that the computer's total agrees with his; however, such a check left to the operator should not replace an enforced periodic check.

Computer-center operators of high ability are needed who can deal with the various emergencies that may arise. They must be able to initiate the correct type of fallback and recovery action. However, human operators in the computer room make the system vulnerable to some extent, and controls should be devised to check their actions. They may load the wrong disks or tape, execute incorrect routines that could destroy data on file, and so on. The computers must, when possible, examine what their operators do and check that the right disks and tapes have been loaded.

FAILURE-DRILL PROGRAM
The computer operators and also the terminal operators on many commercial systems must be carefully trained in what to do when failures occur. When on-line terminals are used for training, this should include operation in the various fallback modes. A remote office must not panic when the personnel discover that they are cut off from their source of information. In particular, the terminal operators must follow precisely those procedures that will ensure that data are not lost or double entered.

To ensure that the correct procedures are followed, it is desirable to have "fire drills" periodically. A program can be specially written for this purpose, which simulates a machine failure and then checks the terminal operator actions to see whether they are in fact correct. The *failure-drill program* may be written so that it can be evoked from a branch office at the convenience of the supervisors there.

A detailed set of instructions needs to be written for the terminal and computer operators instructing them how to deal with failures. It is the combination of correct operator actions and related program actions that provides the assurance of accuracy when failures occur.

On some systems a variety of different users are affected, and the system designers should specify how they know that a failure has occurred and what action they take. Table 9.1 shows the type of chart that is needed for specifying the various user and staff actions. This chart is for the data-collection system illustrated in Fig. 7.3.

The system designers should try to anticipate all possible sources of trouble and tie the system down with a network of controls that will make it safe from hardware or software errors, from terminal operator mistakes and clerical errors, and from the staff in its own computer room. A well-planned commercial system should be locked in an interlacing set of carefully designed controls on accuracy.

Table 9.1

Type of Failure	How is Failure Detected and by Whom?	What Action is Taken by the Detecting Party. Who is Notified?	What Action is Taken by the People Notified?	Recovery Procedures
Single-station terminal	Detected by *worker*: 1. Light does not come on 2. Repeated request to resend or 3. Rejection of badge or card ⎯ Detected by *I/O Control Group* via excessive exception messages	Notifies *supervisor* or the *shop-floor expediter,* and uses another terminal	1. Inform the *Input/Output Control Group* 2. Inform Maintenance 3. Place an Inoperative sign on the terminal	Repair the terminal and remove the Inoperative sign
Controller for a group of work station terminals	Detected by *workers* (as above) ⎯ Detected by *I/O Control Group* (as above)	Notifies *supervisor* or the *shop-floor expediter.* If he cannot use a different terminal, he fills in a fallback card with his data (as a bypass procedure)	As above. *Workers* are instructed to go to fallback operation (unless another terminal is within reach)	Repair the fault, The fallback cards are collected periodically and sent to the *I/O Control Group* for entry into the computer

Table 9.1 (*cont'd*)

Type of Failure	How is Failure Detected and by Whom?	What Action is Taken by the Detecting Party. Who is Notified?	What Action is Taken by the People Notified?	Recovery Procedures
Line failure to many work station terminals	Detected by *workers, foreman,* or *I/O Control Group*	As above	As above	As above
Foreman's terminal	*Foreman* observes malfunction	Foreman notifies the *I/O Control Group.* Uses another terminal if one is close. Otherwise, obtains necessary information directly from the *I/O Control Group.* Uses printed sheets for modifying schedules or other essential items	1. Inform *Maintenance* 2. Print out listings of data required by the foreman relating to jobs under his supervision 3. Input the foreman's schedule change sheets directly into the system	*Expediter* keeps in touch with the foreman to ensure that his needs are met, and he collects the foreman's schedule change sheets
Line network control unit	Failure is immediately apparent to *computer operators* and all *terminal operators*	*Workers* fill in fallback cards with their data. *Foreman* uses printed sheets for modifying schedules and other essential items		System recovery from checkpoint using journal tape. Worker's data cards and foremen's schedule sheets are punched into cards for rapid entry on restart
Terminal in *I/O Control Group*	Detected by *I/O Control Group* 1. Inability to enter messages 2. Garbled output 3. Error message describing malfunction	Turn power off terminal to direct messages to an alternative terminal	Alternative terminal may be permanently assigned by the engineers until the repair is completed	None
All terminals fail in *I/O Control Room*	As above	*Computer operators* instructed to initiate off-line *I/O* control operations		Error messages printed on computer-room line printer. *I/O Control Group.* data changes delayed if possible, otherwise entered on cards with printed logging for control purposes

Table 9.1 (*cont'd*)

Type of Failure	How is Failure Detected and by Whom?	What Action is Taken by the Detecting Party. Who is Notified?	What Action is Taken by the People Notified?	Recovery Procedures
Tape unit or noncritical disk	Error message to *computer operator*	*I/O Control Group* is notified, and they inform the *shop-floor expediters* that the system will be off the air for 10 minutes	*Workers* delay entry of transactions for 10 minutes. Where labor claim time adjustments are needed, these are recorded for entry by the *I/O Control Group*	System is restarted with a spare disk or tape, after an orderly shutdown. Transactions are then entered after the 10-minute delay
Critical disk or disk control unit	Error message to *computer operator*	*I/O Control Group* is notified, and they inform the *shop-floor expediters* that the system will be off the air until they are notified	*Expediters* instruct *workers* to use fallback procedures and *foreman* to use printed sheets for schedule changes and other essential items	System recovery from checkpoint using journal tap. Worker's data cards and foreman's schedule change sheets are collected regularly and punched into cards for rapid restart
Computer	Immediately apparent to all	As above	As above	As above

10 PROGRAMMED LOCKS AND ALARMS

We shall now turn to the question of making the system secure from unauthorized access.

Security in the noncomputer world involves locks—locked doors, locked store rooms, and locked safes. When we store sensitive data in filing cabinets, we lock up those cabinets and take careful precautions that only authorized people will be able to obtain the key. We try to ensure that the key holders are people whom we trust. If a high level of safety is needed, as with a major bank vault or with the launching of a nuclear weapon, we fit a double lock, and two independent key holders have to be present to unlock it.

PHYSICAL LOCKS
Physical locks are also needed in computer installations, and have been surprisingly absent on some systems. The computer building should be locked and as far as possible burglar proof. There should be secure locks on the store room where sensitive data are kept—tapes, disks, or cards. The computer room should be locked. During operation it should be locked on the inside by the computer operator. The telecommunication facilities should be locked.

In addition to these building locks, the machinery itself should be constructed with locks on critical components. The terminals should have locks on them so that they cannot be used by unauthorized persons, especially at night. The computer power supply should be locked. Units containing sensitive data, such as disk drives and tape units, should be locked. Some such units are lockable; others are not. Some users have devised ways of fitting their own locks to hardware, such as disk drives, that did not have a lock. Last, it is desirable that the program load (IPL) button or its equivalent on the computer should be locked on some installations to prevent an unauthorized person from changing the operating system, because it is into the operating system that many future security features will have to be built.

A general principle in security is that the number of persons *who have to be trustworthy* should be minimized. It is desirable that the computer operator should be trustworthy, but as a check on him he may be prevented from having access to certain tape units or disk drives. Only one senior operator may have the key to certain disk drives (or to the program load button if this is lockable), and all operators may be barred from a logging tape, as we shall discuss later.

When a high level of security is needed, two independent persons may be needed to unlock some components.

PROGRAMMED
LOCKS

On computer systems another form of lock is used, of an entirely different nature. It can be made more secure than locks of filing cabinets. Instead of having one lock on the entire cabinet full of data, we can have very elaborately structured sets of programmed locks allowing different people to read different parts of the information, and the locks cannot be broken by violence. Programmed locks can be thought of as being something like a combination lock on a bank vault, but of any level of complexity that we wish to program into them. Furthermore, the combination can be changed frequently to enhance security. The computer can be programmed to guard its information with the same relentless thoroughness with which it can do anything else.

A person seeking to use the computer or obtain data from it must unlock the mechanisms by the use of appropriate keys. These may be physical keys. The key, for example, may be a card like a credit card with a magnetically encoded stripe. The key may be a memorized code or password. It may be the identification of the individual himself. When it is used, it will usually not open the door to the whole computer system, but will merely enable the user to employ a particular program or particular items of data.

The blocks in Fig. 10.1 show a possible sequence of events when a person is using a terminal. The locks that might be applied at the various stages in the process are indicated. Not all these locks need be used on the same system; however, a secure system should have more than one lock in the chain, so that if any one lock is bypassed, accidentally or deliberately, the data are still secure.

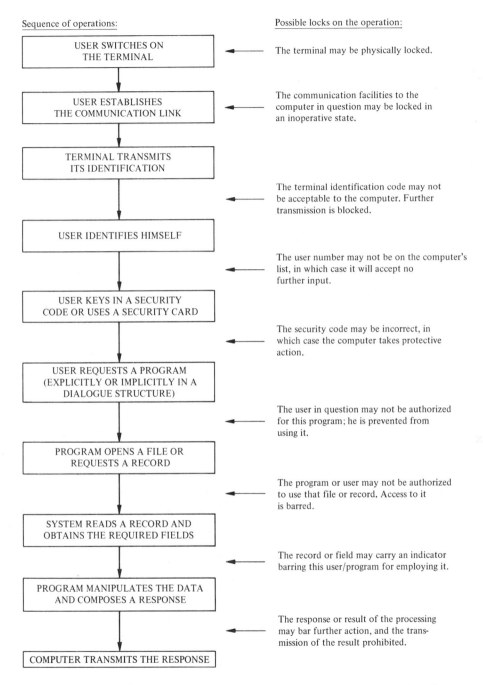

Sequence of operations:

Possible locks on the operation:

USER SWITCHES ON
THE TERMINAL

The terminal may be physically locked.

USER ESTABLISHES
THE COMMUNICATION LINK

The communication facilities to the
computer in question may be locked in
an inoperative state.

TERMINAL TRANSMITS
ITS IDENTIFICATION

The terminal identification code may not
be acceptable to the computer. Further
transmission is blocked.

USER IDENTIFIES HIMSELF

The user number may not be on the computer's
list, in which case it will accept no
further input.

USER KEYS IN A SECURITY
CODE OR USES A SECURITY CARD

The security code may be incorrect, in
which case the computer takes protective
action.

USER REQUESTS A PROGRAM
(EXPLICITLY OR IMPLICITLY IN A
DIALOGUE STRUCTURE)

The user in question may not be authorized
for this program; he is prevented from
using it.

PROGRAM OPENS A FILE OR
REQUESTS A RECORD

The program or user may not be authorized
to use that file or record. Access to it
is barred.

SYSTEM READS A RECORD AND
OBTAINS THE REQUIRED FIELDS

The record or field may carry an indicator
barring this user/program for employing it.

PROGRAM MANIPULATES THE DATA
AND COMPOSES A RESPONSE

The response or result of the processing
may bar further action, and the transmission of the result prohibited.

COMPUTER TRANSMITS THE RESPONSE

Figure 10.1. A possible sequence of events when a terminal is used, and
the locks that could be applied to each stage.

First, the terminal itself might be locked. A physical key is needed on some terminals to switch on their electrical supply, for example. Second, the communication link may be severed or unabtainable. The telephone number that must be dialed may be secret. The communication facilities may be switched off in the evening to prevent unauthorized use. They may be disconnected at the computer center during a period of testing or when security is compromised in some way. This may be done by breaking the line at a communication "patch panel" or by disconnecting a multiplexor or concentrator.

The next possible lock in the sequence relates to the terminal identification. It may be designed to transmit an identification number to the computer, and the computer will proceed no further until it has positively identified the terminal. Following this, the operator identifies himself. He may transmit an identification number, and again the computer will proceed no further if this number is not on its list. To verify that the operator is who he says he is, he may have to type in a secret code, password, or security number. Only when this has been done correctly will the computer permit the dialogue to proceed.

An application program must now be assigned to the user. He could be assigned a series of application programs as the dialogue proceeds. The program library may be protected so that only users on an authorized list can use each program. If the user in question is not on the list, he will be prevented from having access to that program.

The program will request data from the files on the basis of the user's input. Here another check could be made to see whether the program or the user is entitled to read, or to modify, that file. If not, the file will not be accessed.

The data concerning who is entitled to read, or modify, a record may be stored on the record itself, as we shall illustrate in more detail later. In this case the data are read into the computer before the censoring process is applied. If correct authorization is not established, the processing will proceed no further.

In some cases the inhibition of a response to the user may be dependent upon the *result* of processing the data. The information may only appear to be sensitive after the calculations have been performed, and the application program may have its own mechanism for preventing release of the data.

ALARMS   To keep burglars out of a building or bank vault, the locks on the windows and doors will be backed up by burglar alarms. The physical locks on the computer room or telecommunication facilities can be used with alarms that both scare in-truders and increase the likelihood of their being caught. Similarly, the pro-grammed locks in the computer system can be backed up by surveillance methods to detect anyone who is attempting unauthorized entry.

Some systems sound an alarm bell at the computer console when a pos-sibly serious violation is detected, and the operator is instructed what action to take when this occurs. Some systems send an immediate message to a central security officer's terminal, giving full details and possibly sounding a bell there also. Some systems inform a suitable authority at the user's loca-tion. All three types of alarm action may be employed.

The existence of the alarms, but not the details of how they work or what triggers them, should be well publicized to act as a psychological de-terrent.

RELATIONSHIPS
FOR WHICH LOCKS
MAY EXIST
Restrictions may be placed on the relationships between five different entities on a normally working system—the users, the terminals or input/ output devices that are used, the application pro-grams, the data sets or elements of data, and the volumes such as tapes or disks on which the data are recorded. Locks may exist on any of these rela-tionships, and alarms may be used to bring attention to any suspected violation.

Figure 10.2 summarizes the relationships that may be locked:

1. The user himself may be identified and locked out of the terminal, or out of the pro-gram, data, or volume he requests.
2. A specific terminal may be considered in an insecure area and locked out of certain programs, data, or volumes.
3. A program may be prevented from accessing certain data or volumes.
4. Certain data may have a high security classification and so be prevented from being stored on any volume that has a lower classification.

The locks may be based on security classification levels, on the indivi-dual entities or groups of entities, or on time. These are indicated by the letters L, I, and T, respectively, in Fig. 10.2.

If security classification levels are used, the five types of entities may each be assigned a classification, such as CONFIDENTIAL, SECRET, and so on. If a user is not security cleared for SECRET information, he will not be permitted to use a terminal classified for SECRET work, or permitted to use any program, data, or volume classified SECRET. SECRET data may not be transmitted to an unclassified terminal. If a volume is not labeled SECRET, SECRET data may not be written on it. And so on. As indicated in Fig. 10.2, any of the relationships may be based on such classification levels. There may be any number of levels.

Much greater precision is obtained by basing the relationships on individual users or entities. User A is only permitted to use program B, data C, and volumes D and E. Program X is only permitted to access data Y and Z. Or a certain file, volume, or program is labeled so that it can only be used by the person who created it. Some such schemes result in the need for large authorization tables, as will be discussed in the next two chapters. To lessen the size of the tables, the individual persons, items, or data entities can be arranged into groups, and the locks based upon groupings.

Last, the system may have time locks. Like a bank vault door, access may be permitted only at certain times of day. A *nocturnal* intruder will not be able to access data even if he knows the necessary passwords or security codes. A terminal in a secure area on the prime shift may be classified as insecure on the other shifts. If a person is detected trying to use a magnetic-stripe card key on a terminal out of hours, he will immediately trigger an alarm.

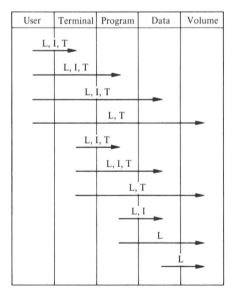

L = Based on security *levels*.
I = Based on *individual* items or persons, or groupings of these.
T = Based on *time*.

Figure 10.2. Relationships covered by locks and alarms.

11 IDENTIFYING THE TERMINAL USER

When an on-line system is operated with terminals, the first essential in making the system secure is to *identify* the person at the terminal.

There are three ways in which a person can be identified:

1. *By some physical personal characteristic.* For example, a device could be used for reading and transmitting his fingerprints or thumbprint, and the computer would have a program for identifying this. Again, his voice could be transmitted to the computer speaking certain prearranged digits or words, and the computer would have a program for recognizing his voice, comparing his speech against a stored "voiceprint." A variety of other physical characteristics of a person might be employed. Research is taking place on such schemes. They are the least used and usually the most expensive of the three types of ways of recognizing a person.

2. *By something that he knows or memorizes.* He could memorize a password, secret number, or answer a prearranged set of questions. Techniques of this type require no special hardware. They are the least expensive of the three, and can be made to be reasonably but not absolutely secure.

3. *By something carried.* For example, a badge, card, or key. He inserts the badge into a terminal badge reader, or the key into a lock on the terminal.

1. IDENTIFICATION BY PERSONAL CHARACTERISTICS

There are many physical characteristics by which a person may be recognized; if not uniquely, at least with a very low probability of error. Many patents have been obtained for devices that would record an identifiable human measurement. Some of these are expensive, for example fingerprint or thumb-print readers. Some are improbable, such as smell detectors, lip print readers, and devices for measuring the shape of the head.

With all devices for recognizing physical characteristics of a person there is a major difference between *identification* of the individual and *verification* that he is who he says he is. With fingerprints and voiceprints, identification of the individual has been much more widely studied than verification. Veri-fication, however, is *much* less expensive—the computer merely has to make a binary decision: YES, he is who he says he is, or NO, he is not. The best way to use physical recognition, therefore, is to make the individual enter some form of coded identification and then use the recognition process to check it. In comparing a person's thumbprint with a given thumbprint, for example, a simple optical comparison can be made of the center of the prints (where the distortion is least); this is far less expensive than attempting to analyze the whorls on the print.

MEASURES OF EFFECTIVENESS   There are two types of errors that any verification device can make: (1) a *false rejection* in which the person is who he says he is, but the device rejects him, and (2) a *false acceptance* in which the device accepts an impostor. We may, therefore, discuss two measures of effectiveness of a device: (1) the *probability of false rejections,* and (2) the *probability of false acceptances.* With most techniques, if we lower the probability of false acceptances, this tends to increase the probability of false rejections.

VOICEPRINTS   The attraction of using a *voiceprint* to identify the terminal user is that no special terminal equipment is needed—merely a telephone. The user speaks a predetermined phrase, possibly the digits of a code number, and a device at the computer converts the sound into a pattern of bits. It compares the pattern of a particular speech sound with the pattern previously stored for that user. As the user's voice differs somewhat from time to time, it must extract certain sound characteristics and compare these, using permissible limits of variation. The analysis of human speech is complex and is a technology that is still devel-oping. Some experimental voice-recognition systems are now in use on com-mercial systems.

Speakers tend to vary the speed of different parts of their speech. A first step in speaker recognition is to adjust the timing of the utterance to bring it in line with the sample with which it will be compared. When this "time-warping" has been done, the variation in pitch (rate of vibration of the vocal chords) and variation in intensity (loudness) can be compared with the sample. Other characteristics of the speech may also be time-warped and compared with the reference sample—for example, the vocal tract emphasizes certain frequencies in the speech called "formants" (Fig. 11.1). In Bell Telephone Laboratory experiments, it was found that the comparison of the pitch, intensity, and time-warp was good enough for practical speaker verification. Inclusion of the formants added greatly to the cost and only slightly to the accuracy. The device used in the Bell Telephone Laboratory was adjusted so that the *probability of false rejection* and *probability of false acceptance* were both 1.2%. (The probability is 1.0% if the formants in Fig. 11.1 are included in the comparison.)

The voice recognition operation *by itself* does not therefore identify the speaker, although voiceprints were used as legal evidence in the United States in 1972 to convict a murderer. Used in conjunction with another identification means, such as the person giving a secret security number (with speech input?), voice recognition could provide a high measure of security.

Further development of voice-recognition techniques will occur, and it seems possible that this may become a standard security technique in the future. One day you may be admitted through locked doors by speaking to them, but a substantial improvement in the state of the art is needed for this to be so.

With any technique for identifying a person we must ask the question: What methods can an impostor use? With speech recognition, he might learn to mimic the speaker. Bell Telephone Laboratories measured the effectiveness of mimincry by hiring the best mimics available from top New York talent agencies. These mimics, after much practice under ideal conditions, achieved a *false acceptance* rate of 42% (but only 27% when formants were used as in Fig. 11.1). The average person, however, cannot mimic effectively. The impostor might, under appropriate circumstances, use a tape recording of the speech of the person he is trying to impersonate.

A potential problem with voice recognition is that a person may not be recognized when he has a cold or hangover. If the range of acceptable parameters is enlarged to increase the likelihood of accepting users with colds (forget those with hangovers!), then the *probability of false acceptance* is increased.

On large terminal networks the need to transmit the human voice would add substantially to their cost. They are designed as *digital* links concentrating the transmission of many intermittently used terminals. The usable characteristics of the human voice might be digitized at the terminal for transmission over the digital network, but the advantage of needing no terminal equipment for identification other than an ordinary telephone is then lost.

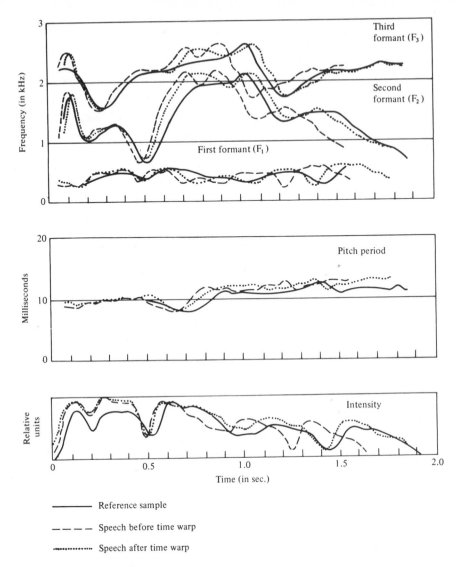

Figure 11.1. A Bell Telephone Laboratories device for identifying a person by means of his speech; time warps his utterance to bring it into registration—as much as possible—with a reference sample. This adjustment of the timing is necessary because there are always variations in the speed at which a person repeats a phrase. In the specimen above, five characteristics of the speech are compared with the reference sample. In this case, the speaker is not an imposter. With this device, the *probability of false rejection* and the *probability of false recognition* are both 1.0%. (*Reproduced with permission from Reference 1.*)

HAND
GEOMETRY

It is surprisingly rare for two people to have hands of the same shape—sufficiently rare, in fact, that hand shapes may provide a better means of recognizing individuals than voiceprints. A device that makes use of this fact is shown in Fig. 11.2 on page 142. The user places the four fingers of his right hand in the grooves shown and pushes his hand forward against the peg between his middle fingers. The device measures the lengths of his fingers.

An analysis of the finger lengths of over 4000 people was made by the Stanford Research Institute [2]. It indicated that if the four finger lengths of one hand are used for identification of a person, the *probability of false recognition* is on the order of 0.5 per cent if the measurement tolerance is ±1.5 mm (±0.06 inch) and on the order of 0.05 per cent if the measurement tolerance is on the order of ±0.75 mm (±0.03 inch). The *probability of false rejection* is very low.

The Identimat 2000 uses an intense light that makes the fingertips translucent and then measures the light transmission of the fingertips. This prevents a person with long fingernails from being rejected, and makes it very difficult to cheat the device by wearing a carefully made glove.

2. IDENTIFICATION BY SOMETHING KNOWN

Computer data may be protected in a less expensive fashion by requiring a would-be user to identify himself by giving a password or other information that he uniquely should know.

A low-level approach to the problem is to use a *password*. On many time-sharing systems the terminal operator creates and maintains his own file. He writes a password on that file, or possibly multiple passwords on different sections of the file, and his file cannot then be read by anyone who does not type in the correct password. The terminal user is free to change the password with which he has locked his files at any time he wishes. Such a scheme is in use today on a variety of different systems and is successful in protecting the files from most persons who would like to pry into them from a terminal. Most of these schemes, however, cannot be regarded as being highly secure, because an ingenious and persistent invader can generally obtain the password, and in many cases has. All users of the data file employ the same password. In some cases the password file itself in the computer has not been password protected! Passwords will usually keep out the casual intruder, but not one who is determined.

CHANGEABLE
SECURITY CODES

For a reasonable measure of security it is desirable to provide *each* terminal user with a different security code. He must type this code into the terminal. The computer will then check what the individual using that code is permitted to do. Safer still is a scheme in which the user keys in his own personal identification number, and follows this with his issued security code. The computer then checks that this security code has in fact been issued to the person with that number. The security code must be changed periodically. On some systems it is changed once per month. All terminal users must be instructed to keep their code to themselves and not let anyone else know what it is.

In one large corporate system in which it is vital to protect the information in the data base, the users must type in first their personnel number and then a security code number, which may contain any combination of letters, digits, or special characters. The computer checks that the person with the personnel number has in fact been issued *that* security code. A new security code is mailed to each user in his monthly pay packet. The code is on a detachable piece of card with nothing else written on it. The receiver is instructed to detach this piece of card immediately. Then if he loses the card with the security code on it, anybody finding it is unlikely to associate it with the correct personnel number. The user can be issued a new security code whenever he wants it. If he feels that security has been compromised in any way, for example, by someone seeing his security code perhaps over his shoulder as he types it in the terminal, he can ask immediately for a new security code.

Another scheme that makes successful use of memorized numbers is that for the cash-dispensing machines in use by the banks in some countries. The user inserts a "cash card" into the machine in the street to obtain money, and as he does so he keys in a number that should be known only to himself. If the number is not the one authorized for that particular card, the machine will keep the card and not give out any money.

In a location where mail theft is easy, it should be assumed that it will occur if made worthwhile. One organization in the United States lost a substantial sum attempting to set up cash dispensing machines—it mailed both the card and the user's number, and both were stolen.

INHIBITING DISPLAY
OF SECURITY CODES

Security codes may lose much of their security if a terminal prints the code. They may be more secure when the terminal is a visual display unit. It is of value to have a switch or key on a terminal with which the printing or display can be inhibited during the typing in of the security code. Even on a visual display terminal, it is useful to prevent the security code being displayed when it is typed in, as this lessens the chance of the code being observed by another person. This is possible on some of today's terminals, but not on others. On some, the computer can request a security code and then inhibit printing or display at the terminal. *Automatic* inhibition of printing or display is clearly preferable to relying on the operator to do it.

Some terminals attempt to hide printed security codes by overprinting them with other characters. This approach is much less satisfactory than inhibiting the printing.

The terminal sign-on procedure should be made as easy as possible for the user. He should not be left bewildered as to what he is supposed to do. It is a good idea to design a simple sign-on dialogue in which the computer asks for the security numbers it needs. The advantage of clarity for the user can be combined with the inhibiting of the display of security numbers; thus,

TERMINAL: TYPE YOUR PERSONNEL NUMBER

(The computer instructs the terminal to inhibit printing or display.)

USER: 053731 (not displayed)
TERMINAL: TYPE YOUR SECURITY CODE

(The computer instructs the terminal to inhibit display again.)

USER: PZ054 (not displayed)
TERMINAL: PROCEED

The security code should be sufficiently short so that the operator will memorize it. If he does not memorize it, he will often compromise security by writing it down, or by taking out a card with the code on it, which he may leave lying about.

ONCE-ONLY   The disadvantage of the password or security code
CODES   schemes is that the code can be given to another
                         person without any physical loss by the giver and
without anything having to be duplicated. There is no physical evidence of the other person's possession of it. Many terminal users write down their passwords or security codes. A would-be intruder can often find them on calendars or desk diaries. He may be able to find the detachable card mentioned above in a person's wallet.

Password or security code schemes can be protected from the intruder who has casually or deliberately learned another person's number by the use of *once-only codes.* With these a password or security code becomes invalid as soon as it has been used once. Wiretapping or distant observation of an operator's actions would not enable an intruder to break in. The operator is provided with a list of numbers rather than one number. If he receives a detachable card in his pay packet, it may contain 64 numbers rather than one (and no other identification). After he has used one of the numbers, he must then use the next. He will be told not to cross off the numbers on the card when they are used, so that if the card becomes lost it will not tell an intruder which number to use. He may make a note in a pocket diary of how many numbers he has used.

In one system the terminal gives the user the option of renewing his password at each terminal session.

SECRET NUMBERS   Another way to employ a nonrepeating number is to instruct the user to enter only certain digits, these being selected by the computer. Suppose that each user memorizes a 10-character number, word, or phrase. Let us call it a "secret number" and make it different from the user's personnel number or social security number so it cannot be found out by obvious means. It can contain any letters or characters, and to make it easier to memorize the user may be permitted to compose his own number. It should be possible to change the number at any time. When signing on, the user would be instructed by the computer to type certain characters, say, the second and eighth characters of the number. A different pair of characters would be selected each time.

To make the task of the would-be intruder more difficult, the sign-on procedure should require both a memorized number and a changeable written number (security code). The sign-on dialogue may be as follows:

TERMINAL: TYPE YOUR SECURITY CODE
USER: AR*21
TERMINAL: TYPE THE FIRST AND SEVENTH CHARACTERS OF YOUR SECRET NUMBER
USER: P6
TERMINAL: PROCEED

The security of user identification can be increased up to a point by increasing the complexity. For some systems memorized numbers and once-only codes will be too complex, and a careless user will make mistakes. *If the sign-on procedure becomes too difficult, security becomes compromised because the users find insecure ways of overcoming the difficulty.* A balance is needed, and the best solution depends upon the degree to which the terminal operators can be disciplined.

Any serious use of security code numbers must be accompanied by rigorous controls, and by a serious attempt to catch any person who is using another person's code, quickly and automatically. If the majority of users think that there is a high probability that they will be caught when they attempt to enter the system with another person's code, this will be a great psychological factor in deterring such invalid entry.

QUESTION-AND-ANSWER SEQUENCE Another technique that has been used in conjunction with passwords, locks, badges, security codes, and the like, is to have a question-and-answer sequence when the user signs on, in which the computer asks the user a number of personal questions. He has previously stored these questions in the system, and the questions are selected in such a way that only he is likely to give the right answer to them. They are questions to which he is not likely to forget the answer, as he might indeed forget his password or security code. Such questions could be: When is your wife's birthday?, What is the first name of your grandmother?, What is your Aunt Mary's maiden name? Passwords that need a fixed response, such as "Betty," requiring the response "Tomlinson," have been stored in the computer by the user along with the correct answers. When the terminal user signs on and keys in his personal identification number, the computer asks him questions, selected from a small list of such questions, to check that the right person is in fact at the terminal. It may not ask the same question every time, and this precludes the possibility of another person being able to observe his answer to all the questions. This sign-on procedure has the advantage of being easy to use, but the disadvantage of being somewhat lengthy in operation. It does not give a high degree of security if the questions are such that a persistent intruder could find out the answers to them, as with the first two questions above.

3. IDENTIFICATION BY SOMETHING CARRIED

KEYS AND BADGES For centuries man has unlocked his house door by means of a key. He can similarly unlock a terminal. Many terminals have, often as an optional feature, a key like a car ignition key. With modern electronics, however, the key can be much more complicated. A card or badge can contain information optically or magnetically encoded that is used to identify the owner. Some terminals have both a lock to disable them at night, and a card reader to identify the operator.

Optically encoded cards or badges are less secure than magnetically encoded ones because the encoding can be seen. One terminal used an identifi-

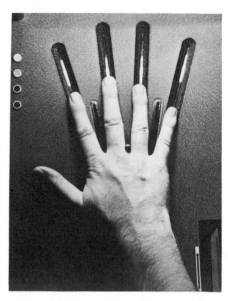

Figure 11.2. The Identimat 2000 identifies an individual by measuring the relative lengths of his fingers. A better method than voiceprints? *Photographs courtesy Identimation Corp.*

Figure 11.3. Identification of a person with a magnetic-stripe card at a credit-authorization terminal in a shoe store.

Figure 11.4. A magnetic-stripe card reader which can be attached to various terminals in order to identify the user.

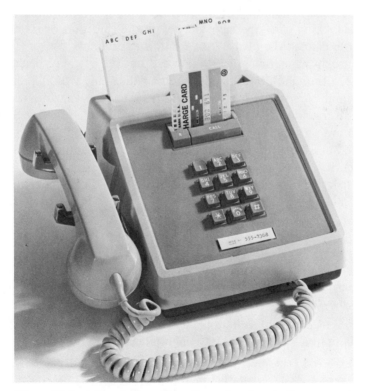

Figure 11.5. A Touch-Tone ®credit-card reader, similar to a card-dialer telephone, for identifying the card holder and inputing data, developed by *Bell Laboratories Record. Photograph courtesy A.T. & T.*

cation card for security with user data encoded in black and white marks, optically sensed, and a Xerox copy of the card was found to work equally well! A card the size of a credit card with information recorded on a magnetic strip has been in use for a variety of applications. Such a card has been used with machines like the credit-authorization terminal in Fig. 11.3. A card reader, such as that in Fig. 11.4, has been attached to a variety of conventional terminals for operator identification purposes. Fig. 11.5 shows a card-dialer telephone adapted to read a punched identification card and transmit its number in the form of Touch-Tone ® pulses [3].

A magnetic-strip credit card or identification card cannot be duplicated as easily as can a key. An organization with money to spend could, however, set up a facility for duplicating such cards, or an individual with skill and patience could produce a duplicate card in his basement.

Keys, machine-readable badges, and credit cards all have the disadvantage that the key or card could be lost or stolen. The user could fail to remove it from the terminal after the transaction is complete. If a sign-on action is used along with a badge or card, the user could forget to sign off. On some secure installations a fence has been placed around the terminal with a self-locking gate openable only with the card that operates the terminal. The user cannot then leave his card in the terminal.

The use of magnetic cards is likely to spread. They have been very useful in practice, although nobody would pretend that they would keep out a very ingenious and persistent invader, any more than an apartment lock would keep out an ingenious and determined burglar. They are better than no lock at all, and are particularly effective if used with appropriate burglar alarms, as we shall describe later. They are more secure when combined with a memorized security code, so that both are needed to gain access to the system. Some installations using the Identimat 2000 (Fig. 11.2) have backed up its use with an identification card reader.

REFERENCES

1. R. C. Lummis, "Speaker Verification: A Step Toward the 'Checkless' Society," *Bell Laboratories Record*, Bell Telephone Laboratories, Murray Hill, N.J. (September 1972).

2. D. R. Cone, "Personnel Identification by Hand Geometry Parameters." Stanford Research Institute (1969). Available from Identimation Corporation, Northvale, N.J.

3. Terry Prince and Dan Miller, "A Telephone for the 'Checkless' Society," *Bell Laboratories Record*, Bell Telephone Laboratories, Murray Hill, N.J. (September 1972).

12 IDENTIFYING THE MACHINE

When machines intercommunicate, it is sometimes a security requirement that one machine can positively identify the other.

FALSE CONNECTIONS

Machine identification is needed where telecommunication switching equipment is used. Some switching mechanisms occasionally make a wrong connection and have no means of recognizing their error. Again, on a line interconnecting many terminals, a polling mechanism may occasionally set up a connection with an incorrect device because noise on the line has changed his address. (This can happen when a parity check alone is used to detect noise errors, because telecommunication noise often changes more than one bit.) When a connection is established by human dialing, the likelihood of error is far greater.

On a well-designed system misconnections will be infrequent. However, on some systems with sensitive or classified information misconnections have been a considerable embarrassment. In keeping with Murphy's Law the machines sometimes obtain the wrong number at the worst possible time! In one corporation a list of executive appraisals was transmitted to the wrong terminal; it quickly found its way to a Xerox machine. It is desirable to determine which machine one is connected to before sending sensitive data to it.

SECURE AND
INSECURE
TERMINALS

A reason on some systems for positive terminal identification is that some terminals are in an area that is designed to be secure, whereas other terminals are not. Only trustworthy or security-cleared personnel may be able to enter a certain building or a certain room. The terminals in this room are secure, and so the computer as part of its security procedure needs to identify the fact that it is communicating with these particular terminals. We may, in fact, divide the whole of a far-flung system into areas that are secure and areas that are not. In Fig. 12.1, for example, those components within the dotted circles are secure areas. All the components that are not within dotted circles can be thought of as being insecure. To obtain a low-cost communication-line configuration, it may be desirable that terminals in secure areas be on the same communication line as terminals in insecure areas. This is illustrated in Fig. 12.2. A private branch exchange may have both secure and insecure terminals attached to it, and similarly a control unit or concentrator may have both, as shown in Fig. 12.3.

On many terminal systems today the computer knows the address of the terminal with which it is communicating. It may poll, for example, a terminal of a specific address. Even when a general poll is sent to a control unit on which any of the attached terminals may respond, the computer still knows

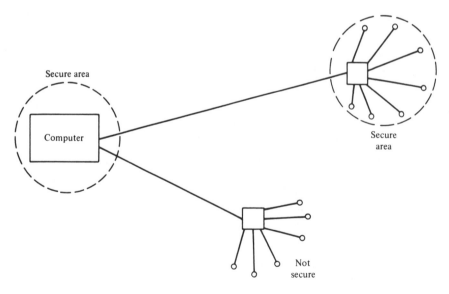

Figure 12.1

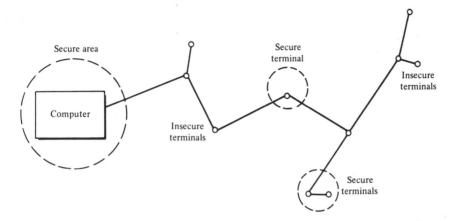

Figure 12.2

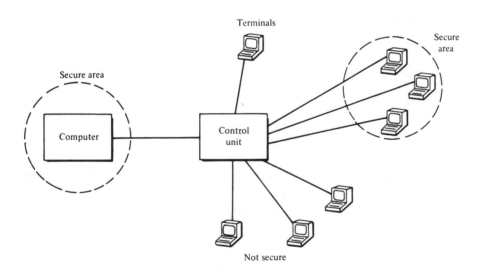

Figure 12.3

the address of the answering terminal, because this address precedes the text that is sent back. The computer then reads a table that tells it which terminal address it should treat as secure and which insecure.

Unfortunately, however, it is possible on some systems for a person wishing to gain unauthorized access to the system to switch the address of some of the terminals. This is possible with certain line configurations only. In Fig. 12.3, for example, the cables from the control unit to its visual display terminals could be switched, so that a terminal which the computer has listed as being in a secure area now becomes one in an insecure area. This perhaps would not have been possible if the control itself had been in a secure area, as in Fig. 12.4

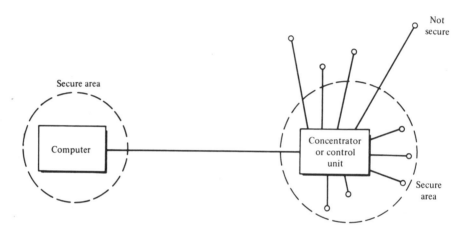

Figure 12.4

The security code for terminal identification is installed in such terminals in tamper-proof circuitry. No terminal can be completely safe from tampering, and a would-be intruder might obtain a terminal and change its security number. To do so, however, and to substitute the communication link from the original terminal to the imposter terminal would require considerable skill and knowledge of the system, which should be difficult to come by.

On some systems containing sensitive data, positive terminal identification is not used. The system relies entirely on some technique for identifying the user rather than the terminal or its location. It is sometimes an advantage in configurating a system, especially on a leased-line network, to *avoid* having a positive means of terminal identification as described, because, then, if a terminal fails, one terminal can be quickly interchanged with another, and this can improve the overall availability of the system.

PUBLIC DIAL-UP SYSTEMS

On some systems data are sent to a computer or obtained from it using the switched public network. Sometimes portable terminals are used. A salesman with a terminal the size of a briefcase may dial a computer from a call box or from his home, using an acoustical coupler. An imposter, knowing the requisite user number or codes, could dial the computer from anywhere. In one instance maintenance men on strike sabotaged a system for a month by dialing in and transmitting invalid signals. To prevent unauthorized access, the system should require that the terminal itself be uniquely and positively identifiable.

Again, some terminal control units are designed to collect and store data so that a computer can dial them at intervals and request that they transmit the data collected. The transmission may occur at night when the telephone rates are cheap. In this case it is desirable that the terminal control unit should automatically check the identification of the machine that dials it; otherwise, anyone could dial the machine and make it transmit its collected data.

TERMINAL IDENTIFICATION RESPONSE

On some systems the computer can send a message to the terminal asking it to identify itself. On others the terminal automatically sends its identification number when it transmits for the first time on a switched network line.

Two levels of identification numbers are found. The lower level is simply to identify the terminal without giving protection from deliberate felonious interchanging of terminals. The higher level provides for the transmission of a security code that is installed in tamper-proof circuitry so that it would be difficult to interchange terminals.

The IBM 2770, for example, can be equipped with either level of automatic identification. The former level is referred to as an *identification feature*. The terminal transmits an 8-bit character twice. The computer, under program control, can then identify a legitimate 2770 system. The identification character is specified by the user and wired into the terminal by his customer engineer. The more secure level of identification is referred to as a *security identification feature*. With this, the above identification character is transmitted twice and followed by three security characters. These can be almost any distinct 8-bit characters forming a unique sequence, which is built into the terminal when it is manufactured.

Without these features the terminal would have requested permission to transmit, after a dial-up connection was established, by sending an ENQ character, as follows:

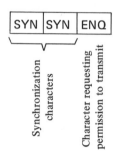

With the security identification feature the five characters described above are transmitted before the ENQ character; thus,

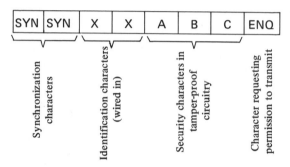

13 STRUCTURES OF AUTHORIZATION SCHEMES

When the user of a computer has been identified, the computer must check what he is authorized to do. On many systems he will be authorized to use some of the programs, but not all of them. He will be authorized to have access to certain files and be withheld from others. He may be permitted to read certain files, but not to update them or modify them. In other cases he may be permitted to enter data, but not to read what is there. A table may state what each user is authorized to do, or possibly there may be separate autoorization records for each user. The authorization procedure on some systems is very simple; on others it is highly structured and complex.

STRATIFICATION VERSUS COMPARTMENTALIZATION Different kinds of structures are possible in the design of the authorization system.

First, the information may be divided horizontally into security strata or levels such as Top Secret, Confidential, and so on. We shall refer to this as *stratification* (Fig. 13.1).

The security levels may be labeled with names such as "ABC Corporation Internal Use Only," which will inform employees that it must not be divulged outside, or "ABC Management Use Only," or "ABC Corporation Registered Users Only," which would mean that a registered-users list would be maintained by security procedures external to the computer.

Second, it may be divided "vertically" among different users, groups, or departments. This has been referred to with the (awful) word "*compartmentalization*" (Fig. 13.2).

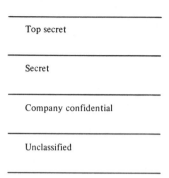

Figure 13.1. Stratification.

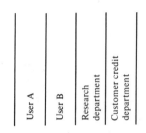

Figure 13.2. Compartmentalization.

When compartmentalized security is built into a system, it will be the designer's job to build impenetrable fences between the compartments. User A must not be able to gain access to user B's data or programs. Within each compartment there may be separate security levels which are employed by the users of that compartment. This type of security would normally be used on time-sharing systems to isolate the users. It is often necessary on multi-programming systems in which different jobs can run concurrently in different partitions. One partition may be running a highly classified job requiring maximum security protection, while other partitions have jobs with no security requirements and programs that could be insecure.

AUTHORIZATION TABLES   Third, authorization tables of some form may be used, which indicate what each user is permitted to do (Fig. 13.3), or which give other permissible relationships of the types indicated in Fig. 10.2.

An authorization table or algorithm may indicate what *transaction types* the user is permitted to enter, or it may relate to some other aspect of system

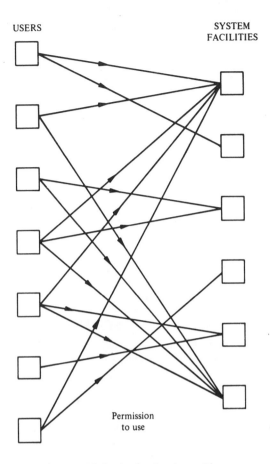

USERS

SYSTEM
FACILITIES

Permission
to use

Figure 13.3. Authorization tables.

use, such as what programs he is permitted to use, which data sets he is permitted to read, and which he is permitted to modify:

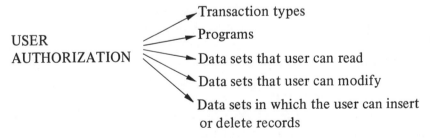

USER
AUTHORIZATION

Transaction types

Programs

Data sets that user can read

Data sets that user can modify

Data sets in which the user can insert
or delete records

In its simplest form we may divide the users of the system into a small number of categories. The application programs that the operator is permitted to use will depend upon his categorization. By such a scheme, certain application programs or certain files may be barred from certain categories of users. The category of user will be determined either by the password or security code that he keys in, by the badge or card that he inserts into the terminal, or possibly by terminal address itself or terminal location. On some airline systems, for example, the card a user employs to sign on with indicates that he falls into categories such as supervisor, reservation agent, trainee, person giving a demonstration, and so on. In a similar fashion, the category of authorization might be derived by an algorithm from the security code that is typed in.

Rather than basing the authorization on category of user, it will be desirable on some systems to base it on the individual himself. In this case, a table will be needed that relates the authorization to the user. When there are many users, a user file will be maintained, and once a user is identified his record will be read from the file to see what he is permitted to do.

LOCKS ON DATA RECORDS   Fourth, a security control may be placed in the data records, or filed along with a record indicating who is permitted to read each record, and who is permitted to modify them. This control may be placed in the records themselves, in the directory (index) used for addressing the records, or in a separate table.

PASSWORDS   As we commented earlier, the use of simple passwords should not be regarded as highly secure. It probably has about the same level of security as the normal locking of a filing cabinet with a key.

The combination of a password system with other precautions can build up a high level of security. One such system stores highly secret information along with unclassified data, both accessible to terminal users. Only terminals *in a secure area* can have access to the secret information, and then only if the correct document number and password are used.

In another system some users were found to be casual in their approach and often did not bother to lock their files with a password. In this case the system locks them, making up its own password and informing the user what password it has created. Only when the creator of the file returns and types in this password will the system permit access to the files. If the user loses the password, he can gain access to the file by contacting a security officer.

Sometimes a password permits communication between one user and another. Just as one person can give the key of his filing drawer to another, so a group of users can share access to a common document or file by knowing the password.

To lock the files in a more secure manner, the password scheme should be linked positively to the identification of the terminal user and to the surveillance procedures that will be described in Chapter 16 for policing the activities of the terminal users. The password system should be designed so that the password cannot be obtained by the computer-center operating staff, but can only be accessed or changed by the security officers concerned with the system.

A password scheme tends to be used when the file is employed only, or primarily, by the person who created it. On many systems the file is set up for use by many persons, and a password would not give good security because too many people would know the password. In this case the user must be positively identified, and the records must contain information saying which users are permitted to read, modify, or purge them. The types of authorization tables that are used for this will be discussed in Chapter 14.

STRATIFICATION   When stratified security is used, it should carry over beyond the computer room to documents, data volumes, peripheral machines, and personnel. Each page of computer listings or terminal printouts that has a high security classification should be marked with this. It should be labeled "Top Secret," "ABC Company Confidential," or whatever name has been given to its security level, and the pages should be numbered to ensure that none are removed. The data volumes such as tapes and disks should be labeled with the classification of the most secure data on the volume. A computer room operator may not be permitted to load or unload a "Top Secret" volume. This will be mounted on a *locked* drive by suitably cleared personnel. Similarly, programs will be assigned security classifications, and those with a high classification will be put through an appropriate clearance procedure. Some terminals, remote printers, or peripheral computers may be designated with low security clearances, and no data of a higher classification will be used with them.

The personnel employed will be graded according to the strata of data they can handle. No person will be permitted to see documents of a higher stratum than his own, or to handle programs or data volumes of a higher level. He may not be permitted to use terminals that are cleared for a high security level. The locations of some terminals and other machines may be accessible only to persons of an appropriately high clearance.

The security levels may thus apply to

1. Data records
2. Programs

3. File volumes—disks, tapes, or card decks containing data or programs
4. Disk drives and tape units
5. Terminals
6. Locations where classified data, volumes, or machines exist
7. Computer listings
8. Manuals and other operating or supporting documents
9. Terminal users or machine operators
10. Other personnel

When security stratification of this type is employed, the computer operating system should be designed to work with it. The operating system becomes an essential part of the security armor, and we shall discuss it further in Chapters 17 and 18. A secure operating system will prevent data of a given classification from going to a terminal of a lower classification, or being written on a disk or tape of a lower classification. Its output writer will ensure that all listings are labeled with security level and page number. It will ensure that a classified program is only used by a person with a high enough level of authorization, and that a program cannot gain access to data of a higher level than itself.

Ideally, the handling of security strata in this way should be built into the operating system or computer control program as an integral but optional part of its operation. Sometimes it is necessary to use an operating system written without such features, and additions or modifications have to be made to it. The security protection can be built entirely into the application programs, but this, as we shall discuss later, does not give such a high measure of protection.

The IBM Operating System/360 can be ordered with a *resource security feature*, which is discussed in Chapter 18. Among other measures, it has provisions for up to eight security strata. When using this, all printed (or spooled) output is labeled with a security classification, page number, date, and (optionally) time. The user selects his own names for the eight security strata. The system controls the maximum level of data that can be written on any disk or tape. A disk not labeled "Top Secret" or higher cannot have "Top Secret" data written on it. It controls the programs that the system will fetch, add, or replace for a user on the basis of his security level, and also controls which data sets he may read or write. Similarly, it controls what data may be displayed on terminals. Data of a given classification cannot be displayed on a terminal with a lower classification.

The use of the security strata usually extends to all documents in the organization, not merely to those involved with the computer.

MORE COMPLEX   Simple stratification, or simple compartmentaliza-
STRUCTURES   tion, can be implemented without necessarily in-
                    curring a high overhead in the computer system.
The more elaborately structured authorization schemes are often advocated,
and in some of these the overhead can become substantial.

Simple compartmentalization and stratification can be combined in one
system (Fig. 13.4), still without incurring a high level of overhead.

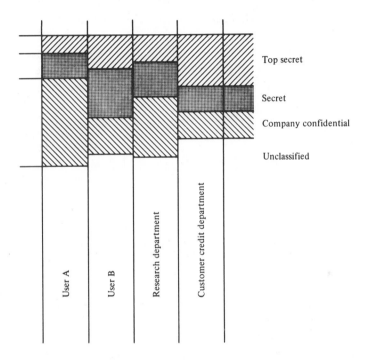

Figure 13.4. Simple stratification and compartmentalization, combined,
need not incur a high level of overhead in the computer system—as do
some more elaborate authorization structures.

The reason for more elaborate structures is that the same data or programs are to be shared between many users of different types, and it is
desirable to restrict the users differently as to what they may see or do. In
some cases a single record may be accessible by a variety of persons differing
in their needs, and separate *fields* within the record may be restricted differently. The simple schemes are rather like locked filing cabinets with drawers
being restricted to different users and different security categories. With a
computer the authorization can be much more intricate than that; different

items in the same document can be restricted to different users. The main reason for wanting to do this is so that a data base can be employed for multiple purposes.

Many files on commercial systems are established for one application. These can usually be made secure without elaborate authorization tables and without having to write security control information on the records. There is a growing tendency to build data bases that integrate the data needed for many purposes and that provide a bank of information which can be used for answering a variety of different questions as they arise. In the data base environment of the future an organization's data elements will be stored in a largely non-redundant application-independent manner. On such data bases, security controls must be an integral part of the data management system, and tables such as those discussed in Chapter 14 will often be needed.

14 AUTHORIZATION TABLES
      AND THEIR USE

When the security system uses more elaborate structures than simple stratification or compartmentalization, tables may be used to indicate what an identified user is permitted to do, or which users are permitted to read which records. This chapter discusses the structure and use of such tables.

The authorization tables may be short and simple, or they may be so lengthy that careful attention must be paid to their structure to avoid excessive overhead. The need for highly complex authorization schemes should be questioned.

USER   A basic form of authorization table has an entry for
TABLES   each user stating what he is entitled to do. Such a
                  table may give the security code assigned to each
user and a field indicating his category of authorization, as in Fig. 14.1

The computer's first operation would be to check the security code or password. Rather than using one category of authorization, it may be desirable to structure the authorization table according to the facilities that may be used or the actions that may be taken. The authorization table may list for each items such as the following:

1. Programs that he may use.
2. Types of transactions that he might enter.
3. Data sets that he may read.
4. Data sets that he may modify.
5. Categories of data within a data set that he may read.
6. Categories of data that he may modify.

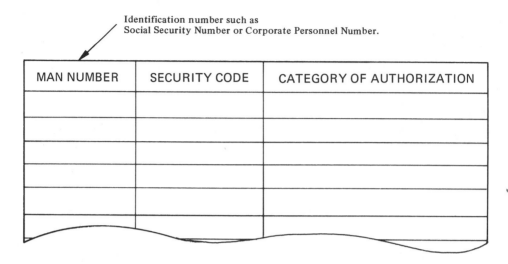

Figure 14.1

Figure 14.2 illustrates a table that gives the *types of transaction* that a user may enter. It relates to a commercial system on which there can be up to 160 different transaction types. One bit is used for each of these 160 transaction types, saying whether or not the user in question has been authorized to enter this transaction type or not. Before any transaction program is processed, this table will be inspected.

In Figure 14.2 one single bit is employed to say whether a user is authorized to enter that transaction type. It may be desirable to have more than one bit. For example, one bit might relate to reading the files with that transaction type, another bit might relate to writing or updating the files. Another bit on one such system indicates whether or not the user in question has the *capability* to update these particular files. He may be authorized to update them because he is in a high position in the organization in question, but he may not have had sufficient training with this transaction type. It is undesirable that he should be permitted to modify the records until he has had the necessary training, because he might damage the records. It is very important on the system in question that the training of the terminal operator is done very thoroughly and that the standards involved in this are adhered to. Sometimes, computer-assisted instruction techniques using the same terminal are employed for the training.

Figure 14.3 shows an authorization table that is again related to 160 different transaction types but now uses three bits for each transaction type,

MAN NUMBER	SECURITY CODE	160 AUTHORIZATION BITS

One bit for each transaction type.

Figure 14.2

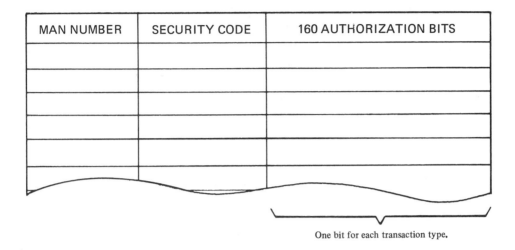

MAN NUMBER	SECURITY CODE	AUTHORIZATION TO READ RECORD
		AUTHORIZATION TO MODIFY RECORD
		CAPABILITY TO MODIFY RECORD
MAN NUMBER	SECURITY CODE	AUTHORIZATION TO READ RECORD
		AUTHORIZATION TO MODIFY RECORD
		CAPABILITY TO MODIFY RECORD
MAN NUMBER	SECURITY CODE	AUTHORIZATION TO READ RECORD

For each of 160 transaction types

The authorization bits could be encoded with two bits per
user for each transaction type, as follows:

    00 = No permission
    01 = Permission to read records
    10 = Authorization to modify records but no capability,
           hence permission granted to read but not write
    11 = Permission to modify records

Figure 14.3

one giving the authority of the individual in question to read the records associated with that transaction, the second indicating whether he has authority to modify the records, and the third indicating whether or not he has completed the required training that permits him to update the files. It is impossible for him to look at the files unless he types in the correct security code and also has had the authorization to read these files. He cannot update the files without the correct security code and also the appropriate *authorization* bit and *training* bit.

DATA-BASE
CONTROLS

Control of a data base can be better maintained if the file is secured by a central authority, a data base administrator, or a security officer. Security on some data bases is left in the hands of individual "file owners." The file owner has the responsibility of controlling who will see the information in his file, and to do this he employs lockwords, authorization bits in the records, or authorization tables.

The lockwords or table entries may refer to (Fig. 14.4):

1. Complete files
2. Volumes—disks or tapes
3. Individual records
4. Groups of records or record categories
5. Individual fields in a record type
6. Categories of fields in a record type (the categories could possibly relate to more than one separate file)
7. Group items (segments, tuples) in a data base, or combinations of these. Relations, or combinations of relations in a normalized data base [1].

The control *could* refer to individual fields within individual records, but the overhead associated with so fine a structuring may be too great.

The lockwords or authorization bits for data-base protection must be linked to the user. They could relate to

1. Individual user
2. Group or category of users
3. Security level
4. Application program
5. Terminal or terminal location
6. Time of day
7. Transaction type
8. Combinations of these

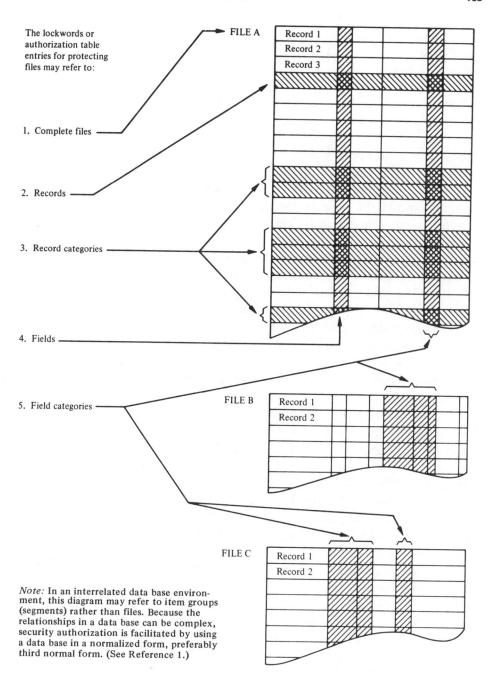

The lockwords or authorization table entries for protecting files may refer to:

1. Complete files

2. Records

3. Record categories

4. Fields

5. Field categories

FILE A

Record 1
Record 2
Record 3

FILE B

Record 1
Record 2

FILE C

Record 1
Record 2

Note: In an interrelated data base environment, this diagram may refer to item groups (segments) rather than files. Because the relationships in a data base can be complex, security authorization is facilitated by using a data base in a normalized form, preferably third normal form. (See Reference 1.)

Figure 14.4

Bits or lockwords for controlling access to files may reside in the records themselves, or may be in a separate table. They may be a part of the directories or indexes used for addressing the files.

COMPLEXITY OF MAPPING   Authorization, then, is basically a mapping function. Users must be mapped with data records or fields. The users may be mapped with programs or transaction types. Programs or transaction types may be mapped with data. Terminals or physical locations may also be involved in the mapping.

When many users *share* the data on the files, the mapping becomes more complex. When the records contain fields that differ in their sensitivity, it becomes more complex still. Some systems require complex mapping, whereas others can use a simple approach, as illustrated by Figs. 13.1 and 13.2. Any operating system designed to provide security for a wide variety of computer systems must be designed so that an appropriate level of complexity of mapping can be introduced at *system generation* time. A small savings-bank system, for example, needs to be secure, but does not need the elaborately structured authorization tables that could be needed in a corporate information system. Even a corporate information system may have a relatively well-defined and fixed assortment of data, and a relatively small number of user classes, compared with general-purpose shared-file time-sharing systems.

In general-purpose systems and in loosely defined information systems, new data sets of entirely unpredictable formats may be introduced at any time. New categories of users may be introduced. The file-addressing methods may change. The mapping mechanism in such cases must be entirely flexible. When there is *any* likelihood of change, it would be shortsighted to base an authorization scheme on fixed user relationships.

Even when this level of flexibility is not needed, the authorization categories of users will change periodically on most systems. The mapping mechanism must therefore be designed so that changes can be made easily but securely. It should be designed so that only the security officer can make such changes, and no one else.

EFFICIENCY OF MAPPING   To map the users directly to the data records, or fields within records, might require an excessively complex mapping function. A large commercial system might have a data base of 10^{10} bits and thousands of potential users, say 5,000, of whom several hundred might be on line at once. The data base might contain 10^8 separate data fields. To indicate whether a given user was authorized to read, write, or purge a field would require 2 bits. Hence, to give a complete authorization table for all fields and all users would require $2 \times 5000 \times 10^8 = 10^{12}$ bits. This is clearly not practical, and the reader should note that some of today's commercial systems have a data base more than 10 times larger than this example.

If each user, on the other hand, had an authorization record related to *transaction types* and needed 2×160 bits, as in Fig. 14.3, this would require $5000 \times 2 \times 160 = 1,600,000$ bits. This, with the security codes, could be contained on one cylinder of a disk drive with an average access time of 10 to 20 milliseconds.

It might be decided that on a data base of this size it would be reasonable to use one disk pack for the security provisions. On one typical disk this would permit the designer of the security techniques to use approximately 10^8 bits for his tables and have an average access time of 30 milliseconds, say.

The user table could relate to transaction types, as above, or it could relate to programs, every user requiring specific authorization for any program that he might employ. In addition to such measures, however, it is necessary on some systems that the authorization scheme relate the user to the data records which the transaction type or program employs. When this is the case, the efficiency of the mapping becomes of concern, and to reduce the size of the tables, some form of grouping must be used.

On some systems the users may be grouped together. On others the data records may be grouped for authorization purposes. In grouping the users together, for example, all the clerks in one office may be categorized as being in the same group. The group would be handled with one entry in the authorization table. In grouping the records together, the records categories shown in Fig. 14.4 might be categorized as one group. A personnel file, for example, might be grouped by department, rank (first-level manager, second-level manager), or field category (salary information, appraisals, etc.).

Figure 14.5 shows the type of tables that may be employed with user groups and data groups. When a user first keys in his user number, a record is read from a *user authorization table* giving his *security number* and *user group*. The computer instructs the user to key in his security number to see whether it matches. The computer may also check the terminal identification and verify that a person with the number in question should in fact be at that terminal. The person may be permitted to use one of several terminals, and so Fig. 14.5 shows a *terminal group* number. If these checks confirm that the person is authorized to use a machine in that terminal group, then the *user group* number is employed for any further checks.

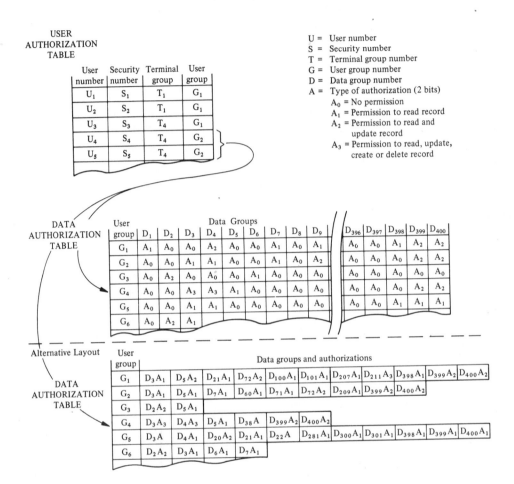

Figure 14.5. Authorization tables with user groups and data groups.

When the program being employed by that user attempts to read or write a record, the authorization program ascertains which *data group* the record is in. From the *data authorization table* in Fig. 14.5 it can then obtain the type of authorization for that *user group* and that *data group*. The type of authorization is again given by two bits, this time indicating whether the user is permitted to read, write, or create and delete, records.

The lower form of data authorization table in Fig. 14.5 might be used when most user groups are allowed access to only a small portion of the data groups. The upper form of table might give lower storage requirements when user groups are permitted to access a high proportion of the records.

ZONES AND   For authorization purposes, many files on com-
CATEGORIES IN DATA   mercial systems can be divided into *zones* and *cate-*
                             gories. Zone refers to a *group of entities about*
which data are stored, such as customers and accounts handled by a branch
office, or employees in a given office; *category* refers to a *type of data stored*
about those entities such as customer information, sales figures, salary, and
so on. There will usually be many categories of data about the entities in any
particular zone; for example, there may be many types of records stored
concerning the business in one branch office.

À person using the data bank may be permitted to see many categories
of information, but be restricted to a particular *zone*. He may, for example,
be permitted to see most of the information relating to his own branch office,
but not information of the same categories relating to other branch offices.
On the other hand, a person using the data bank for statistical purposes may
be authorized to see only certain *categories* of information, but he may be
permitted to see these in all or most zones. He may be authorized to look at
all the expenditure figures in the corporation.

The size of the authorization tables can be reduced substantially by dividing them into categories and zones. Figure 14.6 shows tables for a case
with 100 categories. The zone figure in the upper table may refer to a single
zone or a group of zones. Two bits for each of the 100 categories again indicate whether the user is authorized to read, write, or create and delete, the
records.

The upper table in Fig. 14.6 might relate, for example, to a system used
for the administration of the sales operations of a corporation. Terminals are
used for many different functions in the sales offices, regional headquarters,
and head office. A central data bank is maintained of sales and customer information. A salesman can have access to records relating to his own activities
and customers, but nobody else's. His territory may be one zone in the authorization scheme. A branch manager can see records relating to all the salesmen in his branch—several contiguous zones—and may see information in
categories other than those which the salesmen can see. The regional office
accesses the records of many branch offices, and so on. The zone field in the
upper table of Fig. 14.6 therefore shows the upper and lower limits of the
group of contiguous zones. The first two digits of a zone, for example, may
indicate the branch office. Alternatively, it may refer to a numbered zone
group that is specified elsewhere. Individual salesmen are allowed and instructed to modify certain of their own records; they must not be permitted
to change other salesmen's records. The table is therefore based on individual
users, not user groups.

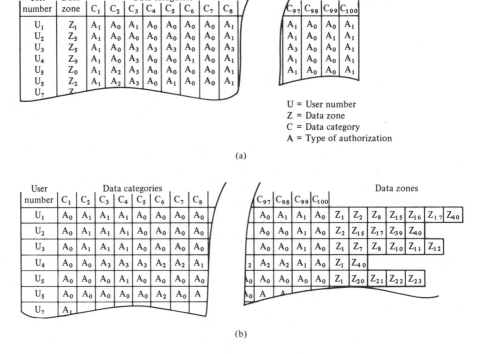

Figure 14.6. Two data-access authorization tables with *type* of data classified into "categories" and data about different areas classified into "zones."

A zone entry in the upper table may relate to one zone, a contiguous group of zones (all zones beginning with the digits *xx*), or to *all* zones of a given type. On some systems it will be necessary to link the user number to a varying number of separate zones or zone groups. The second table format in Fig. 14.6 would permit this.

MORE COMPACTED FORMS OF TABLE   Various forms of authorization tables can be used in which neither the users nor the data are deliberately grouped to lower the table size, but the table is designed to take advantage of similarities in user sets for different data. In many systems there is a substantial commonality between the authorizations granted for different fields or records.

Consider, for simplicity, a scheme with ten data items and four users. Figure 14.7 shows which users are permitted to see which items. Item R_1 can be read by all the users. Item R_2 can be read by user number 2; R_3 by users numbers 1, 2, and 3; and so on.

The authorization scheme assigns a *class* and a *level* to each item. In this simplified illustration three classes will be necessary: A, B, and C. For a large and finely structured file, several hundred classes may be needed, though often the number is much less. Each user is given an *authorization level* for each class. In this illustration the numbers 0 through 4 are the numbers of the levels; 0 means that the user is not permitted to read data of that class. A digit higher than 0 means that the user is authorized to read data of that class, provided its level is not higher than the digit in question.

The table in Fig. 14.8 states what each user is authorized to read. User number 2, for example, can read data of class A, at all four levels; he can read data of class B at level 1 but not at higher levels, and cannot read any data of class C.

The levels and classes assigned to the data are written on the file either alongside the data or in an associated table. They are shown in Fig. 14.9. Using Figs. 14.8 and 14.9, the reader may reconstruct the permissions shown in Fig. 14.7.

Data items	R_1	R_2	R_3	R_4	R_5	R_6	R_7	R_8	R_9	R_{10}
Users with permission to use these records	1 2 3 4	2	1 2 3	2 3 4	1 2 3 4	2 3	3 4	3	1 3	1

Figure 14.7

USER AUTHORIZATION TABLE	Classes		
	A	B	C
User number 1	2	0	2
User number 2	4	1	0
User number 3	3	3	1
User number 4	1	2	0

The level numbers for each class

Figure 14.8

Data items	R_1	R_2	R_3	R_4	R_5	R_6	R_7	R_8	R_9	R_{10}
Class	A	A	A	B	A	A	B	B	C	C
Level	1	4	2	1	1	3	2	3	1	2

Figure 14.9

Given the requirements shown in Fig. 14.7, the algorithm for constructing the tables in Figs. 14.8 and 14.9 could operate as follows. Scan the data items in Fig. 14.7 from left to right, examining first those with the maximum number of users. Scanning first for items with four users, data items R_1 and R_5 are found. Assign the first "class" to these (class A), and give it level 1. Data item R_5 has the same set of users and so is also assigned class A, level 1. The first is R_3. Its three users (1, 2, and 3) are a *subset* of the group (1, 2, 3, and 4) previously found. The data item will also therefore be assigned class A, but now with level 2. The users who are authorized to see class A items with level 2 will also be able to see class A, level 1 items R_1 and R_5. Continuing the scan, item R_4 has a user group (2, 3, and 4) that is also a subset of the class A, level 1 group (1, 2, 3, and 4). However, class A cannot be assigned to it, even at a higher level; otherwise one of its user groups, 4, would then be able to see item R_3, which is not permitted. A new class, B, is therefore assigned to item R_4 at level 1.

Now scan for items with two users. The first is item R_6, and all its authorized users are a subset of the group that can see R_3 (class A, level 2). R_6 will therefore be assigned class A, level 3. Continuing the scan, item R_7 has a user group (3 and 4) which is a subset of those for R_4. It is therefore assigned class B, level 2. The users of item R_9 are not a subset of the highest of class A or class B. They are therefore assigned class C.

Last, the single-user items are assigned to classes of which they are a subset: R_2 to class A, level 4; R_8 to class B, level 3; and R_{10} to class C, level 2.

Figures 14.7 to 14.9 referred to reading the data only. Authorization for modifying it is also necessary and may utilize the same class assignments. Figures 14.10 and 14.11 add *write levels* to the *read levels* of the previous figures.

USER AUTHORIZATION TABLE	Classes					
	A		B		C	
	Read	Write	Read	Write	Read	Write
User number 1	2	1	0	0	2	1
User number 2	4	2	1	1	0	1
User number 3	3	0	3	2	1	0
User number 4	1	0	2	1	0	0

Figure 14.10

Data item	R_1	R_2	R_3	R_4	R_5	R_6	R_7	R_8	R_9	R_{10}
Class	A	A	A	B	A	A	B	B	C	C
Read level	1	4	2	1	1	3	2	3	1	2
Write level	1	2	1	1	1	2	2	2	1	1

Figure 14.11

When a similar operation is carried out on a large file, 16 levels (4 bits) are usually sufficient. The user groups often form natural subsets and this commonality keeps the numbers of separate classes small. A data item may be protected by 4 bits for read levels, 4 bits for write levels, and perhaps 8 bits for classes:

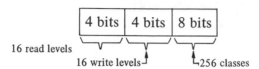

Two bytes per data item are thus employed. If the data item is a record of 100 bytes on average, this will represent an overhead of 2 per cent of the file volume. If the data items are *fields* rather than records, the overhead may be higher. A number of variations on this theme are possible.

FLEXIBILITY　　　　　　　A more intricate form of authorization table, such as the previous one, can save storage space and possibly processing time. On the other hand, it is substantially more difficult to change the authorizations. When the users and their permissions change, the levels and classes may need to be recomputed. On a large system they can change frequently, and so a simpler form of table, such as that in Fig. 14.6, is usually preferable. It is often desirable that the system security officer be able to alter the authorization in real time.

A primary consideration in data base design is that the techniques used should be adaptable so that modifications can be made to the data organization without forcing any rewriting of the application programs. The security authorization procedures should be similarly adaptable.

REFERENCES

1. Normalization and third normal form are discussed in Section I of the author's book *Computer Data Base Organization* (Prentice-Hall, 1974). The original papers on relational (normalized) data base organization were the following:

2. E. F. Codd, "A Relational Model of Data for Large Shared Data Banks," *Communications of the ACM*, 13, 6 (June 1970), 377-387.

3. E. F. Codd, "Further Normalization of the Data Base Relational Model," in *Data Base Systems,* Randall Rustin, ed., Prentice-Hall, Inc., 1972.

15 CONTENT-DEPENDENT PROTECTION

The locks discussed in the previous two chapters have been direct and positive. A user is either allowed to employ a certain program or he is not; a user is either allowed to access a given file or data element, or he is not.

In some computer systems the authorization process is more complicated than that and depends in some way upon the *contents* of the file or the results of the processing. A requestor may, for example, be authorized to request salary information up to but not exceeding $300. If he attempts to read a record with a salary over $300, he will either be denied access or told "over $300."

Again, he may be permitted to ask certain questions about the data, but not others. He may, for example, access a record giving number of convictions, and not be permitted to ask how many, but merely whether a person has one or not.

He may be allowed access to any of the fields in a record individually, but not be permitted to see the relationship between certain fields. For example, researchers may be using a medical data base with data about mental illness. The records giving details of patients' histories contain the patients' names. Some users will access the names. Some will access the medical details. However, the researchers are not permitted to associate a name with the medical details. It is permitted to ask "what are the ages of the patients who received thorazine?" but not "what are their names?"

Access must therefore be denied on some systems on the basis of

1. Content of a record
2. Form in which a question is asked
3. Relation between certain fields, or contents of those fields

Where authorization is to be based on the values of fields or combinations of values, a set of qualification expressions may be stored for each file, or in a relational data base for each relation. A program, which has been referred to as an *arbiter program,* will have the task of reading the data requested, applying the qualification expressions to it, and deciding whether or not the user can be given the information he requests. Where the user is not permitted to read all of the fields he has requested, some of the fields may be suppressed, modified, or garbled before he is given the data. The arbiter program itself must be highly protected.

One of the problems of content-dependent protection is that high overhead can occur in terms of processing time and time to access the authorization tables. In order to minimize this a procedure is needed that can handle the majority of transactions simply and that can only invoke the more elaborate forms of authorization for the few transactions that need it.

E. F. Codd [1] has suggested a step-by-step authorization procedure similar to the process in Fig. 15.1. The access control is based on a user code, which will indicate the class or identity of the user and the operation requested (Read, Update, Delete, Insert). The user code, referred to as X in Fig. 15.1, is the argument which is used to search the authorization tables. Tables exist for files, generations of data, fields within the files, field combinations, and attributes of fields and requestors that affect the qualification expression. Twelve tables may be used corresponding to the twelve security interrogations of Fig. 15.1. The interrogations are arranged in a sequence of increasing complexity so that approval or denial can be decided upon as fast as possible.

In Fig. 15.1 whenever one test yields the answer "NO" the following test is carried out. The sequence is arranged so that the tests alternate between attempted denial and attempted approval. The exact nature of the interrogations and their associated tables would differ from one installation to another, as also would their sequence. The first tables interrogated should be small enough to fit into the computer's main memory. The tests should be arranged so that most transactions can be authorized with the first one or two tests.

Codd [1] designed his authorization procedure to operate with a relational data base using *relations* and *domains* rather than the files and fields of Fig. 15.1. (See references at the end of Chapter 14.) The authorization tables in such a case are declared as relations and are stored and retrieved like any other relation.

1. Are all *files* mentioned in the request unconditionally accessible to X?

    (YES) ─────────────────────────────────────── ► APPROVE

    (NO)

2. Is there a *file* mentioned in the request which is unconditionally prohibited to X?

    (YES) ─────────────────────────────────────── ► DENY

    (NO)

3. Are all *generations* mentioned in the request unconditionally accessible to X?

    (YES) ─────────────────────────────────────── ► APPROVE

    (NO)

4. Is there a *generation* mentioned in the request which is unconditionally prohibited to X?

    (YES) ─────────────────────────────────────── ► DENY

    (NO)

5. Are all *fields* mentioned in the request unconditionally accessible to X?

    (YES) ─────────────────────────────────────── ► APPROVE

    (NO)

6. Is there a *field* mentioned in the request which is unconditionally prohibited to X?

    (YES) ─────────────────────────────────────── ► DENY

    (NO)

7. Are all *field combinations* mentioned in the request unconditionally accessible to X?

    (YES) ─────────────────────────────────────── ► APPROVE

    (NO)

8. Is there a *field combination* mentioned in the request which is unconditionally prohibited to X?

    (YES) ─────────────────────────────────────── ► DENY

    (NO)

9. For each sensitive field combination mentioned in the request is there a *field qualification expression* and do the values of the fields lie within the constraints approved for X?

    (YES) ─────────────────────────────────────── ► APPROVE

    (NO)

10. For each sensitive field combination mentioned in the request is there a *field qualification expression* for which the values of the fields lie outside the constraints approved for X?

    (YES) ─────────────────────────────────────── ► DENY

    (NO)

11. For each sensitive field combination in the request is there a *qualification expression relating attributes of the requestor and values of the fields in question,* and are the constraints satisfied?

    (YES) ─────────────────────────────────────── ► APPROVE

    (NO)

12. For each sensitive field combination in the request is there a *qualification expression relating attributes of the requestor and values of the fields in question,* for which the constraints are not satisfied?

    (YES) ─────────────────────────────────────── ► DENY

    (NO)

13. Inform the user that his request is denied on the basis of lack of information in the system (as opposed to being explicitly forbidden).

Figure 15.1. An authorization procedure based on successively more complex questions. Most requests will be dealt with by the first few questions. Only occasional requests will need the entire procedure. *(Based on a memorandum of E. F. Codd which applied such an approach to relational data banks [1]).*

STATISTICAL   Some data banks are used for statistical purposes,
DATA BANKS   and a variety of questions such as the following may
be answered using the system: What proportion of
convicts are rearrested, What is the average salary of branch managers and
what is its standard deviation?, What is the proportion of bad debts for each
customer category?, and What is the correlation between social attitude test
results and job performance?

When private personal information is stored, there can be a major difference between a *dossier* data bank and a *statistical* one. In the former the enquiries will be to obtain facts about specific individuals or entities, and access
to the data will be controlled by authorization procedures such as those described in the previous chapters. In a statistical bank the user should be able
to scan all the records, but should not be able to associate the facts with a
specific individual, and possibly not with a specific office, factory, product,
or other entity. Instead he should be able to obtain aggregate values and cor-
relations. The distinction between these two types of data banks has been
much stressed in the Congressional hearings on privacy [1]. Note, however,
that some data banks that store full details about the entities they relate to
are used in both a statistical manner and to provide specific details.

In a statistical data bank the names of the individuals (or other entities)
about whom data are recorded may be omitted. Often, however, this is not
possible because the records are needed for other purposes. The names may
be garbled or, better, the statistical user may be locked from access to them.

MISUSE OF   A major problem associated with the statistical data
STATISTICAL   bank is that the user can sometimes *deduce* infor-
DATA BANKS   mation he is not intended to know by phrasing
questions in certain ways. The query language will
usually permit him to scan the files for information that fulfills certain conditions. On some systems he is permitted to ask for mean and standard deviation values but not explicit values. He is prohibited from asking for the
maximum or minimum values of certain items, for example salary. Nevertheless, he may be able to obtain certain explicit values by selecting the conditions which must be fulfilled in the scan so that only one item is included in
the sample. In one corporate information system it was relatively easy to
obtain certain individuals' salaries by such a procedure. More sensitive information can be obtained from other data banks, for example psychiatric data,
debts, and police convictions.

If the browser in a statistical data bank can use it freely, there is much that he can deduce about individuals—so much in some cases that the distinction between statistical and dossier data banks was referred to by Paul Baran in a Congressional hearing as "illusory" [2]. A different form of safeguard is necessary on statistical data banks from that on dossier data banks, and must be based upon the results of the user's file searches and on the quantity of activity he is carrying out. Such safeguards will make it difficult to obtain information about individuals, but not necessarily impossible.

Suppose that a user wishes to find the income of a certain person he knows. He knows many facts about the person and asks the computer questions such as "How many people in the data bank have the following properties?

Sex: male
Age: 42
Education level: Ph.D.
Marital status: Bachelor
Place of residence: Chicago
Profession: Consultant."

The machine may respond with 36. The user then asks, "How many people have the following properties?

Sex: male
Age: 42
Education level: Ph.D.
Marital status: Bachelor
Place of residence: Chicago
Profession: Consultant
Salary exceeds $60,000."

The machine says 27. The user then repeats the question with salary $50,000. The machine says 33. He tries $40,000. The answer is 36. $45,000 also gives 36. $46,000 gives 35. The user then knows that this person's salary is greater than $45,000. Similarly he may find that the person's salary is less than, say, $48,000.

The user may then try to add other factors he knows about the person in question to narrow down the field, for example, "Degree subject: physics." Relatively rare factors, such as "Nationality: Norwegian," would speed the search.

If the answer to any such search is 1, the user has hit the jackpot and may phrase a variety of other questions about the person, using the same parameter set with one added condition. Many variations on this theme are possible if the user has unlimited access to the data bank. He can find out much information about an individual, even if the individual's name and other identifying characteristics are deleted or inaccessible.

One approach to this problem is to prevent responses being given by the system when the sample size is too low. When the computer scans the files, it will count the number of items that fulfill the request. If this number is less than a given figure, say, 10, it will not print or display the result, but instead will state that the sample size is too low. The minimum sample size used will differ with different files. If the sample size is zero, the user may not be told this, as to do so would enable him to narrow down a maximum or minimum value by asking multiple questions.

Controls based on sample size do not give complete protection of the data, as can be seen in the above example. They may be supplemented by controls that monitor the activity of each user. A log of all user activity may be kept and statistically summarized. The summary may highlight areas of unusual activity, activity in which the user asks many similar questions, and particularly activity that results in small counts in producing the answers. An algorithm based on these factors may be devised for any particular data bank with the intent of drawing attention to possible threats. It is possible that manual inspections of the activity log will do more than automated scans to reveal improper use of the data. Publicized spot checks of the activity log may be used to discourage would-be intruders.

Such safeguards help greatly, but do not render the statistical data bank immune from misuse.

REFERENCE

1. E. F. Codd "Access Control Principles for Security and Privacy in Integrated Data Banks". An IBM internal memorandum.

2. U.S. Congress. The computer and the invasion of privacy—hearings before a subcommittee of the Committee on Government Operations, House of Representatives, 89th Congress, Second Session, U.S. Government Printing Office, Washington, D.C., 26-28 July 1966.

16 ALARM AND SURVEILLANCE PROCEDURES

It is desirable that any persons contemplating an invasion of the files, either through reasons of curiosity or through malicious intent, should be deterred by the thought that there is a high probability that the system will detect them and immediately take some form of action. The psychological deterrence of knowing that the system has effective burglar alarms is great.

Like other deterrents, they should be highly publicized. Burglar alarms can be more effective than on a house or a bank because the would-be intruder usually does not know what triggers them or what the resulting action will be. A computer is capable of a wide variety of detection techniques and responses. Furthermore, alarms can be designed so that it is almost impossible for the intruder to disable them, unlike those on a building. The system designer must be alert to methods of disabling the alarms. Some houses have been equipped with elaborate electronic burglar alarms that automatically contact the police over the telephone. In some of these cases it is not even necessary for a burglar to cut the telephone lines; the alarm system fails to make contact if the telephone is ringing. All the burglar needs to do is dial the number of the house, and as long as the telephone is ringing he is safe.

REAL-TIME SURVEILLANCE Surveillance procedures on a computer system can be of two types, real-time and non-real-time. A well-protected system will have both.

The real-time checks will detect violations of security procedure such as the following:

1. User types in an invalid identification (personnel number or social security number).
2. User types in a security number that does not conform to his identification.
3. User employs a terminal for which he is not authorized.
4. Terminal is not identifiable as one that should be connected to the system.
5. User requests a program he is not authorized to use.
6. User sends a transaction type he is not authorized to send.
7. User tries to read data he is not authorized to read.
8. User attempts to modify data he not authorized to modify.
9. User takes some action at a *time* when it is not permitted.
10. User attempts to gain access to a highly secure region such as the authorization tables.
11. User exceeds a specified amount of activity at his terminal.
12. User takes more than a given number of incorrect actions at a terminal.

Many of the above violations will occur accidentally. The user miskeys a number or a transmission error occurs. Most terminal users make occasional mistakes. The action of the computer, therefore, on receiving the first unauthorized request will be to ask the user to reenter it. If the computer then receives a correct number, it will allow the user to proceed. If it receives the same unauthorized number, the user may be inadvertently trying to do something he is not supposed to do, but without malice aforethought. If a new number that is also unauthorized is entered, the user may be trying to break into the system by trial and error. If the terminal is unidentifiable, if the user is attempting to reach the authorization tables, or if anything is astray with the security officer's terminal, this may be a serious indication of felonious intent.

FOUR TYPES
OF REACTION

When a second violation in succession is detected the computer can take one of the following actions:

1. It can caution the user and give him only one more chance to take a correct action.
2. It can lock the terminal keyboard in such a way that it can only be unlocked by an appropriate authority. As it does this, it will notify a person responsible for security.
3. It can refuse to accept new input for a period, perhaps 1 minute, and then start again. This would impede a user trying to obtain passwords with some high-speed trial-and-error scheme.
4. It can "keep the user talking" while preventing him from obtaining any sensitive data or from modifying any data or programs in the system. At the same time it will contact a person responsible for security in hope that the miscreant will be caught red-handed.

On some commercial systems the second of the above approaches has proved successful. If the terminal locks, the user has to go to his office manager, who can arrange for it to be unlocked. This means that users are generally careful to type their codes correctly the second time.

On time-sharing systems there is often no office manager to assist, and so locking the keyboard may be too extreme an action. It can lock out a user who is genuine but mistake-prone. In this case the third approach may be used, the 1-minute delay lessening the likelihood of trial-and-error invasion. The number of password or security-code violations should be counted, and the user cautioned that he will be locked out if he exceeds a certain number.

Figure 16.1 shows a possible sequence on a system that does not lock the terminal. The computer in this case checks the terminal identification, the user's identification, and a once-only security number. If the user identification is invalid or his security number is not correct, the computer notifies the user that his sign-on procedure has not met the requirements. The computer then ignores the terminal for 1 minute. If the user has committed two violations in succession, a security officer is notified, and the activities of the user may be monitored. If the terminal being used is not a valid one, more serious action will be taken. The computer will ignore the terminal and alert the security officer. It will only do this after several transmission retries in case the misidentification was caused by a transmission error.

Figure 16.2 shows another approach, which is more secure and could be used on an in-house commercial system. Here the keyboard is locked if the user types invalid numbers twice in attempts to sign on. A record of the violation is written on the file so that it can be inspected by an office manager or security officer when the terminal is to be unlocked again.

If the user is not authorized to employ the terminal he attempted to sign on at, he will be notified of this and told that a security officer has been informed. If he attempted to use data for which he has not been authorized, he will again be cautioned that a security officer has been informed, and if he persists in trying to gain access to unauthorized data, the terminal keyboard will be locked.

There are many variations on this theme, varying in their complexity and degree of security.

SECURITY STAFF

When the system detects what may be an attempted breach of security, who does it inform? A system for commercial operation may inform two categories of persons, a security officer at a control location with overall responsibility for security, and a person at the location where the suspected attempt

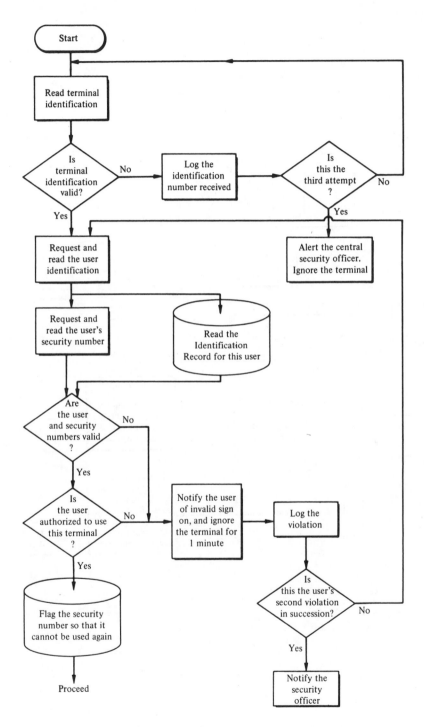

Figure 16.1

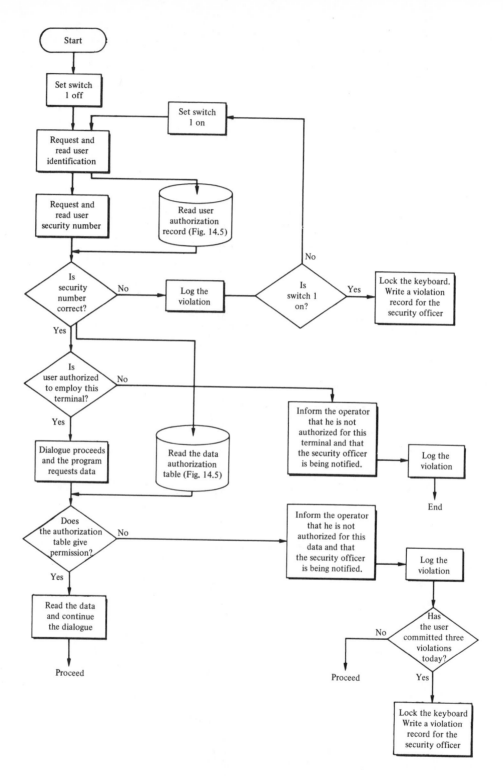

Figure 16.2

takes place. The latter person may be an office manager charged with maintaining security in his location. The system may have a means for attracting his attention, such as flashing a light or sounding a buzzer. In addition to this, it may send a message to his terminal giving details of what has happened. The flashing light and buzzer alone do not give a high measure of security because the would-be felon can always insert a dead bulb or disable the buzzer. He could also introduce a natural-looking fault into the office manager's terminal. The office manager may quickly call a repair man, but the felon might have 2 hours or more in which to raid the data base. Alarms alone are never enough. They must be backed up by locking the miscreant out of sensitive files.

The would-be intruder may devise some operation of use to him that can be carried out when the office manager or his terminal are temporarily not monitoring his activities. He may be trying to find a correct password or security code by trial and error. If he knows that information about this activity goes to the central security officer as well as his own office manager, he is unlikely to think that putting his office manager's terminal out of action will be likely to protect him.

SECURITY LOGS AND OFF-LINE SURVEILLANCE The central security officer may be an expert on the system's security, whereas the local office manager is usually not. The computer should be programmed to produce listings of each day's security-procedure violations and also statistics about them that could rapidly highlight unusual activity. These should be organized into whatever format best enables the experienced eye of the security officer to spot anything unusual.

In remote locations the person who is responsible for security, such as the office manager, may also receive listings of security-procedure infringements. To enliven the office manager's interest in security, he might be billed for the cost of violations from his location that add to system expense in any way.

The designers of the system should apply the full range of their ingenuity to trying to devise methods of breaking in. The logs and security reports should then be devised to give the best chance of detecting any such attempts. For example, when a system allows a terminal operator one mistake at a time in keying in passwords or other items, the would-be intruder may proceed by trying one password at a time, in an attempt to find the right one. He may intersperse correct entries between his attempts, and may wait a long time between different tries. If he found a security card with 64 numbers, as discussed in Chapter 9, he might try them one at a time interspersed with valid entries. Activity such as this should be highlighted on the security officer's report. Anticipating such an attempt, the designer of the surveillance procedures should make the system count the number of misentered items of one person, and stop him when he reaches a given, low, number.

Some systems record not only the procedure violations, but *all* the requests for sensitive data or all the modifications made to a file. If some doubt about security arises, the security officer can examine this log. The log of file requests may, again, be analyzed by the computer and statistics produced. The printouts for the security officer will highlight periods of unusually high activity on given files.

On a statistical file too many successive similar questions may indicate that a user is attempting to obtain other than statistical information, as was discussed in Chapter 15. This would particularly be so if there were a large number of requests resulting in answers with a small count of items summarized in the answer. The security report may include *graphs* of file usage, which quickly accentuate areas of excessive activity.

Sudden departures from the norms may be picked out automatically from the activity log, and the security officer will use these to decide whether somebody could be tampering with the system. As far as possible, the would-be intruder should be given little time to practice.

COMPUTER-ROOM OPERATOR

Another log should record the actions of the computer-room operator. He should never be left free to feel that he can take any action he chooses with the system. The computer-room operator has been a key person in some break-ins. The log may be kept on a drive or printer which is locked so that the operator cannot tamper with the log. Examination of the log will ensure that he has not inserted his own programs or made use of utility file dumps or other routines that bypass the operating system. It will record the loading and unloading of data volumes.

AUTHORIZATION TABLES

It is of particular importance to maintain extremely tight security over the authorization tables and the file lockwords. If the would-be invader can change these, most of his problems are solved. No one should be given the authority to read or change these records except the file owners or the security officers. If any change is made, the appropriate file owner or security officer will be sent details of that change the following day. Such changes might be detected on a nightly run by comparing last night's authorization records and file lock tables with those of tonight. If any unauthorized person has managed to make any change to these, it will be detected quickly.

It is recommended that a history should be kept which logs all changes made to these security records, indicating who made the change and where it was made.

17 SECURITY IN SYSTEMS PROGRAMS

No system can be regarded as secure unless both the hardware and the systems programs were designed for security. Some hardware-software combinations that were not originally designed for security were subsequently made more secure by means of a series of modifications and additions—like burglar proofing a house.

The hardware additions have included *positive identification* of terminals and other components, *fetch protection* to prevent a program in one user's partition of main memory reading information from another user's partition, and *operator logs* of such a nature that no operator action can go unrecorded. Table 17.1 lists the features that are included on terminals for security reasons. Features recommended for future computers include lockable tape and disk drives, and remote tape and disk drives, so that volumes can be mounted in the volume library or elsewhere without being handled by the computer operator.

Table 17.1 Features Included on Terminals for Security Reasons

1. Physical lock and key.
2. Keyboard which is lockable by the computer.
3. A unique terminal identification number which will be transmitted on receipt of a command from the computer
4. Operator's identification card reader (e.g., for magnetic stripe credit card or ID card).
5. A means of automatically checking a data message before printing or displaying it to ensure that it has not reached the wrong terminal.

Table 17.1 Features Inlcuded on Terminals for Security Reasons (*cont'd*)

6. A key which enables the operator to prevent the printing or display of items entered (e.g., security code).
7. Automatic prevention of the printing or display of certain input items, either by terminal editing or computer control.
8. Automatic erasure of data in control unit buffers.
9. Cryptographic enciphering and deciphering.

SECURITY SYSTEM

The software presents a more complex problem. In addition to sealing any potential security leaks in the internal workings of an operating system, it is necessary to link it to a security system that will carry out the identification, authorization, and surveillance discussed in Chapters 10 to 16. The security system may be an integral part of an operating system, or it may be a series of tasks that the operating system performs like any other task. It must, however, be designed in such a way that no input job or message can escape the scrutiny of the security programs.

The advantage of having a security system which is a separate addition to the operating system is that the requirements for security and privacy differ substantially from one installation to another. A computer used in a research environment is quite different in its requirements to one that maintains commercial files, and a military or intelligence computer has much tighter requirements than either. A system with a statistical data base needs different protection than one with a dossier data base. Different data management systems have different built-in security aids. However, all these use the same operating system.

There should be five aspects to the security built into the systems programs:

1. *Identification.* The identification of a terminal user must be established (as discussed in Chapter 11). The terminal being used may also be positively identified (Chapter 12). On a batch job not submitted at a terminal, the job card will carry the identification code.
2. *Authorization.* The security software must establish whether the user/terminal is authorized to do what is being attempted (as discussed in Chapters 13 and 14).
3. *Alarm.* When security procedures are violated in a manner that appears deliberate or unnecessarily careless, an appropriate authority should be notified immediately. Would-be intruders should be made aware that the system has burglar alarms.
4. *Surveillance.* Details of all procedural violations must be logged, and statistics or charts of how the system is being used will be compiled. Both should be perused by the system security officer each morning.

5. *Integrity.* The operating system and the security programs must be designed in such a way that they cannot be compromised by ingenious techniques. Many modifications have been made to OS/360, for example, to make tamper-proof versions of it. The operating system and security programs must link together in a manner that cannot be compromised. As ingenious new techniques become apparent for bypassing the security facilities, the programs have to be modified to seal the leak, and this is likely to be a continuing process.

One segment of the security system will be attached to the input/output software, and another segment may be attached to the file-handling software, as shown in Fig. 17.1. An incoming job or message will be checked by a security program before it gains access to the application programs. The security program will determine the *identification* of the user and/or of the terminal from which the message comes, and will determine whether he/it has *authorization* to access the program requested. An authorization check may also precede any file access. If the authorization is dependent upon the content of the record or records requested, the security program will check the contents before releasing the information to the application program.

The two security routines in Fig. 17.1 may have the capability to contact a security officer in real-time. They may contact him to sound an *alarm* if security violations are suspected. He may be given the ability to inspect the violation log or other records collected for *surveillance* purposes from a security-officer terminal, as shown in Fig. 17.2. The security officer must have the capability to inspect and modify the authorization tables, and this capability must be rigorously withheld from anyone else.

OPERATOR LOG

To reduce the likelihood of the operator doing harm to the system, all operator actions are logged. They should be logged in such a way that there can be no break in the log. The log is usually printed on the console typewriter. Such a log could have a break in it and might be feloniously modified, even if the entries are numbered. A safer method is to record it on a locked or remote device.

SOFTWARE INTEGRITY

The software must be written in such a way that users cannot bypass the security features. The incoming jobs and messages must not be able to enter the system except via the input/output software with its security protection, and the programs must not be able to access the files except via the file-management software with *its* security protection.

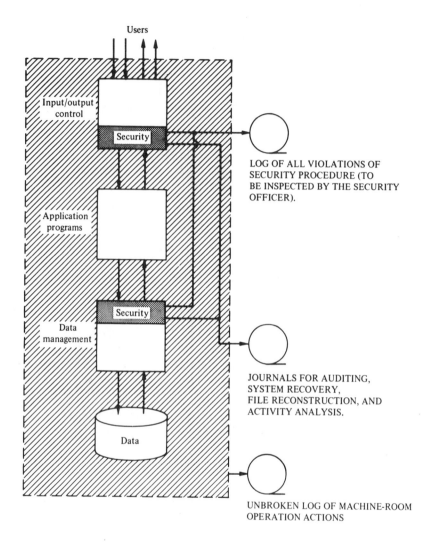

Figure 17.1. Jobs or transactions from the system users must not be able to escape the scrutiny of the security modules that check user and terminal identification and user and program authorization, and that write the logs shown.

Most modern computers isolate the *application programs* (problem pro-grams) from the *supervisory programs* (monitor, executive, or control pro-grams). The supervisory programs handle all input and output, all interrupts, and the scheduling of operations. It is essential to ensure that the user pro-grams stay in application-program state and cannot by any ingenious method

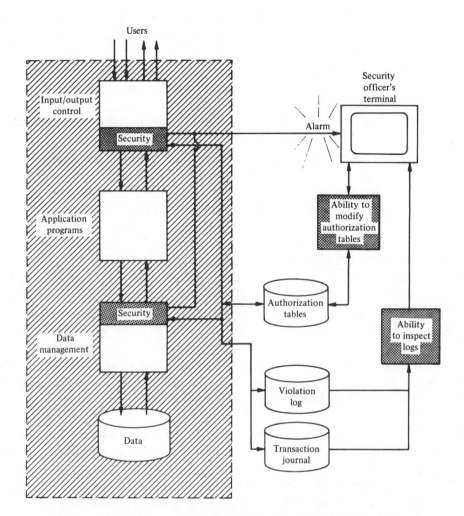

Figure 17.2. The security officer with a real-time terminal may be alerted immediately of suspected security violations, and may be given the ability to inspect the violation and activity logs from his terminal. He must be able to inspect and modify the authorization tables.

get into supervisory state. If they can once get into supervisory state, the security controls can be bypassed. In most computers there are certain instructions that can only be executed in supervisory state. On the IBM 360 and 370 these are referred to as *privileged* instructions, and include input and output instructions, storage protection instructions, LOAD PSW (Program Status Word), and Set System Mask. It is essential to ensure that the users cannot find any way to execute privileged instructions.

The user must not be able to modify the supervisory programs in any way. In most computers the area of memory occupied by the supervisory programs is protected so that nothing in that area can be overwritten. However, it is always desirable that the user should not be able to *read* items in that area; otherwise, if he has enough knowledge, he may be able to read passwords, security codes, or other items that would enable him to compromise the system. On some systems ingenious programmers have accomplished this.

Most computers use multiprogramming so that several programs may be executing together. This improves the overall efficiency and permits high throughput on real-time systems. It is necessary on a secure system to stop one such program from interfering with another. *Storage protection* facilities are in use in almost all systems to prevent any one such program from modifying another program or any data it stores in its partition. However, many systems do not have a means of stopping a program in one partition from *reading* information in another partition. The *fetch-protection* feature mentioned at the start of this chapter is designed to prevent this unauthorized reading. It is a simple extension of storage protection to protect storage from reading as well as writing. The operating system must be written to support fetch protection.

On some defense-related systems, classified programs or data have run in one partition of a multiprogrammed system while unclassified programs use another, simultaneously. On such a system fetch protection is clearly essential.

Another method of compromising software is to cause an error of such a nature that the response the system takes to the error reveals sensitive information. Thus an ABEND (abnormal end) storage dump may take place, revealing the contents of a partition that may contain passwords or a segment of an authorization table. On some operating systems the ABEND dump has been modified so that it does not print items protected by fetch-protection or other means.

Classified information may be left in main memory after the job is completed. A secure operating system will automatically overwrite it.

PATCHING THE LEAKS The phrase is sometimes used that a supervisory
IN AN OPERATING or operating system has "holes" or "leaks" in it,
SYSTEM meaning that a sufficiently knowledgeable operator
can compromise its security with methods such as those described previously. Three methods of dealing with this situation are common:

1. Ignore it, assuming that the programmers will not be sufficiently motivated or sufficiently clever to find the leaks.
2. Control the programmers, as discussed in Chapter 34.
3. Seal the leaks, or buy a sealed version of the operating system.

Sealing the leaks is highly skilled work, if only because of the uncertainty of knowing whether they have all been found, and because of the high level of ingenuity of certain programmers in finding new leaks. The only way to test the effectiveness of a leak-sealing operation is to employ a small team of highly skilled systems programmers to attempt to compromise the system. They must be highly motivated to succeed. While the white-hat programmers seal the leaks, the black-hat programmers look for more leaks. This dual operation has been highly successful in some installations, but only a rare installation can afford it.

Modifications made to the IBM OS/360 for security purposes included

1. Software support for the *fetch-protection* hardware feature to ensure privacy between the regions of different users.
2. The automatic clearing of hardware buffers when a device is deallocated so that their contents cannot be read by subsequent users.
3. The automatic clearing of each core block when it is returned to the system after an application program has used it.
4. The automatic overwriting of temporary data sets (which are created by the operating system) when it scratches them. With the automatic overwrite (PURGE) it merely deletes them from the volume's table of contents (VTOC).
5. The forced termination of any program step that causes an ABEND by a violation of protection (attempting to read or write a protected area of memory that the program does not have access to) or of privileged operation (attempting to use an instruction that can only be used in privileged mode).
6. The ability to sound the console alarm when a security violation occurs. The operator can read which job has caused it.

LINKAGE TO
SECURITY ROUTINES

The "leak-proof" operating system will be connected to the security routines shown in Figs. 17.1 and 17.2. These may be part of input/output or file-management packages. On the other hand, they may be written independently of other packages. The entry to them will be in supervisory state so that it cannot be bypassed.

In the 360 Operating System an *exit* is placed in the operating system at each point where a security function is performed. This exit usually consists of placing an option code into a register issuing a supervisor call (SVC) via an EXECUTE command. After the routine has made appropriate checks, it returns control to the instruction after the exit if the checks were successful; otherwise, the routine ABENDs, terminating the job or job step. Using the exit approach, only a few lines of code are added in line in the operating system module. Most of the functional code is in the supervisor call. For infrequently used operations a transient supervisor call is used, with the routine not resident in main memory. Frequently used routines, such as that to check a job's authorization code, will normally be resident in main memory.

The linkage techniques should be chosen to have minimum impact on the operating system modules and hence on maintenance.

The security routines may be quite simple and present little overhead, if the identification and authorization procedures used are simple. Simple procedures are adequate for many commercial systems. The security needs of different types of users vary widely, and a security system designed to meet the needs of everybody is likely to be complex and have significant, though not necessarily intolerable, overhead.

Chapter 18 describes a system that meets the needs of a wide variety of users.

18   A GENERAL-PURPOSE
SECURITY PACKAGE

As an example of a general-purpose software package that incorporates the functions discussed, this chapter describes a feature available with IBM's Operating System/360-MVT. It is called the Resource Security Feature and operates on a 360 or 370 with *fetch-protection* hardware. It can meet the needs of a variety of users and has withstood attack from highly skilled system breakers.

SECURITY LEVELS AND   All *users, terminals, programs, data sets,* and *vol-*
ACCESS CATEGORIES   *umes* (tapes and disks) are defined to the security
system, and the system controls the relationships between them. It employs an authorization scheme that uses both *stratification* and *compartmentalization,* as discussed in Chapter 13. The user can define eight strata or hierarchical *security levels,* as shown in Fig. 18.1a, and up to 30,000 *access categories,* as shown in Fig. 18.1b. The hierarchical levels relate to users, terminals, programs, data sets, and volumes. Every user, terminal, program, data set, and volume will be given a security level or else may remain *undefined.* The access categories relate to users, terminals, programs, and data which they *need to know.* The access categories may include the need-to-know categories for each user, and that is why there are so many of them. Frequently, however, individual users are grouped together, and an *access category* relates to the group rather than to individual users. All members of the group are permitted identical access to the same resources. They may be members of a department, a project team, a management class, or merely colleagues sharing a file.

STRATIFICATION

up to eight security levels

COMPARTMENTALIZATION

up to 30,000 access categories.
Groups of categories may be defined that
overlap and/or nest.

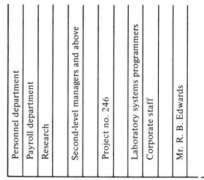

Each user, terminal, program, data set,
and volume is assigned a security
level. The terminal security level
may change with the time of day.

Each user, terminal, program, and data set
(not volume) is assigned one or more access
categories or category groups.

(a)   (b)

Figure 18.1. Security levels and access categories used by the resource
security feature of IBM's Operating System/360.

Authorization is controlled in three ways:

1. When a system resource (terminal, program, data set, or volume) is used, the using
   entity must have a *security level* as high as that of the resource.
2. When a terminal, program, or data set is used, at least one of its access categories must
   match one of the entity using it. For example, a data-set access category must match
   that of a program using it; a program access category must match that of a job using it;
   and the job access categories are derived from those shared by the terminal and the
   individual user.
3. When a data set is used, authorization tables will be checked to ensure that the user, or
   user and program, have permission to read, modify, or delete the data.

**MAIN
FEATURES**

The following are the main features of the system
[1]:

1. Identification

(a) The system gives the ability to uniquely identify each user, whether he is a batch user or a terminal user. A security profile will be established for each user, and will reside in the computer's main memory while he is using the system to permit authorization of his actions.

(b) Every system element (user, terminal program, data set, and volume) can be defined to the system so that each is uniquely identifiable.

(c) An interface is provided to terminal-oriented subsystems so that the security provisions can apply to each of their on line users.

2. Authorization

(a) The ability exists to determine all resources to which a user can have access, and to decide what mode of access (i.e., READ or READ/WRITE) he is allowed.

(b) The ability exists to group system elements (users, data sets, programs, or terminals) that are of like type in order to form an *access category.*

(c) The ability exists to restrict access to data sets, programs, and terminals on the basis of at least 30,000 *need-to-know* or *access categories.*

(d) The ability exists to restrict access to data sets, programs, and terminals on the basis of eight hierarchical *security levels.*

(e) The ability exists to control which programs the system will fetch, add, or replace for a user on the basis of his *security level, access categories,* and *need to know.*

(f) The ability exists to control access to data sets (in both READ and READ/WRITE mode) for a user on the basis of his *security level, access categories,* and *need to know.*

(g) The ability exists to restrict the use of a data set to only certain programs.

(h) The ability exists to restrict the display of data on terminals on the basis of user *security level,* terminal *security level,* time of day, *access categories,* and *need to know.*

(i) The ability exists to control the maximum *security level* of data that will be recorded on a direct access or tape volume.

(j) The system has a defined interface to allow a program to control data at the *field* level, by name. This control is by *security level* only.

3. Alarm

(a) When certain security procedure violations occur, an alarm will be sounded at the computer console and a message giving details will be sent immediately to the security officer's terminal.

4. Surveillance

(a) The system maintains an audit log, the contents of which (i.e., the types of data collected) are determined at SYSGEN time (i.e., when the system is initially generated).

(b) The system will generate lists of security-procedure violations and reports summarizing the violations, which can be specified by the security officer.

(c) The system can generate reports concerning system usage.

5. Integrity

(a) A secured version of the 360 Operating System is provided, with the resource security feature incorporated in it.

(b) The system can overwrite (PURGE) sections of direct access storage after a data set is scratched to prevent subsequent users of the same storage from compromising security by examining residual data.

(c) Each user's programs and data are protected from both reading and writing by other user's programs while they are resident in main storage.

(d) The facility can be provided to label all printed output (including spooled output) with its security classification, page number, date, and time.

(e) No data can be written on a volume (tape or direct access) that does not have a security classification as high as that of the data, or higher. Thus all data that can be taken away, in print or volumes, are labeled with their security classification.

6. Features for the Security Officer

(a) The system provides a centralized point of control at a communications terminal that accepts commands only from security personnel.

(b) The system can print lists, on a high-speed printer or at the security terminal, describing the secured resources and their relationships to one another.

(c) A set of terminal commands is provided for the security personnel, which enables them to modify the security relationships in a real-time manner. Using the security terminal they can define system elements and describe access categories.

SECURITY OF USERS When a user employs a terminal, he will identify himself either by means of a dialogue in which the system asks for security information, or else he may key the security information in directly. When he submits a job without using a terminal, he will identify himself by parameters in the JOB statement (the first card in the deck). In either case, the security system obtains the user's last name and two initials, and a five-character code word. It checks that the code word has in fact been issued to that user, and, if so, reads a user's authorization profile into main memory. If the code word has not been issued to that user, a security violation will be recorded and the job will not be processed. The authorization profile contains a *security level* and a set of *access categories* for the user.

SECURITY OF TERMINALS

Each terminal is also defined to the system as having a security level and a set of access categories.

The security level can change with the time of day, which provides a time lock. Up to 15 periods of time can be defined and a security level specified for each. A terminal used for top secret work during part of the day when high security precautions are taken, for example the area is guarded, can also be used for unclassified work in the evening when the precautions are relaxed.

When a user signs on, he is identified, and if his security level is lower than that of the terminal, the system will lock the terminal. Similarly, if none of his access categories matches any of those assigned to the terminal, the terminal will be locked. In either case the security violation will be recorded.

The job will then have either the user's security level or the terminal's security level, whichever is lower. It will have those access categories common to both the terminal and the user. These remain in main memory while the job is processed. The terminal's security level will not change (with time) until the job is terminated. New information occurring during processing might, however, change the security level or access categories that the job has. No data will be displayed on the terminal which has a security level higher than that for the job in question, or which does have at least one access category that matches one of the job access categories.

SECURITY OF PROGRAMS

Similarly, each program is defined to the system as having a security level and a set of access categories.

All programs that can be executed must be members of data sets on disk *(load modules* in the program library). Before any program is loaded into main memory for execution, a security check is made. If the security level of the job is less than that of the program or if its access categories fail to match, the job will terminate with a security violation. The security level and access categories of the program are stored in main memory along with those of the job while the program is executed.

Whenever an attempt is made to add a program to the library or to replace or delete a member, a security check is made, consisting of three tests.

First, the user must be listed on an authorization table as being permitted to take the action in question. Second, the security level of the job making the attempt must be as high as that of the program in question. Third, at least one access category of the job in question must match one of the program. If any of these tests fail, the action is prohibited, an alarm message is sent to the security officer, and a security violation is recorded.

Some programs may be *uncontrolled.* In this case they are freely accessible by anyone authorized to use their data set. Normally, assemblers, compilers, and certain utilities are uncontrolled. On some systems many application programs will be uncontrolled.

SECURITY OF TEMPORARY DATA SETS
The 360 Operating System has two classes of data sets, temporary and permanent. Temporary data sets are created by the operating system to help in the processing of a job. When the job is terminated, they are scratched. Permanent data sets are created by the system users and remain permanently in the files until the users or system staff removes them.

Security of the temporary data sets is entirely in the hands of the operating system. The operating system gives each temporary data set a name, which includes the name of the job that created it and the time that the job was read by the reader. No job that does not have the same job name and time field will be permitted access to the data set.

Normally, when a job is terminated, the 360 Operating System SCRATCHes that job's temporary data sets by removing their names from the volume's table of contents (VTOC). In a secure environment, this action is not enough; the data set must be over-written entirely (PURGED) to ensure that the residual data cannot be read in an unauthorized fashion. The Resource Security System PURGEs all temporary data sets when they are finished with, except those which are unclassified.

SECURITY OF PERMANENT DATA SETS
The permanent data sets have a table associated with them saying which users may CREATE, READ, READ/WRITE, and SCRATCH each data set. Some data sets, in addition, have an entry in the table saying which programs may access them. Each data set is also assigned a security level and a set of access categories. The authorization to use permanent data sets is controlled exclusively by the security officer. He alone can create and modify entries in the data-set authorization table.

Data sets are described as *user restricted* and *program restricted.* Before access is permitted to user-restricted data sets, three tests must be satisfied.

First, the job requesting the access must have a security equal to that of the data set, or higher. Second, at least one of the job's access categories must match one of the data set's. Third, the data set's authorization table must say that the user in question is permitted to READ, READ/WRITE, CREATE, or SCRATCH the data set, whichever is the case. Before access is permitted to program-restricted data sets, the same three tests are made and, in addition, a fourth one. The program requesting the data must be on the data set's authorization table. If any of these tests fail, access is prohibited, the job is terminated, an alarm message is sent to the security officer, and a security violation is recorded.

Only the security officer is permitted to remove permanently (PURGE) data sets.

SECURITY
OF VOLUMES
Each volume used by the system can be assigned a security level. It must be physically labeled with this security classification. If no security level is assigned, the volume is assumed by the system to be unclassified. No data of a higher security level than that of the volume may be written on any volume.

SECURITY OF
PRINTED OUTPUT
All printed output will be labeled with the following information:

1. The highest security level of the data used in the job.
2. Optional header information, specified by the user.
3. Time and date of printing.
4. Page x of y (e.g., page 4 of 7). This feature is optional.

SECURITY
BY ASSOCIATION
In addition to the authorization described above, a special relationship can be defined between a program and a data set that changes the output security level. If a program so defined processes certain critical fields, the output may be given a security level higher than that of either the data set or the program. Conversely, if the program processes *only* certain fields, the output may be given a lower security level than either the data set or the program.

ALARM
Each attempted violation will terminate the job that caused the violation, or lock a user out of a terminal. In addition, certain types of violation attempts will cause the security officer to be notified immediately at his terminal, and an audible alarm will be sounded at the computer console.

SURVEILLANCE   The system maintains a log of all attempted security violations, giving the circumstances surrounding the attempt. This log is maintained on a direct-access file, which the security officer may inspect at any time. The security officer is provided with a sample program, which will generate reports from the log. It is expected that the nature of the reports will be varied from time to time or from one installation to another, and so the program may be modified to individual requirements.

In addition to recording violations, the system can record the normal use of controlled resources. The system can produce listings or statistics of items such as

> Initial access to each permanent data set.
>
> Initial access to each temporary data set.
>
> Modification of all programs that have been defined as members of controlled program libraries.
>
> Execution of all programs that have been defined as members of controlled program libraries.
>
> All modifications to system data sets.

SECURITY OFFICER   The security officer, in addition to his surveillance
DIALOGUE   function, must define for the system each of the controlled elements. He must define the security levels and access categories. He must set up and maintain the authorization tables. He will create and delete data sets. Many changes in users, data sets, authorization, and other features will occur. He must be able to enter these changes into the system. To permit this activity, the system provides a command language, which the security officer may use at his specially designated terminal.

There will normally be only one terminal that accepts the security officer dialogue, and a high level of security should surround this terminal. Before the security officer begins a session, he must *sign on* and correctly enter an identification word originally composed by himself and a code word originally composed randomly by the computer. If he signs on incorrectly twice, he is locked out of the system; an alarm sounds at the computer console and the security-officer terminal is not unlocked until a new program load (IPL) is performed. When the security officer signs on successfully, he is asked whether he will change his identification word or have his code word changed for the next time. Subversion of the security-officer sign-on procedure must be made extremely difficult. When the security officer finishes with the terminal, he must sign off. He is automatically signed off if his terminal remains inactive for a given period of time.

By means of a DEFINE command, the security officer may define

1. *Time periods.* The number of the time period is entered (1 through 15), and its starting and ending time.
2. *Security levels.* The number of the level is entered (1 through 8), and the name of the level, for example, FOR INTERNAL USE ONLY or COSMIC TOP SECRET.
3. *Users.* The user's name and initials are entered along with his security level. One or more time periods may also be defined for the user. If none are defined, the user can use the system at any time.
4. *Terminals.* The number of the terminal is entered along with its security level. A different security level may be entered for each time period.
5. *Programs.* The name of the program is entered along with its security level (and several other options).
6. *Data sets.* The name of the data set is entered along with its security level (and several other options).
7. *Volumes.* The number of a tape or direct access (DASD) volume is entered along with its security level.
8. *User groups.* A user group number is entered and the names of the users in the group are entered.
9. *Terminal groups.* A terminal group number is entered along with the terminal numbers in the group.
10. *Program groups.* A program group is similarly defined.
11. *Data-set groups.* Similar.

The defining of *groups* of users, terminals, programs, and data sets can save the security officer much work in entering and modifying their authorizations. Five examples of the DEFINE commands are

```
DEFINE PERIOD 3 AS 0900 THROUGH 1300.

DEFINE LEVEL 2 AS "FOR INTERNAL USE ONLY".

DEFINE USER "ROPLEY ES" AT LEVEL 2, PERIOD 3.

DEFINE FILE SYS1.LINKLIB AT LEVEL 8 ON DISK01.

DEFINE USERGRP26 TO CONTAIN USERS "MARTIN JT", "ROPLEY ES",

        "BLANAGAN JE".
```

Other commands enable the security officer to create files, assigning ownership to them, and to SCRATCH (delete from volume table of contents) or PURGE (overwrite with zeros) any file. He may add items or delete items from groups. He may request that new code words be issued to users. Listings of any security definitions may be requested. Changes may be made in any definitions. Users or user groups may be authorized to access one or more resources or resource groups, and the authorizations may be changed.

Some examples of these commands are

AUTHORIZE USERGRP26 TO FILES ACCT71, ACCT72.

AUTHORIZE USER "ROPLEY ES" TO DESGRP25, TERMINAL 012.

DELETE USER "BLANAGAN JE" FROM UGRP26.

LIST AUTHORIZATION OF FILES AUTHORIZED TO USER "ROPLEY ES"

SEQUENCED BY LEVEL.

OPERATION   The Resource Security Feature is a *system task* in the operating system, just as the operating system's *readers* and *writers* are system tasks. It is designed so that its execution cannot be controlled by the computer operator or users. It is automatically started before any users tasks at IPL time (Initial Program Load time). It cannot be terminated without stopping the operating system.

The system maintains a standby security data set. If there is an unrecoverable input/output error on the primary security data set, an automatic switch is made to the standby. All WRITE operations to the security data set write both copies.

INSTALLATION   Different installations have widely differing security requirements. An installation that requires minimal security checks should not have to pay in system overhead for all the features described above. The security system can therefore be configured when the operating system is generated (SYSGEN time), and there is a substantial variation in main memory and disk requirements from one system to another.

Features not constantly in use, such as all those involved with the security officer's dialogue, are not resident in main memory. They are called in as transient tasks when needed. On the other hand, all the facilities needed for the authorization of a job are retained in main memory throughout the processing of the job, to minimize processing time.

If software security is introduced to an existing installation it is generally preferable to do it in stages rather than make everything secure at once. Suddenly having all the files secured, and having the terminals locking like rat traps every time their operators make errors in procedure, can be too troublesome. The feature permits a gradual implementation by allowing the terminals, programs, data sets, and volumes to be *undefined resources* at the start. One by one they will be defined by the security officer as the users become accustomed to security. When permissible, it is also desirable that the system should run under OS/360-MVT for a while and become used to it before adding the security feature.

PERFORMANCE   The feature requires a 256K System 360 or 370, or larger, with direct access space equivalent to about 15 to 20 2314 cylinders. On a typical installation it has used about 20K bytes of main memory, but this figure varies somewhat with the number of resources secured. The overall degradation of processing time varies with the degree of security, the size of the authorization tables, and the nature of the jobs being processed. The degradation on typical installations has ranged from 5 to 10 per cent. On installations with particularly complex or severe requirements it has been higher.

REFERENCE

1. "System Description Manual for OS/MVT with Resource Security," IBM Manual No. GH20–0967, International Business Machines, Poughkeepsie, N. Y., 1972.

19 CRYPTOGRAPHY

A year after the first telegraph was invented, Samuel F. B. Morse published a commercial code entitled "The Secret Corresponding Vocabulary" and declared in its publicity that "secrecy in correspondence is far the most important consideration." A flurry of activity in cryptography took place after the introduction of the telegraph. England's *Quarterly Review* in 1854 commented, "The clerks of the English Telegraph Company are sworn to secrecy, but we often write things that it would be intolerable to see strangers read before our eyes. This is a grievous fault in the telegraph and it must be remedied by some means or other."

In today's computer systems handling sensitive data, cryptography can be used to protect both transmitted data and data stored on files and tapes. Since World War I, much has been written about cryptography and code breaking. The subject, however, has drastically changed its nature with the advent of computers. When a computer or computer-like logic can be used to do the coding, an immeasurably more complex form of enciphering can be used. On the other hand, the computer will now be used to aid in the decrypting and to search at high speed through very large numbers of possible transformations. In balance, if both sides act prudently, the sender is generally better off as a result of computing technology, provided that the person doing the code breaking does not have enormous resources or endless time available to him.

When the transmission is between computers, the machines can scramble the data in a truly formidable fashion. On the other hand, when the data are transmitted to or from terminals, the terminal or its control unit must have the logic for enciphering and deciphering. This can add substantially to the system cost. Computer-to-computer cryptography can be made more secure.

WHERE IS
CRYPTOGRAPHY
USED?
It has been estimated that the American intelligence community spends more than $1 billion a year on the interception and analysis of enciphered messages [1]. On the other hand, only a minor use of cryptography is found in industry. This ratio may be out of balance if industrial espionage is as widespread as some authorities have stated [2].

Provided that secure enciphering algorithms are available, cryptography can be used in computer systems with little difficulty and little expense. That it is not used on commercial systems today as much as might be expected may be due to the shortage of persons knowledgeable in the subject. Most cryptography professionals have gained their experience in circles in which the know-how has a top secret classification, or higher classification too high to be nameable. They cannot employ their knowledge for commercial work. The National Security Agency has given even the simplest techniques a high classification. It is highly desirable that the commercial world should build up its own expertise in computer cryptography and be free to disseminate it.

With a few important exceptions, cryptography is rarely used on today's commercial real-time terminals. This situation will probably change, but first it needs inexpensive and secure cryptoboxes for data transmission to come on the market. Meanwhile, the identification and authorization procedures described in earlier chapters are proving to be an adequate safeguard for most purposes. Cryptography is sometimes used for non-real-time message transmission. Devices are available for encryption and decryption on telegraph links, and few special-purpose computer terminals employ cryptography hardware.

Cryptography is occasionally used with batch transmission of highly sensitive data. This is normally on a computer-to-computer link with the coding and decoding done by programming so that no special hardware is needed.

Sensitive data may also be enciphered when sent by mail or delivery van on a reel of tape or disk pack. A routine for decoding it as it is read need not necessarily take much computer time, and this is the best way to protect it from being read during its journey. Certain data in the tape or disk store could be encoded to safeguard against theft, but this is not normally done except in some military installations. It is thought that normal theft precautions suffice.

On some special systems, cryptography is the *only* adequate way to safeguard the data. This is the case, for example, with certain banking systems that have *cash dispensers* controlled by teleprocessing. One English bank has many hundreds of cash dispensers set in bank walls on the streets. A user inserts a bank card with his account data encoded on a magnetic stripe. He keys in a unique "secret number," and then keys the sum of money he requires. The information is transmitted over leased telecommunication lines to a central computer where the customer's record is kept. The terminal, as an additional check, sends details of the cash remaining in it. If all is in order, the computer will send back to the terminal a figure for the new amount of cash. This indicates to the terminal that it should dispense the cash requested. Cryptography is used to safeguard the message to the computer and its response. It must clearly be done with a high measure of security or the English public (who have a national talent for bank robberies) could get rich quick by wiretapping! Each terminal contains many thousands of pounds (Fig. 19.1).

In certain circumstances, the enciphering of sensitive data can add greatly to its security. We may see encryption techniques used much more in the future.

The laws relating to industrial espionage do little to protect the firm that has its valuable data copied and removed. No physical item need be stolen when a tape or disk is copied. Several attempts to convict persons who have copied and sold valuable data have failed. Enciphering the data could have prevented the loss.

**TYPES OF
CODES**

If cryptography is worth using at all, it should be used well. The use of poor-quality cryptography is sometimes tempting and if employed could give a false sense of security.

One method of encryption that has been suggested for terminals, for example, is to scramble the letters on the type element (such as that on a Selectric typewriter golf ball). Only by fitting the appropriate type element would the message be made readable, and this type element would be carefully safeguarded. This simpleminded form of encoding would be very easy to crack. It could form half an hour's entertainment for a person with no special cryptanalysis skills.

We should assume that a person trying to crack a cryptography code will use a computer. Of the encoding devices that have been used in telegraphy, some give a high measure of security, but most use a code that, in the computer age, is relatively easy to break.

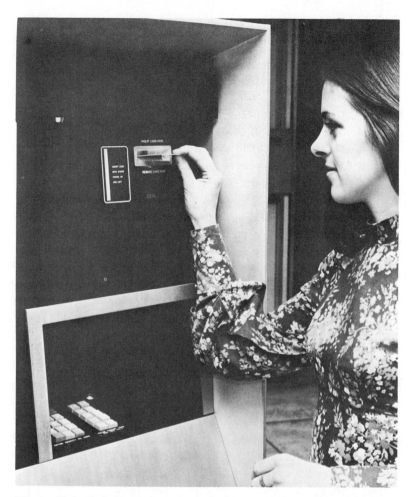

Figure 19.1. Cash-dispensing terminals (shown above and below), set in the walls of bank branches, send a teleprocessing message to a remote computer to ask whether they should give a customer the cash that she is requesting. If the customer has enough money in her account, the computer sends back an affirmative message. The secure way to protect such transmission is to use cryptography.

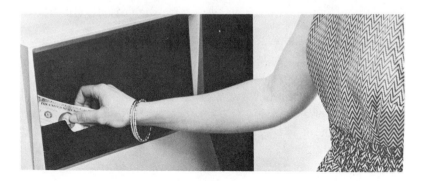

Some classes of enciphering that have been used traditionally but are no longer safe with the advent of computers include

1. *Substitution.* The replacement of message characters with other characters in a one-for-one manner, or replacement of single characters or groups of characters with other groups of characters using the table look-up process.
2. *Transposition.* Changing the order of the characters in the message.
3. *Arithmetic manipulation.* Transforming groups of bits in the message with some simple arithmetic process.
4. *Repetitive addition of a key.* The characters in the message are transformed by combining them with a fixed key supplied by the sender.

Using the power of a computer, much more elaborate transformations than these are practical. Algorithms of great complexity can be devised for randomizing the message in such a way that it would be almost impossible to unscramble it without knowledge of how the algorithm worked. With a good encoding method the intruder should be unable to decode the message *even when he knows how the algorithm works,* because it would take him too long to obtain the key that is used with the algorithm.

Two classes of cipher that were widely used prior to development of computers were the Vernam system [3], in which the contents of a key are repetitively combined with the text characters to be transmitted, and the Vigenère system, which employs character-substitution tables. Both are well described in Kahn's excellent book *The Codebreakers* [1]. Several variants on Vernam and Vigenère systems have been in common use, and Tuckerman demonstrates in a fascinating report [4] how they may be broken using a computer. Tuckerman breaks them using an APL (Iverson Language) terminal. In some of his examples he assumes that the codebreaker possesses a segment of text and the same text enciphered. In other examples he assumes that only the cipher is available.

In general the system designer should regard with high suspicion *any* enciphering method that was employed prior to the computer age, with the exception of the use of one-time keys, which we shall discuss shortly.

VALUATION OF SECRECY SYSTEMS   A number of different criteria can be used to judge systems for encryption. Claude E. Shannon, the communication-theory pioneer, developed a mathematical treatment of secrecy systems, and in a classic paper [5] lists the following five criteria as being the most important. As in many aspects of systems design, there is some incompatibility between the most desirable features.

1. *High degree of secrecy.* Some systems, for example those employing a key used once only, have absolute theoretical secrecy. Other systems can yield a diligent cryptanalyst some information, but do not yield a unique "solution." Those that do yield a unique solution differ widely in the amount of work needed to obtain it and in the amount of material that must be intercepted. Good enciphering techniques require a very high *work factor* for deciphering.

2. *Smallness of key.* The key must be sent to the transmitting and receiving locations by some method that cannot be intercepted. In military and espionage circles the key has often been memorized. In the past it has generally been desirable that the key should be small. Now, with disk and magnetic tape storage, a scheme with a very large key can be practical. It is still convenient, however, to use a relatively small key that can be *easily and frequently changed.*

3. *Simplicity of enciphering.* Complex mechanisms for enciphering and deciphering can be expensive. In the past it has been desirable that the mechanisms should be simple. Now elaborate mechanisms can be built with programming and with microelectronic circuitry. It is still desirable that they should be fast and neither delay the transmission process nor consume an excessive amount of computing time or main memory space.

4. *Low propagation of errors.* In some types of cipher an error occurring in the transmission of one character leads to a large number of errors in subsequent characters. This is the case, for example, when the result of deciphering one element of a message is used as the key for deciphering the next element. It is desirable to minimize this error propagation.

5. *Little expansion of message size.* In some secrecy systems the size of the message is substantially increased. This is sometimes done to invalidate the use of statistical techniques in deciphering. It is desirable to minimize message expansion.

Shannon showed that when encrypting natural language these five criteria cannot be met simultaneously. If any one of them is dropped, the other four can be met fairly well. For data-processing usage we are likely to drop criterion 2 or 3, either employing our storage capability to give a very long key or else employing our computing capability to achieve a complex enciphering process. Because computers are available to the enemy, the work factor for deciphering must be extremely high.

TIME AVAILABLE FOR BREAKING THE CODE   If an intruder has a very long time available for breaking a code, he is more likely to succeed. Again, he is more likely to succeed if he has a very large amount of text to work on. The computer system should be designed so that whenever possible it minimizes the time available to the codebreaker. This can be done by designing the enciphering program so that it can be changed at suitably frequent intervals, and employing a key for deciphering that is also changed frequently.

The system should minimize the amount of data that the codebreaker has to work on. Data that are not sensitive should not be enciphered. Repetitive English phrases should not be enciphered. It is advisable to substitute numbers or character sets for phrases that are frequently used, before the data is enciphered—a technique also valuable for the compaction of data stored or transmitted.

On some systems the time available for cracking the code can be made very short. With the cash-dispensing terminals, for example, the key is changed frequently so that a thief would have to break the code before the next key change. Data on certain types of files are scanned every night, and could at that time be reencoded with a different program or key.

On the other hand, some commercial data retain their value for a very long time. Data concerning oil drillings or mineral prospecting, for example, could be of great value to a thief, and in some cases may retain their value for years. The thief has plenty of time to break the code. In such cases cryptography should only be an adjunct to other methods of preventing the data from being stolen, and an enciphering method might be used that cannot be cracked by computing techniques, for example, the use of a *once-only key.*

ONCE-ONLY
KEYS

One of the simplest and most effective techniques is to use a key sufficiently long that it is only employed once. A Vernam system [1] employing a key that is never repeated has been in use for military communications for many decades.

A Cipher-Printing Telegraph System used by the U.S. Army Signal Corps reads two five-channel paper tapes. One contained the information to be sent, coded conventionally, and the other was a tape of similar form having characters punched in it at random, and with every tenth character numbered so that the tape could be set to any designated starting position. This was referred to as the key tape. It was prepared in advance, and both the transmitting station and the receiving station needed to have identical copies of it. A simple electromechanical device then combined the bits on the two tapes and perforated a new tape containing the message so encrypted. The cipher-message tape prepared in this way was sometimes transmitted over telegraph lines and sometimes delivered by messenger or mail. If the key tape was short and repeatedly used, it was possible to break the code or messages transmitted. However, if the key tape was used only once, the code was regarded as unbreakable. Sometimes the key tape would be on a roll 8 inches in diameter.

Over telegraph lines operating at 45 words per minute, this would have taken 7 hours to transmit. With a key tape this long, it was almost impossible to break the code used, even if the key tape was used a number of times. On some machines two key tapes were used that could operate in different positions relative to one another.

With computer-to-computer transmission, such a technique can give the highest level of security with little programming. The sequence of characters in the key can be very long—several million. The equivalent of the telegraphic key tape might now be an entire disk pack filled with random numbers. Both the sending installation and the receiving installation have the same disk pack. The message is transmitted in fixed-length blocks of, for example, 100 characters. The bits in these are binary added (or EXCLUSIVE OR'ed) with blocks of 100 characters taken sequentially from the key disk pack. This would be simple, quick, and virtually uncrackable if the contents of the key disk pack were changed frequently.

In using such a method it is essential that the sequence of characters in the key is not generated in such a way that it would be easy to predict future characters in the sequence. No well-known mathematical algorithm should be used for generating the key characters. Some German secrets were deciphered in World War II because the messages were encoded with a string of digits from an internationally known table of random numbers. There are innumerable ways of generating characters so that they will be *completely* unpredictable. One could, for example, take a scratch tape that has recently been generated by another unrelated run and which will be different every day and use that as a sequence of hundreds of thousands of seeds to a random-number generating process. Some systems have employed an electronic noise generator, such as a Geiger-Müller tube, or a device, such as a thyratron, that produces thermal noise.

KEY LEVERAGE   In the preceding example the key is used in a simple manner. It is possible to make a given quantity of key encode a larger quantity of data by utilizing it in a more complex way. This is referred to as *key leverage*. The key may be made to go further by a variety of different methods. Suppose that instead of adding one segment of key to the data, two or several segments are added or subtracted. These segments are selected by some addressing mechanism that is reproducible at the receiving machine. The addresses may themselves come from a segment of the key.

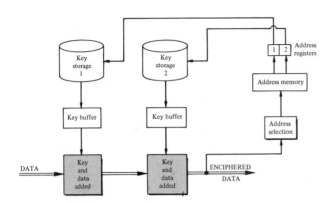

Figure 19.2 There are many computer variations of the Vernam once- only tape system.

Figure 19.3. An address-selection mechanism for the address memory in Fig. 19.2. One thousand messages of one thousand characters each can be sent before a pair of addresses is repeated. If these address registers were used with three key storages, one million messages of one thousand characters each could be sent before a set of addresses was repeated.

Message	Character number	Address memory position 1	Address memory position 2
000	000	000 001 002 ↓ 999	000 001 002 ↓ 999
	001	000 001 002 ↓ 999	001 002 003 ↓ 000
	002	000 001 002 ↓ 999	002 003 004 ↓ 001
	003	000 001 002 ↓ 999	003 004 005 ↓ 996
	998	000 001 002 ↓ 999	998 999 000 ↓ 997
	999	000 001 002 ↓ 999	999 000 001 ↓ 998
001	000	001 002 003	000 001 002

The mechanism illustrated in Fig. 19.2, devised by R.O. Skatrude [6], combines two segments of the key with the data. Another section of memory contains data used for addressing the key storage. An address-selection mechanism selects a pair of positions in the address memory, which gives addresses of sections of the key.

The address memory may contain, for example, 1000 addresses of key storage, all different, and randomly arranged. Different pairs of addresses will be selected in such a way that no pair is repeated for a long time. The address-selection sequence in Fig. 19.3 might be used, for example, to give non-repeating pairs of addresses for 1 million characters or blocks of characters. After 1 million address pairs have been used, the address memory will be reloaded with a new set of random characters. At less frequent intervals the massive key will be changed.

There are endless variations on this theme. With a sufficiently long key the transmission can be made as secure as desired.

CRYPTOGRAPHIC HARDWARE   In the future, cryptography at terminals is perhaps more likely to be done by hardware than software.

Cryptography at the computer center could be performed either by programming or by special cryptographic hardware. At the time of writing, it is usually done by programming. Advantages of using special hardware are that it could be made immune to possible tampering by the systems programmers, and that for complex enciphering it can be immensely more efficient.

Figure 19.4 shows a hardware enciphering technique which is considered to be extremely secure. The enciphering technique is employed by an IBM device called Lucifer [7]. Lucifer can be used in conjunction with any conventional terminal as shown in Fig. 19.5. The device enciphers and deciphers messages of any length in groups of 128 bits; this is done under the control of a cipher key of 128 arbitrarily chosen bits. The key can be furnished from either a 16-byte plug-in read-only store module which would be changed at suitably frequent intervals, or else from a magnetic-stripe card like a credit card which authorized users could carry. If the latter method is used, the computer that receives the enciphered transmission must have a means of retrieving the identical key from its files. To accomplish this, the user identification may be transmitted from the terminal before enciphering begins.

In the deciphering process, the steps are performed in the reverse sequence. The device contains a circuit that can distinguish between plain text and cipher text, so it can receive a mixture of the two.

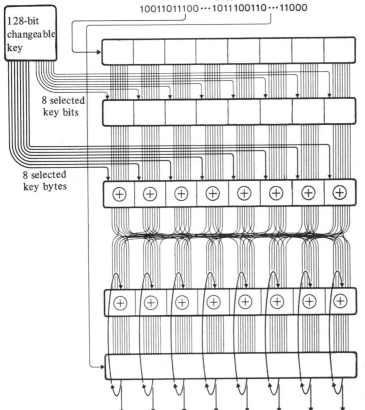

INPUT
10011011100 ··· 1011100110 ··· 11000

128-bit changeable key

8 selected key bits

8 selected key bytes

1. The message to be enciphered is read in in blocks of 128 bits (16 bytes).

2. It is split into two halves of 8 bytes each.

3. According to the value of each of 8 selected bits from the key, one of two different nonlinear transformations is performed on each of the 8 bytes in the top half.

4. The 8 bytes in the top half are then added to 8 selected bytes from the key with modulo-2 addition.

5. The 8 bytes are scrambled.

6. The 8 bytes in the bottom half of the block are then added to the top half.

7. The above six steps are then repeated with the two halves interchanged and with different selected key bits.

8. After 16 such rounds, alternated with 15 interchanges, the encipherment of this block of message is complete.

Figure 19.4   The operation of the cryptography module shown in Fig. 19.5.

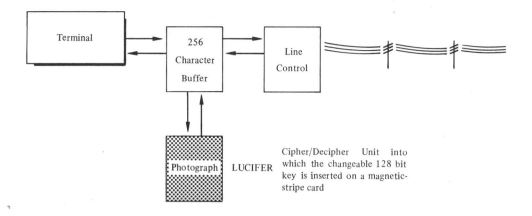

Cipher/Decipher Unit into which the changeable 128 bit key is inserted on a magnetic-stripe card

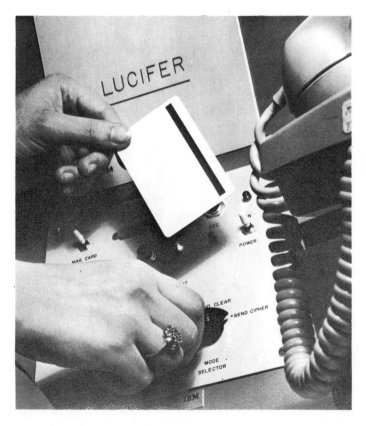

Figure 19.5 Use of a hardware cryptography module. *(Courtesy IBM.)*

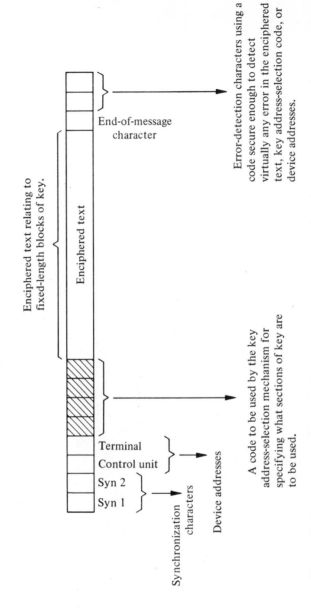

Error-detection characters using a code secure enough to detect virtually any error in the enciphered text, key address-selection code, or device addresses.

End-of-message character

Enciphered text relating to fixed-length blocks of key.

Enciphered text

A code to be used by the key address-selection mechanism for specifying what sections of key are to be used.

Terminal
Control unit

Syn 2
Syn 1

Synchronization characters

Device addresses

Figure 19.6. Block structure for synchronous transmission of enciphered text. Conventional transmission control software could be used.

CRYPTO-PROTECTED   If concern over security and privacy in data banks
VAULTS   increases, we may see the emergence of systems
                         in which the computers and data banks are in a
secure vault, and all transmission to and from them is protected by cryptography. The users may all have different keys, which are frequently changed,
and transmission from one user to another is via the computer so that the
users never know each other's keys. If the technology develops in this direction, hardware cryptography will become common. The current developments
in *large-scale-integration* (LSI) circuitry are naturally suited to cryptographic
modules. Cryptography may become a standard extension of secure operating
systems, such as those discussed in the previous two chapters.

TIGHT   A wiretapper attempting to break a cipher may de-
DISCIPLINE   liberately cause errors on the communication line
                         and observe the recovery action that takes place.
To stop this technique from being of any value, when an erroneous block is
retransmitted it should be enciphered in the same way as the previous block,
using the same position of the key. A line control procedure that detects
block errors and causes identical retransmission of any erroneous block
would be suitable. The transmission buffering and retransmission process are
separated from the enciphering process.

Each enciphered message or record may contain a code that goes to an
address-selection mechanism such as that in Fig. 19.2. If, then, any loss of
synchronization occurs, as with a computer failure, the code will specify
exactly what sections of key are to be used. Figure 19.6 shows a transmission
block that contains such a code, and that could be used with conventional
forms of synchronous transmission.

The enciphering process should be isolated not only from the transmission mechanism but from all other segments of the program design. The
biggest disadvantage of cryptography is that it can generate an alarming degree of confusion if it is not carried out simply, and tightly controlled. The
procedures for recovery from errors and machine failures must be designed
so that there is no loss of synchronization between the enciphering and
deciphering process. The keys used must be carefully and securely controlled.
When data on files are enciphered with changing keys, an audit trail must
record past keys in such a way that data reconstruction can be automatically
carried out.

Everything that can possibly go wrong with the system must be tested out with the enciphering and deciphering mechanisms. Use of the cryptography techniques must be made as simple as possible. Cryptography should only be used where it is really needed. The systems designer should remember this axiom:

CRYPTOGRAPHY + LOOSE DISCIPLINE = CHAOS

REFERENCES

A bibliography on cryptography is at the end of Chapter 20, page 242.

1. D. Kahn, *The Codebreakers*, The Macmillan Company, New York, 1967, p. 684.

2. P. Hamilton, *Espionage and Subversion in an Industrial Society*, Hutchinson Publishing Group, Ltd., London, 1967.

3. A. S. Vernam, "Cipher Printing Telegraph Systems for Secret Wire and Radio Telegraphic Communications," *Journal of the AIEE*, Vol. 45, 109–115 (1926).

4. B. Tuckerman, "A Study of the Vigenère-Vernam Single and Multiple Loop Enciphering Systems" IBM Report No. RC2879, Thomas J. Watson Research Center, Yorktown Heights, N. Y., 1970.

5. C. E. Shannon, "The Communication Theory of Secrecy Systems," *Bell System Technical Journal*, Vol. 28 (Oct. 1949).

6. R. O. Skatrud, "A Consideration of the Application of Cryptographic Techniques to Data Processing," Fall Joint Computer Conference, 1969, AFIPS Press.

7. IBM Research Reports, Vol. 7., No. 4 (1971). Published by IBM Research, Yorktown Heights, New York. (An issue on cryptography.)

20 PROGRAMS FOR ENCIPHERING DATA

The subject of cryptography has become shrouded in mystique because of its espionage and National Security Agency connotations. One consultant is quoted by the Diebold Group as saying, "It is all but insane for the vast majority of business, except perhaps five or ten in total to consider these techniques because of the extreme difficulty." Other experts say that virtually any cipher produced by the "amateurs" in a data-processing team could be cracked by using professional techniques.

In reality a basic level of data enciphering is no more difficult than other accomplishments in contemporary software, and can add substantially to the security of sensitive data. Programs of the type illustrated at the end of this chapter encipher data securely enough for *most commercial operations.* When the highest security is needed, a system with a once-only key of millions of characters, discussed in Chapter 19, may be used. The enciphering illustrated at the end of this chapter probably could be broken by a handful of the world's most expert cryptanalysts using computers. It is also true to say that modern bank vaults could be opened by the world's top safe-breaking experts. Fortunately, the majority of persons we seek protection from are neither expert cryptanalysts nor expert safe breakers. A criminal confronted with the codes at the end of this chapter will normally set about stealing the program and the key rather than attempting to break the code.

Theoretically and in practice, the cipher produced with a once-only key can be unbreakable if the key is suitably safeguarded. It is often, however, cumbersome and inconvenient for both the sending and receiving parties to be provided with an entire tape or disk of key, and a simpler method is sought using a computer algorithm for scrambling the data.

The programs discussed in this chapter can be entirely self-contained with the exception of a key, which can be on one punched card or magnetic-stripe credit card. Hence they are simple to use. An application programmer wishing to use them can simply write CALL CIPHER in his program.

For purposes of illustration we shall discuss in the beginning of the chapter a number of coding methods, which by themselves give quite inadequate security. Only when the techniques are suitably combined is the cipher unlikely to be broken by a team skilled in the techniques of cryptanalysis. Although all the programs in this chapter would keep out a casual intruder, only the last one should be regarded as secure enough to protect valuable commercial data. None of them would be good enough for secrets sought by the KGB!

A set of principles to be used in devising cipher programs is given at the end of the chapter. The first factor to remember is that the enemy may have available to him powerful computers and plenty of time.

In selecting an enciphering technique it is necessary to assess how much time the codebreaker might have available to him. In some systems he will have less than 24 hours because the key or program is changed every day and real-time deciphering is needed, as with the bank terminals discussed in Chapter 19. In other cases he may have a year or more, for example with a commerical tape that retains its value.

Second, it is necessary to assess how much effort that codebreaker might expend. He may expend very little effort to obtain personnel records, but a massive amount of effort to obtain unique trade secrets.

PROGRAMS   This chapter discusses enciphering algorithms and gives examples of them programmed in PL/I. PL/I has been chosen for this because of its conciseness and readability. When the routines discussed are used frequently and high efficiency is needed, it might be better for a skilled programmer to use Assembler Language.

The text to be enciphered is referred to as TEXT and the enciphered message is referred to as MESS throughout the programs. The text is read and the messages are generated in blocks of 48 characters.

USE OF A   A much less secure variation on the Vernam once-
RANDOM-NUMBER   only key theme generates the "key" continuously,
GENERATOR   using some form of random-number generator. The sending and receiving parties generate a long string of pseudo-random numbers, which are combined with the data to be sent.

The following sections of PL/I codes, for example, would accomplish this:

Preliminary:

```
DCL (TEXT,MESS,ALPH) CHAR(48);
ALPH=
 'ABCDEFGHIJKLMNOPQRSTUVWXYZ1234567890-.,)(:;"=+ ?';
 S=23518967;
```

Enciphering Routine:

```
GET EDIT (TEXT)(A(48));
DO K=1 TO 48;
N=INDEX(ALPH,SUBSTR(TEXT,K,1));
CALL RANDOM (S,R); J=R*48;
L=J+N; IF L>48 THEN L=L-48;
SUBSTR(MESS,K,1)=SUBSTR(ALPH,L,1);
END;
```

Deciphering Routine:

```
DO K=1 TO 48;
L=INDEX(ALPHA,SUBSTR(MESS,K,1));
CALL RANDOM (S,R); J=R*48;
N=L-J; IF N<1 THEN N=N+48;
SUBSTR(TEXT,K,1)=SUBSTR(ALPH,N,1);
END;
PUT EDIT (TEXT)(A(48));
```

CALL RANDOM (S,R) invokes a random-number generator that initially requires a seed S, and which produces a new seed S and a near-random number R.

The random-number generator should be made up by the programmer. Well-known forms of random-number generators should be avoided. It does not matter if the numbers generated follow a nonuniform distribution. Some possibilities are the following, where S is Fixed Binary:

1. $S=S*65539$; $R=S*.465661E\text{-}9$; IF $(R<.76 \ \& \ R>.69)$
   THEN $S=S+(R-.69)*723$;
2. $R=MOD(S, 77317)/86437$; $L=L+17$; $S=S*L*3742.7$;
3. $S=S*3750217$; $R=MOD(S/172751, 5671)/7327$;

A programmer could amuse himself by trying a variety of unusual random-number generators. He should always test their output very thoroughly before using them, however, to make sure that they produce a suitably varied string of numbers with no repetitive cycles.

UNPRINTABLE MESSAGES The preceding example was programmed in such a way that it always produces printable characters. A more efficient type of coding can manipulate the data in binary form and produce an enciphered bit stream that does necessarily contain valid characters. Such an enciphered message has the disadvantage that it cannot be transmitted with some of today's terminals. A line control procedure is needed that can transmit a binary bit stream. Some can accomplish binary transmission, and some cannot. A binary bit-stream cipher message cannot be directly printed. Most terminals can only print those resulting characters that happen to be members of a printable character set.

Code for binary enciphering could be similar to the following:

Preliminary:

```
DCL (S,R) FIXED BINARY(31);
DCL E CHAR(4) BASED(P);
DCL M FIXED BIN(31);
P=ADDR(M);
DCL (TEXT,MESS) CHAR(48);
S=23518967;
```

Enciphering Routine:

```
GET EDIT (TEXT)(A(48));
DO K=1 TO 48 BY 4;
E=SUBSTR(TEXT,K,4);
CALL RANDOM (S,R);
M=M+R;
SUBSTR(MESS,K,4)=E;
END;
```

Deciphering Routine:

```
DO K=1 TO 48 BY 4;
E=SUBSTR(MESS,K,4);
CALL RANDOM (S,R);
M=M-R;
SUBSTR(TEXT,K,4)=E;
END;
PUT EDIT (TEXT)(A(48));
```

A complete listing of the programs for enciphering and deciphering with these routines is given in Appendix A (Programs 1A and 1B).

INSECURENESS OF
FIXED ALGORITHMS
The main disadvantage of the preceding methods of enciphering is that once an intruder obtains the algorithm, all is lost. Such is the case for any algorithm with no changing component, no matter how complex.

It is true that the initial seed employed could be varied. However, using a computer, the intruder may be able to try all possible numeric seeds unless a very large value of S is used. He may also find a mathematical method of working backward from the result of the randomizing process.

In Auguste Kerckhoffs' classic book *La Cryptographic Militaire*, 1883, he established the principle that *the enemy should be assumed to know the encoding techniques*; the security must rest with a key that is frequently changed. The principle is valid today with computer systems.

The key can be changed perhaps once per day, and the key and algorithm are chosen such that the work needed to determine the key cannot conceivably be completed in one day, even with the aid of the most powerful computing systems.

This is the case with the cash-dispensing terminals mentioned previously. The numbers transmitted are encoded using complex manipulation of a small key. It is estimated that if a would-be felon wished to decode the messages sent, even if he knew the encoding algorithm exactly, it would take many months of work on the world's most powerful computer to determine the key. The key is changed every day, and so he would be many months too late.

If a cryptobox is used attached to a terminal, a criminal may be able to buy one and find out how it works, or he may be able to obtain its drawings or the diagnostic procedures which the engineers use to test that it is functioning correctly. Many engineers will be needed to service such devices. The intruder may simply transmit from the terminal and record the enciphered transmission.

Although the intruder may be able to find out the enciphering algorithm, to obtain even a small key by trial and error can take an extremely long time. Suppose that a key of 12 alphabetic characters is employed. Then 26^{12} different keys are possible. If the intruder using a computer is able to test them at the rate of 1 per microsecond, he will take an average time of

$$\frac{26^{12}}{2} \text{ microseconds} = \frac{26^{12}}{2 \times 10^6 \times 60^2 \times 24 \times 365} \text{ years}$$

that is, 1513 years.

A key of 20 alphabetic characters would require 3×10^{14} years.

Complete trial and error will clearly never be used in solving cryptograms other than the simplest. The art of the cryptanalyst must be to find shortcuts that avoid full trial and error. Consequently, the encoding technique must do everything possible to prevent shortcuts working.

In the following examples the key is a string of 48 different characters. One of the characters is a blank. The 48-character set may be arranged in any sequence, for example,

```
NY+BTGV FCED18WS:)X564AQZ,.-OLOPIKJM=U9732?"(;HR';
```

There is thus no possibility of the encoder selecting a verbal or numeric key that can be guessted.

In the following program, the text is read in 48-character blocks (any length could have been used) and is manipulated using this key. The first example uses a letter-for-letter substitution. This, as discussed in Chapter 19, would be insufficiently secure by itself. The characters in the block are therefore taken in a random sequence, the sequence depending upon the order of the characters in the key. Thus,

Preliminary:

```
    DCL (TEXT,MESS,ALPH,KEY) CHAR(48);
KEY=
  'NY+BTGV FCED18WS:)X564AQZ,.-OLOPIKJM=U9732?"(;HR';
ALPH=
  'ABCDEFGHIJKLMNOPQRSTUVWXYZ1234567890-.,)(:;"=+ ?';
    DCL M(48);
    DO K=1 TO 48;
    M(K)=INDEX(KEY,SUBSTR(ALPH,K,1));
    END;
```

Enciphering Routine:

```
GET EDIT (TEXT)(A(48));
DO K=1 TO 48;
N=INDEX(KEY,SUBSTR(TEXT,K,1));
SUBSTR(MESS,M(K),1)=SUBSTR(ALPH,N,1);
END;
```

Deciphering Routine:

```
DO K=1 TO 48;
N=INDEX(ALPH,SUBSTR(MESS,M(K),1));
SUBSTR(TEXT,K,1)=SUBSTR(KEY,N,1);
END;
PUT EDIT (TEXT)(A(48));
```

The cryptanalyst, attacking the resulting code, may examine the frequency of usage of characters. The relative frequency of usage of characters in conventional English is given in Fig. 20.1. If the cryptanalyst knows that English is being sent, he may use this table to guess which letter is which. He will use trial and error, combined with a computer program for the uncertain letters.

There are several defenses against this technique. First, the text may be preprocessed to disguise the easily identifiable letters such as E, T, O, J, K, Q, X, and Z. Second, the letters may be taken two at a time, each pair being substituted for a different pair. The cryptanalyst may then look for common (and uncommon) letter pairs. To prevent this, the letter pairs enciphered should not be letters that are adjacent in the text, but letters that may be many characters apart, with positions selected at random.

Letter	Relative frequency
E	13.05
T	9.02
O	8.21
A	7.81
N	7.28
I	6.77
R	6.64
S	6.46
H	5.85
D	4.11
L	3.60
C	2.93
F	2.88
U	2.77
M	2.62
P	2.15
Y	1.51
W	1.49
G	1.39
B	1.28
V	1.00
K	0.42
X	0.30
J	0.23
Q	0.14
Z	0.09

Figure 20.1. Relative frequency of letters in English text. *(Data from reference 3.)*

DEFENSE
IN DEPTH

Certain persons in an organization must be given the cipher key. Like a key that locks up physical valuables, it should only be given to persons who can be trusted. The possibility is always present, however, of the key falling into the wrong hands or being misused.

A principle that should be employed in computer cryptography is that a person who has misappropriated the key should not be able to crack the system if he does not know the enciphering method. Conversely, a person who knows the program but does not have the key should not be able to decipher the data. *The management responsible for security must then ensure that no person can obtain both the program and the key.* Programmers will never be given the key, and steps will be taken to ensure that key holders cannot be given the program. Both the key and the program will be closely guarded, and both may be changed at suitably frequent intervals.

Adopting this principle, and assuming that either a person processing the key or a person with knowledge of the program can be diabolically clever, *none of the programs given so far in this chapter is sufficiently secure.* A fixed algorithm with no key is inadequate, and a program that uses its key in a simple way is inadequate, even if the key is complex.

We must manipulate the key in a much more complex way, but must do so without unduly lengthening the execution time.

The next example uses the 48-character key to form a two-dimensional substitution table for pairs of characters. The characters in the table are thoroughly scrambled using random-number generaters. Figure 20.2 shows a table used for encoding. It is unlikely that any pattern will be detected in the sequencing of characters in the table. Using the table, any pair of the 48 characters may be converted into another unique pair. To convert them back again in the deciphering process, another table is used, shown in Fig. 20.3.

These two tables are formed from the key by the following PL/I code, which refers to them as ENCODE and DECODE, respectively.

```
DCL (TEXT,MESS,ALPH,KEY) CHAR(48);
DCL (ENCODE,DECODE)(48,48) CHAR(2);
DCL L(2);
DCL X(48,48,2) FIXED BINARY;
S1=23518967;
S2=50173031;
KEY=
 'NY+BTGV FCED18WS:)X564AQZ,.-OLOPIKJM=U9732?"(;HR';
ALPH=
 'ABCDEFGHIJKLMNOPQRSTUVWXYZ1234567890-.,)(:;"=+ ?';
```

	A	B	C	D	E	F	G	H	I	J	K	L	M	N	O	P	Q	R	S	T	U	V	W	X
A	FE	4Y	JO	GX	EZ	O1	AP	2?	81	-=	1Z	P(	TP	II	.B	O7	:7	G:	G)	:F	2E	5Y	GO	K
B	CR	LH	SX	SU	1W	A?	Y,	KE	RS	DJ	1K	Q.	7	E8	GK	+-	O;	77	M"	PW	6L	P1	FH	P7
C	1	OX	.M	V1	)Q	4O	?:	T!	(4	V4	8	;T	EI	MF	4P	ON	?I	27	UW	Z8	.G	"V	KG	P
D	A8	;=	57	WZ	3T	1C	Q2	RO	.(	HI	S8	Y1	QC	-V	WU	DK	SY	9J	YD	-1	PA	FO	ZT	PH
E	M-	.?	DO	G+	T-	F?	-4	Y	6?	ZY	5=	G-	;O	PZ	E:	8T	?X	UJ	CO	FY	XR	Z(	LS	,R
F	BL	R)	L7	L3	OT	2X	"(	-Y	D8	S5	SC	W6	+S	)=	MO	9	R3	XD	9	9S	ZW	WO	S;	L
G	F	-J	:Z	WX	2H	WA	D;	,7	PV	2,	F(	5)	FO	CQ	M?	QG	(O	,C	ZL	TQ	ON	V?	M2	VK
H	JA	(Y	6C	9X	ZE	UE	OY	SQ	RU	,O	NN	H?	PT	I3	S2	1"	NE	TX	Q;	,N	LB	NM	NY	?S
I	FI	,9	(P	C9	8F	82	30	WL	.I	L2	JW	5C	11	OZ	G5	BR	1Q	LF	WR	-.	1V	?6	T(	YW
J	?C	VU	ED	VL	S"	8=	6U	JT	JN	G4	LU	1)	=R	?E	.1	+X	44	9G	GD	=O	03	M1	7:	7"
K	GZ	7P	ZR	,J	V7	(	-L	2.	.T	3	L(	?2	2M	.S	A	54	MB	=?	7.	1+	-"	HV	5P	V=
L	FW	ZG	VG	-?	18	R2	;1	T=	2	O.	)	WY	90	7H	8L	B=	KO	YZ	R+	4R	E3	5	U8	.P
M	KW	FJ	51	GI	1R	)M	D	5M	IG	F"	-G	.O	(8	XM	RY	Z7	N+	ZH	TR	6=	G.	MW	9Q	S9
N	99	6Q	UQ	ZN	VW	TO	WO	OK	;N	O4	9W	"4	16	H(	((	HA	6P	4L	DA	.O	-	I+	R(	3D
O	6	AI	JJ	U6	SI	CC	,W	DH	SH	Y2	BW	"D	.,	4B	(C	W2	39	NL	JY	.2	EF	J-	+T	YN
P	)9	DM	=T	O6	:L	SW	O8	EG	OQ	60	47	7B	KY	=B	VN	5;	IV	KJ	Q8	YT	,F	OI	OB	JL
Q	9T	PU	=3	Y5	"2	T+	Y8	(.	P:	3J	R,	FP	CM	HJ	GL	UO	3H	)	RR	Z,	MA	LN	R=	6O
R	T9	GM	;K	?J	ET	TN	Q4	PB	?L	NU	T2	W	Y9	5T	6)	7=	?	Q	8G	(V	1(	K=	55	OP
S	=L	NQ	6K	)V	B1	E	EB	7;	S1	8W	F9	1-	IR	G"	DO	,G	X(	"H	5:	2V	L=	K-	IS	S.
T	YJ	Y+	-C	VA	;;	8N	E7	+P	QB	AO	-P	2;	:6	BG	NR	-+	UV	9"	IO	PY	.=	3I	8.	HW
U	4O	GO	4-	Y6	"	Y:	=(	DU	..	W3	N	=	S:	,	+Q	IP	.K	)T	:+	D6	O=	NV	+G	Z4
V	3E	(	5K	V8	AL	EH	AN	D:	QO	Z	UO	2Z	Y;	-T	T3	6,	G8	PF	W(	=2	.-	PK	."	"C
W	(P	=9	-Z	E1	2J	.7	4U	MQ	1=	Z	:V	=O	?M	D3	)L	(+	;-	N)	1B	31	?P	?U	P3	13
X	V.	XI	7O	FF	5O	;J	CN	VQ	GA	P-	:R	Q3	B7	E(	W"	A6	C1	4?	FK	QQ	I	7(	R"	+6
Y	+V	J5	SO	AJ	,)	4"	LW	NC	74	,V	F)	Y3	C7	JF	PX	DR	6N	:	2O	T,	H8	VT	V:	M=
Z	AC	-A	VO	.D	1?	76	KK	V	FZ	M	;D	S(	36	,B	B3	U4	7T	Z=	W?	O=	WN	)	;	YK OU
1	U1	N	GP	A7	8:	U?	O-	-Q	GU	U	W-	O8	59	.)	3M	BE	9E	HG	88	M5	),	=,	X:	N?
2	TL	K2	:"	A=	,4	IQ	.	"3	FM	S6	A;	8P	D+	"T	1F	HP	GC	XT	H3	O?	UA	5S	T6	4E
3	QV	R6	OA	SR	B5	EA	K)	,H	UT	IH	9Z	D5	OI	9?	?-	T:	+K	"8	-(	L)	Q6	:Y	DV	A
4	+7	WE	=	QZ	X"	DY	W5	JQ	.J	;	JP	,,	5A	XO	64	Q=	XW	Q)	(;	(Q	GE	RA	7?	YO
5	UN	UY	+	E;	9N	,Y	2P	U(	-,	XL	8?	U.	7G	ZX	+?	O)	ZK	+.	+9	BN	(N	1A	8V	F7
6	I7	80	DX	FB	KC	PR	SA		8+	2N	93	F3	)C	PS	Q"	V(	AW	O4	IR	ZM	KL	62	,=	GW
7	3F	NH	W,	P=	OC	17	6	J6	2U	63	KX	Y4	OB	(-	9=	=C	C4	6D	=)	=1	AK	L1	T5	OX
8	"A	ZB	C-	5-	SM	QF	KO	J,	7-	-S	"O	Y"	7A	CA	+3	UL	YA	;,	Y?	.	(=	RF	8	8O
9	IL	V(	(F	TZ	94	49	2(	ZO	R9	O5	Z5	6(	O)	X2	,O	IT	J7	XY	):	7M	Z-	OL	SV	FD
0	:D	+U	Z;	6F	T	-E	6P	KF	JR	EJ	TG	71	15	(:	8)	=+	UP	OS	E=	?D	;P	;	4,	RP
-	RP	)Y	GB	VI	X=	7I	+O	Z.	CX	.Q	4G	X;	=V	H"	;Z	,K	U9	,	KM	C"	I-	5F	7I	1G
.	2B	;?	NZ	:H	,:	N5	9M	D9	F5	;X	)?	(G	MI	5D	Q?	-H	;.	5F	69	TV	2	GT	4	2G
,	R	==	=6	ZS	EL	XE	V+	PL	4+	-)	H9	:T	CD	5Z	A(	:.	U=	::	XJ	+;	F-	K+	UD	OS
)	6W	46	YI	DT	LX	+R	7L	.+	E+	H;	,;	O9	,6	5L	X-	BV	XU	6Z	SL	LM	8Y	GG	23	PQ
(	C	=A	LV	EP	KI	VO	3G	I?	43	WW	LJ	56	J(	,1	BJ	TF	-X	5	:N	78	EO	NW	ES	+=
:	"B	;F	F2	X4	19	O3	O	9B	"+	)7	)6	LD	J3	BC	J:	=Q	OQ	MN	,T	D7	PU	OV	=W	"-
;	RK	3Y	;2	8C	2W	WC	M)	JH	A)	P.	(U	)W	H-	4I	QP	+(	9.	TR	)U	N2	L?	W4	,I	3)
"	VJ	:M	C	:E	WT	YS	G;	H=	F+	DL	:S	W7	6I	NO	GF	VY	=8	5W	3P	.F	JC	SO	12	41
=	=E	H+	BP	MJ	A.	YB	7D	AS	=U	4J	7E	BH	5(	MO	H	34	B4	6A	DZ	+C	LL	AV	FU	)8
+	-O	X1	WP	,D	3Z	7Q	EM	9O	G,	1P	GY	1.	ZA	CE	2T	UH	+:	C?	5Q	;"	H7	RW	G3	1X
	3C	?W	QX	1E	M+	-K	M;	J;	ZJ	C=	Y)	?A	4.	QA	D"	D:	P6	IE	5O	I(	4H	CV	BA	)S
?	VX	R4	IA	,+	2A	K?	;6	(S	,L	G	N-	7C	"5	S7	NX	XF	D(	1I	RQ	V2	9:	RK	W+	)5

Figure 20.2. The "ENCODE" table for enciphering data produced from a 48-character key. As an example of its use, the letter pair "BD" would be converted into ";=". Note: A program such as that in Fig. 20.4 does not encipher adjacent letter pairs—only letter pairs that are well separated.

```
Y   Z   1   2   3   4   5   6   7   8   9   0   -   .   ,   )   (   :   ;   "   =   +       ?

.;  (J  98  X)  DF  02  X6  A,  5B  TS  79  ?Y  P5  (M  9D  -3  25  V)  (I  TD  .H  X5  )2  :
I=  "I  -R  H6  4Z  28  8U  RX  Z"  N,  (5  MV  PI  EE  FT  H5  LU  CS  )(  ?+  ;H  T1  MP  U,
P)  QH  5G  :B   X  2Y  N8  M:  QJ  RJ   P  ?0  9F  VC  LG  ?F  OM  OH  "6  ":  -8  .F  .Y  M8
:9  (B  35  RZ  ZU  V,  =J  84  MU  ?:  KU  QW  4=  0A  RL  M7  UX  9,  CO  )"  ))  1T  =M  OM
-;  AE  LC  CI  )F  U3  J+  ?3  GV  LK  0Z   "  QE  73   0  7S  ND  K;  XO  RE  P"  ;7  .W  D2
C+  =I  N0  C8  HQ  Q+  RM  =5  US  :1  WD  KR  -M  6B  Z)  6H  H,  L;  R8  G7  +1  37  -2  GN
R   -U  :?  J0  3:  Z9  Y.  I4  5U  HD  V3  9Y  24  :C  "X  )1  38  -6  (X  75  VR  J)  "E  0P
E4  M6  UG  4N  ST  J=  XZ  ,"  K,  5R  VM  0-  :4  X,  UR  "S  ??  00  7K  V9  I"  :0  SP  (W
D)  =;  BI  0Y  6G  J9  (K  A:  GH  +)  JM   0  VP  H0  D.  IM  (2  A-   +  ;3  ,R  MZ  ,P  X3
ZD  L"  "1  VZ  +N  70  )F  YG  )J  7Z  8,  6"  7)  EQ  0U  "J  B6  PJ  KN  4C  CY  ;S  C(  CJ
OK  SJ  BX  E2  +4  KB  0.  (D  (T  ;)  XP  Q9  V9  X.  F;  B;  42  G9  :A   T  7J  ?9  0F  KT
:=  B5  :2  3?  LT  S3  ;Q  MR  7V  0P  P2  CW  4V  (?  2K  DW  J"  UC  CK  TT  0H  F"  ,.  FY
PP  T;  WH  6J  SK  V;  S+  P?  8(  D?  PD   V  FG  N1  HE  D1  AD  AM  95  ).   .  :8  M3  R0  4M
KQ  =G  IM  1N  3=  0D  Q0  F=  W8  ,X  WR  22  J2  DI  09  QN  B.  NS  GQ  5J  I:  89  V"  SZ
AZ  :J  X?  T4  N"  5.  0+  3K  86  7R  ?4   J  L+  JD  ?1  ER  )I  JI  G1  4(  :P  8E  ,5  J?
RH  =-  8S  )0  2+  ;U  07  2C  TY  T.  JX  C3  E-  R:  TU  1M  .3  IK   ?  0T  -B  H2  XN  G
KH  .C  :W  ,3  ?=  ZC  ZF  D,  S-  RG  HY  6+  CL  8B  4F  HP  U-  0;  00  Q7  B9  PG  K1  MD
B8  ()  FC  MS  FQ  32  2-  YQ  M4  :G  N3  (6  ,S  K8  T9  45  W=  4)  +0   -  0,  Y0  =Y  U)
WQ  CP  DN  P,  S4   K  XQ  +F  A9  R7  0D  72  )R  4;  2=  5V  +W  Y-  F:  G(  I0   M  3B  J8
(F  BT  XG  X+  3Q  J4  U;  ?B  B1  8I  6S  =:  ;5  6T  :;  HB  (Z  FA  61  U+  HT  PC  U"  6V
6M  10  )0  YY  ",  3S  PE  2K  HX  9+  X7  (9  NG  Z+  BS  FU  AT  W:  =X  ;W  U2  A+  C)  J.
26  FV  FR  IU  ?Q  X8  MG  3P  0(  QK  8H  KA  N7  LP  ,(  ?7  2D  +2  00  .X  N=  ,M  F.  UZ
?"  Y=  DG  7N  NA  DD  K.  ""  3"  B)  P;  0,  7+  TF  CB  S,  BM  ;V  0(  A2  0F  AF  ?;  )A
"0  ;L  0-  :U  KV  FX  TJ  N;  5,  F8  XC  SF  I.  NK  0E  HL  4:  2Q  T7  Z0  ;E  K4  KD  HH
QD  A4  52   S  ZZ  53  LQ  BU  8A  LI  L:   R  UU  9)  ZP  LB  IC   1  ++  VB  4S  =7  YF  NB
QR  HN  =H  9(  HS  0E  F1  ,-  XH  8J  A3  0+  3.  5N  XS  "=  "B   4  S=  9U  21  -N  YF  58
0G  H.  BZ  L4  B?  +H  9C  FL  PM  5"  YV  QY  JG  SB  8X  3A  4Q  (,  M,  IW  K:  6.  ,A  ZQ
D=  )D  0R  3+  MY  GR  CT  1,  V6  H:  XK  BD  ?,  B+  EN  JB  06  -0  ;0  .N  L9  WG   B  BQ
EV  VD  +"  I)  "L  T?   E  +J  .8  9L  IL  7U  )-  ?G  AG  66  0S  40  JU  EW  ?5  E,  ?(  V-
LZ  DF  MX  9;  R.  DQ  F,  CG  E6  .6  )K  )G  +D  CZ  IZ  02  "G  "M  )N  WF  JK  ,?  2I  XB
?.  )H  UI  =F  B,  0"  .9  ,Z  6:  )B  =.  T8  Z6  AX  BN  VH  M9  :0  DS  .A  )3   7  ;P  H0
K7  V5  9R  B:  K9  YL  2S  C.  "9  E.  EX  1U  3(  4B  MH  1H  4T  11  "N  L-   J  (H  :0  G=
CH  MM  RV  3X  8;  3;  3V  97  U:  YX  SD  L0  +,   H  I2  B2  3N  N4  7,  TM  LE  :-  C2   F
-F  ?V  (L  I,  N:  YR  GS  =4  9I  L5  KS  3Q  U7  H)  7F  ;G  B(  C:  4K  TC  :(  I;  6;  ";
-5   S  RD  P4  RC  .5  G6  +A  0C  EC  1J  ,2  B"  BF  UB  IJ  ,Q  5?  5X  F6  S?  .:  NP  =N
.V  2F  --  IF  0:  65  AA  -I  U5  14   Y   D  AB  1:  :X  "7  +Y  "P  3,  TK  04  ,U  ?8  ?T
MT  5H  H1  )X  WS  C6  7W  I5  2P  C;  Q:  E?  "?  .4  R5   3  ML  JE  IY  LR  6X  DC  VV  NT
87  NF  XA  L6  "K  NJ  5+  =Z  ?)  NI  I6  ?N  R?  K5  CF  WK  3-  TH   I  9A  A0  9P  7Y  AU
 W  0G  Q5  ;C  9H   L  E9  A1  33  AY  )Z  "Z  3L  HM  (0  "Q  W9  +E  B7  AB  P9  +I  LY  6Y
"U  -9  ?R  I8  )4  YU  SN  :3   X  Y(  FU   U  U"  X9  5I  ID  2L  +Z  L,  -W  1;  K3  BT  6F
(1  T0  8P  -:  ="  L.  .R  C5  HU  VF  (A  SG  .L  TA  N.  10  D-  4X  0U  68  1S  E5  (7  B:
".  YM  DB  =K  Z:  01  :5  P3  MK  KP  HC  )+  0"  29  8D  G2  F4  =S  8K  :)  JZ  B-  MC  ;B
.Z  HZ  XV  +8  0I  +5  GJ  ;A  8M  3U  ::  :K  Z3  ME   Q  3W  M.  VF  0W  0(  WI  QT  WV  ()
ZV  0P  ;M  0,  P0  2)  AQ  FS  B0  ?Z  4H  K6  )P  91  ?H  QM  IX  67  1Y  +L  8-  BB  +M  UK
+P  =P  YC  W)  0?  :,  FN  SE  Z1  6-  M(  9K  W.  ;I  ?0  1D  P+  0L  4A  9-  0I  HK  4W  K7
-7  0J  "F  9V  CU  :I  Y7  7X  ;+  JS  S)  N6  W1  HF  B0  VS  :0  G?  T"  2"  Z2  SS  30  D5
WM  8"  0J  96  WJ  W;  K(  J1  ,Y  0V  BY  T)  83  0U  ")  E)  0L  TW  B-  ,E  :4  H4  A"  .U
```

Figure 20.2 (cont'd)

	N	Y	+	B	T	G	V		F	C	E	D	1	8	W	S	:	)	X	5	6	4	A	Q
N	KH	XO	3J	T5	FB	?F	OP	B1	5+	GX	,2	1S	2N	FT	UZ	5(	S(	:4	P	.Z	QY	2H	GV	)N
Y	WH	2U	(-	9?	7P	K+	P"	HE	?L	=J	TE	F4	;=	U)	LL	QD	V3	B-	R9	VA	?)	BA	8)	O1
+	QM	BT	;Y	.2	FQ	DE	G,	;I	I"	YF	I)	M2	TK	T6	W?	5M	SU	O;	2T	5,	OQ	I,	+U	4F
B	?Y	F=	F)	PI	R;	C-	"Y	A,	D6	,N	GS	1;	SW	.Q	9N	.1	2C	86	?4	7A	.F	NO	--	IT
T	?.	TP	WD	ZT	"L	V.	VY	FO	,B	52	ER	D)	+D	PF	F"	3H	L,	RU	R2	NR	.T	(7	(U	+"
G	-U	6J	WU	NT	KO	V)	CL	?P	-M	64	HP	1W	X-	SB	+2	O:	8R	O4	1T	1C	3I	K-	,3	PG
V	VU	91	AY	P)	T.	7E	.	HZ	ZV	V	Y3	W3	UI	W5	"	W9	KW	DS	1"	)S	?T	-L	V=	A3
	KU	9-	C5	2	"K	J?	OM	H6	AG	A(	53	O-	:Y	W8	LR	ZO	?A	RQ	7(	R(	G7	:Z	X3	,"
F	Z,	Y	6S	.O	P(	O"	8:	?8	DX	,,	UO	Z4	O2	EI	"4	OX	TA	5J	P?	R.	DO	,Q	+W	F8
C	HY	1+	T=	N:	"9	Q2	.C	C"	1R	FO	80	+.	FD	D;	F;	KF	.G	M6	9X	LI	CH	"J	AZ	MD
E	QH	Z	:)	P1	.W	U4	:"	FS	AA	N+	.B	3A	D	+D	B4	6+	D"	3E	F,	V-	?(	X2	ZE	-E
D	(E	SD	-4	O2	"A	SJ	Z3	GM	X9	M,	CJ	4W	)+	,;	9F	98	AO	Z2	PF	N.	R7	:3	(M	YY
1	.M	LD	=F	ES	+B	;O	DC	AC	5Z	QX	DW	)M	MI	IA	-	IS	8F	)G	B+	CM	;T	X"	6)	=+
8	5C	GQ	2"	YR	O6	QV	DV	KC	8X	2F	NB	IF	FL	S1	7N	KD	=M	X=	4V	2Z	":	.7	AD	SP
W	V(	XI	(S	KO	:?	X6	EN	Y)	AL	OL	"3	)L	EB	JS	J(	FP	1Q	L;	Q4	R"	A)	+	Q6	OD
S	:N	F"	MF	IB	8A	59	)	2Y	6=	:B	W(	;6	=:	1P	3.	+	K"	X	,Z	V2	9T	=Y	H=	RO
:	39	FU	Q+	?:	P3	RA	WY	RY	;S	:9	OE	HV	.-	E1	:U	MU	9"	S9	W1	SS	76	(X	6I	9.
)	RW	K	8I	8W	O?	SA	:A		KL	KY	U	)?	YI	LJ	OO	2+	9	";	=D	2A	LG	OR	I;	R4
X	O?	88	PJ	1K	RH	DA	A?	3C	4X	I-	97	C6	X+	,1	DG	CB	,-	2.	85	;O	=.	::	.6	C
5	F.	DQ	4"	E3	W7	OI	Z7	VL	I.	6:	+:	L3	MO	ZL	G4	JF	5;	X?	+A	WR	4-	)R	;5	1)
6	O	DU	XX	(J	W2	50	72	AO	"O	4.	74	TU	MN	7O	LF	J2	MT	K:	5A	L(	)3	B)	PX	U3
4	:8	L7	3K	Q=	2O	JJ	JC	W.	(;	Q7	YH	R6	8-	6D	V;	3S	=?	3(	O:	PK	O4	QJ	ZY	GP
A	3W	Q8	60	W	.:	IX	DT	OK	:T	N8	F3	SN	V5	7Y	FG	G6	;K	?W	1,	M4	R=	;+	5-	N
Q	BS	6R	OU	?2	TG	;N	HX	RR	3R	NG	.J	44	QI	O9	YS	HH	(	EC	5S	S+	BN	(1	5=	TX
Z	C.	RL	:(	11	D9	AK	2J	JW	IZ	.4	EA	S=	KA	;)	DD	?N	CG	9)	5H	N,	R)	3B	YO	D4
,	8B	GB	-8	KQ	TY	I+	4D	NU	54	.5	+3	6Q	62	9J	C7	)W	4+	U1	.H	7X	PV	WO	6A	=R
.	,:	5G	R5	(N	8P	UM	AX	G2	V	67	87	,I	L+	WT	-+	XS	P,	"M	.K	4O	+1	M	E=	LB
-	K?	:S	PB	+;	EE	LE	?3	"R	U,	C8	-P	(:	LS	==	K1	7Q	+8	-3	O)	D8	8+	CU	:I	OH
O	N"	+R	;R	7=	Z:	WA	CZ	OI	MG	;O	U(	OS	ZU	B6	GN	V"	7	1U	;E	S	JP	FC	JT	IV
L	RO	47	"=	AF	A2	OQ	DJ	4)	61	-Q	E,	J"	93	OL	HI	S)	EP	OW	J5	N)	UB	BN	EV	(?
O	1F	X4	G-	,	FN	BU	F(	?"	VD	SE	9(	CE	):	X8	VF	CY	+H	2P	N4	EX	XQ	AU	=,	5N
P	O	=5	HT	C=	MA	C1	-I	XC	LQ	ZS	D(	XR	J+	1:	C+	H	=O	-=	9K	WK	GO	OC	GA	O;
I	8,	C)	+)	1I	HC	DM	D-	UX	AI	2E	MC	.N	R?	8T	="	EO	4	(O	BX	,(	M"	N;	BO	M3
K	.X	WZ	Q3	A;	"-	OB	XG	4S	:5	;L	SX	PD	KB	;;	),	3M	O"	94	92	CV	CS	;9	U7	8V
J	4,	AT	63	O(	5X	5"	A"	OO	BM	?J	JO	JB	90	8Z	3?	ZK	ZO	7J	S,	"N	2M	J=	DY	7C
M	VH	Z;	=	(W	"8	BR	9H	JZ	I2	MQ	G+	BP	)P	7"	Y?	E8	B"	FM	NM	HM	YU	?M	:M	)=
=	=V	ZW	X(	PL	HL	?7	XK	C4	6N	J	SO	Y2	IW	FJ	(R	;Z	YL	NF	F-	KF	TM	-D	D2	P4
U	JR	4(	BO	6Y	,P	I1	BJ	J1	)U	3	w=	HU	O7	5B	OD	DB	2X	S;	Q)	7G	GJ	GW	?,	.?
9	"H	MR	S5	=Q	AR	:K	-K	SF	KS	DI	5)	H.	E:	+N	()	XM	YD	AP	.(	M1	S.	F9	7S	OK
7	-V	5	A4	MX	;X	"F	EK	MB	X5	MY	GT	T:	F7	Y,	L"	N?	QA	J:	9U	CD	:=	KP	D1	"Q
3	9R	LY	O8	DZ	OV	W+	9G	JK	L6	OP	UL	NW	XW	-?	JU	4L	6(	=6	?I	4Y	J7	I(	9Z	LX
2	T;	JO	:V	)8	KR	);	T?	IL	C:	8	2K	?E	W"	FI	PO	OH	1L	A	N9	1Y	V6	(K	"W	GD
?	X1	SB	O5	31	43	:	VG	QR	FF	R+	O.	8M	EZ	K5	SZ	=O	1G	K.	1O	:O	IE	RX	FB	O.
"	3O	L8	13	-O	;	NS	N	EU	JM	T-	+L	O	PH	Z?	OX	EJ	C2	"D	E4	81	OJ	FY	?	O6
(	P6	8(	P;	(9	WI	"S	B9	BV	KG	J	NX	Q?	UR	7M	SV	LZ	=9	;B	OS	M=	L9	"O	O,	7V
;	6X	MV	T,	)K	ZM	G"	4M	VO	,K	8.	D5	GG	=(	38	4?	WF	,T	VZ	L-	PP	9	.S	K2	SH
H	B7	?5	41	L=	:,	7I	)6	O=	WB	Y8	FV	HO	)7	9V	1M	IO	D.	Z6	7Z	Z.	)F	9=	U	ZC
R	OT	49	Y+	SQ	SM	42	=G	OY	1V	AB	)O	PY	EM	L2	SI	D3	KX	-S	UE	8H	QN	TL	")	YZ

Figure 20.3. The "DECODE" table for deciphering data that have been enciphered with the table in Fig. 20.2. As an example of the table's use, the character pair ";=" would be converted back into the letters "BD". The program in Fig. 20.4 employs such a table.

```
Z   ,   .   -   O   L   O   P   I   K   J   M   =   U   9   7   3   2   ?   "   (   ;   H   R

DN  TH  "2  +Z  UG  VQ  PC  5   )I  ;J  IJ  R:  ?O  A5  E5  2W  (8  J6  9,  ;7  U5  IN  ZZ  ,6
JE  7?  C   HF  GH  )   2I  TT  ;.  MP  SO  32  R   B5  OG  ,   B;  4C  OA  45  BH  F5  9Q  OM
.U  D?  H)  PT  OZ  -O  5O  (+  VN  V,  5F  E   PO  "T  8U  -W  22  3D  "B  I:  PW  7   R=  SL
BB  NZ  OA  =P  M7  UH  WP  HR  S6  4K  )2  QK  NP  ,O  H:  LP  S   A.  6T  A:  ZD  )5  )T  +=
WD  S:  IK  NV  "P  3L  EF  MH  P9  ?K  HJ  Y.  CP  I3  AQ  QZ  ED  O+  ?-  N2  7K  LC  =T  (
BL  PS  UC  KM  Z)  ,C  Y1  +Q  IM  WC  -1  5V  ZN  1H  RJ  M5  G(  X.  .3  (4  L.  )9  R1  8Q
Y=  JY  Y-  ND  8?  C(  V:  IG  QP  3X  Z5  OB  M-  QT  2   7L  58  TS  Z9  VC  TP  :W  VK  1B
JV  R-  T8  UN  G:  XF  ,E  9C  ;,  XA  =7  +S  LU  O(  PF  +6  ).  .   U.  ;P  OE  FK  J4  .B  YG
5Q  UP  T"  Y9  K   RI  =W  RV  2-  HO  NY  NC  26  +5  -C  ,9  A7  Z-  )C  1   C9  B:  .   V8
4Q  RG  ZQ  CT  7O  1E  E7  +T  (Y  F6  U"  ;   P7  :L  51  L?  A   6P  AJ  XV  OO  2)  9;  3O
EH  "?  +C  FO  47  =8  ,X  5U  R   HB  :.  ."  A=  FH  Q1  K=  AV  UA  NJ  G   YT  =X  ,M  "F
YJ  D+  DZ  :2  9S  L:  4N  9M  )(  X   .O  ?Q  65  W,  ,A  G=  XN  (V  TO  LO  6K  KZ  8G  1O
7+  N(  OJ  TD  4;  V7  FA  VB  :7  Q   6?  VJ  T7  A1  .=  LO  TW  =Z  ,O  1J  Y:  G!  1.  7T
TC  XE  73  =C  L1  )Y  GP  6;  2(  .R  ?S  ?C  Q"  WL  1A  T(  (G  4B  -   R3  MM  ?;  UY  ;F
UF  GO  E   "(  25  GY  ;"  TB  "1  AM  KI  VM  W:  SC  KN  5.  )"  E;  R   95  ?H  "U  XT  V+
D,  -R  NK  J8  X,  WE  (3  N6  WS  99  8   2R  :;  7F  TF  )E  4U  57  XH  )H  H2  ?+J  3Z  ,U
3;  F.  +O  2:  3-  9Y  P   IQ  =N  =1  O:  6C  OT  7B  U?  WJ  3G  8D  GC  "C  NO  R,  B2  .P
,F  EY  N1  J,  P5  T3  M9  YC  23  G3  +G  G;  S7  ?B  .Y  -J  X;  4=  7,  ,?  ZP  8K  .O  BF
N5  8N  "V  Q(  X7  E)  BC  OY  (=  K7  9P  14  ;U  (D  DH  6   2B  FF  OE  ,G  ;G  J.  7U  6B
K9  O   40  YO  J9  89  ?   -A  6.  .,  BY  T1  6F  7-  ;M  "G  1D  (A  =3  M?  9B  -T  )B  .,
-6  M)  84  :G  (2  2,  DP  Q   9,  O=  H7  ZH  C,  DO  2?  FZ  MZ  YV  VI  ;C  OR  G?  2B  B3
XU  E2  ..  GE  JN  21  =-  2O  6G  +X  4T  7R  69  PZ  F9  IY  P=  -G  9O  LN  IC  -H  +?  B?
M+  1   "6  BZ  .D  -5  C3  UD  C?  OV  AH  UQ  B(  U2  ",  M8  )1  F?  L   A3  9:  6"  PN  V4
?1  (O  J-  H1  Q:  5Y  IP  X)  F2  YN  H4  HW  P:  CN  WM  F+  3T  :X  3V  ))  T4  5L  3F  S?
3Y  66  Y"  CW  NI  Y4  9E  NF  ,4  Y7  =;  +I  6,  ?V  K3  8J  E+  LV  8=  O)  (T  O-  Z"  2D
TQ  L4  MO  T5  OW  ;(  2=  2S  29  7H  H8  ;1  V1  ?B  :D  ;8  ;-  JG  -2  3U  :1  P8  (F  36
H-  L   IU  TI  JL  4:  5K  J;  -X  5W  ?U  ("  96  L5  Q;  SK  -Z  HK  Y6  Y;  HQ  Q.  Z1  34
U9  6Z  UV  1-  G1  "7  1X  JX  U-  VS  VO  AE  ZP  (Q  "+  I8  (,  5R  O3  X:  N7  QW  M;  ;?
H9  JH  LM  A+  :H  O8  ;V  3=  =S  G8  CA  OF  LW  KV  ML  4J  GI  35  OC  YX  OG  :6  .I  M
SG  I?  -:  GK  V9  U=  :+  H,  A9  U6  XP  (.  AS  P8  83  G)  -)  ((  IR  33  19  ZX  )X  ,O
"X  O9  TN  Y5  ;Q  (B  ,J  U:  ST  QL  2G  N=  TJ  PQ  H+  CX      SY  ,+  K8  ,)  ME  ?6  HO
,Y  I   XL  KT  Z=  .V  8L  YM  PU  8;  K4  B   Z+  QO  +,  BK  6V  7.  UW  :-  CI  6   )Q  A-
W-  W;  II  6-  VP  8Y  3"  -B  NA  E(  :O  M.  ZF  16  79  F-  VT  4   OC  ZB  ;A  .+  JD  75
Q5  P-  QU  F   YK  8E  HN  VV  :P  GZ  =4  7;  2;  ?=  O+  ;H  6O  6U  ,L  3,  5I  CB  ++  V?
I   DK  I4  BG  1?  K(  Z   :J  )O  RP  CO  D=  5D  RE  RD  =K  JQ  EW  DR  )J  ZA  FX  NQ  9C
T6  +V  CC  -F  ?D  T)  (C  71  1N  S-  9I  Z8  O   T   G.  T9  O1  MK  MW  :4  .A  1=  .)  5F
RZ  W6  UT  JA  T7  US  UU  D7  YB  VP  4H  XY  B,  Q,  O7  PB  3N  ,S  3Q  )Z  U8  BD  H"  WO
3D  +-  ??  ZG  ;;  KJ  XZ  BQ  2V  9D  ;3  7D  I=  -Y  "Z  O3  8"  I7  VW  Y(  K;  4P  7:  1H
4G  BI  56  Z(  L)  =2  ,N  =)  ,R  37  4I  (6  BW  Q-  AN  9A  QO  .;  +K  77  OU  ;2  K,  T9
PM  HG  FW  Y   PA  CF  5P  XB  A6  ?+  Q9  )D  +Y  -9  68  RB  +F  RC  )V  )-  :   +E  U+  8S
-"  2Q  (P  )A  UJ  DF  F:  WW  NH  +(  M:  +M  CQ  4E  K6  .F  7)  W)  6F  H2  (5  "I  S2  QF
=   OO  TO  F   4A  JI  )4  9L  ,8  B2  -N  WG  TV  =U  ,5  OS  4F  ON  LK  EQ  (T  C;  +P  FL
W4  +4  BF  DL  T2  U;  3+  6M  H(  F?  ?O  OG  RK  F1  N3  O5  2L  HA  (H  -.  .L  B.  LH  -,
7B  6H  WV  UK  46  ZJ  -;  =F  =H  "5  (L  SB  3:  -(  RT  XJ  7W  "   YW  6W  15  T+  N-  WX
VE  ,V  TD  S3  :W  KK  ""  LA  T   5?  M(  9+  GU  H5  2Z  VX  -7  G9  3   GF  ON  55  NN  WN
CO  K)  YA  YE  :Q  :F  QB  9W  +9  :E  H   G   ZI  5T  24  HS  48  LT  W   ?9  S4  ET  J)  27
RM  H3  =A  P.  :C  BB  =L  XD  J3  YQ  H;  ,7.1Z  P+  3)  NL  QQ  EG  ,=  RS  +7  =B  ?X  YP
CK  =I  5:  1B  12  ".  ?G  F6  MS  OF  IO  6L  MJ  ,H  17  8O  S"  G5  1(  (Z  AW  UO  P2  XO
```

Figure 20.3 (cont'd)

```
DO I=1 TO 48;
DO J=1 TO 48;
K=I+J; IF K>48 THEN K=K-48;
X(I,J,1)=I; X(I,J,2)=MOD((I+J),48);
END;END;
DO K=1 TO 48;
DO I=1 TO 48;
CALL RANDOM(S1,R); J=CEIL(R*48);
L=X(J,K,*); X(J,K,*)=X(I,K,*); X(I,K,*)=L;
END;END;
DO K=1 TO 48;
DO I=1 TO 48;
CALL RANDOM(S2,R); J=CEIL(R*48);
L=X(K,J,*); X(K,J,*)=X(K,I,*); X(K,I,*)=L;
END;END;
DO I=1 TO 48;
DO J=1 TO 48;
ENCODE(I,J)=SUBSTR(KEY,X(I,J,1),1)||SUBSTR(KEY,X(I,J,2),1);
DECODE(X(I,J,1),X(I,J,2))=SUBSTR(ALPH,I,1)||SUBSTR(ALPH,J,1);
END;END;
```

The following enciphering and deciphering routines employ the tables so formed. Using the tables, the enciphering and deciphering operations are fairly short:

Enciphering Routine:

```
GET EDIT (TEXT)(A(48));
DO K=1 TO 48 BY 2;
I=INDEX(ALPH,SUBSTR(TEXT,K,1));
J=INDEX(ALPH,SUBSTR(TEXT,K+1,1));
SUBSTR(MESS,K,2)=ENCODE(I,J);
END;
```

Deciphering Routine:

```
DO K=1 TO 48 BY 2;
I=INDEX(KEY,SUBSTR(MESS,K,1));
J=INDEX(KEY,SUBSTR(MESS,K+1,1));
SUBSTR(TEXT,K,2)=DECODE(I,J);
END;
PUT EDIT (TEXT)(A(48));
```

The complete programs are Programs 2A and 2B in Appendix A.

The cryptanalyst may now look for common letter pairs, such as TH, ST, OR, and so on. We can stop this by pairing *nonadjacent* characters and encoding them. In the following variation of the preceding example the characters are paired in an arbitrary sequence that depends both upon the key *and* upon a random-number generator:

Preliminary Routine:

```
DCL N(48)
DO K=1 TO 48;
N(K)=INDEX(KEY,SUBSTR(ALPH,K,1));
CALL RANDOM(S3,R); J=CEIL(R*48);
N1=N(J); N(J)=N(I); N(I)=N1;
END;
```

Enciphering Routine:

```
GET EDIT (TEXT)(A(48));
DO K=1 TO 48 BY 2;
I=INDEX(ALPH,SUBSTR(TEXT,N(K),1));
J=INDEX(ALPH,SUBSTR(TEXT,N(K+1),1));
SUBSTR(MESS,K,2)=ENCODE(I,J);
END;
```

Deciphering Routine:

```
DO K=1 TO 48 BY 2;
I=INDEX(KEY,SUBSTR(MESS,K,1));
J=INDEX(KEY,SUBSTR(MESS,K+1,1));
SUBSTR(TEXT,N(K),1)=SUBSTR(DECODE(I,J),1,1);
SUBSTR(TEXT,N(K+1),1)=SUBSTR(DECODE(I,J),2,1);
END;
PUT EDIT (TEXT)(A(48));
```

The preliminary routine sets up a table $N(K)$ that determines which positions each character to be paired will be selected from. A would-be-intruder having a knowledge of the program cannot determine the character sequence without having the key. A person possessing the key cannot determine the character sequence without a knowledge of the program and its random-number generater.

A clue may be provided the cryptanalyst by blank sections in the text. The table in Fig. 20.2 encodes a pair of blanks as "3O". This clue may be removed by substituting random characters for all strings of blanks. Thus,

```
DO K=1 TO 48 BY 2;
IF SUBSTR(TEXT,K,2)='  ' THEN DO;
CALL RANDOM(S1,R); I=CEIL(R*48);
CALL RANDOM(S2,R); J=CEIL(R*48);
SUBSTR(TEXT,K,2)=ENCODE(I,J);
END;END;
```

Program 3A in Appendix A employs the above enciphering technique. The spaces between and after the words in the deciphered text are still clear, but strings of blanks appear as meaningless jumbles of characters.

Blanks are still dangerous because a blank is the most common "character" in text, and the blanks can give away the lengths of words. For this reason, characters paired with blanks may be translated into multiple different pairs so that the blanks cannot be found with a frequency count.

COMPARING ENCIPHERED AND NONENCIPHERED TEXT

Usually, the most powerful shortcut the cryptanalyst can take is to obtain a segment of text in both its enciphered and nonenciphered form. Comparing the two, especially with the aid of a computer, will tell him much about the enciphering process, and reduce his work factor to a fraction of what it would otherwise be. When the secret Pentagon papers on the Vietnam War were stolen and published in the *New York Times* in 1971, the U.S. Government protested to the *Times* that the publication would give foreign governments knowledge of cryptographic codes because they could compare old diplomatic messages published in the *Times* with their enciphered originals. Three types of protection must *all* be used against cryptanalysts seeking to compare enciphered and nonenciphered text:

1. Efforts must be made to prevent a "clear" version of data that have been enciphered becoming available. Data that have been made available should not subsequently be enciphered.

2. When there is a danger of an intruder comparing data enciphered and nonenciphered, the enciphering method should be designed so that both the program and the key used can be changed frequently.

3. The enciphering method should be sufficiently complex that even if the intruder does have a sample of the results it gives he will still not be able to establish a deciphering method. The same word or phrase in the text should produce different ciphers at different times.

TO AVOID
REPETITIVE
ENCODING

To protect against the comparing of clear and enciphered text, the enciphering method may be designed so that an identical segment of text produces different codes at different times. There are many ways of doing this. A serial number may be worked into the randomizing algorithm or into the mechanism for constructing the ENCODE and DECODE tables. A number giving the date and time of origination may be sent with the message, and this may be employed in encoding and decoding.

The previous enciphering routine always produces the same code for the same line of 48 characters of text. This repetition could be avoided by selecting the character pairs to be encoded differently for each line. The enciphering routine in Fig. 20.4 uses a two-dimensional table, $N(a, b)$, for selecting the characters to be encoded. The character pairs to be encoded with the ENCODE table of Fig. 20.2 are the $N(K, M)$th character and the $N(K + 1, M)$th character, where K is the number of the character in sequence within a line of 48 characters, and M is the number of the line in sequence with a block of 48 lines. The $N(a, b)$ table is developed in the preliminary routine along with the ENCODE and DECODE tables. The encoding process takes no longer than in the previous example. The complete programs are 4A and 4B in Appendix A.

It is sometimes desirable to have a block of code self-contained, as in this example, so that it can be decoded without any other external variables, such as serial number or time. However, if a changing external variable were worked into the enciphering, breaking the code could be more difficult. The attacker might use a technique such as introducing transmission errors so that he obtained two or more different messages containing identical text.

The routine in Fig. 20.4 is probably secure enough for most commerical purposes, especially if the seeds in the program, S1, S2, and S3, are changed frequently, and the key is changed frequently. The lines of code that generate random numbers may also be changed. If the data have extremely high value for a long time, such as oil-drilling results, the program should not be used without additional forms of protection.

A CHALLENGE
FOR THE READER

Figure 20.5 contains a passage from Shakespeare (of some relevance) enciphered with the routine in Fig. 20.4. The reader who is interested in cryptography is challenged to try and decipher it. Nobody has succeeded *yet*! The deciphering routine is given in Appendix A, Program 4. The key was changed. The enciphered code in Fig. 20.5 is long enough to attack with statistical methods.

```
(NOFIXEDOVERFLOW):LPC:PROC OPTIONS(MAIN);
ON ENDFILE (SYSIN) GO TO FIN;
DCL(S1,S2,S3,R) FIXED BINARY(31,0);
DCL (TEXT,MESS,ALPH,KEY) CHAR(48);
DCL (ENCODE,DECODE)(48,48) CHAR(2);
DCL L(2);
DCL N(48,48);
DCL X(48,48,2) FIXED BINARY;

/*** SET UP ENCIPHERING TABLES *********************************************/
    S1=23518967;
    S2=50173031;
    S3=72735419;
  KEY=
   'NY+BTGV FCED18WS:)X564AQZ,.-OLDPIKJM=U9732?"(;HR';
  ALPH=
   'ABCDEFGHIJKLMNOPQRSTUVWXYZ1234567890-.,)(:;"=+ ?';
    DO I=1 TO 48;
    N(I,*)=INDEX(KEY,SUBSTR(ALPH,I,1));
    DO J=1 TO 48;
    X(I,J,1)=I; X(I,J,2)=MOD((I+J),48);
    END;END;
    DO K=1 TO 48;
    DO I=1 TO 48;
    R=MOD(S1,66103)/66103; S1=S1+312754**(R+1);
    J=CEIL(R*48);
    N1=N(J,K); N(J,K)=N(I,K); N(I,K)=N1;
    J=CEIL(MOD(S2,73937)/1541.1); S2=S2+J*121767;
    L=X(J,K,*); X(J,K,*)=X(I,K,*); X(I,K,*)=L;
    END;END;
    DO K=1 TO 48;
    DO I=1 TO 48;
    J=CEIL(MOD(S3,38692)/806.1); S3=S3+J*513778;
    L=X(K,J,*); X(K,J,*)=X(K,I,*); X(K,I,*)=L;
    END;END;
    DO I=1 TO 48;
    DO J=1 TO 48;
    ENCODE(I,J)=SUBSTR(KEY,X(I,J,1),1)||SUBSTR(KEY,X(I,J,2),1);
    DECODE(X(I,J,1),X(I,J,2))=SUBSTR(ALPH,I,1)||SUBSTR(ALPH,J,1);
    END;END;

/*** ENCIPHERING ROUTINE ***************************************************/
  A1:DO M=1 TO 48;
    GET EDIT (TEXT)(A(48));
    DO K=1 TO 48 BY 2;
    I=INDEX(ALPH,SUBSTR(TEXT,N(K,M),1));
    J=INDEX(ALPH,SUBSTR(TEXT,N(K+1,M),1));
    SUBSTR(MESS,K,2)=ENCODE(I,J);
    END;
    PUT EDIT (MESS)(SKIP,A(48));
    GO TO A1;
```

Figure 20.4. A fast enciphering routine that produces the code shown in Fig. 20.5. The equivalent deciphering routine is in Program 4B in Appendix A. It could be made more secure by encoding larger blocks, increasing the complexity of the ENCODE and DECODE tables, using three-dimensional tables, randomizing the output, and incorporating a number into the randomizing algorithms that is different for each transmission.

```
OUKIMIWFG+G94L5IUAD81JBAWG9=Q.H745MLFP14IY7):RI:
2OS"4LI+H6S9NKILILO.=B:=Q"511JWVJBWF,TP27L1SMSM+
4JW)4L5F1CF"LG-YP?BMW)MLB6F(O=P24LJO+FGOO85=KID:
:XT O:-?WVWB?E1BGL-QLYLG5Z"::3B(VBKWFBAAB=7D:-V
ZI.=WGI8=7FPKIO3:OWGB.IBKI51KII4(LWFWFCCGOBAB(,:
SB8B1JW)8PO:I.="WF4O;P?E12I,H F-B;H3M4BA=7HXP71O
7B864LAXFQ75;HWF,:I=-QO8BOZ3B(4VG5,TI84VCOHE9YIG
O84LJB2H(V)SMAG=55B6FPOOIG+IML(ZSCAB-VWFJY14-4AZ
BAWVW2=BODG=,:1J=.WFOF092UUS)2;.4L-VJJQ:OILO1(I
:8WFB6BAO9I,BAO=U34L)R12SZW)IIBVBQ1OWF5=+ S7G=?E
Q+OHJJS"TD.FB)14GV,"B)-4KTSB,:,TILW 18:R.OG4)NIG
H 7+MOH3S"HZW2)5M=(V)E=+USZI-Y=O6)-?:RZIS"5?UC82
GD1JTD(;WVDG-LML::PO-4?EOUK3FA:R-?O6)SW2BDIGU9FW
I Q.?EZH-F1JBKW2)E7+:EILCYWF4 W)OOO==Q:OQSH6I)WN
Q2L1IL1,2=O8WV=Q-77:I,=OS"I 4ZQ:DYHSEW-?Q?1J)=2W
.OM+NB4G,:4LW2HZZI=Z1JZII,4JFQ)EE.O1TDWF4:+(:=Q.
H3-?;HFJ7:Z88:1J-L4 BX51WVLB?E;HM+BO1CI4D:WFI+8B
KIMY=7-?-?)NMA1J89GQFWO8KIOKBAWG7SP??E?EI-WV?(?E
W2 IWH4AS2O7:XE.7MWFAB O-YKI++)2="-?FWJBWF=Z9==7
IL1J,NH+H.ZZ4FABIL=.WF4L(84JW2?EC,WFQ.Q?,X.OFQT(
::WF1JB 9LO")-G=1+WI-4ODRI=7-XJO7QWFHJBOBXP)BA)K
?EWVWFIG XO=;1M+CJ="HX7LCY+IO6:OFPWFI6EC7M X.OOD
W )R-?WFOAD.SZ:8EP)N=O.)I4,TO6MLWFMA:=IG=OL4Y+1O
ILI+55QSS91C,TEP.F OILAZ+BB(,TIC;.:OS"11S)IG,NFQ
BOHFYAS"SBBA-4SNW)14WF.JMY+BCO4LG:M+O=OM:EGC,:IG
NOCD2O-X4L2?C4IGB +(-=+(Y,WGD:B HOOU-4W6:O4LW2PF
F-ILI6FQI 82KIHEO6Q.C8)B-?WFOUZ3:X)K,:-?NGOM4?OI
)R82-Y,:(8GCF(WGD56)HS1J)?,"L=O7;:FQ8BU.7ZO1BA14
CNODIGBAFAZ )RC8(V1C)?=O7MB6W):R51;P7GW2S98I+(W
WO)E=?,:::M=O9Z3:=OP-?1C+Y4:-;N-SZ-?=?C8I W2-?WF
G5WFJO)Z12O55?H ?EU?LGU"Z5P7I,Z3Z;W24LWOO?O?=ZC+
4LS9-4O8W2I+CMJOBXBM.=B2WFHSZ,PS)RO4M+O=OU.=)EI4
GP-V4L8BSB:O19Q"MYO.WFO4U3M+4F.9BKHSKH8BIG-?C(Q4
.)-?-L:OT3O5WB8B3GQ:="W2Y,FWL, "WF1OS"B8ZK-L14NJ
OHQ;PC,(OWI(-4 BAE.O=EC::FH-Y+BFHIGH?97)E.=W2I3
)EIG:OW)4ZFP-?(+:XBA?EBX45BAO?-L?EH?OUJ,ILL,IYWF
O6U9+OPSFQKIT4IL I8=BIL8:O5WFO=:O:8CYUXWVL,=CQ1WF
IG1L12G5)B+FKI4 ,TK3IGBA="=7I6O"KI4IIGM?WV,"=B9S
FWB6C:F"BAPEQU-XBAIL11MIFPTE6OM+:OQSILWFWF14)F1O
-FLCL+WFTOUXFPWFHXL=SBO6WOUBHQ4L-WI,9=BDL=?E,:CN
MYI6AV:RWFOP1C4LO8UA.FIB+ BXQM;:?E2?WF(-;EWVILOV
:YC8GDWF5ZDYS76)WVCM9=-W6)IG1JML4LI6WF;8I :YF6OD
SB-SHZZI:R:XV5UK?FS9O9W)82F(11KISC-YEC55PFYA5F-?
WFL4CNJOWGOU="FPSZ:=WHQFI8-LP9B8H3BKO?Q?2O XW IG
)-WVJOL,AOFKU6PG=QQUWFODNBCDIG7G5YWVLU---45F;:1J
JBCMW)B6HZHZ8"1OI,BA4OIGI)B.:OH3MNMSS"WFI6TEI+J,
4VMSB6?EO.T(KIFWFP9=G4L4-451)?O9WF?E1J=QS")WWG=A
NVI,ILO?WF=QZ;QFFKBOS"SB,:LC.Q124LAY())EKI?EFQWV
```

Figure 20.5. A challenge for cryptoanalysts. The code shown is a passage from Shakespeare enciphered with the routine in Fig. 20.4 (with its key changed). The deciphering program is Program 4B in Appendix A. Programs such as these encipher and decipher quickly, are easy to use, and are safe enough for most commercial purposes. They would not be adequate for high-level military security. The reader who is interested in cryptography is challenged to decipher this passage from Shakespeare.

```
CDWF1J,TGDSB(ZO:+I9G-?;4WFQ?Z;G:75BMGO=Q)RO+89L4
MLZCWVO604+D:OIHGD,:MYO.B8WF)-WFW)8B;PH ,MFP9X89
O6B4-YIL5?CPMIM=;4-4H6B6OMGVI O4IG1CWFG+=BQS8B(Z
)NFH-JW2:OWVGO?E=O:RBH);4LFAUL82O8Q3,:BAO4Q:C)5F
S"7M+(JO)RCMIHOZJYSB1JL=Z5I,OH Y,TSO-?KI;:-?CKAB
O=7+WFPRMLG9WF84;HECC8::ILW))W4LQ::814+F8MP7FJIG
?E1JIBZ BA="8ICMZNS"HS4L=7PSSB2?AB1,-F:OM+Q:,T)Q
829:0?55"-IG(-?EIB1S1C,TWVSB:8H O=S"3XML1+)R-YJO
4ABAI61J;655SZU3B=D?MST.MS6)+BH3S"="(Z1LOT4LIG"-
9X;QML,THSF"?EP7FKW =QIL:ONBW (D+(WF;4FWI1?EZ;O4
I4I.?E="3XS"3XHS1J-4MY-9O8B IGBXU37O)GOD4 U)?E+
1N)EKI(DB6P74Z)CWFLC4L=;L4D:HJWF6)S9S"BDB(I=BDJY
)E:=KI-?FQFK8PSOI,UC8BB TB7ZHSZ IGK3K3WVC)FH-7Z
-451H311W WFLC)-(DW)P94:CMS2H71OW2B(WFMOL=S=L16)
Q3NW)R7=CM-?Q2W W2L1ZUW =QY,-LILT84S1JS2=Q(F3X8I
8BHG1J)ZJYQ"I 4LWFPQ4LWFGVML)-J"MLQUFWBX7LJ,SZFH
7NWO)-K3:X1,(DC8CPKIJ,G414,TS"O=WFB6WOFW7Z1.1S=O
NJILR(T9B(1JSR1J1CJYO=P?(DYAGVL4WF,:UXF?1JF6EPS"
OLI OD-YPSS2O8HZZ88B(V=AM+FW7Y1JR6WV-V(Z-YQ?4V:B
E.:O,:Q?4ZH+W2Y+:=)BOL=B1J-VWFCM8BB ?EZ;B6LCIG(V
WFIB(VS"OGHE4L5FKIO?U"8BZ,O?O6Z,IL X45:XM+)-O4BO
M=?E-4.OMRZIPS1N7+G:ZK=ZH2W)14Z+WV?ECMPF)W+USBW
J"PE82BA=?-4HM,:GLG+514L?ES2H6FP5D.OW)U"IGL+42S2
JQRI-L.)B6:O)EL1PS4 MIM+FWP7BA,:.JBH+UIGU6lJ-4LY
IGHQG1IGIGHMP72JQSILUAW2H6(DWOFJ8R;M;PPCH3IL1J55
TD2YO=-?-7-?Q?QE1J7U1JMOWFMOYA?E)5O4W 6)="GZ-?O6
B9-FOG)==OFP8B;.)C4LBCWFF7WF(VCMO6BAC+ASNJT SB8I
WF4LGLR2ILO6HEWOABJOCMB;LG:4P9,:U3H.,:EWMSS"BX?E
Z8EX)EK3C=F7WX1J;H-QZ;9A,:K3WVJ)UXP)14-WS9S2IR?E
MI+(,TFPG4=QM=OULY)K931,T(1J+Q4MR2WBIG-YILU9L4:1
BABCM==82J-?TGW FW=Q;.,:)?C297)28:+IOUD9MRHSW22?
BAUSQSFW=ZP6C:LC1JIGFW8:FP1EWO2O,:MIKII WF77O=4L
W2.F9YG1D:PS-QSRFW971SLU5PC8RAS9(D9LMO4LWFU6W28B
PS-QKIHECWZO1JWI1,8R82(D.OS7GDWVB6D8:7I41OK3YWWG
WV,TFWK3(Z="IN=QO:I 7)8:+UO92?FDW I:W)BXCO(VA81J
:7BX4Z)=JOZ5WV+Q-?F.I8-4M;H3O?O8:N3?,:72?(11LY+:
Δ J,:OMYWFW)M=Z3,:7QCJ:ETOAQGQLU?EJR1LBMO7O:=",:
="BA-?JPBAW)1.RX4VBAIG?EHX42WVHGO?Q?CM()KIGIS9Y,
W2R+F7SBBX;P51MRS"MLHG1J-Y1OMNI=LC+FB )WS"WV)ENJ
CY8RO9,"W)4J=OI+BAPE+UM+HGWFNJ-?B )2LJ::WO OZ,BX
WFODWFFQL+ILF9Q34FSZ=7RHWFG2OLQSWFMLIGT 514L,:BH
12)R=QHSCN-?OOJ,-45ZFW)EN-CM-LI6B-MO=ZW2.Q1JIBQF
BOL4:OJO-?(),:KIMLZOWFI EWQS,:5F7Q"-::B(-4S"SB4L
1JWIIG9G"-6DMSQ?:OQ.+FW)?E=Z.)(-W BHB8O?I,FT?EIL
:O-J1C-?(P1,)5WOPFMYW)C8SB77ILU1O?FJO:IB2OB655F3
Δ QU7QWVSB(V14O5O1(?WFDJIGSBO?=Z8214J,(F4V=;+ )T
WFWF9=KI9:H2FPDJHE4L-QT S"4L)?J,1J(ZWFO9(ZOP+N:8
IGJYIB-FYΔ+I1JILH6S"WFC2WVOMO?VAY,F(=ΔWV.9":B BL
```

Figure 20.5 (cont'd)

```
PS84MRWFFABOUWB LC)-L+W2H6M(JYH GQ9=WFSB=Q-L4JW)
O=QU:8IL1,OH554L;HW H FJ4LF(4LW2OJ8214Q.S9JFSB--
SBG=W2(VIL7Q-92JT)WGBAWVB6=Z5FGMO87MC)-?IG1O-4-?
W2:OBA77DJLY;PNBL4LGGVWFWFBMIN829=550?Z5:74L?(9:
.=(DV71S4LI,-VQ?);W2MRTDWFFW:=HF1,WFC2HZ-L7+4LQU
-?7):=IL51ZCOOCNBA118BA81JW2;?1JU3Q.C+Z4W2:OFHLC
W 9GHS75,N7UONI.:E-4085Y1S(DY,Q+NK)NW2WF)2+S=?1,
AK14ILDJ3?H .OK3Z1+(QS(FOU1AQ3Z51BS"H682-W-LI-BK
Z3MYSB-WWG=73QON?E-4RT4L45FWHX8BO?-=Z3HSH?7M8B4L
(-BLU3QU+YB(WV)RI6SBHE-4KI?EU3O:1J=B4WHO1C(Z-?,T
1JG+GI;HAO82IBQ.7 ML4ZY,82Q?,:WFCY4L?ELU+(NBL=.O
ODILWF1JKIWH-JI,Q.FPC)B.ODG+C=S"DJ)EB9="OTWFBXQ.
FDCCZ1Z,?E1,-?QSI:QUIGB9SB-?9X4L)=4C-70?08?EETNJ
(V;7W28BHJILPF:X8DO7C,:=:=ILG HO-YN-HQ+IZ3SBJO-V
MOS"EC-HB6FWWV1NB(Q?D:FK="IG2?HG=;HQWVKLH311C=ZB
84H682WFL=AZZI(ZFW9=JY1S+:-4?EFQ82BA7Q(F4LWOOM?E
+I(-L3WVWV::G+MY4GB4L=72W)OOBAM+U3FPO3:XO?4LJOB6
1JO=)?DJ)3JOOGRX82PEFWGC;6U)BX:ROD,:I4;11JBKM=BD
S914,"(D6=:XW))WWFIGJ";ZIG4LWFPF1C-41BHS)NOTQ")-
L=)5+IGAP6MTB6G=D:1JMYWF,TW2(??EF?-=CMILHM8BAY51
ILA.8:C2FJ1S-X1JSOQWC:CM?E:RPGW)S9.Q7LO8BK4L4LIL
(P)R1JILZI8BB)L114O8:=MOMLJ"OI?E4HGD1,I8O=WFKIZ"
S9W2HONB2Y:0047OM=B ILWO8BQ,1J;()-M= X550H-YAB;M
FWO6WOWF83MYIL,TI,-QWGIBP2F.,:E94L)2WFF-FW(V-?KI
?EGO1OMLHMH6JCBA82.OH+0?HZ-4CJB6H6B 1J-?)=,NI-C,
2=B6W2M+BA7:I6(ZO84L X77FPB6,MEC(-WFO?=Z4 BOKIEC
WF5F?E?E(I:G?EUX(-O?(-7ZMOS2GO::,:U"CMZIF3WFC+P?
(+8BAQBOC"83QWH6OVQ.WF)BW)N,WF-WHF51C4,TS2)-,:PE
O8WFWFI81JZIQUC"HEWF,:G:-LHZ5?8:2?;M4Z;ZI-Y,(DWF
,:JY:8(-77ILWF+(SBB6-YG )27L+NMRBKU6WF(FN,:=2=I+
AXKI(V:OWO5ZUXY,JOC=WVQ?O4W)4FF2W?8B)?-?Q:82U1;P
O7WI-QWB72,:724JWK75IL GBK-??E"T-?(Z+ISZ-4OUW21J
O6:RG ?EW)4:RIS"BCWVUX-LB ODBA=7F( ":OQSH ;.)K:O
O?UC=QK3(-WF-XAOIGWFBM=ONBW)URH3O=F?MOCNU3:84IBX
QFHZ4AUXWI;HWVGDWF9:O8H 4V6)DJRAWF1J=7O"-Y-7BMI+
WFZO4LU1-?1J,;ZIFWL4BA4:UC-3QU=Q-Y2OO?IGQ:HGBDF3
=BFWC(.=ZMT =ZWVK3W)BA?E-Q)5,:COCYF5CY-4L1)-SBBO
9GWG-LW)WFWF2A9S-OFP GN?BO.61,20WV=QWFHZWV+NS"EW
WF2OWF;QHS89BXNJ4HQRLJWF4IFJ O4VWVWB=B-4WF=O7:OA
Q?2=-JSB4LC8KIJY:87;,:7QBKNRDY,T9AC=,TS78:(-K3W)
2YJ,WV9B GEW-JWO-7H B H3KIFT1282?EW2W)K3B(BKMY-?
L4WV1C?EPF)59G4VWFH CM-?Z+I.KI:OA8COW)BD1CGMIL)E
7:-YJB4 141SOI20BX)C4LQU104 SBKIC4S"R+G2HJMYMNWV
MY-4I44L1+QF97TE8BS"W ;6 IS"-Q9742L=O89XCM)EZ8M=
OAD;?EIG+,L1C+WF?EA9FA,T2OWFO?=OFWFWGV,:)=;1PGB6
8BBALG=B,"ABUXCJIG1S(DWF42CKIG8BGD:=IGIG-QZ5BAIB
5FHZB6B 827:I4Z3IG1,-7W))EWV12CCILOIMI4LW2M?C,S"
IB-L?EWF=OWOB(TYM+M+OMM=-?141J7LFW:8CO,::R(GWFCN
```

Figure 20.5 (cont'd)

```
+IO"WG-?Q+O=;L:O.O9GJOI8BOG O.4L)Z-4=Z4L)Z?EKIWB
R6,IC::XG4?FOI14?EFH?EHEWF-?Z3S34M)211SZQU-JSZ2=
)-G-.=-40OF(;QBH1,S2T(ZEBAA)(DW)SBFQ;6ILI6Q.O8BK
ILOT(GS9W2B6OY7GAYWFC,GPM(MYWVW2)BQ2H Q?Z5GJQFIL
ILZ3.JIG1J55CC:O82W)WGO?SB14-J7)KHOIB(K36)WFMAAG
S2KI;M8B5FFW4O75H6(PWF7P7Y1OZI?EIL:OMIFYWF()SZ1J
QSO?)ZPSG ?E1,;4-QB6=OQ:JY4VWFW)WB4LFA1.C=4LBAQ(
-Y=?QSM+BCO=S"1JO:MSWVO6SB="IG?EEC-1MOL1WGPCOU=O
IB-?MRS"F(8=CMHXWFB(L,G-C 72?EGCFW7 HF?EKI,TCM)E
Z3-?WFWF-4I,?EZRP71JML-?I:ZF-O;4CM)EQ.JOO:DJ2H4F
X:8BI)WFW2CPUUFPL4BMI,S2HX10B K3C2WO5?-4JOQ.ILB6
NB9=JO)E(VL4WFY,B)KI(-5FW2H3C,?EP7KI)-5142(ZH 3Q
+IGJWFQRO4(V.,U3FJBALC12P7Y,)2FH-4AZWFIHBAW)CM7Z
Z+-LHZ)=1ODJ4Z1C1JSBB2BKSB12H6SBQ?ML4 ?EB7HQW)4W
,:J,OD-?9H=OFW5F51SBH3H ZHILFT?EB6WFFPHJFWZ1H+IL
4PQUC=82LGZ34FJOO:Z8="O?Q,8BKIZI4FO+4 W)7+IB1JIG
S"BA4LH ODIAI=HO="2?FK4ZBAW2WV2012--G4:XMO1J.O4L
NJ(8I JYB(BAO=S"14W C89O1C9A(V:RW412WFWF8B84G+4L
BKWBU9Q:8X;QB )RKI)=BH4ZW24OSBWB1,-L9GIL OMABO)W
1H-?B67+IG4M-YO614IB(-IL(ZZ ,T(Z=OCMSBWF1,CMC)3X
WFRI8IQ"KIJOMR=B4LI+8U1JW2WVCJKI(O X;(4LO6SZ=7BM
WIOI+US9BK1JS91O1GFK?E+(GC-?P7U3)=;HI B;W2(VB6SB
B 8"KI7MJOBOO?O?G+BA8.ZO1JIGHS+(;WF55B6:OT 4 H2
4LA9LGI,O?B MYU"S"IGMYB.WVO?HMHMCY82(VODQ:;1G44L
O4LC4?BAFJ2?W)1SIGOVW)I,LG.=14Z+OUG 5YC+NBC8M+K3
L14C=Q:X7:PF8BILABH 4OHGM+WFO4="J-;4WFWV-JI KIW2
ZII4S9-VM+G+UAWFMN2O,:A8BO;P-?HX-?)5V 10+(WF2?FV
(-8B8:L14L:OC8(ZZCHE?EQ.4L-?F2=QWFYA)WW2GOWICMWI
ZI=7-L,:LCFP3XOUU3)-FW=;(FH3IG:=8:EPC8?EIB)SBXO8
=ZB64VKI;PW)FPI+)?EWQRH PED:=OM=ILBX1HMO4AH6S"W)
WFLGMLMACMFJLY7LODJU;1-?9H)EWVWKSB?E?EPO7M1J1JA9
MIGLB WF8:BMC2?FKIO8W2IG4LC"55+BF?WOG2=O1,8P)5L1
7QP7BA.OH68BWFS"BL(VWF2O+(L1SOO8W)C)QFB6IGMO42S7
SBHFF?3L18Q?WFB6J,IG4L);U9B ILL47L9G:OO.W).OKIOL
WVWFMLFA+FQ.-Q=BL=4Z1JWOWF=;I WV9SLGKIMAO4L=55IB
S"4L4LO8M5)WW)N BOB6BMPB7Z;1C814:N-LQ.82-4X:OD1J
O5=EJOL=WFUSI+?E-4H6CNUC4VWV8BWFL4KI=O(ZHX;H-?I-
IGP)O=NJ(--1OD+O:8O1D;WF1JL4?E IILS2O?12WF":8"KI
7L1JF(JOM4O?RKG=C+?E,TB7Q382.J-JHZCMHS=OWFHSO4BW
IB1OLGABI61LP7,NWFO.Z3=BOGO?WFH J)WFL+Z Q"MAR2WF
)--YFRIG?E14OUH +(M(LCWVWF5FH6+N(V:=W)A9DJC8;:E.
7:SZ=7F(O614(DWF6)89IGIN:X-O;HU3Q"4ZSB?ESZ.=CMWF
-??ED:SB?EMLKN=QB)WFA.PFAB+I1CBXGI14QUU1QS)RIGO8
K3-V)ECNJYO5=XIGUXWH-JPCD:12OFHZ1J4L.FIG:OWKWV8B
C,WFL4GJF3+KK3,TN,B99SB(W2WF,TBXBLO=HTWFI,GP)=1C
1AHZWF)-OGRQ+(+F:OZ8(-?EL=O:AX824L=BOG1,Q.ECILJ,
OD.FIL4M-V+I)-CN(-YAU3UXT2-4+(7+(DA.=?Z,,:L4)R1S
4 =71+S7ZK)N-?OV-QC)B(ILWOWF4LHJ)E-?:8S)QU511,-=
```

Figure 20.5 (cont'd)

**ADDITIONAL
SECURITY**
Many other features could be added to such a program to enhance its security. Letters at the top and bottom of Fig. 20.1 could be substituted with unique letter pairs before enciphering. Additional randomizing processes could be added to the cipher produced.

The program uses a two-dimensional substitution table. We could equally well have used a three-dimensional table, which operates on three randomly chosen characters at a time. An N-dimensional table could have been used, which operates on groupings of N characters, although storage requirements rise rapidly with more than three dimensions.

The 48 characters in our key can be arranged in $48! = 1.24 \times 10^{61}$ different ways. Even if we only use 26 of them, there are $26! = 4.03 \times 10^{26}$ different groupings. However, if numeric information only is sent, it is desirable to shuffle the character sequence, include randomizing routines along with the table look-up operation, or have tables of more than two dimensions.

When alphabetic text is transmitted, the decipherer may have a method of searching for commonly used words. In data-processing systems we should avoid transmitting repetitive phrases. We must be careful not to give other clues, for example repetitive fields giving the same number or code, numbers with many zeros, or the encoding of blank characters, control characters, and so on. The decipherer will usually know where to look for control characters, and so all such characters (start of message, end of message, error responses, etc.) should be sent in clear.

There are an almost infinite number of methods for enciphering, given a computer or computer-like logic. In most cases on commercial systems the would-be intruder will not be an expert cryptoanalyst nor will he have massive computing facilities at his disposal for long periods of time. An ounce of protection may be worthwhile. The references at the end of this chapter contain a variety of enciphering techniques, but the reader should be cautious of any that were devised before the advent of fast computers.

Now that we have examined some specimen algorithms, let us summarize some principles.

PRINCIPLES WHEN
ENCIPHERING DATA

1. Assume that a would-be intruder may be able to steal the program or obtain knowledge of the algorithm used. Devise a form of encoding that is undecipherable even when the enemy knows the enciphering method.
2. Employ a key that can be changed at suitably frequent intervals.

3. Change the key sufficiently frequently that an intruder is unlikely to obtain it by computing methods, given that he has the enciphering method, even if he uses the fastest computers available.

4. Make the key sufficiently complex that it cannot be obtained by trial-and-error methods using the fastest computers.

5. Do not trust the persons to whom the key is given. Make the enciphering *program* sufficiently complex that a person possessing the key, but not the program, cannot make use of it even if he has access to the fastest computers.

6. Devise external security procedures such that no person gains access to both the key and the program.

7. Write the program so that it can easily be changed if its security is compromised, for example, by changing a pseudo-random-number generator or seed embedded in the program.

8. Do not use a key that might be guessed, for example, alphabetic words or numbers that have other meanings.

9. Process the messages being sent, before enciphering, so that no clues reside in the encoded message that will lessen the work needed in trial-and-error deciphering. For example, substitute random characters for blank fields; remove strings of zeros; change letters such as E, T, O, Q, Z, Y, J, and K in alphabetic text so that statistical letter counts cannot be used; substitute numbers or short codes for commonly used phrases; remove repetitively used words.

10. Avoid *conventional* techniques such as conventional random-number generators. The expert codebreaker will have less chance if unconventional or eccentric routines are used.

11. If known characters such as *end of record* or *end of transmission* are used, send these in clear (unenciphered).

12. Avoid transmitting obvious or repetitive messages of which the codebreaker can guess the meaning.

13. Assess the vulnerability from active wiretapping causing specific messages to be sent or repeated.

14. Assess the vulnerability from an intruder seeing the enciphered form of records of which he *already knows the contents.*

15. Assume that the intruder will be able to obtain some past text along with its enciphered form. This information should not enable him to discover the enciphering method in time for him to make use of his knowledge.

16. If the data enciphered are valuable to the enemy a long time in the future (as with oil-survey data), encipher them with the combination of a once-only key and a complex algorithm. Back up the enciphering with a high level of physical security.

17. A programmer or analyst devising an enciphering technique *must* be familiar with the methods the cryptanalyst will use in trying to break the cipher. (Read reference 11.) Programmers sometimes tend to think their algorithms are secure, when in fact they could be broken by an amateur cryptanalyst.

BIBLIOGRAPHY

1. C. E. Shannon, "The Communication Theory of Secrecy Systems," *Bell System Technical Journal*, Vol. 28 (Oct. 1949).

2. A. S. Vernam, "Cipher Printing Telegraph Systems for Secret Wire and Radio Telegraphic Communications," *Journal of the American Institute of Electrical Engineers*, Vol. 45, 109–115 (1926).

3. H. F. Gaines, *Cryptanalysis*, Dover Publications, Inc., New York, 1956.

4. M. Givierge, *"Cours de Cryptographie."* Berger-Levrault, Paris, 1925.

5. D. Kahn, *"The Codebreakers,"* The Macmillan Company, New York, 1967. A comprehensive history of secret communication. Informative, entertaining, and well worth reading.

6. R. O. Skatreid, "A Consideration of the Application of Cryptographic Techniques to Data Processing," Fall Joint Computer Conference 1969, AFIPS Press.

7. H. F. Friedman, *Military Cryptoanalysis*, War Department, Office of the Chief Signal Officer, Washington, D.C., U.S. Government Printing Office; series of papers from 1939 to 1943.

8. J. S. Galland, *An Historical and Analytical Bibliography of the Literature of Cryptography* (Northwestern University Series in the Humanities, No. 10), Northwestern University, Evanston, Ill., 1945.

9. General Luigi Sacco, *Manuel de Cryptographie* (translated by J. Bres), Payot, Paris, 1951.

10. D. Terrett, *The Signal Corps: The Emergency (to December 1941)*; G. R. Thompson, D. R. Harris, P. M. Oakes, and D. Terrett, *The Signal Corps: The Test (December 1941 to July 1943)*; D. R. Harris and G. R. Thompson, *The Signal Corps: The Outcome (Mid 1943 Through 1945)*, Department of the Army, Office of the Chief of Military History, U.S. Government Printing Office, Washington, D.C., 1956 to 1966.

11. J. M. Wolfe, *A First Course in Cryptanalysis*, 3 vols., Brooklyn College Press, Brooklyn, N.Y., 1943.

12 A. Sinkov, *Elementary Cryptanalysis, A Mathematical Approach*, Random House, Inc., New York, 1968.

Most papers on computerized cryptography have been in the *National Security Agency Technical Journal*, which is classified and unobtainable.

21 STEGANOGRAPHY

Steganography is a word used in intelligence circles to refer to the conceal-ment of the existence of data or messages. The methods of steganography are invisible inks, microdots in which a page of print is photographically reduced to a dot the size of a typewritten period, and schemes in which messages are hidden in apparently innocuous text. The first letters of certain words, for example, might spell out the hidden message. Techniques are available for hiding data in radio transmissions, and for transmitting long messages in a single short spurt of high bandwidth.

Computers can make data vanish magically with one line of PL/I code; for example,

```
UNSPEC(MESS) = UNSPEC (MESS)& REPEAT ('10111111'B79);
```

What has happened is that it has been converted into characters which cannot be printed, and normally print as blanks. A substantial number of bit combinations in most 7-bit and 8-bit codes form no printable character. The enciphering routines in Chapter 20 that add a binary bit pattern or number to the text produce a message of which only certain characters are printable.

The following text was encoded with the routine shown after it:

CIRCULAR 2444 FROM TOKYO 1 DECEMBER ORDERED LOND

ON, HONGKONG, SINGAPORE AND MANILA TO DESTROY PU

RPLE MACHINE. BATAVIA MACHINE ALREADY SENT TO TO

KYO. DECEMBER 2 WASHINGTON ALSO DIRECTED DESTROY

PURPLE, ALL BUT ONE COPY OF OTHER SYSTEMS, AND

ALL SECRET DOCUMENTS. BRITISH ADMIRALTY LONDON T

ODAY REPORTS EMBASSY LONDON HAS COMPLIED.

```
A1:GET EDIT (TEXT)(A(48));
    DO K=1 TO 48 BY 4;
    E=SUBSTR(TEXT,K,4);
    CALL RANDOM (S,R);
    M=M+R;
    SUBSTR(MESS,K,4)=E;
    END;
    PUT EDIT (MESS)(SKIP,A(48));
    GO TO A1;
```

(See Program 1A in Appendix 1.)

That part of the resulting message which was printable was as follows (printing blocks of 48 bytes):

```
T 8            ? .V      D         L          4L* Y  Y>

  "    $  Y    E         6        $   W  _   A U

  D ;          C         :     X  0          U   12

9>H       8  Y       - A  |        "  ( 5  Y ' |     9 )

   <    2      = X +  F@             ?        C@  *

   < Z6 Y    P   Z   ,C            AS       K "

 (&    1           2             3  D5  4  F_        N
```

VANISHING TRICK Readable characters appear sporadically in the previous enciphered message. A coding technique can be used which ensures that *none* of the characters in the enciphered data are printable.

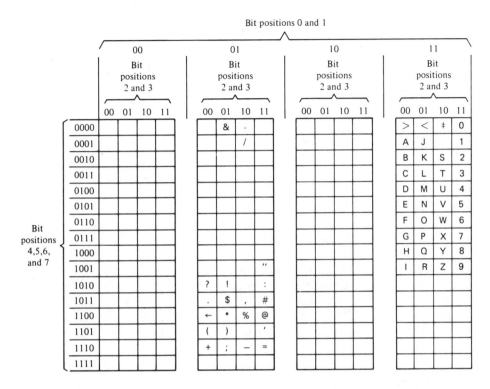

Figure 21.1. The characters that may be printed by a conventional printer in EBCDIC code. To make the data unprintable, change the second bit (bit position 1) to a 0.

Figure 21.1 shows the bit assignments of the characters that are normally printed in EBCDIC code. If the enciphering process renders a fully printable character set, it may be made unprintable by changing the second bit in each character into a 0 bit.

To make a character declared as C "disappear," the following statement is used:

```
UNSPEC(C) = UNSPEC(C) & '10111111'B;
```

The resulting character C is then unprintable. To render the character printable at a later time, the following statement may be used:

```
UNSPEC(C) = UNSPEC(C) | '01000000B';
```

When fixed-length messages are being used, a similar operation can be applied to the entire message. A PL/I statement for making a message of 80 characters, declared as MESS, unprintable is

```
UNSPEC(MESS) = UNSPEC(MESS) & REPEAT('10111111'B,79);
```

And for making it printable again:

```
UNSPEC(MESS) = UNSPEC(MESS) | REPEAT('01000000'B,79);
```

Using these on the program that enciphered the Shakespeare in Fig. 20.4, we have

Enciphering Routine:

```
GET EDIT (TEXT)(A(48));
DO K=1 TO 48 BY 2;
I=INDEX(ALPH,SUBSTR(TEXT,N(K,M),1));
J=INDEX(ALPH,SUBSTR(TEXT,N(K+1,M),1));
SUBSTR(MESS,K,2)=ENCODE(I,J);
END;
UNSPEC(MESS)=UNSPEC(MESS)&REPEAT('10111111'B,47);
```

Deciphering Routine:

```
UNSPEC(MESS)=UNSPEC(MESS)|REPEAT('01000000'B,47);
DO K=1 TO 48 BY 2;
I=INDEX(KEY,SUBSTR(MESS,K,1));
J=INDEX(KEY,SUBSTR(MESS,K+1,1));
SUBSTR(TEXT,N(K,M),1)=SUBSTR(DECODE(I,J),1,1);
SUBSTR(TEXT,N(K+1,M),1)=SUBSTR(DECODE(I,J),2,1);
END;
PUT SKIP EDIT (TEXT)(A(48));
```

Seven-bit ASCII code may similarly be made unprintable by changing the sixth bit in any character to become the same as the seventh. Some of the resulting characters will be ASCII *control* characters, and so the enciphered code can only be transmitted by systems that can send "transparent" data.

A person tapping a communication line which is transmitting unprintable characters may be led to believe that nothing is being transmitted (although not if he has a type of terminal which makes chugging noises when it receives unprintable characters). Only with the correct deciphering routine will anything be printable.

The systems analyst may be tempted to store data in unprintable code without cryptography. This is a mistake, as it may be apparent to an intruder what has happened and it can easily be rendered printable. The technique should only be used when it is an adjunct to secure enciphering.

HIDING ONE DATA   A similar technique may be used to hide data in
STREAM IN ANOTHER   what is otherwise an innocuous-looking message or
record. All the blanks or spaces in a message could be converted into unprintable characters.

In the following section of PL/I program, for example, the data to be hidden are referred to with the name SECRET—an 80-character item. It is to be hidden in data called TEXT, and the resulting character stream is referred to with the name MESSAGE:

```
GET EDIT (SECRET)(A(80));
UNSPEC(SECRET)=UNSPEC(SECRET)&REPEAT('10111111'B,79);
K=0;
DO I=1 TO 10;
GET EDIT (TEXT)(A(80));
MESS=TEST;
DO J=1 TO 80;
IF SUBSTR(TEXT,J,1)=' ' THEN DO;
IF K>79 THEN GO TO FIN; K=K+1;
SUBSTR(MESS,J,1)=SUBSTR(SECRET,K,1);
END;END;
PUT SKIP EDIT (MESS)(A(80));
END;
```

If the PUT instruction is an instruction to print, TEXT is printed with no trace of SECRET.

To print the hidden data, the following instructions would be given:

```
DO I=1 TO 10;
GET EDIT (MESS)(A(80));
DO J=1 TO 80;
X=SUBSTR(MESS,J,1);
IF SUBSTR(UNSPEC(X),2,1)='0'B THEN DO;
UNSPEC(X)=UNSPEC(X)|'01000000'B; PUT EDIT (X)(A(1)); END;
END;
END;
```

Once again, if the secret data are worth hiding, they should be enciphered first, in case an intruder finds out what is going on. For example,

Enciphering and Hiding:

```
GET EDIT (SECRET)(A(48));
DO K=1 TO 48 BY 2;
I=INDEX(ALPH,SUBSTR(SECRET,K,1));
J=INDEX(ALPH,SUBSTR(SECRET,K+1,1));
SUBSTR(SECR,K,2)=ENCODE(I,J);
END;
UNSPEC(SECR)=UNSPEC(SECR)&REPEAT('10111111'B,47);
M=0;
DO I=1 TO 10;
GET EDIT (TEXT)(A(48));
MESS=TEXT;
DO J=1 TO 48;
IF ((SUBSTR(TEXT,J,1)=' ')&(M<80)) THEN DO;
M=M+1;
SUBSTR(MESS,J,1)=SUBSTR(SECR,M,1);
END;END;
PUT EDIT (MESS)(A(48));
END;
```

Deciphering and Printing:

```
DO I=1 TO 10;
M=0;
GET EDIT (MESS)(A(48));
DO J=1 TO 48;
Y=SUBSTR(MESS,J,1);
IF SUBSTR(UNSPEC(Y),2,1)='0'B THEN DO;
UNSPEC(Y)=UNSPEC(Y)|'01000000'B; PUT EDIT (Y)(A(1));
M=M+1;
SUBSTR(SEC,M,1)=Y; END;
END;
END;
DO K=1 TO 48 BY 2;
I=INDEX(KEY,SUBSTR(SECR,K,1));
J=INDEX(KEY,SUBSTR(SEC,K+1,1));
SUBSTR(SECRET,K,2)=DECODE(I,J);
END;
PUT SKIP EDIT (SECRET)(A(48));
```

22 RECOVERY TECHNIQUES

There is a variety of possible circumstances that could lead to a computer system being damaged. Some are common occurrences. Some are dramatic events that one hopes will never happen. The hardware may become severely damaged. A copy of a program may become lost. The data on the files may become damaged. For all such occurrences there must be a contingency plan. Sometimes the plan is simple common sense, like storing an up-to-date copy of all programs away from the computer site. Sometimes it needs much forethought and advanced planning such as writing special programs for recovery purposes.

The recovery process must be a by-product of the daily data-processing operation. As with a living creature, the system must be designed so that it recovers naturally from injuries. A small injury should be repairable easily and quickly with little or no effect on performance. A catastrophic injury, such as an entire file being destroyed, will need more drastic measures, and the system will have to stop part of its work temporarily while the damage is rectified.

To neglect the detailed planning of recovery techniques is to ask for trouble, because the history of computers is filled with catastrophes, big and little. In a surprising number of installations recovery techniques have been neglected, but other installations have recovered quickly from total disasters. One Friday afternoon the $9 million computer center in San Antonio controlling Volkswagen's distribution was gutted by fire. The entire 175,000-square-foot building was destroyed (Fig. 22.1). The aluminum castings of the computer and its peripherals melted. An intensive emergency operation went

Figure 22.1

into action. New machines were airlifted from IBM factories in widely scattered locations. Tapes were recovered from a fireproof vault and time was purchased on a nearby installation to initiate file recovery procedures. Fourteen engineers worked through the night to install and test a rapidly assembled system in a nearby basement. A rush order was executed for 200,000 punched cards, and by 8:00 a.m. on the Tuesday after the fire the system was fully operational. A Volkswagen spokesman commented that their dealers might never have known about the fire if they had not read about it in the newspapers.

Every data-processing manager should ask himself whether he could do the same.

In such a disaster new machines can be shipped in, and programs can be recovered from a remote storage. It is imperative to know of a similar machine installation where emergency time may be purchased. Backup procedures are necessary to bridge the temporary period when the machines are unavailable. Of particular importance, however, are the file recovery procedures. When the files are damaged, there must be some way of reconstructing the data that have been lost.

TWO CATEGORIES   There are two types of file damage. In one a few
OF FILE DAMAGE   fields or records may be harmed; they can be cor-
rected relatively quickly, providing there is some means of knowing what the correct records should be. In the other, an entire file is destroyed or a large segment of a file; the damage is too extensive to be corrected by manual methods. One hopes that the latter massive file damage will never occur. Every precaution should be taken to prevent it happening. On many installations it will not occur. However, it would be folly to assume that it will not. A reconstruction program must be in existence to deal with the eventuality of massive file damage. In this chapter we shall discuss massive reconstruction first, and then we shall consider the reconstruction of isolated fields or records.

Table 22.1 lists some of the possible causes of file damage with the less probable causes at the bottom of the table. Where file damage is concerned prevention is far better than cure, and the table lists the primary means of prevention along with the chapters in this book where they have been discussed. It will be seen that the most common causes of harm, the first five on the list, damage single fields or records. Those which cause massive damage can be prevented most of the time.

In one installation massive file damage was caused after a program-testing session that continued through the night, because the wrong files were loaded on to the machine. In other cases a disk had been dropped and bent, and was unloadable. On one real-time system the wrong files were loaded and contained out-of-date information in what otherwise appeared to be valid records. The wrong records were updated for many hours with an extremely high transaction throughput before the process was stopped. Because it was a real-time system, the run could not be repeated with the same input.

On a well-run installation such eventualities (it will be thought) should never occur. In reality they have occurred, occasionally, on installations that were thought by their managers to be well run. Instances of sabotage to files have occurred on installations where sabotage was thought to be too improbable to consider.

Table 22.1

Causes of Damage to Files	Extent of Damage				Main Means of Prevention
	Field	*Entire record*	*Group of records*	*Entire file*	
1. Keypunch error	✓				Use of verifier Batch validation checks On-line data entry and checking
2. Terminal operator input error	✓				Good dialogue design On-line validation checks Prevent unauthorized terminal use Design cross-checks that will catch the wrong item at a later time
3. Data transmission error	✓				Powerful error-detecting code
4. Card chewed up by machine		✓			Good card-handling procedures Good maintenance of card readers
5. Program error	✓	✓	✓	✓	Thorough program testing
6. Accident during program testing	✓	✓	✓	✓	Do not use live files when testing If programs are under test on a live system, bar them from the live files
7. Wrong volume loaded and updated			✓	✓	Good library procedures Mandatory checking of volume labels
8. Computer operator error		✓	✓	✓	Thorough operator training Foolproof and clearly documented operating procedures
9. Mislaid tape				✓	Good library procedures
10. Defective tape or disk	✓	✓	✓	✓	Buy good quality products Adequate tape-renewal policy
11. Theft of tape or disk				✓	Physical locks and alarms Tight library procedures
12. Embezzlement	✓				Tight accounting controls Segregation of functions Tight control of the programmers Disciplined program promotion
13. Playful maliciousness				✓	Discipline Tight control of programmers Prevent unauthorized terminal use
14. Fire			✓	✓	Good fire-prevention procedures Fireproof tape and disk storage
15. Sabotage					Physical locks and alarms Good morale Security police

It is essential, therefore, to have the ability to reconstruct files that are damaged so extensively that manual restoration methods are out of the question. Massive file reconstruction methods need not necessarily be slick so that they can be applied immediately. Emergency overtime working may be needed. However, they do need to be planned and to have programs written for them, and to have appropriate logs or dumps made during operational running if these are needed for the reconstruction process. Such measures are an essential insurance policy.

GRANDFATHER, FATHER Reconstruction procedures are generally easier on **AND SON TAPES** batch systems than real-time systems. A new file is usually created on a different disk or tape. Figure 22.2 gives a typical example. Last week's Product Master File is run with the tape of new orders and a new Product Master File is read in the invoicing run, and a new Customer Master File is written. To give the ability to recover from any errors or unforeseen catastrophes, last week's files are retained. The tapes are sometimes referred to as *father* and *son* tapes, the father tape being the input to the run and the son tape being the new output. To be extra safe, the input to the previous run is also kept, and this is called the *grandfather* tape. Some installations retain earlier members of the family tree, but usually grandfather, father, and son are thought to be sufficient. The old grandfather tapes are reused for new data. Because the tapes are retained, entire runs can be repeated if they are found to be faulty or if the new tapes are damaged in some way. As a precaution against fire, theft, incompetent operators, or malicious deeds, the older tapes needed only for reconstruction purposes should be stored away from the computer installation, preferably in a fireproof strong room.

ISOLATED When corrections to single records or small groups **CORRECTIONS** of records are needed, the batch run may not be repeated. Instead, the corrections are saved for the next run, perhaps on the following week. The batch totals, input validation, and calculation checks described in Chapter 6 will be applied to the correction items along with the new input.

CHECKPOINTS It is desirable not to have to repeat the whole of a batch run when something goes wrong if it can be avoided. This is especially true when the run is long. For this reason *checkpoints* are built into the run at appropriately short intervals. If a machine failure occurs or a fault is detected, it is necessary to rerun the work from the

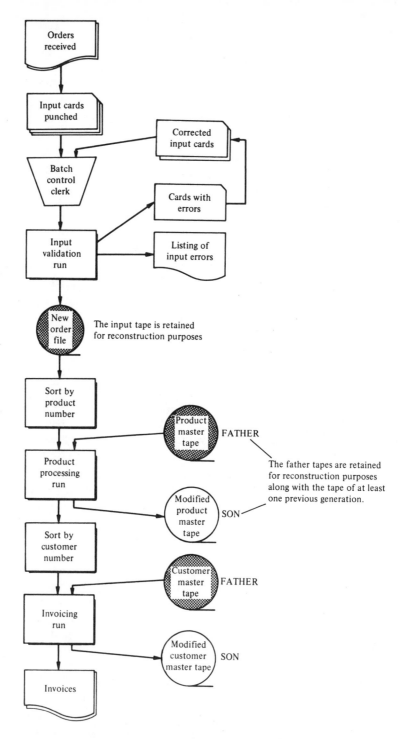

Figure 22.2. A batch-processing operation for handling customer orders, showing the tapes retained for reconstructing data if they become damaged.

last checkpoint, not from the beginning of the entire batch. When a check-point is reached, the batch totals up to that point will be recorded along with any other information necessary to restart the run. Any checks which can be performed to test the accuracy of the run up to that point will be completed.

UPDATING FILES IN PLACE

When files are recorded on disk or other direct-access device rather than tape, the possibility arises of updating them in place with the new fields over-writing the old. There are two main reasons for wanting to update the file in place. First, on a file in which only a low proportion of items is modified it may save time. When a tape is read, and an equivalent new tape is created, *every* record must be read and written. On many batch runs less than one tenth of the items change, and so it is advantageous not to have to spend time on the unchanging majority. The time saved could be substantial. Second, the items need not necessarily be in sequence, and so the need to sort them is avoided. The access mechanism can skip in no predetermined sequence from one item to another. In the operations illustrated in Fig. 22.2, the New Order File has to be sorted twice, first into the sequence of the Product Master File, and then into the sequence of the Customer Master File. These sorts are time-consuming and could be avoided if the Product Master File and Customer Master File were updated in place on direct-access devices. A calculation of the overall timing and costs would reveal whether updating in place gives a more economical form of batch processing.

The disadvantage of updating in place is that the grandfather-father-son sequence does not exist. During a run the previous versions of the modified records are lost. The run therefore cannot be reexecuted in the event of trouble. A different means of reconstructing records is needed.

IN-LINE PROCESSING

The same problem applies to what is referred to as *in-line processing* or *single-transaction processing* illustrated in Fig. 22.3. Here each transaction is completely processed and the relevant files are updated at one time. To achieve this, the files must all be on direct-access devices. An advantage of *in-line* operation is that the transaction cycle time is cut to a low figure. With batch processing a transaction may have to wait for a week or a month be-fore the point in the batch cycle where it can be processed comes around. With in-line processing it can be handled immediately.

FILE DUMPS

A means of massive file reconstruction must be planned for in-line processing, or for batch proc-essing with items updated in place. To provide this, the files that are directly

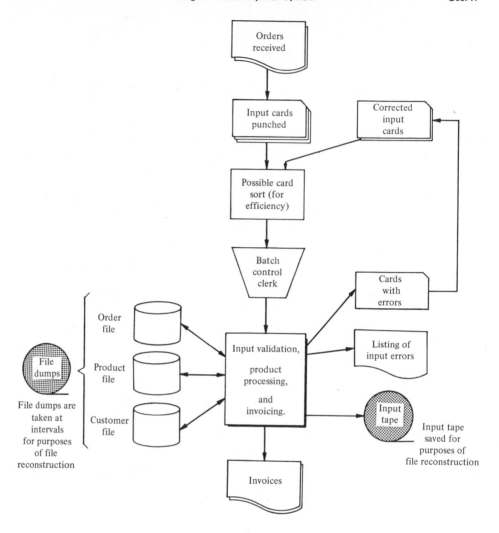

Figure 22.3. An in-line processing operation equivalent to the batch-processing operation shown in Fig. 22.2. Periodic file dumps must be taken and the input preserved.

accessed and overwritten must be dumped periodically. The input transactions used since the last file dump must be retained. The files can then be reconstructed by a program that uses the last file dump and the input transaction tapes. Any corrections that may have been made to individual records in the files must be recorded on the input tape so that these can be reconstructed also.

The program for file reconstruction should be written and tested *before the installation is first put into operation*. It is during the first weeks of operation that file catastrophes are most likely to happen because of unforeseen program bugs or operators unfamiliar with their jobs.

REAL-TIME
SYSTEMS

Real-time systems, such as that illustrated in Fig. 22.4, do not have the controls in input which are a feature of batch and in-line systems. The transactions are entered at remote terminals, and while input validation checks are applied, as described in Chapter 7, there is no batch control clerk or input/output control group.

To achieve file reconstruction, the files are dumped periodically and a journal is kept of the changes made to the file since the last dump. Many of the input messages do not result directly in file records being updated. The terminal operator carries on a dialogue with the system, which results in the answering of his queries, searching of sections of file, updating of information in the files, or creating of new records. When one record is updated, there may be several messages to and from the terminal, forming the dialogue that accomplishes this action. On most systems, therefore, it is not desirable to record individual input messages for file reconstruction; it is better to log the changes that are made to the files.

A transaction journal is usually kept, however. In Fig. 22.4 such a journal is shown, kept by the network control computer. There are several reasons for journalling transactions as well as a file actions. First, it can form the means for recovery from computer failures. The transactions in it may be reprocessed without having to be reentered by the terminal operator. As discussed in Chapter 9, the transaction journal may be the means of ensuring that no transaction is lost or double entered during the period of failure.

Journals will be discussed in more detail in the next chapter.

DUPLICATE
FILES

Some systems keep duplicate copies of critical data on the files. When the system updates these data, it updates both copies. If one file becomes temporarily unavailable, or if one copy of the data becomes damaged, for example by a read/write head crashing on a track, the second copy is immediately available. Unfortunately, this does not provide protection from program errors, because these will usually damage *both* file copies. It is not, therefore, a substitute for the transaction and file-action journals. Its advantage is in providing immediate backup where this is important. On most real-time systems it is worthwhile to duplicate a portion of the files, if only the program

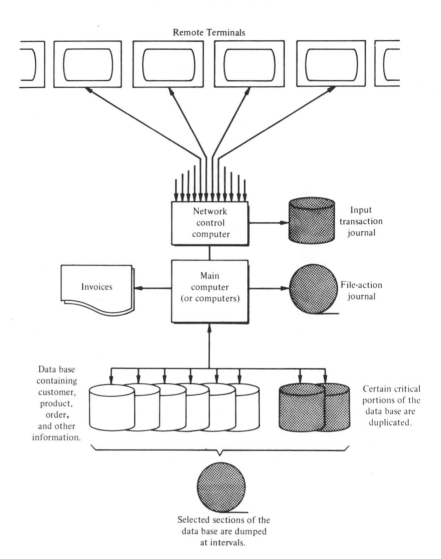

Figure 22.4. A real-time system for doing the same work as the systems in Figs. 22.2 and 22.3 (and other work). The data base is too large to dump regularly in its entirety, so portions of the data base are copied at varying intervals. File actions are logged rather than complete input transactions.

files. The files that are most critical to continuous operation are usually a small proportion of the total. Conversely, on most systems there is no need to duplicate *all* the files, although total file duplication does exist on some systems.

A problem with real-time file duplication occurs when a file that is being updated is temporarily unavailable; when it returns to operational state, it must be quickly updated with the items it missed. There are several approaches to the recovery operation. First, it may be performed from the file-action journal. This, however, may place a temporarily heavy load on the file channel. Furthermore, it does not take care of the case when the records in question were damaged. Second, the copy that did not fail may be written on the duplicate volume. This, however, may be a lengthy operation, and the copying procedure is not straightforward as it must be done while new transactions are themselves changing the file. An approach taken on some systems is to save the file recovery operation until the evening when the real-time work ceases. This approach is viable when there is a low probability of both files being harmed independently on one day.

Sometimes only files that are not updated in real-time are duplicated, such as files of programs and data which may be modified at night.

LARGE   When a system has small direct-access files, there is
DATA BASES   no difficulty about copying the files periodically
                     onto tape or disk and retaining this for recovery
purposes. A long time is needed, however, to copy a large data base, and data bases in use are becoming larger at a rapid rate.

Suppose that with a fast device the data base can be copied at the rate of 300,000 characters per second. One billion characters can be copied in just over 1 hour. The largest data bases in commercial use today contain about 100 billion characters. It would take more than 2 weeks working for an entire night shift to copy them. It is predicted that still larger data bases are needed and that the hardware will become available to hold them. Five or ten years hence we shall probably see direct-access data bases of 10^{12} characters or more.

Reconstruction of such enormous files is a formidable task to contemplate. Several factors become apparent. First, the entire set of files may never be copied regularly, as would a small set of files today. The data base may be divided into vital and nonvital records, and only the vital areas will be copied regularly. Different parts of the data will have different copying cycles. At one extreme, some of the data may be unchanging and will only be copied once. Some of the data may never be copied because they will quickly be replaced with new data. Some of the data will change only rarely, such as the addresses of persons and firms, and it will only be copied rarely, if at all. At the other extreme, some files that are vitally important to the day's operations will be copied every night so that a quick recovery can be made if they should be harmed.

Much of the data will change sufficiently infrequently that it is quicker to create the backup copy by updating an earlier copy than by duplicating the files. The file-activity journal may be employed for this purpose in an off-line batch-processing operation that goes on continuously in support of the real-time system.

In future generations of systems, it would seem desirable to construct the hardware for very large data-base systems in such a way that the data in it are protected from fire, flood, and theft, as it would be in a strong, locked, fireproof, waterproof cabinet.

DAMAGE TO　　　　　　　So far in this chapter we have discussed damage to
ISOLATED RECORDS　　　large areas of files. Now let us turn our attention to
　　　　　　　　　　　　　the reconstruction of single items.

Whereas massive file reconstruction should be a rare event, the correction of single fields or records may be needed frequently. This may be because of terminal operator errors, incorrect input documents, program errors, or possibly because of a reason inherent in the application, such as customers changing their minds. On some installations it has been difficult to tell where the file errors originate, but they are certainly present. On some real-time systems, especially those with a high degree of multiprogramming, the programs never become fully debugged. Rarely occurring and almost untraceable coincidences in the data and timing trigger program errors that cause incorrect file updates. The imperfections are rare enough to live with, provided that file errors can easily be corrected when they are found. The correction process itself, however, *may be a security loophole* and needs to be carefully controlled.

Isolated errors may be found by error-detection procedures such as those in Chapters 6 and 7. They may be found by terminal operators using the files. On a batch operation the error may be corrected at the next appropriate point in the batch cycle. On some real-time systems, however, it may be desirable to correct the error as quickly as possible.

In a batch operation, details of the error will be printed out by the program that detects it. A transaction designed to correct that record will be punched, and such corrective transactions may precede a normal batch run. It is important that the batch accuracy controls be maintained throughout the correction operation. (The controls shown in Fig. 6.4, for example.) The clerks in the input/output control section (Fig. 6.3) will have procedures to ensure that this is so. The control and hash totals will be appropriately adjusted and recorded. The user department will be notified of the change if the change originates from them and not if it originates in the input/output control section's own keypunching. If the control totals kept by the user department are affected, these must be changed accordingly.

RECORD CORRECTION In real-time systems the records directly accessible
IN REAL-TIME SYSTEMS can be made only too easy to correct from a terminal. The problem is not correcting the record, but maintaining adequate control over this process.

Systems will have different reasons for adopting particular procedures for dealing with damaged real-time records. The procedures may permit records to be corrected by one of three groups of persons:

1. The terminal operator who originally created the record or entered the data. Alternative operators at a branch location may also be permitted to change the records for that location, if the location has overall responsibility for its own records.
2. The file owner. One person may have overall responsibility for a file and its usage. He must be notified of any errors that are found in it, and must be responsible for correcting them, with appropriate controls.
3. A special group whose function it is to deal with errors in the system. This group will be familiar with all the errors arising in the system and the ways to minimize them.

On systems in which embezzlement is a danger, the prime concern will be with control of any changes. On many real-time systems, however, this is not a concern, and the prime need is to correct wrong records as quickly and easily as possible. On a police system for keeping track of emergency calls and police operations, for example, the sole concern is to keep the files representing the current status as accurately as possible. A history log will be kept along with tape recordings of all telephone calls, but this will not normally be used for file reconstruction, as events move too rapidly. At the other extreme, if an error is found in a record containing financial data, the record will be flagged to indicate that there is an error and the new value may be recorded elsewhere. The field in question will be updated later when tight control procedures can be assured. In some cases an entire record may be found to be garbled because of an earlier program error. It may be possible for a new record to be created immediately for that account, but without values recorded in certain fields. If the values are known, they may be entered, but must be marked to indicate that they have not been through the necessary control procedures. The security technique will not allow the entry of cash values without the indication that they are uncontrolled.

A case that illustrates this is a savings-bank system in which a customer comes in with a passbook. The passbook contains the balance from the last time the entry was made with the passbook. When the teller attempts to retrieve the customer's record, he receives only an error indication. Upon investigation it is found that the record has become garbled. The teller takes the customer's money, or possibly pays him money not exceeding the limit allowable in such circumstances. He records the transaction using his terminal off-line, and the passbook is marked with details of the transaction but with the new balance. A code character may be printed to indicate what has happened. The cash involved must be entered into the system so that the controls on the teller cash totals work correctly. If the damaged record is not reconstructed before the balancing run takes place, the totals will not agree, and the group responsible for accuracy control must record the reason why. The shell of the record with the correct account number may be reconstructed by this central group as soon as the damage is done. The group should attempt to establish the reason for the damage (damaged disk track, program error, invalid account number) and find out whether any other records have been affected. The controlled reconstruction of the contents of the record may have to await the evening's file-scanning operations.

On systems in which data relating to customers are kept, it is usually important that the local sales office should correct any mistakes which *they* have made or which arise from the sales situation. Mechanisms for detecting some of these may be built into the processing, as discussed in Chapters 7 and 23. For example, an airline reservation system attempts to detect duplicate bookings. If a duplicate appears to be found, the system does not delete the second copy itself or even adjust the seat inventory. Instead it refers the matter to the agent who made the bookings. His customer may have deliberately made a duplicate booking or may even be flying twice. The agent must call his passenger and clarify the issue. The computer can be programmed to insist that this be done.

On the other hand, if the error in the customer data appears to have been made by the computer system and not to be the fault of the branch operator, it should be corrected by the central authority without disturbing the branch operator.

In a data-collection system there is usually a central authority responsible for accuracy control. A valuable and practicable scheme for a factory system is to use specialists in a control room, as shown in Fig. 7.3, whose job is to sort out the problems. Of the five examples of error messages to the control room, given in Fig. 7.4, only the one below might have been caused by an error on the file:

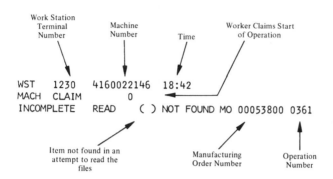

The control specialist would investigate the cause for the message. The computer is attempting to read a record for manufacturing order number 00053800 and cannot complete the file access. The cause may be that there is no record for this manufacturing order number. The number may have been entered incorrectly by the shop-floor terminal operator, either now or earlier when the record was created. If the control specialist finds this to be the case, he will reenter the number correctly or create a correct record for that number, whichever is required. The cause may have been that a programming error had destroyed the requisite record or at least its identification number. The specialist will explore the extent of the damage and correct it from his terminal.

No other person will be allowed to change records in this way. File locks should prevent them from doing so. The changes made by the control specialist must be automatically recorded in such a way that a log of all such changes can be inspected, and in a way that facilitates massive file reconstruction operations should they be needed.

CAUTION OVER
FILE CORRECTION
PROCEDURES

Although the facility for easy modification of erroneous records is necessary, it can easily become abused and so presents a danger. A casual attitude can lead to this facility being employed when more difficult or thorough operations are called for. The author came across one instance in which a stockbroker had balancing controls on his system, and considerable problems were caused when the balance was not correct at the end of the day. It was often out by a small sum. Rather than leave work late, the staff would make minor adjustments to the records so that the totals balanced. When such a practice gains a foothold, integrity is lost.

23 JOURNALING AND FILE BALANCING

In different places in the previous chapters we have mentioned different reasons for journaling (logging) system activity and for off-line scanning of the files. These processes form an important part of the techniques for maintaining security, accuracy, and privacy in on-line systems. In this chapter, we shall summarize the reasons for journaling and file-scanning, and stress that the different requirements should be met in an integrated fashion. The scanning and copying of the files and the processing of the system journals constitute a background of off-line activity which, where necessary, should be planned and operated like a small batch-processing installation in its own right.

REASONS FOR JOURNALING
Journals (logs) are used on an on-line system for some or all of the following reasons:

1. To provide an audit trail which will enable an auditor to follow the history of a transaction.
2. To permit recovery when it is found that a user has incorrectly updated or deleted a record, and that record has subsequently been used or processed elsewhere.
3. To investigate the causes when a record is found to be faulty.
4. To assist recovery from massive file destruction.
5. To assist in correcting the file when it is found that a faulty program has been damaging data.

6. To correct false information which has been sent to system users.
7. To monitor procedural violations in an attempt to highlight possible breaches of security.
8. To assist in correct recovery from a system failure.
9. (Not necessarily related to security.) To monitor the way the system is being used as an aid to design and installation management.
10. To recover from a loss of a journal.

TWO TYPES
OF INFORMATION
JOURNALED

On some systems, two types of journal are used; these are shown in Fig. 9.2 as the *transaction journal* and the *file-action journal.* The former contains information related to the incoming messages and, possibly, the outgoing messages. The latter contains information related to the updating of the files. Many systems record both sets of information in the same journal—the same magnetic tape, for example—and this is sometimes referred to as an *audit trail,* although the functions described here extend beyond those required by a traditional audit trail.

There are two main reasons for having a separate transaction journal and file action journal. The first is that keeping separate journals enhances system efficiency. The system must be synchronized to the journaling operation and if all journaling is done on one tape the system performance may be degraded to an extent that is unacceptable. The processing of the journals is also done more quickly if the transaction and file-action journals are separate. This is especially so when the file is updated long after the transaction is received. (On many systems with real-time enquiries there is no need for real-time updating.) The second reason for keeping separate journals is that it may be thought desirable to recover if one of the journals is itself damaged. If the message journal is separate, the file-action journal can be reconstructed from it. If the message journal is lost, its more important functions may be performed (with more difficulty) using the file-action journal.

WHAT SHOULD BE
ON THE JOURNALS?

Table 23.1 lists the data that might be recorded on the journals, and suggests which data should be included for different purposes.

Journaling, like everything concerned with security, can be taken too far. To be able to deal with all eventualities leads to complexity in the journal processing programs, and to degradation of the system performance. Do we, for example, want to send corrected information to users whom we discover were earlier given wrong information because of errors on the files? If this is to be part of the recovery process, we have to store details of enquiry messages on the transaction journal. Do we want to plan for recovery from the loss of a journal? Can we dispense with automated correction of errors on some files, and leave the correction operation to the file users?

Table 23.1. Data Which May be Recorded for Journaling

KEY: √ = Yes
P = Possibly
I = At specified intervals

	To provide an audit trail for an auditor to follow the history of a transaction	To permit recovery when it is found that a user has incorrectly updated or deleted a record	To investigate the causes when a record is found to be faulty	To assist recovery from massive file destruction	To assist in correcting the file when a program has been damaging data	To correct false information which has been sent to system users	To monitor procedural violations to highlight possible breaches of security	To assist in correct recovery from a system failure	To monitor the way the system is being used (as an aid to design)	To recover from the loss of a file-action journal
Transaction journal										
Incoming enquiry transaction							√		√	
Incoming update transaction	√	√	√				√		√	√
Transaction type		P	P				√	√	P	
Transaction number	√	√	√				√	√	√	√
Originating terminal	√	√	√				√	√	√	√
Originating operator	√	√	√				√	√	√	√
Time and date	I	I	I				I	√	I	I
Response to enquiry transaction							√		√	
Response to update transaction	√	√	√				√	√	√	√
Indication that response was received correctly	√	√	√				√	√	√	√
Procedural violations on input							√			
Record of start and end of file reconstruction									√	
Note of completion of update									√	
File-action journal										
Transaction number	√	√	√		√			√		
Time and date		I	I	√	I					

The above information may be all on the same journal.

Table 23.1. Data Which May be Recorded for Journaling (*cont'd*)

KEY: √ = Yes, P = Possibly, I = At specified intervals	To provide an audit trail for an auditor to follow the history of a transaction	To permit recovery when it is found that a user has incorrectly updated or deleted a record	To investigate the causes when a record is found to be faulty	To assist recovery from massive file destruction	To assist in correcting the file when a program has been damaging data	To correct false information which has been sent to system users	To monitor procedural violations to highlight possible breaches of security	To assist in correct recovery from a system failure	To monitor the way the system is being used (as an aid to design)	To recover from the loss of a file-action journal
File-action journal (cont'd)										
Addresses of items updated	√	√	√	√	√			√		
Contents of items before they are updated	√	√	√	√	√			√		
Contents of items after they are updated	√	√	√	√	√			√		
Note of completion of update	√	√	√	√	√			√		
List of programs used for update			√		√					
Full contents of any records created			√	√	√			√		
Full contents of any records deleted			√	√	√					
Details of any indexes opened or closed			√	√	√			√		
Procedural violations deleted during update or processing							√			
Contents of items corrected, before correction	√		√	√				√		
Contents of items corrected, after correction	√		√	√				√		
Indication of start and end of a correction run	√		√	√				√		

The above information may be all on the same journal

One view of the journal is that it should record historically all values that all fields have in each record, so that the state of the record at any previous point in time can be recreated, or an update history of the record can be reconstructed. Such a journal may be thought of as "logically" as a three-dimensional set of values—a set including the value of each attribute of each entity at each update. The journal may be stored in a compact form. For many systems, however, this complete recording of each update level is unnecessarily burdensome.

How much the journaling is expected to accomplish determines what data will be recorded on the journal tape or tapes. The column "To assist in correct recovery from a system failure" in Table 23.1 is perhaps a list of the minimum requirements for secure systems. In this list, the transactions are journaled, not the dialogue messages which are used in composing transactions; only the *update* transactions are journaled, not the enquiry transactions. On most systems, journaling the inquiry transactions more than doubles the normal overhead caused by journaling, and often this type of journaling is considered unnecessary. Without journaling the inquiry transactions, a system can accomplish the other most important functions of journaling—including the recovery from damaged files, the finding of faulty programs and the updating of transactions found to be faulty, and the journaling of procedural violations.

A transaction journal which does include enquiry transactions has a variety of other uses related to monitoring and analyzing the system's performance. It may be used for billing purposes. The security officer may refer to it if he is checking on how the system is being used. System load statistics and performance statistics can be produced from it. The input and output transmissions may be time stamped to help provide a measure of system response times. The traffic-volume measurements will be used to optimize the teleprocessing network.

**FILE
SCANNING**
On systems that update records by direct-access methods an important technique for control purposes is the scanning of the files, off-line, when the day's work is done. File scanning can achieve several diverse ends. It can be used to look for security violations. It can be used to balance the files as a check on accuracy. Undesirable circumstances of a variety of different types can be searched for. The file can be dumped to make file reconstruction possible in the event of massive data loss.

These functions should all take place on the same run. If a file-scanning run is attempted at all, the maximum benefit should be derived from it. On real-time and in-line systems it is only when the controls discussed in the previous chapters are combined with the file-scanning operations that a truly safe interlocking set of controls can be built.

**OPERATIONS CARRIED
OUT ON THE FILE-
SCANNING RUN**
The following types of operations can be carried out on the file-scanning run:

1. Establish Cash Balances

In a system handling cash records, cash totals will be added during the scanning of certain files. In addition to obtaining an overall cash total, the totals for various departments or groups may be added. For example, the cash for each branch in a bank or the cash for each sales office will be totaled. The totals obtained will be balanced to the totals from the previous scan or to the totals accumulated during the day. Thus, if the file is scanned every day the following relationship should hold: *today's cash total = yesterday's cash total + cash credited to records today − cash debited from records today.* The totals of the cash debited and credited during the day will be accumulated as part the day's processing. This, itself, will be balanced prior to the file-scanning run. The cash takings of a bank teller, for example, will be agreed to the total the computer gives for that teller. The file-scanning run will then ensure that the records are correct.

2. Inventory Controls

Items other than cash may be controlled in a similar manner. With cash the balancing run is usually performed every day, but with other items it may be done less frequently, although sometimes a daily balancing run is done with goods inventories.

In a typical billing or warehouse system using direct-access files, the goods inventory record is updated as each item is billed. The field giving the quantity in stock is changed as each item is billed or as new stock comes in. A control on this type of record may use a field giving the *old in-stock quantity* the last time an inventory-updating run was performed. This additional field may be used in two ways. First, it provides a safe means of restarting a run after a computer failure or program error has occurred. The run may, if necessary, be restarted from the beginning, ignoring the now incorrect current in-stock quantity, and starting again from the old in-stock quantity. Second, the file-scanning run will add all the old in-stock quantities as well as all the new. It will check that the total of the *old in-stock* fields equals yesterday's new in-stock total. The updating run will keep an overall total of the additions and also of the deletions; the equation *today's new total = yesterday's old total + today's additions − today's deletions* must balance.

3. Hash Totals

Hash totals may be balanced in the same way as cash totals or totals of tangible items. One reason for using hash balances is to ensure that no record has been damaged, for example, by a programming error. A second reason is to provide a control on the adding of new records or the deletion of records.

Account numbers, for example, or record identification numbers may be added during the file-scanning run. If no new records have been created in the file, the totals of these numbers should be those obtained last time. This gives assurance that no records have been accidentally destroyed. When changes have been made, the balance is checked: *hash total on this scan = hash total on previous scan + hash total of items added — hash total of items deleted.*

4. File Reconstruction

To protect against massive data loss, as we discussed earlier the files must be copied at intervals, and rebuilt if necessary from that copy using the file-action journal. The copying is done on the file-scanning run. In fact, some analysts regard the other items on this list as by-products of the file-copying run.

5. Single-Record Checks

The file records can be designed so that accuracy tests can be applied to single records. The checks may involve a hash total and error-checking field for the record as a whole. They may include self-checking numbers, range tests, and the other accuracy tests discussed in Chapters 6 and 7. The record may be tested using these checks when the file scan is made. This test is of less value than the others in this list, but may be applied without much extra cost if the file is being scanned anyway.

6. Check for Undesirable Circumstances

It is sometimes valuable to scan a file to check for undesirable circumstances. On some real-time systems there are checks that can be made in real-time or when the transactions are processed.

One such check on an airline reservation system is a check that duplicate bookings do not exist. It is an important check because they often exist in reality. A man may telephone several times, and this accidentally results in duplicate bookings being entered. His secretary may call and duplicate the booking that he has made. Sometimes passengers deliberately make bookings on more than one flight because they are not sure what time they will fly. If not found, duplicate bookings can result in empty seats on the planes. The author came across one case in which the same passenger was booked 16 times. To detect suspected duplicates, the computer must compare passenger names and sometimes other passenger details on the same flight and also on other flights to the same destination. This can only be done economically in an off-line scan.

Different applications have widely differing sets of circumstances that may be checked for.

7. Policing Operator Actions

It is often desirable to check that the operator is doing what he is instructed to do. In some systems the operator, or branch office manager, may stand to benefit in some way by "beating the system." Once again it may not be desirable to police the operators' actions in real-time, if only because of response-time constraints. The off-line scan may be used.

8. File Activity Measurement

It is possible to use the file-scanning run to produce statistics on file activity. Such statistics are often used in reorganizing the files. They may also be used for security purposes. The security officer, examining the statistics each morning, may spot unusual activity, which causes him to investigate.

Some embezzlements have been based on inactive accounts. In one case a bank employee checked the files for accounts that had not moved for 5 years. Assuming that the probability of a transaction arriving for the accounts in the near future was very low, he closed the accounts, keeping the money. It was easy to do. A computer activity scan might draw the attention of management to movement in long-inactive accounts.

This and the previous item can also be accomplished by processing the journals.

9. Management Reports

The same file scan may be used for preparing certain types of management reports.

10. *Creating Summary Files*

The files for management-information systems or files for planning purposes are used in entirely different ways from those on operational systems.
They must be organized for unstructured enquiry patterns and often for information retrievals based on multiple keys. Inverted files are sometimes used,
with multiple indices. To make possible the response times needed, the information in the files may be reduced to a summary form. The data for the summary files, or a highly condensed version of the records, may be compiled
during the daily scanning operation.

WHEN THE BALANCE   The balancing controls that form the first three of
IS WRONG   the preceding items are an important technique for
          ensuring accuracy on a system that updates files by
direct-access methods.

When the balances agree, the operations managers have a comfortable
feeling that all is well. An embezzler wanting to falsify the data must change
the balancing run at the same time as changing the transaction processing,
and the programs for both can be made inaccessible.

The question must be asked, however, what is to be done when the balances do not agree? The answer to this is different on different systems and
needs to be worked out in detail when the controls are being planned.

There must be some means of narrowing the search necessary to find the
error. It is not practicable to search the whole file in looking for it. The scanning run should therefore be divided into slices, each scanning a small segment
of the file and taking the various balances for that segment. The entire file
should also be balanced. If there is an error in the overall balance, then segment balances will be inspected to find the segment in error. This might
contain perhaps 100 records, and it must then be determined which of these
is in error.

On some systems it is possible to find which individual records are in
error by means of a program applied to the faulty segment. This could apply
various accuracy checks to the records in the segment. The program may go
to the detail records or file-action journal in an attempt to reconstruct the
records in error. If the customer-account *old balances* in a segment are correct
(as they should be if they were made to balance on the previous file scan),
the program may examine the items posted to that account since the previous
scan. Again, in an inventory file an extra field may be used in each record
to give the total of the additions and deletions. This field is checked only

when the file scan is out of balance, and it may indicate which record has caused the problem.

When tight controls are needed, there should be strict discipline relating to the file balancing. In some systems it has proved difficult to find the cause of the out-of-balance situation, and the problem has been sidestepped by artificially adjusting the totals. Sometimes this has been done with a suspense account, and sometimes by modifying the data records themselves. Any such casual practices destroy the system integrity. When the system is being planned, a correct way of dealing with imbalances must be devised and programs written to make it easy.

SYSTEMS WITH LARGE FILES   The time taken to scan files of, say, 10 million bytes will not be great. However, in the largest commercial data bases it would be impractical to scan the entire files every day. The data base must therefore be divided into sections that are scanned and sections that are not. In some applications the scanning operations need apply to only a small proportion of the total data base. The data base may be organized to speed up the scanning operation.

More critical than the machine time may be the human time in rectifying errors. Several systems have reached the alarming state in which new errors are being found at a faster rate than the old ones can be corrected. This indicates a failure in system testing, in terminal operator procedures, or in input/output control, which must be dealt with firmly.

The file scans are sometimes planned on a cycling basis to give the staff more time to correct errors, should they be found. A file may, for example, be divided into five parts, and one part scanned on each of the five nights of the workweek.

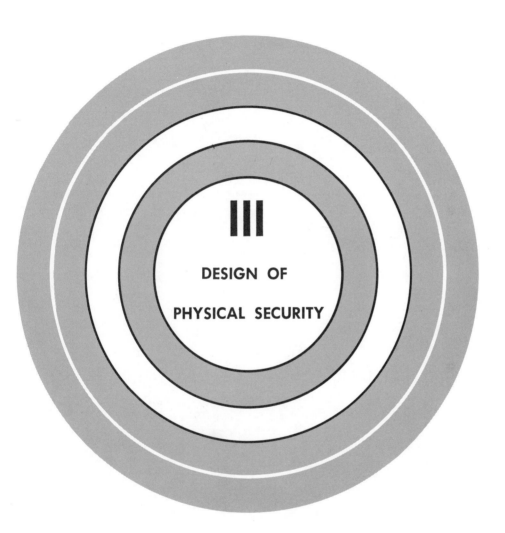

III

DESIGN OF
PHYSICAL SECURITY

24 LOCKS, VAULTS, AND PROTECTED AREAS

The technical controls discussed in Section II need to be supplemented by physical controls. Locked doors, theftproof vaults, fire precautions, guards, and burglar alarms are familiar to the traditional security specialist. Such precautions are very important in critical computer installations, but are sometimes surprisingly neglected.

Physical security should be of concern not only for critical areas such as the computer room and volume library, but for every aspect of system development and operation, as illustrated in Fig. 24.1. A person planning a technical assault on the system may start with the system design documents, the programming paperwork, or the program decks. He may obtain listings from the garbage cans, or make adjustments in the private branch exchange that connects communication lines to terminals. Much of the physical protection needed requires the same techniques as that for conventional office security. Computer installations raise a few special problems, such as the control of magnets and wiretapping. Specialists on plant security should be contacted to advise on intruder and fire protection. The references at the end of this chapter and Chapters 25 and 26 discuss the construction of physical security aids in more detail.

Specialists use the term *defense in depth* to mean that multiple layers of safeguards must be penetrated by the would-be burglar or other intruder. For a computer system the same term also implies that the intruder must overcome the technical controls discussed in Section II as well as physical defenses.

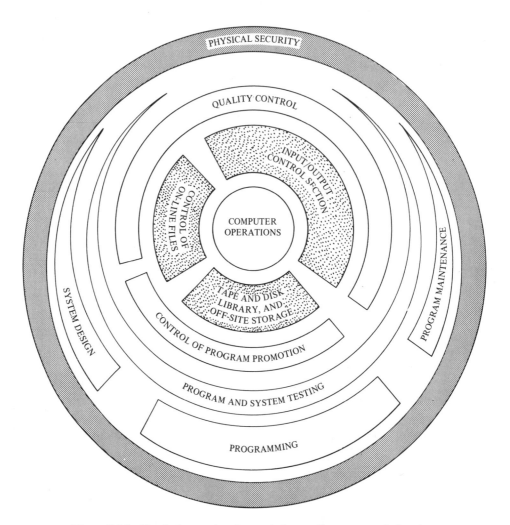

Figure 24.1. Physical security is needed on all aspects of the data-processing operation [1].

As with other security aids, the most effective safeguards are the most costly, and expenditure on physical security must be related to the overall security plan and budget.

PERIMETER   Three layers of *physical* defenses can be used. First,
BARRIER   there can be a perimeter barrier such as a wall or
                       fence. Second, there are the walls, windows, doors,
and ducts of the building itself. Third, there are locked cabinets and vaults.
Each of these three layers can be equipped with intruder alarms.

If the perimeter barrier is not guarded, it may not keep out a determined intruder. It may only delay him. If it is equipped with an intruder alarm (Chapter 25), it can give early warning of his presence, and this may be its most valuable function. A perimeter fence acts as a psychological deterrent to lesser intruders and is effective in keeping out mobs (who have posed a serious threat to some computer installations). Many vital computer installations are in buildings with no perimeter barrier.

BUILDING　　　　　　　Strong locked doors and secure windows are an
DEFENSES　　　　　　essential part of the defenses of a building. How-
　　　　　　　　　　　ever, many self-respecting burglars would not go through a door or window even if it were open. They expect them to have burglar alarms. Many buildings can be entered via manholes, storm drains, utility tunnels, openings in elevator penthouses, and the like. The roof of a building is sometimes ill protected because it seems difficult to reach. In fact, burglars can reach the roof of most buildings that are not too high, and once there they can work at leisure, out of sight, cutting holes into the air-conditioning ducts or through the roof itself. Sometimes the fire escape provides access to the roof.

Burglars sometimes cut through the common wall between two buildings. This wall is often thin and vulnerable. Probably the most likely intruders into computer centers, however, will use surreptitious means of entry rather than entering by force. A person who is at the center during the day can often disable a window catch or a self-closing fire exit door.

GUARDS　　　　　　　Some buildings employ guards and patrols. As will
AND PATROLS　　　　be discussed in Chapter 25, the effectiveness of a
　　　　　　　　　　　guard can be greatly enhanced if the building is wired with appropriate electronic detectors. Without these, a stationary guard will not know what is going on in the premises, and careful intruders can hide from a patrolling guard. (An intruder knowledgeable in electronics can use his own radio device to detect when the guard is on his way.)

Although there is much to be said for locating a computer center in a guarded building, it is questionable whether the center itself should have a guard. There should only be one entrance, and during working hours a receptionist at the door should act as a guard. After working hours the center should be securely locked with effective intruder alarms, and all valuable data and programs should be in burglar-proofed safes, vaults, or store rooms. Expenditure on intruder proofing is often better than expenditure on a guard. Some data-processing centers that employed a guard have subsequently reconsidered this decision.

It is essential that the receptionist and computer operator know what to do when challenged or disobeyed by an intruder. A hidden button to summon help is advisable.

When a guard is employed, it pays to obtain him from a good firm. Do not hire the cheapest available. He should be given detailed instructions and monitored carefully to see that he follows them and stays alert. More often than not it is possible for an intruder to bluff his way past the guard. The guard must beware of bogus repairmen, bogus telephone company men, and so on. In some cases the intruder only has to say that he is the general manager and the guard greets him like an affectionate dog wagging its tail at a burglar. In larger corporations guards trained and supervised by a corporate security service are generally better than those from outside the corporation.

INNERMOST
LAYER
Of the three layers of physical defenses the perimeter barrier is usually the least effective in keeping out a determined intruder. The building with its locked doors and, perhaps, guards may also be ineffective. The innermost layer of defense, the burglar-proof safes and store rooms, is very important. Sometimes this innermost layer is neglected on the naive assumption that the other two layers will keep out thieves.

Business Management, October 1965, contained an interview with an industrial spy. The article indicated that it is not difficult to recruit professional business spies. A good one can earn over $10,000 a month and can generally gain entrance to protected buildings with ease:

> He was hired once by an oil company to steal oil exploration maps from a competitor. These maps are developed after millions of dollars worth of geological tests. They tell the company in what new spots oil is likely to be found. They are the most jealously guarded of oil company secrets.
>
> Mitchum bribed a half a dozen armed plant guards to let him in a side door. He walked into a vice-president's office, photographed the maps he was told to get, and walked out. "To this day," he said "that company thinks that my client simply got to the oil first because of better research."

This very expensive theft could have been prevented by $1000 spent on a good safe and intruder alarm. Unfortunately, it often takes a disastrous loss before appropriate precautions are taken.

In most organizations the malefactor does not need to be a professional. The safeguards can be penetrated by an ingenious amateur with sufficient observation and planning. More often than not he can enter the building during the day and wait in the men's room for nightfall; he can open most cabinets with a small crowbar, or better, the cabinet where all the keys hang is often easy to penetrate. A short course in locksmithing [4] will often enable him to enter the tape store leaving no trace. The lock stores in New York City, for example, are not permitted by law to sell blank master keys, but in actuality a would-be intruder has no difficulty buying them. If the lock proves difficult, he can often force the doorframe apart sufficiently with a car jack. If he knows how to operate it, he can usually switch the computer on to copy tapes or disks. If there is a patrolling guard, he can wait for the next visit and then go to work in the interval. The main prerequisites are time, patience, and sufficient observation.

To keep out such intruders, a small expenditure is necessary on intruder alarms, and attention is needed to locks, doors, doorframes, vents, and windows. Valuable data should be locked in a burglar-resistant cabinet or area.

LOCKS   Locks provide one of the cheapest forms of protection, but often inadequate locks are fitted and insufficient care is taken in the safeguarding of keys. For critical doors, locks should be selected which cannot have their keys duplicated at a lock store. The lock should be of the type that carries a guarantee that the key pattern is not available as a standard commercial key blank. Combination locks are generally preferable on safes, chests, vaults, etc., and locks classified Group 1, Group 1R, or Group 2 by the Underwriters Laboratories, Inc., should be used. The first six references at the end of this chapter have detailed information concerning locks.

Many computer centers today fit locks operated by cards with magnetic encoding, rather than conventional keys. Some such locks can be highly selective as to which cards they accept and which they reject.

SECURE   There are four categories of burglar-resistant places
STORAGE   within a building. They are

1. Safes and protective containers
2. Vaults
3. Record storage rooms (larger than a vault but generally less safe)
4. Closed areas (in which people work)

Safes and vaults can also be made fire resistant so that their contents survive if the building is totally destroyed by fire. Storage rooms can be made to protect their contents from a less-than-total fire.

Detailed specifications exist for the construction and properties of safes, protective containers, vaults, storage rooms, and closed areas. Insurance underwriters and government agencies have carried out thorough testing of safes, containers, locks, doors, and methods of building construction. If physical security is taken seriously, attention should be paid to these.

SAFES AND CABINETS   Safes and record cabinets fall into two categories—those which are primarily designed to be fire resistant, and those which are primarily designed to be burglar resistant. Two types of standard labels are used by the U.S. Safe Manufacturers' National Association, indicating that the safe complies with one of the Association's specifications for (1) a fire-insulated safe or (2) a burglary-resistive chest. The labels are shown in Fig. 24.2.

The number in the top left-hand corner of the label is the specification, and details of the specifications used can be obtained from the Association. The number in the bottom right-hand corner is the *class* of safe or cabinet.

FIRE-RESISTANT CONTAINERS   There are five classes of fireproof containers in the United States. Their protective capabilities are defined by the Underwriters' Laboratories, Inc., and are listed in Table 24.1. To meet this specification, the containers are given three types of test: a fire-endurance test, an explosion test, and a fire-and-impact test.

The temperature in a fire increases with time, and in most buildings fires follow the curve shown in Fig. 24.3. The scale on the right-hand side of Fig. 24.3 shows the temperature at which various items melt or are damaged, and hence indicates how long after the start of the fire the damage occurs. When a safe is tested, the temperature of the furnace in which it is placed is raised as in Fig. 24.3, and the temperature of the interior is measured. To pass the test the inside temperature must not exceed 350°F at any time, and the papers inside must not "crumble with ordinary handling" and must be "decipherable by ordinary means."

In the explosion test the container is placed in a furnace already at 2000°F to see whether the explosive pressure development inside it causes any crack or opening.

In the fire-and-impact test, the safe is preheated for a given time, and then dropped 30 feet onto a hard surface and reheated upside down. The heating times are specified in Table 24.1. Class D and E containers do not have this test and so should not be used above the ground floor in a building in which the floors might collapse.

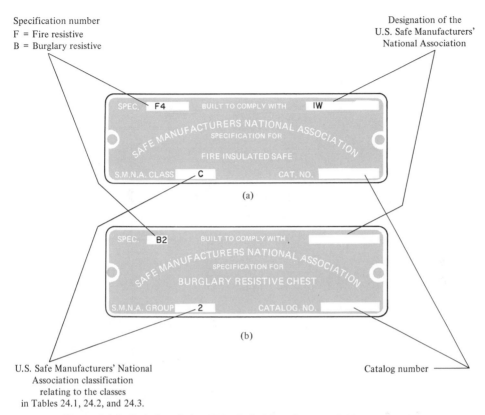

Specification number
F = Fire resistive
B = Burglary resistive

Designation of the
U.S. Safe Manufacturers'
National Association

U.S. Safe Manufacturers' National
Association classification
relating to the classes
in Tables 24.1, 24.2, and 24.3.

Catalog number

Figure 24.2. Labels of the U.S. Safe Manufacturers' National Association for (a) fire-insulated safes and (b) burglary-resistive chests.

Magnetic tapes can be harmed by fire at temperatures below 350°F. The Class 150 specifications are intended for the storage of magnetic volumes. They normally achieve their protection by means of a "safe within a safe." It should be noted that tapes in some of the other classes of safes *have been destroyed* in fires.

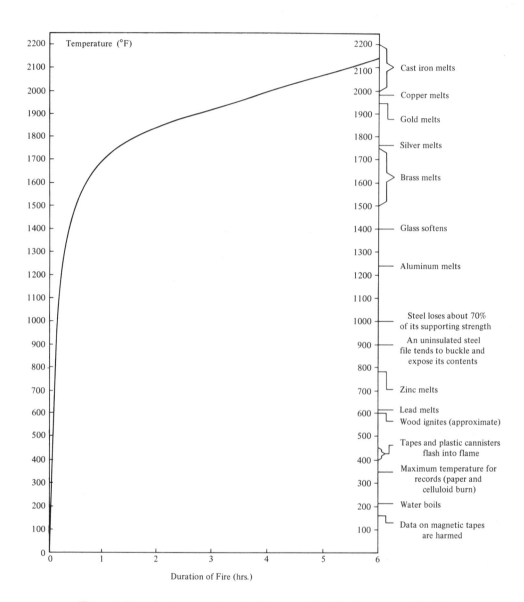

Figure 24.3. The temperature in the area of a fire increases with the duration of the fire. The scale on the right shows the effect of different temperatures.

Table 24.1. Classes of Fireproof Safes and Record Containers*

Class A –Effective in withstanding:

1. A standard fire test for at least 4 hours (reaching 2000°F); the interior temperature, 1 inch from walls or door, is not to exceed 300°F either during the period of fire exposure or when cooling while inside the furnace after the fire exposure;

2. A sudden heating without producing an explosion sufficient to cause an opening into the interior;

3. An impact due to falling 30 feet in the clear after being heated for $\frac{1}{2}$ hour, and reheating for $\frac{1}{2}$ hour in the inverted position after the impact without destroying the usability of papers or records stored inside.

Class B –Effective in withstanding:

1. A standard fire test for at least 2 hours (reaching 1850°F); the interior temperature, 1 inch from walls or door, is not to exceed 350°F either during the period of fire exposure or when cooling while inside the furnace after the fire exposure;

2. A sudden heating without producing an explosion sufficient to cause an opening into the interior;

3. An impact due to falling 30 feet in the clear after being heated for 45 minutes, and reheating for 1 hour in the inverted position after the impact without destroying the usability of papers or records stored inside.

Class C –Effective in withstanding:

1. A standard fire test for at least 1 hour (reaching 1700°F); the interior temperature, 1 inch from walls or door, is not to exceed 350°F either during the period of fire exposure or when cooling while inside the furnace after the exposure;

2. A sudden heating without producing an explosion sufficient to cause an opening into the interior;

3. An impact due to falling 30 feet in the clear after being heated for $\frac{1}{2}$ hour, and reheating for 1 hour in the inverted position after the impact without destroying the usability of papers or records stored inside.

Class D –Effective in withstanding:

1. A standard fire test for at least 1 hour (reaching 1700°F); the interior temperature in the center of any compartment or $7\frac{1}{2}$ inch maximum from any wall is not to exceed 350°F either during the period of fire exposure or when cooling while inside the furnace after the fire exposure;

2. A sudden heating without producing an explosion sufficient to cause an opening into the interior.

Class E –Effective in withstanding:

1. A standard fire test for at least $\frac{1}{2}$ hour (reaching 1550°F); the interior temperature in the center of any compartment or $7\frac{1}{2}$ inch maximum from any wall is not to exceed 350°F either during the period of fire exposure or when cooling while inside the furnace after the fire exposure.

2. A sudden heating without producing an explosion sufficient to cause an opening into the interior.

Class 150 Containers:

A special set of specifications relates to containers in which the temperature must not exceed 150°F. For example, a *Class 150 One Hour* container is one in which the temperature will not exceed 150°F in a 1-hour fire. Class 150 containers are needed when magnetic cards, tapes, or disks are stored.

---

*Specifications for the protection against fire, explosion, and impact, defined by the Underwriters' Laboratories, Inc.

BURGLARY-RESISTANT CONTAINERS The testing of burglar resistance is more interesting. The specifications for burglary-resistant safes, defined by the U.S. National Bureau of Casualty Underwriters and listed in Table 24.2, relate only to burglars using brute force. The more intelligent safe breakers study the mechanisms of the safe and devise ingenious methods of manipulating them.

Table 24.2. Classes of Burglar-Resistant Safes and Record Containers*

Class B:

Generally any fire-resistive container with a body of steel or iron less than $\frac{1}{2}$ inch thick and with a door of steel or iron less than 1 inch thick.

Class C:

A container with a body of steel at least $\frac{1}{2}$ inch thick and with a door at least 1 inch thick.

Class E:

A container with a body at least 1 inch thick and with a door at least $1\frac{1}{2}$ inches thick. If the container has two steel doors, one in front of the other, each must be at least $1\frac{1}{2}$ inches thick and the body then must also be $1\frac{1}{2}$ inches thick.

Class F:

This classification is based on performance specifications which require that the container be tool resistive for 30 minutes. The container must have a steel door at least $1\frac{1}{2}$ inches thick, and the body must be at least 1 inch thick. Any current production money safe to meet this classification will bear the Underwriters' Laboratories, Inc., "Tool Resisting Safe TL-30 Burglary" label. Older safes carrying the Underwriters' Laboratories TR-30 and X-60 labels also meet this classification. However, the newer TL-30 classification requires that the money safes resist drilling with carbide drills, whereas the older classifications had no such requirements because carbide drills were not generally used by burglars at the time the older safes were being built.

Class H:

This classification is based on performance specifications which require that the container be tool- and torch-resistive for 30 minutes. The container must have a door at least $1\frac{1}{2}$ inches thick and a body at least 1 inch thick with 3-inch minimum reinforced concrete around the body. Present production safes which meet this classification will carry the Underwriters' Laboratories, Inc., "Torch and Tool Resisting Safe TRTL-30 Burglary" labels. Older safes carrying TX-60 labels will also meet this classification. However, the TRTL-30 will have protection against carbide drills whereas the older safes were not required to have carbide drill resistance.

Class I:

This classification is based on performance specifications which require that the container be torch- and tool-resistive for 60 minutes. The container shall have a door at least $1\frac{1}{2}$ inches thick and the body at least 1 inch thick with torch protection around the entire body. Containers carrying Underwriters' Laboratories, Inc., "Torch and Tool Resisting Safes TRTL-60 Burglary" or Underwriters' Laboratories, Inc., "Torch, Explosive and Tool Resisting Safe TXTL-60 Burglary" meet the Class I requirements. In addition to torch and tool resistance, the TXTL-60 has been tested to satisfy that it will withstand severe explosive attacks.

*Specifications for construction or the protection afforded, defined by the U.S. National Bureau of Casualty Underwriters.

Safes are described with the terms *burglary resistive* and *robbery resistive*. Robbery resistive means that the contents are secure if the thief does not attack the body of the safe itself. Burglary-resistive safes can withstand an attack by crowbars, giant wedges, cutting torches, explosives, carbide drills, and other tools, in accordance with their specifications.

If it is sufficiently worthwhile to break into a given safe, a determined thief can usually buy one of the same type and practice on it. Safe mechanics (who advertise in the Yellow Pages) have drawings of many of the important mechanisms. The ingenious thief can employ hypersensitive electronic listening devices to open combination locks. He can use acid and heat, and can X-ray the locks to study their mechanisms. The skilled safe mechanic can open many combination locks without any tools.

Several U.S. Government agencies in the 1950s decided that commercial specifications for burglar resistance were inadequate to protect classified data, and the General Services Administration set up its own federal specifications. Table 24.3 lists the General Services Administration classes of security containers. Each class contains up to five tests: fire resistance (normally Class C in Table 24.1), time for forced entry (working fast!), time for *surreptitious entry* (meaning any method that does not use brute force), time for manipulating the lock (trying all combinations as rapidly as possible), and radiological attack (X-rays or other radiation).

VAULTS   A vault is a nonremovable construction built permanently into the premises. It generally has a larger capacity than a safe and if properly designed will protect its contents, even if the building is completely destroyed by fire. It is usually constructed of iron, steel, or strong masonry, and has an iron or steel frame and door with a combination lock.

The National Fire Protection Association defines a vault as follows:

A completely fire-resistive enclosure, to be used exclusively for storage. *No work is to be carried on in the vault.* The vault is to be so equipped, maintained and supervised as to minimize the possibility of origin of fire within and to prevent entrance of fire from without. The construction is intended to provide not only a factor of safety for structural conditions, but also to prevent the passage of flame or the passage of heat above a specified temperature into the vault chamber for a stated period, and to permit withstanding stresses and strains due to the application of a fire hose stream while the unit is in a highly heated condition without materially reducing its fire resistance. Vaults are classified as "six hour," "four hour" or "two hour."

Table 24.3. General Services Administration Classes of Security Containers*

Class 1. Insulated security filing cabinet affords protection for:

   30 man-minutes against surreptitious entry
   10 man-minutes against forced entry
   20 man-hours against manipulation of the lock
   20 man-hours against radiological attack
    1 hour Class C fire protection (see Table 24.1)

Class 2. Insulated security filing cabinet affords protection for:

   20 man-minutes against surreptitious entry
    5 man-minutes against forced entry
   20 man-hours against manipulation of the lock
   20 man-hours against radiological attack
    1 hour Class C fire protection (see Table 24.1)

Class 3. Noninsulated security filing cabinet affords protection for:

   20 man-minutes against surreptitious entry
    0 man-minutes against forced entry
   20 man-hours against manipulation of the lock
   20 man-hours against radiological attack

Class 4. Noninsulated security filing cabinet affords protection for:

   20 man-minutes against surreptitious entry
   20 man-minutes against forced entry
   20 man-hours against manipulation of the lock
   20 man-hours against radiological attack

Class 5. Noninsulated security filing cabinet affords protection for:

   30 man-minutes against surreptitious entry
   10 man-minutes against forced entry
   20 man-hours against manipulation of the lock
   20 man-hours against radiological attack

Class 6. Noninsulated security filing cabinet affords protection for:

   30 man-minutes against surreptitious entry
    0 man-minutes against forced entry
   20 man-hours against manipulation of the lock
   20 man-hours against radiological attack

---

*Specifications for construction or the protection afforded, defined by the U.S. National Bureau of Casualty Underwriters.

As with safes, some vaults are designated primarily for fire protection, some primarily for burglar protection. Appendix C gives the Department of Defense specifications for the construction of vaults used in industry for storing classified documents. The National Fire Protection Association gives specifications for fire-proof vaults and discusses where best to locate a vault in a building [12].

The door of the vault is critical and the Underwriters' Laboratories, Inc., has specifications for doors:

> Vault doors classified as 2, 4 and 6-hour fire retardants shall be effective in withstanding standardized fire exposures for the periods indicated before a temperature of 300°F is reached during the fire exposure and 350°F after the fire exposure, two inches from the unexposed face when installed in accordance with directions accompanying the door. The fire resistance shall not be materially reduced by application of a standard hose stream.

Approved vault doors bear the label of the Underwriters' Laboratories, Inc., or that of some other recognized testing authority.

The walls of the vault should have the same fire rating as the door. Materials giving 2- and 4-hour resistance are illustrated in Fig. 24.4.

The National Fire Protection Association recommends that vaults should not exceed 5000 cubic feet in size.

RECORD STORAGE ROOMS   A record storage room is larger than a vault, but is usually far less resistant to fire, flood, or burglars.

If vital records are kept in a vault, the vault is protection enough; if they are kept in a storage room, they should be inside fireproof, burglar-proof cabinets. The storage room should have sprinklers or other automatic fire extinguishers, and the construction should minimize the likelihood of fire spreading into it from outside.

The National Fire Protection Assocaition [12] gives recommendations for the construction of record storage rooms, and recommends that their size should be limited as follows:

1. Rooms containing only paper records shall not exceed 50,000 cubic feet.
2. Rooms containing plastic-based records in noncombustible containers shall not exceed 10,000 cubic feet.
3. Rooms containing plastic-based records in combustible containers shall not exceed 5000 cubic feet.

CLOSED
AREAS
Certain rooms or areas in which persons work may be designated closed areas and firmly locked so as to keep out intruders. The computer room should be a closed area. The area should have only one entrance, and this should have a guard or receptionist during working hours. The door will often have a "panic bar" so that employees can leave but not enter. Sometimes employees can enter by means of a card lock, or lock into which a code must be keyed.

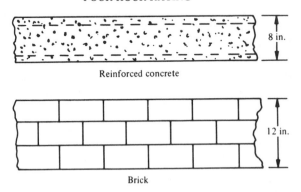

FOUR-HOUR RATING

Reinforced concrete   8 in.

Brick   12 in.

Hollow concrete masonry, not approved for 4-hour rating

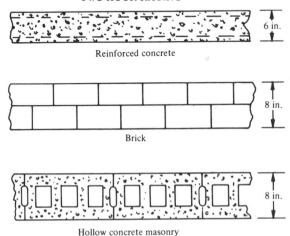

TWO-HOUR RATING

Reinforced concrete   6 in.

Brick   8 in.

Hollow concrete masonry   8 in.

Figure 24.4. Material used in walls of 2- and 4-hour vaults.

Appendix C gives the Department of Defense guidelines for the physical construction of closed areas.

ALARMS   Safes, vaults, record storage rooms, closed areas, and the building itself should all have their physical properties supplemented by alarms—alarms both for fire and burglars. Alarms and their use are discussed in Chapter 25.

REFERENCE

1. This diagram was suggested by J. J. Wasserman, "Plugging the Leaks in Computer Security," *Harvard Business Review* (Sept.-Oct. 1969).

BIBLIOGRAPHY

Locks

1. Underwriters' Laboratories, Inc., "Combination Locks," National Board of Fire Underwriters, Chicago, May 1961.

2. Underwriters' Laboratories, Inc., "Key Locks," UL 437, National Board of Fire Underwriters, Chicago.

3. Underwriters' Laboratories, Inc., "Standard for Tamper-Resistant Doors, Class T-20," UL 720, National Board of Fire Underwriters, Chicago.

4. Whitcomb Crichton, *Practical Course in Modern Locksmithing*, Nelson-Hall Company, Chicago, 1965.

5. T. H. Johnstone, "Locks and Locking Mechanisms," *Industrial Security,* July 1963, p. 21.

6. "Trends in Lock and Key Design," *Security Gazette,* Oct. 1961.

Safes

7. Underwriters' Laboratories, Inc., "Burglary Resistant Safes," UL 687, National Board of Fire Underwriters, Chicago.

8. Underwriters' Laboratories, Inc., "Fire Resistance Classification of Record Protection Equipment," No. 72, National Board of Fire Underwriters, Chicago, July 1952.

9. Underwriters' Laboratories, Inc., "Security File Containers," UL 505, National Board of Fire Underwriters, Chicago.

10. Safe Manufacturers' National Association, Incorporated, *Handbook for the Industry,* New York, 1956.

11. E. T. O'Connor, *Value of Records and Protection of Records,* The Mosler Safe Company, New York, Dec. 1962.

Vaults

12. National Fire Protection Association, "Standards for Protection of Records," Pamphlet 232, Boston, 1967.

13. Underwriters' Laboratories, Inc., "Fire Resistance Classification of Vault and Fire Storage Room Doors," UL 155 and UL 669, National Board of Fire Underwriters, Chicago, Dec. 1941.

14. L. E. Yont, "Protection of Vital Records," National Storage Company, Inc., Cleveland, Dec. 1963.

15. U.S. Department of Defense, Office of Civil Defense, "Protection of Vital Records," FG-F 3.7, U.S. Government Printing Office, Washington, D. C., July 1966.

16. U.S. Department of Defense, "Industrial Security Manual for Safeguarding Classified Information," DOD5220.22-M, Appendix IV, "Outline Construction Specifications for Storage Vaults," U.S. Government Printing Office, Washington, D.C., Sept. 1, 1969.

17. U.S. Government General Services Administration Interim Federal Specification AA-D-00600a(GSA-FSS), Door, Vault, Security, U.S. Government Printing Office, Washington, D.C.

General

18. R. J. Healy, *Design for Security,* John Wiley & Sons, Inc., New York, 1968.

19. Factory Mutual Engineering Division, *Handbook of Industrial Loss Prevention,* McGraw-Hill Book Company, New York, 1959.

20. National Bureau of Casualty Underwriters, "Manual of Burglary Insurance," New York, 1963-1964.

21. National Industrial Conference Board, "Theft Control Procedures Manual," New York, 1954.

22. U. S. Department of Defense, "Industrial Security Regulation," DOD5220.22-R, U.S. Government Printing Office, Washington, D.C., 1969.

23. U.S. Atomic Energy Commission, *AEC Security Manual,* U.S. Government Printing Office, Washington, D.C.

24. R. J. Healy, "Safety and Security: Industrial Buildings," Building Research Institute, Washington, D.C., March-April 1967.

25. R. L. Holcomb, *Protection Against Burglary,* Davis Publishing Company, Santa Cruz, Calif, 1962.

26. D. E. Bugg, *Burglary Protection and Insurance Surveys,* Stone and Cox Limited, London, 1962, 1966.

25 ELECTRONIC SECURITY DEVICES AND SYSTEMS

There is a wide variety of electronic security devices, and the number of such devices will probably increase as a result of current research. Electronic aids to security are perhaps less used than they should be because they are not widely understood. It is curious to reflect that many organizations employing the most advanced electronics for data processing protect their vital installations with a guard who is unaided by technology and who is remarkably ineffectual.

Although electronic systems can greatly improve physical security, it is important that a "gadgets" or James Bond approach to security be avoided. The total security requirements (including all aspects of security) need to be assessed, and an overall system designed that will maximize the protection that can be bought *with a given budget.* In particular, the feeling that electronic devices of themselves buy security should be avoided. Protection in depth is needed, and electronic alarm and surveillance devices may be part of such protection.

In this chapter we discuss first the devices that may be used for alarm and surveillance, and then the ways they may be linked into a security system.

TYPES OF DETECTION DEVICES
Many detection devices are available, each of which detects a single type of physical phenomenon. Each situation must be analyzed to determine which types of devices will be most effective. Unlike the senses of a man, the detection devices will never become tired, but a knowledgeable intruder may be able to put them out of action.

The types of detection devices used include:

1. Fire Detectors

Fire detectors used in data-processing areas are of two types, heat detectors and smoke detectors (See Fig. 26.1). A common type of heat detector is the fusable-link above the ceiling water nozzles in sprinkler systems. The link melts when the heat becomes intense and water sprays into the room.

Electrical-equipment fires are normally localized, at least until they set fire to combustible materials and spread. The fusable link and other heat detectors will usually not detect the fire until it has done a considerable amount of damage. Smoke detectors, on the other hand, will detect the smoke from an electrical fire quickly and so are far more effective detectors for computer rooms. Unfortunately, smoke detectors tend to give false alarms, especially if people smoke in their vicinity. The more sensitive their adjustment, the better able they are to detect fire, but the more likely they are to give false alarms. The false alarms may not matter if they merely alert a computer-room operator or a guard who is able to take protective action. They would be expensive, however, if they triggered the automatic operation of extinguishers. Fire will be discussed more fully in Chapter 26.

2. Breaking an Electrical Circuit

An electrical circuit may be designed to detect the opening of a door, breaking of a window, or the opening of a storage unit or telephone junction box. On some openings a microswitch is used. On windows, current-carrying tape or wire is used. Sometimes tape or wire is used on the surfaces of walls, ceilings, or doors. If the circuit is broken, a relay will close, which activates an alarm. Switches are particularly important on emergency exits to ensure that the exit doors are closed. Without this protection a would-be intruder can place a tiny obstruction in the doorway to prevent the door from completely closing so that it can be opened from the outside.

Simple microswitches can be taped by a thief so that they remain closed. To avoid this, magnetic switches are sometimes used. A cheap magnetic switch can be compromised by taping a magnet close to it. A more expensive variety relies on the magnetic flux balancing between the fixed and the moving component. Any external magnet will unbalance the flux and sound the alarm.

The knowledgeable intruder can compromise *simple* circuit-breaking alarms by shorting a wire across the point at which the break would occur, but he cannot do this with more expensive impedance-bridge devices.

3. Making an Electrical Circuit

The presence of an intruder may cause a microswitch to be closed. The switch may be under a floor panel or a mat. Outside a switch mechanism may be under gravel. The intruder switching on a light or the power to the computer may also close an alarm circuit.

4. Interruption of a Light or Laser Beam

Light focused into a parallel beam is shone across a room, passageway, or entrance onto a photoelectric cell. When an intruder breaks the beam, an alarm circuit is closed.

If a simple light beam is used, the intruder may compromise the system by shining a bright flashlight on the detecting cell. This can be prevented by using a modulated beam. The light source and receiver are modulated by the same frequency, and the substitution of a different light source will be detected.

The beam of light may bounce to and fro between mirrors, as shown in Fig. 25.1. Mirrors have been used to completely surround an object with light beams.

Lasers are occasionally used rather than ordinary light beams. Their monochromatic beams give very little dispersion, and so long path lengths can be used to fill a large area or corridor. Also, a detector of the monochromatic beam can be used that makes it extremely difficult to substitute false signals.

5. Use of Ultraviolet or Infrared Beams

Light beams may be seen by a cautious intruder. He may blow a thin cloud of cigarette smoke into the area. For this reason, beams with frequencies above or below that of visible light are sometimes used in a similar manner to light beams. Lasers can also be used at the ultraviolet and infrared frequencies.

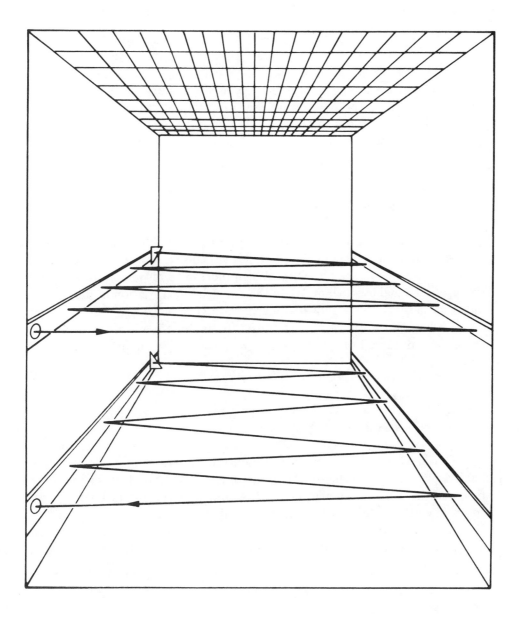

Figure 25.1. Use of light beam (or laser, ultraviolet, or infrared radiation) for protecting a room.

6. Detection of Sound and Vibration

Microphones are sometimes used to detect sound in an area. Sound above a preset level may automatically trigger an alarm. A guard at a control station with an amplifier and speaker may be able to listen to the sound.

Sometimes a contact microphone is used on the surface of a wall. This will detect tapping (even when muffled) that might indicate an attempt at false entry. Microphones can only be used in quiet areas, and tend to be subject to false alarms.

7. Ultrasonic and Radar Detectors

Devices using ultrasonic or radar waves are employed to detect movement within a room or corridor. The devices consist of a transmitter and receiver, sometimes in the same unit. When there is no movement in the room, the received signal is constant. When there is a sudden variation in the received signal, an alarm circuit is activated. Large rooms can be covered with one unit.

Such a device can be used to ensure that there is no person in the machine room or tape library when it is closed, and no person in the PBX at any time.

8. Variation in an Electric Field

One device for detecting the presence of a person employs an electric field. A person near an electrical conductor absorbs some of the energy in the field and this operates an alarm circuit. A similar effect occurs when a person approaches the antenna of a VHF radio; if it is receiving a weak station, a change in the sound may be heard. The conductor can be a wire sounding a doorway or other item. Both capacitance and magnetic detectors are used.

9. Magnet Detectors

Because of the concern over magnets being used to erase tapes or disks, a magnet detector may be used. When a magnet moves within 10 yards or so of the device, it will trigger an alarm circuit. The device would detect a magnet in somebody's pocket even in a crowded room.

10. Identity Card Readers on Doors and Gates

Small devices which read an encoded number on cards or badges can be fitted onto doors or gates and can admit users who display an approved number. The device in Fig. 25.2 reads a magnetic stripe card, the size of a credit card, and transmits its number over telephone wiring to a computer. The card may be the same card as that used with terminals. The computer checks the number to see whether the owner of that card is permitted to open that door at that time. Use of stolen cards will be detected. A 10-digit identification number is used, which is generated by a cryptographic procedure.

The same device may be used for monitoring the night watchman patrol.

11. Closed-Circuit Television

Television cameras are sometimes placed at strategic locations and produce a picture on a screen at a guard post. The guard may be able to switch the image from one camera to another. A camera for transmitting a close-up of an employee's badge is sometimes used at an entrance, as well as a camera for showing his face.

When the camera views an area, the guard may be able to change its position by remote control. It can have a pan (horizontal rotation) and tilt control, and, if desirable, a remotely controlled zoom lens (which can narrow the angle of view for close-up shots or move out for wide-angle shots).

12. Theft Detectors

A number of companies market a tag or adhesive tape that can be attached to an item and sensed remotely by an instrument. If the item is stolen, the instrument will detect its being carried through the door. Most such tags accomplish this by radioactivity. One company markets a tape/disk label that is permanently attached and will send out a detectable signal when it is carried, even in a briefcase. This can be used to prevent tapes from being stolen or "borrowed" for copying (Fig. 25.3).

13. Time-Lapse Cameras

A nonelectronic device used for security purposes is a time-lapse camera This is a movie camera that takes one frame every 30 seconds or so. The film,

Figure 25.2. An IBM magnetic stripe card reader installed on a system controlling access to doors, gates, storage vaults, etc. Only the right card at the right time will open the locks.

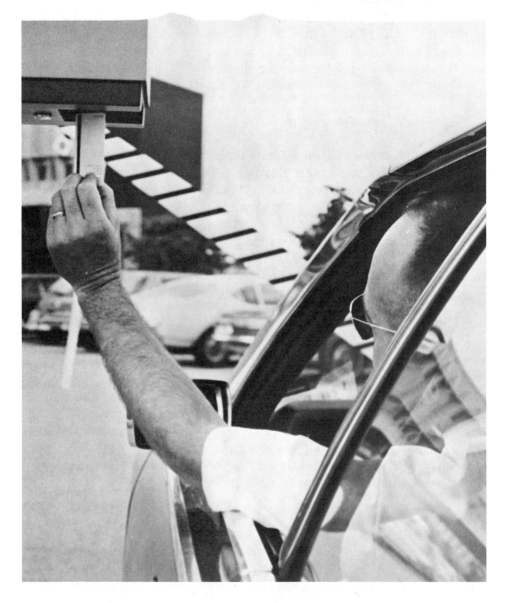

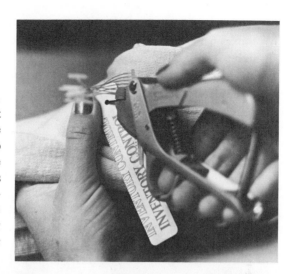

Figure 25.3. Shoplifter detection. The two pillars at the right and left foreground detect any merchandise with a sensomatic tag attached to it that is being removed from the store. The upper photograph shows the tag being attached to the merchandise. A similar scheme can be used to prevent theft of tapes or disk packs. *Courtesy Sensomatic Electronics Corp.*

when developed, can be played back to see who was in an area at a given time. An inexpensive Super 8 camera can be used and one small roll of film lasts all night. The camera may be left running for the whole of an overtime shift.

The installation and wiring of such devices needs to be done in a secure manner and the manuals referenced at the end of this chapter provide a valuable guide to this.

POSSIBLE ACTIONS OF THE ALARM CIRCUIT   The alarm circuit when triggered by these detection devices can initiate a variety of different types of action. They include

1. *An alarm can be sounded in the room where the incident occurs.* A fire alarm may sound loudly to warn the staff in the area. An intruder alarm may be intended to frighten the intruder. A magnet detector may be intended to warn the computer-room staff.

2. *A door can be locked so that the intruder cannot escape.* At the same time authorities are notified so that they catch the man red-handed. The door of the tape store, for example, may lock in this way. Some security experts have recommended a double-entry doorway to a data-processing area, as shown in Fig. 25.4. If the person does not have an authorized badge, or is carrying a magnet or a stolen tape, the interlocking door will not open from the inside, and the man is trapped until a security officer releases him. There may be television and voice communication with the interlocked area. Security authorities generally recommend against "mantrap" devices such as that in Fig. 25.4 on the grounds that innocent employees will sometimes be caught. It is also possible that a man may be trapped when there is nobody to release him. (Perhaps a bag of food should be left in the area!)

3. *An alarm can sound at a guard post in the same building.* When the computer room or other areas are unmanned, the alarm circuits must warn some outside authority. A guard post is sometimes equipped with a console at which the various electronic aids to security terminate. In this manner the operations of the guard can be made more effective. The guard post is often in the same building as the detection equipment. If the guard is alone, he may have to lock the doors and go to investigate when the alarm circuits are triggered.

4. *The guard's console may be in a separate building.* One guard with electronic aids may supervise a complex of buildings, as indicated in Fig. 25.5. The guard must have the means to summon outside help quickly. A leased telephone line is often permanently connected to the local police station. The guard may use this for calling police help, but also the equipment may automatically sound an alarm in the police station. If the guard is attacked, the police will be automatically alerted. If the leased telephone line is cut, they will be alerted.

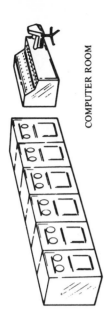

COMPUTER ROOM

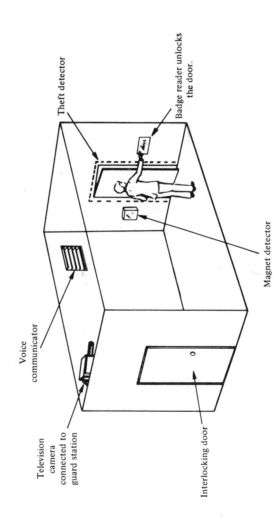

Theft detector

Badge reader unlocks the door.

Magnet detector

Voice communicator

Television camera connected to guard station

Interlocking door

Figure 25.4. A double-door entry system that controls access to the computer room. A questionable recommendation.

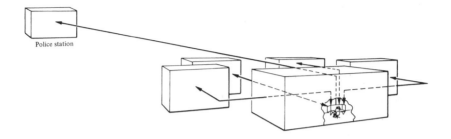

Police station

Figure 25.5. Instrumentation from a complex of buildings is sometimes linked to a central guard console with a leased line to the police station that can sound an automatic alarm in the station.

5. *The equipment can alert the police directly.* Some intruder detectors automatically sound an alarm in the police station, again using a leased telephone line. The police, who must be familiar with the premises, send a patrol to investigate. Sometimes an independent security organization is used for this purpose, often the company which installs the equipment.

SECURITY SYSTEMS

Many organizations employ a security "system" in which a variety of devices, such as fire detectors, intruder detectors, and door locks, is linked to a guard's console. By using such a system, a high level of security can be achieved with low manpower. Manpower is used to react to unusual situations rather than to patrol the building routinely, and can be made much more effective. In some buildings, the devices are on-line to a small monitoring computer.

The National Fire Protection Association defines a *Central Station System* as follows [8]:

A system, or group of systems, the operations of which are signaled to, recorded in, maintained and supervised from an approved central station, in which there are competent and experienced observers and operators in attendance at all times whose duty it shall be, upon receipt of a signal, to take such action as shall be required under the rules established for their guidance. Such systems shall be controlled and operated by a person, firm, or corporation whose principal business is the furnishing and maintaining of supervised protective signaling service and who has no interest in the protected properties.

The security system is usually used for an entire office building or plant, rather than just a computer facility. A building that is already protected in this way can be a suitable building in which to site a vital computer center.

It is desirable to plan the security system in an integrated fashion and to avoid isolated gadgets or gimmicks. The first step is to completely define the protection that is needed from fire, flood, and intruders. A system for meeting these needs can then be designed either by a vendor's staff, consultant, or security specialist. Cost estimates will be established, and approval of the concept can then be sought from management. If the concept is approved, technical specifications can be drawn up and different vendors invited to submit technical proposals.

The tasks that should be considered in the design of a security system include

1. Fire detection and action to control any fires that occur.
2. Intruder detection and action to catch intruders and limit the damage they do.
3. Detection of other problems, for example, water seepage.
4. Control of employee entrances. The door may be unlocked from the guard console when an employee is identified or unlocked automatically by a computer. He may be identified by means such as those in Chapter 11, or television cameras may be used to compare his face with a photograph on an identity card, or a photograph filed at the guard console.
5. Control of emergency exit and loading bay doors.
6. Contact with guard patrols (by key stations or two-way radio).
7. Maintaining an unbroken log from intruder detectors or other devices so that inadequate surveillance by the guard will be detected (guard asleep; guard being bribed).
8. Detection of equipment faults and the summoning of maintenance staff.
9. Control of employee evacuation in emergency, using loudspeakers or evacuation horns.
10. Some time-sharing systems run unattended except during prime shift—some systems providing APL service, for example. In the future more use will be made of unattended computers. Certain complex computers, such as certain telephone exchanges, run *entirely* unattended except for maintenance. A remote console for an unattended computer may be incorporated in the guard's console. Its use must be made very simple, and its main purpose will be to indicate when maintenance staff needs to be called.

Figure 25.6 summarizes the electronic equipment that may be incorporated into a security system.

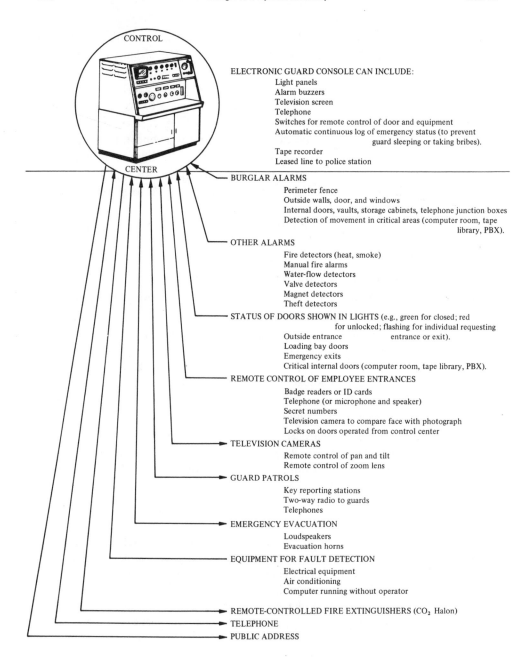

CONTROL

CENTER

ELECTRONIC GUARD CONSOLE CAN INCLUDE:
Light panels
Alarm buzzers
Television screen
Telephone
Switches for remote control of door and equipment
Automatic continuous log of emergency status (to prevent
                                 guard sleeping or taking bribes).
Tape recorder
Leased line to police station

BURGLAR ALARMS
Perimeter fence
Outside walls, door, and windows
Internal doors, vaults, storage cabinets, telephone junction boxes
Detection of movement in critical areas (computer room, tape
                                                      library, PBX).

OTHER ALARMS
Fire detectors (heat, smoke)
Manual fire alarms
Water-flow detectors
Valve detectors
Magnet detectors
Theft detectors

STATUS OF DOORS SHOWN IN LIGHTS (e.g., green for closed; red
                      for unlocked; flashing for individual requesting
Outside entrance   entrance or exit).
Loading bay doors
Emergency exits
Critical internal doors (computer room, tape library, PBX).

REMOTE CONTROL OF EMPLOYEE ENTRANCES
Badge readers or ID cards
Telephone (or microphone and speaker)
Secret numbers
Television camera to compare face with photograph
Locks on doors operated from control center

TELEVISION CAMERAS
Remote control of pan and tilt
Remote control of zoom lens

GUARD PATROLS
Key reporting stations
Two-way radio to guards
Telephones

EMERGENCY EVACUATION
Loudspeakers
Evacuation horns

EQUIPMENT FOR FAULT DETECTION
Electrical equipment
Air conditioning
Computer running without operator

REMOTE-CONTROLLED FIRE EXTINGUISHERS (CO_2 Halon)
TELEPHONE
PUBLIC ADDRESS

Figure 25.6. Possible components of an electronic security system.

Many detectors may be wired to the console and, as with a teleprocessing system, there are several ways of connecting them. They may be connected to privately installed wiring or to telephone company wiring. They may be directly connected on the console on point-to-point lines. On a large system, point-to-point lines incur a high wiring cost, and some means may be used for connecting many detectors to one line. One method attaches the devices to a looped line. The device cost is increased because there must be some means of identifying which signal comes from which device. The reliability of the system is somewhat lower because a failure (deliberate break) of the loop disables many detectors. Another method employs a remote multiplexor. In another scheme a computerized telephone exchange (PBX) scans the devices. In some systems radio links are used.

However the interconnections are organized, the scheme needs to be planned as an integrated system with compatible equipment. Like a computer system, it needs to be modular and expandable.

Increasingly, small computers themselves will form a part of security systems. IBM Controlled Access System, for example, uses a software package on a System/7 to control entrance doors, parking lot gates, etc., with on-line magnetic-stripe card readers and other detection devices. With such a system entrance through each door can be restricted to specific individuals at specific times. Entry to certain doors may need the presence of two individuals. Unusual activity can be reported. Use of lost or stolen cards and tampering with doors will be detected. The system may also have on-line burglar alarms, fire and smoke detectors, lighting controls and controls for heating, ventilation, and air conditioning. The cost of such a system may only be justifiable in a large building or complex.

Reliability is of prime importance in a security system. The equipment may exist for months with no emergency occurring. If it does not function correctly when the moment of truth arrives, it is useless. For this reason the capability to test its correct functioning must be built into the system, and it must be tested constantly.

BIBLIOGRAPHY

1. Detex Watchclock Corporation, "Plant Protection Manual," New York, 1965.

2. Underwriters' Laboratories, Inc., "Central Station Burglar Alarm Systems," UL 611, National Board of Fire Underwriters, Chicago, December 1956.

3. Underwriters' Laboratories, Inc., "Connectors and Switches for Use with Burglar Alarm Systems," UL 634, National Board of Fire Underwriters, Chicago, December 1962.

4. Underwriters' Laboratories, Inc., "Holdup Alarm Systems," UL 636, 4th ed., National Board of Fire Underwriters, Chicago, 1958.

5. Underwriters' Laboratories, Inc., "Local Burglar Alarm Systems," UL 609 and UL 610, 3d ed., National Board of Fire Underwriters, Chicago, Nov. 1950.

6. Underwriters' Laboratories, Inc., "Installation, Classification and Certification of Burglar Alarms," UL 681, National Board of Fire Underwriters, Chicago, June 1965.

7. Underwriters' Laboratories, Inc., "Intrusion Detection Units," UL 639, National Board of Fire Underwriters, Chicago, April, 1964.

8. National Fire Protection Association, "Central Station Protection Signalling Systems," No. 71, Boston, 1967.

26 FIRE AND ACTS OF GOD

Fire protection must be of major concern to any data-processing manager, especially when his installation is essential to the running of an organization. Probably the most worthwhile reading matter on fire protection is the set of pamphlets published by the National Fire Protection Association [1-11].

Fire is not the only type of catastrophe that can destroy an installation. Apart from natural disasters, one installation was destroyed when an aircraft crashed into it, one fell through the floor to the room below, and several have been destroyed by bombs. One organization located its computer securely in the basement. However, a giant mobile shovel dug a large pit in the adjacent lot. The machine came too close to the edge, toppled, rolled down the side, and crashed through the foundation of the building, landing in the middle of the computer room.

As well as minimizing the likelihood and extent of disaster, an essential part of the protection process is to plan the means of recovery.

The protective measures that are necessary include:

1. *Choice of site to minimize likelihood of disaster.* Few disastrous fires originate in a well-protected computer room. They are more likely to spread to it from the outside.
2. *Air-conditioning and other ducts designed so as not to spread fire.*
3. *Positioning of equipment to minimize damage.*
4. *Good housekeeping.* No storage of records or flammables in the computer room. Tidy installation.
5. *Hand-operated fire extinguishers immediately available.* Clearly marked. Regularly tested.

6. *Automatic fire extinguishers installed* in such a way that they are unlikely to cause damage to equipment or danger to personnel.

7. *Fire detectors* give alarm inside computer room and to external authority; start automatic fire extinguishers after a delay to permit human intervention.

8. *Emergency power-off switch* clearly marked, always unobstructed. All personnel must be familiar with all power-off procedures.

9. *Emergency procedures posted.* All personnel must be familiar with them and know exactly what to do when fire starts.

10. *Personnel safety measures* in building layout and emergency procedures.

11. *All records stored outside computer room.*

12. *Important records stored in fireproof cabinets or vaults.*

13. *Records needed for file reconstruction stored off the premises.*

14. *Up-to-date duplicate of all programs stored off the premises.*

15. *Contingency plan* for use of equipment elsewhere should the computers be destroyed.

16. *Ask insurance company and local fire department to inspect the facility.*

CHOICE OF SITE

Ideally, the computer should be in a separate fireproof building. Often this is not possible, and when the computer facilities have to share a building, it should be a fire-resistive sprinklered building. The computer area should be chosen to minimize fire, water, and smoke hazards from adjoining areas. Common walls with other activities should have at least a one-hour rating and effective fire breakers. Windows through which fire can enter should be avoided. Air-conditioning or other ducts should have fire dampers [8, 9].

COMPUTER ROOM

Walls, floors, raised floors, acoustical wall tiles and ceiling, and doors should be fire resistive. The walls enclosing the computer room should extend from the structural floor to the true ceiling, and the doors should be kept closed. The floor of the room above the computers should be made watertight, as far as possible, to avoid water damage to equipment. The pamphlets of the National Fire Prevention Association give details of fire-resistive materials and construction methods that should be used [1, 9, 12].

Good housekeeping and cleanliness in the computer environment are important in minimizing fire risk. Lint from moving paper and cards is particularly flammable. A bursting operation produces substantial lint. It should be cleaned up regularly and not allowed to collect under the false floor. Paper and cards should be stored outside the computer room as far as possible. So also should magnetic tapes and disk cannisters, which have a low flashpoint. Flammable items, such as solvents and floor waxes, should be stored elsewhere.

The furniture should be noncombustible. Wastepaper should be removed frequently. An equipment fire caused by a breakdown in insulation is not likely to spread far if there are no combustible materials around it. It is recommended that smoking in the computer room be prohibited. Some organizations allow it, in which case sufficient safe ashtrays must be provided.

Waterproof covers placed over the equipment when not in use will protect it from water seepage from higher floors or from sprinklers going off. The covers should be readily accessible for emergency, and employees should know where they are.

If possible the computers and peripheral units should be positioned in the computer room so that a fire in part of the room will not destroy the means to continue processing. For example, where two computers are used they should be well separated, possibly in different rooms. Tape or disk units may be divided into two groupings rather than all clustered together. A duplexed, real-time configuration should have similar components physically separated.

HAND-OPERATED EXTINGUISHERS　　A computer area should have both hand-operated fire extinguishers and automatic extinguishers. Carbon dioxide fire extinguishers are used for electrical fires [5, 6]. Some installations also have soda-acid fire extinguishers for combustible materials such as paper. The extinguishers should be clearly marked, for example with a red painted area on the wall, and the path to them should be unobstructed. The marking should state what type fire the device should be used for. The extinguishers should be checked periodically for correct operation in accordance with their manufacturer's instructions. There have been many instances of extinguishers failing to operate, or being empty, when a fire occurred.

AUTOMATIC EXTINGUISHERS　　There are three types of automatic extinguishing systems normally used. One uses overhead water sprinklers and the other two flood the area with a fire-extinguishing gas, carbon dioxide or Halon, from pressurized tanks.

1. Sprinklers

The National Fire Protection Association recommends that any computer room that contains combustible material should have a sprinkler system [1]. Insurance companies often insist on sprinklers also. The main problem with sprinklers is that water can damage the data-processing equipment. In some installations the risk of damage from the sprinkler system is greater than the risk of damage from fire. The reconditioning needed by sprinklered equipment can put some installations out of action for a time, and there is a risk to personnel caused by water with electrical systems. To lessen the damage, electric power should be cut off prior to the application of water. When an operator is in control, the normal delay between the outbreak of fire and the operation of sprinklers should give him time to shut off the power. If a computer is running unattended, automatic power shutdown is desirable, before the sprinklers start. For this reason a "dry" sprinkler system is recommended in which the sprinkling action is triggered by a fire detector that first shuts down the power and permits time for operator intervention.

On some installations without automatic power shutdown, operators leave the computer unattended while they have dinner or coffee. This practice is especially prevalent on a terminal-based system on which the operators do nothing for long periods. It is clearly a risk. Only installations designed for unattended operation should be left unattended.

Reference 2 gives details of sprinkler installation.

2. Carbon Dioxide (CO_2)

Systems that flood an area with carbon dioxide avoid water damage but pose great risks to personnel. The gas is odorless, colorless, and potentially lethal. It is essential that personnel should be drilled to leave the room very quickly when carbon dioxide flooding is about to occur. Recommendations of fire-protection authorities should be followed precisely when installing carbon dioxide flooding systems. Reference 3 is an essential guide.

Safeguards when carbon dioxide flooding is used include proximity of exits, a built-in delay before the release of gas to give time to exit (or to give time to stop the release), available oxygen bottles, and "buddy" systems in which each person must ensure that a specified colleague exits safely. One installation, apparently following the advice of a consultant, installed gas masks. As carbon dioxide flooding works by removing oxygen from the area, gas masks give no protection. (One widely distributed consultant's report recommends gas masks with carbon dioxide flooding!)

For an *unattended* installation automatic carbon dioxide flooding is probably the best form of protection.

3. Halon

Flooding the area with a halogenated extinguishing agent normally causes no harm to equipment and is less dangerous to personnel than carbon dioxide. Halon at a concentration of less than 10 per cent extinguishes fire and can be breathed by man. At temperatures above 900°F it decomposes into chemicals that *are* dangerous, but the staff have much more time to evacuate than with carbon dioxide flooding. Unfortunately, Halon is much more expensive than carbon dioxide.

The National Fire Protection Association [4] describes the hazards to personnel of undecomposed Halon 1301 as follows:

Undecomposed Halon 1301 has been studied in humans and found to produce minimal, if any, central nervous system effects at concentrations below seven percent for exposure of approximately five minutes' duration. At concentrations of seven to ten percent effects such as dizziness, impaired co-ordination, and reduced mental acuity become definite with exposure of a few minutes' duration; however, these effects are not incapacitative for exposures of one minute or less. At concentrations above 10 percent, these effects increase in intensity and may become incapacitating with exposures longer than about one minute. At concentrations of the order of 15 to 20 percent, there is the risk of unconsciousness and possibly death if the exposure is prolonged, although no subjects have actually lost consciousness as a result of exposure to 10 to 15 percent concentrations of Halon 1301.

Personnel should not attempt to remain in an area following discharge of Halon 1301 in concentrations above seven percent and furthermore it is recommended that they do not remain in an area for more than four or five minutes even though agent concentrations are below seven percent. Within the first 30 seconds of exposure to Halon 1301 little effect is noticed, even when concentrations of 10 to 15 percent are inhaled. At these levels, this amount of time appears necessary for the body to absorb a sufficient quantity of the agent to bring about the onset of effects. However, at higher concentrations the onset of symptoms may occur within a few seconds and since an individual may be quickly incapacitated by these higher levels, concentrations greater than 15 percent should not be used where there is any chance of human exposure.

The effects of exposure to Halon 1301 may persist for a short period of time following exposure; however, recovery may be expected to be rapid and complete. Halon 1301 would not be expected to accumulate in the body even with repeated exposures.

Anyone suffering from the toxic effects of Halon 1301 vapors should immediately move or be moved to fresh air. In treating persons suffering toxic effects due to exposure to this agent, the use of epinephrine (adrenaline) and similar drugs must be avoided because they may produce cardiac arrhythmias, including ventricular fibrillation.

Fortunately, whereas undecomposed Halon is ordorless and colorless, the dangerous decomposition products have a sharp acrid odor even in minute concentrations of only a few parts in a million. This odor gives personnel who remain in the area warning that they should leave before the concentrations become dangerous.

The longer the exposure of Halon to the fire, the greater will be the proportion of decomposition products. It has been shown in tests that if the agent is discharged quickly the fire is extinguished faster and the production of decomposition products is minimized. It is advantageous to design the system for the fastest practical flooding. With such equipment fires can be extinguished very quickly.

Halon is five times heavier than air. By itself it would sink to the bottom of the room and not extinguish flames in higher locations. However, once it is thoroughly mixed with air, it does not settle out. The discharge nozzles must therefore be designed so that they produce a well-mixed atmosphere.

Table 26.1 lists 10 safeguards necessary when Halon flooding is used.

Table 26.1. Ten Safeguards for Personnel Needed When
Halon Flooding Is Employed*

The steps and safeguards necessary to prevent injury or death to personnel in areas whose atmospheres will be made hazardous by the discharge or thermal decomposition of Halon 1301 may include the following:

1. Provision of adequate aisleways and routes of exit and keeping them clear at all times.
2. Provision of the necessary additional and/or emergency lighting and directional signs to ensure quick, safe evacuation.
3. Provision of alarms within such areas that will operate immediately upon detection of the fire.
4. Provision of only outward swinging self-closing doors at exits from hazardous areas, and, where such doors are latched, provision of panic hardware.
5. Provision of continuous alarms at entrances to such areas until the atmosphere has been restored to normal.
6. Provision of warning and instruction signs at entrances to and inside such areas.
7. Provision for prompt discovery and rescue of persons rendered unconscious in such areas. This may be accomplished by having such areas searched immediately by trained men equipped with proper

*Reproduced from the U.S. National Fire Protection Association pamphlet on Halon [4].

Table 26.1. Ten Safeguards for Personnel That Are Needed When
Halon Flooding Is Employed *(cont'd)*

breathing equipment. Self-contained breathing equipment and personnel trained in its use and in rescue practices, including artificial respiration, should be readily available.

8. Provision of instruction and drills of all personnel within or in the vicinity of such areas, including maintenance or construction people who may be brought into the area, to ensure their correct action when Halon 1301 protective equipment operates.

9. Provision of means for prompt ventilation of such areas. Forced ventilation will often be necessary. Care should be taken to really dissipate hazardous atmospheres and not merely move them to another location. Halon 1301 is heavier than air.

10. Provision of such other steps and safeguards that a careful study of each particular situation indicates are necessary to prevent injury or death.

FIRE DETECTORS

Many installations do not employ carbon dioxide or Halon flooding even when a high level of security is needed. Sprinklers are common, as many insurance companies insist upon them.

Fire detectors are needed to operate the sprinklers or gas-flooding equipment automatically when the installation is unmanned, or to warn the operators of fire when the installation *is* manned. Fires are unlikely to occur in a well-constructed computer room when the machines are not running and the power is off. Fires that occur when the machines *are* running can usually be put out with hand-operated equipment if detected quickly enough. Often the fire procedures and equipment are designed so that the operator can usually avoid having the sprinklers or flooding equipment go off, because the sprinklers cause damage and gas flooding is expensive.

As discussed in Chapter 25, two types of fire detectors are used, heat detectors and smoke detectors. Heat detectors tend to be ineffective with localized fires such as those in electronic equipment; smoke detectors give the alert much earlier. Electrical fires usually start with a breakdown in insulation or a component overheating. Arcing occurs, and the heat in the local area is quite intense, vaporizing material and generating smoke. Left alone, the fire may do considerable damage, but does not easily spread into a general conflagration. There will be much smoke, but the room temperature will not rise appreciably, especially if the room is air conditioned. A smoke detector will alert the operator quickly, and the fire can usually be put out with a hand extinguisher. It should be put out as quickly as possible to minimize equipment damage. A sprinkler system, triggered by the melting of fusable links in the sprinklers, will not detect the fire for a long time. Much damage may be done before the sprinklers operate, and more after they operate.

Figure 26.1. A typical Halon installation in a computer room. A CO$_2$ installation needs about 10 times as much gas to put out a fire and, consequently, requires much larger gas tanks and is dangerous to personnel. (*Courtesy Fenwal, Inc.*)

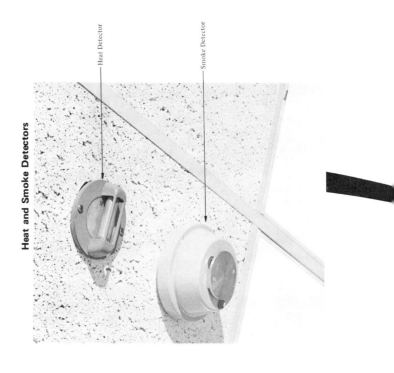

Heat Detector

Smoke Detector

Heat and Smoke Detectors

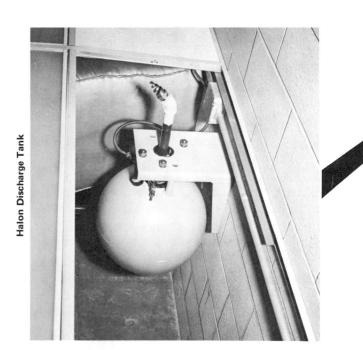

Halon Discharge Tank

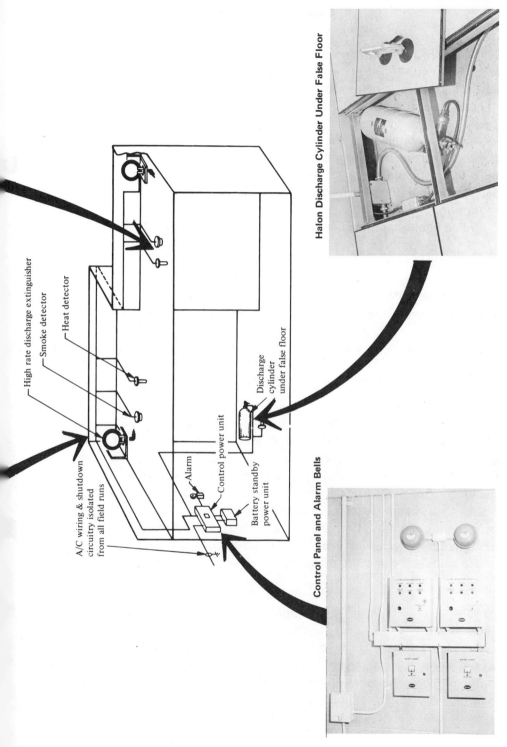

High rate discharge extinguisher

Smoke detector

Heat detector

A/C wiring & shutdown circuitry isolated from all field runs

Alarm

Control power unit

Battery standby power unit

Discharge cylinder under false floor

Halon Discharge Cylinder Under False Floor

Control Panel and Alarm Bells

317

The sensitivity of smoke detectors may be varied. If the threshold is set low, there will be false alarms occasionally. Nevertheless, it is desirable to detect equipment fires as soon as possible. For this reason many installations tolerate the occasional false alarm, but it is vital to ensure that the detection does not release a fire extinguishing agent immediately. When the detector merely alerts an operator, the threshold should be set low. A false alarm need not necessarily interrupt computer operations. There will be less likelihood of false alarms if smoking is prohibited in the area of the smoke detectors. Fire detectors should be placed under the raised floor as well as on the computer-room ceiling.

The smoke (or other) detectors should initiate four actions:

1. They should sound an alarm to alert the operator.
2. They should flash a light or give some other indication as to which of the detectors sounded the alarm.
3. An alarm should sound in a remote location such as a guard post or a headquarters location.
4. The alarm may trigger automatic extinguishing equipment, but not until after a delay sufficient to allow the operator to intervene. The air-conditioning and the power should be shut off before the automatic extinguishing begins.

INSTRUCTION TO OPERATORS   The operators and all persons normally in the computer area should be fully familiar with what to do if fire starts or the alarm sounds. They must be trained in the use of the hand extinguishers. A notice should be posted giving the emergency procedures. Exhibit 26.1 gives an example of such a notice. It relates to a system with smoke detectors, no automatic extinguishers, but a permanent communication line connecting the fire-detection equipment to a headquarters location or guard post. The trouble signal referred to in this notice sounds if this communication line fails.

POWER-OFF PROCEDURE   The computer-room emergency power-off switch and power panel should be clearly marked and always unobstructed. Everyone in the computer room should know their whereabouts and should be instructed in their use. All switches should be labeled. Emergency lighting, which comes on when the main power is cut off, should be installed.

FIRE PROCEDURES

IF FIRE ALARM SOUNDS

1.　Check the lights under the alarm to see which zone has the fire
　　condition.
2.　Silence the alarm by opening indicator unit door with key nearby
　　and flicking the switch in upper right, marked "Gong", from
　　"on" to "off".
3.　Check floor plan posted on inside of fire indicator door for location
　　of detector heads:

　　(a)　If machine room ceiling or air conditioning rooms have
　　　　shown fire signal, these have overhead units - go to the
　　　　area involved and look for flashing light in the detector
　　　　heads - source of smoke should be evident.

　　(b)　If machine room underfloor has shown fire signal, remove
　　　　floor tile involved with plunger available in Customer
　　　　Engineer room.

4.　If fire or smoke is detected, shut off all power for the machines.
5.　If you can handle the fire condition, do so immediately - if you
　　doubt you can handle the situation, call the fire department
　　immediately at RH4-1000 - have someone outside the building
　　to direct the firemen.
6.　Call the building superintendent's office to advise him of the
　　fire condition, tel: 7215. If emergency occurs at other than normal
　　business hours, call the building superintendent at his home,
　　tel: MU4-0999.
7.　If needed a doctor can be obtained from tel: PL1-0100.
8.　Headquarters personnel will contact you regarding the emergency.

IF TROUBLE SIGNAL SOUNDS

This indicates trouble in the fire indicator telephone connection to
headquarters.

1.　Silence the buzzer by opening the indicator unit door and
　　flickering the switch marked "Gong" from "on" to "off".
2.　Check that no fire actually exists.
3.　Headquarters personnel will contact you and handle the
　　situation.

Exhibit 26.1

Pulling the emergency power-off switch may result in damage to certain equipment, and damage to certain records in the files may result. For this reason the power should be turned off in an orderly manner whenever there is time. A notice should be posted giving the orderly and emergency power-off procedures. Exhibit 26.2 is an example of such a notice, giving three alternatives for a computer room with an IBM 360 Model 40 and Model 50. The red Emergency Power handle on the console of each computer in the installation is wired so that it removes power from *both* computers and their peripherals.

**PERSONAL
SAFETY**
A first aid kit must be available in the computer room. Instruction in the first aid that might be needed should be a regular part of the safety program. The telephone number of an available doctor should be clearly posted. Personnel should be warned that the wearing of certain jewelry and loose clothing can present a safety hazard.

**FIREPROOF
STORAGE**
Fireproof storage for important programs and data was discussed in Chapter 24. This and the means of recovery discussed in Chapters 22 and 32 are vital.

**EXPERT
ADVICE**
The advice of fire experts is usually available free from the installation's insurance company and sometimes from the local fire department. The installation should be checked by such authorities when possible. Some municipal fire departments provide free security audits.

REFERENCES

1. National Fire Protection Association, "Protection of Electronic Computer/Data Processing Equipment," Pamphlet No. 75, Boston, 1968.

2. National Fire Protection Association, "Standards for the Installation of Sprinkler Systems," Pamphlet No. 13, Boston, 1968.

3. National Fire Protection Association "Standards for the Installation of Carbon Dioxide Systems," Pamphlet No. 12, Boston, 1968.

EMERGENCY POWER-OFF PROCEDURES

Three alternatives:

Procedure 1.   This alternative is the one which will cause no damage
                to the systems' hardware or data files. It should be
                used whenever there is sufficient time to allow the
                units to be disabled.

                a.   Press Stop on the Model 50
                b.   Disable the 2314
                c.   Unload all tape drives
                d.   Press Power Off on the Model 50
                e.   Press Stop on the Model 40
                f.   Disable all 2311s
                g.   Unload all tape drives
                h.   Press Power Off on Model 40
                i.   Pull Emergency Power on Model 40 (Takes care
                      of both systems)
                j.   Pull Main Line Switch at Panel Box

Procedure 2.   This alternative is for crash emergency, where the power
                must be removed from the system or systems as quickly
                as possible without regard for possible damage to
                equipment or data.

                a.   Pull Emergency Power at the Model 50, or ⎫ Drops both
                      Pull Emergency Power at the Model 40   ⎬   Systems
                b.   Pull Main Line Switch at Panel Box   ⎭

Procedure 3.   This alternative is for use where all power to the
                systems must be removed immediately. This is almost
                certain to cause subsequent damage to the systems.

                a.   Pull Main Line Switch at Panel Box

Exhibit 26.2

4. National Fire Protection Association, "Standards for the Installation of Halon Systems," Pamphlet No. 12A, Boston, 1971.

5. National Fire Protection Association, "Standards for the Installation of Portable Fire Extinguishers," Pamphlet No. 10, Boston, 1968.

6. National Fire Protection Association, "Recommended Good Practice for the Maintenance and Use of Portable Fire Extinguishers," Pamphlet No. 10A, Boston, 1968.

7. National Fire Protection Association, "Standards for Protection of Records," Pamphlet 232, Boston, 1967.

8. National Fire Protection Association, "Standards for Air Conditioning Systems," Pamphlet No. 90A, Boston, 1968.

9. National Fire Protection Association, "Installation of Fire Doors and Windows," Pamphlet No. 80, Boston, 1968.

10. National Fire Protection Association, "Central Station Protection Signalling Systems," Pamphlet No. 71, Boston, 1967.

11. National Fire Protection Association, "Standard for Proprietary Protective Signalling Systems," Pamphlet No. 72D, Boston, 1967.

For a complete list of National Fire Protection Association literature, write to National Fire Protection Association, 60 Batterymarch Street, Boston, Mass. 02110.

27 SABOTAGE

The computer has occasionally been a target for antiestablishment rebels, antiwar protestors, and rampaging students. This has resulted in a number of serious sabotage attacks on computer centers. To some persons the computer has become a symbol of mindless authoritarianism (and this attitude is made worse by the erroneous utility bills and abusive printouts from the credit agencies); to others it represents Orwell's "Big Brother"; to still others it represents a fear of unemployment.

Some organizations developed their first major concern for computer security at the beginning of the 1970s when computer sabotage became highly publicized. At that time, a few computers were wrecked by bombs and many were threatened. Many student groups marched ineffectually on computer centers. Protestors from Students For a Democratic Society succeeded in erasing 1000 magnetic tapes at Dow Chemical. (The press said 10,000 tapes.) For many organizations the era of the showcase data-processing installation was over. Large signs proudly indicating the computer center were taken down, and the policy of displaying this corporate status symbol in a shop-window installation changed to a policy of minimum visibility.

Reports of sabotage against computers have been exaggerated by the press, by security consultants, and by firms with gadgets for sale. A typical report which was repeated in various publications said that ". . . a magnet the size of a quarter can destroy a library of up to 50,000 tape reels in minutes" [1]. In fact, it is likely to take at least $\frac{1}{2}$ minute per volume, or about 50 man-days in total. In spite of the scare talk, computer sabotage remains one of the deadliest of threats to the security of a corporation with advanced data processing. There are far more bombings than the public realizes because most are kept out of the press. Between January 1, 1969, and April 15, 1970, there were 4333 bombings, 1475 attempted bombings, and 35,126 recorded bomb warnings in the United States (see Fig. 27.1). At the time of writing the Federal Bureau of Investigation is quoted as saying that they are occurring at the rate of 433 per month [2] (averaging more than one every 2 hours). Most major businesses have been threatened, but few of the threats are aimed at data processing.

Mob action is also a serious threat to computers. The shift in social attitudes may well increase the likelihood of sabotage.

Sabotage sometimes also comes from the inside. It ranges from the disgruntled factory worker stuffing a peanut-butter sandwich into his badge reader to the data-processing employee methodically damaging the system. In one frightening case a dissatisfied employee erased virtually every file and program that his company possessed. For a time it was doubtful whether the management could keep the company in business. In another case computer maintenance staff who were on strike sabotaged an insurance company's teleprocessing system by dialing paper tape terminals and transmitting false control messages that prevented the control computer from polling and reading the data on the tapes. This sabotage action continued for a month before the cause was discovered.

There are several organizations with the stated objective of doing harm to computers. One is the International Society for the Abolition of Data-Processing Machines, which claims to have several thousand members. It publishes a *Manifesto*, as do other such societies. The actions they recommend mostly fall into the category of nuisance or minor loss rather than catastrophe.

PROTECTION   As with other aspects of security, protection has three facets:

1. Minimize the probability of it happening.
2. Minimize the damage that will occur if it does happen.
3. Plan fast and effective means of recovery.

The approach to *preventing* sabotage by outsiders is twofold. First, minimize the likelihood of them wanting to do it. Second, make it as difficult as possible and especially make the most dangerous methods difficult.

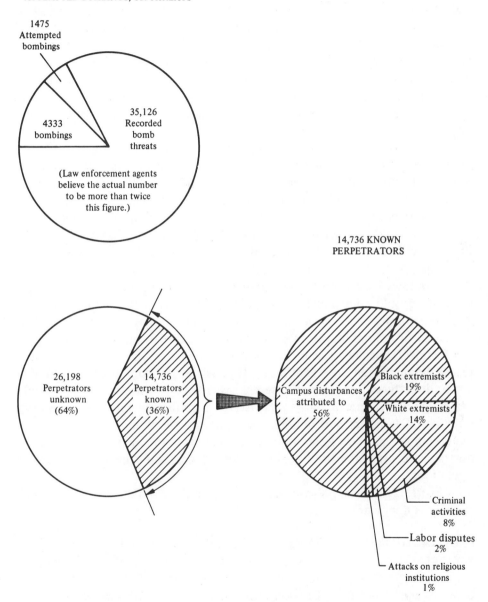

40,934 RECORDED BOMBINGS,
ATTEMPTED BOMBINGS, OR THREATS

1475
Attempted
bombings

4333
bombings

35,126
Recorded
bomb
threats

(Law enforcement agents
believe the actual number
to be more than twice
this figure.)

14,736 KNOWN
PERPETRATORS

26,198
Perpetrators
unknown
(64%)

14,736
Perpetrators
known
(36%)

Campus disturbances
attributed to
56%

Black extremists
19%

White extremists
14%

Criminal
activities
8%

Labor disputes
2%

Attacks on religious
institutions
1%

Figure 27.1. A survey of bombings and bomb threats in the United
States from January 1, 1969, to April 15, 1970 (a vintage year!).
Average: One actual or attempted bombing every 2 hours. The
majority of bombings were directed at business establishments.
(Source: U.S. Treasury, Firearms Department.)

SITE   The likelihood of sabotage can be minimized by
LOCATION   attempting to keep a vital computer center out of
sight. The outside troublemaker should not know
it is there. If possible, the site should be away from areas where a high level
of radical activity occurs, such as near certain campuses or in the center of
troubled cities. If a mob is likely to march on the corporate headquarters, it
might be better to locate vital computers away from the headquarters location. Certainly shopwindow and showcase locations should be avoided. Community groups should not be given tours of the facility.

The computer room should be made as inaccessible as possible. There
should be only one entrance to it, and this should be securely locked or
guarded. Doors used for emergency exits or for equipment loading should
open only from the inside and should be kept closed. If the organization has a
guarded compound, the computer may be located inside it. Advantage should
be taken of any plant security measures already in force. A site may be available where there are already guards or patrols.

The secure computer room should not have outside windows. Ground-
floor windows have been bricked up in some computer rooms. Ground-floor
locations should be avoided if there is a choice. If violent sabotage is of concern, the computer room or vital storage should not have an outside wall. A
truckload of ammonium nitrate explosive (available from farm supply stores
as a fertilizer) backed up against the wall could destroy the facility, and hand-
placed bombs could do severe harm. If possible, the computer room should
not be directly under a flat roof, as explosives or fire bombs on the roof could
destroy vital equipment. For this reason it is preferable not to use one-story
buildings. The rooms surrounding the computer room and the floors immediately above and below should be controlled, and one of the easiest ways to
do this is to use these the floors for programmers and other data-processing
operations.

Figure 27.2 shows a recommended site for a computer room in which
security is important.

PROTECT UTILITY   The air-conditioning vents should be carefully con-
SERVICES   trolled. In some installations they are in obvious
and unprotected locations. The air conditioning
could easily be put out of action, but much more drastic, one of the easiest
ways to destroy a computer room is to empty a drum of gasoline down the
air-conditioning vent. On reaching the air-conditioned facility it will atomize
and probably explode.

Protection is needed for the power and communication lines into the
building. Specially reinforced conduits may be used and the lines may be

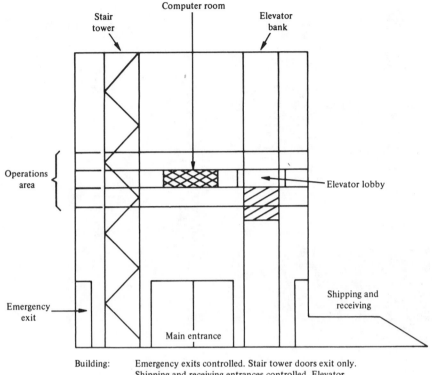

Building: Emergency exits controlled. Stair tower doors exit only.
Shipping and receiving entrances controlled. Elevator
stops selectively locked out.

DP Operations area:
Visitors contained in elevator lobby pending
identification. Rest rooms locked. Floors immediately
above and below the computer room are controlled.

Computer room:
Ideally, room within a room. One entrance only. Minimal number of authorized
entrants. Controlled locks (e. g., card key) on main
entrance. All other egresses fitted with "Exit Only"
hardware.

Figure 27.2. A computer location selected for security. (*Reproduced
with permission from IBM's "Guidelines for Protection and Control in
a Computer Environment."*)

duplexed. Power transformers and other equipment may be specially protected. In some installations it would be extremely easy to disrupt the power
or communication lines. Figure 27.3 shows a leased-line "patch panel" for a
real-time computer system in which security is vital. It is not in a locked
cabinet and is away from the computer in a relatively insecure area. Pulling

Figure 27.3. The unlocked leased-line "patch panel." To disable the system, pull out the plugs. This photograph was taken on a system for which loss of the communication lines would have been catastrophic.

out the plugs at a critical moment would disable the system. Often the private branch exchange that serves the computer is overlooked as a security risk. It is often remote from the computer site and in an unlocked room. A secure private branch exchange should be firmly locked and have detectors that sound an alarm if any movement is detected in the room.

DAMAGE BY INSIDERS   An insider bent upon sabotage, and particularly a member of the data-processing staff, may be able to do more harm than an outsider. Care should be taken with disgruntled employees. Psychological security is important and is discussed in Chapters 33 and 35. It is particularly important to ensure that the programs cannot be tampered with on the operational system (Chapter 34) and that access to the important data records is controlled. Employees other than those who *must* know should not be aware of the location of the backup data storage.

MAGNETS   Magnets have been used to erase tapes and disks;
                       however, the story that tapes inside their cannisters
have been erased by boy scouts walking through an installation with magnets
in their pockets is simply not true.

The world's largest permanent magnet would have to be closer than 4 to
6 inches from the surface of the tape in order to erase it [3]. The most powerful pocket magnet that could normally be bought in a store would have to
be even closer. The world's largest electromagnet would have to be closer
than a few feet. Using a magnet that could be carried in the pocket, an intruder would have to take each tape from its cabinet. The cabinets for sensitive
data should be strong and firmly locked.

The SDS protestors who erased the Dow Chemical tapes had to unspool
each tape from its reel. They erased the front part of each tape only, but that
included the tape label and so made the tape unreadable. To erase a thousand
tapes in this way was a lengthy operation.

A highly sensitive device is on the market for detecting a magnet at a
distance. It may be worthwhile to install one of these in the tape storage, connected to a suitable alarm. However, the money would probably be better
spent on burglar-proof cabinets. The saboteur could do harm to tapes and
disks without magnets.

RADIATION   Another scare story concerns electromagnetic radia-
                       tion. There have been instances of radar signals
causing instantaneous computer errors. The computers in question were in
the direct path of a powerful radar with no intervening structure, for example, at an airport. This is a very rare occurrence. If the electromagnetic signal
strength is less than 1 volt per meter, the radiation will cause no problem.
The solution to the problem can be as simple as grounding the metalwork in
the facility, or at worst, erecting a grounded metal screen (like window
screening).

Alarmist reports have claimed that a specially equipped truck in the
street outside a computer installation can use powerful radiation to erase
tapes and disks. This is not possible. The worst that such an expensive device
could accomplish would be to cause sporadic computer errors or errors in
main memory, both of which would be automatically detected. It would
hardly be worth the effort.

COMPREHENSIVE   Thorough protection against sabotage could be ex-
PROTECTION   tremely expensive—so expensive that few nonmili-
                       tary organizations would consider it. Thorough
protection must assume that the saboteur is highly intelligent, prepared to

use violent methods, and intends to cause the maximum level of damage. Fortunately, these three characteristics seem highly unlikely to coincide on nonmilitary systems. If it is assumed that they will not coincide, protection is possible at a reasonable cost.

The saboteur who is prepared to use violent methods rarely seems to be intelligent enough to maximize the effect of his violence. He is usually an outsider who is unfamiliar with the data-processing details. Only rarely have bomb explosions put a computer center out of action, and generally they have not destroyed the data files. If the data files are destroyed, the saboteur is unlikely to destroy the backup copies when they are properly protected. The damage caused by violent sabotage has been far less than that caused by fires, and generally recovery is easier.

The highly intelligent saboteur, such as the disgruntled data-processing employee, is rarely prepared to use violence. He is usually not familiar with the technology of bombs, and is usually intimidated by the prospects of violence. He generally believes that more damage can be done by destroying data or changing programs. Intelligently thought out safeguards can substantially limit the destruction he can cause.

Most saboteurs do not make a planned attempt to put the installation out of action completely. Most acts of violence are token gestures intended to damage, but not to eliminate the possibility of recovery. Rampaging mobs might cause temporary chaos, but not permanent harm. The disgruntled employee usually also makes a token gesture, and his actions are wounding, not lethal.

MINIMAL SABOTAGE POSTURE   Some managements seem to have dismissed sabotage protection, apparently with the thought, "If they're going to get us, they're going to get us!" More realistically, a fairly low-cost posture can be taken about sabotage if we assume that intelligent inside knowledge, capability for violence, and lethal intent do not coincide.

The following items (some of which have mentioned before) should be regarded as a necessary minimum on any installation in which security is of importance.

1. The computer center should have *low visibility* so as to discourage outside attention. There should not be signs indicating its whereabouts.
2. A vital system should not be in a shopwindow or showcase installation. If it is too late to move it from a plate-glass ground-floor installation, then heavy fabric or plastic mesh drapes should be used, secured in tracks at the top and bottom. The glass may be replaced with "storm plastic" glazing.

3. The computer site should be selected with security in mind, if possible. Preferably it should not be on the ground floor or top floor of a building. The floors above and below it and any surrounding area should be protected. It should be sited in a secure compound or guarded building if possible.

4. Vital equipment should be away from windows.

5. When the site is being planned, security and sabotage protection should be discussed with the architect.

6. Air-conditioning inlets should not be in locations where they are obviously vulnerable.

7. If a night watchman patrols the building, he should pay special attention to the computer center.

8. Effective intruder and fire alarms should be used, wired directly to the building guard or local police.

9. Effective locks should be used on the computer and storage power supply and on the storage cabinets. The tape/disk storage should be especially well protected.

10. The floor or building should have one entrance only. All persons entering should be checked by a guard or receptionist. (Often a guard solely for the computer center does not seem justified.)

11. Frequent checks should be made that it is not possible to enter through rear exits such as fire escapes, or through windows or vents.

12. Open-shop operation should not be used.

13. All visitors should be escorted at all times.

14. Tours of the facilities (stockholders, boy scouts, community clubs) should be banned.

15. Demonstrations to outsiders should be avoided if possible. If they are unavoidable, they should be carefully controlled. A glamorous demonstration room with projector will help keep the visitors away from the sensitive locations.

16. The programs should be carefully controlled, as discussed in Chapter 34. The methods of control should prevent unauthorized programs from ever being used with sensitive data files.

17. The morale of the staff should be watched carefully by all managers. Staff who might cause deliberate damage usually have an obvious chip on their shoulder. Special care should be taken with anyone who is fired. It is often advisable to make him leave the premises immediately.

18. The means must be available to reconstruct records if they become damaged, as discussed in Chapter 22.

19. A vital-records program must be active (Chapter 32). Records needed for this and for general record reconstruction should be securely stored in a different building, and only persons who need to know should be aware of its location.

20. The availability of a backup computing facility should be available in case of disaster, and the programs should be tested on it.

21. The local police should be familiar with the installation and aware of the concern over its security.

FUTURE
SYSTEMS

Future generations of computers will be designed with security problems in mind. Possibly the best way to attack the problem would be to have all input/output units and possibly the operator console remote from the computer. The computer, like the telephone exchange, could be in a highly secure room without people present except for maintenance. The tapes and disks may be loaded on machines in the volume library by a librarian following the instructions of the remote operator. No other person would normally have access to the volume library. The backup or vital record store may also have volume reading units in it. There may be several volume libraries and several operators remotely connected to the computer by teleprocessing. Such an arrangement could make sabotage more difficult and make a higher level of collusion between individuals necessary in order to commit fraud.

REFERENCES

1. Mel Mandell, "Computer Scare Talk," *New York Times,* May 9, 1971.

2. E. P. McGuire, "Target for Terrorists, *The Conference Board Record,* Aug. 1971. pp. 2-8.

3. "Guidelines for Protection and Control in a Computer Environment" (loose-leaf binder), International Business Machines, Poughkeepsie, N.Y., 1971, pp.2-3.

28 COMMUNICATION-LINE WIRETAPPING

With wide use of data transmission the possibility exists that wiretapping will occur. This has been frequently mentioned in public discussions on security in computer systems.

ACTIVE AND PASSIVE WIRETAPPING Wiretapping can be either active or passive. Active wiretapping means that the intruder sends his own data on the line. Passive wiretapping means that he listens only and does not originate any data on the communication line. To carry out active wiretapping, he would normally have to have a terminal and modem compatible with the type of transmission that was taking place on the communication line. Even then, the authorization controls and file locks could make it very difficult or impossible for him to access the precise part of the data base that he is interested in.

Some particularly ingenious forms of active wiretapping have been mentioned in the Congressional hearings on privacy and the alarmist books and articles on computer security. For example, "piggyback" entry into the system refers to the interception of communications in such a way that modifications are substituted for messages that would otherwise occur in the normal man-machine conversation. Often a legitimate user is inactive for a substantial period of time between his sign on and sign off, and during this time an active wiretapper could send messages that would be accepted by the computer. Again, he may be able to cancel the user's sign-off signals completely, so that he can continue operating in the user's name. Such techniques, however, require ingenuity and much technical knowledge. They would be very difficult to accomplish and, while admitting that they are possible, the author can find no instance in which *active* wiretapping has actually occurred in practice.

Passive wiretapping on the other hand can be done with relatively inexpensive equipment. A cheap tape recorder can be used to record the signals passing over a communication line, in such a way that all the data can be reconstructed. In fact, the same tape recorder can be subsequently connected to a terminal with the appropriate modem, and the terminal can be made to print or display the characters that were being transmitted. The data contents, however, can be reconstructedwithout using an actual terminal.

A person tapping the flow of data might have to listen for a very long time on most systems before he finds any information that is of particular value to him. The combination of wiretapping with other techniques may, however, produce results. For example, wiretapping could be used to obtain the security code that the security officer uses to access the system. Using this code at a normal terminal, the wiretapper could then change the authorization codes or file locks in the system and, hence, obtain free access to the data base. With a high degree of ingenuity and a cheap tape recorder, passive wiretapping could help crack the system.

METHODS OF PROTECTION   How can we protect ourselves from wiretapping? First, we might use scramblers. These are devices much seen in World War II movies for the protection of telephone calls. They scramble the signal in an analog fashion. They would be used on the communication-line side of the modem, and would scramble and descramble its output just as can be done with voice. In the computer age they do not provide a major degree of security. The enscrambling method is relatively simple, and it would not present too much difficulty to translate a recording of what is sent into the correct data signals.

Second, we can use the cryptography methods discussed in Chapters 19 and 20. This is, in effect, scrambling in a digital rather than an analog fashion. It can be made much more secure than the use of scramblers and is *essential* to certain systems.

Third, teleprocessing control procedures have been devised that could make *active* wiretapping extremely difficult. The procedures discussed in Chapter 12 are in use to identify a terminal. An ingenious wiretapper could imitate the response that such a terminal would give. To prevent him doing so, the control procedures could require an *authenticity check* in each message. Unlike the *identification check* now in use, it would be different in every message. It may be two characters, or so, derived from such items as

1. A code derived from certain characters in the previous message.

2. A code derived from synchronized message counters.

3. A code combining the readout from a simple clock mechanism and an identification code.

Today, teleprocessing control procedures normally contain an identification check, not an authenticity check, because active wiretapping is not yet a sufficiently serious problem.

Last, we can attempt to make the lines difficult to tap. Scramblers or cryptography devices may be thought too expensive for many commercial terminals. There are steps, however, that should certainly be taken to protect those points in a user's premises where a line is vulnerable to tapping.

TAPPING
PUBLIC LINES

For most of the length of a communication line, wiretapping is singularly difficult to accomplish. Figure 28.1 illustrates a typical communication link. A computer in the building on the left of the diagram is connected to terminals in that building and, by the long-distance link, to the terminals in the building on the right-hand side of the diagram.

The wires leave the building in a fairly thick cable that houses many wires. This is buried under the street in this illustration, and may be a multiwire cable. It would be extremely difficult to gain access to it under the street. An intruder cannot simply lift the manhole covers and go to work. Even if he did, he would probably not be able to obtain the cable book that tells the telephone company engineer which pair of wires is which, unless he operated in collusion with the appropriate telephone company employee.

This cable, after traveling some miles, goes into the telephone company local central office. At this location switching occurs, or the wires are connected to a leased line to the distant location. Again, it would be extremely difficult to carry on any wiretapping in the local central office unless in collusion with a telephone company employee. A high degree of security is normally maintained in such locations, but bribery of employees is always possible.

In Figure 28.1, shielded multiwire cable goes from the local central office to a toll office from which long-distance calls originate. The signals in question are then sent over a microwave link to a toll office many miles away. The microwave link may carry several thousand voice channels all multiplexed together. It would be possible, given appropriate equipment, to intercept the microwave beam, but it would need exceedingly expensive equipment to record it and to demultiplex it so that the data signals traveling over one of the

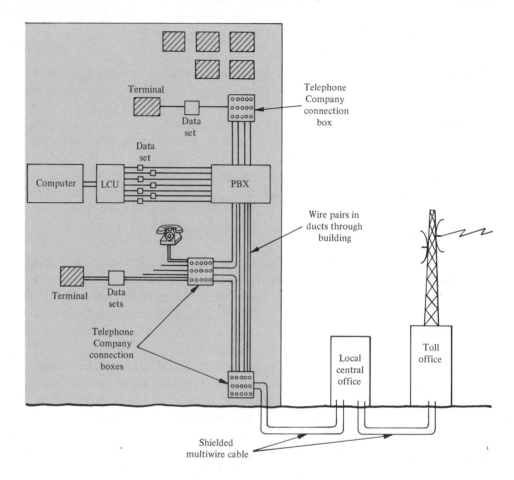

Figure 28.1

many voice channels could be interpreted. The line then travels on to the next toll office over coaxial cable, this time hanging from poles in the street, but again carrying several thousand voice channels all multiplexed together. Once again, eavesdropping on one particular voice channel would be virtually impossible for an intruder who did not have resources such as those of the National Security Agency. The call then travels to the local central office of the receiving location, again on a shielded multiwire cable buried under the street. The last link from the local central office to the building where the receiving terminals are housed is over multiwire cable hanging from poles in the street. This might be a little easier to intercept, but still far too difficult for it to be a practical consideration for most persons who might wish to invade a data-processing system.

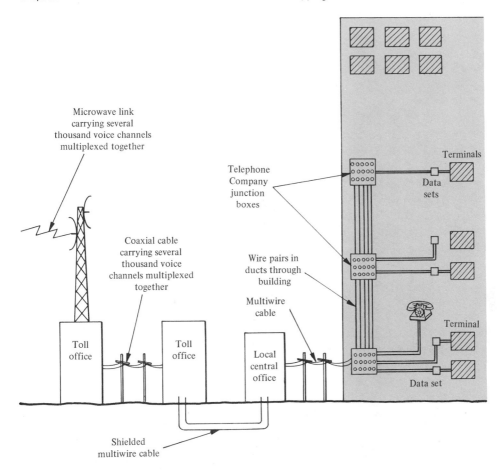

Figure 28.1 (cont'd)

**TAPPING ON THE
USER'S PREMISES**

A reason why telephone lines are unlikely to be tapped in the streets is that they are usually so easy to tap when we get *inside* the buildings—either the building on the left-hand side of the diagram or the building on the right-hand side. Here the cable enters telephone company connection boxes. The many pairs of wires are now separated and connected to terminal screws. They are usually clearly labeled. Figure 28.2 shows a typical telephone company connection box. From this connection box, pairs of wires travel through ducts in the building to the rooms in which the terminals are housed, or, in the building on the left-hand side of Fig. 28.1, to a private branch exchange. These wires will probably have to go through several more connection boxes before they reach their destination. In the private branch exchange, once again the

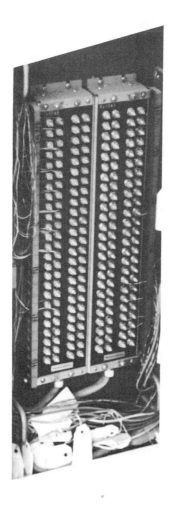

Figure 28.2. Telephone lines can be tapped inside rather than outside the users' premises. A typical junction box in an office building is usually unlocked or insecure (left). The wiring inside the junction box is easy to connect to so that data signals can be taken to an unauthorized and remote extension.

wires are exposed in such a way that they could easily be tapped, and the telephone numbers of the extensions to which they go are very clearly labeled.

If an intruder wanted to tap these lines, the easiest place for him to do it would be at the telephone company junction boxes. He could wire across the terminal screws in such a way that the signal would be picked up, perhaps on the terminal in his own office or perhaps on a different floor of the building, which is owned by a different organization. Usually the job is made easy by the fact that the wires are clearly labeled, as in Fig. 28.3. Often the terminal screws used for data wires are marked with a distinctive color.

The second easiest place for him to do it would be in the private branch exchange, where once again he could wire a connection between the appropriate wires. A connection between his own line and the tapped line could be made at the back of a panel in such a way that the maintenance men might not detect it for many months (Fig. 28.4). He could arrange the tap so that he could dial it on the public network, and do his eavesdropping far away in

Figure 28.3. Data lines are usually clearly labeled for the would-be wiretapper.

Figure 28.4. A wiretap hidden in a normally unseen part of a PBX. The eavesdropper can dial the wiretap from outside on the public network and can record the data transmitted.

comfort and safety. In many office buildings the private branch exchange is unlocked.

The third place where he could tap the wires would be in the ducts as they pass through the building. However, this would be much more difficult. He would have to break holes in the plaster, and he would have considerable difficulty in identifying the correct wires out of the large bunches of wires that travel through the building.

Clearly then, if we want to take some measure to protect ourselves from wiretapping, the first step is to make sure that all the telephone company junction boxes and private branch exchanges carrying the data in question are locked up. They may, for example, be in locked rooms or closets, or the panels over these junction boxes may be padlocked. It is a good idea to fit some form of burglar alarm so that if the locks are broken a signal would be sent over the telephone wires and sound an alarm. The computer system itself could be designed to detect whether the junction boxes or private branch exchange had been broken into. In some defense agency buildings the wires have been in pressurized cases so that any tampering would cause a pressure leak, but such a scheme is probably not cost justifiable on commercial installations.

In general, if the user can maintain security over the wiring within his own building, then telephone-line tapping becomes difficult to accomplish. A telephone operator or repairman casually listening in is not going to hear state secrets, but merely the unintelligible swish of data. There may, of course, be intruders with sufficient technical resources and persistence to accomplish external tapping. The Germans in World War II tapped transatlantic telephone calls, unscrambled them, and listened freely to Churchill and Roosevelt. However, persons wanting access to nonmilitary computer files are likely to look for easier schemes.

29 ELECTROMAGNETIC RADIATION AND SYSTEM EAVESDROPPING

In addition to passive wiretapping, a number of other forms of system eavesdropping are possible.

The newspapers and Congressional hearings have contained stories about "superspy trucks" [1] equipped with sensitive receiving equipment that can pick up radio waves emitted by computing equipment or terminals, and hence can steal computer data. Before an intruder needs to go to this extreme, however, he has many simpler means of eavesdropping open to him.

WASTEPAPER   The wastebins in a computer room often contain information of interest to a would-be intruder. They may contain carbon copies of listings that include sensitive data. They often contain file dumps or program listings. The wastebins used by the programmers may be even more revealing. They can indicate details of the operating system in use, and of its security procedures or lack of them. They can indicate file organization and application-program structures. Perhaps most important, they can give file passwords or authorization codes. Items of interest can also be read from discarded typewriter or printer ribbons or carbon paper.

An infiltrator can often pick items out of wastebins during the day. If he cannot do this, he can usually buy the waste in quantity from garbage collectors. As a source of information, it is more fruitful than days of electronic eavesdropping.

The protective measures are simple. Every wastebin should have a locked lid with a slot in it, and all waste should be shredded at the end of the day. The shredding operation itself must be made secure.

VISUAL
EAVESDROPPING
A security code may be learned by watching a display screen or printout over somebody's shoulder.
A desirable security feature on terminals is the ability to supress printing or display when the code is typed in. This might be done automatically under program control, the computer requesting the security code and then inhibiting display at the terminal. Even with such a feature, an intruder may observe the operator's keying the security code. The terminal operators should be told to be cautious about their security codes being observed, especially by visitors.

Modern telescopes are very powerful. Terminals at which security is of concern should not be situated near windows where they might be overlooked with telescopes.

CAMERAS
Cameras should be forbidden in areas where security is of concern. Even when they are forbidden, it is usually easy to bring a camera in. The best way to take a camera past a guard who checks for them is to carry two cameras; one is handed over to the guard and the other is hidden. The person responsible for security should remember that cameras can be very small, or alternatively they can have telescopic lenses. An amateur photographer with a powerful telephoto lens might be able to capture sensitive data from the other side of the street, if the desks or machines are positioned so as to facilitate this. Such a camera, using ultra-fine-grain film can photograph a typewritten document at a distance of 300 feet, and high enlargement can render it readable. Figure 29.1 illustrates this. If there can be no camera within 500 feet, the documents probably cannot be made legible with *amateur* equipment.

BUGGING
DEVICES
A bug which detects sounds and transmits them by radio can be very small, can be attached out of sight behind a picture frame or under a desk, and can be bought for $25. U.S. Federal law prohibits the sale of most bugs except to police, but they are readily available abroad and in the form of kits. One manufacturer's catalogue has a bug that can be placed in a telephone handset. Particularly insidious is the briefcase with a built-in recorder under a false bottom. The microphone on one inexpensive model is situated in the lock and cannot be seen; the recorder is switched on by setting the ordinary-looking briefcase handle in a particular position. Its user could, for example, set it to record while he leaves the room at a strategic moment.

While bugs are most likely to be used for recording conversations or meetings, it is possible to tell what some machines are printing, punching, or

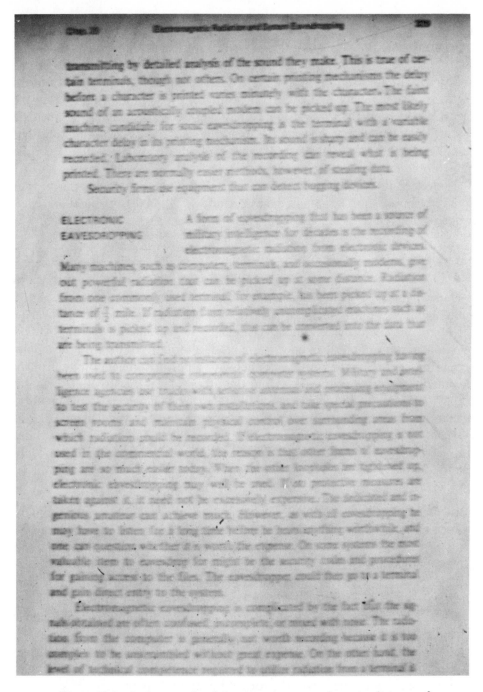

Figure 29.1. A photograph of the opposite page taken at a distance of 240 feet through a window. Photograph was taken by using a Pentax Spotmatic camera and a Celestron 5 telescopic lens. The text was just readable on the original negative.

transmitting by detailed analysis of the sound they make. This is true of certain terminals, though not others. On certain printing mechanisms the delay before a character is printed varies minutely with the character. The faint sound of an acoustically coupled modem can be picked up. The most likely machine candidate for sonic eavesdropping is the terminal with a variable character delay in its printing mechanism. Its sound is sharp and can be easily recorded. Laboratory analysis of the recording can reveal what is being printed. There are normally easier methods, however, of stealing data.

Security firms use equipment that can detect bugging devices.

ELECTRONIC EAVESDROPPING   A form of eavesdropping that has been a source of military intelligence for decades is the recording of electromagnetic radiation from electronic devices. Many machines, such as computers, terminals, and occasionally modems, give out powerful radiation that can be picked up at some distance. Radiation from one commonly used terminal, for example, has been picked up at a distance of $\frac{1}{2}$ mile. If radiation from relatively uncomplicated machines such as terminals is picked up and recorded, this can be converted into the data that are being transmitted.

The author can find no instance of electromagnetic eavesdropping having been used to compromise *commercial* computer systems. Military and intelligence agencies use trucks with sensitive antennas and processing equipment to test the security of their own installations, and take special precautions to screen rooms and maintain physical control over surrounding areas from which radiation could be recorded. If electromagnetic eavesdropping is not used in the commercial world, the reason is that other forms of eavesdropping are so much easier today. When the other loopholes are tightened up, electronic eavesdropping may well be used. If no protective measures are taken against it, it need not be excessively expensive. The dedicated and ingenious amateur can achieve much. However, as with all eavesdropping he may have to listen for a long time before he hears anything worthwhile, and one can question whether it is worth the expense. On some systems the most valuable item to eavesdrop for might be the security codes and procedures for gaining access to the files. The eavesdropper could then go to a terminal and gain direct entry to the system.

Electromagnetic eavesdropping is complicated by the fact that the signals obtained are often confused, incomplete, or mixed with noise. The radiation from the computer is generally not worth recording because it is too complex to be unscrambled without great expense. On the other hand, the level of technical competence required to utilize radiation from a terminal is not too high. The single serial data streams transmitted at a low rate make the job of the professional eavesdropper or skilled amateur relatively easy. The radiation from a typewriter-like terminal can be converted into data without expensive equipment, providing the receiver can be close enough. Typewriter-like terminals differ widely in the amount of radiation they transmit, and hence in the closeness necessary for a receiving antenna.

Some devices transmit the same signal repetitively. Most visual-display terminals, for example, continually scan the screen, refreshing the image. A signal containing the data on the screen may therefore be retransmitted hundreds of times. Repetition makes it possible to reconstruct a very weak or noisy signal, and hence a signal recorded a long way from the terminal. It is by using repeated transmission of the same data that such noise-free photographs are obtained from planetary spacecraft, with transmitters of only 10 watts, many millions of miles away in space. The contents of a visual-display screen can similarly be reconstructed from radiation detected at a substantial distance. The cost of the necessary equipment, however, is high. Vital data such as security codes should not be displayed on the screen, and they will then not be transmitted repetitively.

The first line of defense against electromagnetic eavesdropping lies with the equipment manufacturer. Machines can be designed so that the level of radiation they emit is not high. Until the late 1960s terminal designers usually gave no thought to radiation; consequently, some of the devices on the market radiated with high intensity. The manufacturers are now aware of the problem. Nevertheless, it is uneconomical to build hardware on which radiation has been almost eliminated. The radiation from a well-designed terminal today could be picked up with inexpensive equipment at a distance of 20 feet; to pick it up at 200 yards would be highly expensive. For some devices a curve has been produced estimating the cost of detecting radiation at different distances. Typical curves are those in Fig. 29.2. For a terminal designed for low emission of radiation the cost of electromagnetic eavesdropping becomes extremely high at distances over, say, 150 feet. A large truckfull of equipment is needed.

The computer user can take several measures to protect himself if he feels that electromagnetic radiation is a serious concern. First, he should avoid selecting a terminal that radiates like a shipping beacon. He may obtain a rough estimate of the shape of a curve, such as those in Fig. 29.2, that applies to his terminals. He should then ensure that inexpensive detection equipment cannot come close enough to his terminals to cause trouble. Terminals handling sensitive data can be located toward the center of the building, rather than against the outside walls. Security should be maintained on the floors

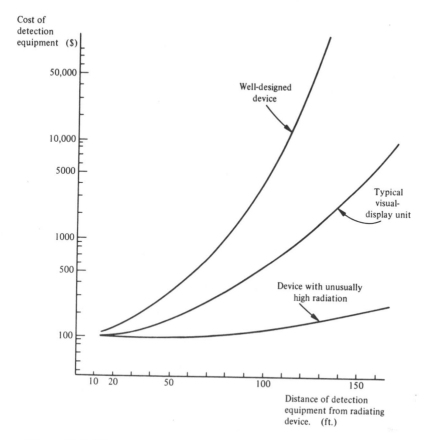

Figure 29.2. If a device such as a terminal is designed to emit little radiation, the cost of electromagnetic eavesdropping rises rapidly with the
distance of the eavesdropper (upper curve).

above and below. Often the best location to pick up radiation is the adjacent
office to that in which a terminal is used. It may be advisable not to place a
sensitive terminal in an office next to one owned by a different organization.
Such precautions apply particularly to the terminal *operated by a security
officer.* If the terminals are designed as with the upper curve in Fig. 29.2, the
user can be sure that transmission through the air is not being picked up if
there is no truckload of equipment with antennas within 120 feet.

In addition to traveling directly through the air, electromagnetic emana-
tions also travel along fortuitous conductors, such as water pipes, power lines,
and the metal in building structures. It is often difficult to tell where the
radiation will be detectable without measuring it. Simple physical changes
can substantially lower the detectable emissions, such as moving the terminal

to the other side of the room, erecting electrical screening, which can be as inexpensive as the metal mesh of window screens, moving cables or conduits, grounding all metalwork, and filtering the power distribution box. In future years the specialists in physical installation of computers may become familiar with the simple techniques that can limit the risk of electronic eavesdropping.

ELECTROMAGNETIC BUGS   The electromagnetic eavesdropper, like the sonic eavesdropper, can accomplish his objectives easily if he can plant a bug close to the devices in question. The bug would detect radiation and retransmit it, usually on a different frequency that can be picked up nearby on an inexpensive radio. A small bug might be placed, for example, inside a modem, and a receiver in a car or the building next door could print out everything the modem transmits. In a secure installation a careful search is needed for bugs which pick up sound or radiation. Equipment exists which can be used to detect bugging devices, and many security agencies use it.

REFERENCE

1. Mel Mandell, "Computer Scare Talk," *New York Times,* May 9, 1971.

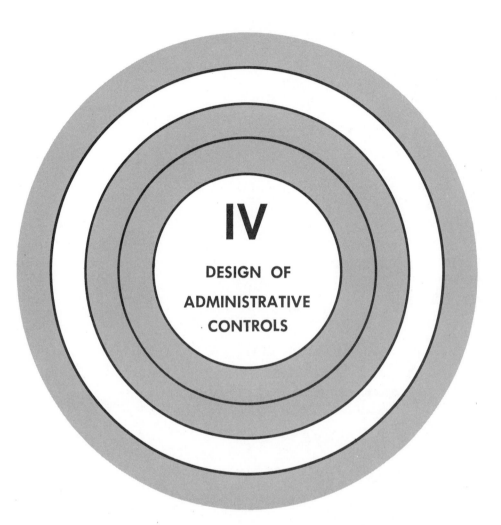

IV

DESIGN OF
ADMINISTRATIVE
CONTROLS

30 WHO IS RESPONSIBLE FOR SECURITY?

The responsibility for security divides into two entirely separate areas: the responsibility for the *design* of security techniques and procedures, and the responsibility for the day-to-day operations, given that design.

In both areas the overall responsibility lies with top management. Top management should be made aware of how vulnerable their organization is if disaster should strike its computer system. Sometimes they are not aware of the extent of their vulnerability, and it is the duty of the data-processing manager to make this clear to them.

Top management should see that an overall strategy for security is established and that a methodology is designed to comply with this strategy. They should make it known that in day-to-day operations they are concerned that the security procedures be strictly enforced. The strategy for security should be a sound, continuing one, not, as has often been the case, one based on current fads or reactions to emergencies.

In one system the security objectives are stated as follows:

1. Ensure the integrity and accuracy of the data required to plan and control the enterprise.
2. Provide for the privacy of proprietary, personal, privileged, or otherwise sensitive data.
3. Protect our employees from unnecessary temptation to default on their responsibilities to the firm.
4. Protect our employees from suspicion in the event of defalcation by others.
5. Protect and conserve corporate assets from the hazards of fire, storm, rising water, misappropriation, misapplication, conversion, vandalism, riot, or war.

6. Ensure the ability of the enterprise to survive hazards and function adequately after survival.

7. Protect management from charges of imprudence in the event of any compromise of security.

Such objectives need to be translated into terms of who will be responsible for the detailed implementation, and what their budgets will be. The responsibilities of the data-processing department are clearly only a subset (although a most critical one) of the overall responsibility for security.

RESPONSIBILITIES   In the design areas the responsibilities for security
FOR SECURE DESIGN   may be divided as follows:

1. *Overall coordination.* The data-processing manager must understand the overall security philosophy and appoint people responsible for the design of aspects of it. He should appoint one man as the overall coordinator of the design for security. This man may also be responsible for one or more of the detailed areas that follow.

2. *Responsibility for technical design.* A systems analyst should be responsible for those parts of the design for security which affect the computer hardware and its programs. His work will cover such aspects as positive identification of the terminal users and terminals (Chapters 11 and 12), the structures of authorization schemes (Chapters 13 and 14), the use of cryptography (Chapters 19, 20, and 21), programmed locks and alarms (Chapters 10 and 16), the controls built into the use of statistical files (Chapter 15), security in systems programs (Chapter 17), the operating system (Chapter 18), file-scanning operations (Chapter 23), surveillance methods (Chapter 16), accuracy controls (Chapters 6, 7, and 8), controls on periods of failure (Chapter 9), wiretapping and system eavesdropping (Chapters 28 and 29), and methods of recovery, file reconstruction (Chapter 22), and journalling (Chapter 23).

3. *Responsibility for procedural controls.* One man must establish the operating procedures and controls that are to be used. He must specify the procedures governing the operation of the computer room, the functions of the input/output control sections and quality-control groups (Chapters 6 and 7), and the tape and disk library procedures. He must specify what controls will protect the data during the conversion process. He must liaise with the users to establish bypass procedures during periods of computer failure, and determine what backup facilities are to be used in case of catastrophe. He must arrange for insurance of the system and its data.

4. *Responsibility for controls on programs and programmers.* One man must establish the controls on programs and programmers to prevent authorized programs or modifications being used in such a way that they can access sensitive data or do harm to the system. This is achieved partly by software controls and partly by procedural controls (Chapter 34). The procedures for control of promotion of programs to the operation system must be established (Fig. 34.6) and procedures for program testing specified.

5. *Responsibility for physical security.* Another person must concern himself with physical security, including the fire precautions, physical locks and alarms, guards if any, cameras for surveillance, and physical precautions against internal wiretapping, electromagnetic and other eavesdropping, theft, and sabotage (Section III).

6. *Responsibility for external administrative controls.* A person, probably outside the data-processing department, should have the responsibility for overall administrative controls such as the vital-records program (Chapter 32), the management of classified data (Chapter 31), the determination of what should be classified, and the backup procedures in user departments in case of catastrophic system loss.

7. *Auditors.* Internal auditors should check every aspect of the system design that relates to accuracy and security (Fig. 37.1). They should ensure that the system *can* be audited fully and should liaise with the systems analysts to develop appropriate audit trails and other technical aids to auditing, such as pseudorecords and pseudotransactions to check for correct program operation. They should prepare a checklist for future audits (Appendix D).

SYSTEM   To maintain tight security in any building or orga-
POLICEMEN   nization, policemen are needed. This is true also if
                      the data-processing system is to be highly secure.
The system may need physical guards on some terminal locations, and possibly also on the computer center. It may need a security staff to keep out intruders, make sure that tape or disk stores are locked, attempt to prevent wiretapping in the building, and so on. The cost of guards, however, is high, especially if the guards are to be effective (which often they are not). A limited security budget is often better spent on good door locks, burglar alarms, and technical safeguards (Chapters 24 and 25).

Whether or not guards are employed to protect the computer installation physically, a system with sensitive data needs a different form of policemen who check on the data aspects of the system.

Their functions will be to ensure that terminals and files are being used correctly, to maintain the authorization tables, to investigate procedure violations, to survey the violation logs and statistics, to carry out periodic spot checks and audits, and so on.

The activities for monitoring security take place with different time cycles; for example,

1. *Real-time monitoring.* When a sign-on or other terminal procedure is violated in an apparently serious manner, action should be taken immediately. As discussed in Chapter 16, the computer may lock the terminal keyboard or may "keep the culprit talking" while a security officer is notified. The security officer for this purpose will be a local manager at the terminal location.

2. *Daily monitoring.* The system will produce logs of procedural violations and of system activity. These may be processed to produce statistical reports or to highlight abnormal activity. Graphical representations may be used to reveal unusual activity patterns. The actions of the computer-room operator should also be logged in an unbroken fashion. These logs and reports will go to a central security officer each day, and he should check them for anything suspicious.

3. *Spot checks.* Spot checks may be made at random intervals to see that the correct procedures are being followed. These checks may apply to any aspect of the system where security is of concern, such as the computer room, the user departments, the program-testing sessions, and so on. The security manager or the auditors may carry out the spot checks.

4. *Periodic audits.* Thorough audits of various aspects of the system's functioning should be made at intervals. There should be audits of the input/output control procedures, the file accuracy, the physical security, and so on. Audits will be discussed in Chapter 37. The internal auditors should be responsible for carrying them out.

RESPONSIBILITIES
FOR OPERATIONAL
SECURITY

In maintaining security of day-to-day operations the responsibilities may be divided as follows:

1. Data-Processing Manager

While delegating specific security responsibilities, the data-processing manager should make it clear to all that he is personally concerned that the security procedures be adhered to in a tightly disciplined manner.

2. Security Administrator

A security manager or representative should be appointed to oversee all aspects of day-to-day security administration. He operates in accordance with standards and directives provided by the security design staff. He observes variances from standards and takes corrective action.

The security administrator may be the sole person who can access the system's authorization tables saying who can use what programs and data, and the file password tables. He will have details of what each user is authorized to read or change on the files. He will be responsible for issuing passwords or security codes, for changing the authorization tables, and for ensuring that these are used correctly.

He will examine the logs of procedural violations each morning, along with the console operator's log, the statistics on system activity, the reports from the guards, the list of overtime work, and any other items that might give a clue to security infringements. He will take action on excessive procedural violations.

He may set up a security training program. He will counsel the data file owners or user groups with terminals installed, receiving their details of authorized users.

An important function should be his assessment of the effectiveness of the techniques employed. He will become aware of methods of breaching security. Based on these and the continually changing technology, he should review with the security design staff new methods for enhancing security.

3. Local Security Officers

In a system with terminals in remote locations, there may be a security officer in each of these locations. A suitable person with another job, such as office manager, may be given the responsibility for systems security in that location. He will take instructions from the main security officer.

The system will send him listings of all detected procedural violations that occur in his location. He will be informed immediately when a procedural violation that appears as though it could be deliberate is detected. When the system detects two violations in succession, it may lock the terminal in question and the local security officer will have to unlock it (Figs. 16.1 and 16.2).

He will be responsible for seeing that the staff at his location does not violate procedures, write down their security codes on calendars, forget to sign off at their terminals, and so on.

4. File Owners

In addition to having a security officer for each *terminal location,* there may be also one who has the responsibility for the security of each individual *file.* He is sometimes referred to as the file owner. He will maintain a list of persons authorized to read or update his file, or to read certain records or fields in it. An individual requiring permission to access an item on the file must obtain it from the file owner. The owner will often restrict his permission on a need-to-know basis.

When file-scanning runs are used for accuracy and security purposes, the file owner will review the results. When errors are found, he may be the only person permitted to modify the erroneous items. The file owner will usually have responsibility for file accuracy as well as file security. He will be responsible for data reconstruction should the file be destroyed.

5. Line Managers

All line managers should be responsible for seeing that their subordinates use secure procedures, do not leave classified items lying around, and generally adopt a security-conscious attitude. They should be responsible for identifying persons working under them who might be a potential risk.

6. Auditors

As was commented earlier, the internal auditors should make spot checks and regular thorough reviews of all aspects of security. Like the security administrator, they should report weaknesses in the security system to the designers and review possible improvements with them.

7. All Staff

"Security is everyone's responsibility."

31 MANAGEMENT OF CLASSIFIED DATA

In maintaining security and confidentiality of data, a computer system should not be considered in isolation from the remainder of the organization in which it is used. The organization should have a set of procedures relating to classified information, and the data-processing procedures should form a part of this overall scheme.

The overall system would be faulty if data that are kept securely in the computer and its files are badly protected as soon as they leave the computer room, or, alternatively, if the computer forms an unsafe link in an otherwise secure system.

CLASSIFICATION CATEGORIES Corporate-wide security programs usually divide the data into security levels as in the left-hand side of Fig. 18.1 (stratification), and, as described in Chapter 18, the software may employ the same stratification.

In a corporation four categories likely to serve the corporate needs are

1. *Unclassified.* These are documents over which special precautions are taken. As much material as possible should be unclassified.
2. *For internal use only.* This designation restricts documents to use within the corporation. It may not be used for purposes unrelated to the corporation's business. Manuals of procedure, technical papers, and employee listings may have this classification. In some corporations internal telephone directories are For Internal Use Only. The category may be planned such that documents need not be kept under lock and key and no restrictions apply to reproducing or mailing them.

3. *Corporate confidential.* This designation refers to data that could be detrimental to a person or to the company if improperly disclosed. It is made available only to those individuals with a need to know because of their job or position. Such information must be kept under lock and key and carefully safeguarded. It may be reproduced only when necessary for a specific operation. Precautions must be taken when mailing it or destroying it.

4. *Registered confidential.* This designation refers to highly confidential information that must be closely controlled and accounted for. Such documents may be seen and possessed only by a specific list of individuals who must take action based upon the data or who need to see them because of their position. Selected persons will have the job of controlling Registered Confidential documents. They will keep records showing the whereabouts of each copy, and no copy may be reproduced. All holders of such documents will be accountable for them and responsible for their safekeeping. The destruction of the copies will be controlled and recorded.

Some corporations have other types of categories, including

1. *Personal and confidential.* Can only be seen by the person to whom it is addressed.
2. *Project confidential.* Can be seen only by persons on a specific project. The Registered Confidential category above could serve this purpose equally well by using a list of recipients concerned with that project.
3. *Secret and top secret.* These categories relate to the clearance of individuals and are used in military and government projects. Only a person with Secret or Top Secret clearance can see documents which fall into that category. Often a lower level is used, sometimes called Restricted, and for certain special purposes levels higher than Top Secret are used.

REGULATIONS THAT SHOULD BE SPECIFIED   Corporations or other organizations using such document classifications normally have a manual stating the regulations that must be observed with each category of document. These regulations should extend to all aspects of data processing in which classified data are used. The instructions given to employees concerning classified data should deal with

1. *Responsibility.* What are the responsibilities of different persons in seeing that the regulations are observed?
2. *Distribution.* How is distribution of the confidential items controlled?
3. *Reproduction.* What rules govern the reproduction of classified data? Reproduction of highly sensitive data should be prohibited by Xeroxing, photography, copying in the computer room, or by other methods.
4. *Locks, keys, and storage.* What data must be kept under lock and key? What form of storage cabinets and locks should be used?

5. *Mailing.* What precautions must be taken when sensitive data are mailed?

6. *Typing.* What precautions are taken when classified documents are typed? Ribbons and carbon paper, for example, should be shredded.

7. *Tapes and disks.* How are tapes, disks, and other storage media to be kept and controlled?

8. *Transmission.* What precautions are necessary when classified data are transmitted by Telex, teleprocessing, facsimile, or other means?

9. *Screen displays.* What regulations govern the display of sensitive data on computer screens?

10. *Verbal communication.* What rules apply to verbal communication of classified data, including lectures and presentations?

11. *Updating documents.* What procedures relate to the updating of documents or computer files? What happens to obsolete copies of documents?

12. *Destruction of documents and records.* What action is taken when classified documents are destroyed? Paper documents should be shredded, and data on tape and disk should be erased.

13. *Lost documents.* What action is taken when documents are lost?

14. *Backup procedures.* How can backup procedures safeguarding the accidental loss of computer data be made secure?

15. *Enforcement.* What steps are taken to ensure that the regulations are enforced?

16. *Audits and spot checks.* Audits of the functioning of the data security system should be carried out periodically, and, more frequently, spot checks should be made. The employees must be convinced that security is serious.

REGISTERED DOCUMENTS   Special control procedures are needed when registered confidential documents are handled. The U.S. Department of Defense Industrial Security Manual [1] specifies details of how sensitive documents should be handled, and is worthwhile reading even for nondefense contractors. Many corporations have their own strict procedures for handling registered documents. Figure 31.1 diagrams a typical control procedure.

The procedure in Fig. 31.1 requires that a manager at each location where registered confidential documents are handled should be designated a "Recorder." When his location originates such a document he gives it a *Record Control Number* and creates two identical punched cards, called *Control and Receipt cards* for each person who will have possession of the document. The cards give the document's *Record Control Number,* its title, the date it will be reclassified, and details of the employee who will receive it. One card is sent with the document to recipient; the other goes to the Recorder at the receiving location. When the recipient receives the document, he signs the card

ORIGINATING LOCATION

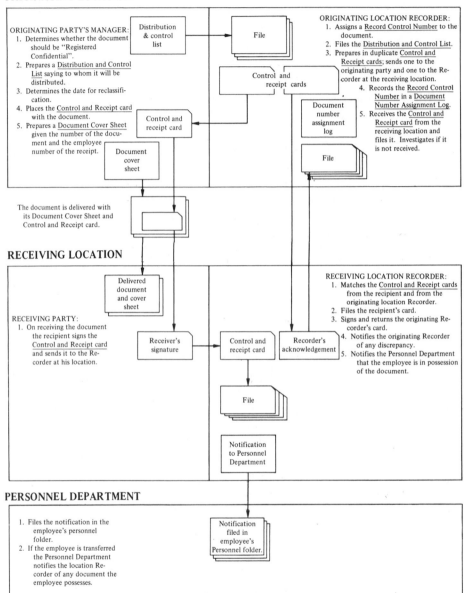

ORIGINATING PARTY'S MANAGER:
1. Determines whether the document should be "Registered Confidential".
2. Prepares a Distribution and Control List saying to whom it will be distributed.
3. Determines the date for reclassification.
4. Places the Control and Receipt card with the document.
5. Prepares a Document Cover Sheet given the number of the document and the employee number of the receipt.

Distribution & control list

File

Control and receipt cards

Control and receipt card

Document cover sheet

Document number assignment log

File

ORIGINATING LOCATION RECORDER:
1. Assigns a Record Control Number to the document.
2. Files the Distribution and Control List.
3. Prepares in duplicate Control and Receipt cards; sends one to the originating party and one to the Recorder at the receiving location.
4. Records the Record Control Number in a Document Number Assignment Log.
5. Receives the Control and Receipt card from the receiving location and files it. Investigates if it is not received.

The document is delivered with its Document Cover Sheet and Control and Receipt card.

RECEIVING LOCATION

RECEIVING PARTY:
1. On receiving the document the recipient signs the Control and Receipt card and sends it to the Recorder at his location.

Delivered document and cover sheet

Receiver's signature

Control and receipt card

Recorder's acknowledgement

File

Notification to Personnel Department

RECEIVING LOCATION RECORDER:
1. Matches the Control and Receipt cards from the recipient and from the originating location Recorder.
2. Files the recipient's card.
3. Signs and returns the originating Recorder's card.
4. Notifies the originating Recorder of any discrepancy.
5. Notifies the Personnel Department that the employee is in possession of the document.

PERSONNEL DEPARTMENT

1. Files the notification in the employee's personnel folder.
2. If the employee is transferred the Personnel Department notifies the location Recorder of any document the employee possesses.

Notification filed in employee's Personnel folder.

Figure 31.1. Control of registered documents.

and gives it to the Recorder. The Recorder matches the two cards, signs them to acknowledge that the document was received, files one card, and sends the other back to the Recorder at the originating location. If after a specified period of time the Recorder at the originating location has not received the card, he must investigate to determine what has delayed it. He files the *Control and Receipt cards,* and maintains a log of the documents that originate at his location.

A manager in the department that originates the document will determine who should have copies of it—as few people as possible—and he will draw up a distribution list. He will also set a date when the classification of the document should be reviewed. It is desirable to downgrade the classification when possible. The number of items that are registered confidential should be kept to a minimum.

Throughout its life, a registered document has a cover sheet attached to it. This sheet gives the document number and the number of the employee who has possession of it. This employee must keep the document locked up and see that it is never reproduced. The detection of illegal reproducing of documents may be enhanced as follows: All Xerox or other copying machines at a location using registered confidential documents may have transparent labels attached to their glass so that they print a unique number on all documents reproduced by them.

An employee possessing a registered document may move his work location or leave the company. To keep track of documents when employees move, the personnel department records the possession of any registered documents in the employees' personnel records.

If the document is later declassified or downgraded, all of the documents in Fig. 31.1 will be stamped to indicate the change. This may be done automatically if the document has a preestablished reclassification date.

DATA-PROCESSING CONTROLS

Controls such as those specified here must be carried through into the computer center when classified data are processed, transmitted, or when they reside on the computer files. The techniques outlined earlier enable the appropriate security to be maintained.

The administrator who is responsible for document security at the location in question must work with the data-processing manager, or his security expert, to ensure that the controls are adequate. The data-processing organization is then responsible for informing the computer users of the security features and controls available, and for applying them.

As with paper documents, all classified computer data must be labeled to show its classification. The classification will be encoded on tape and disk records, and must be written prominently on all printouts and displays. Each page of a Corporate Confidential printout should contain a heading line saying CORPORATE CONFIDENTIAL, possibly with a line of asterisks on each side to make the heading stand out. Information printed at terminals or displayed on a screen should be similarly labeled.

A file owner, or data base administrator, should establish an inventory of all his classified data files, showing the classification of each. A list of all users of classified data should be maintained. These operations ought to be functions provided by the data base software.

The librarian must continue the chain of controls if classified material is stored on tape, disk, or other storage media. All classified items must be labeled with their classification. The librarian should establish inventory controls for all classified items, and maintain a log of the usage of each which can be reviewed by auditors or security representatives.

The controls must extend to classified programs—their design, preparation, operation, maintenance, and documentation. A log should be kept of the use of classified programs. On some systems, *all* of the programs are regarded as sensitive and are subject to tight controls. This type of system will be described in Chapter 34.

AUDITS   To ensure that the procedures are being adhered to they should be formally monitored. The data-processing-center security officer should review the usage of files and programs on the system. He should check that no program has been run without authorization. All unexplained stoppages and interruptions should be accounted for or reported to the appropriate management. The security officer should review the log of procedural violations as discussed in Chapter 16.

A formal audit of all registered documents should be carried out periodically. The Recorders (Fig. 31.1) should send each recipient a list of the documents charged to him, and request his signature confirming that he has them. The instructions regulating registered documents may also tell the Recorders to check a certain percentage of individuals in person and to log the results, reporting any lost documents.

REFERENCE

1. "Industrial Security Manual for Safeguarding Classified Information" (DOD 5220.22 —M), Department of Defense, Washington, D.C.

32 VITAL-RECORDS PROGRAM AND SYSTEM RECOVERY

Separately from the security classifications in Chapter 31, certain data may be categorized as *vital records.* These are records which are thought essential to the continued functioning of the corporation. Special care will be taken to protect them. A program has been established in many organizations, sometimes referred to as the *vital-records program,* to identify those records which are "vital" and to establish means of safeguarding them.

As with the control of classified records, the regulations governing *vital* records apply throughout all aspects of the system. The controls on the files are a subset of the total.

OBJECTIVES

The vital-records program sometimes has an overall statement of mission such as:

> To protect the organization's ability to fulfill its responsibilities to its owners, employees, and customers, and to resume operations within a period of time reasonably consistent with its functions [1]

To protect the data in accordance with such a mission, it is necessary to

1. Identify those records which are vital to the organization's continued operation.
2. Establish measures to protect them.
3. Establish the means to reconstruct records within a reasonable time if disaster should strike.

**EXTENT OF
PROTECTION**

These objectives leave scope for argument, mainly on three grounds. First, what levels of disaster are we talking about? Second, what is a reasonable time for recovery? And third, what records *are* vital to the organization's continued operation?

Everyone will agree that the disasters should include fire, flood, and human carelessness. These disasters are relatively localized. Should we also include war, nuclear attack, and intelligent sabotage? (Most sabotage, fortunately, is unintelligent and hence is unlikely to destroy both the records and the means of recovery.) Small corporations usually ignore the prospect of war and nuclear attack. Some large corporations take it very seriously, believing themselves to be an essential part of the fabric of society that must survive. To protect against nuclear attack some organizations have duplicate well-separated computer centers. Some merely site their computers or backup storage away from supposed target areas. Some rent storage space in nuclear-proof vaults deep underground, such as that at Iron Mountain. Some rent space merely for records, but a few have operational facilities underground.

The time for recovery depends upon what the records are used for. Some types of record, although vital, can be inaccessible for a month without having a severe effect on operations. In other cases it is highly expensive for the data to be unavailable. The overall cost incurred by data not being available should be estimated, along with the cost of reconstruction procedures, and a reasonable time for recovery determined.

**WHAT IS
VITAL?**

The types of records that are considered vital vary widely from one organization to another. For cost reasons it is generally desirable to limit the amount stored in the vital-records program. Many individuals tend to think *their* records are vital when, in fact, the organization could survive quite well without them. On the other hand, for efficient reconstruction it is sometimes necessary to create and store some records that would not exist without the vital-records program. Intelligent judgment is needed as to what records are vital. The approach may be to decide what *functions* are absolutely essential, and then look for specific records which enable these functions to be carried out.

The responsibility for determining what is vital should usually be made outside the data-processing department by the user departments. Data processing is, after all, only a service function.

In engineering development the vital records are those which enable the project to continue after a disaster such as a fire. The project manager should ensure that enough data are stored at appropriate intervals. An instruction to engineering management in one organization states that when a project reaches the cost-estimating stage, functional specifications, bills of material, and drawings should be sent to vital-records storage. At intervals thereafter, based on the manager's judgment, details of modification of further work should be stored.

GRADATIONS   Should there be two classes of records: *vital* and
OF VITALNESS?   *nonvital?* Or should there be several classes with
                        differing degrees of vitalness? The National Fire
Protection Association defines four categories [2]:

> **Class I: Vital records.** Records that are essential to the mission of the equipment, are irreplaceable, or would be needed immediately after the fire and could not be quickly reproduced. Examples might include key programs, master records, equipment wiring diagrams, and certain input-output and memory data.

> **Class II: Important records.** Records that are essential or important but which, with difficulty or extra expense, could be reproduced without a critical delay of any essential missions. Some programs, wiring diagrams, memory and input-output data have this level of importance.

> **Class III: Useful records.** Records whose loss might occasion much inconvenience but which could readily be replaced and which would not be an insurmountable obstacle to prompt restoration of operations. Programs and procedures saved as examples of special problems are typical of records in this category.

> **Class IV: Nonessential records.** Those records which on examination are found to be no longer necessary.

The Association states that all records should be assigned to one of these categories, and specifies the degree of protection required for the categories as follows:

1. RECORDS KEPT WITHIN THE COMPUTER ROOM

The amount of records kept within the computer room shall be kept to the *absolute minimum* required for efficient operation. Nonessential records shall not be kept in the computer room.

Any records regularly kept or stored in the computer room shall be provided with the following protection:

(1) Class I (Vital) or Class II (Important) records shall be stored in Class C or better records protection equipment. [See Chapter 24.]

(2) Class III (Useful) records on paper-based or plastic materials shall be stored in metal files or cabinets.

(3) Class III (Useful) records on metal-based material require no special protection.

2. RECORDS STORED OUTSIDE THE COMPUTER ROOM

To the maximum extent consistent with efficient operation, all record storage shall be outside the computer room.

In the record storage room:

(1) Class I (Vital) and Class II (Important) records shall be stored in fire-resistive rooms. The degree of fire resistance shall be commensurate with the fire exposure to the records, but not less than two hours. [See Chapter 26.]

(2) Unless the records are contained in metal files, cabinets or other noncombustible containers, records storage rooms shall also be provided with an automatic sprinkler system.

(3) Class III (Useful) and Class IV (Nonessential) records do not require any special fire protection unless these records are stored with vital or important records. In such a case the requirements for the most valuable records apply to all records.

(4) The records storage room shall be used only for the storage of records. Spare tapes, however, may be stored in this room if they are unpacked and stored in the same manner as the tapes containing records. All other operations including splicing, repairing, reproducing, etc., shall be prohibited in this room.

Portable extinguishing equipment for record storage rooms or areas should be installed in accordance with the NFPA Standard [3].

When records are kept in cases, boxes, or other containers, protection shall be that required for the highest level of damageable media in the total assembly of records and containers.

3. DUPLICATE RECORDS

The best protection for records consists of storing duplicate records in separate areas not subject to the same fire:

(a) All Class I (Vital) records shall be duplicated on the same or different media and the duplicates stored in an area which is not subject to a fire that may involve the originals, preferably in a separate building.

(b) Whenever practical, Class II (Important) records shall be similarly duplicated and stored.

(c) Class I (Vital) records not duplicated shall be protected in accordance with NFPA Standard on the Protection of Records [4].

Many organizations with data-processing records to store do not use multiple categories of vitalness. They claim that to categorize in this way complicates the whole operation and makes it more expensive. It is better to have a two-category system. Either a record is vital or it is not. The organization can function without it, or it cannot. Typically, less than 2 per cent of all records are vital. Without this clear-cut distinction, too much is stored, the protection site is inundated, and people tend not to support the program.

The two-category system appears to have worked well in practice.

COMPUTER PROGRAMS   The computer programs that are used in an organization are themselves often "vital," and copies of the programs must be stored accordingly. Many programs are continuously under development or are frequently modified. It is important that the copies stored be up to date. It is sometimes impractical to store every modification. One organization has the rule that a complete operational set of programs should be stored every 3 months. The package stored must consist of items such as

1. The most recent coding on magnetic tape.
2. A complete set of test data on magnetic tape, with the results it should produce.
3. A listing of symbolic and actual coding, flow charts, and diagrams, on paper or tape.
4. Details of the required computer configuration, input/output units, and operating system.
5. Complete documentation, including program description and purposes, record formats and block lengths, recording densities, special symbols or formulas, the balancing and accounting controls used, and data recovery instructions.
6. Preprocessing instructions and procedures, including control cards, switch settings, tape unit addresses, and so on.
7. Processing instructions such as halt registers, error procedures, and checkpoint and restart procedures.

When such a package is stored, the previous one is also kept for safety, but the one before that is discarded. Sometimes only part of the package, for example the coding and listing, is changed.

Often computer data and programs can only be of value when a machine and operating system of the correct configuration are available. An essential part of the program may be to determine where this can be obtained if disaster has struck the machine originally used. It may be available from a different organization, perhaps at night and on weekends. There may be an arrangement that the manufacturer shall replace the computer within an agreed time after any disaster. Whatever the circumstances, backup computer availability should be planned, and it must be ensured that the backup machine have the necessary features.

HOW WILL THE RECORDS BE PROTECTED? To some extent there is a trade off between convenience and safety. It is convenient to store the data at the computer center, but this may not protect them from a fire or planned sabotage. The safest storage, the remote nuclear-proof vault, is the least convenient. Off-site storage not too far away is often the best compromise.

Because of the convenience factor, vital records may be divided into those which are highly unlikely to be needed again and those which normally will be needed. The latter category may be stored within easy access of the computer center, though preferably not in the same building. The former category goes on what will normally be a one-way trip to a secure vault.

Effective protection usually means duplication and dispersal of the copies. Sometimes multiple copies of records are dispersed by the very nature of their function. Engineering documents, for example, may be duplicated and sent to persons on a distribution list. A disaster is highly unlikely to destroy all copies. Sometimes the persons on the distribution list are all in the same building, and in this case one copy may be deliberately sent away from the premises. When there is no natural dispersal, the records may be deliberately copied. A second copy will be written on the relevant computer runs. Sometimes the son-father-grandfather tapes or the transaction journals and file dumps are all that is needed.

Vital records are stored in a variety of different forms. Computer listings are bulky and may only be stored when the retention period is fairly short. Magnetic tape is the most commonly used medium and is the cheapest form of archival storage. Often microfilm and microfiche are used for documents.

ADMINISTRATION   The vital-records program needs to be carefully administered. It is not sufficient to just dump the material. A listing must be maintained of everything that is stored. Details of how all important items are to be retrieved or reconstructed must be available. One person must be assigned the responsibility for the routine operation of ensuring that everything is stored as scheduled and is *easily retrievable.*

It is important that the program should be the result of continuing, rational reevaluation of risks and requirements. Sometimes a flurry of vital-record activities is triggered by a catastrophe striking nearby. The staff sometimes waits cynically for the management pressure to "blow over," and then all is quiet again until the next crisis. Crisis-by-crisis operation is almost always inadequate. It often gives management a feeling of security when little security exists. The auditors should check the vital-records program periodically and ensure that it is of continuing effectiveness.

TESTING   The vita-records program and recovery procedures often have only one chance to prove themselves: when disaster strikes. It is desirable that the recovery capability should be tested prior to this event. The only truly effective way to test it is to simulate a disaster.

A disaster test may be an all-embracing operation that takes place at night or on weekends. Alternatively, specific postdisaster problems may be isolated to test various aspects of the recovery procedures during daily operations. Some typical test problems might be

1. Reconstruct records of all customer orders and indebtedness, and prepare the necessary invoices.
2. In a bank: reconstruct the customer account details.
3. Reconstruct the following payroll information for employees in a given location: basic salary rate, year-to-date earnings, tax and benefits, and balance in stock purchase and savings programs.
4. Reconstruct the cash position, including the status of all working funds and a breakdown of cash balances.
5. Produce documents giving the current status of specified development projects.
6. Assume that all the programs have been destroyed in the computer center. Run with the backup copies.
7. Carry out specified runs on the computer facility that will be used if there is a disastrous fire.

8. Assume that a certain critical programmer is killed. Take over his work (without his assistance)!

Different installations will have many different problems of a similar nature. Operating such tests not only verifies that the recovery facilities work, but also, and perhaps equally important, involves people in recovery problems and makes them sharply aware of what is needed so that they will be likely to plan and cooperate better.

REFERENCES

1. "Guidelines for Protection and Control in a Computer Environment," International Business Machines, Poughkeepsie, N.Y., 1971.

2. National Fire Protection Association, "Protection of Electronic Computer/Data Processing Equipment," Pamphlet No. 75, Boston, 1968.

3. National Fire Protection Association, "Standards for the Installation of Portable Fire Extinguishers," Pamphlet No. 10, Boston, 1968.

4. National Fire Protection Association, "Standards for Protection of Records," Pamphlet 232, Boston, 1967.

33   THE DANGER
        WITHIN

Using the methods in Section II, the technical locks and alarms on a computer system can be made at least as effective as those on a bank vault. However, few people today would claim that information stored in a commercial (non-military) computer system is in fact safer than items stored in a bank vault. Our prime reason for mistrust of the former is not the technology, but the *people* who program, operate, and manage the system. To many people, the holders of the keys and combinations of the bank vault seem more responsible than the recently hired, casual, brilliant, argumentative, but indispensible systems programmers.

Most computer systems are appallingly vulnerable to their own staff, and for this more than any other reason data security can never be absolute. There are, however, protective measures that can be taken, widely differing in nature. These are the subject of this and the following two chapters. Used in combination with the accuracy and security controls discussed in Section II they can reduce the risk to a very low level. Few computer installations today, however, have good personnel security.

POTENTIAL   Attack on the security of the system may come
CULPRITS   from a variety of different types of personnel.
                 For example,

1. Complete outsider
2. Normal terminal user
3. Computer engineer

4. Telephone company engineer
5. Engineer for equipment attached to the system
6. Application programmer
7. Systems programmer
8. Machine-room operating staff
9. File-handling staff
10. Designated file owners
11. Security officer
12. System designers
13. Data-processing manager

Some of these persons are clearly more dangerous than others. The systems programmers, for example, are among the most dangerous. The data-processing manager himself might be a potential criminal. Some of the most ingenious computer crimes that have come to the courts have been master-minded by a data-processing manager. If a person wants to pull off a once-in-a-lifetime robbery and retire, the best opening step could be to become the data-processing manager of a suitable organization.

**ENFORCE
COLLUSION**
If we take any category of personnel from the above list *by itself,* it is possible to devise technical controls that will keep those persons out of data they are not authorized to access. When a complete set of such controls is in use, a person wanting to break into the system is forced into collusion with personnel of a different category. An application programmer must act in conjunction with a systems programmer; an authorized terminal user must act in conjunction with a telephone company engineer; or a data-processing manager must act in conjunction with the machine-room operator. The controls can enforce *multiple* collusion in many cases.

A person is much more likely to misuse the system when he can do it alone than when he has to take the risk of seeking a partner in crime. This is especially true when the required partner does not sit next to him, but works in a different department. Embezzlement or intrusion can therefore be made far more difficult by dividing the system responsibilities, and designing the system controls so as to enforce collusion between persons with different jobs. The persons with different jobs should then be kept as far apart as possible.

People who are very close associates should not be employed in positions in which they could jointly break the system. Some banks will not employ husband and wife together in the same department. If the husband handled corporate assets and the wife programmed the corporation's computer, it might be even more dangerous.

A basic rule of internal control in accounting is that no single employee should be allowed complete control over all important stages that a transaction passes through. When possible, several employees should be involved at serial stages. The work of any employee must be checked by others who handle the transaction at other stages, or who handle connected transactions or control totals. As an additional safeguard, the type of transactions that employees handle may be changed periodically, and if there are any grounds to suspect an employee, his functions will be changed.

The proportion of manual operations in the handling of transactions is much lower with computers than it was before. With on-line or real-time systems, or systems with an integrated data base, it is lower than with batch systems. The scope for including many clerks in a series of operations to avoid deliberate falsification is reduced. On the other hand, the collusion necessary for falsification can be made far more difficult. It must usually be between persons with different disciplines, such as programming and accounting. The controls to prevent it can be more thorough and complex.

With a computer the first step toward preventing collusion is to separate completely the data-processing staff from the staff who handle the organization's assets. The accountants and clerks will not be permitted to write programs and will not be allowed into the computer room. They should be kept out of other rooms where data-processing functions take place, such as programming, keypunching, and input/output control. Overtime and working after hours should be controlled to lessen the chance of improper measures being taken then.

The interface between the users and the data-processing function must be precisely defined and controlled in such a way that it both clarifies the operation and presents a barrier to persons wishing to falsify the data. There are two types of interface between a computer and its users: first, that in which the user submits documents for processing, usually in batches, and, second that in which the user employs a terminal directly. The interface in the first case should be an input/output control section, such as that in Fig. 6.3. This group (or person) will enforce the use of the batch totals and other controls discussed in Chapter 6. The terminal and its real-time programs will be the interface in the second case, and these will be backed up by the use of the accuracy checks, totals, and balancing controls discussed in Chapters 7 and 23. Unauthorized persons will be prevented from using the terminals, as discussed in Chapters 10 to 14. An input/output control group (or person) on real-time systems will monitor the use of the controls and ensure that all totals balance.

A second division of functions should be between the input/output control group and the computer operating staff. The input/output control group has the job of ensuring that no items are lost or fraudulently converted by the operating staff. The programs will print out details of all transaction totals and hash totals for checking by the input/output group. Where sensitive data are handled, the system should be designed so that the operators cannot modify the application programs, as we shall discuss in Chapter 34.

The files of data must be carefully controlled. On systems in which embezzlement is a possibility, the users should not handle the decks of cards nor be allowed into the keypunch room. All tapes and disks should be returned to the tape library immediately after use on a preestablished schedule. They should only be issued to authorized persons and their use should be carefully documented. The issuing and return of tapes may be controlled by the input/output control section (or person).

On some systems such controls are taken very seriously; on others there is little or no need for them. One computing science professor reviewing this book referred to them as "paranoia." The controls need to suit the environment.

All check signatures must be authorized by an appropriately high level of management. Many other items may need authorization in exactly the same way as before the introduction of data processing. Large items and other exceptional occurrences may require the special attention of management. With a computer system, the machine may be programmed to detect all cases which need special authorization and ensure that they have it. The computer may print on certain checks that a second signature is needed. An employee, however, often has little difficulty in forging a manager's initials on a check. The history of white-collar crime is full of such cases. The computer may therefore be programmed to communicate with the managers who give authorization. It may produce listings of items needing authorization for the managers in question. Better, it may communicate with the managers directly by means of a terminal. Details of items requiring authorization are placed in the terminal queue for a manager. He must check the queue periodically and respond to the computer, saying whether he gives his authorization to the items. To bypass this process, the felon must be in collusion either with the manager in question, who then risks being caught, or with the computer programmer. And as we shall discuss in Chapter 34, we can make it difficult for the programmers to falsify or modify the programs.

The procedure would be enhanced by making it possible for the transactions to be authorized by more than one manager and by programming the computer to select the manager. This would make collusion between clerk and manager unsafe. The clerk would not know which manager would authorize the item, and the manager may not know which clerk the item had come from.

Enforcing the independent decisions of two persons when highly critical actions are needed is a technique that is used on many systems (data processing and other). Two persons must authorize a large check payment. A copilot checks the landing procedure on an airliner. When a terminal operator is handling police emergency telephone calls, the computer automatically informs the section supervisor of certain classes of emergency.

In a very different world, on the U.S. systems for launching a nuclear attack, decisions of human participants at various critical points are duplicated or triplicated. More than one person, each operating independently, must press the button. On the Primary Alert System two launch-control officers in a concrete missile-control capsule deep underground each receive a coded message. They take down the code and decode it independently. Only when it is confirmed that the two have the same reading can the countdown commence.

Similarly, in the Strategic Air Command bombers flying toward preassigned targets with a load of hydrogen bombs, three independent members in each crew must individually copy down a coded go-ahead message. The message must be matched to a code that the individual carries, and the three must agree that this is in fact a go-to-war instruction. Otherwise, the planes cannot pass a certain "fail-safe" point. In no instance does the launching of an attack hinge upon one person who might accidentally or deliberately give the go-ahead instruction.

USE OF
COMPLEXITY
One factor that can help in preventing intrusion into computer systems is that the systems are becoming exceedingly complex. A large amount of knowledge is needed to break into a reasonably protected data bank. This knowledge itself must be protected. One of the principles of safety should be that we *permit no one man to have all the knowledge that he needs to break into the system.*

If you are planning a bank robbery, the first obstacle you meet is that you do not know how the burglar alarm and other security precautions work. You do not know where the keys are kept. The same must be true on the computer system, and here the complexity factor is on the side of the "white hats." The passwords, authorization procedures, file locks, audit, and alarm techniques raise considerably the level of knowledge needed to break into the system. Details of how these facilities work must as far as possible be kept secret, and knowledge of them is restricted to as small a number of people as possible. Most contemporary operating systems and other software are sufficiently complex that only an expert can tamper with them. Such experts exist in most installations, but the knowledge is restricted to a few skilled programmers. Details of the file addressing, communication line organization, and control program mechanisms, if these are different from standard manufacturers' products, should not be made available to persons with no *need to know*. There is a case to be made out for an organization designing its own authorization schemes, for example, rather than using any that might eventually be available in a computer manufacturer's software. If the design is unique, the workings can be kept secret, whereas anything in a manufacturer's software will be open knowledge.

DIVISION OF   It is important, then, not only to divide the *re-*
KNOWLEDGE   *sponsibilities* on a system where security is of
          concern, but also to divide the knowledge of the
system that individuals have.

The manuals specifying how the application programs, authorization procedures, and other aspects of the system work should be carefully locked up and handled as classified documents. For a break-in to occur a person not in collusion with other groups of people would have to go to great lengths to educate himself in areas other than his own. The more the knowledge of the system is fragmented, the more collusion is necessary for planning an invasion. This can make a system extremely difficult to break into, and can increase the probability of the culprit being caught. Technical secrecy is only desirable, however, when the system has information that really needs to be protected.

The designers of a sensitive system, the data-processing manager, and the man responsible for security should check through the list of people at the start of this chapter and ask themselves the question, "With our system, how are we protecting ourselves from this category of person?" If necessary and practical, they should limit the actions that each person is permitted to take; they should limit his access to the system and his knowledge of the security procedures and of those aspects of the system that can be tampered with. He should then be separated, as far as possible, from persons with whom he could enter into collusion.

TRUST   Having said all of this, there are some persons
          whom it is necessary to be able to *trust*. It is
impractical to assume otherwise.

Some individuals have to be trusted with the management of operations, with the management of security, and with the system design. Some systems programmers may have to be trusted. It is generally necessary to have means of overriding security measures when malfunctions occur. There will always be some individuals who *could* break into the system if they were so minded.

On a well-designed system, however, the persons who have to be trusted will be kept to a minimum. If it is necessary to trust every application programmer, the system is badly designed from the security point of view. *System security should be designed to depend on the integrity of as few people as possible.*

BACKGROUND CHECKS The individuals who have to be trusted should have their backgrounds carefully checked. There is a tendency in some firms today to avoid investigations of a person's past. Such investigations seem contrary to current views relating to the privacy of individuals, which the computer industry has been made painfully aware of. It will be ironic if in a computerized society the computer practitioners are the one group that must forfeit privacy.

Accountants, bank and trust officers, and auditors have traditionally had to demonstrate an untarnished background. Persons in these professions are frequently bonded, meaning that an insurance company accepts responsibility for the person's integrity in his work. The same caution is necessary on computer systems in which security is of major concern.

The minimal group of individuals who can compromise the system without collusion should then be selected with great care. Ideally, they should be employees of long standing whose integrity is well known. In the computer world, however, this is often not possible. When there is any doubt, background checks should be carried out and key individuals bonded. Background checks should only be entrusted to a responsible company. Many investigating firms are far from responsible and, in the words of one reviewer of this book, to use them is "an invitation to tramp over the civil liberties of the investigatees."

34 CONTROL OF THE PROGRAMMERS

Unless appropriate precautions are taken, any system is vulnerable to its programmers.

Manuals and books on security in other areas comment on the types of personality that might constitute a security risk. Peter Hamilton [1] for example, lists the following characteristics that such a person may have: quiet, reserved, generally introverted, a misfit, lack of hobbies, lack of real friends, but exceptional ability at job. Unfortunately, in the programming field such sets of characteristics often describe the most indispensible men! In one high-prestige installation, in the author's experience, the key systems programmer worked with bare feet on his desk, had hippie-like clothes and attitudes, and displayed an overt scorn for authority. However, he alone could make the intricate modifications to the operating system that were deemed necessary. A security risk? Possibly, but they could not manage without him.

One reviewer of this book, who is in industry, made the comment about the previous story:

> It would be appropriate to comment on the stupidity of a management that let itself into this situation—independent of the personal habits of the key man, the existence of such a person is mismanagement in the extreme.

A reviewer who is a university professor made the comment:

> I suspect that there are an awful lot of irresponsible bankers, generals, and politicians around (with short hair) relative to the number of irresponsible system programmers.

Is it, then, possible to design controls by means of which an installation can protect itself from its own programmers?

Certainly it is; tight controls can be designed. However, in doing so it is necessary to give up certain procedures that are popular in some installations today. For example, it must not be possible for a programmer to patch a program in an operational system in an uncontrolled fashion. Programmers "hands-on" use of the machine must be prohibited while sensitive files are loaded, and this includes the program library (which may be the most sensitive of all). The use of certain utilities must be prohibited. For example, an IBM 360 Service Aid called Superzap (IMASZAP) is found very helpful in some installations. It enables a systems programmer to make object changes to a program without reassembling, to change the Volume Table of Contents (VTOC) of a disk pack, or to make direct modification of data in a file. The general use of such a program cannot be permitted in an installation designed for tight security.

The restrictions on programmers do not necessarily mean a loss of efficiency in an installation. On the contrary, low efficiency can result from sloppy procedures. More tightly controlled procedures should be designed to improve efficiency and provide programmers with services, as well as limiting the likelihood of damage.

The introduction of controls may be unpopular with programmers happy in their undisciplined methods. The average systems programmer left to his own devices will end up with a desk four feet deep in paper and a set of programs covered in undocumented patches. Nothing could be more dangerous to system security.

FOUR PRINCIPLES   There are four principles that apply to a system handling sensitive data. We shall state these and then discuss how they can be translated into practical reality.

1. It is a standard requirement in accounting that responsibilities should be divided between different groups so that no single person can commit fraud without being detected. The same principle should be applied to programming. The programming and operational work should be divided into slices handled by different groups. The division should be planned so that no single programmer can fraudulently modify the processing of a transaction or break a sensitive file without being detected.

2. On a system dedicated to a specific set of applications, only authorized programs may be run, which have been thoroughly tested, documented, and inspected. These programs must reside on the systems files and can only be placed there by a tightly controlled procedure.

3. All programmers should be prevented from handling the computer-room hardware when sensitive data or programs are loaded.

4. Programmers must be made fully aware that their work is being monitored and that audit trails will make it possible to pin the blame for any malfunction.

PROVIDE A
SERVICE

The division of responsibilities in the programming team that is needed for security reasons can usually be accomplished by the very desirable method of providing services for the programmers. Division of labor can increase programmer productivity and at the same time be part of the design for security.

In many early computer installations, programmers operated the machine. The operating procedures became increasingly complex and it became desirable to have specialist operators. To enhance machine-room efficiency, *closed-shop* installations became common, with programmers submitting jobs but not being allowed into the machine room. This provided a service for the programmers that improved overall efficiency. It also improved security. It was the first step in protecting a system from its own programmers.

Again, on early computers the programmers wrote their own input/output code. They addressed files directly, writing instructions for the seek and read operations. The programmers productivity was later improved by giving them standard software for carrying out the input/output operations and the file accessing. Such software, primarily intended to provide a service, forms the basis for security measures.

Figure 34.1 illustrates the way application programs can be constrained by security features in the software. On one side the application programs are constrained by data-management software. The application program can no longer address the files directly, by itself. It must employ routines into which can be built the checking of authorization tables or passwords, as discussed in Chapters 13, 14, and 18. On the other side the application programs are constrained by the software for input/output control, and this also can contain security features. The input/output software may, for example, identify a system user and check that he has permission to use the application program in question.

Different groups of programmers will be responsible for the input/output software, the data-management software, and sensitive application programs. The specifications and listings of these three types of software should be classified and securely locked away. The interfaces (shown in Fig. 34.1) will be very clearly specified, and only the interface details will be available to the application programmers.

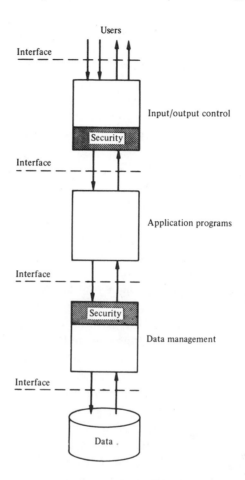

Figure 34.1. On a secure system, the application programs are constrained on the one side by the input/output software and on the other side by the data-management software. Both have built-in security features. Different groups are responsible for input/output software, data management software, and application programs. The specifications and listings of these three types of software are classified and carefully controlled, but the interfaces shown above are precisely documented and widely understood.

SYSTEM
MACRO LANGUAGE

A variety of other services may be made available to the application programmer, having a primary objective of saving him work and a possible secondary objective of improving the design for security. Such services may be provided by means of a package of subroutines, a macro language, or the employment of microprogrammed routines. Whatever method is used, the technique can be very powerful for building the security defenses.

A macro language is used on many commercial real-time systems, making it possible for programmers of little experience to write code for a highly complex system by providing them with powerful macro instructions written for the system, each of which causes a specified function to be executed. The macro language makes registers transparent to the application programmer, provides input/output routines for him, and gives him standard interfaces to various subprograms. However, while the macro language greatly helps the application programmer, it also controls him, and this is essential. Prior to compilation, the code is scanned to ensure that the programmer cannot violate register conventions, cannot write input/output operations other than by using the macros provided, cannot write non-reentrant code, and cannot bypass the security routines.

This concept of using mandatory macros or subroutines is highly flexible, greatly facilitates debugging, and makes tight control possible.

SEGREGATION OF   Financial data in commercial transactions are often
COMMERCIAL PROGRAMS handled by a variety of programs. The programs
                             must have checking facilities, as discussed in Chapter 6, to ensure that no transactions are lost and to balance the cash and accountable items. A balancing run is often separate from the processing runs. A bank, for example, scans its files at the end of each day to ensure that the records of the day's transactions balance and agree with the cash position and that the total cash in the accounts is what it should be.

The circles in Fig. 34.2 represent the programs in a system. The dark circles and connecting line are the series of programs that handle one sensitive transaction. The system must be designed so that if *one* of these dark circles is changed, fraudulently, the fraud will be quickly detected. To get away with it, he must modify *two or more* programs so that the deviations compensate. He may, for example, post a false amount of cash to his own account while ensuing that the cash in hand remains the same, and modify the balancing run so that the excess in his account is not added into the balance. Figure 6.4 shows one interpretation of Fig. 34.2. The interpretation will be widely different on different systems and the programs are often all part of the same

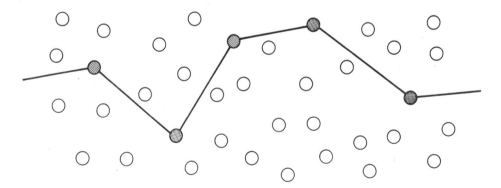

Figure 34.2

run, rather than separate runs as in Fig. 6.4. Some of the circles may represent application programs; others represent operating system or supervisory programs, or subroutines or macro expansions that provide a service to the application programmer.

Having segregated the controls in this way, the work of writing the programs must then be divided between different persons or, preferably, different groups, so that fraud cannot be committed without collusion between the groups. The groups should be kept apart. The detailed documentation and program listings of programs that a malefactor might have reason to modify must be classified and kept securely locked up.

SELF-CONTAINED   On a real-time system or other system using a data
MODULES   base in an integrated fashion, there will be a complex set of relationships between the work of different programmers. This is illustrated in Fig. 34.3. The figure shows the same circles as Fig. 34.2, and the thin lines represent logical interactions that could occur between them. A structure of this type presents serious problems for program development and maintenance. The work of one programmer considerably affects the work of the others. When he makes a change to one of the circles in Fig. 34.3, details of the change must be communicated to the programmers indicated by the arrows in the diagram. Figure 34.3 shows only a few circles; in reality there could be many hundreds, and the pattern of interactions between them would be very complex. Programmers constantly make changes during the development of a system, both to their programs and to the data specifications. Programs tend to grow and develop rather like the growth of a city. It is of fundamental importance that the changes be quickly communicated between programmers, and that the programmers act upon them. However, if the interactions are as haphazard as in Fig. 34.3, there will often be too many for effective control to be maintained.

Figure 34.3

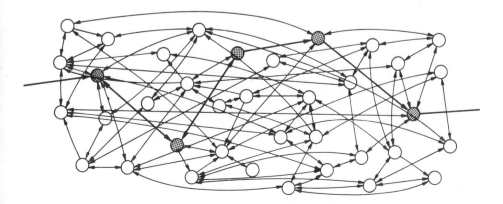

Part of the solution to this problem is to divide the programs into self-contained units. This is illustrated in Fig. 34.4. It is rather like making sub-assemblies in mechanical engineering. The behavior of each subassembly is clearly defined, and the way it fits into the rest of the machinery is specified in detail. This done, the subassembly can be designed and constructed independently of the remainder. The units of program in Fig. 34.4 are small enough for two or three men, or even one man, to handle them. The interactions within this unit are relatively easy to control. The unit is insulated as completely as possible from the other units. The interface between the unit and the rest of the system is very clearly defined. However much program modification occurs within the unit, every attempt will be made to avoid

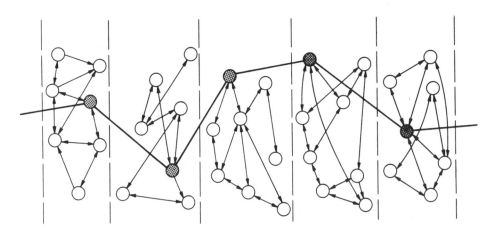

Figure 34.4

modifying the interfaces between the units. When interface modifications become essential, they will be thoroughly documented and communicated to all programmers who need to know. The programmers will have a relatively small number of changes to keep up with, instead of the deluge that would have resulted from the amorphous structure of Fig. 34.3.

This necessary process of division into subassemblies can be employed to enhance security. The units are selected in such a way as to ensure that a fraud can be committed only by the modification of programs in more than one unit and such modification is then made difficult by maintaining tight security over the internal working of the units. Without collusion a programmer will have knowledge only of the interfaces between units.

Separate units of program on a typical system may include the terminal control program, the input editing and accuracy-checking routines, the filing balancing runs, the routines for recording and inspecting check totals and hash totals, the authorization procedures, the routines for journaling and processing journals, the auditors' programs, the routines for checking volume labels, the file-addressing routines, and segments of application program common to different transactions.

Security procedures, once again, can fit naturally into the process of development and maintenance, rather than being an unwanted obstruction.

USE OF A CENTRAL CONTROL GROUP   A second technique for dealing with the problem represented by Fig. 34.3 is to set up a central control group. The control group, illustrated in Fig. 34.5, has the function of maintaining an overall knowledge of the system and controlling all changes that are made. The control group is familiar with the design estimates of memory, channel utilization, and other critical factors. It reviews all program and data specifications before programs are written, and so has an overall knowledge of the programs in the system. Any requests for changes of specifications or changes in working programs would be reviewed by the control group. The control group on some systems modifies the specifications as needed, thus relieving the programmers of a job they dislike. It communicates all changes to the persons who need to know about them.

Figure 34.5

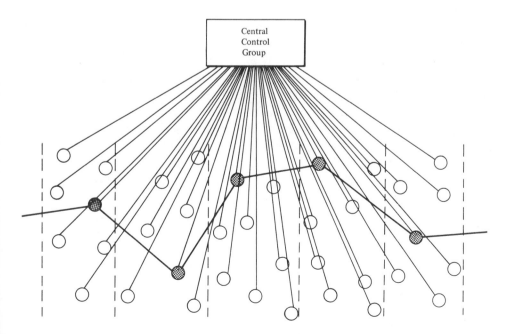

Central
Control
Group

On large real-time and data-base systems, the control group has proved to be invaluable in directing the progress of what could otherwise be an unwieldly monster. Once again, this technique can become part of the design for security. When the control group reviews initial program specifications and their modifications, they will be conscious of the constant need to improve security. Programmers, on the other hand, will be aware that their specifications or proposed modifications *are* being reviewed by a central group. This will be a deterrent to mischief.

INSPECTION OF PROGRAMS The control group on many systems today works only with program and data *specifications.* It could go one step farther and inspect the *code* that is written. Any inexplicable segments of code, apparently unused statements, or unexplained switches or branches would be queried. In some organizations it is a function not of a central group, but of first-level managers or group leaders to inspect the code with security in mind.

Whenever it is done, if a programmer knows that his code is going to be inspected, this will form a major psychological deterrent.

PROGRAM TESTING The next line of defense is a well-planned and carefully controlled program-testing procedure. Again the key to security is division of responsibilities. The programmer should not provide his own test data for any but his initial tests. On systems dedicated to a specific set of applications, it is common to find a centralized group with the function of providing program-testing data and specifying test cases to be run. The testing will be organized and the results checked by a central group.

On a system where accuracy is of importance, testing has to be done very thoroughly indeed. Any shortcuts in this area will lead to trouble. Testing becomes a major operation on real-time systems where multiple combinations of transactions may be handled simultaneously and vast numbers of possible timing relationships exist. An organized operation is needed for flooding the system with transactions for an extended period of time in a multithread manner.

From the programmer's point of view the testing group takes some of the work off his shoulders and provides a service for him. At the same time, however, they control him. His programs must do exactly what they were intended to do. Any attempt to modify transactions in a felonious manner would be caught quickly.

PROGRAM
LIBRARY

When programs finally gain the seal of approval of the testing group, it is necessary to ensure that nobody modifies them thereafter. If modifications are necessary, the changed program must be recycled through the testing process. After programs have been tested, they should be placed by the testing group into a program library. This may be on tape or disk. It should store all approved modifications to programs with details of who programmed and who authorized the modification. The library system can thus reveal how any program arrived at its current state and what it looked like at any time in the past. It provides a backup in case an object program is lost or damaged, and retains an earlier working version of programs in case the latest version proves unexpectedly faulty. Tight security needs to be maintained over the program library tapes or disks so that their contents cannot be read or modified by unauthorized persons.

Once again, the program library offers a work-saving service to the programmer. He is relieved of the chore of maintaining card decks. He can recompile simply by submitting change cards. Again an essential security feature is built out of a valuable service.

PROGRAM
RESIDENCE FILE

Perhaps the most important aspect of program security on a system dedicated to specific applications is the program residence file. It is essential that the only programs used with live data on such a system are those which have been through the inspection and testing procedures, and which reside in the program library. Any possibility for bypassing these procedures must be sealed. If it is possible for anyone to run an unauthorized program with the live data files and not be detected, or to modify a program residence file, then the other precautions become worthless.

Many real-time and data-base systems use two (or more) computers. The operational work takes place on one machine, while compiling, testing, maintenance, and off-line runs take place on the other. The other machine also serves as a standby, so that if the operational machine fails, its functions and peripheral units can be switched to the standby machine. In such a system *no* programs are run in the operational machine other than those in the authorized program file. Other systems will run a mixture of secure and insecure programs and must contain a mechanism to ensure that only the secure ones can obtain the sensitive data. In either case there needs to be a mechanism in the security software for ensuring that no programs other than those from the secure program residence file can be used with sensitive data. Tight security is easier to achieve in the two-computer system in which one computer is dedicated to secure operations. In the future, operating systems are likely to become available that will permit highly secure operations and insecure general operations to coexist safely in the same machine.

LEAKPROOF
OPERATING SYSTEMS

In any security scheme it must be assumed that some of the programmers are diabolically clever. If there are ways of circumventing the security barriers in the programs, they are likely to find them. The computer operating systems that were available in the 1960s were not written with tight security in mind, and a variety of ingenious ways could be found to bypass protection routines, password schemes, and the like. To do so needed Assembler Language coding and a knowledge of the operating systems detailed enough to daunt the majority of programmers. Exceptionally clever programmers could slip through the holes.

In the early 1970s these deficiencies were taken seriously, and versions of operating systems were produced which were intended to be leakproof. No doubt the techniques for making systems programs secure will become better understood and will become a standard part of the requirements for such software. It is necessary also to design the macro instructions, microprograms, and subroutines for specific systems in such a way that they cannot be compromised.

In a highly sensitive system it should be assumed that leaks still exist. If only a person is clever enough to find the technique, he can write a program that will slip through the defenses. The controls should be designed in such a way as to maximize the probability of his being caught in the attempt, and would-be intruders should be intimidated by being told that they will be caught and disciplined. *Bypassing the defenses must not become a game for the programmers.*

Another line of defense is desirable. Controls should be set up to ensure that undesirable programs cannot reach the live system.

PROMOTION OF
PROGRAMS TO
LIVE OPERATIONS

The promotion of programs to the program residence file is a highly sensitive operation and needs very careful control.

On IBM's Advanced Administrative System, which maintains a data base of customers, orders, accounts, commissions, and other items for IBM's Data Processing Division, eight steps are required for the promotion of a program to the live system. To minimize the likelihood of collusion in this sensitive operation, eight different people or groups participate in the process, although on a smaller system, similar control may be maintained with fewer people. They are:

1. *Programmer.* The programmer initiates a request to promote his program or modification to the live system by filling in a *Promotion Sheet.* This states the purpose of the change. It lists any necessary prerequisites. It gives the name of the module and its *Historic Job Number,* which is used in the program library maintenance system to identify the different versions of the different programs.

2. *Programmer's manager.* The Promotion Sheet is signed by the programmer's manager, who must approve the program and take steps to ensure that it does what is specified *and nothing more.*

3. *Testing control group.* The central group which controls testing must sign the sheet to signify that the program has passed through all phases of testing and met the requisite standards.

4. *Application control group.* A central group approves the applications of the system and authorizes the program and data specifications as in Fig. 34.5. This group gives the authorization to move the tested program to the live program residence file.

5. *Operations group.* A utility program moves the new module to the live program file. This utility is run by the system operations group who can only use it with the authorization of the application control group. It produces a record of all program modules placed on the system residence file.

6. *On-line control group.* The on-line control group is concerned with the system performance. They measure mean response time and mean time between system interruptions. When new programs are introduced, there is a risk that system performance will be degraded. The risk is minimized by spreading the changes over time, and retaining the capability to switch to an earlier mode of operation. The group will stop changes if they seriously degrade system performance or reliability. The decision to exercise a new program module is made jointly by the application group.

7. *Functional group.* A group concerned with the function that the module relates to (e.g., accounts receivable) then checks the operation of the module to ensure that it does what they want.

8. *Terminal users.* The system using the module is then exercised by a group of terminal users to ensure that it is satisfactory for the users, that it does not adversely affect the man-machine interaction, and that it cannot be misused by a terminal operator. This is the final acceptance. All the above groups sign the sheet. The new module then comes into operational use (Fig. 34.6).

SUMMARY OF SEGREGATION METHODS

The segregation of responsibilities is a key to security in programming, as elsewhere. To conclude this chapter, here is a list of the types of segregation that can exist on a secure system.

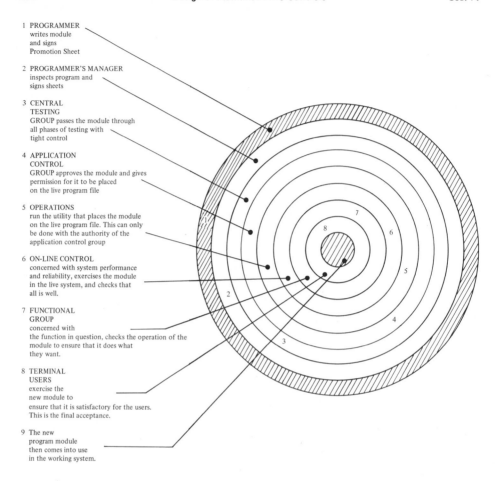

1 PROGRAMMER
writes module
and signs
Promotion Sheet

2 PROGRAMMER'S MANAGER
inspects program and
signs sheets

3 CENTRAL
TESTING
GROUP passes the module through
all phases of testing with
tight control

4 APPLICATION
CONTROL
GROUP approves the module and gives
permission for it to be placed
on the live program file

5 OPERATIONS
run the utility that places the module
on the live program file. This can only
be done with the authority of the
application control group

6 ON-LINE CONTROL
concerned with system performance
and reliability, exercises the module
in the live system, and checks that
all is well.

7 FUNCTIONAL
GROUP
concerned with
the function in question, checks the operation of the
module to ensure that it does what
they want.

8 TERMINAL
USERS
exercise the
new module to
ensure that it is satisfactory for the users.
This is the final acceptance.

9 The new
program module
then comes into use
in the working system.

Figure 34.6. A sensitive operational system needs a number of layers of
insulation to protect it from the programmers.

1. The systems programmers will not write application programs using sensitive data. The
application programmers will not write systems programs.
2 It is not possible for users to access application programs except via the input/output
control software, and this will contain security features, including a user identification
and authorization check.
3. It is not possible for an application program to access the data files except via the data
management software, and this will contain security features, including password or
authorization check.
4. On a dedicated commercial system no user is permitted to use a program that he himself has written.
5. No programmer will be permitted to operate the computer system.

6. The operator will not be told the functions of the programs he is running. Program decks, tapes, and disks will be labeled with an alphanumeric number, but not with anything that indicates the function.

7. On a dedicated commercial system no program will be run that does not reside on the authorized program file. Elaborate control will be maintained over the promotion of programs to this file, to check that such programs are authorized, fully tested, and independently inspected.

8. The programmers will be provided with a set of macros, subroutines or microprograms, which provide them with valuable services but control the way they handle certain operations. Input/output and other security-sensitive operations may be handled *only* by means of the macro language or subroutine library.

9. Users of the system do not specify its programs in detail, but liaise with specialists or programmers who carry out this function.

10. Program specifications are centrally approved by a control group.

11. Specifications for data-base records or files are centrally approved, possibly by the same control group that approves data specifications.

12. Data for final program testing are not generated by the programmer of the routine in question, but by a specialist or group set up for that purpose.

13. Testing will not be carried out by the programmer, but by a central group that controls the operation tightly.

14. All programs and modifications to programs will be kept centrally by a program library maintenance system. Programmers will be relieved of the necessity to keep program decks, and an *audit trail* of program modifications will be kept, saying who authorized them and who specified and programmed them.

15. The operations groups handling the live running of the system may be separate to an operations group for testing and support functions.

16. The application programs for a sensitive transaction will never *all* be written by the same programmer.

REFERENCE

1. Peter Hamilton, "Espionage and Subversion in an Industrial Society," Hutchinson, London, 1967.

35 PSYCHOLOGICAL SECURITY

Some computer installations have an "atmosphere" of security, which has nothing to do with locked doors, police guards, or background checks. The Department of Defense Security Manual has detailed instructions for security clearances of personnel, but these alone are not enough. Psychological security lies in the attitudes of the employees. A security-aware observer going into an installation lacking in psychological security can detect it quickly, like a real-estate evaluator smelling dry rot.

In addition to the measures discussed in Chapter 34, eight steps are essential in the maintenance of psychological security.

1. Information and Training

The personnel in an installation should have their security responsibilities made clear to them. When a man moves from unclassified work to work involving confidential or other classified data, the new responsibilities must be clearly explained to him.

(a) He should understand the rules for the locking up and safeguarding of classified data.
(b) He should understand the rules about reproducing, destroying, mailing, and modifying classified data.
(c) He should understand the rules relating to verbal discussion of classified data.
(d) The nature and value of the data should be explained to each employee, and the methods by which an intruder might compromise it should be discussed.

(e) Special procedures for terminal sign on or for the submission of classified jobs must be taught.

The object of security education must be to obtain security *by consent.* It should never be imposed without reason. Security *must* be seen to be reasonable and necessary, and the procedures must be designed so that they do not cause unnecessary inconvenience.

The staff should be instructed not only to be meticulous in their own personal obesrvation of the security rules, but to keep an eye on their colleagues also and correct them if they omit the requisite precautions.

The rules of security should be written down simply and each employee should have a copy. It is essential to explain the requirements verbally, however, rather than merely give an employee a document to read. Each manager should explain security to his subordinates and stress that concern with security is a necessary part of their job.

2. Ensure That Security Is Taken Seriously

In many organizations security is laughed at behind management's back. Employees dismiss it as "a lot of red tape." Classified reports are left lying around or taken home. Desks are not locked. Worse, it becomes an entertainment to break into the computer system. A programmer will enjoy demonstrating his prowess at taking illegal actions at the terminal.

Management must demonstrate that it is serious about security. Employees must be immediately apprehended for any breaches of security. A sharp reprimand is necessary for any employee who breaks the rules. If an employee knows that he will be in trouble when caught, he will be less likely to make a game of slipping through the security controls Otherwise, some programmers, by their very nature, will tamper with the terminals and play tricks with the coding.

3. Monitoring the Observance of Security Rules

Security, being negative by nature, is possessed of a natural inertia. Left alone it will become forgotten until some event jolts it back into consciousness. If no such event takes place, carelessness and lethargy will set in. The procedures will be forgotten.

One security specialist tells the story of how, posing as an intruder, he walked into a prohibited computer room, going through the normally locked

door by tagging behind an operator. The operator challenged him and he refused to leave, indicating that he wanted to take certain tapes. The operator,
caught by surprise, audibly asked, "What am I supposed to do now?" This
would be the reaction in many computer centers.

The staff can only be kept alert to security procedures by repeated spot
checks and monitoring. A manager or security officer should walk around
occasionally after hours to see whether desks are unlocked and whether
classified documents are left lying around. If he finds classified documents,
he should remove them, and the individuals responsible for them should be
summoned on the following day. Similarly, terminal procedures should be
physically observed as well as mechanically monitored. The secure maintenance of tapes and disks should be checked. Random tests should be made to
see whether emergency procedures will be observed. A manager or security
officer should check that security codes are not being written down in insecure places, and so on. Some installations have assigned individuals the task
of seeing whether they can break into the system.

All employees must know that management is not only serious but *alert*
about security breaches.

4. Morale

When morale is low, the risks to security become high. Employees
become casual. Some become antagonistic and on occasions have done deliberate damage to computer systems. Some employees prepare to leave the
corporation. The computer profession is notorious for its job hopping. Some
may prepare to take valuable information with them.

It should be recognized that low morale is dangerous on an installation
that is vital to the functioning of a corporation. It is a situation that data-
processing staffs are particularly prone to. It may be caused by sudden budget
cuts, by failures in development progress, or by sudden "decommitments" to
schemes that had earlier enthused the technologists. It may be caused by
sheer bad management or by absence of good personnel policies relating to
pay, promotion, hiring and firing, working conditions, and the like. Poor personnel policies or poor management may worsen morale problems that have
some other cause. The prospects of advancement may suddenly seem dim in
the firm to the ever-restless computer professionals.

Line management must concern itself with morale. Good leadership can
often solve morale problems.

It usually pays to separate the development staff from the staff that runs
and maintains a vital installation. The development group is more moved by

tides of fortune, is more prone to sudden decommitments, and is more likely
to contain creative but troublesome employees.

5. Knowledge of Individual Employees

It is possible that the greatest single threat to a computer installation is
the disgruntled employee. There are many cases in which one employee has
damaged a computer installation. Usually it happens accidentally, as when an
airline-reservation data bank was partially destroyed by an employee loading
the wrong tapes to restore the files after a test session. Occasionally it has
happened deliberately, as when an air force major destroyed a set of inventory records. Many cases are recorded of employees selling classified data,
and doubtless far more are unrecorded.

Individual misdemeanors, other than the skillfully planned crimes, tend
to occur when employees are low in morale, emotionally upset, or badly over-
worked. To minimize their likelihood, managers should know each person
who works for them and keep closely in touch with them. When possible, the
manager should understand his employees extramural activities. The misfits
will usually be apparent. When a hitherto loyal employee turns against his
employers, the intelligent manager will usually have ample warning of it and
may be able to take action—either taking steps to improve the employee's
morale or, failing that, moving him to an area in which he is less likely to
cause harm.

6. Care When Firing Employees

There have been several cases of programmers who were fired, damaging
the programs before they left, or, sometimes worse, modifying the programs
to damage data. An often-quoted case is that of a fired programmer modifying a payroll routine to cause havoc on a subsequent payday.

If a data-processing employee is fired, he should be asked to leave the
premises immediately and not be given chance to vent his wrath on the
programs.

7. Controlling Outsiders

When persons are temporarily employed from outside the organization,
they must be made to conform to the installation's security rules. Outsiders

can constitute a security risk. They include persons such as temporary secretaries, programmers, and consultants. They can sometimes cross the boundaries that are erected between different groups and hence could be used in either an internal or external attempt to compromise the system. In highly critical areas, part-timers or temporary employees should be avoided if possible.

8. Higher Management

As far as possible it is desirable that the higher levels of management should set the examples in security. However, in some organizations the higher levels of management are the first to break the security rules. Indeed, the higher the position of the manager, the less likely it is that he will obey such rules. Security professionals recognize the danger that top management leave their papers lying about and forget to lock their safes.

The answer to this lies in surrounding higher levels of management with a security screen. Secretaries and personnel assistants should be responsible for the security of the managers for whom they work, locking away their documents. Items that would be particularly valuable to a would-be intruder, such as system design and programming specifications, can usually be kept out of the hands of high management.

Top management should be occasionally briefed, if possible, on the security threat to computers and how dangerous it might be. Sometimes they will be only too well aware of it. They should review the protective measures employed and endorse them. Security ought to start at the top.

36 PSYCHOLOGY OF THE SYSTEM BREAKER

Many studies have been done of the psychology of criminals, and particularly the *white-collar criminal* [1-6, 9-12]. The facts that emerge from them are fascinating. Do they give any clues about the malefactors that could lead to better design for security?

LONERS   One conclusion of criminologists which is highly relevant to systems design is that most embezzlers, unlike some other categories of white-collar criminals, usually work alone [1]. Sutherland [2] concludes that "the ordinary case of embezzlement is a crime *by a single individual* in a subordinate position against a strong corporation." Top management criminals, on the other hand, such as antitrust violators, usually work in compact with one another. Petty embezzlement is startlingly common in some corporations where the controls are lax. In one investigation, lie detector tests were given to *all* employees in a group of Chicago banks and showed that 20 per cent of the employees had stolen bank property. The results indicating guilt were supported in almost all cases by confessions.

The controls that have been discussed which enforce collusion will prevent most *casual* embezzlement, at least where it relates to data-processing operations. There is still much scope for petty crime beyond the reach of the computer in many organizations.

Although it is true that most embezzlers work alone, collusion has occurred in a substantial proportion of the crimes, and is most likely to be found when management has a lax attitude toward employee honesty. If it is made known that management takes a very serious view of petty dishonesty and is on the alert for it, the establishment of collusion between appropriate people will be difficult and risky.

In many cases an employee was encouraged to commit fraud because he knew that his supervisor or his management in general was dishonest. The oldest maxim of the con man is that "you can't cheat an honest man."

If an employee knows that his supervisor is "on the take," he often feels that he can do the same, and that it will not matter too much if his supervisor finds out. It is often in such circumstances that collusion begins. The supervisor does find out, calls the miscreant into his office, and instead of firing him or admonishing him, cautions him to be careful. As trust develops between the two, they may then cooperate on a crime that needs collusion.

CORRUPT DEPARTMENTS   An atmosphere in which controlled crime is acceptable can rapidly pervade an entire department or an entire organization. The Knapp hearings in 1971 revealed an amazingly broad base to bribery in the New York police. The young policeman learned the methods when he first became a cadet and was expected to conform to them. The higher the rank, the higher was the accepted proportion of the profits. A *New York Times* editorial claimed that the extreme public outcry over the hearings did not change the level of the "take" by 1 cent, so deeply engrained was it as a way of life. The same pervasiveness of crime is found in some department stores, factories, and other organizations. In some cases the installation of a computer system with tight controls has upset the applecart. Just as management did not know how sloppily their inventory was being kept until they installed a computer, so they were ignorant of the generality of petty embezzlement, which the computer prevented.

In the cases in which collusion *has* occurred, it is usually collusion within one department—often between the manager of the department and his staff. In a case quoted by Jaspen and Black [3] as being typical, a control clerk is troubled by his own petty thefts and confesses to his superior, the credit manager. The manager closes the door and the clerk expects the worst. However, the manager says calmly, "I'm not going to turn you in. Forget this conversation. And don't discuss it with anyone else. You see, this department just can't afford a scandal—I've been embezzling for years, myself. We're in this thing together." Jaspen claims that such collusion *within a department* is common.

On this evidence the system designer might anticipate collusion within any one department and plan the controls so that they can only be bypassed if there is collusion between widely separated departments. The data-processing departments should be well separated from those that handle the corporation's assets. The surveys of convicted embezzlers indicate that *inter-departmental* collusion is rare.

MOTIVATION　　　　　　The reasons why the embezzler commits his crime are very diverse—as diverse as human nature itself. However, it is noticeable from the surveys of convicted embezzlers that *very few are professional criminals.* Almost all started off honestly and drifted into crime. Some started to steal or defraud small amounts because it was so easy. The controls to prevent theft were blatantly ineffectual, and the temptation was too much. Some started to steal because they entered a crooked department and were taught the habit by their peer group. Some developed a hatred for the organization they worked with or felt that it had cheated them and that they must redress the balance. The most common motivation, however, is that a person drifts into financial trouble and cannot obtain the money any other way. His trouble may be caused by gambling. In some cities in the United States it is increasingly likely to be caused by drug addiction. The surveys show, however, that by far the most common cause is heavy social expenditure. The person is living beyond his means and feels that his social commitments cannot be cut back. His neighbors and associates are wealthy, and he is too proud not to keep up with them. His income may have temporarily dropped, and he feels that he will "borrow" from the till until he is in a better financial position.

Although there are departments in some firms that are rife with corruption, most major embezzlers are alone. The frame of mind in which most fraud is committed is too personal or too casual for the wrongdoer to want to be a member of a carefully organized team, such as that which could crack a computer system. The miscreant is solving his own personal problems in his own personal way.

In the vast majority of cases he did not originally set out to be a criminal, and, indeed, does not think of himself as a criminal. He normally rationalizes his activity in terms that reduce his guilt feelings. A study by Cressey [4] lists the following typical quotations:

> "They didn't give me the raise I was due for last year"; "they're a big firm, they can afford it"; "they're covered by the insurance"; "everyone is on the fiddle here, so why not me too?"; and "I've put in more work than they've paid me for."

Cressey concludes:

> Trusted persons become trust violators when they conceive of themselves as having a financial problem which is non-sharable, are aware that this problem can be secretly resolved by violation of the position of financial trust, and are able to apply to their own conduct in that situation verbalizations which enable them to adjust their conceptions of themselves as trusted persons with their conceptions of themselves as users of the entrusted funds or property.

In other words, he concludes that three elements are present:

1. The embezzler has a personal financial problem and is ashamed to ask anyone for help.
2. He knows an appropriate embezzlement technique.
3. He can overcome the protests of his conscience by means of rationalization.

The studies of white-collar theft suggest that it is extremely difficult to tell the goats from the sheep. The thief is often the last person anyone would believe capable of committing fraud. His honesty (until caught) often appears impeccable. It has often been a severe shock and disillusionment for executives when a close associate or subordinate has been convicted, and has shaken their faith in their ability to judge the honesty of their fellowmen.

The United States Fidelity and Guarantee Company made a study of 1001 embezzlers. Of them, 846 were white-collar workers and the rest blue collar. They came from all types of occupations and held all types of positions, indicating clearly that no area is immune to embezzlement. Table 36.1 shows a breakdown of the white-collar section of the sample [3]. The company drew a composite picture of the average male embezzler: age 35; married with one or two children; lives in a respectable neighborhood, probably

Table 36.1

Type of Employee	Men		Women	
	Number	*Percentage*	*Number*	*Percentage*
Executives and professional	261	37.6	26	17.2
Sales	190	27.4	37	24.5
Clerical	142	20.4	73	48.3
Government	52	7.5	7	4.7
Labor officials	50	7.1	8	5.3
Totals	695*	100	151	100

*The sample also contained 150 male and 5 female blue-collar workers.

buying his own home; has been employed by his firm for 3 years and has been stealing for 8 months; is in the top 40 per cent of the nation's income distribution; average total take is 120 per cent of salary. The picture of the average female embezzler is similar except that she takes somewhat less and has been at it for a somewhat shorter time. The figures have risen in recent years, and the insurance company expects them to continue rising.

The white-collar thief often works very hard, and he is often very ambitious. In a study of thirty such persons in Leyhill Prison [5], John C. Spencer makes the following observations:

> The outstanding characteristic of these thirty men is their upward mobility. This observation was an unexpected one: It did not constitute a basic assumption underlying the study. I had expected to find in my sample a much larger group of men in leading commercial and financial positions and with a superior social and educational background.
>
> This upward mobility is closely related to what also appears to be an outstanding feature of their personality, their ambition, their drive, their desire to mix with people of higher social position than their own and to give their children an expensive private education, and their willingness to take financial risks in the process. In contrast to their own ambitions and even reckless behavior, I continually noticed the apparent stability and security of their siblings as they discussed their family histories. They lived more expensively than their brothers and they often spoke of their brothers' ability to stick to a routine task without ambitions for success and achievement. Their families had, with one exception, no record of criminal convictions so far as I could learn.
>
> ...They were, in general, popular members of social groups. Club membership was considered important mainly for the social prestige which it carried and for the opportunity of mixing with people of superior status. It was all part of the same process of upward mobility for which the expensive house and automobile and other symbols of status were also thought to be necessary. A small number of the sample took part in the social life of church and chapel. All the evidence points to the fact that they kept separate the norms of the different groups to which they belonged, particularly those of employment, recreation, and family.

Spencer goes on to emphasize the noticeable absence of feelings of rejection and emotional deprivation commonly found in studies of other types of criminal.

The president of a firm of management consultants who specialize in investigations of fraud and related crimes, Jaspen [3] stresses how well the white-collar thief appears to blend with the crowd:

Generally friendly, he would seem to be the first person you would trust and the last you would suspect of wrongdoing. Above average in intelligence, he usually is the hardest worker in the establishment. Once involved in fraud, he seldom suggests new methods of business operation for fear that a radical change in procedure would result in his exposure. Except in rare instances, his home life is exemplary. He is, in the phrase of the mid-twentieth century, the ideal organization man, or so he seems.

But there is another world which the white collar thief inhabits. It is the world of the white collar thief's conscience. In most cases his greatest fear is exposure and the ridicule and loss of status that would invariably follow. Once he has begun his peculations, he will continually be on his guard. Often he is the first employee in the office and the last to leave. He may even eat his lunch at his desk.

MUDLERS AND INCOMPETENTS

Another important conclusion of the studies of white-collar crime is that a large proportion of embezzlers are muddlers and incompetents. This is certainly not true in all cases, but the superbly clever heist of the movies and crime novels appears to be rare in reality. If the system controls will catch the *unintelligent* or the *casual* attempt at crime, they have dealt with most of the problem. Most embezzlers simply do not have the ability to change the balancing programs and other controls discussed in Section II. *If they know that these tight controls exist, they will look elsewhere for opportunities.*

Much white-collar crime is of a petty nature in which a clerk or store-keeper uses an obvious loophole. Much starts as ill-thought-out "borrowing" from the till; the perpetrator has vague intentions of paying the money back, but gets into steadily deeper water. Much crime is suddenly carried out by an executive or employee with emotional problems, rather than being coolly planned in detail over an extended period. In scanning the details of typical embezzlements one is amazed time and time again at how easy the crime was and how long it continued before detection. The fact is that most control systems for preventing embezzlement are woefully inadequate.

In one case a banker, wishing to give a helping hand to everybody, had loaned far more money than he was legally permitted to lend. The bank had a serious shortage, and for 5 years the manager moved items from one account to another in an attempt to hide the deficit. His methods never worked and the shortage became steadily greater, with one borrower alone owing the bank nearly $1 million. The bank manager worked excessively long hours, and never stole money for his own needs. For 5 years the board of directors never suspected anything wrong, and the bank examiners did not check thoroughly enough to find it. The bank manager omitted critical overdrafts from his listings and hid the revealing ledger cards. The manager's haphazard attempts to help everybody continually made the situation worse until the deficit reached enormous proportions. The bank eventually collapsed. It did not even have an excess fidelity insurance policy, which would have protected it at low cost.

REVENGE   A subconscious motive of many embezzlers appears to be revenge against the organization that employs them. They develop a hatred of the organization and believe that it has been unfair to them, but still work there because they are comfortable or need the income. Sometimes the person in question has a serious persecution complex. Sometimes he has genuine grievances against his employers. When an expense account is not fully paid, he may determine to obtain the money from his employers by some other method. He may feel that he has been unfairly demoted or has not received the raise he deserves. The pressures placed on executives in some large corporations are such that some are bound to be hurt. Sometimes such an executive, who has hitherto been a model employee, commits a startling crime. Sometimes the drop in an executive's income or his inability to meet his financial commitments triggers such a crime. Sometimes an executive is expected to cut an impressive figure in his community on a salary that is far from adequate.

The sudden crime that is based on emotion is rarely well planned. The perpetrator is likely to be caught if good controls are in use. Such crimes, again, rarely involve collusion.

A dramatic illustration is the story of Richard Crowe, the assistant manager of a Broadway branch of the National City Bank of New York. He was 41 years old when he committed a crime that made banking history. Prior to that he had led an exemplary life. He was an intelligent man, but the crime he committed was so ill planned that he could hardly have expected to have succeeded uncaught.

Crowe had many social commitments. He was a hard-working, model citizen. He was a director of the Community Chest, director of the Chamber of Commerce, treasurer of the Red Cross, cochairman of the Salvation Army, Boy Scout committeeman, director of the U.S. Volunteer Lifesaving Corps, member of the Police Athletic League, president of the Richmond County Bankers Association, president of Group Seven of the New York State Bankers Association, and president of the Stapleton Board of Trade. He helped raise funds for a variety of charitable activities.

The bank encouraged these activities but did not adequately cover the expenses. Crowe's salary was not high, and his activities caused him to mix constantly with persons much wealthier than himself. He was married, with three children, and lived in an inexpensive house on Staten Island on which he was paying off the mortgage. His expenses slowly began to exceed his means. He had been told by his bank that he would be made manager at some not-too-distant date, but this seemed increasingly unlikely to him, as the manager at his branch was about the same age.

He described his feeling prior to committing the crime in an article in *Cosmopolitan* [6].

> I guess I got cocky and big-headed; the public servant business went to my head. But I was never home at night—I had too many places to go—and when I was home, I was irritable with my wife and children. I suppose the out-of-pocket expenses were worrying me. They were terrific. Some nights, going to a formal dinner, I had to spend twenty-five dollars or more for flowers for the hostess and getting my tails and white tie in shape, cab fares, tips, etc. Before long, I had to begin borrowing. At that time, too, I was trying to pay off the mortgage on my house. All told, when I ran off to Florida, I owed about $35,000, including the mortgage. If I had been sensible, Hon [his wife] and I could have sat down and figured out a way of liquidating these debts. But I wasn't sensible; I was caught up in a maze of what I thought were important activities, and I was most concerned with keeping up that big front.
>
> After months of keeping everything bottled up inside me, I found out I couldn't do it anymore. One day—that Wednesday in March, as I stood there in Lawler's [a favorite bar] —everything exploded. I suddenly got disgusted with myself for leading such a phony life, trying to keep up with the Joneses. And I transferred the blame from myself to the bank—I somehow held the bank responsible for the situation I was in.
>
> I thought, What am I going to do?
>
> And then I thought, I'll fix their wagon, good.
>
> And that was how I decided to take the money.

After work one Friday, Crowe went to the bank's vaults with a large leather suitcase and stuffed it with nearly $1 million in cash and government bonds. He hurried because he was nervous of being discovered. When he had finished, he hastily jammed the lock on the vaults. He did not lock the suitcase securely enough and as he raced to leave the bank it burst open. Tens of thousands of dollars scattered down the staircase. He rushed around picking them all up and compressed them into the overstuffed case. He agitatedly fastened a strap around the case and then as he was leaving he saw the cleaning women checking in. Hoping he had left no money on the staircase, he caught the 5-cent ferry to Staten Island.

If Crowe had flown to Brazil, he might have lived happily ever after, but in fact he had no well-thought-out plans. He stayed at home over the weekend and did not tell his wife what he had done. He hid nearly $700,000 in the attic of his house. He hid $50,000 in the family cemetery plot. He sent some money to friends and hid some in his parent's house. On Sunday evening he told his wife he was going on a business trip and flew to Florida. A week later he was arrested in the washroom of a Daytona Beach nightclub.

TECHNICAL   With computer crime there is one factor that is dif-
INGENUITY   ferent from the traditional world of the embezzler.
          The persons who are involved with computers can, by their very nature, be devilishly ingenious. To some of them a complex electronic system, which is supposed to be difficult to break into, presents an irresistible challenge. We find a form of system cracking that may be quite unrelated to crime. The engineer or programmer wants to break into the system for the same reason that the climber must reach the top of a higher mountain—"because it is there." Bypassing the system's controls represents a form of intellectual entertainment, and the technician who achieves it will joyfully demonstrate his prowess to his close colleagues. The prospect of breaking into a data bank offers a challenge, and success in obtaining information illicitly is exciting—often much more exciting than their legitimate job.

PLAYFUL   We have, then, a major category of system breaker
MALIGNANCY   who does not have criminal intent so much as play-
          ful malignancy.
    A number of persons throughout the world have learned how to make free telephone calls by means of ingenious electronic tricks. *Esquire* interviewed some of these, and their comments revealed well the attitude of the playful malignant [7]:

> You'll find that the free-call thing isn't really as exciting at first as the feeling of power you get from having one of these babies in your hand.

He was referring to a small box of electronics for transmitting the telephone toll signaling frequencies.

> I've watched people when they first get hold of one of these things and start using it, and discover they can make connections, set up crisscross and zigzag switching patterns back and forth across the world. They hardly talk to the people they finally reach. They say hello and start thinking of what kind of call to make next. They go a little crazy.
> He decides to check out London first (from California). He chooses a certain pay phone located in Waterloo Station. This particular pay phone is

popular with the phone-phreaks because there are usually people walking by at all hours who will pick it up and talk for a while.

(Persons who misuse the telephone network in this way are referred to as "phone-phreaks.")

> He presses the lower left-hand corner button which is marked KP on the face of the box.
>
> "That's Key Pulse. It tells the tandem we're ready to give it instructions. First I'll punch out KP 182 START which will slide us into the overseas sender in White Plains. I hear a neat clunk-cheep. I think we'll head over to England by satellite. Cable is actually faster and the connection is somewhat better, but I like going by satellite. So I just punch out KP Zero 44. The Zero is supposed to guarantee a satellite connection and 44 is the country code for England. Okay . . . we're there. In Liverpool actually. Now all I have to do is punch out the London area code which is 01, and dial up the pay phone. Here, listen, I've got a ring now."
>
> I hear the soft quick purr-purr of a London ring. Then someone picks up the phone. "Hello," says the London voice.
>
> "Hello. Who's this?" Fraser asks.
>
> "Hello. There's actually nobody here. I just picked this up while I was passing by. This is a public phone. There's no one here to answer actually."
>
> "Hello. Don't hang up. I'm calling from the United States."
>
> ..."Isn't that far out," he says grinning at me. "London. Like that."

Some of the phone-phreaks are even further out, and the ultimate challenge of the expert is to place a call around the world and back to the caller.

> "I'll tell you how I did it," one interviewee says." I M-F-ed Tokyo inward, who connected me to India." [MF refers to the multifrequency tones used for long-distance signaling.] India connected me to Greece, Greece connected me to Pretoria, South Africa, South Africa connected me to South America, I went from South America to London, I had a London operator connect me to a New York operator, I had New York connect me to a California operator who rang the phone next to me. Needless to say I had to shout to hear myself. But the echo was far out. Fantastic. Delayed. It was delayed twenty seconds, but I could hear myself talk to myself."
>
> "You mean you were speaking into the mouthpiece of one phone sending your voice around the world into your ear through a phone on the other side of your head?"
>
> "That's right. I've also sent my voice around the world one way, going east on one phone, and going west on the other, going through cable one way, satellite the other, coming back together at the same time, ringing the two

phones simultaneously and picking them up and whipping my voice both ways around the world back to me. Wow. That was a mind blower."

"You mean you sit there with both phones on your ear and talk to yourself around the world," I said incredulously.

"Yeah. Um hum. That's what I do. I connect the phones together and sit there and talk."

"What do you say? What do you say to yourself when you're connected?"

"Oh, you know. Hello test one two three," he says in a low-pitched voice.

"Hello test one two three," he replies to himself in a high-pitched voice.

"Hello test one two three," he repeats again, low-pitched.

"Hello test one two three," he replies, high-pitched.

"I sometimes do this: Hello, *hello,* hello, *hello,* hello, *hello"* he trails off and breaks into laughter.

The interviewee in this case was a frustrated engineer who drives a Volkswagon bus with an entire switchboard in the back, and a computerized generator of multifrequency signaling tones. He would pull up at an isolated phone booth on a lonely country road, snake a cable out of his bus, hook it into the phone and play for hours.

"I do it for one reason" he explained to the interviewer.

"I'm learning about a System. The phone company is a System. A computer is a System. Do you understand? If I do what I do, it is only to explore a System. Computers. Systems. That's my bag. The phone company is nothing but a computer."

Another interviewee explained how he had a great affection for the equipment of some of the small independent telephone companies because *"Things break down in interesting ways."* He could "M-F himself" into an independent's switching system and use its idiosyncrasies to obtain "Marvelous leverage over the Bell System."

The mentality of the "phone-phreaks" is not uncommonly found among programmers. A diabolical cleverness is combined with an immense desire to employ it illegally and obtain information they should not have. A locked-up data bank provides an almost irresistible challenge.

"Did you ever steal anything?" says one interviewee in the *Esquire* article.

"Well yes, I—"

"Then you know! You know the rush you get. It's not just knowledge, like physical chemistry. It's forbidden knowledge. You know. You can learn about anything under the sun and be bored to death with it. But the idea that it's illegal. Look: you can be small and mobile and smart and you're ripping off somebody large and powerful and very dangerous."

In one situation a computer programmer discovered how to obtain the passwords that protected the classified files in a system. He wrote a program of immense ingenuity to print out all these passwords.

Eventually, his illegal access to passwords and files was not sufficiently satisfying. He began to change the passwords and antagonize users by indicating that he could obtain their passwords. Although he was causing trouble, he basically meant no harm to the system, any more than the phone-phreak means harm to the telephone company. As the Esquire article put it: the disgruntled inventor needs the system he attacks the way a lapsed Catholic needs the Church, and the way Satan needs a God.

The *London Sunday Times* [8] reported a case where a programmer entertained himself by introducing an automatically multiplying error into a system. At first it was small and of little consequence, but it steadily grew. It proved difficult to find and a specialist from a computer security firm was called in. He described it as "hell to unravel," and before it was eventually found the company's accounts were out by $1,800,000!

COMBINED TALENTS

Fortunately, it appears to be rare that the ingenious engineer or programmer who tinkers with the system is bent upon embezzlement. He usually does not have the social pressures of the executive or the banker, and his status symbols are of a different, less expensive, type. If he did plan a computer robbery with care and patience, he would be likely to succeed. Also, fortunately, the ingenious tinkerer is usually entirely disinterested in accounting. The tally sheets, suspense accounts, and balances remain a mystery to him. He is preoccupied with his technology.

If such a man went into partnership with the financially pressed accountant, the combination could be highly dangerous. It is well to keep them apart.

The combination of talents needed for computer fraud are most likely to be found in the broad-ranging systems analyst or the data-processing manager. It is the latter who is most likely to be able to organize the collusion that would be needed to break into a well-planned system. In a long-term operation the loopholes needed to break into the system may be deliberately *designed* into it by a systems analyst. It is important to involve the auditors at the design stage. The mechanisms of control should be designed so that no one man, including the data-processing manager, has a free hand.

Just as an atmosphere of corruption can pervade a department, so the habit of tinkering with the system can spread among the programmers or engineers. It can become a challenge in which each employee tries to outdo his colleagues. It is important to stop it immediately if it begins. The security surveillance methods discussed in Section II should be designed to detect any misuse of the system or invalid entry, and management should make it clear that they regard such tinkering as a serious offence. Do not allow the tinkerers to develop their expertise.

DIVERSITY   For all we have said in this chapter about the most common types of embezzler, human psychology can constantly surprise us by its diversity. There will be many cases that lie outside the norms. It is the intriguing job of the designer of security procedures to try to outguess the tricks that human nature can play.

REFERENCES

1. Gilbert Geis, *White-Collar Criminal,* Atherton Press, New York, 1968, p. 16.

2. E. H. Sutherland, *White-Collar Crime,* Dryden Press, New York, 1949, p. 231.

3. Norman Jaspen and Hillel Black, *The Thief in the White Collar,* J. B. Lippincott Company, Philadelphia, 1960.

4. D. R. Cressey, *Other People's Money: The Social Psychology of Embezzlement,* The Free Press, New York, 1953.

5. J. C. Spencer, "White-Collar Crime," in Tadeusz Grygier, Howard Jones, and J. C. Spencer, *Criminology in Transition,* Tavistock Publications, London, 1965.

6. "The Insecure Executive," in Norman Jaspen and Hillel Black, *The Thief in the White Collar,* J. B. Lippincott Company, Philadelphia, 1960.

7. Ron Rosenbaum, "Secrets of the Little Blue Box," *Esquire,* Oct. 1971.

8. "Is This the Perfect Crime?" *Sunday Times,* London, July 3, 1971.

Other Recommended Reading

9. E. H. Sutherland and D. R. Cressey, *Principles of Criminology,* J. B. Lippincott Company, Philadelphia, 1966.

10. Daniel Bell, "Crime As an American Way of Life," in *End of Ideology,* The Free Press, New York, 1960.

11. Walter Bomberg, *Crime and the Mind,* The Macmillan Company, New York, 1965.

12. D. R. Cressey, "The Respectable Criminal: Why Some of Our Best Friends Are Crooks," *Trans-action* 2, March-April 1965.

37 AUDITORS

As teams of accountants and government investigators continued to delve into the affairs of bankrupt Equity Funding Corp. of America last week, the biggest insurance swindle in memory—and one of the biggest swindles of any kind in history—began to come into hard focus.

What officials managed to confirm was truly shocking. Fully 58 per cent of the 97,000 policies listed on the books of an Equity Funding life-insurance subsidiary were indeed nonexistent, and thus the reinsurers who purchased the dummy policies had spent millions of dollars for—quite literally—nothing. The shock wasn't limited to the insurance business.

In a larger sense, the manner of deceit in the Equity Funding affair may have an even greater impact on the business world than the fraud itself. As the bizarre tale has unfolded, two facts have become painfully clear: Equity Funding executives used company computers as a key tool in the fraud—probably on a grander scale than ever before—and neither standard auditing practices nor Wall Street analysis was sophisticated enough to detect it. Considering that everyone from stockholder to tax collector depends heavily on audited data, this is a serious problem, indeed.

The company put the scheme into effect precisely *because* auditors have not adjusted their methods to doing business by computer.

—Newsweek, April 23, 1973

The auditor's responsibility is to assess whether the assets of an organization are adequately protected. This responsibility is discharged through the examination of the financial records of an organization for the purpose of expressing an opinion on them. The examination may be described as the process by which the auditor assures himself that the financial records are fairly stated in accordance with generally accepted accounting principles and that these principles have been consistently applied from year to year.

Since the primary function of an auditor is to examine the financial records and express an opinion on them, the techniques and procedures used in an audit are not specifically designed to disclose fraud. The auditor is constantly aware of the possibility that fraud may exist and that in some instances it may be significant enough to have a material effect on the fair representation of the organization's financial position. However, if the auditor had to assume responsibility for uncovering all irregularities and defalcations, he would have to extend the scope of his examination to a point where the cost of the audit would be prohibitive.

The auditor must rely on the organization's internal control procedures to minimize the likelihood of fraud and irregularities. He does have a responsibility to examine the internal controls and assure himself that these procedures are adequate and comply with accepted auditing standards. If an auditor does not review internal control procedures and fraud is subsequently uncovered, he can be held liable through negligence in the performance of an audit.

Internal controls in a manual accounting system are well documented and easy to follow. General principles have been established—separation of duties, audit trails, approval levels, etc.—to minimize opportunities for fraudulent behavior. Records are always visible and a hard-copy record of each transaction is usually available for the auditor to trace through the accounting procedures. With the increased use of computers in financial processing, an audit trail is no longer immediately visible. Records are kept on magnetic storage devices and the traditional set of accounting records are no longer hand posted, visible, and available for immediate examination.

The auditor must now develop a new set of disciplines and processing techniques to audit computer records and to verify the adequacy of internal controls. Two approaches have been used for the auditing of computer records:

1. Auditing around the computer, and
2. Auditing through the computer.

The first approach is usually the easiest for the auditor. He examines the transactions entering the computer and the outputs generated by computer processing to make sure that all transactions were processed correctly. He may go as far as preparing test transactions and sending these through the processing procedures. However, he has to also prepare reversing transactions so that the test amounts are not permanently recorded on the financial records of the company.

The second approach, auditing through the computer, uses computer programs to perform some of the audit functions. An example would be using computer programs to randomly select records from a file to examine or to print confirmation notices, etc. Auditing through the computer usually implies the use of special computer programs to audit the status of a computer file.

Independent of the auditing approach, there are tools and techniques which can assist the auditor. Some techniques can automate parts of the auditing process. Before discussing these, however, it is important to stress that no technique can replace the attention, intuition, and judgment of an *experienced* auditor. His experience enables him to quickly evaluate the adequacy of internal control procedures. His questioning of people leads him to system weaknesses more surely than any automated procedure or fixed-response questionnaire.

For the auditor to be more responsive to management's desire for a computer system that is sufficiently controlled, he should participate during the design of a new computer-assisted financial information system. Adequate controls should be built in to the system during the design phase.

AUDITING AT THE DESIGN STAGE   In determining the adequacy of internal controls in an automated system, auditors have traditionally been concerned with reviews of the computer room operations. They have been concerned with the possibilities of errors arising from fraud, human carelessness, stupidity, and bad supervision. They have investigated whether correct procedures are being adhered to and have made spot checks on transactions, following the history of a transaction from its origin, through the various stages in its processing. With computer systems human frailty may be as damaging at the *design* stage as at the operation stage, and it is clear that the auditor can be of great use when the system is being planned and its checks and balances are being designed.

The more automated the system, the greater the need for the auditors to be concerned with the design. With a fully real-time system or a system with a highly integrated data base, auditor involvement at the design stage is more important than on a batch-processing system. A highly automated system can do much of the work of the auditor by enforcing the use of the accuracy checks, security procedures, and balancing controls. In addition, the system must provide evidence for the auditors that the checks are in fact in use. It must provide a means for ensuring that the programs are doing what they were intended to do, and it must provide a way for the history of individual transactions to be reconstructed.

Not all auditors have adapted to the dramatic changes in emphasis and technique brought by the new forms of automation. Washbrook, in his book on auditing computerized systems [1], puts this as follows:

> Frequently, there was no overall plan, and this, coupled with the mystery of the new electronic machines and mountainous paperwork, caused many auditors to retire from the battle. This "walk away" from the problem by the auditors took two main forms. Sometimes an outright refusal by the auditors to accept as an analytical adjunct to that system. The other reaction was for auditors to latch on to some aspect of the output with which they were relatively familiar as an auditable point, either in relation to original input, or by some other means. Thus, computer processing was not generally accepted as an opportunity for auditors to improve their function by making the computer an audit tool.

Washbrook goes on to say that although auditors have had difficulty in adapting to the new systems, systems analysts are often unfamiliar with the needs of auditing:

> Systems analysts, on the whole, are not usually audit minded. They automatically build in the necessary controls to support their own technicalities, but for auditing purposes, it is necessary that an audit trail is established, and that the accuracy of the records can be tested at particular points. These facilities need to be built in at the design stage, they will not just happen. Conversely, the auditor can be of tremendous help to systems analysts in highlighting such aspects as legal parameters, which would not necessarily emerge from a directly logical analytical approach. There are many accounting conventions which are not basically logical, and which it may be possible to computerize in a more efficient manner. Systems analysts are often not sure just how they can improve on custom and practice, without offending against

legal requirements, or making the work of an auditor unnecessarily difficult. The auditor is in an excellent position to be of help here, but he must be on guard against being biased towards conventionality at the expense of progress.

Clearly, the gap between the know-how of the systems analyst and that of the auditor must be bridged. It is necessary that management appreciate this problem and ensure that it is bridged at the planning stage.

The auditor's requirements must be built in at the design stage; they cannot be added on afterward without substantial expense in modifying the programs and often changing the system configuration. The more fully automated and integrated the system, the more this is true.

Ideally, the partnership of the systems analysts and the auditor should be a highly creative one. The technology is changing so fast that the systems analysts should not slavishly copy existing methods when designing a new system. The changes ahead, such as increased capability of telecommunication networks, radically different file organization techniques, massive main memories and virtual memories, intelligent terminals, more powerful software, and so on, will continue to bring about changing methodology in the future. Given the new technology, the analyst must devise the most logical ways to use it, and the auditor can help in this by telling him what factors have special accounting or legal significance. Together they may be able to devise ways of eliminating today's manual procedures and of building the auditing requirements into the system.

In the Bell System the objectives set for internal auditors relating to computer system design were as follows [2]:

1. Develop new computerized audit techniques and have them built into the system wherever possible.
2. Develop control requirements and techniques, and emphasize to the systems design staff the need for an adequate control system.
3. Evaluate the effectiveness of the control system while it is still in the design process.
4. Evaluate all other areas, such as system testing and conversion, where controls are essential.

It is important that the auditor does not assume design responsibility. He must set objectives for the design of the controls and later must evaluate the design. If he designs the controls himself, he will end up auditing his own work, and will thus lose his objectivity. Similarly, he must not be responsible for enforcing the procedures, but must judge the effectiveness with which somebody else enforces them.

PRECONVERSION
AUDITING
The Bell System used the term "preconversion auditing" to relate to data-processing design and testing prior to cutover. Wasserman [2] refers to the auditor at this stage as a "devil's advocate on behalf of top management." He provides management with an appraisal of the controls on a system before it is cut over. There will sometimes be a difference between the viewpoints of the designers and the auditors, and then management must listen to both sides, assess the potential exposures and the costs of lowering them, and decide which viewpoint shall be followed.

Severe errors have sometimes crept into the operation of converting to a new system. One organization lost $2.8 million during conversion. Part of the internal auditor's work must be to see that conversion is tightly controlled. An important requirement at the design stage is to ensure that the system will be fully *auditable* when it is operational. The source documents and hard-copy printouts that auditors used to employ may not be part of the system, especially on a real-time system. New audit techniques must be built into the programs and procedures, as will be discussed next.

AUDITING THE
OPERATIONAL SYSTEM
Once the system is operational the auditing should serve two purposes. First, it should locate any problems, risks, bad practices, or security exposures, and, second, it should serve warning to any persons who defraud or compromise the system that they are likely to be caught. To accomplish these ends, the auditing should consist of spot checks at random intervals, as well as more complete inspections, which are preannounced.

The auditing should encompass all possible security exposures in an installation. As we have stressed, it is desirable to approach these in an integrated and balanced fashion. If one aspect of security is overstressed and another ignored, the system is not secure. The auditing must therefore check both the system and the users of the system. It must check physical security and technical security. It must check the procedures and controls, and how people are employing them. Program testing, program maintenance, and program promotion need to be checked. The tape library and on-line storage must be audited, and so must the computer operators. All the areas in Fig. 37.1 need to be audited.

This takes the auditors into territories that have been unfamiliar to some of them. Data-processing physical security, for example, is a specialized area, new to some, and it may be desirable to call in a specialist. Several firms offer a "security audit."

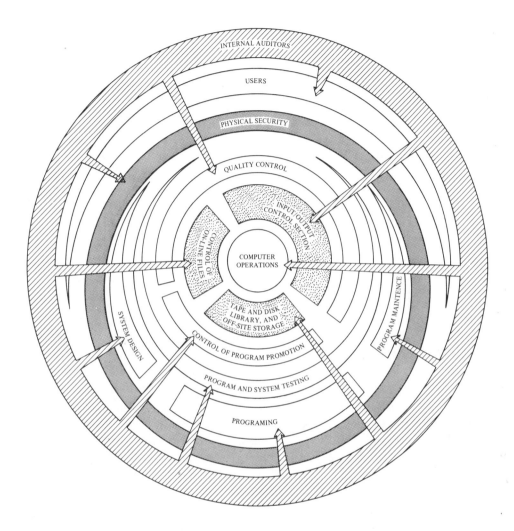

Figure 37.1

INTERNAL
AUDITORS

Undoubtedly the best way to audit a computer installation is to have an internal auditing group that specializes in data processing. This is a very important step in protecting an installation. Members of the group must be experienced and well trained in computing techniques. The group should have specialists in physical, technical, and psychological security. It should have access to legal counsel. The group may or may not be a section of the corporate internal auditing department. However, it must be external to the data-processing department, and under no circumstances should it report to the data-processing manager. No member of the data-processing department should be on the auditing team.

The head of the computer auditing team should be familiar with all aspects of computer security and should coordinate the checks made by his subordinates. He should work with the user department, with corporate and data-processing management, and with the corporation's security staff if there is any. He must have the authority to mandate changes, and to modify and add to the data-processing procedures and standards.

AUDITING   There are a number of techniques that auditors can
TECHNIQUES   use on an operational system:

1. General Questioning

The auditor will often start by asking questions to establish the general level of security and attitude toward security in an installation. By walking through the facilities and talking to people he can learn much and obtain a feel for the exposures an installation faces. If he finds that he can walk through the computer room or tape library without being challenged, he knows that something is wrong. He may ask a file owner what he will do if the file is destroyed, or ask the computer operator what he will do if the machine catches fire. He may ask the programming manager how he prevents unauthorized program modification, and ask some terminal users if they can think of any ways of reading files they are not authorized to read. He can ask a variety of "What if ...?" questions, and often the answers will point out areas where he must ask questions in greater depth.

2. Questions and Checklists

Auditors use checklists of questions and items to be examined in an installation. These help to ensure thoroughness, and ensure that items are not forgotten. Some specimen checklists are given in Appendix D. Items on these checklists are assembled from the auditors' checklists in use today in several different organizations. They may act as guidelines in drawing up checklists for auditors. The items that ought to be on the checklist differ from one organization to another and should be compiled with specific needs in mind.

The subjects covered by auditors checklists should include

(a)   Controls on personnel for fraud protection
(b)   Controls on sensitive programs
(c)   Controls on new programs and changes
(d)   Input/output controls
(e)   Accuracy controls
(f)   Quality control
(g)   Tape and disk library
(h)   Security of remote terminal access
(i)   Software security
(j)   Computer-center operations
(k)   File reconstruction capability
(l)   Physical protection of records
(m)   Physical security for theft protection
(n)   Fire precautions
(o)   Precautions against other physical disasters
(p)   Disaster contingency plan
(q)   Documentation
(r)   Department administration
(s)   Equipment accountability and billing
(t)   Charges to user departments
(u)   Insurance

The checklists should be regarded as aids to the auditor, never as a substitute for the judgement of an experienced data processing specialist in auditing the computer environment.

3. Spot Checks

The auditors make spot checks of such items as the computer operator's log, the records of the Input/Output Control Section, the quality-control reports, logs of security procedural violations, and the tape library log. The spot checks will ensure that the files are being balanced as required and that, in general, the security requirements are not being bypassed.

For this purpose the auditors should have a clear write-up of all the balancing controls, validation procedures, and other means of controlling accuracy and security.

4. Sampling

The auditor can use sampling techniques to test for procedural weaknesses. In traditional fashion they can select a few transactions and follow what happened to them, in as far as the computer records permit. They can select certain customer orders and follow through the records of the ordering, inventory depletion, and delivery, and check that the accounting entries are correct. They can select certain customer accounts and check with the customer that the recorded status of the account is correct. They can check physical inventories of items against recorded inventories, and so on.

To follow the history of a transaction completely, the auditors may need certain records that might not otherwise by kept in such a way that reference to them is easy. This used to be done by printing out the items or by punching them onto cards and thus leaving an *audit trail.* Today it can be done equally well by storing the records on direct access devices as control files so that they can be displayed or printed at a terminal. In the early days of magnetic storage, auditors were deeply concerned that records were not visible. Mainly for this reason, auditors insisted on the audit trail. Some auditors insisted that it should be called a "management trail" rather than an "audit trail," because it is as much needed by management as by auditors.

The best way of providing both auditors and management with record visibility is to store the records in such a way that they are accessible randomly at terminals. When this is too expensive, or incompatible with earlier processing, facilities for printing the required items fairly quickly from tape or disk must be provided. Given the capability to display records when needed, the audit trail can become a sequence of reference numbers indicating the sequence in which items were posted to the files.

5. Use of Erroneous Transactions

An effective way to test the system's validation controls is for the auditor to feed in invalid transactions and see whether the system detects them.

The following are some types of invalid items that the auditors might try out on an accounts payable program:

(a)   Quantity invoiced exceeds quantity ordered by 10 per cent but within $300.00.

(b)   Quantity invoiced exceeds quantity ordered by $300.00 but within 10 per cent.

(c)   Invoice quantity multiplied by invoice unit price is greater than invoice quantity multiplied by purchase order unit price.

(d)   Setup and/or miscellaneous charge billed although not specified on purchase order.

(e)   Tool order invoiced although sample tooling has not been approved by receiving inspection.

(f)   Advice price invoice exceeds acceptable limit.

(g) Discount terms on invoice less than that on purchase order.

(h) Invoicing against an order that has been canceled.

(i) Invoicing for an order not on the purchase order master file.

(j) Unit measure on invoice does not agree with that on purchase order. (Should be done for more than one unit of measure.)

(k) Invoicing of transportation charges for purchase order terms FOB Destination.

(l) Duplicate payment of invoice paid previously.

(m) Duplicate payment of invoice paid in same machine run.

(n) Collect freight charge (via a consignee memo) for purchase order terms FOB Destination.

(o) Duplicate freight charges (i.e., collect charges and invoice charges for same shipment.)

(p) Adjustment to invoicing and/or receiving quantities. (If accepted, they should be listed on exception reports.)

(q) Unit of measure routines working correctly for debit memos.

(r) Quantity rejected on debit memo greater than quantity invoiced.

(s) Debit memo processed but no corresponding order on purchase order master file.

Some of these tests should also be tried for multiple-invoicing situations. For example, the auditor may wish to submit an invoice whose quantity is within the 10 per cent overshipment limit, but when combined with a previous billing exceeds the 10 per cent limit.

A list similar in principle but different in detail may be used with other types of program.

6. Attempt Security Violations

Just as the feeding of subtly invalid transactions by an outsider is an excellent test of the validity checks, so a deliberate and intelligent attempt to violate security can be the best test of security procedures.

Unfortunately, the traditional auditor often does not have the type of personality one might select in a prospective burglar. The auditing group might employ a person who seems to have natural talents in circumventing security procedures. There is a certain type of person who seems to have little difficulty in walking into a normally locked computer room behind a person who is entering it officially, and then walking off unnoticed with a pile of classified tapes. There are certain persons with a type of technical ingenuity that are almost sure to find a way of bypassing the programmed locks.

On some systems in which security is of high importance, a *counter-security group* has been employed for an extended period and has proved very effective in finding security loopholes, which were later closed. Unfortunately, on most systems finding the loopholes does not require great ingenuity.

It is quickly apparent to an outsider that the operators forget to lock their terminals, their security codes can be read when they are entering them, the fire escape door can be prevented from closing so that it gives easy access from the outside, the guard does not read the entry passes, and so on.

The auditing group should use countersecurity staff to test physical security, to steal confidential documents, to check the guards, and to carry out the more difficult and extended operation of penetrating the system technically.

7. Test Records, Pseudotransactions and a Mini-Company

The auditors should have certain records in the files solely for auditing purposes. These records are updated by pseudotransactions that are entered into the system by the auditors. The fictitious records and transactions are processed by the same programs that process the operational transactions. They are used to check that the programs are functioning correctly and have not been tampered with. The false records and transactions will be included in the batch totals and balancing runs when possible. If actual cash is being balanced to the computer totals, a correction will be needed.

A common method of checking a system has been to execute a complete run using an auditor's test deck. A method that is in some ways more effective is to slip auditor's transactions in with the other transactions on an operational run. Some auditors have a collection of records representing a complete system or complete corporation in miniature. This has been referred to as a *pilot system* or *mini-company*. A separate set of output reports and statistics may be produced for the pilot system. A complete subset of a company's data-processing may be carried out with it, like running a miniature company. In some systems, auditors transactions may be included on every run of a given type. The payroll, for example, may contain fictitious employees for whom all the payroll operations are performed each week with the exception of actually paying them.

The auditor's transactions will sometimes be entered at the user departments. They give a means of continuously testing the system and checking on quality control. Erroneous and reject transactions will be included to see how they are handled. The auditor should similarly enter transactions from terminals.

The *pilot system* or *mini-company* is particularly important during conversion to a new system. The same records will be retained and the same transactions processed before cutover to ensure that the new system works correctly, and after cutover to ensure that no errors have been introduced.

8. Special Programs

Because of the absence of printed documents to check, the auditor will need his own programs. These are especially important on on-line and time-sharing systems. The auditor should define what he wants to have checked and the programs for performing the checks should, if possible, be written outside of the data processing department. The programs used may take actions such as the following:

(a) Print records which the auditor selects, for checking.

(b) Print every nth record.

(c) Print all records which meet certain selected criteria.

(d) Take two copies of a master file for different days or weeks and print the differences, for checking.

(e) Take the *transaction journal* and *file update journal* and ensure that the files correspond to these.

(f) Carry out a file balancing operation.

(g) Carry out a year-end check—for example, read the 12 monthly payroll input tapes, perform the payroll calculations and print any discrepancies.

(h) Print a list of all persons added to the payroll, for checking. (A New York City welfare computer paid fake paychecks to 40,000 nonexistant youth workers over a period of nine months: total theft, $2.7 million.)

(i) The auditor should keep original copies of programs, rerun them on a surprise basis, and compare the results with current programs.

EXTERNAL AUDITS
The implication of what we have said is that external audits will be much more dependent on the internal auditing than they used to be. This is because the *system* assumes much more importance than individual transactions, and because most auditors' controls must be built in at the system design stage. If there were no internal auditors, the external auditors would have to pay many visits and be involved in auditing system design.

Some systems must meet the requirements of outside bodies, such as regulatory commissions, bank examiners, etc. Certified public accountants must be able to audit computerized records of assets, liabilities, income, and expense for the annual statements. The Internal Revenue Service needs to check that income and expenses are properly stated. Other auditors, such as those for Department of Defense contractors, will want to check the correct allocation of funds.

The external auditors will need to consider whether the internal auditing procedures are effective and to what degree they can rely upon them. This will depend upon what checks are programmed into the system and built into its procedures.

Many organizations use external auditors or consultants to check certain security and control aspects of their systems. This is done largely because of the lack of sufficiently professional expertise within their own organization that is independent of the data-processing department.

REFERENCES

1. H. Washbrook, *Management Control Auditing and the Computer,* William Heinemann Ltd., London, 1971.

2. J. J. Wasserman, *"Plugging the Leaks in Computer Security," Harvard Business Review,* Sept.-Oct. 1969.

Other Recommended Reading

3. Price Waterhouse and Company, "Management Control of Electronic Data Processing," IBM Manual No. F20-0006, International Business Machines, White Plains, N.Y., 1970.

4. A. B. Flielink, *Auditing Automatic Data Processing—A Survey of Papers on the Subject,* Elsevier Publishing Company, Amsterdam, 1961.

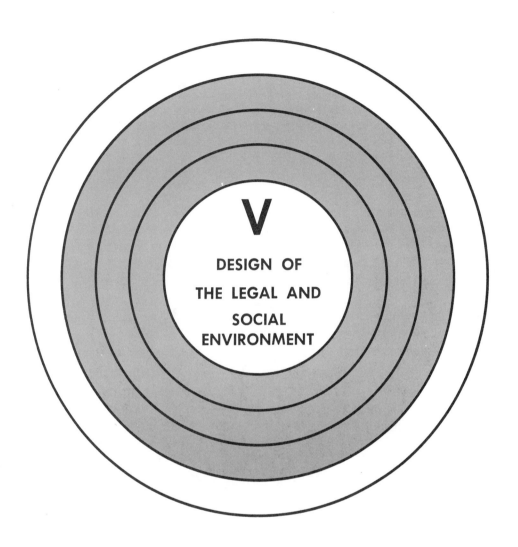

V

DESIGN OF
THE LEGAL AND
SOCIAL
ENVIRONMENT

38 SOCIETAL CONTROLS

There has been much discussion in the press and in governmental hearings about the effect of computers on the lives of people. Often ignoring the beneficial aspects, the media have talked much about computer errors and invasion of privacy. It has been common to find dramatic headlines such as:

The Death of Privacy
Don't Tell It to the Computers
Cheating the Vote-Counting Systems

Senator Sam J. Ervin has stressed how an organization may seize on a data-processing technique with the best intentions of achieving some laudable goal, but in the process violate the privacy of an individual's thoughts or activities. He went on to say:

> The computer industry, the data processing experts, the programmers, the executives—all need to set their collective minds to work to deal with the impact of their electronic systems on the rights and dignity of individuals.
> While there is still time to cope with the problems, they must give thought to the contents of professional ethical codes for the computer industry and for those who arrange and operate the computer's processes.
> If self-regulation and self-restraint are not exercised by all concerned with automatic data processing, public concern will soon reach the stage where strict legislative controls will be enacted, government appropriations for research and development will be denied. And the computer will become the

villain of our society. It is potentially one of the greatest resources of our civilization, and the tragedy of slowing its development is unthinkable [1].

K.G. Bauer in a discussion of policy decisions facing the designers of a computer data bank [2] pointed out that we now have a

special but fleeting opportunity. . .to explore the issue of privacy with objectivity and in some leisure. . .the public's fears of dossier-type police information systems have been thoroughly aroused; left unchecked they may become so strong as to in fact prevent the creation of any publicly supported information systems. The reactions to proposals for a Federal data center are a case in point. Were such blanket prohibitions to be imposed the development of socially useful information-sharing would be enormously impeded. Furthermore, without public trust, information systems could well be fed so much false, misleading or incomplete information as to make them useless. Thus it becomes imperative not only to devise proper safeguards to data privacy, but also to convince the public and agencies which might contribute to a system that these safeguards are indeed being planned, and that they will work.

LEVELS OF CONTROL

The technical controls we have discussed in this book make it possible to lock up the data securely in computer files and control most of the errors in input and processing. Having done this, there is still the matter of questionable design philosophy—the outer ring in Fig. 3.1. Systems analysts, if they are alert to social concern about computers, can design systems that avoid the major abuses—do not leave passengers stranded at airports, cut off old ladies' electricity, or print abusive letters to subscribers who do not warrant them.

Thereafter, the controls pass out of the hands of the computer system designers to higher authority.

Systems controls at the lower levels, as we have seen, are definable and can be designed in a more-or-less fail-safe manner. But lower-level systems are merely components of larger systems. The output of an inner subsystem is part of the input to its surrounding system. There may be many inner systems in an outer. Each level has its checks and controls. In many instances the checks take into account the relationship between the components, which, as a set, provide the inputs.

Eventually we reach a system level at which the lives of people and the fortunes of corporations generate input. The output is the input to the supersystem, the society in which we all live. Some of the subsystem outputs or sets of outputs may be damaging to society. How can we identify them, and what checks and controls can be applied here? The control mechanism must now consist of people. The detection of undesirable system behavior must come from the human beings affected and must generate feedback that modifies the system operation.

In the computerized society of the future it is essential that this feedback mechanism be sensitive. We do not know exactly what effects the massive use of computers is going to have. We want to take advantage of them in every way we can. But in allowing this new world to evolve, we must apply flexible and effective systems controls so that it evolves in such a way as to make society a better environment to live in. We must react to complaints in a sensitive manner and take action accordingly.

CONTROLS THAT INVOLVE PEOPLE
If the technical safeguards exist to lock *unauthorized* persons out of the data files, the controls then become concerned with who is *authorized*.

A privacy violation results from an inappropriate combination of three items: an item of information, a person obtaining it, and a purpose to which that person will put the information, officially or otherwise. Our objective is to establish a checking system that will prevent the creation of an undesirable set of these three items. We can seek to eliminate any one of them. We can limit information to a subset of all possible items, limit persons to a subset of all possible people, or we can restrict the information to those persons who can put the information to use.

Limiting the information that is stored, or where it is stored, is a decision that is in the province of the system designer. Designing the structure of the mechanisms authorizing different persons to obtain data from the files is also a technical problem. Designing the administrative or societal controls that govern who may be authorized to use the data, and for what, is a problem that is usually beyond the direct reach of the system designer. It involves the rules that are made in a corporation, the controls that are imposed upon a government department, and the laws in a society that govern the use of data banks and computers. In the absence of adequate laws, the rules and controls that organizations adopt are especially important.

LEGITIMATE INFORMATION
There is no information about people that cannot for some particular purpose be justifiably collected. Once that purpose is served, however, retention of all the details is indefensible. If the citizen to whom they pertain provided them for one purpose, they ought not to be used for another without his consent. Some of the laws that have been proposed stress that data in a data

bank should be used only for the stated purpose, and that old data should be destroyed. Lacking such laws, government agencies or other bodies should provide their own rules.

The Census Bureau provides standards in this respect. Other agencies might observe similar rules regarding disclosure. The Census Act states that "information furnished" the Census Bureau will be (1) examined only by "sworn officers and employees" of the Bureau or of the Department of Commerce, its parent organization; (2) used only for "the statistical purpose for which it is supplied"; and (3) "compiled in such a manner that the data supplied by an individual. . .cannot be identified."

The Census Bureau once refused President Truman's request for information because he was not a sworn employee. Lesser officials will have to suffer such indignities with understanding, not anger.

Policing the agencies will be difficult, especially if the types of laws discussed in Chapter 39 are not passed. One method is to limit the information they can collect. The Internal Revenue Service should be restricted to financial facts. If it needs confirmation, say, of a taxpayer's medical history, it might ask the Department of Health, Education and Welfare to evaluate his status according to IRS rules and send back an answer, rather than to provide all the details so that the IRS can do its own evaluation. To achieve these limited interchanges, the various agencies must know each other's file-content classifications so that they can ask for feasible answers.

**CONTROLS OVER WHAT
DATA ARE COLLECTED**   The next type of control relates to what data are collected. The working environment in which some data are gathered is simply not conducive to precision.

Information has to be organized into patterns relevant to its ultimate use. This, however, is very seldom the form in which it is most cheaply collected for insertion into files. Take the case of a credit agency that wants to offer its clients relevant case histories, including adverse information such as litigation. The best way for the agency to obtain this information is to go through all court records, updating its files on each individual accordingly. Because the agency is storing results for future use, the scrutiny associated with an immediately relevant item will be absent. A few errors will get through even conscientious operatives, and *there is no immediate check.*

Some errors of commission will be picked up by programming checks built into the system. Errors of omission are more slippery. A court case may be recorded as pending long after its disposition if the system has no self-purging mechanism that automatically warns of incomplete records due for updating.

In addition to patent errors, large files also accumulate two other kinds of troublesome material—the decaying and the unevaluated. The former is characteristic of biographical details. Information gets less reliable the farther away it is from the source. References and testimonials, to say nothing of college degrees, lose their relevance as their subject grows older. The facts remain facts in the environment of their collection, but they may be inappropriate in the context of the use to which they are put. But, as Reich informed a Senate committee, "every normal human reaction is going to be to give more weight to those things in the file than. . .the maker of the file ever meant" [3].

The difference between the concept at the initial collection and the ultimate use is relevant in such matters as storing the results of personality tests, attitude appraisals, and encoded results of interviews. The fate of an individual should depend on a reexamination by an appropriate means at the time of the decision, not by the translation of an inappropriate finding from a different investigation.

The press has frequently protested that the FBI holds untold amounts of unevaluated data about individuals, such as rumors and grudge reports. The FBI's Uniform Crime Reports are based on police investigation as opposed to any decision of a court, coroner, jury, or other judicial body. In other words, the facts could be legally wrong. This would not matter much if there were a constant relationship between arrests and convictions, or arrests and crimes, and the statistics were used merely for guiding general policy.

The American Civil Liberties Union has frequently protested the "widespread use of incomplete and unexplained" police records.

> We have been deeply troubled by the adverse consequences to an individual flowing from the recording of an arrest not followed by indictment or convictions, where the true nature of the conduct leading to arrest (such as peaceful participation in civil rights or peace marches) is not disclosed. In our correspondence over the past few years with the FBI about the arrest record problem it has been clearly established that too frequently local law enforcement officials report arrests to the FBI but fail to report later disposition of the case. Countless persons against whom charges have been dropped or who have been acquitted must still suffer the harsh consequences of a wrongful taint of criminality when seeking employment or other privileges. These problems are even more grievous in the all-too-common case today of those arrested for the valid exercise of constitutionally protected rights. No reliable procedure exists for differentiating such arrests in present FBI records from arrests made for the normal incidents of criminal conduct. [4].

A Senate subcommittee chaired by Senator Sam Ervin in 1971 revealed that the Defense Department maintains a file giving details of constant surveillance of the American Civil Liberties Union and other bodies, such as the National Association for the Advancement of Colored People. The Central Index of Investigations in the Defense Department then contained 25 million cards, each relating to a personality (one sixth of all adult Americans) and 760,000 relating to organizations and incidents in the United States. On an average day, 12,000 requests for information in this file were processed and 20,000 additions and changes were made. Former agents testified to the Committee that information they collected was often passed on to other government departments and local police.

Many of the people who are listed in the Defense Department files of potential troublemakers have done nothing wrong yet, and would be shocked to find their names in the file. Many people would be equally shocked to find what certain credit-bureau computers say about them under the heading of "moral hazards." Extramarital affairs, homosexuality, heavy drinking, and other social observations are recorded on the grounds that they might affect the credit risk. Approximately half of all Americans have dossiers in the credit-bureau computers, and some of the information is collected by dubious methods. A vicious comment from an apartment doorman who was not tipped could lead to a black mark on the record.

Controls are needed over what data are collected.

STATISTICAL FILES VERSUS DOSSIERS   It is important to separate the concept of statistical files from the concept of dossiers about individuals. From the point of view of privacy protection, they are entirely different. Many of the uses to which the information in government and research data banks will be put are statistical. In statistical files the identification of the individual should be stripped off. Once that is done the files can be used much more freely. It is still necessary to make sure that people cannot be identified by some other means, such as home location, a high salary, the fact that he has 13 children or cats, weighs 300 pounds, or has a combination of factors that makes him unique. As we discussed in Chapter 15, it is sometimes possible to extract information about *individuals* from a statistical data bank by asking combinations of questions. Sometimes a large number of questions would be needed, and controls can be devised to prevent such interrogation. The controls are more complex and subtle than on the type of data bank in which details about an individual are requested directly. In general, statistical data banks will not reveal the identities of the persons about whom data are recorded.

Not only should names and identifying numbers be removed, but all other information not relevant to the statistical purpose in question. Identifying information is often retained in the file, but users needing statistical information are prevented from accessing it. Data collected from different sources for different purposes are often kept in the same data bank. It may be more secure (and also more manageable) to keep it in separate special-purpose systems and to give a centralized system the capability of interrogating the special-purpose systems. The center can then be the sole organization with access to the files of more than one department, and can be rigorously policed with elaborate security precautions. It concentrates the risk, since it provides the only means by which a dossier can be built up.

All applications for material collating the records of two or more departments would have to be processed through the center and demonstrated to be privacy preserving. The center would strip identifying data from its output, and ensure that intelligence requests did not sneak in disguised as statistical analyses of populations with one member.

The central system only would be able to call other systems; it would not be callable from them. Subversion of a single "peripheral" system would not, therefore, lead automatically to subversion of all the others. Anyone trying to get at the peripheral data banks would have to break into them individually, or go through the well-defended center.

To manage this legitimately, an inquirer would have to establish his need to know and satisfy the criteria for access. The center would be the only body that could authorize the granting of a request for statistical information, and it would set various levels of security classification for different individuals and purposes. No request for information that included identifiers would ever be met.

SOCIETAL
CONSTRAINTS

The larger the overall framework in which a system operates, the more difficult it is to define precisely the objectives and limitations of the system. We are often concerned with defining the limits of the supersystem into which the computer system fits. When societal issues are involved, definition becomes complex, because every system is a component of a larger system. The environment of the Internal Revenue Service's computer is not merely the IRS computer department. It is not merely the IRS. It affects all citizens and is a part of society as a whole.

We cannot define goals and controls unambiguously once the system we are talking about encompasses more than a certain size of environment. What we can do is to set limits which constrain it to certain paths that do not cause damage. As we hurtle into a fully computerized society, there needs to be continuous debate as to what the constraints should be and how the constraints can be interpreted into laws.

REFERENCES

1. Senator S. J. Ervin, "The Computer—Individual Privacy," *Vital Speeches of the Day 33*, Vol. 14, pp. 421–426 (May 1, 1967).

2. K. G. Bauer, "Progress Report to U.S. Public Health Service on Contract PH 110-234," Joint Center for Urban Studies of MIT and Harvard, Cambridge, Mass., Jan. 1968.

3. *The Computer and Invasion of Privacy*, U.S. Government Printing Office, Washington, D.C., 1966, p. 27.

4. *Ibid*, p. 182.

39 LEGAL
CONTROLS

The American Constitution specifies no right to privacy, similar to the right to freedom of speech or right to vote. For a generation of people living in the shadow of Watergate and Orwell's *1984*, this may be a cause for alarm.

The protection of a person's right to privacy—his "right to be let alone" in the historic phrase of Warren and Brandeis—is largely left to the laws of individual States, and only a few have legislated the right to privacy into statutes. Prosser, after a very thorough survey of the cases recognizing any right to privacy, analyzed them into four distinct types of legal action [1]:

1. Intrusion upon a person's physical solitude or seclusion, or into his private affairs.
2. Public disclosure of embarrassing private facts about a person.
3. Appropriating some element of a personality or likeness for commercial use without permission.
4. Publicity that places a person in a false light in the public eye.

Even before the computer age, the law relating to privacy was "a thing of threads and patches" [2]. Most legal problems raised by the computer, however, are not solved by the above categories of law. They often involve the improper use of information *voluntarily* communicated, rather than the improper taking of information. They involve accuracy of data and computer errors. Communications that were previously protected by law are now unprotected; for example, the communication between a psychiatrist and his patient was protected, but the data records in the mental-clinic computer are not, and these records may be even more sensitive than the psychiatrist's knowledge of the patient, because they lack intelligent human interpretation.

Eventually, no doubt, a legal framework will have evolved that relates effectively to computers and data banks. There is cause for concern that it will take too long to evolve. System designers are not waiting until laws exist. The technology is changing so much faster than the development of social mechanisms to cope with it. On the other hand, there is a danger that unduly restrictive laws might be passed that would prevent some of the social benefits of computers.

There have been many proposals for legislation. Many bills have been drafted in the United States and other countries. The proposals range from amendments to the Constitution to administrative regulations. It is easier to say what is required than to determine how to enact relevant legislation. The general form of some of the laws needed is nevertheless clear.

In the United States the bills that have been drafted or passed tend to deal with isolated aspects of the problem, for example, use of information by government agencies, fair credit reporting, and the collection of data on citizens by the Department of Defense. In Britain and some other countries more general bills have been drafted. The British Data Surveillance Bill seeks to establish a register of all data banks to control their use.

A number of general comments seem clear about the legislative proposals. First, there must be a recognition that modern technology allows one man to gain without another necessarily losing. Second, an extension of the concept of private property does not provide a suitable framework for data privacy laws. The computers copy information so that nothing physical need be taken.

Third, it seems as important to legislate concerning *private* data banks as it does about public or government data banks. Many of the horror stories arise from privately owned data banks such as those of credit bureaus, employment agencies, and private detective agencies. It seems reasonable that, like automobiles, computers ought to have to meet certain basic safety and pollution regulations. Data banks used internally within a corporation might perhaps be omitted from legal control, provided that no disclosure of data to outside parties occurs. Guidelines for corporate regulations on the use of computerized data ought to be maintained by the professional bodies. Inadequate safeguards, however, which result in disclosure of sensitive personal data to outside parties, might be met with legal charges of culpable negligence. Corporations who wish to provide information to customers, subscribers, partners in a joint interprise, state, local, or federal agencies, or for publication should be more strictly controlled.

Fourth, to comply with some of the regulations that have been proposed would require a vast amount of work and expense. It is important that society's eventual legal framework for privacy protection is one which lends itself to the maximum automation. The computers must keep check on the computers. Only in this way can the ultimate system be workable. We shall comment on this point again later.

MAIN ELEMENTS OF   We shall now describe the main elements of the pri-
DATA PRIVACY LAWS   vacy laws that have been proposed. In doing so we
                          shall make references to three typical pieces of legis-
lation. The first is the United States' *Fair Credit Reporting Act*, which be-
came law in 1971. Table 39.1 summarizes the main points in it, and Appendix
B.1 contains part of the Act. There have been many proposals to provide this
Act with sharper teeth.

The second is the Federal Privacy Bill introduced by Congressman Koch
in New York in 1973. This proposed a (somewhat costly) method of regulating government usage of data about individuals. Table 39.2 summarizes its
main points, and the Bill is in Appendix B.2.

The third and most comprehensive of the three is the above mentioned
British bill. This is summarized in Table 39.3, and the Bill is in Appendix B.3.

Table 39.1. Summary of the United States
Fair Credit Reporting Act of 1971*

Compilers of credit and "investigative" reports must:

Eliminate from their reports bankruptcies after 14 years and other adverse information after 7 years.

Keep record entries on employment up to date; confirm adverse interview information 3 months before reporting it.

Notify subject that report is being made; whenever employment or credit is denied on basis of report, subject must be advised of reporting agency that issued report.

On request of subject agency must disclose "nature and substance" of material in file (but not file itself); must disclose sources of data; must reinvestigate item at subject's request; if agency does not correct item, must include subject's statement on it.

Maintain "reasonable procedures" to grant reports only to those with "reasonable interest."

Agency must not, without written consent of subject, furnish to government agency more than name, address, and place of employment of subject except when government has "legitimate business need."

---

*See Appendix B.1.

Table 39.2. Summary of the *United States Federal Privacy Bill of 1973**

Any government agency that maintains records on individuals must:

Notify individual that record exists.

Notify individual regarding all transfers of information in files.

Disclose information from such records only with consent of individual.

Record names and positions of all persons inspecting such records, and their reasons.

Permit individual to inspect records, make copies of them, and supplement them.

Remove erroneous or misleading information from individual's file.

Bill creates a Federal Privacy Board to hear complaints on any of above requirements.

Exceptions are made in case of national security and police files.
The President shall report to Congress each year on the number of records exempted in each agency.

*See Appendix B.2.

Table 39.3. Summary of the British
Data Surveillance Bill of 1969*

Registrar
A Registrar shall be established to keep a register of all data banks (including those government, corporations, credit bureaus, private detective agencies, and any persons who sell information)

The register shall contain details of the data kept, the person responsible, the purpose for which they may be used and by whom.

Only data relevant to the stated purpose may be stored.

The register shall be open to inspection by the public and press.

Any person about whom data are stored shall receive a printout of that data and the purposes for which they are kept when the data bank is established.

Thereafter he may obtain a printout of the data, their purposes, and a listing of all receipients on payment of a fee.

Any person may apply for an order that data about him be removed on grounds that they are inaccurate, unfair, or out of date.

If data are found to be inaccurate, unfair, or out of date, all recipients will be notified.

Offences
It is a punishable offence.

not to accurately register a data bank.
to use the data for nonregistered purposes.
to allow access to persons other than those entered on the register.
to aid and abet the wrong use of the data.

Liability
The operator of a data bank is liable for damages when he permits inaccurate data to be supplied that can cause a person harm.

*See Appendix B.3.

The following, then, are proposals for laws that should be considered:

1. Establishment of a Data-Bank Register

A register of data banks should be established. This may be a register solely of those data banks which contain information about people. Some authorities have proposed that *all* data banks be registered, but this seems an unnecessary burden. The registrar would have the task of ensuring that undue harm did not result from the use of the computer systems registered.

The British Data Surveillance Bill stated that the following information would be registered for each data bank:

(a)   the name and address of the owner of the data bank;
(b)   the name and address of the person responsible for its operation;
(c)   the location of the data bank;
(d)   such technical specifications relating to the data bank as may be required by the Registrar;
(e)   the nature of the data stored or to be stored therein;
(f)   the purpose for which data is stored therein;
(g)   the class of persons authorized to extract data therefrom.

It goes on to define the main work of the Registrar:

> If at any time the Registrar is of the opinion that in the circumstances the information given or sought to be given under paragraphs (f) or (g) (above) might result in the infliction of undue hardship upon any person or persons or be not in the interest of the public generally, he may order such entry to be expunged from or not entered in the register.

The register itself would presumably be computerized. To help automate the procedure, precise record definitions for the information to be supplied should be established. It might in the future be a mandatory requirement to transmit the required information, correctly formated, directly to the Registrar's computer, and systems designers might be interrogated by it online (to avoid filling in and transcribing endless documents).

2. Data Stored

Facts, not opinions, should be stored. One hopes that most organizations providing information will value a reputation for accuracy. To ensure that they do, organizations providing a public service should be restricted to factual data and forbidden to disseminate opinion. For example, a credit report might legitimately say the subject lives on Fifth Avenue, but not that he lives in a "wealthy neighborhood." His wife could be described as 36-24-36, but not as "beautiful." The moral judgements that have appeared in some credit files should not be permitted.

3. Publicly Accessible Data Banks

Publicly accessible data banks should hold only data relevant to the purpose in question. Certain opinions and evaluations become facts: school grades, court verdicts, and so on. To hold these, relevance must be proved. The tax authorities should not maintain files on nonfinancial matters irrelevant to tax assessment, such as race, color, or prison records.

The Data Surveillance Bill states, with regard to reaching a decision as to what is permissible in a data bank:

> The Registrar shall be guided by the principle that only data relevant to the purposes for which the data bank is operated should be stored therein, and that such data should only be disclosed for those same purposes.

4. Record of Interrogations

All interrogations of data banks concerning the public should be automatically logged. As discussed in earlier chapters, a logging tape or file is a desirable part of the system design. This tape can be analyzed to find out what uses are being made of the file and to detect trespassers. With some forms of systems controls, processing the log may reveal attempts at unauthorized entry before they have actually succeeded.

The British Data Surveillance Bill says

> The operator of each data bank to which this section applies shall maintain a written record in which shall be recorded the date of each extraction of data therefrom, the identity of the person requesting the data, the nature of the data supplied and the purpose for which it was required.

It seems anachronistic that the bill requires a written record. The log should be kept by the computer and become, itself, another interrogative file in which an interested party may browse with a display screen.

5. Public Inspection of Records

The public should have the right to inspect records the computers keep about them. Probably the best way to protect an individual from misuses of data banks is to show him exactly what the machines have to say about him and give him the right to protest. He must have the right to have erroneous data corrected, to take issue with unfair and irrelevant data, and to request that his past history be forgotten.

Several schemes have been suggested for enabling citizens to see what the computers have to say about them. One is the annual mailing of statements to subjects of data-bank records. Another is the mailing of "exception reports," providing a printout of adverse decisions—such as refusal to grant credit—when these are based on data-bank records and the individual wishes to question the result. In selecting a scheme we must be careful not to generate an excessive amount of work. Possibly the annual mailing of statements would cause too much protest. The authors of the Data Surveillance Bill thought that the following was a reasonable compromise:

> Any person about whom information is stored in a data bank shall receive from the operator, not later than two months after his name is first programmed into the data bank, a printout of all the data contained therein which relates to him. Thereafter, he shall be entitled to demand such a printout at any time upon payment of a fee the amount of which shall be determined by the Registrar from time to time; and the operator shall supply such printout within three weeks of such demand.
>
> Every printout supplied in accordance with this section shall be accompanied by a statement giving the following information:
>
> (a) the purpose for which the data contained in the printout is to be used...;
> (b) the purposes for which the said data has in fact been used since the last printout supplied in accordance with this section;
> (c) the names and addresses of all recipients of all or part of the said data since the last printout supplied in accordance with this section.

Clearly, this cannot apply to military and intelligence data banks and it is doubtful whether it should be applied to all information in police data banks. The British bill made the following exceptions, which apply to the above data-logging requirement also:

(a) data banks which do not contain personal information relating to identifiable persons;

(b) data banks operated by the police;

(c) data banks operated by the security services;

(d) data banks operated by the armed forces of the Crown.

We must not create more work than we can avoid, and so the mailing of printouts will be done automatically by the computers. Interrogation of one's own record may proceed at an office where suitable display screens are located.

6. Challenging Personal Data

The individual should have the right to take issue with personal data stored about him. Under the Data Surveillance Bill the Registrar would handle protests from the public about information contained in the data banks. There must be a tribunal able to determine in detail what the contents should be when the subject and the "data banker" are in dispute. One hopes that most data bankers will value a reputation for accuracy and thus that such disagreements will be few.

The right to protest is expressed in the Data Surveillance Bill as follows:

> Any person who has received a printout. . .may, after having notified the operator of the data bank of his objection, apply to the Registrar for an order that any or all of the data contained therein be amended or expunged on the ground that it is incorrect, unfair, or out of date in the light of the purposes for which it is stored in the data bank.
>
> The Registrar may, if he grants an order under the foregoing subsection, issue an ancillary order that all or any of the recipients of the said data be notified of the terms of the order.

Thus, reacting to the protest will often protect not only the protestor but also other persons about whom data is banked. Such a scheme will do much to keep the computer systems honest and reasonable.

The Federal Privacy Bill goes on to say that persons about whom data are stored may add to the information in their records when they believe that to do so will give a fairer picture. An agency must

1. permit any individual to inspect his own record and have copies thereof made at his expense;

2. permit any individual to supplement the information contained in his record by the addition of any document or writing containing information such individual deems pertinent to his record, and

3. remove erroneous information of any kind.

Each agency may establish published rules stating the time, place, fees to the extent authorized, and procedure to be followed with respect to making records promptly available to an individual, and otherwise to implement the provisions of this section.

7. Public Inspection of Data-Bank Register

The register of data banks should be open to public inspection. The press and other news media play a very important part in keeping a democratic society on the rails. They should certainly be free to criticize and make suggestions about the new world we are building with computers. They, and the public, should have access to the register of data banks (but not, of course, to the personal data stored in them).

The Data Surveillance Bill said

The register shall be open to inspection by the public, including the press, during normal office hours:

Provided that entries relating to data banks operated by the police, the security services, and the armed forces shall be kept in a separate part of the register which shall not be open to inspection by the public.

Once again, the means of inspection may be automated by means of display terminals.

8. Failure to Register Data Banks

Avoiding registration of a relevant data bank should be a criminal offense. The British bill said

1. It shall be an offence, punishable on summary conviction by a fine of not more than £500, or a conviction on indictment by a fine of not more than £1,000 or imprisonment for not more than five years or both, for the owner

or operator of a data bank to which this Act applies to fail to register it in accordance with this Act.

2. If the operator of a data bank...(excluding police, military, and intelligence data banks)

   (a) fails or refuses to send a printout when under duty to do so; or

   (b) permits data stored in the data bank to be used for purposes other than those stated on the register; or

   (c) allows access to the said data to persons other than those entered on the register as having authorized access; or

   (d) fails or refuses to comply with a decision of the Registrar; he shall be liable in damages to the person whose personal data are involved and, where such acts or omissions are wilful, shall be liable on summary conviction to a fine of not more than £500 and on conviction and endictment to a fine of not more than £1,000 or imprisonment for not more than five years or both.

3. A person who aids, abets, counsels, or procures the commission of an offence described in this section or with knowledge of its wrongful acquisition receives, uses, handles, sells, or otherwise disposes of information obtained as a result of the commission of such an offence, shall likewise be guilty of the said offence.

9. Liability

A negligent data-bank operator should be liable for damage. The British bill said

An operator of a data bank to which this Act applies who causes or permits inaccurate personal data to be supplied from the data bank as a result of which the person to whom the data refer suffers loss, shall be liable in damages to such person.

10. Hierarchy of Availability Categories

A hierarchy of availability categories may be registered for a data bank. In many systems data can be classified into various categories according to who can access them. Some categories of persons will be forbidden access to certain categories of data. Some persons may read but not change data. Some may change them but not disclose them. Some data may be disclosed to a limited group under special conditions; the rest may be disclosed with proper safeguards.

What information falls into which category will depend on the organization and its public. A psychiatrist might ask about and record, but never reveal, the sex life of a patient. An insurance company could neither ask for nor record such details, but a market research group might, given suitable safeguards. Interagency transfers might be restricted to the highest common factor of records, the "public" face of an individual, not including his income, marital status, or medical data. Under rare circumstances, however, disclosure might be mandatory to a restricted group of recipients. Typhus carriers and criminals may have to be found quickly, and it would be absurd not to allow one agency to warn another.

Even the courts should be barred from speculative entry into every and any file. If a specific item is sought, a search warrant detailing the requirement would have to be issued. A court would no more be able to call for a speculative look at a whole dossier than to demand a general search of a man's property. The law, then, must specify what data may be elicited, stored, and retrieved by which persons for what purposes.

11. Aged Data

Aged data should be removed. Stanley Rothman's definition of the purpose of privacy is to "prevent the past from interfering with the future." To prevent our history pursuing us indefinitely, aged data should be removed from certain files as time goes on. California has attempted to "erase" juvenile crime records from files of those who have grown older and wiser. Such a scheme is hard to enforce, since other organizations may at a later date distribute the facts gained legitimately before the erasure. The Registrar should have general guidelines for the removal of aged data, and in certain cases should enforce it. The "removal" of data may occasionally mean not complete deletion but rather transferral to an archival category that has restricted access for all but a few with special needs (for example, research).

The Fair Credit Reporting Act states that bankruptcy information should be removed after 14 years and other adverse information after 7 years. Some claim that these times should be shorter.

12. Security

Security procedures should be registered. To minimize the possibility of unauthorized access, those data banks with sensitive data should register the techniques they have employed to secure them. This will ensure that the systems designers consider building appropriate locks on files which require protection.

SUCCESSIVE TIGHTENING OF THE LAWS
The requirements that we have outlined above no doubt contain loopholes. However, the law is an evolving structure and such as those discussed could provide a foundation on which to build. The Data Surveillance Bill is flexible because so much depends upon the office of the Registrar, and this human flexibility is important. As such a set of laws comes into operation, the loopholes we have not foreseen will become apparent and can be sewn up.

It is desirable to make these safeguards as automated as possible; otherwise a massive amount of work could result. If the Registrar, for example, is likely to inspect the interrogation log kept by computer centers, then this log should be in a machine-processable form. The format of the items it keeps should be a format specified by the office of the Registrar. Eventually, it may become a requirement that such logs can be *transmitted* to the Registrar's computer if required. The Registrar's staff can then inspect them on their screens and ask the computer such questions as: On what occasion did so-and-so ask for information?, or, how often has this file been used for this purpose?

The computerized society must eventually frame its laws and safeguards in such a way that computers can police the actions of other computers. Over a period of time appropriate checks and balances will grow up in this fashion, so that we can develop the type of environment we want to live in. Computers can protect us from harassment by other computers.

POLICE
Police, military, and internal security computers are exempted from most of the provisions listed previously. The police argue that this is essential. If you give a suspect access to the police files on him, he can take evasive action and you will never catch him. Many feel that the rising crime rate is more serious than the issue of privacy. This feeling may grow stronger if crime and violence continue their exponential growth rate.

One of the uses of data banks that has given most cause for concern in the United States is the Department of Defense collection of names and dossiers on the enormous number of Americans who have somehow been judged to be a potential internal security risk.

In some countries there has been much misuse of information sources, and other powers, by the police.

Professor Karst says [3],

We can hardly expect the various police departments around the country to refuse to share investigative leads among themselves. Yet there are serious possibilities of abuse. One recent example was the rather interesting use made of an old criminal file of Mrs. Viola Liuzzo, the victim of a murder charged to certain members of the Ku Klux Klan (one of whom was acquitted by a Lowndes County, Alabama, jury). Mrs. Liuzzo's record (her "make sheet," *not* an investigative file) somehow passed from the Detroit police to the Warren, Michigan police, to Sheriff Clark of Dall County, Alabama, and even on to Imperial Wizard Shelton of the KKK. The point is that some policemen, like others in all occupations, can be expected to make improper use of information in police files.

There are organizations of policemen that are highly politically oriented. Karst gives an example of one that engages in extreme right-wing activity, and publishes a newsletter that consists in substantial part of lists of names of persons who have been identified by someone as communists or communist sympathizers, often coupled indiscriminately with the names of persons who support the establishment of civilian police-review boards, and so on.

The leaders of this organization are in responsible police positions. Karst claims that they have access to police files. With the deployment of police computers now planned, they might obtain access to police records all over the country.

There are innumerable other such examples. Geographical distinctions are losing their significance because of telecommunications. For information to be of service, it must not be bound by artificial boundaries prescribed in an earlier age. But if that information is to be a slave, not a tyrant, *logical* divisions must be prescribed and enforced by law. The data banks of police, intelligence, and other government departments must be restricted to the specific purpose for which they are intended. The divisions must restrict personal data to those who need to know them and can be trusted with them, and make the possession or divulgence of unwarranted material a criminal offense.

The Council of the City of Berkeley drafted a resolution controlling the use of the Berkeley Police Department information retrieval system, Miracode. It attempted to control both the nature of the information stored and the designation of the persons who could inspect it.

1. Data included in the Miracode system shall be limited to that:
   (a) Recorded by officers of public agencies directly and principally concerned with crime prevention, apprehension, adjudication or rehabilitation of offenders; and

    (b) Recorded in satisfaction of public duty directly relevant to criminal justice responsibilities of the agency.

2. Without further approval of the Council, the Miracode system shall include only conviction records of persons who have been found guilty at trial or who have pled guilty to any of the follcwing offenses:

    (a) Arson.

    (b) Auto Theft.

    (c) Bombing.

    (d) Burglary.

    (e) Felonious Assault.

    (f) Homicide.

    (g) Kidnapping.

    (h) Narcotics.

    (i) Robbery.

    (j) Sex Offenses.

    (k) Weapons Offenses.

3. The Miracode system shall exclude unverified data such as that emanating from intelligence sources. The intent here is to prohibit the use and dissemination of data resulting from tips, rumors, second-hand allegations or information provided by police undercover agents that has not been substantiated by official criminal justice proceedings.

.

.

.

.

7. Except as otherwise provided herein, access to the contents of the Miracode system will be limited to criminal justice personnel, which is defined to include the following:

    (a) Police forces and departments at all government levels that are responsible for enforcement of general criminal laws. This shall be understood to include highway patrols and similar agencies.

    (b) Prosecutive agencies and departments at all government levels.

    (c) Courts at all governmental levels with a criminal jurisdiction.

    (d) Correction departments at all government levels, including corrective institutions and probation departments.

    (e) Parole commission and agencies at all government levels.

    (f) Agencies at all government levels which have as a principal function the collection and provision of criminal justice information.

Requests from agencies other than these criminal justice agencies to examine the Miracode files will be honored only if such other agency is authorized by law or valid executive directive to do so. The Public Defender has access to criminal history data only for single defendants and only after he appears as attorney of record or is appointed by the Court for that single defendant. Private counsel has access on the same basis as the Public Defender, unless he is a properly certified agent of the individual in a situation not involving litigation.

.

.

.

17. Information from the BPD Miracode system shall not be integrated into any computerized information exchange system without prior Council approval. Before any such integration is done, the Council shall *obtain and approve a detailed list of technical and administrative safeguards for individual privacy and security which are to be included in the computerized system.*

The resolution also specifies the rights of individuals to challenge information which the system holds about them:

6. An individual for whom a Miracode record exists shall have the right to challenge the contents thereof, either by demonstrating inaccuracies which shall, if verified, be promptly corrected, or by supplementary information believed by the individual to be necessary in order to make the contents of the record not misleading.

**LEGAL
ENVIRONMENT**
Corporations are obliged to adhere to certain regulations governing their mode of business. Accounts must be rendered in terms set down by law; workshops and offices must meet health and safety standards; contracts are established within a known framework. Such a legal system has grown in answer to needs, sometimes as a result of blatant injustice. We must establish a legal environment for information systems now to avoid injustices we can already predict. Good systems design, like proper accounting, can be legally enforced.

REFERENCES

1. Prosser, "Privacy," *California Law Review,* Vol. 48, 383-86, 1960

2. A. R. Miller, *The Assault on Privacy,* University of Michigan Press, Ann Arbor, Mich., 1971. (Recommended reading on the laws relating to computers and privacy.)

3. K. L. Karst, "The Files: Legal Controls over the Accuracy and Accessibility of Stored Personal Data," reprinted in *Computer Privacy,* U.S. Government Printing Office, Washington, D.C., 1967, p. 195

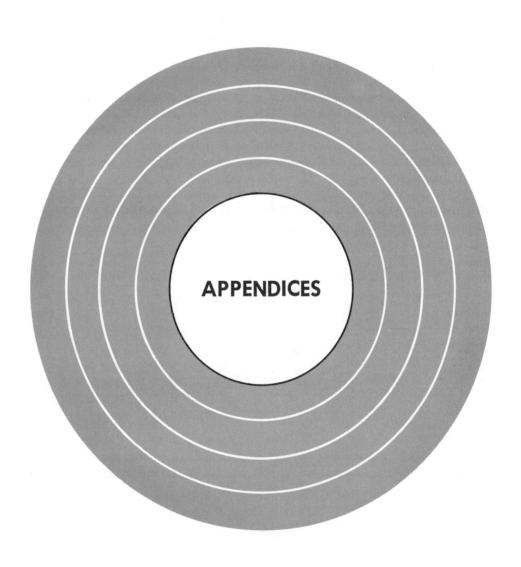

APPENDICES

APPENDICES

A
PROGRAMS FOR
CRYPTOGRAPHY*

```
(NOFIXEDOVERFLOW):LPC:PROC OPTIONS(MAIN);
ON ENDFILE (SYSIN) GO TO FIN;
DCL (S,R) FIXED BINARY(31);
DCL E CHAR(4) BASED(P);
DCL M FIXED BIN(31);
P=ADDR(M);
DCL (TEXT,MESS) CHAR(48);
S=23518967; R=7317;

/***** ENCIPHERING ROUTINE   *******************************************/
A1:GET EDIT (TEXT)(A(48));
   DO K=1 TO 48 BY 4;
   E=SUBSTR(TEXT,K,4);
   CALL RANDOM (S,R);
   M=M+R;
   SUBSTR(MESS,K,4)=E;
   END;
   PUT EDIT (MESS)(SKIP,A(48));
   GO TO A1;

/**** RANDOM NUMBER GENERATOR  *******************************************/
   (NOFIXEDOVERFLOW):RANDOM:PROCEDURE(S,R);
   DCL (S,R) FIXED BINARY(31,0);
   S=S*65539; R=R*S*3105473;
   END RANDOM;

FIN:END LPC;
```

Program 1A

*See Chapter 20

452

```
 (NOFIXEDOVERFLOW):LPC:PROC OPTIONS(MAIN);
 ON ENDFILE (SYSIN) GO TO FIN;
 DCL (S,R) FIXED BINARY(31);
 DCL E CHAR(4) BASED(P);
 DCL M FIXED BIN(31);
 P=ADDR(M);
 DCL (TEXT,MESS) CHAR(48);
 S=23518967; R=7317;

/*****   DECIPHERING ROUTINE    *****************************************/
 A1:GET EDIT (MESS)(A(48));
    DO K=1 TO 48 BY 4;
    E=SUBSTR(MESS,K,4);
    CALL RANDOM (S,R);
    M=M-R;
    SUBSTR(TEXT,K,4)=E;
    END;
    PUT EDIT (TEXT)(A(48));
    GO TO A1;

/****  RANDOM NUMBER GENERATOR   **************************************/
    (NOFIXEDOVERFLOW):RANDOM:PROCEDURE(S,R);
    DCL (S,R) FIXED BINARY(31,0);
    S=S*65539; R=R*S*3105473;
    END RANDOM;

FIN:END LPC;
```

Program 1B

```
  LPC:PROC OPTIONS(MAIN);
   ON ENDFILE (SYSIN) GO TO FIN;
   DCL (TEXT,MESS,ALPH,KEY) CHAR(48);
   DCL (ENCODE,DECODE)(48,48) CHAR(2);
   DCL L(2);
   DCL X(48,48,2) FIXED BINARY;

/*** SET UP ENCIPHERING TABLES ***********************************/
   S1=23518967;
   S2=50173031;
  KEY=
  'NY+BTGV FCED18WS:)X564AQZ,.-OLOPIKJM=U97322"(;HR';
  ALPH=
  'ABCDEFGHIJKLMNOPQRSTUVWXYZ1234567890-.,)(:;"=+ ?';
   DO I=1 TO 48;
   DO J=1 TO 48;
   X(I,J,1)=I; X(I,J,2)=MOD((I+J),48);
   END;END;
   DO K=1 TO 48;
   DO I=1 TO 48;
   CALL RANDOM(S1,R); J=CEIL(R*48);
   L=X(J,K,*); X(J,K,*)=X(I,K,*); X(I,K,*)=L;
   END;END;
   DO K=1 TO 48;
   DO I=1 TO 48;
   CALL RANDOM(S2,R); J=CEIL(R*48);
   L=X(K,J,*); X(K,J,*)=X(K,I,*); X(K,I,*)=L;
   END;END;
   DO I=1 TO 48;
   DO J=1 TO 48;
   ENCODE(I,J)=SUBSTR(KEY,X(I,J,1),1)||SUBSTR(KEY,X(I,J,2),1);
   DECODE(X(I,J,1),X(I,J,2))=SUBSTR(ALPH,I,1)||SUBSTR(ALPH,J,1);
   END;END;

/*** ENCIPHERING ROUTINE *****************************************/
 A1:GET EDIT (TEXT)(A(48));
   DO K=1 TO 48 BY 2;
   I=INDEX(ALPH,SUBSTR(TEXT,K,1));
   J=INDEX(ALPH,SUBSTR(TEXT,K+1,1));
   SUBSTR(MESS,K,2)=ENCODE(I,J);
   END;
   PUT EDIT (MESS)(SKIP,A(48));
   GO TO A1;

/***  RANDOM NUMBER GENERATOR  ***********************************/
   (NOFIXEDOVERFLOW):RANDOM:PROCEDURE(S,R);
   DCL(S,R) FIXED BINARY(31,0);
   R=MOD(S,77317)/80000; S=S+R*1975643;
   END RANDOM;

 FIN:END LPC;
```

Program 2A

```
   LPC:PROC OPTIONS(MAIN);
    ON ENDFILE (SYSIN) GO TO FIN;
    DCL (TEXT,MESS,ALPH,KEY) CHAR(48);
    DCL (ENCODE,DECODE)(48,48) CHAR(2);
    DCL L(2);
    DCL X(48,48,2) FIXED BINARY;

/*** SET UP ENCIPHERING TABLES ***********************************/
    S1=23518967;
    S2=50173031;
  KEY=
   'NY+BTGV FCED18WS:)X564AQZ,.-OLOPIKJM=U9732?"(;HR ';
  ALPH=
   'ABCDEFGHIJKLMNOPQRSTUVWXYZ1234567890-.,)(:;"=+ ?';
    DO I=1 TO 48;
    DO J=1 TO 48;
    X(I,J,1)=I; X(I,J,2)=MOD((I+J),48);
    END;END;
    DO K=1 TO 48;
    DO I=1 TO 48;
    CALL RANDOM(S1,R); J=CEIL(R*48);
    L=X(J,K,*); X(J,K,*)=X(I,K,*); X(I,K,*)=L;
    END;END;
    DO K=1 TO 48;
    DO I=1 TO 48;
    CALL RANDOM(S2,R); J=CEIL(R*48);
    L=X(K,J,*); X(K,J,*)=X(K,I,*); X(K,I,*)=L;
    END;END;
    DO I=1 TO 48;
    DO J=1 TO 48;
    ENCODE(I,J)=SUBSTR(KEY,X(I,J,1),1)||SUBSTR(KEY,X(I,J,2),1);
    DECODE(X(I,J,1),X(I,J,2))=SUBSTR(ALPH,I,1)||SUBSTR(ALPH,J,1);
    END;END;

/*** DECIPHERING ROUTINE *****************************************/
  A1:GET EDIT (MESS)(A(48));
    DO K=1 TO 48 BY 2;
    I=INDEX(KEY,SUBSTR(MESS,K,1));
    J=INDEX(KEY,SUBSTR(MESS,K+1,1));
    SUBSTR(TEXT,K,2)=DECODE(I,J);
    END;
    PUT EDIT (TEXT)(A(48));
    GO TO A1;

/***  RANDOM NUMBER GENERATOR  ***********************************/
    (NOFIXEDOVERFLOW):RANDOM:PROCEDURE(S,R);
    DCL(S,R) FIXED BINARY(31,0);
    R=MOD(S,77317)/80000; S=S+R*1975643;
    END RANDOM;

FIN:END LPC;
```

Program 2B

```
          ON ENDFILE (SYSIN) GO TO FIN;
          DCL (TEXT,MESS,ALPH,KEY) CHAR(48);
          DCL (ENCODE,DECODE)(48,48) CHAR(2);
          DCL L(2);
          DCL X(48,48,2) FIXED BINARY;

/*** SET UP ENCIPHERING TABLES ****************************************/
          S1=23518967;
          S2=50173031;
          S3=71205377;
     KEY=
      'NY+BTGV FCED18WS:)X564AQZ,.-OLOPIKJM=U9732?"(;HR';
     ALPH=
      'ABCDEFGHIJKLMNOPQRSTUVWXYZ1234567890-.,)(:;"=+ ?';
          DO I=1 TO 48;
          DO J=1 TO 48;
          X(I,J,1)=I; X(I,J,2)=MOD((I+J),48);
          END;END;
          DO K=1 TO 48;
          DO I=1 TO 48;
          CALL RANDOM(S1,R); J=CEIL(R*48);
          L=X(J,K,*); X(J,K,*)=X(I,K,*); X(I,K,*)=L;
          END;END;
          DO K=1 TO 48;
          DO I=1 TO 48;
          CALL RANDOM(S2,R); J=CEIL(R*48);
          L=X(K,J,*); X(K,J,*)=X(K,I,*); X(K,I,*)=L;
          END;END;
          DO I=1 TO 48;
          DO J=1 TO 48;
          ENCODE(I,J)=SUBSTR(KEY,X(I,J,1),1)||SUBSTR(KEY,X(I,J,2),1);
          DECODE(X(I,J,1),X(I,J,2))=SUBSTR(ALPH,I,1)||SUBSTR(ALPH,J,1);
          END;END;

          DCL N(48);
          DO K=1 TO 48;
          N(K)=INDEX(KEY,SUBSTR(ALPH,K,1));
          CALL RANDOM(S3,R); J=CEIL(R*48);
          N1=N(J); N(J)=N(I); N(I)=N1;
          END;

/*** ENCIPHERING ROUTINE **********************************************/
     A1:GET EDIT (TEXT)(A(48));
          DO K=1 TO 48 BY 2;
          IF SUBSTR(TEXT,K,2)='  ' THEN DO;
          CALL RANDOM(S1,R); I=CEIL(R*48);
          CALL RANDOM(S2,R); J=CEIL(R*48);
          SUBSTR(TEXT,K,2)=ENCODE(I,J);
          END;END;

          DO K=1 TO 48 BY 2;
          I=INDEX(ALPH,SUBSTR(TEXT,N(K),1));
          J=INDEX(ALPH,SUBSTR(TEXT,N(K+1),1));
          SUBSTR(MESS,K,2)=ENCODE(I,J);
          END;
          PUT EDIT (MESS)(SKIP,A(48));
          GO TO A1;

/*** RANDOM NUMBER GENERATOR ******************************************/
          (NOFIXEDOVERFLOW):RANDOM:PROCEDURE(S,R);
          DCL(S,R) FIXED BINARY(31,0);
          R=MOD(S,77317)/80000; S=S+R*1975643;
          END RANDOM;
```

Program 3A

```
  LPC:PROC OPTIONS(MAIN);
   ON ENDFILE (SYSIN) GO TO FIN;
   DCL (TEXT,MESS,ALPH,KEY) CHAR(48);
   DCL (ENCODE,DECODE)(48,48) CHAR(2);
   DCL L(2);
   DCL X(48,48,2) FIXED BINARY;

/*** SET UP ENCIPHERING TABLES ***********************************/
   S1=23518967;
   S2=50173031;
   S3=71205377;
  KEY=
   'NY+BTGV FCED18WS:)X564AQZ,.-OLOPIKJM=U9732?"(;HR ';
  ALPH=
   'ABCDEFGHIJKLMNOPQRSTUVWXYZ1234567890-.,)(:;"=+ ?';
   DO I=1 TO 48;
   DO J=1 TO 48;
   X(I,J,1)=I;  X(I,J,2)=MOD((I+J),48);
   END;END;
   DO K=1 TO 48;
   DO I=1 TO 48;
   CALL RANDOM(S1,R);  J=CEIL(R*48);
   L=X(J,K,*);  X(J,K,*)=X(I,K,*);  X(I,K,*)=L;
   END;END;
   DO K=1 TO 48;
   DO I=1 TO 48;
   CALL RANDOM(S2,R);  J=CEIL(R*48);
   L=X(K,J,*);  X(K,J,*)=X(K,I,*);  X(K,I,*)=L;
   END;END;
   DO I=1 TO 48;
   DO J=1 TO 48;
   ENCODE(I,J)=SUBSTR(KEY,X(I,J,1),1)||SUBSTR(KEY,X(I,J,2),1);
   DECODE(X(I,J,1),X(I,J,2))=SUBSTR(ALPH,I,1)||SUBSTR(ALPH,J,1);
   END;END;

   DCL N(48);
   DO K=1 TO 48;
   N(K)=INDEX(KEY,SUBSTR(ALPH,K,1));
   CALL RANDOM(S3,R);  J=CEIL(R*48);
   N1=N(J);  N(J)=N(I);  N(I)=N1;
   END;


/*** DECIPHERING ROUTINE *****************************************/
  A1:GET EDIT (MESS)(A(48));
   DO K=1 TO 48 BY 2;
   I=INDEX(KEY,SUBSTR(MESS,K,1));
   J=INDEX(KEY,SUBSTR(MESS,K+1,1));
   SUBSTR(TEXT,N(K),1)=SUBSTR(DECODE(I,J),1,1);
   SUBSTR(TEXT,N(K+1),1)=SUBSTR(DECODE(I,J),2,1);
   END;
   PUT EDIT (TEXT)(A(48));
   GO TO A1;

/*** RANDOM NUMBER GENERATOR *****************************************/
   (NOFIXEDOVERFLOW):RANDOM:PROCEDURE(S,R);
   DCL(S,R) FIXED BINARY(31,0);
   R=MOD(S,77317)/80000;  S=S+R*1975643;
   END RANDOM;

FIN:END LPC;
```

Program 3B

```
      (NOFIXEDOVERFLOW):LPC:PROC OPTIONS(MAIN);
      ON ENDFILE (SYSIN) GO TO FIN;
      DCL(S1,S2,S3,R) FIXED BINARY(31,0);
      DCL (TEXT,MESS,ALPH,KEY) CHAR(48);
      DCL (ENCODE,DECODE)(48,48) CHAR(2);
      DCL L(2);
      DCL N(48,48);
      DCL X(48,48,2) FIXED BINARY;

/*** SET UP ENCIPHERING TABLES ****************************************/
      S1=23518967;
      S2=50173031;
      S3=72735419;
  KEY=
   'NY+BTGV FCED18WS:)X564AQZ,.-OLDPIKJM=U9732?"(;HR';
  ALPH=
   'ABCDEFGHIJKLMNOPQRSTUVWXYZ1234567890-.,)(:;"=+ ?';
      DO I=1 TO 48;
      N(I,*)=INDEX(KEY,SUBSTR(ALPH,I,1));
      DO J=1 TO 48;
      X(I,J,1)=I; X(I,J,2)=MOD((I+J),48);
      END;END;
      DO K=1 TO 48;
      DO I=1 TO 48;
      R=MOD(S1,66103)/66103; S1=S1+312754**(R+1);
      J=CEIL(R*48);
      N1=N(J,K); N(J,K)=N(I,K); N(I,K)=N1;
      J=CEIL(MOD(S2,73937)/1541.1); S2=S2+J*121767;
      L=X(J,K,*); X(J,K,*)=X(I,K,*); X(I,K,*)=L;
      END;END;
      DO K=1 TO 48;
      DO I=1 TO 48;
      J=CEIL(MOD(S3,38692)/806.1);  S3=S3+J*513778;
      L=X(K,J,*); X(K,J,*)=X(K,I,*); X(K,I,*)=L;
      END;END;
      DO I=1 TO 48;
      DO J=1 TO 48;
      ENCODE(I,J)=SUBSTR(KEY,X(I,J,1),1)||SUBSTR(KEY,X(I,J,2),1);
      DECODE(X(I,J,1),X(I,J,2))=SUBSTR(ALPH,I,1)||SUBSTR(ALPH,J,1);
      END;END;

/*** ENCIPHERING ROUTINE *********************************************/
  A1:DO M=1 TO 48;
      GET EDIT (TEXT)(A(48));
      DO K=1 TO 48 BY 2;
      I=INDEX(ALPH,SUBSTR(TEXT,N(K,M),1));
      J=INDEX(ALPH,SUBSTR(TEXT,N(K+1,M),1));
      SUBSTR(MESS,K,2)=ENCODE(I,J);
      END;
      PUT EDIT (MESS)(SKIP,A(48));
      GO TO A1;


  FIN:END LPC;
```

Program 4A

```
      (NOFIXEDOVERFLOW):LPC:PROC OPTIONS(MAIN);
      ON ENDFILE (SYSIN) GO TO FIN;
      DCL(S1,S2,S3,R) FIXED BINARY(31,0);
      DCL (TEXT,MESS,ALPH,KEY) CHAR(48);
      DCL (ENCODE,DECODE)(48,48) CHAR(2);
      DCL L(2);
      DCL N(48,48);
      DCL X(48,48,2) FIXED BINARY;

/*** SET UP ENCIPHERING TABLES ***********************************/
      S1=23518967;
      S2=50173031;
      S3=72735419;
    KEY=
     'NY+BTGV FCFD18WS:)X564AQZ,.-OLOPIKJM=U9732?"(;HR';
    ALPH=
     'ABCDEFGHIJKLMNOPQRSTUVWXYZ1234567390-.,)(:;"=+ ?';
      DO I=1 TO 48;
      N(I,*)=INDEX(KEY,SUBSTR(ALPH,I,1));
      DO J=1 TO 48;
      X(I,J,1)=I;  X(I,J,2)=MOD((I+J),48);
      END;END;
      DO K=1 TO 48;
      DO I=1 TO 48;
      R=MOD(S1,66103)/66103;  S1=S1+312754**(R+1);
      J=CEIL(R*48);
      N1=N(J,K);  N(J,K)=N(I,K);  N(I,K)=N1;
      J=CEIL(MOD(S2,73937)/1541.1);  S2=S2+J*121767;
      L=X(J,K,*);  X(J,K,*)=X(I,K,*);  X(I,K,*)=L;
      END;END;
      DO K=1 TO 48;
      DO I=1 TO 48;
      J=CEIL(MOD(S3,38692)/806.1);  S3=S3+J*513778;
      L=X(K,J,*);  X(K,J,*)=X(K,I,*);  X(K,I,*)=L;
      END;END;
      DO I=1 TO 48;
      DO J=1 TO 48;
      ENCODE(I,J)=SUBSTR(KEY,X(I,J,1),1)||SUBSTR(KEY,X(I,J,2),1);
      DECODE(X(I,J,1),X(I,J,2))=SUBSTR(ALPH,I,1)||SUBSTR(ALPH,J,1);
      END;END;

/*** DECIPHERING ROUTINE ************************************************/
    A1:DO M=1 TO 48;
      GET EDIT (MESS)(A(48));
      DO K=1 TO 48 BY 2;
      I=INDEX(KEY,SUBSTR(MESS,K,1));
      J=INDEX(KEY,SUBSTR(MESS,K+1,1));
      SUBSTR(TEXT,N(K,M),1)=SUBSTR(DECODE(I,J),1,1);
      SUBSTR(TEXT,N(K+1,M),1)=SUBSTR(DECODE(I,J),2,1);
      END;
      PUT SKIP EDIT (TEXT)(A(48));
      END;
      GO TO A1;

    FIN:END LPC;
```

Program 4B

B PROPOSED BILLS RELATING TO PRIVACY AND COMPUTERS*

1. The Fair Credit Reporting Act. (U.S. Public Law 91–508)

2. A United States bill relating to data maintained by government agencies

3. Britain's *Data Surveillance Bill*

1. THE FAIR CREDIT REPORTING ACT
PUBLIC LAW 91-508

"§ 601. Short title

"This title may be cited as the Fair Credit Reporting Act.

"§ 602. Findings and purpose

"(a) The Congress makes the following findings:

"(1) The banking system is dependent upon fair and accurate credit reporting. Inaccurate credit reports directly impair the efficiency of the banking system, and unfair credit reporting methods undermine the public confidence which is essential to the continued functioning of the banking system.

"(2) An elaborate mechanism has been developed for investigating and evaluating the credit worthiness, credit standing, credit capacity, character, and general reputation of consumers.

"(3) Consumer reporting agencies have assumed a vital role in assembling and evaluating consumer credit and other information on consumers.

"(4) There is a need to ensure that consumer reporting agencies exercise their grave responsibilities with fairness, impartiality, and a respect for the consumer's right to privacy.

"(b) It is the purpose of this title to require that consumer reporting agencies adopt reasonable procedures for meeting the needs of commerce for consumer credit, personnel, insurance, and other information in a manner which is fair and equitable to the consumer, with regard to the confidentiality, accuracy, relevancy, and proper utilization of such information in accordance with the requirements of this title.

"§ 603. Definitions and rules and construction

"(a) Definitions and rules of construction set forth in this section are applicable for the purposes of this title.

"(b) The term 'person' means any individual, partnership, corporation, trust, estate, cooperative, association, government or governmental subdivision or agency, or other entity.

"(c) The term 'consumer' means an individual.

"(d) The term 'consumer report' means any written, oral, or other communication of any information by a consumer reporting agency bearing on a consumer's credit worthiness, credit standing, credit capacity, character, general reputation, personal characteristics, or mode of living which is used or expected to be used or collected in whole or in part for the purpose of serving as a factor in establishing the consumer's eligibility for (1) credit or insurance to be used primarily for personal, family, or household purposes, or (2) employment purposes, or (3) other purposes authorized under section 604. The term does not include (A) any report containing information solely as to transactions or experiences between the consumer and the person making the report; (B) any authorization or approval of a specific extension of credit directly or indirectly by the issuer of a credit card or similar device; or (C) any report in which a person who has been requested by a third party to make a specific extension of credit directly or indirectly to a consumer conveys his decision with respect to such request. If the third party advises the consumer of the name and address of the person to whom the request was made and such person makes the disclosures to the consumer required under section 615.

Consumer report or portion thereof in which information on a consumer's character, general reputation, personal characteristics, or mode of living is obtained through personal interviews with neighbors, friends, or associates of the consumer reported on or with others with whom he is acquainted or who may have knowledge concerning any such items of information. However, such information shall not include specific factual information on a consumer's credit record obtained directly from a creditor of the consumer or from a consumer reporting agency when such information was obtained directly from a creditor of the consumer or from the consumer.

"(f)   The term 'consumer reporting agency' means any person which, for monetary fees, dues, or on a cooperative nonprofit basis, regularly engages in whole or in part in the practice of assembling or evaluating consumer credit information or other information on consumers for the purpose of furnishing consumer reports to third parties, and which uses any means or facility of interstate commerce for the purpose of preparing or furnishing consumer reports.

"(g)   The term 'file', when used in connection with information on any consumer, means all of the information on that consumer recorded and retained by a consumer reporting agency regardless of how the information is stored.

"(h)   The term 'employment purposes' when used in connection with a consumer report means a report used for the purpose of evaluating a consumer for employment, promotion, reassignment or retention as an employee.

"(i)   The term 'medical information' means information or records obtained, with the consent of the individual to whom it relates, from licensed physicians or medical practitioners, hospitals, clinics, or other medical or medically related facilities.

"§ 604. Permissible purposes of reports

"A consumer reporting agency may furnish a consumer report under the following circumstances and no other:

"(1)   In response to the order of a court having jurisdiction to issue such an order.

"(2)   In accordance with the written instructions of the consumer to whom it relates.

"(3)   To a person which it has reason to believe—

"(A)   intends to use the information in connection with a credit transaction involving the consumer on whom the information is to be furnished and involving the extension of credit to, or review or collection of an account of, the consumer; or

"(B)   intends to use the information for employment purposes; or

"(C)   intends to use the information in connection with the underwriting of insurance involving the consumer; or

"(D) intends to use the information in connection with a determination of the consumer's eligibility for a license or other benefit granted by a governmental instrumentality required by law to consider an applicant's financial responsibility or status; or

"(E) otherwise has a legitimate business need for the information in connection with a business transaction involving the consumer.

"(a) Except as authorized under subsection (b), no consumer reporting agency may make any consumer report containing any of the following items of information:

"(1) Bankruptcies which, from date of adjudication of the most recent bankruptcy, antedate the report by more than fourteen years.

"(2) Suits and judgments which, from date of entry, antedate the report by more than seven years or until the governing statute of limitations has expired, whichever is the longer period.

"(3) Paid tax liens which, from date of payment, antedate the report by more than seven years.

"(4) Accounts placed for collection or charged to profit and loss which antedate the report by more than seven years.

"(5) Records of arrest, indictment or conviction of crime which, from date of disposition, release or parole, antedate the report by more than seven years.

"(6) Any other adverse item of information which antedates the report by more than seven years.

"(b) The provisions of subsection (a) are not applicable in the case of any consumer credit report to be used in connection with—

"(1) a credit transaction involving, or which may reasonably be expected to involve, a principal amount of $50,000 or more;

"(2) the underwriting of life insurance involving, or which may reasonably be expected to involve, a principal amount of $50,000 or more; or

"(3) the employment of any individual at an annual salary which equals, or which may reasonably be expected to equal, $20,000 or more.

"§ 606. Disclosure of investigative consumer reports

"(a) A person may not procure or cause to be prepared an investigative consumer report on any consumer unless—

"(1) it is clearly and accurately disclosed to the consumer that an investigative consumer report including information as to his character, general reputation, personal characteristics, and mode of living, whichever are applicable, may be made, and such disclosure (A) is made in a writing mailed, or otherwise delivered to the consumer, not later than three days after the date on which the report was first requested, and (B) includes a statement informing the consumer of his right to request the additional disclosures provided for under subsection (b) of this section; or

"(2) the report is to be used for employment purposes for which the consumer has not specifically applied.

"(b) Any person who procures or causes to be prepared an investigative consumer report on any consumer shall, upon written request by the consumer within a reasonable period of time after the receipt by him of the disclosure required by subsection (a) (1), shall make a complete and accurate disclosure of the nature and scope of the investigation requested. This disclosure shall be made in a writing mailed, or otherwise delivered, to the consumer not later than five days after the date on which the request for such disclosure was received from the consumer or such report was first requested, whichever is the later.

"§ 607. Compliance procedures

"(a) Every consumer reporting agency shall maintain reasonable procedures designed to avoid violations of section 605 and to limit the furnishing of consumer reports to the purposes listed under section 604. These procedures shall require that prospective users of the information identify themselves, certify the purposes for which the information is sought, and certify that the information will be used for no other purpose. Every consumer reporting agency shall make a reasonable effort to verify the identity of a new prospective user and the uses certified by such prospective user prior to furnishing such user a consumer report. No consumer reporting agency may furnish a consumer report to any person if it has reasonable grounds for believing that the consumer report will not be used for a purpose listed in section 604.

"(b) Whenever a consumer reporting agency prepares a consumer report it shall follow reasonable procedures to assure maximum possible accuracy of the information concerning the individual about whom the report relates.

"§ 608. Disclosures to governmental agencies

Notwithstanding the provisions of section 604, a consumer reporting agency may furnish identifying information respecting any consumer, limited to his name, address, former addresses, places of employment, or former places of employment, to a governmental agency.

"§ 609. Disclosures to consumers

"(a) Every consumer reporting agency shall, upon request and proper identification of any consumer, clearly and accurately disclose to the consumer:

"(1) The nature and substance of all information (except medical information) in its files on the consumer at the time of the request.

"(2) The sources of the information except that the sources of information acquired solely for use in preparing an investigative consumer report and actually used for no other purpose need not be disclosed *Provided:* That in the event an action is brought under this title, such sources shall be available to the plaintiff under appropriate discovery procedures in the court in which the action is brought.

"(3) The recipients of any consumer report on the consumer which it has furnished—

"(A) for employment purposes within the two-year period preceding the request, and

"(B) for any other purpose within the six-month period preceding the request.

"(b) The requirements of subsection (a) respecting the disclosure of sources of information and the recipients of consumer reports do not apply to information received or consumer reports furnished prior to the effective date of this title except to the extent that the matter involved is contained in the files of the consumer reporting agency on that date.

"§ 610. Conditions of disclosure to consumers

"(a) A consumer reporting agency shall make the disclosures required under section 609.

"(b) The disclosures required under section 609 be made to the consumer—

"(1) in person if he appears in person and furnishes proper identification; or

"(2) by telephone if he has made a written request, with proper identification, for telephone disclosure and the toll charge, if any, for the telephone call is prepaid by or charged directly to the consumer.

"(c) Any consumer reporting agency shall provide trained personnel to explain to the consumer any information furnished to him pursuant to section 609.

"(d) The consumer shall be permitted to be accompanied by one other person of his choosing, who shall furnish reasonable identification. A consumer reporting agency may require the consumer to furnish a written statement granting permission to the consumer reporting agency to discuss the consumer's file in such person's presence.

"(e) Except as noted in sections 616 and 617, no consumer may bring any action or proceeding in the nature of defamation, invasion of privacy, or negligence with respect to the reporting of information against any consumer, reporting agency, any user of information, or any person who furnishes information to a consumer reporting agency, based on information disclosed pursuant to section 609, 610, or 615, except as to false information furnished with malice or willful intent to injure such consumer.

"§ 611. Procedure in case of disputed accuracy

"(a) If the completeness or accuracy of any item of information contained in his file is disputed by a consumer, and such dispute is directly conveyed to the consumer reporting agency by the consumer, the consumer reporting agency shall within a reasonable period of time reinvestigate and record the current status of that information unless it has reasonable grounds to believe that the dispute by the consumer is frivolous or irrelevant. If after such reinvestigation such information is found to be inaccurate or can no longer be verified, the consumer reporting agency shall promptly delete such information. The presence of contradictory information in the consumer's file does not in and of itself constitute reasonable grounds for believing the dispute is frivolous or irrelevant.

"(b) If the reinvestigation does not resolve the dispute, the consumer may file a brief statement setting forth the nature of the dispute. The consumer reporting agency may limit such statements to not more than one hundred words if it provides the consumer with assistance in writing a clear summary of the dispute.

"(c) Whenever a statement of a dispute is filed, unless there is reasonable grounds to believe that it is frivolous or irrelevant, the consumer reporting agency shall, in any subsequent consumer report containing the information in question, clearly note that it is disputed by the consumer and provide either the consumer's statement or a clear and accurate codification or summary thereof.

"(d) Following any deletion of information which is found to be inaccurate or whose accuracy can no longer be verified or any notation as to disputed information, the consumer reporting agency shall, at the request of the consumer, furnish notification that the item has been deleted.

The consumer reporting agency shall clearly and conspicuously disclose to the consumer his rights to make such a request. Such disclosure shall be made at or prior to the time the information is deleted or the consumer's statement regarding the disputed information is received.

"§ 612. Charges for certain disclosures

"A consumer reporting agency shall make all disclosures pursuant to section 609 and furnish all consumer reports pursuant to section 611 (d) without charge to the consumer if, within thirty days after receipt by such consumer of a notification pursuant to section 615 or notification from a debt collection agency affiliated with such consumer reporting agency stating that the consumer's credit rating may be or has been adversely affected, the consumer makes a request under sections 609 or 611 (d). Otherwise, the consumer reporting agency may impose a reasonable charge on the consumer for making disclosure to such consumer pursuant to section 609, the charge for which shall be indicated to the consumer prior to making disclosure; and for furnishing notifications, statement, summaries, or codifications, to persons designated by the consumer pursuant to section 611 (d), the charge for which shall be indicated to the consumer prior to furnishing such information and shall not exceed the charge that the consumer reporting agency would impose on each designated recipient for a consumer report except that no charge may be made for notifying such persons of the deletion of information which is found to be inaccurate or which can no longer be verified.

"§ 613. Public record information for employment purposes

"A consumer reporting agency which furnishes a consumer report for employment purposes and which for that purpose compiles and reports items of information on consumers which are matters of public record and are likely to have an adverse effect upon a consumer's ability to obtain employment shall—

"(1) at the time such public record information is reported to the user of such consumer report, notify the consumer of the fact that public record information is being reported by the consumer reporting agency, together with the name and address of the person to whom such information is being reported; or

"(2) maintain strict procedures designed to insure that whenever public record information which is likely to have an adverse effect on a consumer's ability to obtain employment is reported it is complete and up to date. For purposes of this paragraph, items of public record relating to arrests, indictments, convictions, suits, tax liens, and outstanding judgments shall be considered up to date if the current public record status of the item at the time of the report is reported.

"§ 614. Restrictions on investigative consumer reports

"Whenever a consumer reporting agency prepares an investigative consumer report, no adverse information in the consumer report can be provided to the consumer unless it has been verified in the process of making such subsequent consumer report, or the adverse information was received within the three-month period preceding the date the subsequent report is furnished.

"§ 615. Requirements on users of consumer reports

"(a) Whenever credit or insurance for personal, family, or household purposes, or employment involving a consumer is denied or the charge for such credit or insurance is increased either wholly or partly because of information contained in a consumer report from a consumer reporting agency, the user of the consumer report shall so advise the consumer against who such adverse action has been taken and supply the name and address of the consumer reporting agency making the report.

"(b) Whenever credit for personal, family, or household purposes involving a consumer is denied or the charge for such credit is increased either wholly or partly because of information obtained from a person other than a consumer reporting agency bearing upon the consumer's credit worthiness, credit standing, credit capacity, character, general reputation, personal characteristics, or mode of living, the user of such information shall, within a reasonable period of time, upon the consumer's written request for the reasons for such adverse action received within sixty days after learning of such adverse action, disclose the nature of the information to the consumer. The user of such information shall clearly and accurately disclose to the consumer his right to make such written request at the time such adverse action is communicated to the consumer.

"(c) No person shall be held liable for any violation of this section if he shows by a preponderance of the evidence that at the time of the alleged violation he maintained reasonable procedures to assure compliance with the provisions of subsections (a) and (b).

"§ 616. Civil liability for willful noncompliance

"Any consumer reporting agency or user of information which willfully fails to comply with any requirement imposed under this title with respect to any consumer is liable to that consumer in an amount equal to the sum of—
"(1) any actual damages sustained by the consumer as a result of the failure;
"(2) such amount of punitive damages as the court may allow, and
"(3) in the case of any successful action to enforce any liability under this section, the costs of the action together with reasonable attorney's fees as determined by the court.

"§ 617. Civil liability for grossly negligent noncompliance

"Any consumer reporting agency or user of information which is negligent in failing to comply with any requirement imposed under this title with respect to any consumer is liable to that consumer in an amount equal to the sum of—
"(1) any actual damages sustained by the consumer as a result of the failure;
"(2) in the case of any successful action to enforce any liability under this section, the costs of the action together with reasonable attorney's fees as determined by the court.

"§ 618. Jurisdiction of courts; limitation of actions

"An action to enforce any liability created under this title may be brought in any appropriate United States district court without regard to the amount in controversy, or in any other court of competent jurisdiction, within two years from the date on which the liability arises, except that where a defendent has materially and willfully misrepresented any information required under this title to be disclosed to an individual and the information so misrepresented is material to the establishment of the defendent's liability to that individual under this title, the action may be brought at any time within two years after discovery by the individual of the misrepresentation.

"§ 619. Obtaining information under false pretenses

"Any person who knowingly and willfully obtains information on a consumer from a consumer reporting agency under false pretenses shall be fined not more than $5,000 or imprisoned not more than one year, or both.

"§ 620. Unauthorized disclosures by officers or employees

"Any officer or employee of a consumer reporting agency who knowingly and willfully provides information concerning an individual from the agency's files to a person not authorized to receive that information shall be fined not more than $5,000 or imprisoned not more than one year, or both.

2. A U.S. BILL RELATING TO DATA MAINTAINED BY GOVERNMENT AGENCIES.

93D CONGRESS
1ST SESSION   # H. R. 2998

A BILL

To amend title 5, United States Code, to provide that persons be apprised of records concerning them which are maintained by Government agencies.

By Mr. Koch, Mr. Moakley, Mr. Moss, Mr. O'Neill, Mr. Pepper, Mr. Pettis, Mr. Podell, Mr. Rosenthal, Mr. Roy, Mr. Sarbanes, Mr. Studds, Mr. Symington, Mr. Waldie, Mr. Wolff, and Mr. Won Pat

January 26, 1973
Referred to the Committee on Government Operations

H. R. 2998

IN THE HOUSE OF REPRESENTATIVES

JANUARY 26, 1973

Mr. Koch (for himself, Mr. Moakley, Mr. Moss, Mr. O'Neill, Mr. Pepper, Mr. Pettis, Mr. Podell, Mr. Rosenthal, Mr. Roy, Mr. Sarbanes, Mr. Studds, Mr. Symington, Mr. Waldie, Mr. Wolff, and Mr. Won Pat) introduced the following bill; which was referred to the Committee on Government Operations

---

A BILL

To amend title 5, United States Code, to provide that persons be apprised of records concerning them which are maintained by Government agencies.

1   *Be it enacted by the Senate and House of Representa-*

2   *tives of the United States of America in Congress assembled,*

3   That (a) subchapter II of chapter 5 of title 5, United States

4   Code, is amended by adding immediately after section 552

5   thereof the following new section:

6   **"§ 552a. Individual records**

7   "(a) Each agency that maintains records, including

8   computer records, concerning any person which may be

9   retrieved by reference to, or are indexed under such per-

10   son's name, or some other similar identifying number or

I—O

1 symbol, and which contain any information obtained from

2 any source other than such person shall, with respect to

3 such records—

4   "(1) notify such person by mail at his last known

5   address that the agency maintains or has augmented

6   a record concerning said person;

7   "(2) refrain from disclosing the record or any in-

8   formation contained therein to any other agency or to

9   any person not employed by the agency maintaining

10   such record, except—

11   (A) with permission of the person concerned

12   or, in the event such person, if an individual, can-

13   not be located or communicated with after reason-

14   able effort, with permission from members of the

15   individual's immediate family or guardian, or, only

16   in the event that such individual, members of the

17   individual's immediate family, and guardian cannot

18   be located or communicated with after reasonable

19   effort, upon good cause for such disclosure, or

20   (B) that if disclosure of such record is re-

21   quired under section 552 of this chapter or by any

22   other provision of law, the person concerned shall

23   be notified by mail at his last known address of any

24   such required disclosure;

1 "(3) refrain from disclosing the record or any

2 information contained therein to individuals within that

3 agency other than those individuals who need to ex-

4 amine such record or information for the execution of

5 their jobs;

6 "(4) maintain an accurate record of the names and

7 addresses of all persons to whom any information con-

8 tained in such records is divulged and the purposes for

9 which such divulgence was made;

10 "(5) permit any person to inspect his own record

11 and have copies thereof made at his expense, which in

12 no event shall be greater than the cost to the agency of

13 making such copies;

14 "(6) permit any person to supplement the in-

15 formation contained in his record by the addition of any

16 document or writing of reasonable length containing in-

17 formation such person deems pertinent to his record; and

18 "(7) remove erroneous information of any kind, and

19 notify all agencies and persons to whom the erroneous

20 material has been previously transferred of its removal.

21 "(b) This section shall not apply to records that are—

22 "(1) specifically required by Executive order to

23 be kept secret in the interest of the national security;

24 "(2) investigatory files compiled for law enforce-

1 ment purposes, except to the extent that such records

2 have been maintained for a longer period than reason-

3 ably necessary to commence prosecution or other action

4 or to the extent available by law to a party other than

5 an agency; and

6 "(3) interagency or intraagency memoranda or

7 letters which would not be available by law to a party

8 other than an agency possessing such memoranda or

9 letters in litigation with the such agency.

10 "(c) The President shall report to Congress before

11 January 30 of each year on an agency-by-agency basis the

12 number of records and the number of investigatory files

13 which were exempted from the application of this section

14 by reason of clauses (1) and (2) of subsection (d) during

15 the immediately preceding calendar year.

16 "(d) This section shall not be held or considered to

17 permit the disclosure of the identity of any person who has

18 furnished information contained in any record subject to

19 this section.

20 "(e) Any employee of the United States who under

21 the color of agency authority knowingly and willfully violates

22 a provision of this section, or permits such a violation, shall

23 be fined $1,000."

1   (b) The table of sections of subchapter II of chapter 5

2 of title 5, United States Code, in amended by inserting:

"552a. Individual records."

3 immediately below:

"552. Public information; agency rules; opinions, orders, records, and
    proceedings.".

4   SEC. 2. (a) There is established a Board to be known as

5 the Federal Privacy Board (hereinafter referred to as the

6 "Board").

7   (b) The Board shall establish published rules stating

8 the time, place, fees to the extent authorized, and procedure

9 to be followed with respect to making records promptly

10 available to a person, and otherwise to implement the pro-

11 visions of section 552a of title 5 of the United States Code.

12   (c) The Board shall promptly consider complaints

13 from any person that one or more of the requirements of

14 section 552a (a) of title 5, United States Code, have not

15 been met, with respect to the records specified in such sec-

16 tion, by the responsible agency. The Board upon finding

17 that one or more of the requirements have not been met,

18 shall issue a final order directing the agency to comply

19 with such requirement or requirements, and this order shall

20 be binding on the parties to such a dispute.

21   (d) The Board shall consist of seven members, each

22 serving for a term of two years, four of whom shall consti-

23 tute a quorum. The members of the Board shall be ap-

1 pointed by the President, by and with the advice and consent
2 of the Senate. No more than four of the members appointed
3 shall be of the same political party, and shall be from the
4 public at large and not officers or employees of the United
5 States. Any vacancy in the Board shall be filled in the
6 same manner the original appointment was made.

7   (e) Members of the Board shall be entitled to receive
8 $100 each day during which they are engaged in the per-
9 formance of the business of the Board, including traveltime.

10   (e) The Chairman of the Board shall be elected by the
11 Board every year, and the Board shall meet not less fre-
12 quently than bimonthly.

13   (f) The Board shall appoint and fix the compensation
14 of such personnel as are necessary to the carrying out of its
15 duties.

16   (g) The Board shall hold hearings in order to make
17 findings upon each complaint, unless it determines that the
18 complaint is frivolous. The Board may examine such evi-
19 dence as it deems useful, and shall establish such rules and
20 procedures as it determines are most apt to the purposes of
21 this section, including rules insuring the exhaustion of ad-
22 ministrative remedies in the appropriate agency.

23   Sec. 3. Section 1 of this Act shall become effective on
24 the ninetieth day following the date of enactment of this
25 Act, and Section 2 shall become effective upon the day of
26 enactment of this Act.

3. THE BRITISH DATA SURVEILLANCE BILL

Data Surveillance

A

B I L L

To prevent the invasion of privacy through
the misuse of computer information.

Ordered to be brought in by
Mr. Kenneth Baker, Mr. Ray Dobson,
Viscount Lambton, Sir Harry Legge-Bourke,
Mr. Eric Lubbock, Mr. Stanley Orme,
Mr. Hugh Rossi, Dame Joan Vickers
and Mr. Ben Whitaker

Ordered, by the House of Commons
to be Printed, 6 *May* 1969

LONDON
Printed and Published by
Her Majesty's Stationery Office
Printed in England at St. Stephen's
Parliamentary Press
1s. 3d. net
[Bill 150]   (381853)   44/3

Data Surveillance Bill

ARRANGEMENT OF CLAUSES

A

B I L L

T O

Prevent the invasion of privacy through the misuse of A.D. 1969 computer information.

B E IT ENACTED by the Queen's most Excellent Majesty, by and with the advice and consent of the Lords Spiritual and Temporal, and Commons, in this present Parliament assembled, and by the authority of the same, as follows:—

5   **1.**—(1) A register shall be kept by the Registrar of Restrictive Register of Trading Agreements (hereinafter in this Act referred to as "the data banks. Registrar") of all data banks as hereinafter defined which are operated by or on behalf of any of the following:—

    (*a*) any agency of central or local government;

10   (*b*) any public corporation;

    (*c*) any person exercising public authority;

    (*d*) any person offering to supply information about any other person's credit-worthiness, whether to members of a particular trade or otherwise and irrespective of whether 15   payment is made therefor;

    (*e*) any private detective agency or other person undertaking to carry out investigations into any other person's character, abilities or conduct on behalf of third parties;

    (*f*) any person who offers for sale information stored in 20   such data bank, whether to the general public or otherwise.

[Bill 150]   44/3

(2) The register referred to in the foregoing subsection shall contain the following information concerning each data bank:—

(a) the name and address of the owner of the data bank;

(b) the name and address of the person responsible for its operation;   5

(c) the location of the data bank;

(d) such technical specifications relating to the data bank as may be required by the Registrar;

(e) the nature of the data stored or to be stored therein;

(f) the purpose for which data is stored therein;   10

(g) the class of persons authorised to extract data therefrom.

(3) The owner of the data bank shall be required to register the information referred to in paragraphs (a) to (c) of the foregoing subsection.   The person responsible for the operation of the data bank shall be required to register the information referred 15 to in paragraphs (a) to (g) of the foregoing subsection.

(4) Any person responsible for registering information under this section shall be required to inform the Registrar of any alterations of, additions to or deletions from the said information within four weeks of such alteration taking effect, subject to the 20. provisions of subsection (6) below.

(5) If at any time the Registrar is of the opinion that in the circumstances the information given or sought to be given under paragraphs (f) or (g) of subsection (2) above might result in the infliction of undue hardship upon any person or persons or be 25 not in the interest of the public generally, he may order such entry to be expunged from or not entered in the register.   In reaching a decision under this or the next following subsection, the Registrar shall be guided by the principle that only data relevant to the purposes for which the data bank is operated 30 should be stored therein, and that such data should only be disclosed for those same purposes.

(6) An alteration to the register in respect of paragraph (f) or (g) of subsection (2) above shall be made by application to the Registrar who shall, not earlier than four weeks after receipt 35 of such application, grant or reject the application giving his reasons in writing.

(7) The register together with applications submitted in accordance with the last foregoing subsection shall be open to inspection by the public, including the press, during normal office 40 hours:

Provided that entries relating to data banks operated by the police, the security services and the armed forces shall be kept in a separate part of the register which shall not be open to inspection by the public.   45

480

2.—(1) This section shall apply to all data banks which are required to be registered under section 1 above except for the following:—

    (*a*) data banks which do not contain personal information
5   relating to identifiable persons;

    (*b*) data banks operated by the police;

    (*c*) data banks operated by the security services;

    (*d*) data banks operated by the armed forces of the Crown.

    (2) The operator of each data bank to which this section applies
10 shall maintain a written record in which shall be recorded the date of each extraction of data therefrom, the identity of the person requesting the data, the nature of the data supplied and the purpose for which it was required.

    3.—(1) The Registrar shall submit annually to Parliament a
15 report covering the previous calendar year in which he shall state the number of data banks entered on the register, the number of such data banks which fall within the terms of section 2(1)(*a*) and of section 2(1)(*b*) to (*d*) respectively and the number of instances in which he ordered entries to be amended under
20 section 1(5) or refused an application to alter an entry under section 1(6).

    (2) The Registrar's report may contain such additional information, statistical and otherwise, as the Registrar may think fit.

    4.—(1) Any person about whom information is stored in a data
25 bank to which section 2 above applies shall receive from the operator, not later than two months after his name is first programmed into the data bank, a print-out of all the data contained therein which relates to him. Thereafter, he shall be entitled to demand such a print-out at any time upon payment of
30 a fee the amount of which shall be determined by the Registrar from time to time; and the operator shall supply such print-out within three weeks of such demand.

    (2) Every print-out supplied in accordance with this section shall be accompanied by a statement giving the following
35 information:

    (*a*) The purpose for which the data contained in the print-out
         is to be used, as entered on the register referred to in
         section 1 above;

    (*b*) The purposes for which the said data has in fact been
40   used since the last print-out supplied in accordance
         with this section;

    (*c*) The names and addresses of all recipients of all or part
         of the said data since the last print-out supplied in
         accordance with this section.

Application for amendment or expunging of data.

5.—(1) Any person who has received a print-out in accordance with section 4 above may, after having notified the operator of the data bank of his objection, apply to the Registrar for an order that any or all of the data contained therein be amended or expunged on the ground that it is incorrect, unfair or out of 5 date in the light of the purposes for which it is stored in the data bank.

(2) The Registrar may, if he grants an order under the foregoing subsection, issue an ancillary order that all or any of the recipients of the said data be notified of the terms of the order. 10

Offences.

6.—(1) It shall be an offence, punishable on summary conviction by a fine of not more than £500, or on conviction on indictment by a fine of not more than £1,000 or imprisonment for not more than five years or both, for the owner or operator of a data bank to which this Act applies to fail to register it in 15 accordance with this Act.

(2) If the operator of a data bank to which section 2 above applies—

(a) fails or refuses to send a print-out when under a duty so to do; or 20

(b) permits data stored in the data bank to be used for purposes other than those stated on the register; or

(c) allows access to the said data to persons other than those entered on the register as having authorised access; or 25

(d) fails or refuses to comply with a decision of the Registrar,

he shall be liable in damages to the person whose personal data is involved and, where such acts or omissions are wilful, shall be liable on summary conviction to a fine of not more than £500 and on conviction on indictment to a fine of not more than 30 £1,000 or imprisonment for not more than five years or both.

(3) A person who aids, abets, counsels or procures the commission of an offence described in this section or with knowledge of its wrongful acquisition receives, uses, handles, sells or otherwise disposes of information obtained as a result of the com- 35 mission of such an offence, shall likewise be guilty of the said offence.

Liability for damages.

7. An operator of a data bank to which this Act applies who causes or permits inaccurate personal data to be supplied from the data bank as a result of which the person to whom the data 40 refers suffers loss, shall be liable in damages to such person.

8. The Registrar may make rules relating to the implementation Rules. of any part or parts of this Act and in particular relating to—

    (*a*) the keeping of the register and records referred to in sections 1 and 2 above;

5   (*b*) access by the public to the register referred to in section 1 above;

    (*c*) procedure on hearing objections and argument on a proposal to alter or expunge from the register under subsection 5 of section 1 above;

10   (*d*) procedure on application to alter the register under subsection 6 of section 1 above;

    (*e*) verification of the identity of a person demanding a print-out in accordance with section 4 above.

9. An appeal shall lie to the High Court from any decision Appeals. 15 made by the Registrar under this Act.

10. In this Act, the following terms shall have the meanings Definitions. hereby respectively assigned to them, that is to say—

    " data " means information which has been fed into and stored in a data bank;

20   " data bank " means a computer which records and stores information;

    " operator " means the person responsible for the operation of a data bank and for the introduction into and extraction from it of data;

25   " owner " means the person who owns the machinery comprising the data bank;

    " print-out " means a copy of information contained in the data bank supplied by the computer and translated into normal typescript.

30 **11.** *There shall be paid out of moneys provided by Parliament* Expenses. *any expenses incurred by the Registrar attributable to the provisions of this Act.*

    12.—(1) This act may be cited as the Data Surveillance Act Short title, 969.   commence-
ment and

35   (2) This Act shall come into force on the first day of July 1970. extent.

    (3) This Act shall extend to Northern Ireland.

C

DEPARTMENT OF DEFENSE GUIDELINES FOR THE CONSTRUCTION OF STORAGE VAULTS AND CLOSED AREAS

I. OUTLINE CONSTRUCTION SPECIFICATIONS FOR STORAGE VAULTS

A. Application

The following outline specifications are the criteria for the construction of vaults and strongrooms for use as storage facilities for classified material under the conditions stipulated in paragraph 14 of this Manual. Vaults ordered constructed after 1 July 1966 shall conform to the specifications. Vaults equipped with doors that do not meet Interim Federal Specification AA-D-00600a (GSA-FSS), Door, Vault, Security shall require the supplemental controls prescribed in paragraph 14a(3) (f).

B. Class A Vault

1. *Floor and Walls.* Eight-inch-thick reinforced concrete. Walls to extend to the underside of the roof slab above.

2. *Roof.* Monolithic reinforced-concrete slab of a thickness to be determined by structural requirements, but not less thick than the walls and floors.

3. *Ceiling.* Where the underside of the roof slab or roof construction exceeds 12 feet in height, or where the roof construction is not in accordance with paragraph 2, above, a normal reinforced-concrete slab will be placed over the vault area at a height not to exceed 9 feet.

4. *Vault Door and Frame Unit.* The vault door and frame shall conform to Interim Federal Specifications AA-D-00600a (GSA-FSS), Door, Vault, Security. Pending availability of security vault doors conforming to the Federal specification, vault door and frame unit shall conform to the criteria established in paragraph E. below.

5. *Lock and Locking Parts.* The lock shall conform to Underwriters' Standard No. 768 Group I–R. It shall be equipped with a "top-reading, spy-proof type dial." The Underwriters' label is considered adequate evidence of compliance with these requirements. Axial play on the lever handle spindle shall not exceed 1/16". The locks, lock bolt, door bolt operating cam, and bolt operating linkage connected thereto shall be protected by a tempered steel alloy hardplate located in front of the parts to be protected. Such hardplate to be at least 1/4" in thickness and to be in the Rockwell hardness range of C–63 to C–65. The front plate, edge plates, back plates, and cap sheet shall be of manufacturer's standard construction. The cap sheet of the door will have an inspection plate of such size that its removal will permit examination and inspection of the combination lock and operating cam area without removal of entire back cap sheet of the door.

C. Class B. Vault

1. *Floor.* Monolithic concrete construction of the thickness of adjacent concrete floor construction, but not less than 4 inches thick.

2. *Walls.* Not less than 8-inch-thick brick, concrete block, or other masonry units. Hollow masonry units shall be the vertical cell type (load bearing) filled with concrete and steel reinforcement bars. Monolithic steel-reinforced concrete walls at least 4 inches thick may also be used, and shall be used in seismic areas.

3. *Roof.* Monolithic reinforced-concrete slab of a thickness to be determined by structural requirements.

4. *Ceiling.* Where the underside of the room slab exceeds 12 feet in height or where roof construction is not in accordance with paragraph 3 above, a normal reinforced-concrete slab will be placed over the vault at a height not to exceed 9 feet.

5. *Vault Door and Frame Unit.* See paragraph B4.

6. *Lock.* See paragraph B5.

D. Class C Vault

1. *Floor.* See paragraph C1.

2. *Walls.* Not less than 8-inch-thick hollow clay tile (vertical cell double shell) or concrete block (thick shell). Monolithic steel-reinforced-concrete walls at least 4 inches thick may also be used, and shall be used in seismic areas. Walls back of the exterior wall-faction of the building shall be concrete, solid masonry, or hollow masonry units filled with concrete and steel reinforcement bars.

3. *Roof.* See paragraph C3.

4. *Ceiling.* See paragraph C4.

5. *Vault Door and Frame Unit.* See paragraph B4.

6. *Lock.* See paragraph B5.

E. Vault Door and Frame Unit

Pending availability of an approved vault door and frame unit which conform to Interim Federal Specification AA-D-00600a (GSA-FSS), Door, Vault, Security, the frame unit shall conform to the following specifications:

1. *Vault Door.* The vault door shall be an insulated, steel flatsill, standard, commercial record-vault type door bearing the half-hour label of Underwriters' Laboratories, Inc., (Underwriters' Standard UL-155) and the Safe Manufacturers' Association; and the Underwriters' Laboratories, Inc., approved relocking device label for a relocking device designed to deadlock the door when the lock is under mechanical, explosive or torch attack (right swing or left swing to be specified by purchaser). Door openings shall be standard 32 by 78 inch, normally without day gate. The entrance of the door shall be flush with the finished floor level. The front plate of the doors shall not be lighter than 0.0897-inch (13 gage) steel plate, either riveted or welded to the edge plates. Edge plates and back plates of the doors shall not be lighter than 0.0478-inch (18 gage) steel.

2. *Bolts.* The door and frame shall have not less than five bolts. When the bolts are not located on both jamb sides of the door, the jamb sides not protected with bolts shall interlock with the frame walls of that side.

3. *Hinges.* Each door shall have not less than three heavy ball-bearing or roller-bearing malleable iron, or steel hinges, and shall be hinged right or left as desired.

4. *Locks and Locking Parts.* The lock shall conform to Underwriters' Standard No. 768 Group I–R. It shall be equipped with a "top-reading, spy-proof type dial." The Underwriters' label is considered adequate evidence of compliance with these requirements. Axial play on the lever handle spindle shall not exceed 1/16". The locks, lock bolt, door bolt operating cam, and bolt operating linkage connected thereto shall be protected by a tempered steel alloy hardplate located in the front of the parts to be protected. Such hardplate to be at least 1/4" in thickness and to be in the Rockwell hardness range of C–63 to C–65. The front plate, edge plates, back plates, and cap sheet shall be of manufacturer's standard construction. The cap sheet of the door will have an inspection plate of such size that its removal will permit examination and inspection of the combination lock and operating cam area without removal of entire back cap sheet of the door.

5. *Frame.* The frame shall be of the tongue-and-groove interlocking type constructed of not lighter than 0.0478-inch (18 gage) cold-formed steel, formed from a single length for the soffit. Soffit and jambs shall be continuously welded along the entire intersection. Sills shall be flat and not less in width than the jambs. Frame jambs and soffit shall be insulated with the same material as the door. The frames shall be designed for the thickness of vault wall indicated.

6. *Finish.* The finish for the door, frame, and hardware shall be manufacturer's standard for the type door indicated.

7. *Identification Marking.* Each vault door and frame unit shall have a label or a metal nameplate giving the manufacturer's name, the model and serial number, date of manufacture, and certification attesting that the fire-resistance classification and safety devices conform to these requirements.

8. *Installation.* The vault door and frame unit shall be installed in strict compliance with the approved printed instructions and drawings provided by the manufacturer.

9. *Day Gate.* If desired, the vault door unit may include a day gate of the manufacturer's standard make, and the door frame may be designed to accommodate the day gate. The gate shall be of the swing-in hinged type with not less than 1/2-inch-diameter vertical rods; the gate frame shall be of not less than 3/8" by 1¼" steel members. It shall be equipped with a locking device arranged to permit locking and unlocking of the gate from the inside only.

F. Safety and Emergency Devices

A vault used for the storage of classified material shall be equipped with an emergency escape and relocking device. The escape device, not activated by the exterior locking device, accessible· on the inside only, shall be permanently attached to the inside of the door to permit escape for persons inside the vault. The device shall be designed and installed so that drilling and rapping of the door from the outside will not give access to the vault by actuating the escape device, and it shall meet the requirements of paragraph 3.3.9 of GSA, Federal Specifications AA–D–00600 (GSA–FSS) dated 27 December 1963, concerning an exterior attack on the door. A decal containing emergency operating instructions shall be permanently affixed on the inside of the door. Each vault shall be equipped with an interior alarm switch or device (such as a telephone, radio, or intercom) to permit a person in the vault to communicate with the vault custodian, guard, or guard post so as to obtain his release. Further, the vault shall be equipped .with a luminous-type light switch and, if the vault is otherwise unlighted, an emergency light shall be provided.

G. Structural Design

In addition to the requirements given above, the wall, floor, and roof construction shall be in accordance with national recognized standards of structural practice. For the vaults described above, the concrete shall be poured in place, and will have a minimum 28-day compressive strength of 2,500 psi.

H. Strongrooms

A strongroom, as referred to in paragraph 14*a*(3)(*f*), shall be considered to be an interior space enclosed by, or separated from other similar spaces by, four walls, a ceiling and a floor, all of which are constructed of solid building materials. Under these criteria, rooms having false ceilings and walls constructed of fabrics, wire mesh or other similar material shall not qualify as a strongroom. Specific construction standards are as follows:

1. *Hardware.* Heavy-duty builder's hardware shall be used in construction, and all screws, nuts, bolts, hasps, clamps, bars, hinges, pins, etc., shall be securely fastened to preclude surreptitious entry and assure visual evidence of forced entry. Hardware accessible from outside the area shall be peened, brazed or spot welded to preclude removal.

2. *Walls and Ceilings.* Construction shall be of plaster, gypsum board, metal, hardboard, wood, plywood or other materials offering similar resistance to, or evidence of, unauthorized entry into the area. Insert type panels shall not be used.

3. *Floors.* Floors shall be of solid construction, utilizing materials such as concrete, ceramic tile, wood, etc.

4. *Windows.* Window openings less than 18 feet above the ground or less than 14 feet directly or diagonally opposite uncontrolled windows in other walls, fire escapes and roofs shall be fitted with 1/2" bars (separated by no more than 6"), plus cross bars to prevent spreading or wire mesh fastened by bolts extending through the wall and secured on the inside of the window board. In addition to being kept closed at all times, the windows shall also be opaqued by any practical method, such as paint on both sides of the window, tempered masonite, sheet metal, cement-asbestos board, etc.

5. *Miscellaneous Openings.* Where ducts, registers, sewers and tunnels are of such size and shape as to permit unauthorized entry or visual access, they shall be equipped with man-safe barriers such as wire mesh (No. 9 gauge, 2 inch square mesh) or steel bars of at least 1/2" in diameter extending across their width with a maximum space of 6" between the bars. The steel bars shall be securely fastened at both ends to preclude removal, with cross bars to prevent spreading. Where wire mesh or steel bars are used, care shall be exercised to insure that classified material within the room cannot be removed with the aid of any type of instrument. Door traps shall be dead-bolted inside the room.

6. *Doors.* Doors may be of metal construction or solid wood. When doors are used in pairs, an astragal (overlapping molding) will be used where the doors meet.

7. *Door Louvers and Baffle Plates.* When used, they shall be reinforced with wire mesh (No. 9 gauge, 2 inch square mesh) fastened inside the room.

8. *Door Locking Devices.* Doors shall be secured by either a built-in three-position, dial-type, changeable combination lock, or a three-position, dial-type changeable combination padlock, which is secured to the door by a solid metal hasp.

II.   GUIDELINES FOR THE PHYSICAL CONSTRUCTION OF CLOSED AREAS

A. Application

The following guidance is offered to contractors as a reasonable norm to evaluate the adequacy of existing structural safeguards for closed areas and to provide guidance for construction of new areas.

B. Guidance

1. *Hardware.* Heavy-duty builders' hardware should be used in construction, and all screws, nuts, bolts, hasps, clamps, bars, 2-inch square mesh of No. 9 (Federal Specification RR–F–191 I, June 17, 1965) wire, hinges, pins, etc., should be securely fastened to preclude surreptitious removal and assure visual evidence of tampering. Hardware accessible from outside the area should be peened, brazed, or spot welded to preclude removal. The term "2-inch square mesh of No. 9 wire" which meets the requirements of Federal Specification RR–F–191d, June 17, 1965, hereinafter shall be referred to as "wire mesh."

2. *Walls.* Construction should be of plaster, gypsum wallboard, metal panels, hardboard, wood, plywood, or other opaque materials offering similar resistance to or evidence of unauthorized entry into the area. If insert-type panels are used, a method should be devised to prevent the removal of such panels without leaving visual evidence of tampering. Area barriers up to a height of 8 feet should be of opaque or translucent construction where visual access is a factor. If visual access is not a factor, the area barrier walls may be of wire mesh or other non-opaque material.

3. *Windows.* Window openings less than 18 feet above the ground or less than 14 feet directly or diagonally opposite uncontrolled windows in other walls, fire escapes, and roofs, should be fitted with 1/2 inch bars (separated by not more than 6 inches), plus cross bars to prevent spreading, or wire mesh fastened by bolts extending through the wall and secured on the inside of the window wall. When visual access is a factor, the windows shall be translucent or opaqued by any practical method, such as paint on both sides of the window, tempered masonite, sheet metal, cement-asbestos board, etc. During nonduty hours the windows should be closed and securely fastened to preclude surreptitious removal of classified material.

4. *Doors.* Doors should be of wood or metal construction. If visual access is not a factor, doors with glass panels may be used; however, they should be equipped with wire mesh, fastened securely on the inside of the area. When doors are used in pairs, an overlap molding should be used where the doors meet.

5. *Door Louvers or Baffle Plates.* When used, they should be reinforced with wire mesh fastened inside the area.

6. *Door Locking Devices.* Doors should be secured with a built-in three-position combination lock, a three-position combination padlock with solid metal hasp, a panic bolt, a dead bolt or a rigid wood or metal bar (which should preclude "springing"), extending across the width of the door and held in position by solid metal clamps, preferably fastened on the door casing.

7. *Ceilings.* Ceilings may be constructed of plaster, gypsum wallboard material, panels, hardboards, wood, plywood, ceiling tile, or other material offering similar resistance to and detection of unauthorized entry. Wire mesh may be used if visual access to classified material is not a factor. When wall barriers do not extend to the ceiling and a false ceiling is used, it should be reinforced with wire mesh. (This feature also applies when panels are removable and entry can be gained into the area without visible detection.) When such wire is used, an overlap molding secured by bolts should be used. (The bolts should be peened, brazed, or spot welded.) In those instances where barrier walls of an area extend to the ceiling, there is no necessity for reinforcing a false ceiling.

8. *Ceilings (Unusual Cases).* It is recognized that instances arise so that contractors may have a valid justification for not erecting a suspended ceiling as part of the area, especially in high-ceilinged hangers. The contractor may state that it is impractical to use a suspended ceiling because of his production methods, such as the use of overhead cranes for the movement of bulky equipment within the area. There are also cases wherein the airconditioning system may be impeded by the construction of a solid suspended ceiling. At times, even the height of the classified material may make a suspended ceiling impractical. In such cases, special provisions should be made to assure that surreptitious entry to the area cannot be obtained by entering the area over the top of the barrier walls. Areas of this type should be closely scrutinized to assure that the structural safeguards are adequate to preclude entry via adjacent pipes, catwalks, ladders, etc.

9. *Miscellaneous Openings.* Where ducts, registers, sewers, and tunnels are of such size and shape as to permit unauthorized entry, they should be equipped with man-safe barriers, such as wire mesh or, where more practical, steel bars at least one-half inch in diameter, extending across their width, with a maximum space of 6 inches between the bars. The steel bars should be securely fastened at both ends to preclude removal and should have crossbars to prevent spreading. When wire mesh or steel bars are used, care must be exercised to insure that classified material cannot be removed with the aid of any type instrument. Floor traps should be dead bolted inside the area. Care should be taken to assure that a barrier placed across any waterway (sewer or tunnel) will not cause clogging or offer any obstruction to the free flow of water or sewerage.

D CHECKLISTS AND SUMMARIES

The following checklists and summaries are intended to assist the reader in the design and auditing of procedures for security, accuracy, and privacy; these checklists should also be used to ensure the completeness of these operations.

492

493

Table D.1. A Design Procedure

Procedure	Relevant Chapters
1. Establish the overall control philosophy	1, 5 Table D.31
2. Establish the value of protection and the potential exposures	
Develop tables such as Table 2.1 and 5.1	2, 5
3. Establish a budget for security and accuracy controls	2, 5
4. Establish the responsibility for technical design	
(a) Accuracy controls:	
Determine the accuracy controls on batch operations (Table D.8)	6
Determine the accuracy controls on real-time operations (Table D.9)	7
Determine the error controls for teleprocessing (Table D.12)	8
Determine the controls built into off-line operations (Table D.10)	23
Determine the controls to bridge periods of failure (Table D.11)	9
(b) Security controls:	
Determine the techniques for identifying the terminal users (Table D.16)	11, 12
Determine the structures of authorization schemes	13, 14
Determine whether cryptography should be used	19–21
Determine what locks and alarms will be used to detect an invalid entry	10, 16
Determine the means of establishing security in systems programs (Table D.17)	17
Determine what controls are built into the use of statistical files	15
Determine what controls are built into off-line file scanning operations (Table D.10)	23
Determine surveillance methods	16
Determine what methods will be used to recover from file damage (Table D.21)	22
5. Establish the responsibility for procedural controls	
Determine the nature and functions of the input/output control section	6, 7
Determine how quality control is achieved	
Determine computer room procedures	
Determine tape/disk library procedures	
Determine how conversion to the new system will be controlled	
6. Establish the responsibility for the control of programs	17, 34
Determine the techniques to prevent unauthorized programs from being used (Table D.19)	34
Determine how program maintenance and promotion are controlled (Table D.20)	34
Determine program testing procedures	
7. Establish the responsibility for physical security	
Establish fire precautions	26
Establish physical locks, alarms, guards, and sabotage protection	24, 27
Establish an off-site data storage and means of conveyance	32
Consider precautions against wire-tapping and system eavesdropping	19, 28

Table D.1. (continued)

Procedure	Relevant Chapters
8. Establish the responsibility for administrative controls	30
Establish a vital records program	32
Incorporate controls for classified documents	31
Take out insurance	Appendix E
Establish backup procedures in case of catastrophe	22, 32
9. Involve the auditors	
The auditors should check the controls planned at the design stage	37
Audit trials must be designed, along with other technical aids to auditing	23
All aspects of the system should be audited (Fig. 37.1)	37
A checklist should be prepared for future audits	Table D.28

Table D.2. Table for Assessing Costs of Damage and Level of Protection

Type of File	Modification would permit embezzlement or theft?	Category of intruder that protection is designed for	Intentional					Accidental				
			Effect					Effect				
			Inability to process	Loss of entire file	Loss of single records	Modification of records	Unauthorized reading or copying	Inability to process	Loss of entire file	Loss of single records	Modification of records	Unauthorized reading or copying

A = Accidental

B = Casual entry by unskilled persons

C = Casual entry by skilled technicians

D = Persons who stand to gain financially

E = Well-equipped criminals

F = Organizations with massive funds

0 = Negligible

1 = On the order of $10

2 = On the order of $100

3 = On the order of $1000

4 = On the order of $10,000

5 = On the order of $100,000

6 = On the order of $1 million

7 = On the order of $10 million

Table D.3. Types of Security Exposure

Type of Exposure	Inability to process	Loss of an entire file	Loss of single records	Modification of records	Unauthorized reading or copying
Acts of God					
Fire	✓	✓			
Flood	✓	✓			
Other catastrophe	✓	✓			
Mechanical failure					
Computer outage	✓				
File unit damages disk track			✓		
Tape unit damages part of tape			✓		
Disk, or other volume, unreadable		✓			
Hardware/software error damages file		✓	✓	✓	
Data transmission error not detected			✓	✓	
Card (or other input) chewed up by machine			✓	✓	
Error in application program damages record			✓	✓	
Human carelessness					
Keypunch error			✓	✓	
Terminal operator input error			✓	✓	
Computer operator error		✓	✓	✓	
Wrong volume mounted and updated		✓		✓	
Wrong version of program used		✓		✓	
Accident during program testing		✓	✓	✓	
Mislaid tape or disk		✓			
Physical damage to tape or disk		✓	✓		
Malicious damage					
Looting	✓	✓			
Violent sabotage	✓	✓			
Nonviolent sabotage (e.g., tape erasure)	✓	✓	✓	✓	
Malicious computer operator			✓	✓	✓
Malicious programmer			✓	✓	✓
Malicious tape librarian			✓		
Malicious terminal operator			✓	✓	✓
Malicious user (e.g., user who punches holes in returnable card)			✓	✓	
Playful malignancy (e.g., misusing terminal for fun)		✓	✓	✓	✓
Crime					
Embezzlement			✓	✓	✓
Industrial espionage					✓
Employees selling commercial secrets					✓
Employees selling data for mailing lists					✓
Data bank information used for bribery or extortion					✓

Table D.3. (continued)

Types of Exposure	Inability to process	Loss of an entire file	Loss of single records	Modification of records	Unauthorized reading or copying
Invasion of privacy					
Casual curiosity (e.g., looking up employee salaries)					✓
Looking up data of a competing corporation					✓
Obtaining personal information for political or legal reasons					✓
Nondeliberate revealing of private information					✓
Malicious invasion of privacy					✓

Table D.4. Causes of Damage to Files and the Main Means of Protection

Causes or Damage to Files	Extent of Damage				Main Means of Prevention	Relevant Chapter
	Field	Entire record	Group of records	Entire file		
1. Keypunch error	✓				Use of verifier	
					Batch validation checks	6
					On-line data entry and checking	6, 7
2. Terminal operator input error	✓				Good dialogue design	
					On-line validation checks	7
					Prevent unauthorized terminal use	10 to 16
					Design cross-checks that will catch the wrong item at a later time	7, 23
3. Data transmission error	✓				Powerful error detecting code	8
4. Card chewed up by machine		✓			Good card handling procedures	
					Good maintenance of card readers	
5. Program error	✓	✓	✓		Thorough program testing	34
6. Accident during program testing	✓	✓	✓	✓	Do not use live files when testing	
					If programs are under test on a live system, bar them from the live files.	34
7. Wrong volume loaded and updated			✓	✓	Good library procedures	
					Mandatory checking of volume labels	
8. Computer operator error		✓	✓	✓	Thorough operator training	
					Foolproof and clearly documented operating procedures	
9. Mislaid tape				✓	Good library procedures	
10. Defective tape or disk	✓	✓	✓	✓	Buy good quality products	
					Adequate tape renewal policy	
11. Theft of tape or disk				✓	Physical locks and alarms	24
					Tight library procedures	
12. Embezzlement	✓				Tight accounting controls	6, 7
					Segregation of functions	33
					Tight control of the programmers	34
					Disciplined program promotion	34
13. Playful maliciousness	✓				Discipline	
					Tight control of programmers	34
					Prevent unauthorized terminal use	10 to 16

Table D.4. (continued)

Causes or Damage to Files	Extent of Damage				Main Means of Prevention	Relevant Chapter
	Field	Entire record	Group of records	Entire file		
14. Fire				√	Good fire prevention procedures	25, 26
					Fireproof tape and disk storage	24, 32
15. Sabotage			√	√	Physical locks and alarms	24, 25, 27
					Good morale	35
					Security police	30

Table D.5. Causes of Computer Errors and the Main Means of Prevention

Types of Errors	Means of Prevention	Relevant Chapters
Hardware errors		
Computer or file error	Good hardware design	
Tape error	Powerful error detecting and correcting codes	

Teleprocessing trans-
    mission error
	Powerful error detection and transmission
	   (Table D.12)
		8

Software errors	Good quality software Infrequent changes to new versions Thorough testing	
Errors in application programs	Thorough program testing Control of program patching Control of program promotion (Table D.20)	34 34
Operator errors	Batch controls Foolproof operating procedures Checks built into programs to prevent processing the wrong volume Frequent check of the operator's log Good operator training	6
Data input errors	Card verification Batch controls On-line controls Controls when failures occur File balancing and scanning Use of input/output control group Quality control	6 7 9 23 6, 7 6
Inappropriate program design	Skilled systems analysts	3
Questionable system philosophy	Skilled systems analysts Auditors' participation in the design	3 37

Table D.6. Causes of Breaches of Privacy and the Main Means of Protection

```
       ┌─ Unauthorized access to data
      /    ─ Requires technical and administrative controls
     /
    └───── Authorized access to data
           ─ Requires administrative, societal and legal controls
```

1. UNAUTHORIZED ACCESS TO DATA

Causes of Breach of Privacy	Main Means of Protection	Relevant Chapters
1. Accidental disclosure of private information		
Computer operator error	−Input/output Control Group	6
	−Automatic checks on operating procedures	
User error	−Controls on classified documents.	31
System hardware error	−Hardware designed to prevent output on the wrong device	
	−Terminal identification in teleprocessing	12
2. Theft of listings or documents	−Physical security for theft protection (Table D.24)	24, 25
	−Effective controls on classified documents	31
	−Enforced clean desk policy	
	−Head listings are shredded	
3. Theft of data volume (e.g., tape or disk)	−Tight volume library controls	
	−Physical security for theft protection (Table D.24)	24, 25
	−Instruments which detect removal of a volume	25
	−Tight controls on classified volumes	31
	−Cryptography	19, 20
4. Authorized duplication of a volume	−Tight volume library controls	
	−Tight control of utility programs for duplication	
	−Tight control of classified volumes	31
	−Cryptography	19, 20
5. Authorized printing of a volume	−Tight volume library controls	
	−Tight control of listing utilities	
	−Tight control of classified documents	31
	−Cryptography	19, 20
	−Steganography	21
6. Unauthorized use of terminal	−Positive identification of terminal user (Table D.16)	11
	−Programmed locks, alarms and surveillance based on user identification (Tables D.14 and D.17)	10 to 18

Table D.6. (continued)

Causes of Breach of Privacy	Main Means of Protection	Relevant Chapters
7. Terminal user "masquerading" as another user	—Positive identification of terminal user —Programmed locks, alarms, and surveillance based on user identification	
8. Authorized terminal user "browses" in files not intended for him	—Authorization tables —Programmed lock, alarms, and surveillance based on authorization tables (Tables D.14 and D.17)	13, 14 13 to 18
9. Misuse of a statistical data base—Asking multiple questions to obtain information of nonstatistical personal nature	—Programmed controls to prevent output about too small a population —Surveillance of usage —Detection of excessive usage, to detect trial-and-error exploration	12
10. Switching a connection (e.g., switching on a terminal control unit) between two terminals	—Positive terminal identification —Locked connection panels	12
11. Wiretapping active (in which data is sent on the tapped line)	—Positive terminal identification —Authenticity checks in each message. —Lock up PBX's (Private Branch Exchanges), junction boxes, wiring panels, etc., and install burglar alarms —Cryptography	12 28 28 19, 20
passive (in which data is merely recorded from the tapped line)	—Lock up PBX's, etc. —Cryptography	28 19, 20
12. Submission of unauthorized programs	—All programs must be on the program residence file (program library) —Promotion of programs to the program residence file is carefully controlled (Table D.20) —Control of the programmers (Table D.19)	 34 34
13. "Trap doors" hidden in authorized programs	—Careful inspection of all programs —Control of the programmers (Table D.19) —Psychological security	34 34 35
14. The controls are bypassed by the systems programmers	—Secure operating system —No-break operator's log inspected daily —Control of the programmers —Psychological security	17, 18 34 34

Table D.6. (continued)

Causes of Breach of Privacy	Main Means of Protection	Relevant Chapters
15. Data obtained by dumping main memory, possibly after a contrived error	—Operating system which prevents main-memory dumping of secured data —No-break operator's log inspected daily	17, 18
16. Unauthorized operator actions	—Operating system made secure from operator attempts to access unauthorized data —No-break operator's log, possibly on a locked tape drive, designed for tamper-proof logging —Lock on program load button	17, 18
17. System eavesdropping (bugs, radiation detectors, etc.)	See Table D.7.	29

Table D.6. (continued)

2. AUTHORIZED ACCESS TO DATA

Causes of Breaches of Privacy	Main Means of Protection	Relevant Chapters
1. Misuse of a statistical data bank	—Separate encoding of data that identifies an individual	
	—Programmed controls to prevent output about too small a population	15
	—Surveillance of usage	
	—Detection of excessive usage, to detect trial-and-error exploration	
2. Government agencies misusing their files (Almost 2000 types of government files in the USA contain personal data.)	—Tight governmental controls on agencies	38
	—Data restricted in use to the purpose for which it was collected.	38
	—Laws such as the Federal Privacy Bill (Appendix B)	39
3. Nongovernment agencies misusing their files (Credit bureaus, marketing agencies, detective agencies, etc.)	—Agencies regulated by law	39
	—Only data relevant to the stated purpose may be collected	38
	—Data may only be used for the stated purpose	38
	—Public should be told what information is kept about them	39
	—Laws such as the British Data Surveillance Bill (Appendix B)	39
4. Corporations misusing personnel data	—Employees should be told what information is kept about them and how it is used	
	—Professional codes relating to personal data	
	—Files of personal data restricted (by law?) to use internally in the corporation	
	Laws relating to privacy and data banks may contain provisions such as the following:	39
	1. A register of all data banks containing personal information will be established.	
	2. The register should be open to public (and press) inspection	
	3. Avoiding registration would be a criminal offense	
	4. Facts but not opinions may be stored	
	5. Publicly accessible data banks may hold only data relevant to the registered purpose	
	6. All interrogations of data banks concerning the public should be automatically recorded	
	7. Individuals should be informed automatically of the types of data kept about them	

Table D.6. (continued)

Causes of Breaches of Privacy	Main Means of Protection	Relevant Chapters
	8. An individual should have the right to inspect the data kept about him	
	9. An individual should have the right to take issue with the data kept about him	
	10. A negligent data bank operator should be liable for damages	
	11. Aged data must be removed. Details concerning age of data may be specified for different types of data bank	
	12. Security procedures on sensitive data banks may be subject to inspection	

Table D.7. Types of System Eavesdropping and Main Means of Protection

Type of Eavesdropping*	Main Means of Prevention
Documents casually picked up or copied	Clean desk policy enforced Effective control of classified data
Program listings casually picked up or copied	Clean desk policy enforced Effective control of classified data
Valuable information or listings obtained from waste-paper cans or garbage men	Sensitive documents should be shredded when finished with
Information obtained from carbon paper or typewriter ribbons	Destruction of these should be controlled. Typewriters or terminals which overwrite their own ribbon may be used
Photography	Prohibit cameras on premises
Telescopes or cameras with long-focus lenses	Site terminals away from windows which are overlooked
Wiretapping └─ Public telephone lines (difficult to tap) └─ On user's premises (easy to tap)	Cryptography Lock up PBX (Private Branch Exchange) and install burglar alarm Use computerized PBX Lock up junction boxes (and install burglar alarm) Cryptography
Electromagnetic eavesdropping	Arrange equipment so that eavesdropper cannot come very close to radiating terminals Choice of terminal Physical measures such as screening, grounding metal objects that carry the radiation, filtering power lines
Hidden microphone and transmitter	Have premises checked out by a security specialist
Electromagnetic bug and transmitter └─ in modems └─ in terminals	Have premises checked out by a security specialist

*Types of eavesdropping listed in order of likelihood.

Table D.8. Accuracy Controls on Batch-Processing Systems (Chapter 6)

1 CONTROLS ON INPUT

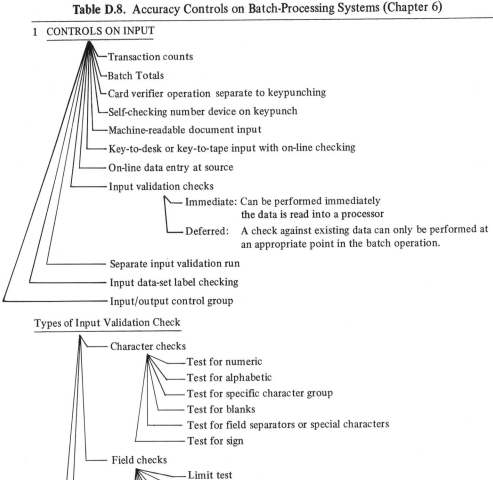

- Transaction counts
- Batch Totals
- Card verifier operation separate to keypunching
- Self-checking number device on keypunch
- Machine-readable document input
- Key-to-desk or key-to-tape input with on-line checking
- On-line data entry at source
- Input validation checks
  - Immediate: Can be performed immediately the data is read into a processor
  - Deferred: A check against existing data can only be performed at an appropriate point in the batch operation.
- Separate input validation run
- Input data-set label checking
- Input/output control group

Types of Input Validation Check

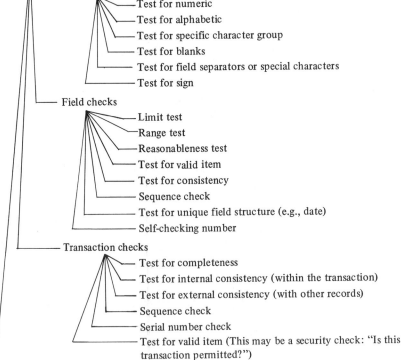

- Character checks
  - Test for numeric
  - Test for alphabetic
  - Test for specific character group
  - Test for blanks
  - Test for field separators or special characters
  - Test for sign
- Field checks
  - Limit test
  - Range test
  - Reasonableness test
  - Test for valid item
  - Test for consistency
  - Sequence check
  - Test for unique field structure (e.g., date)
  - Self-checking number
- Transaction checks
  - Test for completeness
  - Test for internal consistency (within the transaction)
  - Test for external consistency (with other records)
  - Sequence check
  - Serial number check
  - Test for valid item (This may be a security check: "Is this transaction permitted?")

Table D.8. (continued)

Types of Input Validation Check (continued)

└────── Batch checks
- Transaction count
- Batch control total
- Hash totals
- Batch number checks

Separate Input Validation Run before production runs (incorporating the above checks)

        ADVANTAGE: Input data can be repunched before the production runs begin, and correct control totals established

        DISADVANTAGE: Takes extra time

Methods of Input Preparation:

- Keypunching into cards
  - ADVANTAGES: Simple
  - Card handling gives flexibility needed in some operations
- Key-to-tape or key-to-disk
  - ADVANTAGES: Simple
  - Tape cassettes are small and easy to handle
  - Saves card cost
  - Provides faster input to computer
- On-line keying
  - ADVANTAGES: Validation checks applied as the data is being keyed
  - Operator can check a complete record on the screen
  - Computer may provide data from its files, lessening the total keying
  - Dialogue techniques can lessen errors
  - No separate verification operation is needed (generally)
  - DISADVANTAGES: Computer costs
  - Programs and program maintenance is needed
  - Operators idle when the computer is down
- On-line data entry at source location
  - Full-time "dedicated" operator
  - Casual operator

Table D.8. (continued)

Methods of Input Preparation: (continued)

ADVANTAGES:	Data input is controlled at source
	Modification of data from source location is easy
	Source location filing is eliminated
	Validation checks can be applied as the data is being keyed
	Computer may provide data from its files and thus lessen the total keying
	Dialogue techniques can lessen errors
	No separate verification operation is used (generally)
DISADVANTAGES:	Teleprocessing costs
	Programs and program maintenance is needed
	The operation may be more difficult to control

2 CONTROLS ON PROCESSING

- Transaction counts
- Batch control totals
- Hash totals for the batch
- Validation by file reference (Does a record exist for this item?)
- Consistency checks (Does this item agree with previously stored data?)
- Arithmetic checks (Less important today because of machine reliability)
- Controls on rounding errors (separate rounding error account, for example)
- Reasonableness checks
- Suspense accounts (to contain items that for some reason cannot be posted to the normal accounts, thus ensuring that balances can be maintained)
- Scuttle procedures (An erroneous item is set aside to be dealt with after the run, so that the run may continue nonstop. The correct totals and balances must be maintained)
- Artificial transactions with known results (included in the batch to ensure correct processing)

3 CONTROLS ON OUTPUT

- Items counts
- Control totals
- Reasonableness checks
- Trailer labels on data sets
- Control records
- Serial numbers on documents (e.g., checks or invoices)

Table D.8. (continued)

3 CONTROLS ON OUTPUT (continued)

Labels on data sets (e.g., tapes) may contain:

- Label identifier
- File number
- Batch number
- Creation date
- Retention cycle (son, father, grandfather, etc.)
- Volume number (e.g., reel number)
- A count of the records on the reel
- Batch totals
- Hash totals of all important fields

4 INPUT/OUTPUT CONTROL SECTION

Typical responsibilities:

- Receive work for processing from user departments
- Record the receipt of work
- Check document counts and control totals of work received
- Notify user department that the work has been received and indicate whether the counts and totals are correct
- Note any work not received
- Note and initiate action on any improper preparation by the user departments (e.g., failure to provide counts or totals)
- Submit documents to be keypunched or entered into tape or disk
- Check that no documents are lost in the keypunching operation
- Check for results of the input validation run and arrange for erroneous items to be punched or re-entered
- Balance the totals of the input validation run with those provided by the user departments, and record them
- Obtain, and return, necessary tapes and disks from the library
- Submit jobs for processing. Record their submission along with totals and counts
- Receive the output of the processing. Check and record the totals and counts
- If the control figures are incorrect after processing, initiate investigation
- File the run summary

5 QUALITY CONTROL FUNCTION

- Forward the output to the users, bound and burst, with unwanted items removed. Analyze errors by source, type, quantity, magnitude, age, and other factors which might help to control them
- Produce error statistics automatically, to help detect and correct adverse trends

Table D.9. Controls on Real-Time Systems

Types of Control	Main Chapter in which Discussed
Two Essential Categories of Controls ⟨ accuracy controls (listed in this table)	7
security controls (listed in subsequent tables)	
Types of Accuracy Controls (each is expanded below)	
Real-time checks on terminal operator actions	7
Consistency checks applicable later than transaction entry time	7
Accuracy checks applied to data transmission (listed in Table D.12)	8
File balances and transaction balances	7
File scanning operations (listed in Table D.10)	23
Employment of an input/output control staff	7
Careful procedures to bridge periods of system failure	9
Real-Time Checks on Terminal Operator Actions	
Psychological considerations in dialogue design	
(Book: *Design of Man–Computer Dialogues*)	
Select appropriate dialogue structure	
Tailor the dialogue to operator capability	
Avoid confusion	
Avoid operator "channel overload"	
Avoid operator boredom	
Design with appropriate response times	
Fast but nondisruptive error notification	
"Bullet-proof" the dialogue	
Train the operators thoroughly	
Log operator errors and take action when errors are excessive	
Single transaction checks	7
Descriptive readback of items entered	
Character checks	
Field checks	
Limit test	
Range test	
Reasonableness test	
Test for valid item	
Consistency test	
Sequence check	
Special test (as on dates)	
Self-checking fields	

Table D.9 (continued)

Types of Control	Main Chapter in which Discussed
Real-time Checks on Terminal Operator Actions (continued)	
Single transaction checks (continued)	7
Transaction checks	
Test for completeness	
Test for internal consistency	
Test for consistency with file records	
Test for consistency with other transactions	
Sequence check	
Serial number check	
Test for valid item	
Check for a valid sequence of transactions (as with transaction representing the routing of a part in production control)	
Redundant items inserted as a check for contradictions	
Use of machine-readable documents	
Badge	
Cartridge	
Punched card	
Magnetic strips credit card	
Mark-sense card	
Checks Applicable Later Than Transaction Entry Time	7, 23
Operator entering a transaction checks the accuracy of related records previously stored	
An "old balance" is checked when new data is entered	
An historical log is kept of changes to data	
Dialogue checkpoints are used to ensure correct programs in complex data entry	
Consistency of early transactions with the current one is checked	
Group transaction checks	
Periodic item balances (e.g., cash balances)	
Running totals	
Periodic summaries produced for checking at user locations	

Table D.9. (continued)

Types of Control	Main Chapter in which Discussed
File-Balancing Checks	23

Off-line file balance may include the following:

- Establishing cash balances
- Establishing inventory balances
- Hash total balances
- Check for undesirable circumstances
- Preparation of summaries which user or file owner may check

Suspense accounts—Items posted to nonexistent or invalid accounts are temporarily retained in a suspense account so that a balance can be maintained

Correction files— Alterations made to records which are found to be incorrect are logged in a correction file in an attempt to preserve the file and transaction balances

Types of Control	Main Chapter in which Discussed
Input/Output Control Section	7

—may be more than one at remote user locations

Functions:

- Real-time notification of errors not resolved in the man-terminal dialogue (especially useful for data entry terminals which cannot respond alphabetically to their operator)
- Ensures that all balancing operations are performed
- Investigates faulty balances or other error conditions not resolved by terminal operator
- May be responsible for overall accuracy of the data files (file owners, possibly)
- Monitors terminal activity to prevent operators from breaking the rules
- May monitor security controls
- May check that operations occur on schedule
- Application-oriented control functions (e.g., production control monitoring)

Table D.10. Functions Incorporated into Direct-Access File-Scanning Runs

Off-line file scanning and balancing may be linked to transaction entry checks and balancing to provide an interlocking set of controls

Functions which may be included in the scanning run:

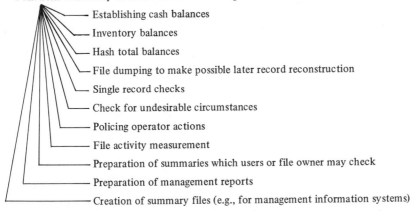

- Establishing cash balances
- Inventory balances
- Hash total balances
- File dumping to make possible later record reconstruction
- Single record checks
- Check for undesirable circumstances
- Policing operator actions
- File activity measurement
- Preparation of summaries which users or file owner may check
- Preparation of management reports
- Creation of summary files (e.g., for management information systems)

Techniques used:

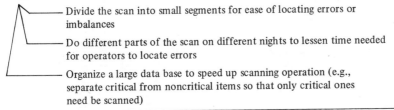

- Divide the scan into small segments for ease of locating errors or imbalances
- Do different parts of the scan on different nights to lessen time needed for operators to locate errors
- Organize a large data base to speed up scanning operation (e.g., separate critical from noncritical items so that only critical ones need be scanned)

Table D.11. Controls to Bridge Periods of Failure (Chapter 9)

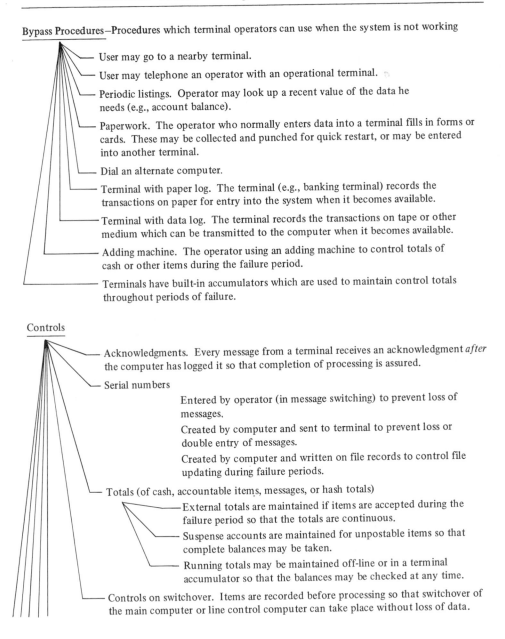

Bypass Procedures—Procedures which terminal operators can use when the system is not working

- User may go to a nearby terminal.

- User may telephone an operator with an operational terminal.

- Periodic listings. Operator may look up a recent value of the data he needs (e.g., account balance).

- Paperwork. The operator who normally enters data into a terminal fills in forms or cards. These may be collected and punched for quick restart, or may be entered into another terminal.

- Dial an alternate computer.

- Terminal with paper log. The terminal (e.g., banking terminal) records the transactions on paper for entry into the system when it becomes available.

- Terminal with data log. The terminal records the transactions on tape or other medium which can be transmitted to the computer when it becomes available.

- Adding machine. The operator using an adding machine to control totals of cash or other items during the failure period.

- Terminals have built-in accumulators which are used to maintain control totals throughout periods of failure.

Controls

- Acknowledgments. Every message from a terminal receives an acknowledgment *after* the computer has logged it so that completion of processing is assured.

- Serial numbers

          Entered by operator (in message switching) to prevent loss of messages.

          Created by computer and sent to terminal to prevent loss or double entry of messages.

          Created by computer and written on file records to control file updating during failure periods.

- Totals (of cash, accountable items, messages, or hash totals)

      - External totals are maintained if items are accepted during the failure period so that the totals are continuous.

      - Suspense accounts are maintained for unpostable items so that complete balances may be taken.

      - Running totals may be maintained off-line or in a terminal accumulator so that the balances may be checked at any time.

- Controls on switchover. Items are recorded before processing so that switchover of the main computer or line control computer can take place without loss of data.

Table D.11. (continued)

Controls (continued)

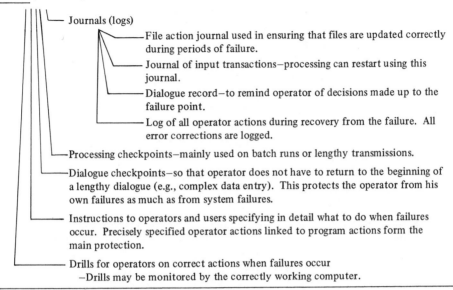

Journals (logs)

File action journal used in ensuring that files are updated correctly during periods of failure.

Journal of input transactions—processing can restart using this journal.

Dialogue record—to remind operator of decisions made up to the failure point.

Log of all operator actions during recovery from the failure. All error corrections are logged.

Processing checkpoints—mainly used on batch runs or lengthy transmissions.

Dialogue checkpoints—so that operator does not have to return to the beginning of a lengthy dialogue (e.g., complex data entry). This protects the operator from his own failures as much as from system failures.

Instructions to operators and users specifying in detail what to do when failures occur. Precisely specified operator actions linked to program actions form the main protection.

Drills for operators on correct actions when failures occur
—Drills may be monitored by the correctly working computer.

Table D.12. Techniques for Controlling Transmission Line Errors

Technique	Usage
1. Ignore line errors	Used where proportion of operator errors is far greater than line errors. Used in verbal message transmission.
2. Common error-detection codes	
Character coding e.g., four-out-of-eight code	Less commonly used today. Less effective than block codes.
Parity checks	Commonly used but of little value (especially with higher speed transmission).
Vertical and longitudinal checks	Commonly used. Simple circuitry. Less efficient than polynomial codes.
Polynomial checks on blocks	Exceedingly efficient block error detection is possible with polynomial codes.
Checks on groups of records	
3. Error detection without automatic retransmission	Manually initiated retransmission is used when the proportion of operator errors is high (e.g., on airline reservation systems).
4. Error detection with automatic retransmission	The safest method, given a good error-detecting code. Some form of message storage is needed at the terminal.
Retransmit one character ——	Echo check.
Retransmit one word ——	Word check.
Retransmit one message or record ——	Probably the most common. Block check on the message or record.
Retransmit several messages or records ——	Possibly checked with a high-order polynomial code.
Retransmit a batch ——	Possibly checked with a batch hash total.
	NOTE: It pays to select optimum block size or batch size.
5. Retransmit at a later time.	For example, after a periodic or daily balancing or policing run
6. Retransmit several times if first attempt fails.	Normally done.
7. Retransmit several times with variable time delays.	To circumvent lengthy periods of line noise.
8. Retransmit with modem switched to lower speed.	Can be done automatically on certain terminals with built-in modems. Otherwise the modem speed may be switched manually.

Table D.12. (continued)

Techniques	Usage
9. Loop check	
Characters returned to terminal	Simple where loop transmission is employed.
Characters sent twice by terminal	Used on in-plant loops with capacity to spare.
10. Forward error correction	Less efficient and less safe than error detection. Used on one-way links and on links with abnormally high error rates such as long-wave and short-wave radio, and telephone-line modems operating at 9600 bits per second.
11. Combination of forward error correction and error detection with retransmission	Forward error correction is added to error-detection schemes when the proportion of retransmission becomes high enough to degrade throughput significantly.

Table D.13. Protective Features on Terminals

1. Features for Security

   Unique terminal identification by the computer
   Lockable keyboard
   Nonprinting feature for use when keying in security code
   Identification card reader
   Cryptography feature
   Physical lock and key

2. Features for Control of Errors (Book: *Systems Analysis for Data Transmission,*
   Chapters 15 and 35)

   Erase, or backspace, key

   Cancel transaction key

   Automatic error detection. The code used for automatic error detection can range from relatively insecure parity checks to virtually error-proof polynomial codes of a high order.

   Automatic transmission when an error is detected (which implies some form of buffer at the terminal)

   Forward error correction

   Transaction logging in the terminal

   Accumulators in the terminal for keeping totals

   Logging facilities and/or accumulators which record details of transactions entered when the computer is inoperative

   A recording mechanism (e.g., tape cassette) for recording transactions when the computer is inoperative, which can later be transmitted to it. This transmission may or may not be automatic

Table D.14. Technical Controls for Ensuring the Privacy of Data

Type of Controls	Relevant Chapter
Privacy, being more than a technical problem, requires:	
Technical controls	
Administrative controls	
Legal controls	
TECHNICAL CONTROLS	
Terminals in secure areas. Guards permit only authorized personnel. Some systems must differentiate between terminals in secure areas and terminals in nonsecure areas.	12
Techniques to prevent eavesdropping and wiretapping. (Eavesdropping techniques that must be guarded against are listed in Table D.7.)	28, 29
Computer room locked and possibly guarded. (See Tables D.24 and D.25.)	
Tight controls on tape and disk library	
Tight controls on usage of tapes and disks (copying must be prevented)	
Programmed locks. (See Table D.17.)	10
Programmed alarms. When an unauthorized attempt to access a program or data is detected, appropriate authorities may be notified immediately. The alarms should be highly publicized.	
Positive identification of the terminal user (See Table D.16.)	11
Positive identification of the terminal	12
Terminal transmits its address or identification	
Terminal transmits security code from "tamper-proof" circuit.	
Positive terminal identification guards against:	
Polling address error	
Faulty line switching	
Deliberate switching of terminal connections	
Unauthorized access to the system	
User authorization	13
For transaction types	
For programs	
For data items which he can read	
For data items which he can write	
For categories of data which he can read	
For categories of data which he can write	

Table D.14. (continued)

Type of Controls	Relevant Chapter
TECHNICAL CONTROLS (continued)	
Locks on data	14
May refer to data as Complete files	
Volumes (disks or tapes)	
Individual records	
Groups of records or record categories	
Individual fields in a record type	
Categories of field in a record type	
Security strata (e.g., confidential, secret, top secret)	
May refer to a user as An individual user	
A group or category of users	
A security level	
An application program	
A terminal or terminal location	
Combinations of these	
Authorization tables map together these two categories	
Controls on statistical data banks may be dependent on the results of inquiries—prohibiting responses when the sample is too small or the enquiries too repetitive	15
Surveillance of the system, noting any violations of security procedure	
Real-time surveillance	
Non-real-time surveillance (from logs which the system keeps)	
(A well-protected system will have both)	
After a second violation in succession of security procedure the system may.	16
Caution the user and give him one more chance only	
Lock the keyboard and notify an appropriate authority	
Refuse to accept new input from that terminal for a period (to impede trial-and-error)	
"Keep the user talking" and inform a security officer so that he might be caught red-handed	
Statistical analysis of security procedure violations to detect unusual activity	16
It should be made known and demonstrated that effective disciplinary action will be taken against security violators	

Table D.14. (continued)

Type of Controls	Relevant Chapter
TECHNICAL CONTROLS (continued)	
Tight control of the programmers should be maintained. (See Tables D.19 and D.20.)	34
All actions of computer room operators should be logged in such a way that there can be no break in the log.	
Cryptography	19, 20
Applied to data transmission	
Applied to data on files	
Steganography—Recording the data so that it cannot be printed on existing devices and hence it appears that no data is present	21

Table D.15. Techniques to Prevent Embezzlement

Techniques	Relevant Chapters
1. Controls on people	33, 34
2. Controls on programmers	34
3. Prevention of unauthorized access	10 to 18
4. Controls on records	Section II
5. Controls on input	6, 7
6. Controls on processing	Section II
7. Controls needed during periods of failure	9
8. Controls on computer room operations	34
9. Controls on documents	31
10. Administrative controls	Section IV
11. Physical security measures for theft protection	24, 25
12. Auditing	37

1. CONTROLS ON PEOPLE

Divide responsibilities so that embezzlement requires collusion between different persons. (No one person should be responsible for the entire processing of a transaction)	33
Minimize the likelihood of collusion by separating departments (the programmers should not normally intermingle with the accountants) and by separating close associates (husband and wife should not be in jobs in which they can collaborate in crime)	33
Divide the knowledge necessary to manipulate the system. (No one man should have all the knowledge he needs to defraud the system. The high level of system complexity can be used to prevent crime.)	33
Segregate the programming responsibilities so that programs cannot easily be modified for embezzlement. (See Table D.19.)	34
Rotate job responsibilities to impede collusion	33
Control overtime working	
Check employee backgrounds where desirable	
Bond employees in critical positions	
Discipline: Ensure that the security and accuracy controls are taken seriously at all levels	35
Monitor the observance of the rules governing security and accuracy	35
Managers should know individual employees well enough to assess any potential security risks	

Table D.15. (continued)

Techniques	Relevant Chapters
1. CONTROLS ON PEOPLE (continued)	
⌐— Outside consultants or contractors should be carefully selected and controlled	
2. CONTROLS ON PROGRAMMERS	
See Tables D.19 and D.20.	
3. CONTROLS TO PREVENT UNAUTHORIZED ACCESS TO THE SYSTEM	
See Tables D.14, D.16, and D.17.	
4. CONTROLS ON RECORDS	
— Determine which records need to be safeguarded against embezzlement	5
— Off-line file balances will be checked for agreement at regular intervals and must cross-check with transations totals, thus forming an interlocking set of controls	23
⌐— Cash balances	
— Inventory balances	
— Hash total balances	
— The file scan also produces summaries which user or file owner may check	
— Checks for undesirable circumstances and invalid conditions are made during the off-line file-scanning run	
— Correction and suspense files are used so that error or exception conditions may be handled without destroying the file and transaction balances	
— Journalling	23
⌐— Transaction log	
— File action log	
— Security violation log	
— Log of all file corrections	
— An historical log of all updates to certain items	
5. CONTROLS ON INPUT	
See Input Controls in Tables D.8 and D.9.	6, 7

Table D.15. (continued)

Techniques	Relevant Chapters
6. CONTROLS ON PROCESSING (The accuracy checks listed in Tables D.8 to D.11 apply here.)	Section II, Chapter 34

— Only programs in the program residence file may be used

— Promotion of programs to this file is vigorously controlled (Table D.20)

— Patching and modification to programs is vigorously controlled

— Reasonableness checks (e.g., to prevent major modification of bank overdraft)

— Validity checks (Is this transaction valid?)

— Consistency tests

— Controls on rounding errors

— Artificial transactions and records (to test that programs are still operating as intended)

— Transaction counts (to detect added items slipped into the input stream)

— Batch totals
    — amount totals
    — hash totals

— Validation by file reference (Does a record exist for this item?)

— New records created are listed for checking by user management

— Secure software to prevent unauthorized use of programs (or data or volumes)

— Alarms in programs to alert security officer to unauthorized activity

— Surveillance of system utilization to detect unusual activity

— Secure software to prevent the bypassing of programmed controls

— "Fetch protection" to prevent a program from accessing items beyond their partition

7. CONTROLS NEEDED DURING PERIODS OF FAILURE ON REAL-TIME	9

SYSTEMS (An embezzler might cause, or expediently utilize, a hardware failure to defraud the system. See also Table D.11.)

— External totals are maintained if items are accepted throughout the failure period so that the totals are continuous

— Transactions are logged at the terminal during the failure period
    — Paper log
    — Data log (e.g., on tape cartridge)

— Every transaction receives a computer acknowledgment

Table D.15. (continued)

Techniques	Relevant Techniques
7. CONTROLS NEEDED DURING PERIODS OF FAILURE ON REAL-TIME SYSTEMS (continued)	
— Transactions are serial-numbered.	
— Running totals may be maintained off-line during normal operation and during failure.	
8. CONTROLS ON OPERATIONS	
— "Open shop" computer room operations should be avoided.	
— Programmer "hands-on" operations should be carefully controlled.	
— No unauthorized persons should ever operate the machines.	
— The machine room should be kept locked, with "panic bar" exits.	
— Overtime working, if permitted, must be carefully controlled.	
— The volume library should be tightly controlled. Tapes or disks may never be borrowed for unauthorized use.	
— Theftproof cabinets should be used for all sensitive volumes.	
— Operator training must be thorough.	
— Operators must be given instructions on how to deal with intruders.	
— An Input/Output Control Section should be used with the functions specified in Tables D.8 and D.9.	
9. CONTROLS ON DOCUMENTS	31
— Checks and negotiable items are handled only by those personnel who are authorized and are responsible for the safety of these items.	
— The storage space for operating manuals, program specifications, and listings must always be locked. (Detailed knowledge of the system is needed for many types of embezzlement.)	
— Classified items (and sometimes nonclassified documents in special categories) have the controls indicated in Table D.22.	
— Accountable or classified items are serial-numbered or page-numbered.	
— The Input/Output Control Group records and controls all computer output.	

Table D.15. (continued)

Techniques	Relevant Techniques
10. ADMINISTRATIVE CONTROLS	Section IV
Different types of systems have different types of miscellaneous administrative controls. Examples are:	
— Checks for more than a certain amount need two signatures	
— Activity on an account that has been inactive for a lengthy period is listed for managerial spot-checks	
— Special authorization is needed for large items. The computer may be programmed to request authorization from one of two or more managers, chosen by the computer to make collusion difficult.	
11. PHYSICAL SECURITY MEASURES FOR THEFT PROTECTION	24, 25
See Table D.24.	
12. AUDITING	
See Tables D.28 and D.29.	37

Table D.16. Means of Identifying the Terminal User (Chapter 11)

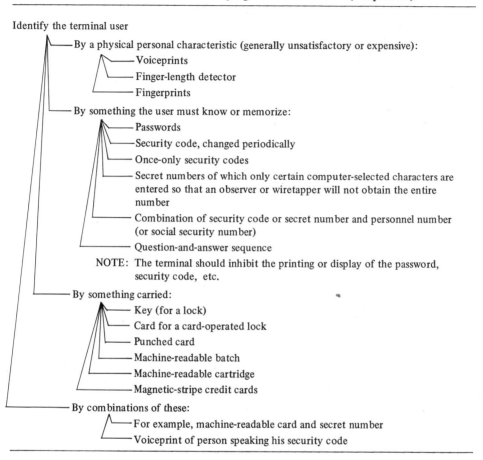

Identify the terminal user

By a physical personal characteristic (generally unsatisfactory or expensive):

Voiceprints

Finger-length detector

Fingerprints

By something the user must know or memorize:

Passwords

Security code, changed periodically

Once-only security codes

Secret numbers of which only certain computer-selected characters are entered so that an observer or wiretapper will not obtain the entire number

Combination of security code or secret number and personnel number (or social security number)

Question-and-answer sequence

NOTE: The terminal should inhibit the printing or display of the password, security code, etc.

By something carried:

Key (for a lock)

Card for a card-operated lock

Punched card

Machine-readable batch

Machine-readable cartridge

Magnetic-stripe credit cards

By combinations of these:

For example, machine-readable card and secret number

Voiceprint of person speaking his security code

Table D.17. The Locks that Can be Applied When a Terminal is Used

Sequence of Operations	Possible Locks on the Operation
THE USER SWITCHES ON THE TERMINAL	← The terminal may be physically locked.
THE USER ESTABLISHES THE COMMUNICATION LINK	← The communication facilities to the computer in question may be locked in an inoperative state.
THE TERMINAL TRANSMITS ITS IDENTIFICATION	← The terminal identification code may not be acceptable to the computer. Further transmission is blocked.
THE USER IDENTIFIES HIMSELF	← The user number may not be on the computer's list, in which case, it will accept no further input.
THE USER KEYS IN A SECURITY CODE OR USES A SECURITY CARD	← The security code may be incorrect, in which case the computer takes protective action.
THE USER REQUESTS A PROGRAM (EXPLICITLY OR IMPLICITLY IN A DIALOGUE STRUCTURE)	← The user in question may not be authorized for this program; he is prevented from using it.
THE PROGRAM OPENS A FILE OR REQUESTS A RECORD	← The program or user may not be authorized to use that file or record. Access to it is barred.
THE SYSTEM READS A RECORD AND OBTAINS THE REQUIRED FIELDS	← The record or field may carry an indicator barring this user/program from employing it.

Table D.17. (continued)

Sequence of Operations	Possible Locks on the Operation
THE PROGRAM MANIPULATES THE DATA AND COMPOSES A RESPONSE	
↓	← The response or result of the processing may bar further action, and the transmission of the result prohibited.
THE COMPUTER TRANSMITS THE RESPONSE	

Table D.18. Cryptography Techniques

LEVELS OF ENCIPHERING ALGORITHM:

<u>Level A:</u>   Can be broken by an intelligent nonspecialist, using a computer, and given sufficient time.

<u>Level B:</u>   Might be broken by an amateur cryptanalyst using a computer.

<u>Level C:</u>   Will probably not be broken by an amateur cryptanalyst unless he has information about its content, but might be broken by professional cryptanalysts.

<u>Level D:</u>   Will probably not be broken by professional cryptanalysts.

(Examples are given in the following table)

NOTE: Most professional cryptanalysts have highly classified government jobs and are unlikely to attack ordinary commercial data. Skilled amateur cryptanalysts are rare. However, only Level C and D algorithms should be employed.

PRINCIPLES FOR ENCIPHERING DATA

1. Assume that a would-be intruder may be able to steal the program or obtain knowledge of the algorithm used. Devise a form of encoding that is undecipherable even when the enemy knows the enciphering method.

2. Employ a key which can be changed at suitably frequent intervals.

3. Change the key sufficiently frequently that an intruder is unlikely to obtain it by computing methods—given that he has the enciphering method—even if he uses the fastest computers available.

4. Make the key sufficiently complex so that it cannot be obtained by trial-and-error methods using the fastest computers.

5. Do not trust the persons to whom the key is given. Make the enciphering *program* sufficiently complex so that a person possessing the key, but not the program, cannot make use of the key even if he has access to the fastest computers.

6. Devise external security procedures that will prevent any person from gaining access to both the key and the program.

7. Write the program so that it can easily be changed if its security is compromised, for example, by changing a pseudorandom number generator, or seed embedded in the program.

8. Do not use a key which might be guessed—e.g., alphabetic words—or numbers which have other meanings.

9. Process the messages being sent, before enciphering, so that no clues reside in the encoded message which will lessen the work needed in trial-and-error deciphering. For example, substitute random characters for blank fields; remove strings of zeros; change letters such as E, T, O, Q, Z, Y, J, and K in alphabetic text so that statistical letter counts cannot be used; substitute numbers or short codes for commonly used phrases; remove repetitively used words.

10. Avoid *conventional* techniques such as conventional random-number generators. The expert codebreaker will have less chance if unconventional or eccentric routines are used.

Table D.18. (continued)

11. If known characters such as *End-of-record* or *End-of-transmission* are used, send these in clear (unenciphered).

12. Avoid transmitting obvious or repetitive messages, the meaning of which can be guessed by the code-breaker.

13. Assess the possibility that active wiretapping will cause specific messages to be sent or repeated.

14. Assess the possibility that an intruder will see the enciphered form of records of which he *already knows the contents.*

15. Assume that the intruder will be able to obtain some past text along with its enciphered form. This information should not enable him to discover the enciphering method in time for him to make use of his knowledge.

16. If the data enciphered is valuable to the opposition a long time in the future (as with oil survey data) encipher it with the combination of a once-only key and a complex algorithm. Back up the enciphering with a high level of physical security.

17. A programmer or analyst devising an enciphering technique *must* be familiar with the methods the cryptanalyst will use in trying to break the cipher. Programmers sometimes tend to think that their algorithms are secure, when in fact they are Level A or Level B above.

METHODS OF ENCIPHERING DATA, AND METHODS OF ATTACKING THE CIPHER

Codes used in the following chart to indicate the quality of the enciphering method when faced with a particular method of attack:

U   = Unsafe

P   = Poor: May possibly be broken by this method of attack.

G   = Good: Will probably not be broken by this method of attack.

G1   = Good for data that retains its value for a short time only.

G2   = Good for data that retains its value for a long time.

S   = Safe: Will not be broken by this method of attack.

Table D.18 (continued)   METHODS OF ENCIPHERING

METHODS OF ATTACK: (All deciphering methods assume the use of a powerful computer)	Unchanging Transforms	
	Level A	
	Simple enciphering algorithms *Single-character substitution* *Character sequence transposition* *Arithmetic transformation* *Repetitive addition of key* *Etc.*	*Combined single-character substitution and character sequence transposition*
Attack by a talented amateur cryptanalyst		
Decipher by trial and error	U	D
Decipher using relative frequencies of letter, letter pairs, words, etc.	U	D
Decipher using mathematical techniques	U	D
Guess words or items and use mathematical techniques	U	U
Obtain clear and enciphered copy of the same past text	U	U
Cause the same text to be re-enciphered (e.g. by requesting retransmission)		
The decipherer might guess the algorithm (or a similar one)	U	U
The decipherer knows the algorithm (theft, or an "inside job")	U	U
The decipherer obtains the key a long time after it was first used		
The decipherer knows the key in advance or steals it quickly		
Attack by a professional cryptanalyst		
Decipher using relative frequencies of letters, letter pairs, words, etc.	U	U
Decipher using mathematical techniques	U	U
Guess words or items and use mathematical techniques	U	U
Obtain clear and enciphered copy of the same past text	U	U
Cause the same text to be re-enciphered (e.g., by requesting retransmission)		
The decipherer might guess the algorithm (or a similar one)	U	U
The decipherer knows the algorithm	U	U
The decipherer obtains the key a long time after it was first used		
The decipherer knows the key in advance or steals it quickly		

Table D.18 (continued)

Unchanging Transforms							Changeable Transforms			
Level B		Level C		Level D			Algorithms which employ an automatically changing parameter (e.g., based on time of day or serial number)		Algorithms in which the operator changes a parameter (once a day, say)	
Single-character substitution with multiple alphabets	Character-pair substitution (As in Program 2 in Appendix 1)	Single-character sequence trans-position followed by character-pair substitution (as in Program 3 in Appendix 1)	Combination of characters with a continually changing random number (as in Program 1 in Appendix 1)	Systems which convert the characters into numbers and perform mathematical operations on them	Systems which convert the text into bit streams and perform multiple shift register operations on them	Complex combinations of the above	Level C algorithms	Level D algorithms	Level C algorithms	Level D algorithms
D	D	G2	G2	S	S	S	G2	S	G2	S
D	D	G1	G1	G1	G1	G2	G1	G2	G1	G1
D	D	G1	G1	G1	G1	G2	G1	G2	G1	G1
U	U	D	D	G1	G1	G1	G1	G1	G1	G1
U	U	D	D	D	D	D	G1	G1	G1	G1
							D	D	D	D
U	U	U	U	U	U	U	U	D	U	D
U	U	U	U	U	U	U	U	U	U	D
U	U	U	U	G1	G1	G2	D	G2	G1	G2
U	U	U	U	G1	G1	G2	D	G2	G1	G2
U	U	U	U	D	D	D	U	D	U	D
U	U	U	U	U	U	U	U	U	U	U
							U	U	U	U
U	U	U	U	U	U	U	U	U	U	U
U	U	U	U	U	U	U	U	U	U	U

Table D.18 (continued)

A once-only key (The same key is not used twice)	*A once-only key with key expansion*	*Key which is changed frequently (say once per day) with Level C algorithm. (Programs 3 and 4 in Appendix 1)*	*Ditto with Level D algorithm*	*Key which is changed frequently with automatically changing algorithm of Level C*	*Ditto with Level D algorithm*	*Algorithm with frequently changed parameter used in conjunction with a key which is frequently changed— Level C algorithm*	*Ditto with Level D algorithm*
	Fixed Transforms Employing a Key			Changeable Transforms Employing a Key			
S	S	S	S	S	S	S	S
S	S	G1	G1	G1	G2	G1	G2
S	S	G1	G1	G1	G2	G1	G2
S	S	G1	G1	G1	G1	G1	G1
S	S	G1	G1	G1	G1	G1	G1
S	S	G1	G1	G1	G1	G1	G1
S	S	G1	G1	G1	G1	G1	G1
S	S	G1	G1	G1	G1	G1	G1
G1	G1	G1	G1	G1	G1	G1	G1
U	U	D	G1	G1	G1	G1	G1
S	S	D	G1	D	G2	G1	G2
S	S	D	G1	D	G2	G1	G2
S	S	D	G1	D	G1	D	G1
S	S	U	D	U	U	U	U
S	S						
S	S	D	G1	D	D	D	G1
S	S	D	D	D	D	D	D
G1	G1	D	G1	D	D	D	G1
U	U	U	D	U	D	U	D

Table D.19. Control of the Programmers: Segregation of Responsibilities
(Discussed in Chapter 34)

1. The systems programmers will not write application programs using sensitive data. The application programmers will not write systems programs.

2. It is not possible for users to access application programs except via the input/output control software and this will contain security features including a user identification and authorization check.

3. It is not possible for an application program to access the data files except via the data management software and this will contain security features including a password or authorization check.

4. On a dedicated commercial system no user is permitted to use a program that he himself has written.

5. No programmer will be permitted to operate the computer system.

6. The operator will not be told the functions of the programs he is running. Program decks, tapes, and disks will be labeled with an alphanumeric number but not with anything that indicates the function.

7. On a dedicated commercial system no program will be run that does not reside on the authorized program file. Elaborate control will be maintained over the "promotion" of programs to this file as a means of ensuring that such programs are authorized, fully tested, and independently inspected.

8. The programmers will be provided with a set of macros, subroutines, or microprograms, which provide them with valuable services but control the way that the programmers handle certain operations. Input/output and other security-sensitive operations may be handled *only* by means of the macro language or subroutine library.

9. Users of the system do not specify its programs in detail but liaise with specialists or programmers who carry out this function.

10. Program specifications are centrally approved by a control group.

11. Specifications for data-base records or files are centrally approved, possibly by the same control group that approves data specifications.

12. Data for final program testing is generated not by the programmer of the routine in question but by a specialist or group that is established for that purpose.

13. Testing will be conducted, not by the programmer, but by a central group which maintains tight control over the operation.

14. All programs and modifications to programs will be kept centrally by a program library maintenance system. Programmers will not have to keep program decks. Instead "audit trail" of program modifications will be kept, and this will indicate who authorized the modifications and who specified and programmed them.

15. The operations groups handling the live running of the system may be separate from the operations group for testing and support functions.

16. The application programs for a sensitive transaction will never *all* be written by the same programmer.

Table D.20. Control of the Programmers: Nine Stages in Promoting a
Program to Operational Use

1. *Programmer* writes module and signs Promotion Sheet.

2. *Programmer's manager* inspects program and signs sheet.

3. *Central testing group* passes the module through all phases of testing with tight control.

4. *Application control group* approves the module and gives permission for it to be placed on the live program file.

5. *Operations group* run the utility which places the module on the live program file. This can only be done with the authority of the Application Control Group.

6. *On-line control*, concerned with system performance and reliability, exercise the module in the live system and check that all is well.

7. *Functional group* concerned with the function in question check the operation of the module to ensure that it does what they want.

8. *Terminal users* exercise the new module to ensure that it is satisfactory for the users. This is the final acceptance.

9. The new program module then comes into use in the operational system.

Table D.21. Data Reconstruction Techniques (Chapters 22 and 32)

Programs and facilities for data reconstruction must be planned well ahead. A "vital records" program should exist in and beyond the data processing department.

Two types of capability needed:

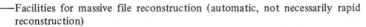

— Facilities for massive file reconstruction (automatic, not necessarily rapid reconstruction)

— Facilities for reconstructing individual records (quick, not necessarily automatic, reconstruction is required)

DATA WHICH MAY BE RETAINED FOR MASSIVE FILE RECONSTRUCTION

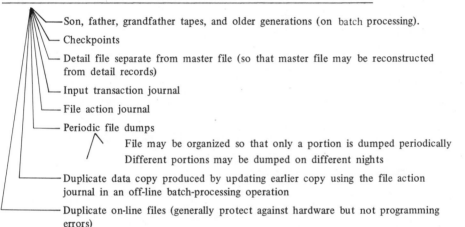

— Son, father, grandfather tapes, and older generations (on batch processing).

— Checkpoints

— Detail file separate from master file (so that master file may be reconstructed from detail records)

— Input transaction journal

— File action journal

— Periodic file dumps

        File may be organized so that only a portion is dumped periodically

        Different portions may be dumped on different nights

— Duplicate data copy produced by updating earlier copy using the file action journal in an off-line batch-processing operation

— Duplicate on-line files (generally protect against hardware but not programming errors)

RECONSTRUCTION OF ISOLATED RECORDS

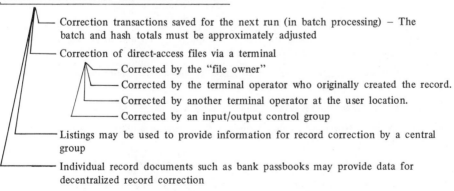

— Correction transactions saved for the next run (in batch processing) – The batch and hash totals must be approximately adjusted

— Correction of direct-access files via a terminal

      — Corrected by the "file owner"

      — Corrected by the terminal operator who originally created the record.

      — Corrected by another terminal operator at the user location.

      — Corrected by an input/output control group

— Listings may be used to provide information for record correction by a central group

— Individual record documents such as bank passbooks may provide data for decentralized record correction

        All balancing controls must be adjusted appropriately

        Suspense accounts may be used to preserve balances

        All changes should be journalled

        Tight security controls needed to prevent unofficial record correction

Table D.22. Controls Needed on Sensitive Documents

Rules are required governing the following aspects of sensitive document usage:

1. What security classification levels are used:

Typical levels in government:	*Typical levels in industry:*
TOP SECRET	REGISTERED CONFIDENTIAL
SECRET	CONFIDENTIAL
CONFIDENTIAL	FOR INTERNAL USE ONLY
RESTRICTED	UNCLASSIFIED
UNCLASSIFIED	
Special category:	Special category:
CRYPTOGRAPHIC	PERSONAL AND CONFIDENTIAL

2. *Distribution.* How is distribution of classified items controlled?

3. *Reproduction.* What rules govern the reproduction of classified data? Reproduction of highly sensitive data should be prohibited—by xeroxing, photography, copying in the computer room and by other methods.

4. *Locks, keys, and storage.* What data must be kept under lock and key? What form of storage cabinets, vaults and locks should be used?

5. *Mailing.* What precautions must be taken when sensitive data is mailed?

6. *Typing.* What precautions are to be taken when classified documents are typed? Ribbons and carbon paper, for example, should be shredded.

7. *Tapes and disks.* How are tapes and disks, and other storage media, to be kept and controlled?

8. *Transmission.* What precautions are necessary when classified data is transmitted by Telex, teleprocessing, facsimile, or by other means?

9. *Screen displays.* What regulations govern the display of sensitive data on computer screens?

10. *Verbal communication.* What rules apply to verbal communication of classified data, including lectures and presentations?

11. *Updating documents.* What procedures relate to the updating of documents or computer files? What happens to obsolete copies of documents?

12. *Destruction of documents and records.* What action is taken when classified documents are destroyed? Paper documents should be shredded, and data on tape and disk should be erased.

13. *Lost documents.* What action is taken when documents are lost?

14. *Backup procedures.* How can backup procedures safeguarding the accidental loss of computer data be made secure?

15. *Enforcement.* What steps are taken to ensure that the regulations are enforced?

16. *Audits and spot-checks.* The functioning of the data security system should be audited periodically, and, more frequently, spot-checks should be made. The employees must be convinced that security is serious.

17. *Responsibility.* What are the responsibilities of different persons in seeing that the regulations are observed?

Table D.23. The Vital Records Program (Chapter 32)

OBJECTIVES

I. Identify those records that are vital to the organization's continued operation.
II. Establish means to protect them.
III. Establish means to reconstruct records within a reasonable time after they have been destroyed (by a disaster, etc.).

GRADATIONS OF VITALNESS

Approach 1 (The recommended approach) Records should be classified as either *vital* or *nonvital.*

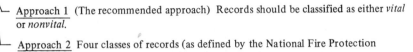

Approach 2 Four classes of records (as defined by the National Fire Protection Association):

(a) Vital records: Essential to operation, irreplaceable or needed immediately after catastrophe and cannot be quickly reproduced.

(b) Important records: Essential to operation, but can be reproduced without critical delay.

(c) Useful records: Inconvenient if lost, but loss would not prevent prompt restoration of operations after a catastrophe.

(d) Nonessential records: Not necessary to replace if lost.

PROGRAM STORAGE

Programs are "vital" items. An up-to-date package should be stored at intervals which may include the following:

1. The most recent coding on magnetic tape.

2. A complete set of test data on magnetic tape, with the results it should produce.

3. A listing of symbolic and actual coding, flow charts and diagrams, on paper or tape.

4. Details of the required computer configuration, I/O units, and operating system.

5. Complete documentation, including program description and purposes, record formats and block lengths, recording densities, special symbols or formulas, the balancing and accounting controls used, and data recovery instructions.

6. Preprocessing instructions and procedures, including control cards, switch settings, tape unit addresses, etc.

7. Processing instructions such as halt registers, error procedures, and checkpoint and restart procedures.

TYPES OF PROTECTION FOR VITAL RECORDS

Dispersion (Multiple copies in existence)

Natural dispersion (many people need a copy)
Planned dispersion (e.g., distribution list deliberately extended to off-site locations)

Duplicate copy is written (often during the run which produces the prime copy). Duplicate is stored off-site

Natural reconstruction capability (e.g., Grandfather–Father–Son tapes)

Table D.23. (continued)

TYPES OF PROTECTION FOR VITAL RECORDS (continued)

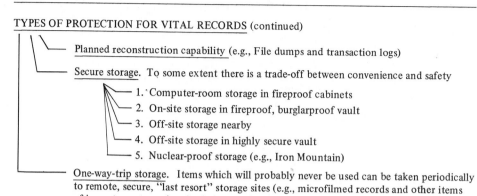

Planned reconstruction capability (e.g., File dumps and transaction logs)

Secure storage. To some extent there is a trade-off between convenience and safety

    1. Computer-room storage in fireproof cabinets

    2. On-site storage in fireproof, burglarproof vault

    3. Off-site storage nearby

    4. Off-site storage in highly secure vault

    5. Nuclear-proof storage (e.g., Iron Mountain)

One-way-trip storage. Items which will probably never be used can be taken periodically to remote, secure, "last resort" storage sites (e.g., microfilmed records and other items of importance to society in the event of total catastrophe)

TESTING

The vital records program *must* work when needed and hence should be tested by simulating disaster

    1. All-embracing test at night or week-end

    2. Nondisruptive sequence of sample recovery problems

Table D.24. Physical Security for Protection Against Theft and Sabotage

FOUR LAYERS OF DEFENSE

- Perimeter barrier
- Building exterior (doors, windows, walls, roof, manholes, storm drains, utility tunnels, fire escape, elevator penthouses, etc.)
- Locked rooms and protected areas
- Burglar-resistant safes, cabinets, and vaults

EACH LAYER CAN HAVE:

- Physical impenetrability
- Guard patrols
- Intruder detection devices
- Reactions to intruder detection:
  - Guards
  - Police
  - Frighten intruder away with siren or bell
  - Trap intruder, as in a double-door "man trap," (not generally recommended)

TYPES OF INTRUDER DETECTION DEVICES

- an electrical circuit is broken
  - microswitch
  - magnetic switch (harder to prevent switch from operating)
- an electrical circuit is made (e.g., microswitch under mat)
- a light beam is broken
- a laser beam is broken (longer beam path between mirrors; false light source cannot be substituted for the beam)
- An ultraviolet beam is broken
- An infrared beam is broken   } advantage: invisible to intruder
- Sound or vibration detector
- Ultrasonic detector of movement in a room
- Radar detector of movement in a room
- Variation in an electrical field detects the presence of a person
- Theft detector. (Items such as tape reels have a special label which will be detected electronically if a person tries to remove an item from the area)
- Closed-circuit TV (sometimes remotely controlled)

OTHER DEVICES

Time-lapse movie camera (e.g., one 8 mm frame every ten seconds) to record who is in an area

Guard console (see Table D.25)

Such equipment should be part of an integrated security plan. Isolated gadgetry should be avoided

Table D.24. (continued)

FOUR TYPES OF SECURE LOCATION

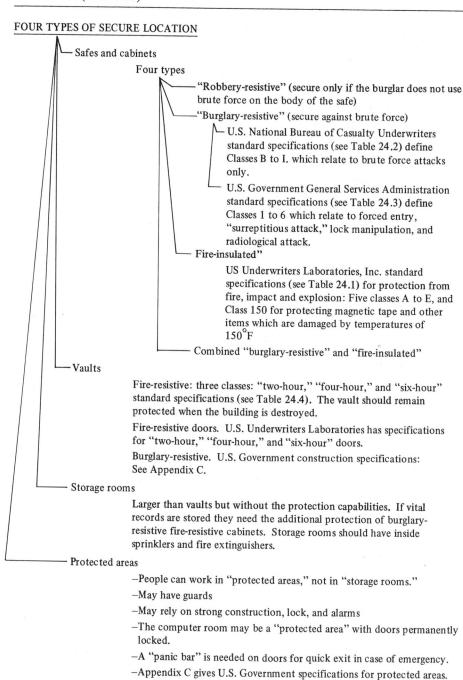

Safes and cabinets

Four types

"Robbery-resistive" (secure only if the burglar does not use brute force on the body of the safe)

"Burglary-resistive" (secure against brute force)

U.S. National Bureau of Casualty Underwriters standard specifications (see Table 24.2) define Classes B to I. which relate to brute force attacks only.

U.S. Government General Services Administration standard specifications (see Table 24.3) define Classes 1 to 6 which relate to forced entry, "surreptitious attack," lock manipulation, and radiological attack.

Fire-insulated"

US Underwriters Laboratories, Inc. standard specifications (see Table 24.1) for protection from fire, impact and explosion: Five classes A to E, and Class 150 for protecting magnetic tape and other items which are damaged by temperatures of $150°F$

Combined "burglary-resistive" and "fire-insulated"

Vaults

Fire-resistive: three classes: "two-hour," "four-hour," and "six-hour" standard specifications (see Table 24.4). The vault should remain protected when the building is destroyed.

Fire-resistive doors. U.S. Underwriters Laboratories has specifications for "two-hour," "four-hour," and "six-hour" doors.

Burglary-resistive. U.S. Government construction specifications: See Appendix C.

Storage rooms

Larger than vaults but without the protection capabilities. If vital records are stored they need the additional protection of burglary-resistive fire-resistive cabinets. Storage rooms should have inside sprinklers and fire extinguishers.

Protected areas

–People can work in "protected areas," not in "storage rooms."

–May have guards

–May rely on strong construction, lock, and alarms

–The computer room may be a "protected area" with doors permanently locked.

–A "panic bar" is needed on doors for quick exit in case of emergency.

–Appendix C gives U.S. Government specifications for protected areas.

Table D.25. Possible Components of an Electronic Security System

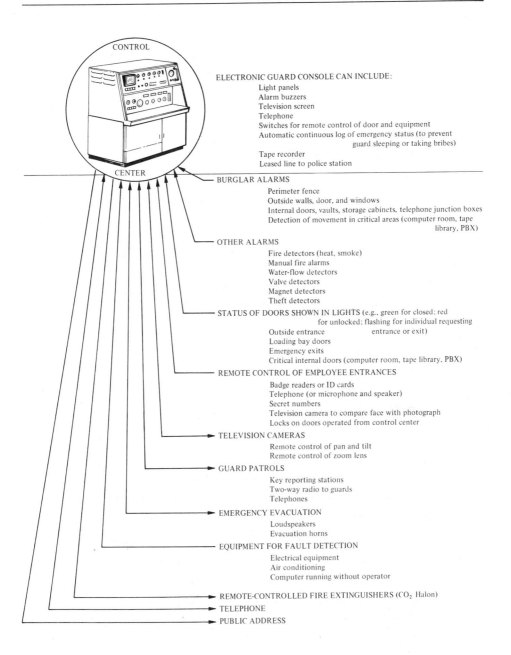

ELECTRONIC GUARD CONSOLE CAN INCLUDE:
 Light panels
 Alarm buzzers
 Television screen
 Telephone
 Switches for remote control of door and equipment
 Automatic continuous log of emergency status (to prevent
          guard sleeping or taking bribes)
 Tape recorder
 Leased line to police station

BURGLAR ALARMS
 Perimeter fence
 Outside walls, door, and windows
 Internal doors, vaults, storage cabinets, telephone junction boxes
 Detection of movement in critical areas (computer room, tape
            library, PBX)

OTHER ALARMS
 Fire detectors (heat, smoke)
 Manual fire alarms
 Water-flow detectors
 Valve detectors
 Magnet detectors
 Theft detectors

STATUS OF DOORS SHOWN IN LIGHTS (e.g., green for closed; red
        for unlocked; flashing for individual requesting
 Outside entrance   entrance or exit)
 Loading bay doors
 Emergency exits
 Critical internal doors (computer room, tape library, PBX)

REMOTE CONTROL OF EMPLOYEE ENTRANCES
 Badge readers or ID cards
 Telephone (or microphone and speaker)
 Secret numbers
 Television camera to compare face with photograph
 Locks on doors operated from control center

TELEVISION CAMERAS
 Remote control of pan and tilt
 Remote control of zoom lens

GUARD PATROLS
 Key reporting stations
 Two-way radio to guards
 Telephones

EMERGENCY EVACUATION
 Loudspeakers
 Evacuation horns

EQUIPMENT FOR FAULT DETECTION
 Electrical equipment
 Air conditioning
 Computer running without operator

REMOTE-CONTROLLED FIRE EXTINGUISHERS (CO_2 Halon)

TELEPHONE

PUBLIC ADDRESS

Table D.26. Protection from Fire and Other Disasters (Chapter 26)

FIRE EXTINGUISHERS

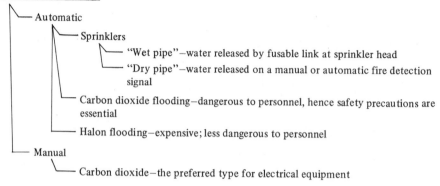

- Automatic
  - Sprinklers
    - "Wet pipe"—water released by fusable link at sprinkler head
    - "Dry pipe"—water released on a manual or automatic fire detection signal
  - Carbon dioxide flooding—dangerous to personnel, hence safety precautions are essential
  - Halon flooding—expensive; less dangerous to personnel
- Manual
  - Carbon dioxide—the preferred type for electrical equipment

FIRE DETECTORS

- Fusable links in sprinkler nozzles—do not detect electrical fires in time to prevent severe equipment damage. Not recommended
- Heat detectors—often do not detect localized electrical fires
- Smoke detectors—the most sensitive but prone to give false alarms. Recommended for use when an operator is present.

Other detection instrumentation—see Table D.25.

OTHER MEASURES NECESSARY

1. Personnel must be trained so that they know what to do about fire.

2. Their knowledge of what to do in case of fire should be periodically tested.

3. Explicit fire instructions must be posted in obvious positions.

4. Power-off instructions must be posted (see Table 26.3).

5. The power-off pull switches must be obvious and unobstructed.

6. The portable fire extinguishers must be obvious, strategically located, and unobstructed.

7. Fire detectors should be tested and extinguishers checked periodically.

8. Emergency escape routes must be well-designed and must be kept unobstructed.

9. Smoke detectors should be in the ceiling, in the air ducts, and under the raised floor.

10. The emergency power-off switch should shut off the air conditioning.

11. The computer room construction should be such as to minimize the chance of fire spreading to the area from outside.

12. Areas adjoining the computer area should be well-protected from fire.

13. The fire detectors should automatically signal an external location (guard post, head office, local fire station) with 24-hour coverage.

14. Combustible materials should be removed from the computer room.

Table D.26. (continued)

OTHER MEASURES NECESSARY (continued)

15. The computer area should be cleaned thoroughly (including the space under the false floor).

16. The materials used in the false floor, ceiling, and computer room facilities should be noncombustible.

17. Thorough contingency planning is needed in case of fire.

18. Duplicate programs and records should be stored away from the area where the originals are stored.

19. Good insurance coverage is needed.

It is recommended that the U.S. National Fire Protection Association pamphlets listed at the end of Chapter 26 be studied.

Other types of disaster should be considered.

— Flood (usually from plumbing failures)

— Storm damage

— Mobs, riots, looting

— Earthquakes

— Explosions and unpredictable catastrophes

See Table D.29, Part 8.

Table D.27. Insurance

For specimen policies, see Appendix E.

Insurance may cover the following losses:

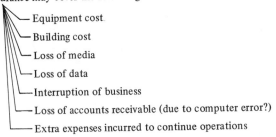

- Equipment cost
- Building cost
- Loss of media
- Loss of data
- Interruption of business
- Loss of accounts receivable (due to computer error?)
- Extra expenses incurred to continue operations

The insurance program should consider the following:

- Fire
- Natural disaster
- Water damage
- Power failure
- Fraud
- Crime
- Sabotage
- Errors

It should be established what security safeguards can lower the insurance premium.

Table D.28. Auditing Techniques

AUDITING TECHNIQUES

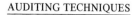

    — External auditors (public accountants, consultants)

    — Internal auditors

          —Must be independent of the data processing group

          —Should cover all aspects of the system and its environment (Fig. 37.1)

    — The data processing manager's auditors and temporarily convened auditing committees

Stages of auditing:

    — Auditing at the design stage (increasingly important as the level of automation increases)

    — Preconversion auditing

    — Auditing of the operational system (requires different talents and knowledge than the two audits above.)

TECHNIQUES

    —Sampling. Selected items—e.g., customer orders—are investigated in detail.—Must be followed all the way back to the source or to the tangible entity; must not stop short at a document or record which could be false (as on Equity Funding).

    —Audit Trial (Also called "Management trial")

        —Maintained by computer so that transaction history may be followed

            — On printed listings

            — On punched cards

            — On serial-access volumes (e.g., tape)

            — On direct-access volumes so that items may be displayed on terminals at random

    — Spot-Checks

          — On records of the Input/Output Control Section

          — On the quality control reports

          — On the operator's log

          — On the transaction journals

          — On the volume library log

          — On the log of security procedural violations

          — Security officer's log

          — Authorization tables

    — Question Lists and Checklists

          Installation-independent checklist

          Checklist compiled for a specific installation.

          Table D.29 gives specimen checklists. Checklists may cover areas such as the following:

          1. Controls on personnel

          2. Controls on sensitive programs

Table D.28. (continued)

Question Lists and Checklists (continued)

      3. Controls on new programs and changes
      4. Input/output controls
      5. Accuracy controls
      6. Quality control
      7. Tape and disk library
      8. Security of remote terminal access
      9. Software security
    10. Computer center operations
    11. File reconstruction capability
    12. Physical protection of records
    13. Physical security for theft protection
    14. Fire precautions
    15. Precautions against other physical disasters
    16. Disaster contingency plan
    17. Documentation
    18. Controls on classified documents
    19. Department administration
    20. Equipment accountability and billing
    21. Charges to user departments
    22. Insurance

Invalid transactions fed to a system to test its validity checks (specimens in Table D.30)

A counter-security group, suitably knowledgeable and ingenious, attempt to bypass the safeguards.

Pseudotransactions, which produce known results, are processed with the live transactions to check that all is working as it should.

Pseudorecords, which are updated and included in the file-scanning runs, to test the file balancing and control procedures

An auditor's test deck is processed to check that the system is working correctly and detecting invalid items.

Table D.29. Specimen Checklists for Auditors

The following checklists are based on actual questionnaires that are in effective use in several different organizations.

Checklists for accuracy control, control of terminal operators, physical theft protection, file construction software features, and control of classified documents are not included as these are dealt with at length in the earlier tables.

Table D.29 is presented on pages 552-574.

Table D.29. (continued)

		Not Applicable	Scope of Review %-Period-Quantity	Satisfactory	Unsatisfactory	Scheduled for Implementation On	Workpaper Reference
1. CONTROLS ON PERSONNEL							
Are responsibilities divided so that fraud cannot be carried out without collusion?							
Are departments and close associates separated so as to minimize the likelihood of collusion?							
Are personnel handling the corporation's assets entirely separate from personnel involved in data processing?							
Are background checks performed on all new hires?							
Are critical personnel bonded?							
Do managers know their subordinates sufficiently well to detect disgruntled employees, or employees who are in trouble; who might be a threat to the installation?							
Can employees who constitute a threat be transferred or dismissed immediately?							
Are critical jobs rotated periodically?							
Are employees cross-trained so that if any critical employee becomes unable to do his job another can immediately take it over?							
Is the level of training sufficiently high?							
Is there a continuing education program?							
Is security included in this program?							
Do all personnel take security seriously?							
Are casual practices—such as leaving classified documents unlocked—to be found?							
Is a "clean desk" policy enforced?							
Controls on programmers—See Table D.19							

Table D.29. (continued)

	Not·Applicable	Scope of Review %-Period-Quantity	Satisfactory	Unsatisfactory	Scheduled for Implementation On	Workpaper Reference
2. SENSITIVE PROGRAMS						

Definition of a "sensitive" program:

A sensitive program is one in which a programmer can, by changing program instructions *only*, misappropriate company assets and conceal the act even though adequate administrative processing controls are in place. They are the programs in the system where important internal control tests are made. The more sensitive areas have been identified as Payroll, Accounts Payable, Fixed Assets, Purchasing, and Inventory Control.

(Note: Although there may be many programs in a given system, such as Accounts Payable, only a small number may contain internal control tests. These should be identified as the sensitive programs. The other programs should not be identified as such. To identify all programs in Payroll, Accounts Payable, etc, as sensitive defeats the purpose of the control which is to establish reasonable protection from programming fraud without burdening the location. Controls over unnecessary programs make the controls costly and less effective.)

1. Is there a control list for sensitive programs identifying the responsible programmer and his manager?

2. Is there adequate separation of maintenance responsibility for sensitive programs between programmers?

3. Are programs and documentation stored in a secure location to prevent unauthorized access? Each storage area should maintain a log that shows the program requestor's name, date, and authorization reference.

4. Is unauthorized patching and changing of sensitive programs prevented, or could a programmer or operator bypass the safeguards?

5. Does an independent party review all requests for updates to sensitive programs, and advise management of questionable changes?

6. Is there controlled maintenance of a history of assembled programs? Local management discretion should be used on the number of documented changes to be maintained, since frequency of change will vary by program.

7. Are there sufficiently frequent unannounced periodic audits of program changes for authorization and documentation?

Table D.29. (continued)

3. NEW PROGRAMS AND PROGRAM CHANGES	Not Applicable	Scope of Review %-Period-Quantity	Satisfactory	Unsatisfactory	Scheduled for Implementation On	Workpaper Reference
1. Are new programs and changes to existing programs reviewed and approved by programming management?						
2. Does a knowledgeable person within the controller's function also review these new programs and program changes and the program documentation on an unannounced basis (at least semiannually)?						
3. Does this review and approval include the final program listing?						
4. Is there an operating procedure covering request for service explaining approvals required, economic justification, and method of notifying requestor of acceptance?						
5. Select a representative sample of permanent and one-time computer jobs and trace for:						
(a) Are all jobs or revisions supported by a written request for DP Service?						
(b) Are requests for jobs properly approved by using department management as well as appropriate information Systems Manager?						
(c) Is economic or other justification adequate?						
(d) Is Information Systems replying to the requestor indicating acceptance or rejection of request within time limits established?						
(e) Are estimate/agreement forms properly prepared and approved?						
(f) Is program documentation adequate and maintained current?						
6. Is there a procedure or practice established that prevents programs from being changed without the knowledge and consent of the user's department?						
7. Review priorities assigned to program requests that have been received but not actioned.						
8. Does "user department" management formally review and approve?						
(a) New programs and program changes during the design phase?						
(b) Data used to test programs and the results of these tests?						

Table D.29. (continued)

3. NEW PROGRAMS AND PROGRAM CHANGES (continued)	Not Applicable	Scope of Review %—Period-Quantity	Satisfactory	Unsatisfactory	Scheduled for Implementation On	Workpaper Reference
(c) New and changed programs after the parallel runs? These reviews should be especially concerned with insuring that there are adequate manual and computer-developed control totals to ensure correct processing.						
9. Is a history maintained of changes to these programs?						
10. Will the Computer Room accept a new or changed program without the above approvals being evident?						
11. Have controls been established to insure that review and approval procedures have not been bypassed? Several techniques that can be used to detect unauthorized changes.						
(a) Control the final program assembly to ensure that the approved program is being used.						
(b) Have a program that compares a controlled duplicate machine language deck to those installed and used in the Computer Room.						
(c) Establish predetermined hash totals (e.g., a count of the number of bits—binary digits—in the program steps) for critical programs to help ensure that the proper programs are used.						
(d) Use predesigned control data to test the program and verify its output.						
12. Are program files maintained that show original write-up in understandable language?						
13. Are systems analysts' reports, coding sheets with comments, printouts, or original programs and program changes retained?						
14. Are these flow charts, coding sheet comments, program printouts, and operator instructions revised each time a program change is made.						
15. What controls exist to ensure that all the above documents are updated at the same time?						
16. Are program tests and debugging supervised and documented?						
17. Is there a complete record of all versions of the programs used during unit and system test, parallel runs, etc.?						

Table D.29. (continued)

	Not Applicable	Scope of Review %–Period-Quantity	Satisfactory	Unsatisfactory	Scheduled for Implementation On	Workpaper Reference
3. NEW PROGRAMS AND PROGRAM CHANGES (continued)						
18. Are they effectively deleted from machine library after finishing development of maintenance testing?						
19. Are patches permitted? If so are they adequately documented?						
(a) Is program (source) listing annotated with patch no., date, and explanation; also has source deck been updated?						
(b) Are operators' instructions revised to include steps to be taken in the event of program failure due to incorrect patches? (Patches are not always tested, therefore failure may occur in the run immediately after adding the patch card.) (No revision to operators' instructions should be permanent as patch may affect the exception routine that is performed infrequently by the computer.)						

Table D.29. (continued)

	Not Applicable	Scope of Review %-Period-Quantity	Satisfactory	Unsatisfactory	Scheduled for Implementation On	Workpaper Reference
4. INPUT/OUTPUT CONTROLS						
1. What controls exist for input of sensitive data from point of origin?						
2. What controls exist for the distribution of output to designated areas?						
3. Are controls established for point of origin review of rejected sensitive transactions?						
4. What type of controls are established for correcting errors in input/output with the point of origin?						
5. Are predetermined totals or item counts maintained within the DP operation and compared with keypunch, unit record, or computer output prior to being sent to the customers? The person maintaining the controls should not be involved in processing the data.						
6. Keypunching—are all important data fields subject to mechanical verification by operators using verifier machines?						
7. Are limit checks included in appropriate programs? On input? On output? Is appropriate action taken when limit checks are violated?						
8. Review the controls listed in Tables D.8 and D.12. Should any of these be added to the controls currently in existence?						
9. Is appropriate segregation of duties in effect for persons who handle sensitive data?						
10. Are data control personnel provided with schedules listing the dates that programs will be run, the due in and due out times, the dates for customers providing input data and the date for distribution of output. Schedulers should monitor the flow of work. *Note:* This will facilitate the flow of work to the computer and reduce idle time awaiting input.						
11. Is the backlog of jobs reasonable? Review for excessive delays.						
12. Is rerun time due to error by operator, programmer, or other Information Systems personnel segregated and charged to department overhead?						

Table D.29. (continued)

	Not Applicable	Scope of Review %–Period-Quantity	Satisfactory	Unsatisfactory	Scheduled for Implementation On	Workpaper Reference
4. INPUT/OUTPUT CONTROLS (continued)						
13. Has responsibility been established for following up all input errors to ensure that they are properly corrected and returned for processing?						
14. Are the exceptions (or significant events) logged by Machine Operators reviewed by management and is action taken?						
15. Are reasons determined and corrective action taken for rerun hours (machine-operator-input-program)?						
16. Are all significant deviations from targets established for "hands on" time rerun checked?						
17. What is done about low utilization machines and over-load situations?						
18. To test the system's validation controls, the auditor should feed in invalid transactions and see what the system does with them.						

Table D.29. (continued)

5. TAPE AND DISK LIBRARY	Not Applicable	Scope of Review %-Period-Quantity	Satisfactory	Unsatisfactory	Scheduled for Implementation On	Workpaper Reference
1. Are magnetic tapes, disk packs, and data cells stored in a closed, dust free, fire resistant, and lockable library area? (Under no circumstances should these items, which have magnetic attraction to paper dust, be used or kept where card equipment or paper cutting devices are used.)						
2. Does the library have a sprinkler system and automatic fire alarm for added protection?						
3. Is there one person who is responsible for administration of the Tape Library? (Either a Librarian or Scheduling Clerk.)						
4. Are all shifts covered for tape library operation?						
5. Is access to the library restricted to authorized personnel only? Key listing maintained?						
6. Is there an inventory list of tapes, disk packs, and data cells? Minimum information should include: (a) Library location (b) Reel or serial number (c) Job or project number (d) Description of data (e) Date created (f) Expiration of retention period (Optimum controls could be achieved by having several listings sorted by (a), (b), (c), and (f) above.)						
7. Is there a tape retention plan (security) which permits the reconstruction of the tape file in the event that the file is inadvertently destroyed?						
8. Is confidential material identified? Stored in locked cabinets within the library? Is there also strict accountability for copies of confidential material?						
9. Are periodic inventories taken and reconciled against previous inventory listings? Are variances resolved or explained?						
10. Are the controls over ordering additional or replacement inventory adequate? (a) Old tapes, disk packs, and data cells should be degaussed or blanked out before they are destroyed.						

Table D.29. (continued)

	Not Applicable	Scope of Review %–Period–Quantity	Satisfactory	Unsatisfactory	Scheduled for Implementation On	Workpaper Reference
5. TAPE AND DISK LIBRARY (continued)						
(b) When new tapes are received in the tape library, the tapes should be recorded as part of the inventory.						
(c) The library manager should certify destruction of all "bad" tapes.						
(d) Lost tapes to be written off should be documented and approved by the library manager.						
11. Is there a secure off-site storage facility for maintaining backup copies of vital data programs, and documentation?						
12. Are there current listings of personnel authorized to sign out:						
(a) Confidential material?						
(b) Nonconfidential material?						
13. Are sign-out logs utilized for material borrowed? Are return dates indicated?						
14. Are borrowed tapes, disks or data cells containing confidential information supported by approvals from both Using and Programming Department Managers? (Generally there is little reason why this information has to be removed from the computer facility.)						
15. Review the procedure for shipments to other locations to determine if:						
(a) The shipment is sufficiently protected from damage? Insured?						
(b) Interlocation billing is rendered if shipping is on a nonreturn basis?						
(c) Shipments are sent directly to corresponding Tape Library?						
(d) Return due date indicated?						
16. Is there an effective procedure for following up "delinquent" returns of borrowed material?						
17. Is there a documented and implemented data retention system to ensure that obsolete material is not needlessly retained?						
18. Determine whether tape reserves or stockpiling of "scratch" tapes by individuals or departments is adequately controlled. (Weaknesses in 14, 15, and 16 could lead to a shortage of tapes for use by the Tape						

Table D.29. (continued)

5. TAPE AND DISK LIBRARY (continued)	Not Applicable	Scope of Review %-Period-Quantity	Satisfactory	Unsatisfactory	Scheduled for Implementation On	Workpaper Reference
Library and could cause the purchase of the tapes that are not really needed.)						
19. Possession of material borrowed from other locations should be documented by:						
(a) Name of requestor						
(b) Date received						
(c) Due date to return						
(d) Lending location						
20. Are separate schedules for teleprocessing tape transceivals maintained and updated on a consistent basis? Does the tape librarian follow up on these schedules to ensure that the tapes are transmitted or received on time?						
21. Review the Master tape replacement operation?						
(a) Is the old Master retained pending run verification?						
(b) Is the old Master monitored by the tape librarian to prevent misuse or premature scratching?						
(c) Is the entire replacement operation performed and controlled by the Tape Librarian?						
(d) Son-Father-Grandfather theory used?						
22. Do operating procedures exist concerning the overall tape library function? Are they adhered to?						
23. Do procedures include periodic review of jobs (programs) using Master or Dedicated tapes?						
24. Select a representative sample of jobs using Master tapes.						
(a) Are programs obsolete?						
(b) Is it necessary to use dedicated tapes?						
(d) Are an excessive number of tapes used?						
(d) Is the retention period in agreement with corporate instructions?						
25. Is there a listing maintained by job number and tape location in the tape library?						
26. Review the operating budget and statements applicable to the tape library (if any). Investigate any noticeable inconsistencies.						

Table D.29. (continued)

	Not Applicable	Scope of Review %-Period-Quantity	Satisfactory	Unsatisfactory	Scheduled for Implementation On	Workpaper Reference
5. TAPE AND DISK LIBRARY (continued)						
27. Do systems and programming managers receive reports for release of tapes and deletion of programs as a result of periodic tape utilization review?						
28. Are job control sheets consistent and do they accurately record the reel numbers used?						
29. Are tape reels clearly identified as to job number, reel number, storage location, etc.?						
30. Determine the accuracy of tape library control records.						
31. Examine tapes in all programming departments and any other departments which use a large amount of tapes. Test check the tape library's records to determine that these tapes have been properly signed out—especially check the records of tapes that have been loaned out for a long time.						
32. Are the following exceptions identified and resolved on a timely basis?						
(a) Tapes on loan in excess of maximum borrowing period.						
(b) Tapes not located in periodic inventories.						
(c) Tapes authorized for release by systems and programming but not found.						
(d) Tapes for which responsible person is not identified.						
33. Check the "programmers hold area" and programming department for any:						
(a) Unauthorized possession of tapes, especially Master or Confidential tapes.						
(b) Stockpiling or nonuse of Scratch and Testing tapes, resulting in a shortage of tapes for use by the tape library.						
34. Determine if any tapes have been restricted for one individual or department's use for an extended period of time.						
35. Follow-up for return of Confidential tape to locked cabinet?						
36. Is there follow-up for release of dormant restricted tapes?						

Table D.29. (continued)

	Not Applicable	Scope of Review %-Period-Quantity	Satisfactory	Unsatisfactory	Scheduled for Implementation On	Workpaper Reference
6. COMPUTER CENTER OPERATIONS						
1. Have computer center operating procedures been written?						
(a) Are they sufficiently descriptive in detail to guide the organization and operation?						
(b) Are they kept up-to-date?						
(c) Does the computer center operate independent of the programming area?						
2. Do operators' instructions for running each job include:						
(a) Identification of all machine components used and purpose?						
(b) Identification of all input/output forms?						
(c) Explanation of purpose of run?						
(d) Detailed input and output disposition instructions?						
(e) Identification of all possible programmed halts and prescribed restart instructions?						
3. Is an operating log maintained to record any significant events and action taken by the operator? (Proper recording would indicate whether operators were following instructions for halts in programs, etc.)						
4. Is the operator log inspected daily by management?						
5. Are the pages of the operator log prenumbered, or is some other method used to ensure total accountability?						
6. Are data control center personnel and operators' assignments rotated? (This not only aids in cross-training, it helps avoid fraudulent manipulation of jobs.)						
7. Are logs maintained to record the CPU meter readings (for both customer and CE meters) at the start and end of each shift? Are variances explained?						
8. Are CE maintenance logs kept current? (These logs are especially important when recording reruns caused by machine failures. This time should be claimed against any additional billable time.)						
9. Are trouble reports prepared when processing is interrupted because of operator or program(mer) error or machine failure? (The reports should indicate what caused the problem and what action was taken.)						
10. Are computer room personnel the only individuals allowed to operate the machines?						

Table D.29. (continued)

	Not Applicable	Scope of Review %–Period-Quantity	Satisfactory	Unsatisfactory	Scheduled for Implementation On	Workpaper Reference
6. COMPUTER CENTER OPERATIONS (continued)						
11. If programmers operate the machine, is this time controlled?						
(a) Are programmers required to obtain written permission from their department manager for all "hands on" time?						
(b) Is management able to determine whether programmers are making excessive tests and assemblies due to poor programming techniques? Is control adequate?						
(c) Are targets for reasonable "hands on" time rerun due to operator or programmer error established?						
12. Are operators denied access to program flow charts, source decks, program listings, etc.? (The operator does not need access to these items to perform his duties. Consequently these items should be maintained outside of the computer room to prevent changes to programs or operation by computer operators.)						
13. Do programmers test their programs with "live data"? Are there procedures in effect to control this?						
14. Are adequate safeguards exercised to ensure that only authorized persons are permitted in computer or machine areas? Are these safeguards effective in practice?						
15. Do operators know what to do when an unauthorized person does come into the machine room and is intent upon stealing something or doing harm?						
16. Do the operators know what to do in the event of fire or other emergency?						
17. Is there a surveilling escort for all visitors?						
18. Are demonstrations controlled?						
19. Are computer operating staff adequately screened before hiring?						
20. Are all computer runs supported by a work request or other written authorizations? (This includes scheduled and nonscheduled production assemblies and tests.)						
21. Are the above approved by management? If not, are there other controls to ensure that *all* computer runs are justified?						

Table D.29. (continued)

	Not Applicable	Scope of Review %–Period-Quantity	Satisfactory	Unsatisfactory	Scheduled for Implementation On	Workpaper Reference
6. COMPUTER CENTER OPERATIONS (continued)						
22. Are there provisions for scheduling of jobs on the system? These provisions would include:						
(a) Due dates of input and output						
(b) Records covering delays in receipt of input; processing of data; delivery of output						
(c) Establishment and adherence to priorities						
23. Is all input data accompanied by control totals, or other control information (such as number of cards, reels of tape and records per tape, etc.)?						
24. Are control totals produced independently by the tape/disk/drum loading program?						
25. Are input, load, and output totals reconciled after processing?						
26. Input errors; Are the users provided with data error listings that report on the accuracy of their input data?						
27. Are there procedures to extend document control to such items as blank checks, stock certificates, etc.?						
28. Is adequate control maintained over the input and output data? (Trace the flow of operational data through the computer and/or machine room.)						
29. Are system utilization and usage reports distributed to management for their review of:						
(a) Operating system reporting						
(b) Productive time						
(c) Program test and assembly						
(d) Operating system generation (Sysgen)						
(e) CE maintenance time						
(f) Programmer "hands on" time						
(g) Demonstration time						
(h) Rerun time						
(i) Idle time						
(j) Power off time						
(k) Other (other location backup, etc.)						

Table D.29. (continued)

	Not Applicable	Scope of Review %–Period-Quantity	Satisfactory	Unsatisfactory	Scheduled for Implementation On	Workpaper Reference
6. COMPUTER CENTER OPERATIONS (continued)						
30. Is "productive time" broken down into scheduled and nonscheduled production? (Periodic comparison of productive to nonproductive time and scheduled to nonscheduled production is necessary to ensure reasonability. The Utilization Reports are also needed to evaluate system effectiveness and profitability; help plan manpower and hardware work loads; provide a basis for scheduling new job capacity.)						
31. Are "turn-around" (time on and time off the system) reports distributed for Management review?						
32. Are procedures for billing charges for computer usage and/or cost allocations, if applicable, based upon operating records?						
(a) Can departmental charges be reconciled back to the usage/utilization reports or turn-around reports?						
(b) Is rerun time caused by programmer, operator, systems personnel or machine error segregated and charged to overhead rather than to the using department?						
(c) If using departments are not charged for computer time, is there a procedure to ascertain the need for regularly scheduled production jobs?						

Table D.29. (continued)

7. FIRE PRECAUTIONS	Not Applicable	Scope of Review %–Period-Quantity	Satisfactory	Unsatisfactory	Scheduled for Implementation On	Workpaper Reference
1. Do the computer room operators know exactly what to do when the different types of fire emergencies occur?						
2. Do the other personnel know exactly what to do when fire emergencies occur?						
3. Are clear and adequate fire instructions posted in all locations?						
4. Are the fire alarm pull boxes and emergency power switches clearly visible and unobstructed?						
5. Are there enough fire alarm pull boxes in the computer area?						
6. Are the machine operators familiar with the different levels of power-off procedure (Table 26.3)?						
7. Are the operators trained periodically in fire fighting?						
8. Are the operators assigned individual responsibilities in case of fire?						
9. How frequently are fire drills held?						
10. Does the machine room have automatic extinguishers of the following types:						
(a) Sprinkler?						
(b) Carbon dioxide flooding?						
(c) Halon flooding?						
11. Does the computer also have portable extinguishers in suitable locations? Are these extinguishers immediately accessible and vividly marked?						
12. If carbon dioxide or halon flooding is used, are the personnel safety precautions adequate?						
13. If sprinklers are used, is a "dry-pipe" arrangement employed coupled to an appropriate fire detection system? And can the operator preempt the sprinkling while he extinguishes the fire manually (to prevent machine damage)?						
14. Is the water supply adequate?						
15. Is the fire detection system adequate?						

Table D.29. (continued)

	Not Applicable	Scope of Review %-Period-Quantity	Satisfactory	Unsatisfactory	Scheduled for Implementation On	Workpaper Reference
7. FIRE PRECAUTIONS (continued)						
16. Are smoke detectors used:						
(a) In the ceiling?						
(b) In the air ducts?						
(c) Under the raised floor?						
17. Are the smoke detectors tested sufficiently frequently?						
18. Are the extinguishers checked sufficiently frequently?						
19. Does the emergency power shutdown switch off the air conditioning?						
20. Is there emergency (battery operated) lighting in the computer room?						
21. Does the fire alarm sound:						
(a) Outside the computer area?						
(b) At a guard station?						
(c) At a headquarters location?						
(d) At the local fire station?						
22. Is there 24-hour coverage of alarm stations?						
23. Can emergency crews gain access to the installation without delay?						
24. Is smoking prohibited in the computer area?						
25. Are the following combustible materials avoided in the computer area:						
(a) Combustible curtains and rags?						
(b) Flammable cleaning fluids?						
(c) Paper and other supplies?						
26. Are the raised floors and hung ceiling noncombustible?						
27. Is the space under the raised floor cleaned regularly to remove fluff?						
28. Is the cleanliness of the computer area adequate?						
29. Are areas adjoining the computer area suitably protected from fire?						
30. Is the computer housed in a suitable building?						

Table D.29. (continued)

	Not Applicable	Scope of Review %-Period-Quantity	Satisfactory	Unsatisfactory	Scheduled for Implementation On	Workpaper Reference
7. FIRE PRECAUTIONS (continued)						
31. Can the walls, doors, partitions, and floors in the computer area resist the spread of fire?						
32. Are tapes and other data storage media stored away from the computer room?						
33. Are duplicate copies of all programs and important records stored away from the computer center?						
34. Is the fire insurance adequate?						

Table D.29. (continued)

8. OTHER PHYSICAL DISASTERS	Not Applicable	Scope of Review %–Period-Quantity	Satisfactory	Unsatisfactory	Scheduled for Implementation On	Workpaper Reference
1. Is the building structurally sound?						
2. Will it withstand hurricanes, high winds, flood, and earthquakes?						
3. Are the building and equipment correctly grounded for protection from damage by lightning?						
4. Will the computer room ceiling protect the room from flood water on the floor above?						
5. Are overhead water and steam pipes eliminated (except for sprinklers)? Are the computers excluded from basement areas which might flood?						
7. Will the drainage system take water away from the computers?						
8. Is there drainage under the raised floor?						
9. Is there a backup air-conditioning system?						
10. Are the air intakes covered with protective screening, and are they well above the street level?						
11. Is mob action or sabotage a probability?						
12. Does the installation have a "shop window," and if so, can the glass be broken?						
13. Have steps been taken to give the installation "low visibility"?						
14. Is the computer room visible from the street?						
15. Does the computer room have self-locking doors with "panic bars" on the inside?						
16. Is access to the building controlled by guards or other means?						
17. Does the installation have good liaison with the local police?						
18. Do the computer room personnel know how to handle unauthorized intruders?						
19. Do the personnel know how to handle telephone bomb threats and other disturbances?						
20. Is an electronic system used to detect intruders, flood water, etc. (see Table D.25)?						

Table D.29. (continued)

	Not Applicable	Scope of Review %-Period-Quantity	Satisfactory	Unsatisfactory	Scheduled for Implementation On	Workpaper Reference
8. OTHER PHYSICAL DISASTERS (continued)						
21. Is protection needed from power failures and "brownouts," and if so, is it adequate?						
22. Is the voltage monitored with a recording voltmeter?						
23. Is protection needed from communication line failures, and if so, are the alternate means of transmission (usually public dial lines) adequate?						
24. If the main telecommunication cable to the building fails, will this remove the alternate transmission capability also?						
25. Are the communication lines monitored for noise, errors, and dropouts?						
26. Are food and beverages banned in the computer room, or confined to a side table?						
27. Is there adequate insurance against:						
(a) Fire?						
(b) Natural disaster?						
(c) Water damage?						
(d) Power failure?						
(e) Fraud?						
(f) Crime?						
(g) Sabotage?						
(h) Errors?						
28. Does the insurance cover all losses including loss of data and loss of business?						

Table D.29. (continued)

	Not Applicable	Scope of Review %-Period-Quantity	Satisfactory	Unsatisfactory	Scheduled for Implementation On	Workpaper Reference
9. DOCUMENTATION						
1. Are there written documentation standards? Are they enforced before new systems are implemented or existing ones changed? Are the following included?						
(a) Systems flow chart showing the portion of the system that the program represents—equipment used, keypunch, unit record, computer, etc.						
(b) Program flow chart—logic of program instructions						
(c) Narrative description—what is the objective of the program? What data is the user receiving?						
(d) Program listing (printout of the source deck)						
(e) Sample of output (listings, cards, etc.)						
(f) Record layouts (data included in tape, disk, and punched card fields, etc.)						
2. Prior to installation, is there a program release sheet, signed-off by the: using department manager; programming manager; DP operations and systems manager(s)?						
3. Are all production programs or projects documented with run instructions? They should include:						
(a) Title and explanation of job						
(b) Due-in and due-out schedules						
(c) Deadline priorities						
(d) Set-up instructions						
(e) Programmed halt and restart instructions						
(f) Checkpoint—restart procedures						
(g) Data control total checks required						
(h) End of job—(take down) instructions						
(i) Disbursement of I/O data						
4. Are there overall operational standards for all projects? Are they kept current?						

Table D.29. (continued)

	Not Applicable	Scope of Review %–Period-Quantity	Satisfactory	Unsatisfactory	Scheduled for Implementation On	Workpaper Reference
10. FINANCIAL QUESTIONS						

1. *Equipment accountability and billing*

   (a) Are physical inventories taken periodically and reconciled to equipment rental invoices? The auditor should perform a physical inventory and reconcile to latest equipment rental invoices.

   (b) Is equipment rental being billed correctly?

   (c) Sample billable time authorizations submitted by DP and compare with additional use billing for systems.

   (d) Sample extra shift authorizations for unit record machines and compare to invoices. Do reports of extra shift usage appear reasonable compared to personnel assigned to second and third shifts and jobs run on second and third shifts?

2. *Accounting*

   (a) Review the bases on which direct and indirect costs are charged to the various phases of the projects. Do these methods appear logical and equitable?

   (b) If the amounts to be charged are based on forecasts, are the forecasting procedures formalized? (Reviewing the adjustments will give an idea of the causes of inaccurate charges.)

   (c) Are adjustments to the charges highlighted, (e.g., via a special account on the departmental operating statements)?

   (d) Are variances analyzed and used as a basis for judging efficiency of the operation?

3. *Funding and charging of costs*

   (a) Does the method of funding require prior approval of all users prior to proceeding through the various phases? (Prior approval probably restricts the ability of the project to perform its function efficiently.)

   (b) Are formalized procedures established to measure efficiency whether it be machine utilization, staffing of departments, or recovery of costs from users?

Table D.29. (continued)

10. FINANCIAL QUESTIONS (continued)	Not Applicable	Scope of Review %-Period-Quantity	Satisfactory	Unsatisfactory	Scheduled for Implementation On	Workpaper Reference
(c) Is the basis for charging out machine costs and overhead consistent throughout the financial cycle?						
(d) Are machine and overhead rates regularly reviewed and are adjustments made to these rates promptly where under/over recoveries differ widely from plan?						

Table D.30. A Specimen List of Invalid Transactions Which Auditors May Feed to a System to Test Its Validity Checks

The following are some of the types of invalid items that the auditors might try out on an accounts payable program:

1. Quantity invoiced exceeds quantity order by 10% but by no more than $300.00.

2. Quantity invoiced exceeds quantity ordered by $300.00 but by no more than 10%.

3. Invoice quantity multiplied by invoice unit price is greater than invoice quantity X purchase order unit price.

4. Set up and/or miscellaneous charge billed although not specified on purchase order.

5. Tool order invoiced although sample tooling has not been approved by receiving inspection.

6. Advise price invoice exceeds acceptable limit.

7. Discount terms on invoice less than that on purchase order.

8. Invoicing is against an order that has been cancelled.

9. Invoicing is for an order not on the purchase order master file.

10. Unit measure on invoice does not agree with that on purchase order. (Should be checked for more than one unit of measure.)

11. Invoicing of transportation charges for purchase order terms "F.O.B. Destination."

12. Duplicate payment of invoice paid previously.

13. Duplicate payment of invoice paid in same machine run.

14. Collect freight charge (via a consignee memo) for purchase order terms "F.O.B. Destination."

15. Duplicate freight charges are received (i.e., collect charges and invoice charges are received for same shipment).

16. Adjustment is made to invoicing and/or receiving quantities. (If accepted, adjustments should be listed on exception reports.)

17. Unit of measure routines working correctly for debit memos.

18. Quantity rejected on debit memo greater than quantity invoiced.

19. Debit memo processed but no corresponding order on purchase order master file.

Some of the tests listed above should also be tried for multiple invoicing situations. For example, the auditor may wish to submit an invoice with a quantity that is within the 10% overshipment limit but that when combined with a previous billing exceeds the 10% limit.

A list similar in principle but different in detail may be used with other types of program.

Table D.31. Forty Common Reasons for Inadequacy
in the Security of Computer Systems*

1. *Unconstrained or inadequately controlled access to the system area.* Very few installations afford a significant deterrent to the entry of persons seeking to steal magnetic storage media, paper output, or cards or damage the hardware.

   How much security is enough is a function of the value of the data, the cost of its protection, the value of intrusion to the intruder and his costs, including punishment.

2. *Vague or inadequately defined responsibilities for the security of data, systems, and programs.* Data and programs are assets just as are other more tangible things. Specific responsibilities for their protection must be firmly established if adequate security is to be achieved.

   In general, the person with physical control of an asset must have the immediate responsibility for the protection of that asset. In the case of data within the DP center, this person is the Center Manager. The internal auditors and the security administrators may and should review the adequacy of the protection afforded the data but, because they do not have physical control over it, they generally cannot be given the primary responsibility for its safety.

3. *Inadequate indoctrination of data processing personnel as to the importance of security and their individual responsibilities in achieving security.*

   Data processing people need to be acutely aware of the importance of their activities to the welfare of the enterprise. People generally respond well to a realization that they occupy positions of great trust and responsibility.

   Their alert, enthusiastic support of the security measures which are put in place is necessary to the achievement of a significant degree of security. Virtually no security measures are effective without the support of most operating personnel.

4. *Inadequate or nonexistent disciplinary measures where security is jeopardized or lost.*

5. *No protection against the destructive activities of disgruntled data processing personnel.* There are a number of instances where employes who were just discharged or who know that they are about to be discharged have destroyed files or modified them for their future benefit— for example, adding their names to the pension rolls or generating an excessively large terminal pay check.

   Prudence dictates procedures for the prompt and complete exclusion of all disgruntled, disaffected people, particularly those having special knowledge of the system, from opportunities to damage or otherwise modify the files or the physical facility.

6. *No data inventory or other measure of the value of the data holdings.* Data and programs are assets with determinable values.

   The proposal to put a dollar value on data on a file-by-file basis is generally greeted with considerable skepticism. It is, however, feasible in most cases and quite often produces rather surprising results.

7. *Inadequate threat assessment.* Such an analysis often leads to the rejection of many things previously considered to be problems and the inclusion of others which are quite important but less obvious.

8. *Operation in the reactionary mode only.* In some systems security measures have been incorporated primarily in reaction to well-publicized problems reported to have been encountered by others. This frequently leads to illogical responses to situations which frequently did not exist or which were so inaccurately described as to be grossly misleading.

   Included in this category are the magnets carried into the machine room which result in the erasure of all magnetic media in the area, the erasure of tapes and packs by airborne radar, and

---

*Robert H. Courtney, Jr. reproduced with permission from *Security Letter* Vol. 1, No. 19,
475 Fifth Ave., New York.

Table D.31. (continued)

the acquisition of proprietary business information by vans parked outside bristling with antennas and microphones eavesdropping on the computer.

Concern for the loss of data in these rather elegant ways can completely mask the attention which is due the pile of proprietary information which may be lying on the loading platform waiting for the trash man.

9. *Signs publicly identifying sensitive DP centers.* Prominent signs that identify the locations of such facilities invite the attention of potentially destructive groups.

It is true that a modestly determined effort by such groups can always result in finding the location of such facilities even if the signs are not there. However, such signs often draw their interest. If there are two potential targets to draw the attention of destructive people in an area, it is probable that they will take on the one whose location is known to them as opposed to disrupting the one whose location has to be determined with some effort.

10. *Inadequate criteria for the selection and implementation of fire detection and quenching systems and their interconnections, if any, with electrical power.*

More consideration frequently should be given to the use of fire retardant walls about areas from within which fire will probably not originate. This will save initial system installation costs and, with some quenching systems, damage from water in the event of fire.

11. *Vulnerable air conditioning installations.* There is a fairly large number of DP center air conditioning installations in which inadequate concern has been shown for the locations of the fresh air intakes.

Considerable disruption or damage can be caused, accidentally or intentionally, through ingestion of undesirable gases and vapors into these. Further, the air intake should be located so as to not invite the attention of those who would disrupt the operation. Some cooling towers are vulnerable in that they can be constructed or located so that a single rifle bullet can disable the water flow and subsequently cause the failure of the system.

12. *Exterior glass walls and windows in vulnerable locations.* The plastic glass substitutes will do a good job of deflecting thrown stones or incendiary materials and their cost is sufficiently low to make their installation economically feasible in most centers.

13. *Inadequate instructions and procedures in the event of fire or fire alarms.* Personnel expected to use fire extinguishers should be trained in their use. It is completely appropriate that they receive some classroom instruction in the mechanics of fire and then be taught to operate hand-held extinguishers followed by practice in allowing them to put out a fire in the parking lot or other suitable areas.

14. *Inadequate plans for protection against smoke damage.* Smoke, particularly that consisting primarily of heavy black particulate matter, can be very damaging and necessitate a lengthy and costly cleanup operation. Most smoke reaching into and damaging data processing systems originates from fires external to the data processing centers.

Fitted plastic covers for all of the equipment, desks, and storage cabinets can do much to reduce smoke damage. They are inexpensive and easily made.

15. *Inadequate protection against water damage.* Water damage can occur as a consequence of leaking roof top cooling towers, leaking roofs—even on new buildings—leaking pipes in the overhead, and the operation of sprinkler systems on floors above the data processing center. As mentioned in the preceding paragraph, fitted plastic covers are invaluable in protecting the equipment against water coming through the ceiling.

16. *Inadequate liaison with the local fire department.* Reaching an understanding with the local fire department prior to the time they are called in an emergency can be very rewarding.

The awareness of the fire department to the particular vulnerabilities of a system to extensive

Table D.31. (continued)

quantities of water coming through the overhead and the desirability of venting smoke in such a way as to minimize the amount reaching the data processing area is highly desirable.

17. *Inadequate liaison with the appropriate police departments.* It is important that DP center management and the plant or facilities personnel for security and a corporate attorney meet with senior representatives of the local police departments.

It is commonly and often erroneously believed that the police may be called to remove any trespassers from the property. They frequently will not do this except under particular, quite specific circumstances. These circumstances must be understood so that the reaction of the persons responsible for calling the police can be appropriate in the light of the particular service to be provided by them.

18. *Inadequate reliance on guards or an inadequate guard force for protection against civil disturbances.* The value of a single unarmed guard at the door as a deterrent against reasonably determined dissident groups bent on damaging or destroying a facility is commonly over-estimated. Similarly, the protection afforded by locked doors, particularly if they delay for entry for even a few minutes, is often overlooked. Dissident groups are quite aware generally that guards are usually unarmed or, if armed, are instructed not to fire.

It is appropriate to make a cost comparison between the cost of a fully effective guard force and the cost of a back-up facility which will afford a limp-along capability in the event the principle facility was lost through civil disturbance.

19. *Failure to include the peculiar requirements of the data processing center in establishing procedures and instructions for responding to bomb threats.* Most large organizations, particularly those which have had bomb threats, have developed a more or less standard response to such threats.

Less commonly, however, they have considered the peculiar requirements of the data processing center under such circumstances. If the established response to a bomb threat is to evacuate the entire facility, then consideration should be given to securing the DP center from intrusion by those who remain in the building.

The more valuable files, particularly including transportation logs, should be identified as part of a bomb threat response plan so that they can be properly protected or backed up, provided that an explosion actually occurs following the threat.

20. *Failure to properly assess the need for protection against power failures . . . or voltage reductions.* It is important to fully understand the peculiar needs of the specific DP center, including anticipated growth in power requirements, if operationally suitable and economically satisfactory solutions to these problems are to be determined.

21. *Too much or too little concern for the ability of magnets to damage magnetic storage media.* The ability of any magnet to erase data decreases very rapidly with distance. As a consequence, even very large magnets cannot damage data at distances in excess of a few inches—say 20 inches to be safe.

Except in unusual circumstances, distances of six to eight inches between the media and even very large magnets should prove adequate protection for the recording medium.

22. *No procedures for the control of portable transceivers.* These receivers will not disrupt data processing equipments. However, some portable transceivers, which provide the capacity for transmitting back to the caller, do have a potential for disrupting data processing equipment if they are operated in the immediate vicinity—such as in the DP center itself.

23. *Inadequately constrained access to terminals.* Terminals which are left unprotected are subject to misuse. Terminals which can be used to access system-managed data should be

Table D.31. (continued)

locked in a secure area or equipped with key-operated power on switches so that they cannot be used except by those who have the proper keys.

Similarly, consideration should be given to means for identifying the operators of the terminals to the system.

24. *Keys, combinations and passwords changed too infrequently.*

25. *Insecure operation of the working tape and disk libraries.* Procedures should be introduced to assure proper authorization of all withdrawals from the libraries, to assure limitation of access to only those people who must have access, to account for all material removed from the library, and to assure protection against fire, water, smoke and damage by disgruntled employees.

26. *Inadequate back-up files.* Relatively elaborate plans for the preparation and storage of back-up files are more common than are fully, or even partially implemented, workable plans.

27. *Failure to use the back-up files.* There is an unfortunately high probability that untested back-up files may be unusable files.

28. *Unavailable or untested back-up facilities.* The probability of incompatibility through configuration differences or feature mismatches is sufficiently great that such tests must be conducted if there is a real dependence on the availability of a back-up facility.

29. *Failure to identify or prioritize critical operations in planning use of back-up facilities and other recovery activities.* Recovery from disasters or major interruptions almost always implies a limp-along or degraded operation. It is important that the temporarily limited capability be expanded on the most critical activities—which is possible only if they have been properly identified.

30. *Inadequate procedures for the delivery of records to archival storage and their subsequent recovery.* Care should be given to the identification of representatives of the delivery service who transport materials to and from the archival storage.

31. *Inadequate control of scratch packs and tapes and other residual data.* Information can be disclosed to unauthorized persons when left on scratch packs and tapes which these persons will subsequently use.

32. *Inadequate attention to the cleanliness and neatness of operating areas.* All of the reasons for having neat, clean operating areas are too numerous to list here. However, they include the fire hazard generated by the accumulation of paper under the raised floor, the potential damage to equipment as a consequence of spilling coffee, milk and hot chocolate into system components, the ease with which various tapes or packs can be removed from the area if large numbers are allowed to accumulate, the fire hazard presented by excess storage of paper supplies, the fire hazards caused by smoking, and the false alarms created in smoke detection systems are just a few of the problems which may be encountered in sloppy operating areas.

33. *Poor procedures for receiving and storing paper supplies.* The receiving platform often affords the potential intruder ready access to the entire facility or opportunity of delivering incendiary materials with which he would destroy the facility.

34. *Exposure of sensitive data in the outgoing paper trash.* Sensitive data should be shredded by an appropriate shredder. As a minimum, boxes of cards should be dumped so that extreme efforts would be required to put them back in the proper groups and sequences.

35. *Inadequate procedures for the protection of programs, run instructions, object decks, etc.* Programs, instructions for their use, object decks and such materials must be afforded the same protection extended to the data.

Table D.31. (continued)

36. *Loose procedures for the control of application programs.* Particular concern must be given to the potential of the disgruntled programmer employee to do extensive damage through unauthorized program modification.

37. *Inadequate and nonexistent procedures for the control of paper output.* It is unfortunately common to see large volumes of sensitive information sitting about in offices and relatively available to large numbers of people. It is difficult to justify extensive security measures in the data processing center if adequate controls are not extended to the paper output from the system.

38. *Inadequate procedures and instructions for system operators.* One person whose disloyalty, poor judgement, or incompetence is most difficult to protect against is the system operator. Special attention should be given to determination of his loyalty, the latitude with which he is given to innovate and modify established procedures and run instructions for programs, and to the possibility of more firmly enforcing a two-operator rule.

39. *Failure to use audit trials or transaction logs as security measures.* An audit trial or complete transaction log can be a very effective security measure if it is properly used as such. Failure to provide a processor for the transaction log may wholly defeat its use as a security measure.

40. *Failure to test physical security measures and operating procedures to see if they are effective.* Reasonably frequent tests of security measures indicate a continuing awareness and concern for security and, for that reason, are in themselves a security measure in that they improve the sensitivity of employees toward security as a continuing problem.

E SPECIMEN INSURANCE POLICIES

Included below are specimen copies of data processing insurance policies offered by two separate companies.

The policies can be classified as "multiple peril insurance." Generally speaking, they insure against loss or damage resulting from *physical* mishaps: fire, lightning, flooding, burst water pipes, earthquakes, and the like. Damage .from student riots or local civil disturbances, from natural flooding and earthquake is generally covered unless the firm seeking insurance is in a particularly high risk area. Then, either no coverage is given, or a separate policy is written. The policies do not provide protection against electrical damage—for example, damage due to a brownout or blackout. A company suffering severe damage, however, may be able to recover their losses by applying to, or bringing suit against, the responsible power company.

The policies are broken down so that one may insure:

1. The "physical plant" or *"hardware"* (i.e., the CPU, terminals, tape drives, key punch machines and the like).
2. *The "media" and information contained thereon.* Thus, if a blank magnetic tape was lost in a fire, it would be replaced blank. If a magnetic tape containing unfilled customer orders and unpaid invoices was destroyed by fire, the value of the tape, plus the value of the lost information would be recovered, *but* only if the (approximate) value of the information had been first specified.
3. *The replacement or reconstruction cost, and the cost of doing business as normal.* The cost of reconstructing a tape of unfilled customer orders and unpaid invoices would be covered by the insurance, as well as the cost of providing normal service. This might involve renting time on equivalent equipment from a nearby company, paying overtime wages for reconstruction, detective work, etc.

A firm may elect any combination of coverage—it may be covered for hardware only, media or information only (say for a company that relied on time sharing for its data processing needs), or it may be covered for all three.

Perhaps the *key* factor in insurance coverage is setting adequate values on the items, particularly media items, to be insured.

Note that certain risks particularly applicable to data processing installations are not covered: damage to media from magnets, damage from power failure (blackout) or power cut (brownout), and damage from software failure.

1. A DATA-PROCESSING POLICY FROM CHUBB & SON INC.

Electronic Data Processing Policy

No. FMP

FEDERAL INSURANCE COMPANY

INCORPORATED UNDER THE LAWS OF NEW JERSEY

CHUBB & SON INC., *Manager* 90 John St., New York, N.Y. 10038

(A STOCK INSURANCE COMPANY, HEREIN CALLED THE COMPANY)

IN CONSIDERATION OF REQUIRED PREMIUM DOES INSURE

Insured

SPECIMEN

Address

This policy covers from   to

Noon, standard time at the address of the Insured as stated above.

1. WHAT IS COVERED AND LIMITS OF LIABILITY

This insurance applies only at the following location and to those Coverages for which a Limit of Liability is shown. This Company shall not be liable under any one Coverage for more than the Limit of Liability specified for that Coverage.

Location

Coverage	Limit of Liability		Property and Interest Covered
A	$	on	Electronic Data Processing Equipment listed in Paragraph 2.
B	$	on	Electronic Data Processing Media including the Information recorded therein.
C	$	on	Extra Expense as provided for in Paragraph 7 (c) not exceeding $ per

2. DESCRIPTION OF ELECTRONIC DATA PROCESSING EQUIPMENT

Quantity	Manufacturer, Serial and Model No.	Amount Insured
		$

Unscheduled Peripheral Equipment $

3. HOW COVERED

All risks of physical loss or damage except as provided in Paragraph 4.

4. LOSSES NOT COVERED

This policy does not insure:

(a) loss or damage caused by error in machine programming or instructions to machine;

(b) loss or damage caused by or resulting from latent defect, wear and tear, gradual deterioration;

(c) loss or damage caused by or arising out of infidelity by an employee of the Insured. A willful act of malicious intent shall be deemed not to be an act of infidelity;

(d) loss by nuclear reaction or nuclear radiation or radioactive contamination, all whether controlled or uncontrolled, and whether such loss be direct or indirect, proximate or remote, or be in whole or in part caused by, contributed to, or aggravated by the perils insured against in this policy; however, subject to the foregoing and all provisions of this policy, direct loss by fire resulting from nuclear reaction or nuclear radiation or radioactive contamination is insured against by this policy;

(e) loss or damage caused by (1) hostile or warlike action in time of peace or war, including action in hindering, combating, or defending against an actual, impending or expected attack, (a) by any government or sovereign power (de jure or de facto), or by any authority maintaining or using military, naval or air forces; or (b) by military, naval or air forces; or (c) by an agent of any such government, power, authority or forces; (2) any weapon of war employing atomic fission, atomic fusion, radioactive force or material whether in time of peace or war; (3) insurrection, rebellion, revolution, civil war, usurped power, or action taken by governmental authority in hindering, combating or defending against such an occurrence, seizure or destruction under quarantine or customs regulations, confiscation by order of any government or public authority, or risks of contraband or illegal transportation or trade;

(f) loss or damage occasioned by enforcement of any ordinance or law regulating the construction, repair, or demolition of any building or structure, nor by the suspension, lapse or cancellation of any lease, contract or order, nor for any interference at the location insured by strikers or other persons with rebuilding, repairing or replacing property or with the resumption or continuation of business.

5. EXTENSIONS OF COVERAGE

(a) **Newly Acquired Property** $100,000 at the location insured on newly acquired property of the kind insured under Coverage A subject to all conditions of this policy. Insurance under this extension shall cease 90 days from the date of acquisition, or on the placement of more specific insurance, whichever first occurs. If newly acquired property is to be covered under this policy additional premium shall be payable from the date of acquisition.

(b) **Transit $** applicable to property insured hereunder while in transit or temporarily located elsewhere within the United States of America and Canada. **The Insured agrees to notify this Company prior to moving any item scheduled in Paragraph 2.**

(c) **Removal** Such insurance as is afforded under Coverage A and B of this policy shall also apply while the property insured is being removed to or from and while at a place of safety because of imminent danger of loss or damage.

(d) **Debris Removal** This policy is extended to cover expenses incurred in the removal of all debris of the damaged property insured hereunder which may be occasioned by loss caused by any of the perils insured against in this policy. In no event shall the additional coverage granted by this paragraph increase the Limit of Liability specified in Paragraph 1.

6. WHAT TO DO WHEN LOSS OCCURS

(a) **Notice of Loss** The Insured shall as soon as practicable report to the Company or its agent every loss or damage which may become a claim under this policy.

(b) **Protection of Property** The Insured's primary duty is to act in every respect as if no insurance existed. The Insured shall employ every reasonable means to protect the property from further damage, including the prompt execution of temporary repairs where necessary for such protection and including the separation of damaged from undamaged property. The Company shall be liable for reasonable expense so incurred to minimize insured loss, but any payment under this provision shall not serve to increase the limit of liability that would otherwise apply at the time and place of loss.

(c) **Proof of Loss** The Insured shall file with the Company or its agent a detailed, sworn proof of loss within 90 days after date of loss.

7. HOW LOSS IS SETTLED

(a) Coverage A, Electronic Data Processing Equipment

The measure of recovery shall be the full cost of repair or replacement; if not replaced, actual cash value on date of loss.

(b) Coverage B, Electronic Data Processing Media and Information therein

The measure of recovery shall be the full cost of replacement or reproduction; if not replaced or reproduced, blank value of media.

(c) Coverage C, Extra Expense

The measure of recovery shall be the Extra Expense necessarily incurred to actually perform the operations normally performed by the Electronic Data Processing System:

(1) following damage to or destruction of property or information insured under Coverage A or B, or

(2) following suspension or reduction of the Insured's ability to use property or information insured under Coverage A or B due to damage to or destruction of the building(s) housing such property, the air conditioning system for such equipment, or the electrical system supplying such equipment, or

(3) for not exceeding a period of two weeks, when due to damage or destruction to the premises housing property insured access thereto is prohibited by order of civil authority

all as a direct result of a peril insured against under this policy.

Subject to the limit specified in Paragraph 1, insurance hereunder with respect to any one loss shall not be limited by the date of expiration of this policy and shall apply for such length of time as shall be required with the exercise of due diligence and dispatch to repair, rebuild or replace such property as has been destroyed or damaged.

Should insurance under this policy apply only to Coverage C, any reference in this Paragraph 7 (c) to Coverages A and B shall be construed as if coverage were actually provided under A and B.

(d) Deductible Clause, Coverages A and B

Each loss separately occurring under Coverage A or B shall be adjusted separately and from the amount of each adjusted loss the sum of $ shall be deducted. If such loss involves Coverages A and B, only one deductible shall apply.

(e) Deductible Clause, Coverage C

The sum of $ shall be deducted from the amount of each loss occurring separately.

8. GENERAL CONDITIONS

(a) Company's Options It shall always be optional with this Company to take all, or any part, of the property at the ascertained or appraised value or to repair or replace any property lost or damaged with other of like kind and quality within a reasonable time, on giving notice within 30 days after receipt of the proof herein required of its intention to do so.

(b) Abandonment There can be no abandonment to this Company of the property insured unless specifically agreed to by the Company.

(c) Property of Others At the option of the Company any loss to property or information of others may be adjusted with and paid to the owner of the property.

(d) Appraisal If the Insured and the Company fail to agree as to the amount of loss each shall, on the written demand of either, select a competent and disinterested appraiser, and notify the other of the appraiser selected within 20 days of such demand. The appraisal shall be made at a reasonable time and place. The appraisers shall first select a competent and disinterested umpire, and failing for 15 days to agree upon such umpire, then on request of the Insured or the Company, such umpire shall be selected by a judge of a court of record in the State in which the insured property is located. The appraisers shall then appraise the loss in accordance with the policy conditions, stating separately the amount of loss, and failing to agree shall submit their differences to the umpire.

An award in writing of any two shall determine the amount of loss. The Insured and the Company shall each pay his or its chosen appraiser and shall bear equally the other expenses of the appraisal and umpire. The Company shall not be held to have waived any of its rights by any act relating to appraisal.

8. GENERAL CONDITIONS (Continued)

(e) **Payment of Loss** All adjusted claims shall be paid or made good to the Insured within 30 days after presentation and acceptance of satisfactory proof of interest and loss at the office of this Company.

(f) **Reinstatement** Any loss paid hereunder shall not reduce the limits of liability.

(g) **Suit Against Company** No suit, action or proceeding for the recovery of any claim under this policy shall be sustainable in any court of law or equity unless the same be commenced within 12 months next after discovery by the Insured of the occurrence which gives rise to the claim. Provided, however, that if by the laws of the State within which this policy is issued such limitation is invalid, then any such claims shall be void unless such action, suit or proceeding be commenced within the shortest limit of time permitted by the laws of such State to be fixed herein.

(h) **Examination Under Oath** The Insured shall submit, and so far as is within his or their power shall cause all other persons interested in the property, including employees, to submit to examinations under oath by any persons named by the Company, relative to any and all matters in connection with a claim and subscribe the same; and shall produce for examination all books of account, bills, invoices, and other vouchers or certified copies thereof if originals be lost, at such reasonable time and place as may be designated by the Company or its representatives, and shall permit extracts thereof to be made.

(i) **Subrogation** In the event of any payment under this policy the Company shall be subrogated to all the Insured's rights of recovery therefor against any person or organization and the Insured shall execute and deliver instruments and papers and do whatever else is necessary to secure such rights. The Insured shall do nothing after loss to prejudice such rights.

(j) **Inspection** This Company shall be permitted to inspect the premises of the Insured at any time during the policy period.

(k) **Protective Safeguards** The Insured agrees to maintain throughout the term of this policy such protective safeguards as were in existence at the time of or installed subsequent to the attachment of this insurance.

(l) **Assignment** This policy shall be void if assigned or transferred without the written consent of the Company.

(m) **Misrepresentation and Fraud** This policy shall be void if the Insured has wilfully concealed or misrepresented any material fact or circumstance concerning this insurance or the subject thereof or in case of any fraud, attempted fraud or false swearing by the Insured touching any matter relating to this insurance or the subject thereof, whether before or after loss.

(n) **Conformance** The terms of this policy which are in conflict with the applicable statutes of the State wherein this policy is issued are hereby amended to conform to such statutes.

(o) **Liberalization** If during the period that insurance is in force under this policy or within 45 days prior to the inception date thereof, on behalf of this Company there be adopted, approved or accepted, in conformity with law, any forms, endorsements, rules or regulations by which this policy could be extended or broadened, without additional premium charge, by endorsement or substitution of form, then such extended or broadened insurance shall inure to the benefit of the Insured hereunder as though such endorsement or substitution of form had been made.

(p) **Benefit to Bailee** This insurance shall not inure, directly or indirectly, to the benefit of any carrier or bailee other than the Insured.

(q) **Other Insurance** Unless otherwise provided herein, it is agreed that in the event other valid and collectible insurance exists on any property insured hereunder at time and place of loss, the insurance under this policy shall be considered as excess insurance, and shall not apply or contribute to the payment of any loss until the amount of such other insurance shall have been exhausted, it being understood and agreed that under this policy the Insured is to be reimbursed to the extent of the difference between the amount collectible from such other insurance and the amount of actual loss otherwise recoverable hereunder.

(r) **Cancellation** This policy shall be cancelled at any time at the request of the Insured in which case this Company shall, upon demand and surrender of this policy, refund the excess of paid premium above the customary short rates for the expired time. This policy may be cancelled at any time by this Company by mailing to the Insured at the address of the Insured on page 1 and to any mortgagee designated in this policy a 15 days' written notice of cancellation with or without tender of the excess of paid premium above the pro rata premium for the entire time, which excess if not rendered, shall be refunded on demand. Notice of cancellation shall state that said excess premium (if not tendered) will be refunded on demand.

THIS POLICY IS MADE AND ACCEPTED SUBJECT TO the conditions which are hereby specially referred to and made a part of this policy, together with such other provisions, agreements or conditions as may be endorsed hereon or added hereto; and no officer, agent or other representative of this Company shall have power to waive or be deemed to have waived any provision or condition of this policy unless such waiver, if any, shall be written upon or attached hereto nor shall any privilege or permission affecting the insurance under this policy exist or be claimed by the Insured unless so written or attached.

IN WITNESS WHEREOF, the said **FEDERAL INSURANCE COMPANY** has caused this policy to be signed by its President and Secretary, but it shall not be valid unless countersigned by a duly authorized representative of the Company

Secretary   _President_

Authorized Representative

2. DATA-PROCESSING POLICIES FROM THE ST. PAUL INSURANCE COMPANIES

The Data Processing Policy has been designed to meet a real need to insure Electronic Data Processing Equipment and other machines related to the data processing operation on a broad "All Risks" basis. It is also designed to provide proper insurance on the very substantial exposure of Media as well as the Extra Expense involved to return to a normal operation after a loss to machines or media and the monetary loss due to Business Interruption.

The coverage is divided into four major sections, as follows:

Insuring Agreement No. 1.   **DATA PROCESSING EQUIPMENT.** This portion insures all equipment and component parts related to the processing unit. A schedule must be obtained of the units to be covered, and it is optional whether all or part is to be insured. Many firms will rent much of the equipment, and in such cases, we are prepared to cover the Difference of Conditions to pick up the responsibility of the Insured. This, basically, would be perils over and above Fire and Extended Coverage. Valuation may be actual cash value or retail replacement cost. Coinsurance of 80%, 90%, and 100% on actual cash value is optional but 100% coinsurance is mandatory on replacement cost basis.

Insuring Agreement No. 2.   **DATA PROCESSING MEDIA.** This section insures physical loss or damage to all forms of media and can include magnetic tapes, perforated paper tapes, punch cards, discs, drums, and other forms of communication related to the data processing unit—in other words, this media picks up the data after it is converted from the source material into a form which is used in the processing system. For example, in the insurance business, when the information from a policy copy is put on a punch card or magnetic tape or perforated tape, it is then in converted form. The daily report or copy of the policy is not covered in this example. The Insured may elect to insure all media or any specific part. Great care must be exercised in developing a risk to determine the proper valuation to be insured on media. We give the Insured the option of valuing on two bases. If they can establish and wish to set a fixed value on each item — for example, so much per reel of tape or so much per punch card — we will accept this valuation and it becomes valued. If no specific valuation is placed, then we pay the actual reproduction cost. Reproduction cost will mean what it would cost to replace the media after a loss. This cost, therefor, must be figured not only on the basis of what it cost to originally produce those records, but the additional expense that must be incurred as a result of a loss. This additional expense can be quite substantial because it may involve working at some other location or on an overtime basis. No coinsurance applies.

Insuring Agreement No. 3.   **EXTRA EXPENSE.** This coverage is designed to insure the extra expense necessary to continue to conduct, as nearly as practicable, the normal operation of business, due to damage to or destruction of the processing system including equipment and component parts and the data processing media therefor. On the surface, this would appear to overlap Agreement No. 2, because it includes media. It was written this way to take care of situations where all media may not be insured, although it should be, and also in situations when the machines are damaged but there is no damage to the media. Here again, it is essential that great care be exercised in developing the proper exposure, not only for the protection of the Insured, but for rating the risk. It will be found that this extra expense item can be very substantial. No coinsurance applies.

Insuring Agreement No. 6.   **BUSINESS INTERRUPTION.** This agreement designed for use with the Data Processing Policy to cover monetary loss resulting from total or partial suspension of operations by reason of direct physical loss to data processing equipment and active data processing media. Perils are all risk using a **valued** business interruption form.

Use of this Agreement, in combination with Extra Expense Insuring Agreement No. 3, rounds out the Insured's recovery program whenever extra expense, while compensating for extra expenses incurred, falls short in replacing production earnings lost when data processing equipment and media control daily production and when a definite loss to earnings can be demonstrated.

DEDUCTIBLES will be available in most states on Insuring Agreements Nos. 1, 2, 3 and 6 from $500 to $100,000 with appropriate credits. ($5,000 to $250,000 in New York)

VALUABLE PAPERS AND ACCOUNTS RECEIVABLE. These two parts tie into the general requirements of a firm and can be included in the contract. The Valuable Papers policy covers the source material plus any other valuable papers. It should be considered at the same time. Accounts Receivable is important since there may be a loss of receivables due to the destruction of the records.

INSPECTION. Each risk must be considered on its individual merits and a complete inspection will be necessary for each risk.

APPLICATION. The Application is designed to not only develop information for our own use, but to load the Insured into a realization of his exposures and assist him in developing the proper amount of insurance. The Information Sheet should be used as a preliminary check of the exposures prior to inspection to determine the desirability of the risk.

RATES. Each risk will be rated individually, but the rates generally are based on the Fire, Extended Coverage, and Vandalism rate plus a loading to take care of the additional perils, plus any possible increase in the fire exposure not previously considered.

TERM. While it is preferable to write policies for only one year because of constant changes in valuations, exposures, equipment and procedures, policies can be written for a term of three years at the term multiple.

PROSPECTS. In addition to the obvious prospects such as insurance companies of all kinds, large manufacturers, banks and finance organizations, there are no doubt many other low hazard classes of risks that have small units of data processing equipment in various forms, which qualify, who also need this type of coverage.

POLICYWRITING PROCEDURE: Although most states in which this Policy is filed have approved the standard coverage forms and the Multiple Peril Policy jacket illustrated in this manual, certain states demand the use of different forms because of filing peculiarities. Refer to Company underwriting rules applicable to each particular state.

APPLICATION FOR DATA PROCESSING POLICY

NAME OF APPLICANT (Include names of all subsidiaries)

BUSINESS ADDRESS

NATURE OF BUSINESS	EFFECTIVE DATE	TERM

RATING INFORMATION

LOCATION 1						LOCATION 2					
CONTENTS FIRE RATE	COINS. %	E. C. RATE	COINS. %	V. & M. M. RATE	COINS. %	CONTENTS FIRE RATE	COINS. %	E. C. RATE	COINS. %	V. & M. M. RATE	COINS. %

THE APPLICANT HAS THE OPTION of insuring only his data processing equipment, or his data processing media, or his extra expense or business interruption, or he may elect to take any two, three or four of the coverages. If desired, the applicant may also purchase these coverages on a deductible basis subject to a minimum deductible of $500.00.

DATA PROCESSING EQUIPMENT: The applicant has the option of insuring all or only part of the equipment, which may be either owned or leased, on an actual cash value basis or on a retail replacement cost basis.

ACTIVE DATA PROCESSING MEDIA: The applicant has the option of (1) specifically scheduling items or groups by types, establishing per-unit agreed values, or (2) blanketing all or unscheduled items into a total single value.

DATA PROCESSING EQUIPMENT
(Attach schedule or list below under "Additional Information")

LOCATION 1				LOCATION 2			
LIMIT OF LIABILITY	OWNED OR LEASED	ACTUAL CASH VALUE	REPLACEMENT COST	LIMIT OF LIABILITY	OWNED OR LEASED	ACTUAL CASH VALUE	REPLACEMENT COST
$		$	$	$		$	$

VALUATION:		*MUST BE WRITTEN WITH 100% COINSURANCE	COINSURANCE:			DEDUCTIBLE:	
☐ ACTUAL CASH VALUE	☐ REPLACEMENT COST*		☐ 80%	☐ 90%	☐ 100%	☐ YES	☐ NO $

DATA PROCESSING MEDIA

LOCATION 1				LOCATION 2			
LIMIT OF LIABILITY	100% COINS. F.C. RATE	ACTUAL CASH VALUE	REPLACEMENT COST	LIMIT OF LIABILITY	100% COINS. F.C. RATE	ACTUAL CASH VALUE	REPLACEMENT COST
$		$	$	$		$	$

LIMIT OF LIABILITY		DEDUCTIBLE	
$	WHILE IN TRANSIT AND WHILE TEMPORARILY WITHIN OTHER PREMISES.	☐ YES	☐ NO $

EXTRA EXPENSE

AGREED "PERIOD OF RESTORATION"	ESTIMATED EXTRA EXPENSE TO BE INCURRED FOR THAT PERIOD	DEDUCTIBLE	
	$	☐ YES	☐ NO $

BUSINESS INTERRUPTION

NO. OF "OPERATING DAYS"	AMOUNT OF INSURANCE	MEASURE OF RECOVERY	DEDUCTIBLE	
PER WEEK	$	$ PER DAY	☐ YES	☐ NO $

ADDITIONAL INFORMATION

Agent, please help your applicant by completing all of the following pages.

MACHINE CHARACTERISTICS, OPERATION AND EXPOSURES

Yes No

1. ☐ ☐ Are any machines enclosed in combustible material, or are panels lined with combustible insulation or sound deadeners?

2. ☐ ☐ Is this installation in a special room, hereinafter referred to as "the room"?

3. ☐ ☐ Are computers equipped with vacuum tubes?

4. ☐ ☐ Does any machine cable or wiring outside the room pass through areas containing combustible material?

5. ☐ ☐ Are all units inside the room governed by a master switch located either inside or outside the room?

6. ☐ ☐ Is an engineer permanently assigned to the room?

7. ☐ ☐ Is the engineer's workshop inside the room?

8. ☐ ☐ Have definite arrangements been made for the use of substitute facilities elsewhere in the event of a shutdown?

9.   Is tape storage (other than tape in use):

    ☐ ☐ a. in a vault?

    ☐ ☐ b. in the computer room?

    ☐ ☐ c. in combustible racks?

    ☐ ☐ d. in approved metal containers in a 2-hour safe?

10.   What kind of tapes are used?

    a. metal ☐

    b. plastic ☐

    c. paper ☐

11.   Is flammable solvent used for tape roller or capstan cleaning:

    ☐ ☐ a. by being brought to the machine?

    ☐ ☐ b. by being applied with an applicator elsewhere?

12. ☐ ☐ Is the solvent kept in 6-oz. cans with spouts?

13. ☐ ☐ Is all flammable solvent kept in glass bottles?

AIR CONDITIONING EQUIPMENT

1. ☐ ☐ Is an electric precipitron provided in the air stream to the room?

2. ☐ ☐ Is the room air-conditioned? If "Yes,"

    ☐ ☐ a. are duct linings combustible?

    ☐ ☐ b. are combustible filters used?

    ☐ ☐ c. are filters oil-dipped?

3. ☐ ☐ Is the compressor in the room or immediately adjoining?

4. ☐ ☐ Is freon used as the refrigerant?

AIR CONDITIONING EQUIPMENT, continued

Yes No

5.   Is fresh or make-up air intake:

☐ ☐   a. within 10 feet of the ground?

☐ ☐   b. screened with ¼ inch or heavier galvanized mesh?

☐ ☐   c. over adjoining buildings or over any combustible material or subject to smoke from near-by stacks (within 150 ft.)?

6. ☐ ☐ Does the system have a control switch in the room or an electric eye or any other automatic shutdown switch?

7. ☐ ☐ Is there any provision for duplication in event of system shutdown?

NOTE: Duplication can be by air, chilled water, or compressor facilities.

WATER DAMAGE

1. ☐ ☐ Is the room subject to accumulation of water from its own level?

2. ☐ ☐ Do water lines other than sprinkler system pipes enter or pass through the room or its ceiling space?

3. ☐ ☐ Do steam lines other than radiator branch lines for the computer room enter or pass through the room?

4. ☐ ☐ Are floor(s) and roof over the room water-tight to prevent entry from above?

5. ☐ ☐ Are there sprinklered areas over the room?

6. ☐ ☐ If the room is sprinklered, are the computers fitted with incombustible canopies to prevent the entry of water from overhead?

COLLAPSE

1. ☐ ☐ Are there unprotected metal supports (posts or beams) above or below the room? If "YES," are they:

a. sprinklered?   ☐

b. unsprinklered? ☐

2. ☐ ☐ Are combustible floors (excluding any pedestal floor) above or below the room? If "YES," are they:

a. sprinklered?   ☐

b. unsprinklered? ☐

3. ☐ ☐ Are there sprinklers above or below the room?

FIRE

1. ☐ ☐ Is the room of combustible material or of any material on combustible studs or supports with wooden floors?

2. ☐ ☐ Is the room near open courts or stairways or in a vertical flueway, receiving or delivery dock or port, or adjacent to a passageway?

3. ☐ ☐ Does the room have a pedestal floor? If "YES," answer a, b, or c below.

a. the floor is metal or incombustible.................... ☐

b. the floor is of treated wood (slow-burning incombustible) ☐

c. the floor is of untreated wood........................ ☐

FIRE, continued

Yes No

4. ☐ ☐ Does the room have combustible curtains or drapes?

5. ☐ ☐ Is the ceiling in the room made of combustible material or situated on combustible supports?
   If "YES," are the combustible surfaces:

   a. unpainted or covered with ordinary paint? ☐

   b. covered with fire-retardent paint?....... ☐

6. ☐ ☐ Is smoking permitted in the room or in an adjoining repair shop?

7. ☐ ☐ Do the watchman's recorded rounds take him to the room while the machinery is not in operation?

8. ☐ ☐ Are adequate carbon dioxide extinguishers available in the room?

9. ☐ ☐ Are gas masks or other self-contained breathing apparatus available for use in the room?

10. ☐ ☐ Is the engineer's workshop inside the room? If "YES," are:

    a. flames or flammable liquids used for any purpose?...... ☐

    b. flammable liquids stored, including flammable cleaner in excess of 1 pint (disregarding 6 oz. cans with spouts)? ☐

11. ☐ ☐ Is the room equipped with smoke detectors?

12. ☐ ☐ Are windows in the room on outside walls? If "YES," do they face or overlook:

    a. the street, and are they at basement or grade levels or within 15 ft. of the ground and not exposed to other buildings? .... ☐

    b. the street, and are they at least 15 ft. (or higher) above the ground?..................................... ☐

    c. other buildings, materials, supplies or structures? (If so, indicate the extent of exposure.)..................... ☐

       (1) light ☐; (2) medium ☐; (3) severe ☐

DUPLICATE PROGRAM TAPES

☐ ☐ Are duplicate program tapes maintained?

☐ ☐ Are they stored in a fireproof vault or safe?

☐ ☐ Are they stored in a building rated as a separate fire risk?

INSURING AGREEMENT No. 1

Data Processing System Equipment

1. **PROPERTY COVERED:** Data processing systems including equipment and component parts thereof owned by the Insured or leased, rented or under the control of the Insured, all as per schedule(s) on file with this Company.

2. **PROPERTY EXCLUDED:** This Insuring Agreement does not insure:
   A. Active data processing media which is hereby defined as meaning all forms of converted data and/or program and/or instruction vehicles employed in the Insured's data processing operation;
   B. Accounts, bills, evidences of debt, valuable papers, records, abstracts, deeds, manuscripts, or other documents;
   C. Property rented or leased to others while away from the premises of the Insured.

3. **LIMITS OF LIABILITY:** See "DECLARATIONS".

4. **PERILS INSURED:** This Insuring Agreement insures against all risks of direct physical loss or damage to the property covered, except as hereinafter provided.

5. **PERILS EXCLUDED:** This Insuring Agreement does not insure against loss, damage or expense caused directly or indirectly by:
   A. Damage due to mechanical failure, faulty construction, error in design unless fire or explosion ensues, and then only for loss, damage, or expense caused by such ensuing fire or explosion;
   B. Inherent vice, wear, tear, gradual deterioration or depreciation;
   C. Any dishonest, fraudulent or criminal act by any Insured, a partner therein or an officer, director or trustee thereof, whether acting alone or in collusion with others;
   D. Dryness or dampness of atmosphere, extremes of temperature, corrosion, or rust unless directly resulting from physical damage to the data processing system's air conditioning facilities caused by a peril not excluded by the provisions of this Insuring Agreement;
   E. Short circuit, blow-out, or other electrical disturbance, other than lightning, within electrical apparatus, unless fire or explosion ensues and then only for loss, damage or expense caused by such ensuing fire or explosion;
   F. Actual work upon the property covered, unless fire or explosion ensues, and then only for loss, damage, or expense caused by such ensuing fire or explosion;
   G. Delay or loss of market;
   H. War risks or nuclear risks as excluded in the Policy to which this Insuring Agreement is attached.

6. **VALUATION:**
   A. ACTUAL CASH VALUE — The following clause shall apply if indicated in the "Declarations": This Company shall not be liable beyond the actual cash value of the property at the time any loss or damage occurs and the loss or damage shall be ascertained or estimated according to such actual value with proper deduction for depreciation, however caused, and shall in no event exceed what it would then cost to repair or replace the same with material of like kind and quality.
   B. REPLACEMENT COST — The following clause shall apply if indicated in the "Declarations": This Company shall not be liable beyond the actual retail replacement cost of the property at the time any loss or damage occurs and the loss or damage shall be ascertained or estimated on the basis of the actual cash retail replacement cost of property similar in kind to that insured at the place of and immediately preceding the time of such loss or damage, but in no event to exceed the limit of liability stipulated in the "Declarations".

7. **COINSURANCE CLAUSE:**
   A. The following clause shall apply if indicated in the "Declarations": This Company shall be liable in the event of loss for no greater proportion thereof than the amount hereby insured bears to the percent indicated in the "Declarations" of the actual cash value of all property insured hereunder at the time such loss shall happen.
   B. The following clause shall apply if indicated in the "Declarations": This Company shall be liable in the event of loss for no greater proportion thereof than the amount hereby insured bears to the percent indicated in the "Declarations" of the actual cash retail replacement cost of all property insured hereunder at the time such loss shall happen.

8. **DEDUCTIBLE:** Each and every loss occurring hereunder shall be adjusted separately and from the amount of each such loss when so adjusted the amount indicated in the "Declarations" shall be deducted.

9. **DIFFERENCE IN CONDITIONS:** It is a condition of this Insurance that the Insured shall file with this Company a copy of any lease or rental agreement pertaining to the property insured hereunder insofar as concerns the lessors' liability for loss or damage to said property, and coverage afforded hereunder shall be only for the difference in conditions between those contained in said lease or rental agreement and the terms of this Insuring Agreement. The Insured agrees to give this Company thirty days notice of any alteration, cancellation or termination of the above mentioned lease or rental agreement pertaining to the lessors' liability.

All other terms and conditions of the Policy not in conflict herewith remain unchanged.

INSURING AGREEMENT No. 2
Data Processing Media

1. **PROPERTY INSURED:** Active data processing media, being property of the Insured or property of others for which the Insured may be liable.

2. **PROPERTY EXCLUDED:** This Insuring Agreement does not insure accounts, bills, evidences of debt, valuable papers, records, abstracts, deeds, manuscripts or other documents except as they may be converted to data processing media form, and then only in that form, or any data processing media which cannot be replaced with other of like kind and quality.

3. **LIMITS OF LIABILITY:** See "DECLARATIONS".

4. **PERILS INSURED:** This Insuring Agreement insures against all risks of direct physical loss or damage to the property covered, except as hereinafter provided.

5. **PERILS EXCLUDED:** This Insuring Agreement does not insure against loss, damage, or expense resulting from or caused directly or indirectly by:

   A. Data processing media failure or breakdown or malfunction of the data processing system including equipment and component parts while said media is being run through the system, unless fire or explosion ensues and then only for the loss, damage or expense caused by such ensuing fire or explosion;

   B. Electrical or magnetic injury, disturbance or erasure of electronic recordings, except by lightning;

   C. Dryness or dampness of atmosphere, extremes of temperature, corrosion, or rust unless directly resulting from physical damage to the data processing system's air conditioning facilities caused by a peril not excluded by the provisions of this Insuring Agreement;

   D. Delay or loss of market;

   E. Inherent vice, wear, tear, gradual deterioration or depreciation;

   F. Any dishonest, fraudulent or criminal act by any Insured, a partner therein or an officer, director or trustee thereof, whether acting alone or in collusion with others;

   G. War risks or nuclear risks as excluded in the Policy to which this Insuring Agreement is attached.

6. **VALUATION:** The limit of this Company's liability for loss or damage shall not exceed:

   A. As respects property specifically described in the "Declarations", the amount per article specified therein, said amount being the agreed value thereof for the purpose of this insurance;

   B. As respects all other property, the actual reproduction cost of the property; if not replaced or reproduced, blank value of media; all subject to the applicable limit of liability stated in the "Declarations".

7. **DEDUCTIBLE:** Each and every loss occurring hereunder shall be adjusted separately and from the amount of each loss when so adjusted the amount indicated in the "Declarations" shall be deducted.

8. **DEFINITIONS:** The term "active data processing media", wherever used in this contract, shall mean all forms of converted data and/or program and/or instruction vehicles employed in the Insured's data processing operation, except all such UNUSED property, and the following

_____,

(insert names of media not to be insured)

which the Insured elects not to insure hereunder.

All other terms and conditions of the Policy not in conflict herewith remain unchanged.

INSURING AGREEMENT No. 3
Extra Expense

1. **SUBJECT OF INSURANCE AND PERILS INSURED:** This Insuring Agreement insures against the necessary Extra Expense, as hereinafter defined, incurred by the Insured in order to continue as nearly as practicable the normal operation of its business, immediately following damage to or destruction of the data processing system including equipment and component parts thereof and data processing media therefor, owned, leased, rented or under the control of the Insured, as a direct result of all risks of physical loss or damage, but in no event to exceed the amount indicated in the "Declarations".

This Insuring Agreement is extended to include actual loss as covered hereunder, sustained during the period of time, hereinafter defined, (1) when as a direct result of a peril insured against the premises in which the property is located is so damaged as to prevent access to such property or (2) when as a direct result of a peril insured against, the air conditioning system or electrical system necessary for the operation of the data processing equipment is so damaged as to reduce or suspend the Insured's ability to actually perform the operations normally performed by the data processing system.

2. **MEASURE OF RECOVERY:** If the above described property is destroyed or so damaged by the perils insured against occurring during the term of this Insuring Agreement so as to necessitate the incurrence of Extra Expense (as defined in this Insuring Agreement), this Company shall be liable for the Extra Expense so incurred, not exceeding the actual loss sustained, for not exceeding such length of time, hereinafter referred to as the "period of restoration", commencing with the date of damage or destruction and not limited by the date of expiration of this Insuring Agreement, as shall be required with the exercise of due diligence and dispatch to repair, rebuild, or replace such part of said property as may be destroyed or damaged.

This Company's liability, during the determined period of restoration, shall be limited to the declared amount per period of time indicated in the "Declarations" but in no event to exceed the amount of insurance provided.

3. **EXTRA EXPENSE DEFINITION:** The term "Extra Expense" wherever employed in this Insuring Agreement is defined as the excess (if any) of the total cost during the period of restoration of the operation of the business over and above the total cost of such operation that would normally have been incurred during the same period had no loss occurred; the cost in each case to include expense of using other property or facilities of other concerns or other necessary emergency expenses. In no event, however, shall this Company be liable for loss of profits or earnings resulting from diminution of business, nor for any direct or indirect property damage loss insurable under Property Damage policies, or for expenditures incurred in the purchase, construction, repair or replacement of any physical property unless incurred for the purpose of reducing any loss under this Insuring Agreement not exceeding, however, the amount in which the loss is so reduced. Any salvage value of property so acquired which may be sold or utilized by the Insured upon resumption of normal operations, shall be taken into consideration in the adjustment of any loss hereunder.

4. **EXCLUSIONS:** It is a condition of the insurance that the Company shall not be liable for Extra Expense incurred as a result of:

A. Any local or State ordinance or law regulating construction or repair of buildings;

B. The suspension, lapse or cancellation of any lease, license, contract or order;

C. Interference at premises by strikers or other persons with repairing or replacing the property damaged or destroyed or with the resumption or continuation of the Insured's occupancy;

D. Loss or destruction of accounts, bills, evidences of debt, valuable papers, records, abstracts, deeds, manuscripts or other documents except as they may be converted to data processing media form and then only in that form;

E. Loss of or damage to property rented or leased to others while away from the premises of the Insured;

F. Error in machine programming or instructions to machine;

G. Inherent vice, wear, tear, gradual deterioration or depreciation;

H. Any dishonest, fraudulent or criminal act by any Insured, a partner therein or an officer, director or trustee thereof, whether acting alone or in collusion with others;

I. Damage due to mechanical failure, faulty construction, error in design unless fire or explosion ensues, and then only for loss, damage, or expense caused by such ensuing fire or explosion;

J. Short circuit, blow-out, or other electrical disturbance, other than lightning, within electrical apparatus, unless fire or explosion ensues and then only for loss, damage or expense caused by such ensuing fire or explosion;

K. Delay or loss of market;

L. War risks or nuclear risks as excluded in the Policy to which this Insuring Agreement is attached.

5. **RESUMPTION OF OPERATIONS:** As soon as practicable after any loss, the Insured shall resume complete or partial business operations of the property herein described and, in so far as practicable, reduce or dispense with such additional charges and expenses as are being incurred.

6. **INTERRUPTION BY CIVIL AUTHORITY:** Liability under this Insuring Agreement is extended to include actual loss as covered hereunder, sustained during the period of time, not exceeding two weeks, when as a direct result of a peril insured against, access to the premises in which the property described is located is prohibited by order of civil authority.

7. **DEFINITIONS:** The term "Normal" wherever used in this contract shall mean: The condition that would have existed had no loss occurred.

8. **DEDUCTIBLE:** Each and every loss occurring hereunder shall be adjusted separately and from the amount of each such loss when so adjusted the amount indicated in the "Declarations" shall be deducted.

All other terms and conditions of the Policy not in conflict herewith remain unchanged.

INSURING AGREEMENT No. 4
Valuable Papers and Records

1. **PROPERTY COVERED:** The Company agrees to pay on valuable papers and records, as stated in the "Declarations".
2. **THIS INSURING AGREEMENT INSURES AGAINST:** All risks of direct physical loss of or damage to the property covered, except as hereinafter provided, occurring during the period of this Insuring Agreement.
3. **LOCATION AND OCCUPANCY OF PREMISES:** See "DECLARATIONS".
4. **PROTECTION OF VALUABLE PAPERS AND RECORDS:** Insurance under this Insuring Agreement shall apply only while valuable papers and records are contained in the premises described in the "Declarations", it being a condition precedent to any right of recovery hereunder that such valuable papers and records shall be kept in the receptacle(s) described in the "Declarations" at all times when the premises are not open for business, except while such valuable papers and records are in actual use or as stated in paragraph 5 of this Insuring Agreement and 1B of Policy General Conditions.
5. **AUTOMATIC EXTENSION:** Such insurance as is afforded by this Insuring Agreement applies while the valuable papers and records are being conveyed outside the premises and while temporarily within other premises, except for storage, provided the Company's liability for such loss or damage shall not exceed ten percent of the combined limits of insurance stated in paragraph 1, nor Five Thousand Dollars, whichever is less.

EXCLUSIONS

THIS INSURING AGREEMENT DOES NOT APPLY:

(a) to loss due to wear and tear, gradual deterioration, vermin or inherent vice;

(b) to loss due to any fraudulent, dishonest, or criminal act by any Insured, a partner therein, or an officer, director or trustee thereof, whether acting alone or in collusion with others;

(c) to loss to property not specifically declared and described in section (a) of paragraph 1, "Property Covered", if such property cannot be replaced with other of like kind and quality;

(d) to loss to property held as samples or for sale or for delivery after sale;

(e) to loss due to electrical or magnetic injury, disturbance or erasure of electronic recordings, except by lightning;

(f) to war risks or nuclear risks as excluded in the Policy to which this Insuring Agreement is attached;

(g) to loss directly resulting from errors or omissions in processing or copying unless fire or explosion ensues and then only for direct loss caused by such ensuing fire or explosion.

SPECIAL CONDITIONS

1. **OWNERSHIP OF PROPERTY; INTERESTS COVERED:** The insured property may be owned by the Insured or held by him in any capacity; provided, the insurance applies only to the interest of the Insured in such property, including the Insured's liability to others, and does not apply to the interest of any other person or organization in any of said property unless included in the Insured's proof of loss.

2. **LIMITS OF LIABILITY; VALUATION; SETTLEMENT OPTION:** The limit of the Company's liability for loss shall not exceed the actual cash value of the property at time of loss nor what it would then cost to repair or replace the property with other of like kind and quality, nor the applicable limit of insurance stated in this Insuring Agreement; provided, as respects property specifically described in section (a) of paragraph 1, "Property Covered", the amount per article specified therein is the agreed value thereof for the purpose of this insurance. The Company may pay for the loss in money or may repair or replace the property and may settle any claim for loss of the property either with the Insured or the owner thereof. Any property so paid for or replaced shall become the property of the Company. The Insured or the Company, upon recovery of any such property, shall give notice thereof as soon as practicable to the other and the Insured shall be entitled to the property upon reimbursing the Company for the amount so paid or the cost of replacement.

   Application of the insurance to property of more than one person shall not operate to increase the applicable limit of insurance.

3. **INSURED'S DUTIES WHEN LOSS OCCURS:** Upon knowledge of loss or of an occurrence which may give rise to a claim for loss, the Insured shall give notice thereof as soon as practicable to the Company or any of its authorized agents and, if the loss is due to a violation of law, also to the police.

4. **ACTION AGAINST COMPANY:** No action shall lie against the Company unless, as a condition precedent thereto, there shall have been full compliance with all the terms of this Insuring Agreement, nor until thirty days after the required proofs of loss have been filed with the Company, nor at all unless commenced within two years after the discovery by the Insured of the occurrence which gives rise to the loss. If this limitation of time is shorter than that prescribed by any statute controlling the construction of this Insuring Agreement, the shortest permissible statutory limitation in time shall govern and shall supersede the time limitation herein stated.

5. **DEFINITIONS:**

   (a) Valuable Papers and Records — The term "valuable papers and records" means written, printed or otherwise inscribed documents and records, including books, maps, films, drawings, abstracts, deeds, mortgages and manuscripts, but does not mean money or securities, or electronic data control tapes.

   (b) Premises — The unqualified word "premises" means the interior of that portion of the building at the location designated in paragraph 3, "Location and Occupancy of Premises" and described in the "Declarations", which is occupied by the Insured for the business purposes stated therein.

6. **CHANGES:** Notice to any agent or knowledge possessed by any agent or by any other person shall not effect a waiver or a change in any part of this Insuring Agreement or estop the Company from asserting any right under the terms of this Insuring Agreement nor shall the terms of this Insuring Agreement be waived or changed, except by endorsement issued to form a part of this Insuring Agreement.

INAPPLICABLE POLICY CONDITIONS

Paragraph 1A, 1F, 1G, 1H, 1I and 1N of General Policy Conditions do not apply to this Insuring Agreement.

All other terms and conditions of the Policy not in conflict herewith remain unchanged.

INSURING AGREEMENT No. 5
Accounts Receivable

1. **THE COMPANY AGREES TO PAY:**

   A. All sums due the Insured from customers, provided the Insured is unable to effect collection thereof as the direct result of loss of or damage to records of accounts receivable;

   B. Interest charges on any loan to offset impaired collections pending repayment of such sums made uncollectible by such loss or damage;

   C. Collection expense in excess of normal collection cost and made necessary because of such loss or damage;

   D. Other expenses, when reasonably incurred by the Insured in re-establishing records of accounts receivable following such loss or damage.

2. **THIS INSURING AGREEMENT INSURES AGAINST:** All risks of loss of or damage to the Insured's records of accounts receivable, occurring during the period of this Insuring Agreement, except as hereinafter provided.

3. **LOCATION AND OCCUPANCY OF PREMISES:** See "DECLARATIONS".

4. **PROTECTION OF RECORDS OF ACCOUNTS RECEIVABLE:** Insurance under this Insuring Agreement shall apply only while records of accounts receivable are contained in the premises described in the "Declarations", it being a condition precedent to any right of recovery hereunder that such records shall be kept in the receptacle(s) described in the "Declarations" at all times when the premises are not open for business, except while such records are in actual use;

5. **LIMIT OF INSURANCE:** The Company shall not be liable hereunder for an amount to exceed the Limit of Insurance stated in the "Declarations".

EXCLUSIONS

THIS INSURING AGREEMENT DOES NOT APPLY:

(a) to loss due to any fraudulent, dishonest or criminal act by any Insured, a partner therein, or an officer, director or trustee thereof, while working or otherwise and whether acting alone or in collusion with others;

(b) to loss due to bookkeeping, accounting or billing errors or omissions;

(c) to loss, the proof of which as to factual existence, is dependent upon an audit of records or an inventory computation; but this shall not preclude the use of such procedures in support of claim for loss which the Insured can prove, through evidence wholly apart therefrom, is due solely to a risk of loss to records of accounts receivable not otherwise excluded hereunder;

(d) to loss due to alteration, falsification, manipulation, concealment, destruction or disposal of records of accounts receivable committed to conceal the wrongful giving, taking, obtaining or withholding of money, securities or other property but only to the extent of such wrongful giving, taking, obtaining or withholding;

(e) to loss due to electrical or magnetic injury, disturbance or erasure of electronic recordings, except by lightning;

(f) to war risks or nuclear risks as excluded in the Policy to which this Insuring Agreement is attached.

SPECIAL CONDITIONS

1. **DEFINITION OF PREMISES:** The unqualified word "premises" means the interior of that portion of the building at the location designated in Paragraph 3, "location and occupancy of premises" and described in the "Declarations", which is occupied by the Insured for the business purposes stated therein.

2. **PREMIUM:** The Insured shall, within twenty days after the end of each fiscal month during the policy period, furnish the Company with a written statement of the total amount of accounts receivable, with deferred payments and charge accounts segregated, as of the last day of each such month.

   The premium stated in the "Declarations" is provisional only. Upon each anniversary and upon termination of this Insuring Agreement, the sum of the monthly amounts of accounts receivable for the preceding twelve months shall be averaged and the earned premium shall be computed on such average at the rate stated in this Insuring Agreement, whether or not such average exceeds the applicable limit of Insurance under this Insuring Agreement. If the earned premium thus computed exceeds the provisional premium paid, the Insured shall pay the excess to the Company; if less, the Company shall return to the Insured the unearned portion paid by the Insured, but such premium shall not be less than any minimum premium stated in this Insuring Agreement.

3. **INSPECTION AND AUDIT:** The Company shall be permitted to inspect the premises and the receptacles in which the records of accounts receivable are kept by the Insured, and to examine and audit the Insured's books and records at any time during the period of coverage and any extension thereof and within three years after the final termination of this Insuring Agreement, as far as they relate to the premium basis or the subject matter of this insurance, and to verify the statements of any outstanding record of accounts receivable submitted by the Insured and the amount of recoveries of accounts receivable on which the Company has made any settlement.

4. **RECOVERIES:** After payment of loss all amounts recovered by the Insured on accounts receivable for which the Insured has been indemnified shall belong and be paid to the Company by the Insured up to the total amount of loss paid by the Company; but all recoveries in excess of such amounts shall belong to the Insured.

5. **INSURED'S DUTIES WHEN LOSS OCCURS:** Upon the occurrence of any loss which may result in a claim hereunder, the Insured shall:

   (A) Give notice thereof as soon as practicable to the Company or any of its authorized agents and, if the loss is due to a violation of law, also to the police;

   (B) File detailed proof of loss, duly sworn to, with the Company promptly on expiration of ninety days from the date on which the records of accounts receivable were lost or damaged.

   Upon the Company's request, the Insured shall submit to examination by the Company, subscribe the same, under oath if required, and produce for the Company's examination all pertinent records, all at such reasonable times and places as the Company shall designate, and shall cooperate with the Company in all matters pertaining to loss or claims with respect thereto, including rendering of all possible assistance to effect collection of outstanding accounts receivable.

6. **DETERMINATION OF RECEIVABLES: DEDUCTIONS** — When there is proof that a loss covered by this Insuring Agreement has occurred but the Insured cannot accurately establish the total amount of accounts receivable outstanding as of the date of such loss, such amount shall be based on the Insured's monthly statements and shall be computed as follows:

   (a) determine the amount of all outstanding accounts receivable at the end of the same fiscal month in the year immediately preceding the year in which the loss occurs;

   (b) calculate the percentage of increase or decrease in the average monthly total of accounts receivable for the twelve months immediately preceding the month in which the loss occurs, or such part thereof for which the Insured has furnished monthly statements to the Company, as compared with such average for the same months of the preceding year;

   (c) the amount determined under (a) above, increased or decreased by the percentage calculated under (b) above, shall be the agreed total amount of accounts receivable as of the last day of the fiscal month in which said loss occurs;

   (d) the amount determined under (c) above shall be increased or decreased in conformity with the normal fluctuations in the amount of accounts receivable during the fiscal month involved, due consideration being given to the experience of the business since the last day of the last fiscal month for which statement has been rendered.

   There shall be deducted from the total amount of accounts receivable, however established, the amount of such accounts evidenced by records not lost or damaged, or otherwise established or collected by the Insured, and an amount to allow for probable bad debts which would normally have been uncollectible by the Insured. On deferred payment accounts receivable, unearned interest and service charges shall be deducted.

7. **SETTLEMENT OF CLAIMS; ACTION AGAINST COMPANY:** All adjusted claims shall be paid or made good to the Insured within thirty days after presentation and acceptance of satisfactory proof of interest and loss at the office of the Company. No action shall lie against the Company unless, as a condition precedent thereto, there shall have been full compliance with all the terms of this Insuring Agreement nor at all unless commenced within two years after the discovery by the Insured of the occurrence which gives rise to the loss. If this limitation of time is shorter than that prescribed by any statute controlling the construction of this Insuring Agreement, the shortest permissible statutory limitation in time shall govern and shall supersede the time limitation herein stated.

8. **CHANGES:** Notice to any agent or knowledge possessed by any agent or by any other person shall not effect a waiver or change in any part of this Insuring Agreement, or estop the Company from asserting any right under the terms of this Insuring Agreement, nor shall the terms of this Insuring Agreement be waived or changed, except by endorsement issued to form a part of this Insuring Agreement.

INAPPLICABLE POLICY CONDITIONS

Paragraphs 1A, 1F, 1G, 1H, 1I and 1N of the General Policy Conditions do not apply to this Insuring Agreement.

All other terms and conditions of the Policy not in conflict herewith remain unchanged.

INSURING AGREEMENT No. 6
Business Interruption

1. **SUBJECT OF INSURANCE AND PERILS INSURED:** This Insuring Agreement covers against loss resulting directly from necessary interruption of business as a direct result of all risk of physical loss or damage from any cause (except as hereinafter excluded) to the following property owned, leased, rented or under the control of the Insured:

   A. Data processing systems, computer systems or other electronic control equipment including component parts thereof;

   B. Active data processing media meaning all forms of converted data and/or program and/or instruction vehicles employed in the Insured's data processing or production operation except the following_____

   which the Insured elects not to insure hereunder.

   This Insuring Agreement is extended to include actual loss as covered hereunder when as a direct result of a peril insured against the premises in which the property is located is so damaged as to prevent access to such property.

2. **MEASURE OF RECOVERY:** In the event such loss or damage results in either a total or partial suspension of business then this Company shall be liable:

   A. for the amount stated in the "Declarations" for each working day during the period of such total suspension of business; or

   B. in the event of partial suspension, for such proportion of the amount stated in the "Declarations" for each working day of total production which would have been obtained during the period of partial suspension had no damage occurred;

   commencing with the date of damage or destruction, and not limited by the expiration date of this Insuring Agreement, as would be required through the exercise of due diligence and dispatch to rebuild, repair or replace such described property as has been damaged or destroyed but in no event to exceed the amount of insurance provided.

3. **RESUMPTION OF OPERATIONS:** It is a condition of this insurance that if the Insured could reduce the loss resulting from the interruption of business,

   A. by complete or partial resumption of operation of the property herein described, whether damaged or not, or

   B. by making use of other property at the location(s) described herein or elsewhere, or

   C. by making use of stock at the location(s) described herein or elsewhere, such reduction shall be taken into account in arriving at the amount of loss hereunder.

4. **EXPENSE TO REDUCE LOSS:** This Insuring Agreement also covers such expenses as are necessarily incurred for the purpose of reducing any loss under this Insuring Agreement (except expense incurred to extinguish a fire), but in the absence of prior authorization by this Company or its adjuster, NOT EXCEEDING THE AMOUNT BY WHICH THE LOSS UNDER THIS POLICY IS THEREBY REDUCED.

5. **INTERRUPTION BY CIVIL AUTHORITY:** This Insuring Agreement is extended to include the actual loss as covered hereunder during the period of time, not exceeding two consecutive weeks, when, as a direct result of the peril(s) insured against, access to the premises described is prohibited by order of civil authority.

6. **EXCLUSIONS:** It is a condition of the insurance that the Company shall not be liable for Total or Partial suspension incurred as a result of:

   A. Any local or State ordinance or law regulating construction or repair of buildings;

   B. The suspension, lapse or cancellation of any lease, license, contract or order;

   C. Interference at premises by strikers or other persons with repairing or replacing the property damage or destroyed or with the resumption or continuation of the Insured's occupancy;

   D. Loss or destruction of accounts, bills, evidences of debt, valuable papers, records, abstracts, deeds, manuscripts or other documents except as they may be converted to data processing media form and then only in that form;

   E. Loss of or damage to property rented or leased to others while away from the premises of the Insured;

   F. Error in machine programming or instructions to machine;

   G. Inherent vice, wear, tear, gradual deterioration or depreciation;

   H. Any dishonest, fraudulent or criminal act by any Insured, a partner therein or an officer, director or trustee thereof, whether acting alone or in collusion with others;

   I. Damage due to mechanical failure, faulty construction, error in design unless fire or explosion ensues, and then only for loss, damage, or expense caused by such ensuing fire or explosion;

   J. Short circuit, blow-out, or other electrical disturbance, other than lightning, within electrical apparatus, unless fire or explosion ensues and then only for loss, damage or expense caused by such ensuing fire or explosion;

   K. Delay or loss of market;

   L. War risks or nuclear risks as excluded in the Policy to which this Insuring Agreement is attached.

7. **WORK DAY:** The words "work day", however modified, whenever used in this Insuring Agreement shall be held to cover a period of twenty-four hours and shall mean a day on which the operations of the Insured are usually performed.

8. **DEDUCTIBLE:** Each and every loss occurring hereunder shall be adjusted separately and from the amount of each such loss when so adjusted the amount indicated in the "Declarations" shall be deducted.

All other terms and conditions of the Policy not in conflict herewith remain unchanged.

IN CONSIDERATION OF THE PROVISIONS AND STIPULATIONS HEREIN OR ADDED HERETO AND OF the premium above specified, this Company, for the term of years specified above from inception date shown above At Noon (Standard Time) to expiration date shown above At Noon (Standard Time) at location of property involved, to an amount not exceeding the amount(s) above specified, does insure the insured named above and legal representatives, to the extent of the actual cash value of the property at the time of loss, but not exceeding the amount which it would cost to repair or replace the property with material of like kind and quality within a reasonable time after such loss, without allowance for any increased cost of repair or reconstruction by reason of any ordinance or law regulating construction or repair, and without compensation for loss resulting from interruption of business or manufacture, nor in any event for more than the interest of the insured, against all **DIRECT LOSS BY FIRE, LIGHTNING AND BY REMOVAL FROM PREMISES ENDANGERED BY THE PERILS INSURED AGAINST IN THIS POLICY, EXCEPT AS HEREINAFTER PROVIDED,** to the property described herein while located or contained as described in this policy, or pro rata for five days at each proper place to which any of the property shall necessarily be removed for preservation from the perils insured against in this policy, but not elsewhere.

Assignment of this policy shall not be valid except with the written consent of this Company.

This policy is made and accepted subject to the foregoing provisions and stipulations and those hereinafter stated, which are hereby made a part of this policy, together with such other provisions, stipulations and agreements as may be added hereto, as provided in this policy.

42 **Added provisions.** The extent of the application of insurance
43 under this policy and of the contribution to
44 be made by this Company in case of loss, and any other pro-
45 vision or agreement not inconsistent with the provisions of this
46 policy, may be provided for in writing added hereto, but no pro-
47 vision may be waived except such as by the terms of this policy
48 is subject to change.
49 **Waiver** No permission affecting this insurance shall
50 **provisions.** exist, or waiver of any provision be valid,
51 unless granted herein or expressed in writing
52 added hereto. No provision, stipulation or forfeiture shall be
53 held to be waived by any requirement or proceeding on the part
54 of this Company relating to appraisal or to any examination
55 provided for herein.
56 **Cancellation** This policy shall be cancelled at any time
57 **of policy.** at the request of the insured, in which case
58 this Company shall, upon demand and sur-
59 render of this policy, refund the excess of paid premium above
60 the customary short rates for the expired time. This pol-
61 icy may be cancelled at any time by this Company by giving
62 to the insured a five days' written notice of cancellation with
63 or without tender of the excess of paid premium above the pro
64 rata premium for the expired time, which excess, if not ten-
65 dered, shall be refunded on demand. Notice of cancellation shall
66 state that said excess premium (if not tendered) will be re-
67 funded on demand.
68 **Mortgagee** If loss hereunder is made payable, in whole
69 **interests and** or in part, to a designated mortgagee not
70 **obligations.** named herein as the insured, such interest in
71 this policy may be cancelled by giving to such
72 mortgagee a ten days' written notice of can-
73 cellation.
74 If the insured fails to render proof of loss such mortgagee, upon
75 notice, shall render proof of loss in the form herein specified
76 within sixty (60) days thereafter and shall be subject to the pro-
77 visions hereof relating to appraisal and time of payment and of
78 bringing suit. If this Company shall claim that no liability ex-
79 isted as to the mortgagor or owner, it shall, to the extent of pay-
80 ment of loss to the mortgagee, be subrogated to all the mort-
81 gagee's rights of recovery, but without impairing mortgagee's
82 right to sue; or it may pay off the mortgage debt and require
83 an assignment thereof and of the mortgage. Other provisions

1 **Concealment,** This entire policy shall be void if, whether
2 **fraud.** before or after a loss, the insured has wil-
3 fully concealed or misrepresented any ma-
4 terial fact or circumstance concerning this insurance or the
5 subject thereof, or the interest of the insured therein, or in case
6 of any fraud or false swearing by the insured relating thereto.
7 **Uninsurable** This policy shall not cover accounts, bills,
8 **and** currency, deeds, evidences of debt, money or
9 **excepted property.** securities; nor, unless specifically named
10 hereon in writing, bullion or manuscripts.
11 **Perils not** This Company shall not be liable for loss by
12 **included.** fire or other perils insured against in this
13 policy caused, directly or indirectly, by: (a)
14 enemy attack by armed forces, including action taken by mili-
15 tary, naval or air forces in resisting an actual or an immediately
16 impending enemy attack; (b) invasion; (c) insurrection; (d)
17 rebellion; (e) revolution; (f) civil war; (g) usurped power; (h)
18 order of any civil authority except acts of destruction at the time
19 of and for the purpose of preventing the spread of fire, provided
20 that such fire did not originate from any of the perils excluded
21 by this policy; (i) neglect of the insured to use all reasonable
22 means to save and preserve the property at and after a loss, or
23 when the property is endangered by fire in neighboring prem-
24 ises; (j) nor shall this Company be liable for loss by theft.
25 **Other insurance.** Other insurance may be prohibited or the
26 amount of insurance may be limited by en-
27 dorsement attached hereto.
28 **Conditions suspending or restricting insurance. Unless other-**
29 **wise provided in writing added hereto this Company shall not**
30 **be liable for loss occurring**
31 (a) while the hazard is increased by any means within the con-
32 trol or knowledge of the insured; or
33 (b) while a described building, whether intended for occupancy
34 by owner or tenant, is vacant or unoccupied beyond a period of
35 sixty consecutive days; or
36 (c) as a result of explosion or riot, unless fire ensue, and in
37 that event for loss by fire only.
38 **Other perils** Any other peril to be insured against, or sub-
39 **or subjects.** ject of insurance to be covered in this policy
40 shall be by endorsement in writing hereon or
41 added hereto.

84 relating to the interests and obligations of such mortgage may
85 be added hereto by agreement in writing.
86 **Pro rata liability.** This Company shall not be liable for a greater
87 proportion of any loss than the amount
88 hereby insured shall bear to the whole insurance covering the
89 property against the peril involved, whether collectible or not.
90 **Requirements in** The insured shall give immediate written
91 **case loss occurs.** notice to this Company of any loss, protect
92 the property from further damage, forthwith
93 separate the damaged and undamaged personal property, put
94 it in the best possible order, furnish a complete inventory of
95 the destroyed, damaged and undamaged property, showing in
96 detail quantities, costs, actual cash value and amount of loss
97 claimed; **and within sixty days after the loss, unless such time**
98 **is extended in writing by this Company, the insured shall render**
99 **to this Company a proof of loss,** signed and sworn to by the
100 insured, stating the knowledge and belief of the insured as to
101 the following; the time and origin of the loss, the interest of the
102 insured and of all others in the property, the actual cash value of
103 each item thereof and the amount of loss thereto, all encum-
104 brances thereon, all other contracts of insurance, whether valid
105 or not, covering any of said property, any changes in the title,
106 use, occupation, location, possession or exposures of said prop-
107 erty since the issuing of this policy, by whom and for what
108 purpose any building herein described and the several parts
109 thereof were occupied at the time of loss and whether or not it
110 then stood on leased ground, and shall furnish a copy of all the
111 descriptions and schedules in all policies and, if required, verified
112 plans and specifications of any building, fixtures or machinery
113 destroyed or damaged. The insured, as often as may be reason-
114 ably required, shall exhibit to any person designated by this
115 Company all that remains of any property herein described, and
116 submit to examinations under oath by any person named by this
117 Company, and subscribe the same; and, as often as may be
118 reasonably required, shall produce for examination all books of
119 account, bills, invoices and other vouchers, or certified copies
120 thereof if originals be lost, at such reasonable time and place as
121 may be designated by this Company or its representative, and
122 shall permit extracts and copies thereof to be made.
123 **Appraisal.** In case the insured and this Company shall
124 fail to agree as to the actual cash value or

125 the amount of loss, then, on the written demand of either, each
126 shall select a competent and disinterested appraiser and notify
127 the other of the appraiser selected within twenty days of such
128 demand. The appraisers shall first select a competent and dis-
129 interested umpire; and failing for fifteen days to agree upon
130 such umpire, then, on request of the insured or this Company,
131 such umpire shall be selected by a judge of a court of record in
132 the state in which the property covered is located. The ap-
133 praisers shall then appraise the loss, stating separately actual
134 cash value and loss to each item; and, failing to agree, shall
135 submit their differences, only, to the umpire. An award in writ-
136 ing, so itemized, of any two when filed with this Company shall
137 determine the amount of actual cash value and loss. Each
138 appraiser shall be paid by the party selecting him and the ex-
139 penses of appraisal and umpire shall be paid by the parties
140 equally.
141 **Company's** It shall be optional with this Company **to**
142 **options.** **take all,** or any part, of the property at the
143 agreed or appraised value, **and** also to re-
144 pair, rebuild or replace the property destroyed or damaged **with**
145 other of like kind and quality within a reasonable time, on giv-
146 ing notice of its intention so to do within thirty days **after the**
147 receipt of the proof of loss herein required.
148 **Abandonment.** There can be no abandonment to this Com-
149 pany of any property.
150 **When loss** The amount of loss for which this Company
151 **payable.** may be liable shall be payable sixty **days**
152 after proof of loss, **as** herein provided, **is**
153 received by this Company and ascertainment of the loss is made
154 either by **agreement between the insured and this Company** ex-
155 pressed **in writing or by the filing with this Company of an**
156 **award as herein provided.**
157 **Suit.** No suit **or action on this policy for the recov-**
158 ery of any claim shall be sustainable in any
159 court of law or equity unless all the requirements of this policy
160 shall have been complied with, and unless commenced within
161 twelve months next after inception of the loss.
162 **Subrogation.** This Company may require from the insured
163 an assignment of all right of recovery against
164 any party for loss to the extent that payment therefor is mad-
165 by this Company.

ST. PAUL FIRE AND MARINE INSURANCE COMPANY
DATA PROCESSING POLICY

DECLARATIONS:

Name and address of Insured

SPECIMEN

FORMER POLICY NO.

A
G
E
N
T

The insurance afforded is only with respect to such and so many of the following Insuring Agreements as are indicated by ⊠. The limit of this Company's liability shall be as stated herein, subject to all the terms of this Policy having reference thereto.

In states where required, the statutory fire conditions are made a part of this Policy.

POLICY PERIOD* FROM	TO	SUM INSURED	RATE	PREMIUM
		$		$

*AT NOON STANDARD TIME AT PLACE OF ISSUANCE AS TO EACH OF SAID DATES.

☐ **1. DATA PROCESSING SYSTEM EQUIPMENT:**

LIMITS OF LIABILITY (Paragraph 3)

A. On property of the Insured in the amount of:
   (1) $_____located at_____
   (2) $_____located at_____

B. On property leased, rented or under the control of the Insured in the amount of:
   (1) $_____located at_____
   (2) $_____located at_____

C. $_____while in transit and while temporarily within other premises.

VALUATION (Paragraph 6)		COINSURANCE CLAUSE (Paragraph 7)		DEDUCTIBLE (Paragraph 8)
☐ A. ACTUAL CASH VALUE CLAUSE	☐ B. REPLACEMENT COST CLAUSE	☐ A. ____%	☐ B. 100%	$_____

☐ **2. DATA PROCESSING MEDIA:**

LIMITS OF LIABILITY (Paragraph 3)

A. On property of the Insured in the amount of:
   (1) $_____located at_____
   (2) $_____located at_____

B. $_____while in transit and while temporarily within other premises.

VALUATION (Paragraph 6)	VALUE OF EACH	LIMITS OF INSURANCE	DEDUCTIBLE (Paragraph 7)
(A) Specified Articles	$	$	$
(B) All Others		$	

☐ **3. EXTRA EXPENSE:** Subject of Insurance and Perils Insured (Paragraph 1):

AMOUNT OF INSURANCE	MEASURE OF RECOVERY (Paragraph 2)	DEDUCTIBLE (Paragraph 8)
$	$	$

☐ **6. BUSINESS INTERRUPTION:** Subject of Insurance and Perils Insured (Paragraph 1):

AMOUNT OF INSURANCE	MEASURE OF RECOVERY (Paragraph 2)	DEDUCTIBLE (Paragraph 8)
$	$ PER DAY	$

COUNTERSIGNATURE DATE	COUNTERSIGNED AT	AGENT

CLASS
PROBLEMS

With questions in Parts A to D below students might be told to either write answers or prepare answers for class discussion. Questions in Parts E and F are perhaps best assigned to small teams of students, in which healthy arguments can develop.

Part A: General Questions
Part B: Questions about Techniques
Part C: Shutting the Stable Door
Part D: Questions Relating to Privacy
Part E: The Design of Specific Systems
Part F: Projects

A. GENERAL QUESTIONS

A.1. What are the distinctions between privacy and data security?

A.2. Why should security, accuracy, and privacy measures all be considered together when planning or revamping a data processing installation? In what ways are their technical solutions interrelated?

A.3. What does the term "exposure" mean? Give a formula for estimating exposure rating. Give two examples of types of incidents which could have the same exposure rating but which differ greatly in their probability of occurrence.

A.4. "The search for security will be a search for inexpensive methods of multiplying the probabilities of unlikely occurrences happening." Give an example of what this statement means. When can such probabilities *not* be multiplied?

A.5. Discuss signs that either data processing management or general management should watch for that could indicate the possibility of recent data processing crime.

A.6. List the ways in which you think auditors should be involved with computer security.

A.7. Take a system with which you are familiar, or an imaginary system, and fill in a chart like that in Table 5.2 (guesses will suffice). Would you modify the form of the table for the system you have selected?

A.8. For the system in the previous question list all of the types of security exposure that you can think of. For each item on the list write rating factors for your estimate of the probability of that incident occurring, and for your estimate of the potential cost of damage that it might cause

A.9. What measures should be taken to protect a commercial system handling financial transactions from its own application programmers?

A.10. How do the methods of controlling the accuracy of input differ between a punched card system and an on-line data-entry system? What are the pros and cons of the two methods if accuracy of input is vital?

B. QUESTIONS ABOUT TECHNIQUES

B.1. List the types of accuracy controls that should be used on a magnetic-tape batch-processing payroll run with punched card input.

B.2. List the types of accuracy controls that you would recommend on a multinational real-time airline reservation system.

B.3. Draw a block diagram showing what steps would be taken by a sales order entry system with remote terminals when it detects that a user has typed in an invalid identity code.

B.4. List the possible causes of damage to data on on-line computer files, and the main means of preventing such damage.

B.5. An on-line data base of 50 billion characters is to be installed to hold details of a large corporation's customers, their orders, and general marketing information. What reasonable measures would you recommend to permit reconstructing this data if all or part of the contents of the on-line files are lost?

B.6. What types of system eavesdropping are possible other than telephone wiretapping? Number your list in order of increasing cost.

B.7. A corporate message-switching system sends messages between many locations across the United States. A few of the messages contain highly sensitive or trade secret information. A central file is maintained of all messages sent. What measures could be taken to protect such a system from telephone wiretapping?

B.8. Specify, in detail, how self-checking numbers operate. Convert the following account numbers into self-checking numbers: 7253, 5100738.

B.9. What controls should be used with rounding errors in a system handling a large quantity of financial transactions?

B.10. List the possible functions of the Input/Output Control Section on a sales order entry and inquiry system, on which remote terminals are employed to build up a data base of customer orders.

B.11. List the types of locks and alarms that can be used to combat unauthorized use of terminals.

B.12. List the various methods of identifying a remote terminal user. Number the methods in order of cost assuming that long-distance voice-grade data transmission links are used.

B.13. Under what circumstances do you think cryptography should be used? Give three examples of systems on which you think cryptography should be used. Give three examples of systems with security problems which you do not think should be solved with cryptography.

B.14. Consider the enciphered English text in Fig. 20.5. What types of approach can you suggest that might be likely to help deciphering the text with the aid of a large computer?

B.15. Consider the program in Fig. 20.4, used to encipher the text in Fig. 20.5. What steps could you take to improve the program so that the enciphered text would be more difficult to decipher?

B.16. What principles should govern the use of cryptography on a commercial computer system?

B.17. What features can be incorporated into terminals for security protection?

B.18. What features are desirable in operating systems for giving security protection? What are typical loopholes in today's operating systems?

B.19. What features should man-computer dialogues have to lessen the likelihood of operators making errors?

B.20. A real-time system may employ off-line runs to enhance the system safeguards. What could be incorporated into such runs?

B.21. A system handling accounts receivable and accounts payable and using magnetic tape is to be converted to an entirely different type of computer using disks. What types of controls should be employed during the conversion process to protect against embezzlement or loss of data?

C. SHUTTING THE STABLE DOOR

The following sections describe some harmful incidents that have occurred on actual computer systems. For each of them specify in as much detail as you can what system controls would have prevented the incidents and would prevent similar incidents from occurring again. Are the controls you suggest reasonable to apply to other such computer systems?

C.1. A data-processing tape librarian became very angry with the organization she worked for and decided to get her own back. She knew that the backup tapes which she sent to a secure off-site store as a protection against disaster would in all probability not be used as it was unlikely that severe damage to the file which a tape backed up would occur before the file was next dumped. She substituted blank or scratch tapes for the master file backup tapes and changed the external labels. After waiting a long enough time to ensure that the master files were without means of emergency reconstruction, she then erased most of the critical on-site files, and left. The company was in serious trouble.

C.2. *The Wall Street Journal* ran an article headlined "Errant Computer Throws Wholesaler's Business into Turmoil," about a wholesale grocer who stated in court that his computer "almost put us out of business. ...When a customer ordered a case of cereal, he might get a whole roomful. And the bill for it might make him think he had bought a shipload." A customer testified that the computer sent him so many items that he had nowhere to store them. Bills were sent out with wrong prices—for example, one bill charged $200 for a $13 case of dog biscuits. "In some cases," the grocer claimed, "it refused to charge at all. The item was shipped, for all intents and purposes, free of charge to the customer." As for stock-control, warehouse workers were likely to be informed that there were no canned peas, when in fact they were piled up to the ceiling.

The system in question was a batch-processing invoicing and inventory control system.

C.3. A programmer in a Minneapolis bank was employed to write a program to inform the bank officers of checks arriving for accounts with insufficient funds. His program worked perfectly except that it ignored his own account. The programmer then wrote many bad checks and the bank computer accepted them. He was eventually caught, but only because one of his checks arrived while the computer was broken down and the checks were being processed by hand.

C.4. $2.7 million was stolen from the antipoverty program of the New York City Human Resources Administration by a group who arranged for the computer to make out pay checks for 40,000 nonexistent youth workers. The false payments continued for nine months. Other less spectacular embezzlements have occurred with fictitious persons being added to payrolls.

C.5. A U.C.L.A. engineering graduate studied a telephone company's computer by posing first as a journalist and later as a customer. He learned enough to place false commercial orders for telephone equipment by keying order-entry codes on his home Touchtone telephone. He picked up the equipment he ordered and sold it through a dummy firm. The telephone company allowed the unpaid bills to accumulate. The district attorney charged that $1,000,000 worth of goods were stolen in this manner.

C.6. One of the largest crimes in history was a recent insurance fraud. A large life insurance company created fictitious life insurance policies and then sold the dummy policies to reinsurers. 58 per cent of all of the 97,000 policies listed on the books were in fact nonexistent, and about $2 billion worth of fictitious policies were sold. The insurance company computer contained details of these policies and the policy numbers were coded in such a way as to identify which were real and which were fictitious policies. The billing program omitted the phony policies when notices were sent out to real policyholders. Using normal actuarial statistics a number of fictitious policyholders were caused to die and false death certificates were created.

Independent auditors checked the system by sampling the computer files and verifying the data against the original hard copies. When auditors asked for hard copy files of the fictitious policies, if the file did not exist they were told they could have it the following day and could meanwhile check the genuine files. Certain employees then created the hard copy the auditors requested in all-night working parties.

An auditor wanted to send letters to a sampling of policyholders so that they could confirm that they did indeed have a policy. The letters were automatically addressed with correct addresses to the genuine policyholders and with false addresses to the fictitious policyholders so that these letters were received by certain employees who responded accordingly.

D. QUESTIONS RELATING TO PRIVACY

D.1. It has been suggested that on critical computers—for example, on a system concerned with the assets of a large corporation—background checks should be made on key data-processing personnel. Some corporations do make such checks. Which of the data-processing personnel do you think should be checked? Specifically what information do you think should be found out about these personnel?

D.2. What would be the advantages and disadvantages of the Data Surveillance Bill (Appendix C) becoming law? Could you suggest improvements to compensate for the disadvantages?

D.3. Suppose that the laws relating to privacy which are suggested in Chapter 39 came into force. What computer systems could be installed to assist in enforcing the laws? Outline a preliminary design of such systems and suggest how the laws might be modified to enable "computers to keep watch on computers."

D.4. By the 1980s when data banks will be far more pervasive than today and will be available at a small fraction of today's cost, some countries will probably have a legal structure designed to protect the privacy of individuals. Legal restrictions similar to those in Chapter 39 may be in force. However, by this time, international data transmission via satellites will have become very inexpensive by today's standards. Some data bank operators may set up "off-shore data banks," which, like today's off-shore funds, will take advantage of the absence of restrictions in particular countries. Some small countries may even try to attract data bank operators just as today they attract certain types of financial operations by their lenient laws. A data bank operator providing information about credit risks, background checks, talent searches, or information for private detective agencies, might find it profitable to set up "off-shore" operations.

What actions might be taken to help prevent this anticipated evasion of national laws?

D.5. In recent years there have been many terrorist attacks on Israelis living abroad and on other Jews. Israel vowed to fight international anti-Jewish terrorism. A useful tool to assist this action would be a data bank system, perhaps in Israel, containing the names and backgrounds of any individuals in other countries, who are suspected of anti-Semitic views or actions. Israeli agents and certain members of Jewish Defense Leagues abroad could have access to such a system by means of commercial cables or international data transmission. One weekly news magazine has suggested that such a system already exists. It is likely that the future will bring other international data bank systems for special policing activities, perhaps by minority groups.

Should such systems be a cause for concern? If so what could be done to control them?

D.6. Figure 27.1 shows a survey of the bombings and bomb threats that occurred in the United States from January 1, 1969 to April 15, 1970 (a vintage period for bomb threats). If the number of bombings and bomb threats become greater than in Fig. 27.1, should the situation be countered by methods that require invading the privacy of potential culprits? What limitations should be placed on police methods using data banks in connection with such a situation?

E. THE DESIGN OF SPECIFIC SYSTEMS

It is suggested that these questions should be tackled in small teams to encourage healthy argument between the team participants. There is no single correct answer to these questions.

E.1.　*A Sales Order Entry System*

The district offices of a sales organization are such to have a small on-line entry system.

Customer orders and other details about customers and potential customers will be entered into terminals cable-connected to a small data collection computer on the same floor. The computer will check and store the items.

A large system at a headquarters location will process the information that is collected by the district order entry computers. To do this it will dial each computer twice a day using the public telephone network, and instruct it to transmit the data it has collected. The transmission will normally last for less than a minute, hence this forms an economical way for the headquarters system to obtain the order information sufficiently quickly.

It is important that the data collected should be accurate before it is processed by the headquarters computer. Furthermore the orders are for expensive items in a highly competitive market and therefore it is important that the data about sales and potential sales be safeguarded. The transmission lines cannot be regarded as secure, especially as the telephone junction boxes and PBX's in the district office buildings cannot be controlled. (Many offices occupy one floor of a building owned by a different organization.)

Question. Specify in detail what measures you would build into the system (i) for accuracy control, (ii) for security.

E.2.　*The Maintenance Man*

A computer maintenance engineer services the data processing installation of a large and highly competitive corporation. He realizes that he could sell a listing of the corporation's customers and prospective customers for a considerable sum of money, and discovers that the computer performs a run which updates the file of customers and prospects every Tuesday morning.

The engineer constructs a tiny radio receiver on a computer circuit card, designed so that he can install it in the computer in such a way that it will cause a failure when he transmits a signal to it. He employs this during the customer file updating run. He is sent for, and uses his utility program to dump the main memory of the computer. The engineer takes the printout to the maintenance room, photographs it with a Minox camera, using several films, and returns with the printout to the computer room.

The fault is corrected and the computer operator shreds the main memory dump as he has been instructed.

The dump contains data about three customers. It also contains the program used for updating the customer files. The engineer types the data about the three customers and uses it to establish that there is indeed a market for such information.

He writes a program which combines his main memory dump program with the routine for accessing the customer files in the program he copied. On the following Tuesday morning he causes another computer failure and runs his new program. It looks to the operator like a main memory dump, but in fact it scans the customer and prospect file printing out details. The engineer returns an old memory dump to the operator who again shreds it.

The engineer's clients are pleased with the information and one offers to pay him a retainer for obtaining such a listing every two months.

Question. What security measures in an installation would have prevented this type of attack?

E.3. *Cash-Dispensing Terminals*

A large bank is preparing to install cash-dispensing machines in the street walls of its branches so that customers may withdraw money from their accounts when the bank is closed. The machines will be connected to the bank's computer center by multidrop communication lines. Such a line is shown in Fig. A.

A customer wanting to withdraw cash from his account inserts his bank card which contains a magnetic stripe readable by the machine. Up to 40 numerals can be inscribed on the card's stripe. The customer keys in the sum he requires. The machine, when polled, sends a teleprocessing message to the computer center. The computer looks up the customer's account record, and transmits a message back to the cash-dispensing machine saying whether or not it should give him the money. If the reply is affirmative the machines dispense the requested sum in dollar bills, and the user's bank account is debited.

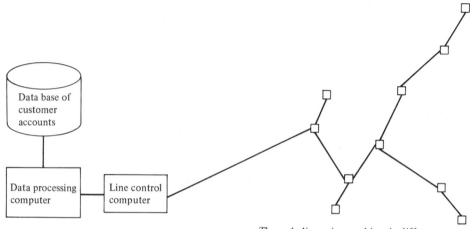

The cash-dispensing machines in different towns are connected to the computer center by means of multidrop communication lines, which the line-control computer polls.

Figure A

All of the machines when loaded contain large sums of money (up to 3000 $5, $10, or $20 bills).

Question. The machines are strong enough to resist physical attack. How else could a major robbery be committed? Specify in as much detail as possible a set of controls which you think would make this system robbery-proof.

E.4. *Electronic Fund Transfer*

One of the Federal Reserve Banks carried out a study on the future of the American payments mechanism. It anticipated that the volume of checks would become too great to be economically absorbed. Credit cards also have problems associated with them, give an alarmingly high cost per transaction (which the consumer pays indirectly and unknowingly), and do little to reduce the overall quantity of paperwork.

The solution is an electronic fund transfer (EFT) system. Using this, the consumer would have a magnetically encoded card with which he would make payments directly. The card would be inserted into an EFT terminal, and the transaction would be transmitted to a bank where the consumer's record would be updated in real-time if he had the funds available.

It was calculated that when EFT becomes as widely used as credit cards are today, the cost per transaction would be a fraction of the cost of using credit cards. It is critical that the cost of mass-produced EFT terminals be low, and estimates of terminal costs below \$300 were made. Most stores, offices, and restaurants would have an EFT terminal. Some consumers might have one in their home. It was thought possible that at some time in the 1980s there might be more than a million EFT terminals in use in the United States.

Question. What would be the security exposures of such a system? Suggest appropriate techniques for building security into EFT systems.

E.5. *Data Base Software*

You work for a large stockbroker who is planning a new information system in which the needs of the market analysts, the requests of management, and the routine processing of customer transactions will be met by the same data-base/data-communications software.

This software will have the following characteristics:

1. Multiple different application files can be derived from the same set of data elements.
2. Redundancy is largely eliminated from the data base because a data element stored once can become part of many different records.
3. Complex relationships between the data elements are made possible by means of pointers, chains, or directories.
4. The data can be used for real-time or batch processing.
5. The data base can be designed to provide answers quickly to *unanticipated* forms of information request.
6. The content and structure of the data base may be changed without having to rewrite the application programs.
7. The software will handle the communication with terminals.

Question. You are asked to specify in detail what security provisions you think a suitable data-base/data-communications software package would have.

E.6. *A Service Bureau*

You operate a small computer service bureau in which there has been little need to pay attention to security. Now, however, you are gaining a type of business in which highly valuable and sensitive information is stored on the customer tapes in your custody. You have read in the newspapers about a case in which employees of a service bureau in Sweden were sentenced to six months in prison for copying information on computer tapes and selling it. Some of your employees are temporary.

Question. What steps can you take to ensure that your employees will not copy data on customer tapes?

E.7. *Future Data Processing Systems*

It has been suggested that data processing systems of the future should not have a computer operator as they do today. The computer should be in a fireproof, sabotage-proof vault visited only occasionally by a maintenance engineer. It should switch itself on in the morning and off at night by means of a time switch. All operative data should be permanently on-line so that there is no tape librarian, or volumes that can be stolen. No volumes would be loaded in the computer room by an operator.

All input and output to the computer would be handled by some form of telecommunications—telephone lines, a wideband network like the ARPA network, rooftop satellite or microwave antennas, and high-bit-rate coaxial cables within the building. Peripheral units such as high-speed printers would be linked to the computer by cables within the building or by longer-distance telecommunication links.

Question. List the features which such a system should have in order to make it feasible and in order to provide a high measure of security.

F. PROJECTS

A useful exercise is to conduct a security audit on your local computer center. If the manager of the computer center grants permission for this exercise ask if he will agree to submit to a 20-minute interview with each participating team, or else appoint a subordinate to do so. Different teams might be sent to different computer centers.

Project 1. Consider the functions carried out by the computer center. Draw up a chart of the possible security exposures and develop a policy for safeguarding such an installation. Draw up a questionnaire for use in conducting a security audit of the installation.

The class, in teams, should then investigate all aspects of the installation's security measures, produce a report of any deficiencies found and list recommendations for improving the safeguards.

Project 2. The same computer center is to be used. This time, however, assume that the computer employs a data base which contains commercial data of considerable value. Loss or theft of the data would cause harm valued at $200,000.

Carry out the same investigation as in Project 1 but with this new assumption.

Project 3. Divide the class into opposing teams such that one set of teams must devise and make presentations of safeguards for the above computer system (with or without fictitious assumptions about the nature of its data base). The other set of teams must assume that the safeguards are implemented and devise means to break into the system or subvert it.

Do not forget that (1) breakins should benefit the intruder in some way. (2) A system designer should not spend a disproportionate amount of time or money protecting items of no value. (3) Some items which appear to have no dollar value, such as personal information about an employee's past, or his salary, may in fact deserve protection for other reasons such as maintaining good employee moral, or maintaining ethical standards within the corporation.

Project 4. The previous project may be based on a system that is described to the students, rather than on a live installation (although much can be learned from a live installation and its physical environment). The following description may be employed, with the class divided into teams and bank robbers:

A large bank serving most of Britain has its computer center in London, and all records of customer accounts for 900 branches are kept in a single data base at the computer center. The average total of the account balances is approximately 60 million pounds sterling. (The figures are fictitious.) A customer can walk into any branch and ask to withdraw money from his account. The bank teller will use a terminal connected to the London computer to determine whether there is sufficient money in the account. The account records will be updated from the same terminal.

The team must determine what procedures must be employed if, for any reason, the terminal is temporarily not working. The telecommunication network employs voice-grade lines. Stored-program concentrators or terminal cluster controllers can be employed. The team must decide what functions should be programmed in these peripheral devices.

INDEX

James Martin is a graduate of Oxford University, England, and holds an M.A. degree in physics. He is also a graduate of the British Institute of Management. He works for IBM on the staff of the Systems Research Institute in New York.

Mr. Martin has designed and worked on many major real-time and data transmission systems including some with world-wide networks. He has lectured on four continents and has broadcast on radio and television in several countries. He was a member of the first Russian-American committee to study possible exchanges in computer skills.

He is well known as the author of the series of best-selling books on computers shown on the front endpapers.